ENCYCLOPEDIA OF INTERNATIONAL COMMERCE

ENCYCLOPEDIA
OF
INTERNATIONAL
COMMERCE

BY WILLIAM J. MILLER

CORNELL MARITIME PRESS

Centreville, Maryland

Library of Congress Cataloging in Publication Data

Miller, William J., 1947-
    Encyclopedia of international commerce.

        1. Commerce—Dictionaries.   2. Foreign trade
regulation—Dictionaries.   3. Commercial law—
Dictionaries.   I. Title.
HF1001.M55   1985   382'.03'21   84-46106
ISBN 0-87033-322-4

Manufactured in the United States of America

First edition

This work is dedicated to

MR. YASUSHI HIBINO

President

Asahi Unyo Kaisha, Limited

CONTENTS

PREFACE

International trade is vital to the well-being of virtually every nation, because no nation is capable of satisfying its material needs beyond the subsistence level entirely from domestic resources.

As a nation's technology advances and educational levels improve, heavy industry and manufacturing are often supplanted by service industries, as evidenced by the economies of Europe, North America, and Japan. The shift to a service economy increases import reliance, especially in the areas of consumer products and basic industrial commodities, such as steel. This transition creates opportunities—in the form of new markets and lower unit costs—but also begets confrontation as lower priced imports displace domestic workers, and charges of unfair competition congeal into protectionist policies.

Unfortunately, the *process* of international trade is often obscured by the graphs and statistical tables used to illustrate and measure volumes of trade. It is important to remember that "trade" is a forest composed of many individual trees. To understand international trade in the macroeconomic sense, one studies data—to conduct trade as a business person, it is essential to understand the mechanics of buying and selling in foreign markets. To the latter end this book is directed.

While teaching a course in export-import management at a Connecticut college several years ago, I confronted the paucity of material published on the practical aspects of trading in the international market. No textbook suited my purpose, so I set about to write one.

My first task was to define my terms—tariffs, non-tariff barriers, shipping terminology, etc. As this labor progressed over many months, it became evident there was need for an encyclopedic reference work which focused upon international trade. My enquiries having divulged no similar work in English, I decided to concentrate efforts upon an encyclopedia.

In selecting entries, it was my intention to provide the reader with a cross section of terminology of the various aspects of international trade—marketing, taxation, shipping, law, accounting, etc. Each entry, it is hoped, is sufficiently descriptive to define the topic adequately, without extraneous detail or digression. Considerable attention has been given to transportation, especially marine transportation, because it is such an integral area. Without transportation there can be no trade, and the overwhelming bulk of trade moves by sea.

International trade is a highly dynamic field within which concepts, terms, and agreements are continually emerging and changing. Great effort was taken to ensure the content of this work was current at time of publication. It is possible that changes may have occurred between final text revision and publication. While this is unavoidable in a work of this kind, I am confident such changes will not impair the overall utility of the book.

In preparing this work, I have drawn upon many resources. I would like to acknowledge the assistance of the following individuals and organizations who aided me in my efforts: AFL-CIO; African Development Bank and Fund; American Association of Port Authorities; American Steamship Owners Mutual Protection and Indemnity Association; American Trucking Associations; American Warehousemen's Association; Amtorg Trading Corp.; Asian Development Bank; Association of American Railroads; Association of Shipbrokers and Agents (U. S. A.); Baltic and International Maritime Conference; Ms. Mary Condellis, Bankers Association for Foreign Trade; Board of Governors of the Federal Reserve System; Messrs. Tom Cole and John Wheeler, Boeing Commercial Airplane Company; Mr. Jean Ste. Jacques, Canadian Embassy, Washington; Council for Mutual Economic Assistance; Customs Co-operation Council; Equipment Interchange Association; Ms. Cesaria Daniello Klayman, European Communities; European Free Trade Association; European Investment Bank; Export-Import Bank of the United States; Mr. Geoffrey Rogers, Federal Maritime Commission; Federal Register, General Services Administration; Financial Accounting Standards Board; Frank P. Dow Company; General Agreement on Tariffs and Trade; Inter-American Development Bank; Internal Revenue Service; International Air Transport Association; International Bank for Economic Cooperation; International Coffee Organization; International Investment Bank; International Lead and Zinc Study Group; International Longshoremen's Association; International Maritime Organization; International Natural Rubber Organization; International Organization for Standardization; International Rubber Study Group; International Sugar Organization; International Tin Council; Japan External Trade Organization; Lloyd's of London; Lykes Bros. Steamship Company; Mr. Robert Gray, Japan-Korea/Atlantic and Gulf Freight Conference; National Foreign Trade Council, Inc.; Office of the U. S. Trade Representative; Overseas Private Investment Corporation; Mr. Thomas Morrow, Port Authority of New York/New Jersey; Mr. Robert Koplowitz, Port of Seattle; Scandinavian Airline System; Mr. Suheil Elias, State Street Bank and Trust Company; Union Pacific Railroad; United Nations Council on Trade and Development; United Nations Statistical Office; U. S. Customs Service; U. S. International Trade Commission; U. S. Department of Commerce; Mr. Frank O'Donnell, Maritime Administration, U. S. Department of Transportation; and many others.

Special thanks are due to Ms. Joanne Ingram, who undertook the heroic task of typing the original manuscript, and to my dear wife, Maura, who endured years of research, editing, and updating.

ENCYCLOPEDIA OF INTERNATIONAL COMMERCE

A

ABANDONMENT. (1) In domestic transportation, the termination of service by a common carrier over a given route; (2) the refusal, by a consignee, to accept delivery of a lot of cargo tendered for delivery; (3) in marine insurance, the act by which the owner of a vessel claims constructive total loss arising from a maritime calamity, leaving the ship to the insurer for such salvage value as may be recovered.

ABATTEMENT FORFAITAIRE. *See* MONTANT FORFAITAIRE.

AB KAI. In German, a term of sale signifying that the goods are sold free at the pier.

AB QUAI. *Synonymous with* AB KAI *(q.v.).*

ABSOLUTE ADVANTAGE. The ability of a country to supply a given product at an economic cost lower than that of a competing nation.

ABSOLUTE CONTRABAND. *See* CONTRABAND OF WAR.

ABSOLUTE ENDORSEMENT. An archaic term not used in modern statutes, it meant an unconditional endorsement of a negotiable instrument. It is replaced effectively by the term General Endorsement. *See* ENDORSEMENT.

ABSOLUTE SPREAD. A provision in a variable rate loan that fixes the upper limit of the premium over prime rate at a specific percentage, e.g., prime plus 3 percent.

ABSORPTION. The performance by a common carrier of special services not provided for in the tariff or included in the freight paid; among such services may be switching, wharfage, or redelivery of merchandise. The performance and/or acceptance of such services may constitute an "improper inducement" on the part of the carrier which may be prohibited by law or regulation.

ACCEPTABILITY. As used in relation to the discount or re-discount of a negotiable instrument at the Federal Reserve, *acceptability* implies that the Bank regards the paper as sound and apt to be collectible upon maturity. Where the Bank has doubts concerning the maker, payee, or endorsers of an instrument, financial statements of the relevant parties may be required.

Acceptability, which is basically a reflection of credit worthiness, is one of two criteria for the discount of an instrument. The other criterion is *eligibility*. *See* ELIGIBLE PAPER.

ACCEPTANCE. A bill of exchange or draft that has been *accepted* upon presentation to the drawee; the acceptance is created upon presentation by stamping or writing the word *accepted* across the face of the instrument, accompanied by the signature of the drawee.

Instruments on which a bank is the acceptor are *bankers' acceptances;* instruments accepted by commercial entities other than banks are *trade acceptances.*

An active market exists for acceptances, which may be discounted at prevailing rates. As a practical matter, bankers' acceptances tend to receive a more favorable discount rate over the trade acceptances of all but the most credit-worthy firms.

See BILL OF EXCHANGE.

ACCEPTANCE AND RETURN. The act of returning an accepted draft or bill of exchange, through banking channels, to the maker to await maturity. Upon maturity, the holder of the instrument would return it to the drawee and demand payment. This process is cumbersome and is often avoided by leaving the acceptance at the bank that made the original presentation to the drawee; upon maturity, the bank will demand payment from the drawee and remit the proceeds to the owner of the bill.

ACCEPTANCE COMMISSION. A fee charged by a bank for accepting a draft on behalf of a customer. By accepting the draft, the bank guarantees payment of the instrument, making the bill more acceptable in the discount market. A bank normally accepts drafts against a prearranged line of credit with its customer.

ACCEPTANCE CREDIT. *See* ACCEPTANCE FINANCING.

ACCEPTANCE FACILITY. *See* ACCEPTANCE FINANCING.

ACCEPTANCE FINANCING. An arrangement by which a bank extends to an exporter or importer a line of credit, known as the *acceptance facility*, to finance the purchase or sale of goods. The borrower draws against the line of credit by drawing drafts, with future maturity dates, upon the bank; the bank will accept such drafts, up to the amount of the acceptance facility, with maturities thirty, sixty, or ninety days hence. The bankers' acceptances so created may be discounted, resulting in cash for the borrower.

The bank, as collateral for the financing provided, may require that the borrower *hypothecate*, or pledge, bills of lading, or warehouse receipts, evidencing title to the goods that have been financed, or otherwise provide acceptable security. Borrowers of high standing may be extended *clean,* or unsecured, credit.

Acceptance financing can be arranged not only through banks but also through specialized financial firms known as *acceptance houses.*

ACCEPTANCE FOR HONOR. *See* ACCEPTANCE SUPRA PROTEST.

ACCEPTANCE HOUSE. A nonbank financial institution that specializes in ACCEPTANCE FINANCING *(q.v.).*

ACCEPTANCE LIABILITY. The aggregate of all drafts or bills of exchange accepted by a bank and outstanding. On a bank's ledger, this liability is reflected as "liability on account of acceptances."

ACCEPTANCE SUPRA PROTEST. An action, also known as *acceptance for honor,* by which a third party accepts a draft or bill of exchange that has been *dishonored*, i.e., repudiated by the party upon whom it was drawn and where formal protest has been made. By accepting the instrument, the third party makes himself responsible for payment of the instrument upon maturity, thereby saving the honor of the instrument, and, by implication, the credit worthiness of the drawer and endorsers of the draft.

The advent of high-speed telecommunications, as well as the availability of other vehicles to preserve the credit worthiness of the maker of a bill, has mitigated the necessity for acceptance supra protest transactions. The practice is regarded as outmoded in advanced commercial centers, although it is still employed in less developed areas.

ACCEPTOR. A person who accepts a draft or bill of exchange. The act of acceptance is performed by writing or stamping the word *accepted* across the face of the instrument, accompanied by the acceptor's signature.

ACCESSORIAL SERVICES. Additional services, over and above transportation of merchandise, performed by a carrier. Such services may include, inter alia, advancing payments to other carriers or service providers, storage, and c.o.d. collections. A charge is normally imposed by a carrier for the performance of accessorial services.

ACCOMMODATION BILL. A bill of exchange or similar instrument to which a credit-worthy party has added its endorsement, usually to enhance the value of the bill as a money market instrument.

ACCOMMODATION BILL OF LADING. A bill of lading issued by a carrier or its agent to a shipper in advance of actual receipt of the goods for carriage. The motives for such action may be to permit the shipper to draw on an expiring letter of credit, or to book a sale during a particular accounting period. The carrier is responsible to the consignees or holders of the bill of lading (*see* Section 7-301 [1] Uniform Commercial Code).

In addition, the issuance of an *on board* endorsement prior to actual loading of the cargo, or predating a bill may be viewed as accommodations by a carrier to a shipper.

ACCOMMODATION ENDORSEMENT. The endorsement of a bill of exchange or other negotiable instrument by a bank or other credit worthy party for purposes of enhancing the acceptability of the instrument in the money market. Generally, the accommodation endorser is not a direct party to the transaction which gave rise to the creation of the instrument. By acting as endorser, however, the accommodation party assumes responsibility for redeeming the instrument upon maturity if the drawee or prior endorsers default. Accommodation endorsements are often provided by established firms for affiliated companies, or by banks for valued clients. *See* ENDORSEMENT.

ACCOMMODATION LINE. The acceptance by an insurance company of substandard risks as an accommodation to a particular broker who has previously provided, and is expected to continue to provide, attractive underwriting business.

ACCOMMODATION PARTY. One who provides an ACCOMMODATION ENDORSEMENT *(q.v.)* on a negotiable instrument.

ACP COUNTRIES. An acronym for African-Caribbean-Pacific countries. The term originated in conjunction with the LOMÉ CONVENTIONS *(q.v.).*

ACQUITTANCE. A document releasing a party from a debt or other obligation.

ACTION IN REM. A form of legal action in which suit is brought against an object, rather than the owner of the object. In rem actions are most common in admiralty jurisdiction.

ACT OF STATE DOCTRINE. A principle of international law that holds that the actions of a state, performed within its own boundaries are not subject to legal review in other countries. Some limitations on the doctrine have arisen in recent years, largely in response to international conventions guaranteeing just treatment of individuals and private property.

As a result of the doctrine, a state normally may not be sued in a foreign court without its consent. In response to wholesale expropriations of American property in Cuba in the early 1960s, U.S. law was amended by the so-called HICKENLOOPER AMENDMENT *(q.v.)*, whereby U.S. courts were empowered to try cases to which a foreign state is a party whenever American property has been expropriated in violation of U.S. law.

The jurisdiction of American courts over suits involving foreign states and state-owned enterprises was further expanded by the FOREIGN SOVEREIGN IMMUNITIES ACT *(q.v.)*.

ACTUAL DISPLACEMENT. *See* DISPLACEMENT.

ACTUAL OWNER. The party having legal title to a vessel, as listed in the ship's registry papers. *See also* DISPONENT OWNER

ACTUAL SOLVENCY. *See* SOLVENCY.

ACTUAL TOTAL LOSS. In marine insurance, a loss where nothing remains of the insured property but debris, or where the property is so situated as to make recovery impossible.

ACTUAL VALUE RATE. A freight rate applicable to certain commodities where, depending upon the actual goods, value may vary greatly. For example, the classification "scientific instruments" may embrace low-value laboratory glassware or high-value precision instruments. In such cases, the shipper must declare the actual value of the merchandise, and his freight rate will be appropriate to the value declared. Commodities subject to actual value rates are specially identified in the tariff.

ADCOM. *See* ADDRESS COMMISSION.

ADDED VALUE TAX. *Synonymous with* VALUE ADDED TAX *(q. v.)*.

ADDITIONAL PRODUCT AID. A feature of the Common Agricultural Policy of the European Economic Community, which provides price supports to EEC producers affected by import competition. The "community preference" mechanism of the CAP eliminates external competition for most items but does not respond for certain products (e.g., durum wheat, olive oil, tobacco) on which duties are low and are fixed under the General Agreement on Tariffs and Trade. Additional product aid payments are applicable on commodities covering only 2.5 percent of EEC agricultural production. *See* COMMON AGRICULTURAL POLICY.

ADDRESS COMMISSION. A commission payable to a third party arising from a contract to charter a ship. Commonly known as *ADCOM*, this is not a brokerage fee but an additional commission paid by the vessel to any third party named by the charterer. An adcom is usually expressed as a percentage of the charter hire of the vessel; the percentage is negotiated between the vessel owner and the charterer. In some cases, the firm chartering the vessel may nominate itself or an affiliated company to receive the adcom, thus resulting in a reduction in actual freight.

ADJUSTED C.I.F. PRICE. A factor in determining the variable import levy imposed by the European Economic Community on grain imports. The adjusted C.I.F. (cost, insurance, and freight) price is derived by assigning a quality factor to grain imported from non-EEC countries so as to put the import on a quality basis comparable with EEC-produced grain. Depending upon its quality relative to EEC grain, the imported grain may be advanced or discounted in value for the application of C.I.F. ad valorem duties. *See* COMMON AGRICULTURAL POLICY.

ADMINISTERED PRICING. A condition in which the prices of certain goods and/or services are determined by governmental authority, supplier cartels (legal or illegal), or trade associations, and not by market forces.

The purpose of administered pricing is to eliminate price competition or to maintain price stability over time. Examples of administered pricing include: price controls imposed by government during periods of shortage or high inflation; setting of rates or fares; and collusion among suppliers and importers to ensure market prices do not fall below agreed levels.

ADMISSION OF SEAWORTHINESS. A clause commonly found in contracts of marine insurance whereby the insurer agrees not to raise unseaworthiness of the vessel as a defense in a claim brought by the policyholder. In olden days, a merchant was obliged to ascertain the seaworthiness of a ship before offering cargo for carriage. The admission of seaworthiness clause relieves the shipper of this burden. *See* SEAWORTHY.

ADMISSION TEMPORAIRE. The temporary duty-free admission of otherwise dutiable merchandise, usually for the purpose of processing into goods for export. The most common vehicles for avoiding duties on such temporary imports are: (1) *importation under bond*—the importer posts a bond with customs to cover duties in the event the goods are not re-exported within a prescribed period; and (2) *drawback*—duties are paid at time of importation and recovered from the customs authorities when the final product is exported.

Regulations governing importations under bond and drawback recoveries vary from nation to nation.

ADMITTED CARRIER. An insurance company that is *admitted*, i.e., licensed to do business, in a given jurisdiction.

AD VALOREM. Literally, according to value. Any charge, tax, or duty that is applied as a percentage of value.

AD VALOREM DUTY. Any duty that is expressed as a percentage of the value of the imported merchandise. Most customs duties, particularly in the developed nations, are ad valorem duties.

ADVENTURE. In marine insurance, any maritime enterprise. The term is most commonly used to denote the risks undertaken by a vessel and her cargo in the course of transiting the seas.

ADVERSE SELECTION. The practice of applying insurance cover only in those cases where a higher than normal degree of loss is contemplated. Inasmuch as adverse selection defeats the object of insurance, which is to spread risk, the practice is discouraged or contractually prohibited in contracts of insurance.

ADVICE. Also known as *advice of fate*, a document issued by a commercial bank to acknowledge receipt of funds or instruments from a third party or to confirm performance of previous instructions. For example, a bank would send an advice to a customer confirming the receipt of funds by wire .

ADVICE OF FATE. *See* ADVICE.

AFFILIATION PRIVILEGE. Tax relief which a firm receives because it controls, is controlled by, or is under common control with another firm. For example, company A derives significant tax credits from investments in new plant and equipment, but does not have sufficent earnings to fully utilize the credits; company B, the parent of company A, has taxable earnings but limited deductions and credits. Because of the affiliation between A and B, company B will use the tax credits of its subsidiary to reduce its own tax liability.

AFFREIGHTMENT. *See* CONTRACT OF AFFREIGHTMENT.

À FORFAIT FINANCING. *See* FORFAITING.

AFOROS. An official value, as compared with actual market value, assigned by customs authorities to certain classes of imported merchandise and used as the basis of computing ad valorem duties. The term is peculiar to a few countries in Latin America, notably Brazil, Mexico, and Uruguay.

AFRICAN DEVELOPMENT BANK GROUP. A multilateral development organization, the first component of which, the African Development Bank, was created in 1963 under the auspices of the United Nations Economic Commission for Africa. The group provides funding to African states and multinational official bodies in Africa to advance industrial, agricultural, and infrastructure development.

Initially, membership in the bank was restricted to African states. To attract participation by industrial nations in African development projects, the African Development Fund was organized, to which nonregional, i.e., non-African, states were admitted. The bank subsequently accepted nonregional members as well.

The bank invests in projects with the object of improving the economic base of a sector or region; while funding terms are concessional, projects must be commercially sound and offer a reasonable likelihood of repayment. The fund concentrates its resources in the neediest African nations.

The authorized capital of the bank consists of 525,000 shares having a par value of 10,000 *units of account* (UA) each. On December 31, 1983, the subscribed capital was UA 5,048,120,000. The unit of account is equal to one SPECIAL DRAWING RIGHT *(q.v.)* (SDR). Prior to December 31, 1977, the UA was nominally equivalent to .88867088 grams of fine gold.

The financial resources of the fund are derived from the industrial countries. The fund issues no shares; voting is proportional to the subscriptions of the members, with one exception: the African Development Bank, which is a subscriber, enjoys fifty percent of the voting power in the fund. This arrangement permits the African states, through their membership in the bank, to have a voice in fund affairs equal to that of the industrial nations.

Total subscriptions to the fund equal 2,168,097,305 *fund units of account* (FUA). The FUA is equal to .921052 SDR.

During the period 1982–86, it is envisaged that bank lending will increase from U.S. $890 million to U.S. $2,188 million; total commitments of the group within this period are expected to reach U.S. $7,259 million. Allocation of the group's sectoral lending during 1982–86 is projected as follows:

Agriculture	33 percent
Transport	22
Public utilities	20
Industry and development banks	11
Social	9
New forms of lending	5

Headquarters of the bank and the fund are in Abidjan, Ivory Coast. In Fiscal Year 1983, members in the bank were:

Regional members:

Algeria	Djibouti
Angola	Eygpt
Benin	Equatorial Guinea
Botswana	Ethiopia
Burkina Fasso	Gabon
Burundi	Gambia
Cameroon	Ghana
Cape Verde	Guinea
Central African Republic	Guinea-Bissau
Chad	Ivory Coast
Comoros	Kenya
Congo	Lesotho

Liberia
Libya
Madagascar
Malawi
Mali
Mauritania
Mauritius
Morocco
Mozambique
Niger
Nigeria
Rwanda
Sao Tome & Principe

Senegal
Seychelles
Sierra Leone
Somalia
Sudan
Swaziland
Tanzania
Togo
Tunisia
Uganda
Zaire
Zambia
Zimbabwe.

Nonregional members:

Austria
Belgium
Brazil
Canada
Denmark
Finland
France
German Federal Republic
India
Italy
Japan

Korea (South)
Kuwait
Netherlands
Norway
Portugal
Saudi Arabia
Sweden
Switzerland
United Kingdom
United States
Yugoslavia.

Subscribers to the fund at the outset of Fiscal Year 1984, with their respective voting powers, were:

Participant	Votes	Percentage
African Development Bank	1,000.00	50.00
Argentina	1.17	.06
Austria	11.24	.56
Belgium	12.32	.62
Brazil	13.35	.67
Canada	110.79	5.54
Denmark	38.21	1.91
Finland	13.09	.65
France	63.24	3.16
German Federal Republic	100.76	5.54
India	8.23	.41
Italy	35.20	1.76
Japan	130.44	6.52
Korea	11.85	.59
Kuwait	14.36	.72
Netherlands	21.12	1.06
Norway	44.93	2.25
Portugal	4.69	.23
Saudi Arabia	36.20	1.81
Spain	11.15	.56
Sweden	62.50	3.13
Switzerland	45.01	2.25
United Arab Emirates	5.28	.26
United Kingdom	47.55	2.38
United States	148.23	7.41
Yugoslavia	9.09	.45

AFRICAN DEVELOPMENT FUND. *See* AFRICAN DEVELOPMENT BANK GROUP.

AGENCY FEE. A charge imposed by a shipowner's local agent for services on behalf of a vessel while the ship is in port; also, the commission paid by a vessel's owner to local sales agents on cargo shipped on the vessel.

AGENCY FOR INTERNATIONAL DEVELOPMENT. A component of the UNITED STATES INTERNATIONAL DEVELOPMENT COOPERATION AGENCY (*q.v.*).

AGENT/DISTRIBUTOR SERVICE. An export promotion service to industry offered by the International Trade Administration of the U.S. Department of Commerce. The object of the program is to locate foreign firms to serve as agents and distributors for American products.

An American firm interested in using the service submits an application, using form ITA-424P, to the Commerce Department giving details of the firm and product he wishes to sell abroad. The completed form is transmitted to an American foreign service post in the target country selected by the exporter; an American trade representative in the target country will seek out interested firms. After about thirty days, the American firm will receive a listing of firms abroad that have expressed interest in the product. A fee of $25 is charged for each country in which the exporter is interested.

Copies of form ITA-424P and details of the program can be obtained by contacting any district office of the U.S. Department of Commerce.

See Appendix C2 for a full listing of Department of Commerce district offices.

AGGREGATE. The maximum exposure borne by an insured party under a contract of insurance during a given time period, usually one year. If, for example, a policy provides for a deductible of $1,000 per occurrence with an aggregate of $5,000, then once the insured party has paid out $5,000 in total, he will not pay the deductible on subsequent claims arising during the policy period, irrespective of the number of claims made against the policy or the amounts involved.

AGGREGATED SHIPMENT. A sum of cargo, bound for a single consignee, which has been assembled over time by a carrier at his premises from smaller lots shipped in from one or more sources. The entire lot will be shipped on to the consignee as a single load. The carrier may impose a charge for performing the ASSEMBLY SERVICE (*q.v.*).

AGGREGATE OF THE INTERMEDIARIES RULE. A provision of the Interstate Commerce Act which states that in those cases where a combination of rates among intermediary points along the route would result in a freight charge lower than the through rate, a shipper may use the lower aggregated rate. This rule applies to rail and water carriers, subject to the act, but not to motor carriers or freight forwarders.

AGGRESSION. Unlawful acts on the part of a state or group of states directed at coercing another state or undermining its sovereignty. Aggression cannot be defined precisely in legal terms suitable for universal use; however, aggressive behavior is defined in some international agreements. For example, the Charter of the Organization of American States defines aggression as "the use of coercive measures of an economic or political character to force the sovereign will of another State and obtain for it advantages of any kind."

Some acts generally denounced as aggression are unlawful confiscation of a nation's property, arrest of its citizens, and interference with diplomatic personnel or premises; threats of attack or total destruction; support of internal subversives, revolutionaries, or rebels by a foreign power (such support may take the form of providing money, weapons, advisors, or sanctuary in the territory of the aggressor; undermining a nation's economy by withholding trade or impeding trade with others, or debasement or corruption of a nation's money; and the use of spies, saboteurs, or agents to infiltrate a nation or stimulate domestic unrest. A nation deemed to be engaged in aggression when it employs third-party surrogates to perform any act that would be aggressive if performed directly.

AGIO. A premium paid in the process of exchanging one currency for another, or for a bill of exchange denominated in a foreign currency.

AGIOTAGE. The practice of speculating in public debt instruments.

AGREEMENT ON GOVERNMENT PROCUREMENT. A multilateral agreement, arising out of the Tokyo Round of trade discussions, which significantly opens government procurement bids to foreign suppliers. Signatory nations are obliged to publish openly invitations to bid, and to apply the same criteria in selecting contractors to national firms and to firms of other signatory states.

The agreement applies to governmental purchases valued at 150,000 SPECIAL DRAWING RIGHTS (*q.v*) or more, excepting contracts for most services, construction, national security procurements, purchases by political subdivisions, and procurements by agencies specifically exempted.

U.S. participation in the agreement was authorized by the Trade Agreements Act of 1979. *See* GENERAL AGREEMENT ON TARIFFS AND TRADE.

AGREEMENT ON SUBSIDIES AND COUNTERVAILING MEASURES. *See* SUBSIDIES CODE.

AGREEMENT ON TECHNICAL BARRIERS TO TRADE. *See* STANDARDS AGREEMENT.

AGREEMENT ON TRADE IN CIVIL AIRCRAFT. *See* AIRCRAFT AGREEMENT.

AGRIBUSINESS. That portion of an economy concerned with the production, processing, marketing, and distribution of agricultural commodities. Included in this group would be manufacturers and suppliers of agricultural chemicals and implements and agricultural credit institutions.

AGRICULTURAL PAPER. Bills of exchange, drafts, and like instruments that arise from transactions in agricultural commodities. Agricultural paper with maturities of nine months or less may be discounted at regional Federal Reserve banks, subject to eligibility requirements contained in Federal Reserve Regulation A. *See* REGULATION A.

AGRICULTURAL TRADE DEVELOPMENT AND ASSISTANCE ACT. Known commonly as P.L. 480, a 1954 act of Congress directed at the long-term improvement of the economies of developing nations through the concessional sale or grant of American agricultural products. The act is implemented by the Foreign Agricultural Service of the U.S. Department of Agriculture through several programs:

1. *Title I* authorizes low-interest, long-term financing of the sale of American farm commodities to developing countries. Such sales are paid in dollars which are used in recipient countries to fund agricultural development, such as irrigation, distribution systems, and technical research and training.

2. *Title II* permits donation of American food products to nations that have suffered natural disasters or famines.

3. *Title III* is divided into two parts: (a) the Food for Peace program, which permits development schemes to be planned on a multiyear basis, and permits forgiveness of dollar obligations incurred under Title I in return for pursuit by the recipient country of defined development objectives, and (b) the Commodity Credit Corporation Export Credit Guarantee Program, also known as GSM-102, which is designed to stimulate exports of American farm products by providing payment guarantees on private financing of export sales. The guarantees are applicable on letter of credit sales to foreign buyers with terms of three years or less.

AGRO-INDUSTRIAL COMPLEX. A national economy in which sustained and significant efforts are directed toward increasing agricultural productivity. Inherent to success of the program is a significant contribution of the national wealth to agricultural projects and vigorous efforts on the part of industries that provide inputs to the agricultural sector.

As a practical matter, a high degree of economic central planning at the governmental level is required to orchestrate the various inputs necessary to achieving an agro-industrial complex.

AIRCRAFT AGREEMENT. A product of the Tokyo Round of Multilateral Trade Negotiations, the

Aircraft Agreement (known officially as the Agreement on Trade in Civil Aircraft) provides that sales of civil aircraft will be free of duty, effective January 1, 1980. The agreement also provides duty-free treatment for flight simulators, and similar equipment. Subassemblies specifically named in the agreement are free of duties as well. In addition, signatories are prohibited from pressuring airlines or aircraft users to buy from any particular supplier, and may not grant or deny landing rights in an attempt to influence purchasers. It is the articulated purpose of the agreement to permit aircraft buyers to select suppliers on the basis of technical and commercial factors.

An aircraft committee was established to ensure compliance and consult on matters affecting the agreement. The United States adhered to the agreement by authority of the Trade Agreements Act of 1979.

See GENERAL AGREEMENT ON TARIFFS AND TRADE; Appendix D8.

AIR WAYBILL. A document issued by an airline as a receipt for cargo and contract of carriage between the carrier and shipper. An air waybill is the effective equivalent of a bill of lading, except that it lacks the feature of being issued in negotiable form. Two types of air waybills are commonly used. A *master air waybill* is issued by an airline for a unitized load of cargo from one shipper to one consignee; a *house air waybill* is issued by an air freight forwarder or consolidator who collects many small shipments to a given city, unitizes them, and ships them intact to his agent in the destination city.

The international air waybill is standard through the world, although air waybills intended for purely domestic use may vary from country to country. A single, uniform air waybill, intended for both domestic and international use, has been adopted by the International Air Transport Association for use by its members; use of this waybill became mandatory January 1, 1984 (*see* figure, next page).

AKTIEBOLAG. A Swedish form of stock company requiring a minimum of three corporators and an initial capitalization of 5,000 kroner. The company may have no fewer than three directors, one-third of whom may be foreigners.

AKTIENGESELLSCHAFT. A form of corporate organization employed in Germany for large or publicly held companies. Identified by the letters *A.G.* at the end of a company's name, this form of incorporation requires the filing of a registration statement with the commercial registrar at the court having jurisdiction over the company's domicile.

At least two persons must serve as incorporators, and a minimum share capital of at least 100,000 marks is required. Shares may be in bearer form, but all shares must have a par value of at least 50 marks; if a higher par value is designated, it must be at least 100 marks, or multiples thereof.

If the firm employs 500 or more persons, worker participation in management, or CODETER-MINATION *(q.v.)*, is required.

ALEXANDER COMMITTEE. A congressional investigative committee that, starting in 1912, enquired into the commercial practices of the maritime shipping industry. The purpose of the investigation was to determine the effects of foreign-flag-dominated shipping cartels upon the waterborne commerce of the United States. After two years of enquiry, the committer came to the following conclusions: that rate conferences are useful in stabilizing service and rates; the international character of the industry is such that unilateral action on the part of the United States would not correct abuses; conferences could be de facto regulatory bodies within the industry, and the conferences themselves could be regulated by legislative action; and certain discriminatory practices should be abolished by law.

The recommendations of the committee were largely accepted and implemented in the Shipping Act of 1916 and creation of the United States Shipping Board, precursor of the FEDERAL MARITIME COMMISSION *(q.v.)*.

ALIEN CORPORATION. See FOREIGN CORPORATION.

ALLIANCE FOR PROGRESS. An economic development program for Latin America sponsored by the Organization of American States (OAS) at the 1961 Punta del Este Conference.

The program called for ten years of concerted efforts directed towards economic growth, social reform, and the relaxation of trade barriers among the American republics. Goals were defined for each developing nation in the region, and their governments pledged substantial resources to the program, to be augmented by economic and technical assistance from the United States.

All members of the OAS, with the exception of Cuba, participated in the program. The Alliance for Progress formally expired in 1972; however, the term is still used to describe U.S.-sponsored aid programs in Latin America.

ALLIED COMPANY ARRANGEMENT. *Synonymous with* COMPLEMENTARY EXPORTING *(q.v)*.

ALL IN. A freight charge that is all-inclusive, i.e., no surcharges or other charges will be added to the quoted rate.

ALLOCATED QUOTA. *See* QUOTA.

ALLONGE. An attachment to a bill of exchange or other negotiable instrument upon which additional endorsements can be placed when no room remains on the instrument itself. The method by which an allonge is to be attached is not specified, other than it must be "permanently affixed."

AIR WAYBILL NUMBER		AIRPORT OF DE-PARTURE	EXECUTION DATE DAY/MTH/YR.	TC	CHGS. CODE	CUR'CY CODE	FOR CARRIER USE ONLY	
AIRLINE PREFIX	SERIAL NO.						FLIGHT/DAY	FLIGHT/DAY
012-8813 3603		JFK	18/2/83			USD		

012-8813 3603

AIRPORT OF DEPARTURE (ADDRESS OF FIRST CARRIER) AND REQUESTED ROUTING	AIRPORT OF DESTINATION	FLIGHT/DAY	FLIGHT/DAY
New York (JFK)	NRT		

NOT NEGOTIABLE
AIR WAYBILL
(AIR CONSIGNMENT NOTE)

ROUTING AND DESTINATION

1/
TO	BY FIRST CARRIER	TO	FROM	TO	FROM
NRT	NW				

BOOKED
ISSUED BY

NORTHWEST ORIENT

Northwest Airlines, Inc.
ST. PAUL, MINNESOTA U.S.A. 55111

2/
CONSIGNEE'S ACCOUNT NUMBER
18574-7

CONSIGNEE'S NAME AND ADDRESS

Mr. K. Imai,
Nihon Trading Corp., Ltd.,
14 Campai Road,
Tokyo, JAPAN

Copies 1, 2 and 3 of this Air Waybill are originals and have the same validity.

It is agreed that the goods described herein are accepted in apparent good order and condition (except as noted) for carriage SUBJECT TO THE CONDITIONS OF CONTRACT ON THE REVERSE HEREOF. THE SHIPPER'S ATTENTION IS DRAWN TO THE NOTICE CONCERNING CARRIERS' LIMITATION OF LIABILITY Shipper may increase such limitation of liability by declaring a higher value for carriage and paying a supplemental charge if required.
Carrier is not liable for the goods until they are received at its town terminal or airport office.

3/
SHIPPER'S ACCOUNT NUMBER
18547-4

SHIPPER'S NAME AND ADDRESS

John Jones,
Great American Export Corp.
111 Fifth Avenue,
New York 10017 USA

Shipper certifies that the particulars on the face hereof are correct and that insofar as any part of the consignment contains restricted articles, such part is properly described by name and is in proper condition for carriage by air according to the International Air Transport Association's Restricted Articles Regulations.

SIGNATURE OF SHIPPER OR HIS AGENT

4/
ISSUING CARRIER'S AGENT, ACCOUNT NO.

ISSUING CARRIER'S AGENT, NAME AND CITY

SIGNATURE OF ISSUING CARRIER OR ITS AGENT

AGENT'S IATA CODE

EXECUTED ON 18/2/83 AT Jamaica, NY
(Date) (Place)

5/
CURRENCY	DECLARED VALUE FOR CARRIAGE	DECLARED VALUE FOR CUSTOMS	AMOUNT OF INSURANCE
USD	none	$675.	none

INSURANCE — If shipper requests insurance in accordance with conditions on reverse hereof, indicate amount to be insured in figures in box marked "amount of insurance".

WEIGHT/ ROUTE/ VALUATION CHARGE PREPAID	COLLECT	ALL OTHER CHGES. AT ORIGIN PREPAID	COLLECT
X			

ACCOUNTING INFORMATION
bill shipper's account

6/
NO. OF PACKAGES RCP	ACTUAL GROSS WEIGHT	Kg./ lb.	Rate Class	COMMODITY ITEM NO.	CHARGEABLE WEIGHT	RATE/ CHARGE	TOTAL	NATURE AND QUANTITY OF GOODS (INCL. DIMENSIONS OR VOLUME)
2	752	L		GCR	752	1.91	L $1436.32	machine fittings 8 cu. ft.

7/ PRE-PAID
PREPAID WEIGHT CHARGE	PREPAID VALUATION CHARGE	DUE CARRIER	TOTAL OTHER PREPAID CHARGES	DUE AGENT	TOTAL PREPAID	FOR CARRIER'S USE ONLY AT DESTINATION
$1436.32		$45.00			1491.32	

R OTHER CHARGES (EXCEPT WEIGHT CHARGE, ROUTE CHARGE AND VALUATION CHARGE)
pick-up charge, Joe's Cartage $ 45.00

COLLECT CHARGES IN DESTINATION CURRENCY

S | COD AMOUNT

T | TOTAL CHARGES

8/ COL-LECT
COLLECT WEIGHT CHARGE	COLLECT VALUATION CHARGE	DUE CARRIER	TOTAL OTHER COLLECT CHARGES	DUE AGENT	COD AMOUNT	TOTAL COLLECT

9/ These commodities licensed by the United States for ultimate destination JAPAN .....Diversion contrary to United States law prohibited

as addressed

HANDLING INFORMATION (INCLUDING MARKS, NUMBERS AND METHOD OF PACKING ETC.)

RECEIVED IN GOOD ORDER AND CONDITION | SIGNATURE OF CONSIGNEE OR HIS AGENT
AT ON

COPY 11 (EXTRA COPY)

012-8813 3603

Air Waybill. Courtesy of Northwest Orient Airlines, St. Paul, MN

ALLOCATION CARTEL. An agreement among firms in a particular industry by which each participant is assigned certain customers or areas within which it will be the exclusive or principal supplier.

ALL PURPOSES. Also known simply as *purposes*, the total time for loading and unloading authorized to a vessel under the terms of its charter party.

ALL RISKS. A form of marine insurance coverage which provides that the insurer will be liable to the policyholder for all risks of loss or damage attributable to external forces, other than perils expressly omitted.

ALL TOLD. An expression used to describe the total deadweight capacity of a vessel, including water, stores, fuel, et cetera, in addition to cargo-carrying capacity.

ALL WATER SERVICE. A service provided by a steamship company whereby the goods are transported from the origin port to the destination port entirely by ship, without intervening overland carriage. For example, an *all water* shipment from Yokohama to New York would travel entirely by sea, usually through the Panama Canal. This type of service is contrasted with *mini-landbridge* service, under which the goods might travel by sea from Yokohama to Los Angeles and then overland by rail to New York. In both instances, the steamship operator would provide a Yokohama-New York bill of lading for the shipment and arrange for overland transportation, if necessary, at his expense. *See* LANDBRIDGE.

ALWAYS ACCESSIBLE. Also known as *reachable on arrival*, a provision in some charter parties by which the charterer undertakes to provide the vessel, immediately upon arrival, a berth at which it may load or discharge.

ALWAYS AFLOAT. A provision in some marine contracts, charter parties, and marine insurance policies that stipulates that the vessel is presumed to perform only in water of sufficient draft. In some contracts, the term *always safely afloat* is used.

ALWAYS SAFELY AFLOAT. *See* ALWAYS AFLOAT.

AMERICAN BUREAU OF SHIPPING. A nonprofit corporation founded in 1862 for the purpose of certifying the soundness and seaworthiness of vessels and other maritime engineering structures. The ABS, along with other recognized classification societies, establishes vessel standards and classifies individual vessels within each class. This system of vessel classification is essential to the marine insurance industry.

To date, more than fifteen thousand vessels of eighty nations have been classified by the American Bureau of Shipping, which maintains its headquarters in New York.

AMERICAN COMPONENTS ASSEMBLED ABROAD. Within the meaning of the Tariff Schedules of the Unites States, Annotated (TSUSA), imported merchandise which was assembled abroad from components produced in the United States and eligible for relief from duties on the value of the American components. Importation of such merchandise is addressed in Item 807.00 of the TSUSA, which defines eligible articles as:

> Articles assembled abroad in whole or in part of fabricated components, the product of the United States, which (a) were exported in condition ready for assembly without further fabrication, (b) have not lost their physical identity in such articles by change in form, shape, or otherwise, and (c) have not been advanced in value or improved in condition abroad except by being assembled and except by operations incidental to the assembly process such as cleaning, lubricating, and painting.

In computing the value for duty of articles under Item 807.00, the full value of the imported article will be reduced by the value of the American components. Because of the identity requirements, articles made abroad from American components which will be transformed, such as bolts of cloth or rolls of metal, for example, would not qualify under this tariff item.

See TARIFF SCHEDULES OF THE UNITED STATES.

AMERICAN DEPOSITORY RECEIPT. *See* INTERNATIONAL DEPOSITORY RECEIPT.

AMERICAN FOREIGN TRADE DEFINITIONS. *See* REVISED AMERICAN FOREIGN TRADE DEFINITIONS.

AMERICAN GOODS RETURNED. A provision, contained in Item 800.00, of the Tariff Schedules of the United States that permits duty-free return of merchandise of American manufacture. In order to qualify for duty-free return, the goods must not have been manipulated or advanced in value, except for the packaging of the product. *See* TARIFF SCHEDULES OF THE UNITED STATES.

AMERICAN HULL INSURANCE SYNDICATE LINER NEGLIGENCE CLAUSE. *See* LINER NEGLIGENCE CLAUSE.

AMERICAN INSTITUTE OF MARINE UNDERWRITERS. An association embracing virtually every insurance company writing ocean marine insurance cover in the United States. The organization serves as a conduit for information on legislative affairs affecting its members, provides data on marine casualties, and certifies marine surveyors.

The association was formed in 1898 and is based in New York.

AMERICAN MANUFACTURING CLAUSE. *Synonymous with* MANUFACTURING CLAUSE.

AMERICAN SELLING PRICE. A method formerly employed in the United States to establish the value for duty of a limited number of imported products. Under the ASP scheme, an imported product's value for duty was based upon the selling price of like products manufactured in the United States, irrespective of the price the importer actually paid.

The ASP mechanism was criticized by both U.S. importers and foreign suppliers, and it was rescinded for imports after July 1, 1980, by the Trade Agreements Act of 1979.

The ASP system is *not* authorized as an alternative method of valuation where the transaction value, constructive value, or deductive value cannot be determined or would be inappropriate. ASP was applied only in those instances where mandated by statute or presidential proclamation under authoriy of Section 336 of the Tariff Act of 1930. The following classes of merchandise were appraised under ASP: 1. Benzoid chemicals and products provided for in Schedule 4, Part 1, Tariff Schedules of the United States, Annotated (TSUSA); 2. Clams in airtight containers provided for in Item 114.04, TSUSA; 3. Footwear products specified in Item 700.60, TSUSA; 4. Knit wool gloves and mittens valued at not over $1.75 per dozen pairs, as provided for in Item 704.55, TSUSA.

See CUSTOMS VALUATION CODE.

AMERICAN TANKER RATE SCHEDULE. A schedule of nominal rates for tanker movements between world ports. Publication was ceased in 1969, and it has been succeeded by WORLDSCALE *(q.v.)*.

ANCILLARY RESTRAINTS DOCTRINE. A principle of U.S. antitrust law, regularly applied in foreign commerce cases, under which actions that might otherwise constitute a restraint of trade may be permitted if ancillary and subordinate to a larger, lawful agreement.

The doctrine was laid down by Justice William Howard Taft in the case of the United States versus Addison Pipe & Steel Company, stating that actions in restraint of trade must be cast down unless "ancillary to the main purpose of a lawful contract, and necessary to protect the covenantee in the enjoyment of the legitimate fruits of the contract, or to protect him from the unjust use of those fruits by the other party." (85 Fed. 271 [5th Cir., 1898].)

ANDEAN COMMON MARKET. *See* ANDEAN GROUP.

ANDEAN GROUP. Originally a subgroup within the now defunct Latin American Free Trade Area (LAFTA), the Andean Group was established by the Cartagena Agreement of 1969. The purpose of the group (also known as the *Andean Common Market* and the *Andean Subgroup*) is to foster economic integration of the member states. In 1984 the membership was composed of: Bolivia, Colombia, Ecuador, Peru, and Venezuela. Panama became an associate member in 1979; Mexico and Argentina often collaborate in group affairs, although they are not formal members. Chile, which was a founding member, withdrew in 1976.

In 1979, to commemorate the tenth anniversary of the founding of the group, the member states issued the Mandate of Cartagena, calling for increased political collaboration. The mandate observes that Andean integration is a prerequisite to a broader Latin American integration; to facilitate this integration, the mandate establishes: an Andean court of justice to ensure legal compliance with the integrative process; the Andean Parliament, which will maintain liaison with the national parliaments of the member states, and will propose legislation to enhance the integration process; and an Andean council, consisting of the foreign ministers of the member states, to harmonize external policies.

ANDEAN SUBREGIONAL GROUP. *See* ANDEAN GROUP.

ANGELL PLAN. A program, devised by James W. Angell, that called for reconstitution of the International Monetary Fund into a world central bank with currency-issuing authority. Under this proposal, individual national currencies would be retained for purely domestic settlements and, to a limited extent, for international settlements under IMF regulation.

The plan itself was received coolly, but the analysis performed by Angell, and the concept of a truly internationalized settlement medium, proved useful foundations in establishment of SPECIAL DRAWING RIGHTS *(q.v.)* by the International Monetary Fund.

ANNECY ROUND. *See* GENERAL AGREEMENT ON TARIFFS AND TRADE.

ANTEDATE. The act of dating a bill of exchange or other instrument with a date earlier than the date of execution. For example, a draft dated December 1, but actually drawn on December 5, would be antedated.

Antedating has no effect upon the negotiability of an instrument.

ANTICIPATED ACCEPTANCE. An acceptance that is redeemed prior to its due date.

ANTIDUMPING DUTIES. An additional duty, over and above ordinary duties, imposed upon imported merchandise sold at less than fair value when such imports are found injurious to domestic industry. *See* DUMPING.

ANTITRUST. Legislation or public policies opposed to the monopolization or domination of a particular product or industry by one firm or a group of firms acting in concert. The object of antitrust laws is to preserve market competition.

In the United States violation of the antitrust laws carries civil and criminal penalties. Victims of monopolies or unlawful combinations may sue in the Federal courts, individually or in *class action* suits, for relief as well as treble damages.

For details of the specific antitrust laws, *see* CLAYTON ACT, MONOPOLY, ROBINSON-PATMAN ACT, SHERMAN ACT.

ANY QUANTITY RATE. A freight rate applicable to a specific commodity irrespective of the quantity shipped, without provision for quantity discounts.

APPARENT GOOD ORDER. The condition of merchandise tendered for shipment or delivery where no damage to packing or other evidence of physical distress is apparent.

ARAB BOYCOTT. An economic boycott of Israel proclaimed in December 1945 by the Arab League to hamper "Jewish industry in Palestine." The boycott came to include not only Israeli firms and products, but firms having economic ties with Israel. A so-called blacklist of such firms was prepared by the Arab League's Boycott Office, and Arab nations are pledged not to deal with any blacklisted company. The proscription applies not only to manufacturers, but to service organizations, such as banks and insurance companies, as well. In response to the Arab boycott of Israel, and economic boycotts involving other nations, part 369 of the Export Control Regulations was invoked in 1965 to require U.S. exporters to report to the Secretary of Commerce any requests from foreign customers to comply with a foreign boycott. The regulations provided that exporters were "encouraged and requested to refuse to take (but are not legally prohibited from taking) any action . . . that has the effect of furthering or supporting such restrictive trade practices or boycotts." On November 20, 1975, the regulations were amended to forbid compliance with the boycott, imposing penalties for compliance. The reporting requirement was retained and, effective October 7, 1976, copies of boycott requests received by American firms and filed with the Secretary of Commerce were made publicly available.

In 1983, the Department of Commerce processed 37,500 boycott requests received and reported by U.S. firms.

ARAB LEAGUE. An association of independent Arab states formed for the purpose of advancing cooperation among the members in political, economic, and social matters. The league, formed in Cairo in 1945, has a permanent council and secretariat. A principal objective of the league since its formation has been to coalesce opposition to Jewish immigration to Palestine, and subsequently the establishment of Israel. In December 1945 the league proclaimed a boycott of "the products of Jewish industry in Palestine" which is still vigorously enforced virtually throughout the Arab world.

ARBITRAGE. The practice whereby foreign exchange or commodities are purchased in one market at lower cost and rapidly traded off in another, higher cost market. For example, if the pound sterling sells for $1.50 in Paris, but only $1.45 in New York, an *arbitrageur* could buy sterling in New York and immediately sell it in Paris at a profit, so long as the cost of performing the transaction does not exceed the difference between the market rates.

ARBITRATION ACT. *See* UNITED STATES ARBITRATION ACT.

ARBITRATION OF EXCHANGE. The near-simultaneous purchase and sale of foreign bills of exchange so as to take advantage of price differentials for such instruments in different money centers.

ARM'S LENGTH PRICE. The price at which a given commodity would sell in a sale between an unrelated buyer and seller. Arm's length pricing is the functional opposite of transfer pricing, in which the buyer and seller are related and the price is influenced by that relationship.

ARM'S LENGTH TRANSACTION. An economic transaction between unaffiliated parties undertaken as a product of commercial negotiation or market forces. Section 482 of the Internal Revenue Code authorizes the Internal Revenue Service to reallocate income to a domestic corporation when transactions with a controlled affiliate are unduly influenced by the corporate relationship.

ARRANGEMENT REGARDING INTERNATIONAL TRADE IN TEXTILE. *See* MULTIFIBER ARRANGEMENT.

ARREST. The restraint of a vessel by legal authority pending settlement of an admiralty suit. An *arrest* in maritime usage is the approximate equivalent of an attachment.

ARRIVAL DRAFT. A documentary draft payable upon the arrival of the goods. Customarily, the draft, without accompanying documents, is presented to the drawee upon receipt in the port of discharge; it must be accepted upon arrival of the vessel carrying the goods, or immediately thereafter. *See* BILL OF EXCHANGE.

ARRIVAL NOTICE. A document issued by a steamship line to the person or firm named in the bill of lading as notify party, advising when the goods will arrive, condition of the merchandise if other than sound, and any charges due.

ARRIVED SHIP. A vessel under charter that has arrived at its point of loading or discharge; LAYTIME *(q.v.)* will begin to accrue from the time of *arrival*. A vessel has *arrived* if it fills three conditions: (1) the ship must have docked at the point of loading or discharge, as provided in the charter agreement; (2) the ship must be ready to commence loading or discharge operations; and (3) appropriate notice of readiness must have been delivered to the shipper or consignee; normally, this notice must be in writing in advance of the arrival of the ship.

ARTICLES OF MIXED STATUS. Merchandise manufactured within a FOREIGN TRADE ZONE *(q.v.)* of components of more than one *status*. The status of merchandise is the product of several factors. An item in a foreign trade zone may possess PRIVILEGED FOREIGN STATUS, PRIVILEGED DOMESTIC STATUS, NONPRIVILEGED FOREIGN STATUS, or NONPRIVILEGED DOMESTIC STATUS *(qq.v.)*.

Upon withdrawal of merchandise fabricated within a zone, the finished product will be assessed duties in accordance with the status of the articles from which it was composed.

ARTIFICIAL CURRENCY UNIT. An international standard of value created by a multilateral agreement. An artificial currency unit (ACU) is not a currency in the conventional sense in that it cannot be used to settle private transactions. An ACU is given a value in terms of a *basket* of various national currencies in fixed or variable proportion.

Unlike national currencies, which are created to settle domestic accounts, ACUs are designed purely for the settlement of international transactions between official bodies.

Although created by official international bodies as reserve assets, ACUs, defined as a mixture of the currencies of major trading nations, tend to be more stable than any single currency. For this reason, some major banks offer accounts and borrowing facilities denominated in terms of the largest ACU, SPECIAL DRAWING RIGHTS *(q.v.)*, and European currency units.

See EUROPEAN MONETARY SYSTEM.

ASEAN. *See* ASSOCIATION OF SOUTHEAST ASIAN NATIONS.

AS FREIGHTED. The process by which surcharges and accessorial charges on ocean freight are computed.

Most ocean tariffs provide for freight to be assessed on cargo by *weight* (usually a ton) or *measurement* (usually a cubic meter or forty cubic feet), whichever provides greater revenue to the carrier. Units of weight and measurement applying to a given commodity will be specified in the tariff. When the *as freighted* method is used, all surcharges will be assessed on the same basis, i.e., unit of weight or measurement, used to compute the base freight. For example, if freight is charged on the basis of the metric ton, then a fuel adjustment surcharge will be assessed for each metric ton.

ASIA DOLLARS. U.S. dollars on deposit in Asian banks.

ASIAN CURRENCY UNITS. A unit of account, employed in some Asian banks, equal to the U.S. dollar. The Asian currency unit arose to circumvent banking regulations which prohibited accounts denominated in terms of foreign currency.

ASIAN DEVELOPMENT BANK. A multilateral development bank formed in 1966 to provide capital to Asian and Pacific countries to expand their economic infrastructure and industrial base. Capital is contributed to the bank by its members, which include both *regional*, i.e., Asian, and *nonregional* states.

At the beginning of 1983, the authorized capital stock of the bank consisted of 716,000 shares, with a par value of 10,000 SPECIAL DRAWING RIGHTS *(q.v.)* each. For the period 1967–82 bank lending exceeded U.S. $11.5 billion, distributed over the following sectors:

Sector	Percentage
Agriculture	29.8
Energy	25.7
Transport & communications	14.1
Development Banks	12.7
Water & sanitation	7.7
Social & education	6.6
Industry & mining	3.4

Membership in the bank and distribution of shares at the outset of 1983 were as follows:

Regional Members

Participant	Shares	Percentage
Afghanistan	1,195	.167
Australia	49,937	6.974
Bangladesh	8,812	1.231
Bhutan	110	.015
Burma	4,700	.656
Cambodia	875	.122
China (Taiwan)	9,400	1.313
Cook Islands	23	.003
Fiji	587	.082
Hong Kong	4,700	.656
India	54,637	7.631
Indonesia	47,000	6.564
Japan	117,500	16.410
Kiribati	35	.005
Korea (South)	43,475	6.072
Laos	246	.034
Malaysia	23,500	3.282
Maldives	35	.005
Nepal	1,269	.177
New Zealand	13,254	1.851
Pakistan	18,800	2.626
Papua New Guinea	810	.113
Philippines	20,562	2.872
Singapore	2,937	.410
Solomon Islands	58	.008
Sri Lanka	5,005	.699
Thailand	11,750	1.641

Participant	Shares	Percentage
Tonga	35	.005
Vanuatu	58	.008
Viet-Nam	6,038	.843
Western Samoa	58	.008

Nonregional Members

Participant	Shares	Percentage
Austria	2,937	.410
Belgium	2,937	.410
Canada	45,143	6.305
Denmark	2,937	.410
Finland	1,175	.164
France	14,687	2.051
German Federal Republic	37,334	5.214
Italy	11,750	1.641
Netherlands	6,462	.903
Norway	2,937	.410
Sweden	1,175	.164
Switzerland	4,037	.564
United Kingdom	17,625	2.461
United States	117,500	16.410

AS LAYTIME. A condition in some vessel charter agreements stipulating that time lost to the vessel because the charterer, shipper, or consignee cannot provide a berth for the ship will count *as laytime*, i.e., LAYTIME *(q.v.)* will begin to run and continue to run until the vessel docks and begins working.

This condition is expressed in some charter parties as "time lost waiting for berth."

See CHARTER PARTY.

AS PER ADVICE. A notation on some bills of exchange and drafts indicating that the drawee has been informed that the bill is to be presented.

ASSAILING THIEVES. Persons employing force in the act of stealing a vessel or its cargo, as contrasted with persons engaged in surreptitious thefts, or members of the ship's company engaged in pilferage.

ASSAY. A metallurgical test performed on metals, usually gold or silver, to assess the degree of fineness or purity. An assay certificate, or the stamp of the assayor in the metal bar, is a customary prerequisite to the sale of bullion.

ASSAY OFFICE BAR. A bar of gold or silver of a specified degree of fineness having undergone examination by a recognized assay office that attests to the stated purity of the metal. Customarily, assay office bars of gold are offered in 400 troy ounce units, while silver is offered in 1,000 troy ounce bars.

ASSEMBLY SERVICE. A service provided by some common carriers whereby small lots of cargo bound for a single consignee are shipped to the carrier's terminal to be aggregated into a single shipment. When a predetermined volume of cargo has been amassed, it is shipped as a unit to the consignee.

This type of service frees the consignee from the inconvenience of multiple, small deliveries and affords a lower per unit cost of transportation due to economies of scale.

ASSET CONVERSION LOAN. A loan that finances the purchase or manufacture of inventory, the proceeds from the sale of which serve to repay the loan.

ASSET CURRENCY. *See* GENERAL ASSET CURRENCY.

ASSIGNED RAILCAR. A railcar that is dedicated to the sole use of a particular firm for a specified period of time.

ASSIST. Inputs to production, including tools, dies, blueprints, designs, or development engineering provided by an American importer to a foreign manufacturer for use in producing merchandise for export to the United States. Such inputs must be declared to U.S. Customs on the first importation of the merchandise into the United States. The value of the assists may be subject to U.S. duties, on the rationale that, had the foreign manufacturer procured the inputs locally, they would have been included in the sale price to the American importer, and would have been subject to duty. In most cases, duty on the value of the assists may be paid upon first importation of the goods, or amortized over the life of the production cycle.

The Trade Act of 1979 removed U.S. research and design work from the category of assists on the grounds that these were *American ideas returned.*

ASSOCIATED FOREIGN CORPORATION. As used in conjunction with the operations of a DOMESTIC INTERNATIONAL SALES CORPORATION *(q.v.)*, or DISC, a foreign corporation in which neither the DISC nor members of the DISC's corporate family own 10 percent or more of the total voting stock, but possess a lesser equity position, which "reasonably furthers a transaction or transactions giving rise to qualified export receipts for the DISC" (Sec. 993-5[d][1], Internal Revenue Code).

ASSOCIATION CAPTIVE. *See* CAPTIVE INSURANCE COMPANY.

ASSOCIATION OF NATURAL RUBBER PRODUCING COUNTRIES. *See* INTERNATIONAL COMMODITY ORGANIZATION.

ASSOCIATION OF SOUTHEAST ASIAN NATIONS. Commonly known by the acronyn ASEAN, a regional cooperation association concerned with the promotion of economic development and trade among the member states.

The group was founded at Bangkok in 1967 by Indonesia, Malaysia, Philippines, Singapore, and Thailand. ASEAN lay dormant until 1976, when an action program was adopted and a permanent secretariat established at Jakarta.

Recent developments include approval, effective July 1980, of tariff preferences on 1,948 items, bringing to 4,325 the number of preferential trading items among the group; adoption of several industrial projects, with at least one project to be constructed in each member state; the signing, in March 1982, of an agreement for commercial and economic cooperation with the European Economic Community; and agreement to establish an ASEAN Agricultural Development Center, to be funded by the United States.

ATA CARNET. A document that can be used to effect the temporary admission of certain items into a country without completing normal customs formalities. The *ATA* is derived from the combination of the French and English terms *Admission Temporaire—Temporary Admission.*

A carnet is issued by the local affiliate of the Paris-based International Chamber of Commerce and is used to cover specific items only. The carnet is valid for multiple uses within a one-year period. In the event the user of a carnet does not re-export the merchandise within the prescribed period, the customs authorities will look to the issuer of the carnet for payment of duties.For this reason, the issuing agencies charge a small fee and ask to be indemnified against duty obligations that may arise.

The United States permits the use of carnets to cover temporary admission of commercial samples, advertising materials, and professional equipment.

Current adherents to the convention permitting use of ATA carnets are:

Australia, Austria, Belgium, Bulgaria, Canada, Cyprus, Czechoslovakia, Denmark, Finland, France, German Federal Republic, Greece, Hong Kong, Italy, Ivory Coast, Japan, Luxembourg, Netherlands, New Zealand, Norway, Hungary, Iceland, Iran, Ireland, Israel, Portugal, Poland, Romania, Senegal, South Africa, Spain, Sweden, Switzerland, Turkey, United Kingdom, United States, Yugoslavia.

ATHWARTSHIP. The condition of lying across the beam of a vessel.

ATTACHÉ. An officer of diplomatic rank, usually assigned to an embassy, but occasionally assigned to a consulate or other mission, for the purpose of studying a specialized area of interest about the country to which he is accredited and reporting to his home government.

Very often, attachés are not career diplomats but are specialists from agencies of government other than the foreign ministry; for example, the Ministry of Trade may assign one of its trade specialists to an embassy abroad as commercial attaché for the purpose of studying the host country for export opportunities.

ATTORNEY IN FACT. Any person who is empowered by another to act in his place. It is not necessary for the person acting as "attorney" to be a lawyer. In most cases, the power to act as attorney is conveyed by the principal in writing. The power of attorney so granted may be limited to the performance of a single transaction, or may be a general power of attorney, thereby permitting the attorney to act for the principal in virtually all matters.

AUTARCHY. A nation that is economically self-sufficient. Efforts toward achieving a state of autarchy usually encompass significant governmental controls over the economy, especially in the areas of international trade and dealing in foreign exchange.

Autarchy is a national policy pursued almost invariably for political reasons, usually in preparation for war.

AUTHORITY TO PAY. *Synonymous with revocable* LETTER OF CREDIT *(q.v.).*

AUTHORITY TO PURCHASE. An instrument used primarily by Far Eastern banks to finance import purchases. The authority-to-purchase instrument resembles, and is often confused with, a letter of credit, although it lacks some of the features of a letter of credit.

The authority instrument directs the negotiating (i.e., advising) bank to purchase the beneficiary's drafts upon the performance of prescribed actions, usually the shipment of merchandise, as evidenced by the submission of shipping documents.

An authority to purchase calls for drafts to be drawn upon the purchaser of the merchandise, rather than upon the opening or advising bank. In the event that the authority instrument does not clearly state that the bank is to purchase the drafts at face value, it is likely that the bank will regard any draft as a collection item. In addition, the instrument may provide for drafts to be drawn "with recourse"; under such circumstances, should the buyer repudiate the draft, the bank will look to the drawer for refund of the sums paid.

In the event that the authority instrument provides for drafts to be purchased at face value and without recourse, and if the instrument is confirmed by the negotiating bank, the authority provides the seller with essentially the same protection as a letter of credit.

Authority-to-purchase instruments have been largely supplanted by letters of credit.

See LETTER OF CREDIT.

AUTOMOTIVE PRODUCTS TRADE ACT OF 1965. An act of Congress that implemented the U. S.-Canadian Auto Agreement, creating a free trade area permitting duty-free movement between the two countries for automobiles and parts used as original equipment. The agreement does not cover replacement parts.

AUTONOMOUS DUTY. A rate of duty imposed by law, as contrasted with concessional duties which arise as the result of treaty or other international agreement.

AVAL. A form of guarantee given by a bank or other party to enhance the value of a negotiable instrument. While an aval acts as an unconditional and transferable guarantee of an instrument, the exact scope or nature of the guarantee may not be evident.

Avals are well established in Continental law and practice, although there is no equivalent to them in the common law countries; accordingly, avals are not recognized, per se, in common law courts, but are imputed to have the features of an endorsement to the instrument.

AVERAGE PROPENSITY TO IMPORT. *See* PROPENSITY TO IMPORT.

AVOIR FISCAL. A tax credit permitted in France to the recipient of dividend income, recognizing that the corporation issuing the dividend has already paid taxes on the income.

B

BACAT. *See* BARGE-ABOARD-CATAMARAN.

BACK LETTER. A letter of indemnity issued by a shipper of cargo to a steamship line to secure issuance of a clean bill of lading where one might not be issued otherwise. For example, a carrier may initially refuse to issue a *clean* bill of lading for cargo which appears to be damaged; a notation to this effect on the bill of lading would normally preclude collection by the shipper under a letter of credit. To prevent issuance of an *unclean* bill of lading, the shipper might provide the carrier with a back letter stipulating that the goods are sound, despite appearances to the contrary, and holding the carrier harmless.

Also, a retroactive clarification of the terms or conditions of a charter party.

BACKSPREAD. In arbitrage, the less-than-customary margin between purchase and sale price.

BACK-TO-BACK LETTER OF CREDIT. A letter of credit raised to purchase goods that will be sold under a different letter of credit. A broker or other intermediary who is the beneficiary under a customer's letter of credit may use that credit as collateral to open a second letter of credit to actually purchase the goods it plans to sell. Under such circumstances, the documentary requirements of both letters of credit must be the same, except that the broker may substitute his invoice for the one supplied by the manufacturer of the goods.

BACKWARD VERTICAL INTEGRATION. *See* VERTICAL INTEGRATION.

BACKWASH EFFECT. An adverse economic condition which arises from excess emphasis upon export expansion. The condition is common among developing countries, which are compelled to expand exports to secure foreign currency with which to fund essential imports. By targeting export industries for expansion, resources are often denied to industries producing for the home market. As a result, domestic manufacturing suffers and industrial self-sufficiency is delayed.

BAD ORDER. A railcar awaiting repair, or otherwise out of service.

BAILEE. A person or firm entrusted with temporary possession of the personal property of another. Possession of the goods by the bailee conveys no title and the bailee must surrender them to the owner upon completion of the purpose that gave rise to the bailment. A steamship carrier, for example, is bailee for the shipper's merchandise.

The law permits *bailees for hire*, such as common carriers and public warehousemen, a lien on the goods for unpaid charges.

BAILEE RECEIPT. A document used in import financing evidencing title to merchandise. The importer executes a bailee receipt as a condition of receiving from his bank negotiable bills of lading, acknowledging the title holder of the goods to be the bank, for whom the merchant serves as agent.

If the merchandise is sold by the importer on an *open account* basis, the invoices will bear the notation "Transferred and payable to the XXX Bank," or similar wording, directing the purchaser to remit to the bank. In a *cash-with-order* transaction, the purchaser's check would normally be deposited with the bank holding the bailiee receipt. Upon settlement of the bank's interest, the balance of the proceeds would be turned over to the importer.

Some banks prefer to use bailee receipts rather than trust receipts when financing imports, because with bailee receipts, the bank retains actual title to the goods, whereas trust receipts convey security interest.

BAILMENT. A contract by which one person (*bailor*) entrusts personal property to another person (*bailee*) for some specific purpose. All contracts for the carriage of goods, for example, are bailments.

BAILOR. A person who temporarily entrusts personal property to another for the accomplishment of a specified purpose. A shipper of cargo is a bailor when he entrusts his goods to a railroad for the purpose of transporting the merchandise to a given destination.

BAKSHEESH. A gift or payment to a business associate or government official in the Middle East in anticipation of, or as an inducement to, completion of a business deal.

The gratuity so provided is not regarded (by the recepient, at least) as a bribe, but as a token of esteem and friendship.

BALANCED GROWTH. National economic growth, as measured by an increase in the popular standard of living, achieved by the coordination of three factors: (1) reduction in dependence upon raw materials production as the primary source of national income; (2) intensification of manufacturing, especially in the area of consumer goods; and (3) stimulation of purchasing power through an intensification of agricultural productivity.

The principles of balanced growth were articulated by the Estonian-born economist Ragnar Nurske (1907–59), who asserted that nations remained poor because capital formation was impeded by low real income; low income also precluded development of a viable market. Nurske saw increased agricultural productivity as a vehicle to expand the disposable incomes of the general population; the concomitant increase in demand would stimulate manufacturing, thereby shifting dependence from low-value raw materials production.

BALANCE OF PAYMENTS. The sum owed to or by a nation as the result of its international transactions during a given time period, usually one year. The balance of payments is calculated by subtracting the nation's total payments to foreigners from total income received from foreigners, and includes not only commercial transactions, but gifts to residents, foreign aid, and sales or purchases of reserve assets such as monetary gold.

The principal components of the balance of payments are: *Balance of Trade account*—which consists of the sum total of merchandise exports (receipts) less merchandise imports (outflows). *Service transactions*—the sum of sales of services (e.g., tourism, insurance, banking, shipping) less purchase of services from foreigners. The product of the balance of trade and service accounts constitutes the balance of goods and services. *Transfer Payments*—this includes sums received or expended without reciprocation, including foreign aid, remissions by foreign workers to their families at home, and gifts. The balance of goods and services, combined with the net transfer payments account constitute the balance on current account. *Capital Transactions Account*—which is the product of investment inflows, less investment outflows. The net capital transactions balance, combined with the balance on current account, are the basic balance, also known as the balance on current account and long-term capital transfers. *Reserve Transactions Account*—represents the net product of a nation's purchase and sale of international reserves (gold, hard currencies, and SPECIAL DRAWING RIGHTS (*q.v.*) issued by the INTERNATIONAL MONETARY FUND (*q.v.*). The net reserve transactions balance, when added to the basic balance, constitutes the official settlements balance for the nation.

For most countries, the balance of trade is usually the largest single factor in the balance of payments.

When a nation's total income from international transactions exceeds expenditures to foreigners during a given time period, the nation enjoys a "positive" balance of payments, or a balance of payments "surplus"; conversely, when expenditures abroad exceed income from foreigners, the nation suffers a balance of payments "deficit" or a "negative" balance of payments. A shortfall caused by a balance of payments deficit must be offset by borrowing or by transfer of official reserves to creditor nations.

To assist nations suffering short-term or chronic balance of payments difficulties, the International Monetary Fund has established various lending facilities.

BALANCE OF TRADE. The sum total, in monetary terms, of a nation's merchandise (i.e., "visible") exports less the value of merchandise imports during a given time period, usually one year. Merchandise imports and exports are contrasted with trade in "invisibles," which are services such as shipping, banking, insurance, and tourism.

If, during the reporting period, the nation exports more than it imports, it is said that the nation enjoys a balance of trade "surplus," or a "positive" balance of trade; if, however, more is imported than exported, the nation suffers from a "negative" balance of trade, or a trade "deficit" (*see* figure).

A trade surplus provides savings to a nation, which may be used to satisfy foreign debt, enhance domestic consumption by increasing imports of foreign merchandise, provide wealth for investment abroad, or create credits in the nation's international reserves. Conversely, a trade deficit, especially if it is chronic, may involve a reduction of the nation's reserves, borrowing to cover the shortfall, or economic controls to reduce imports.

For most countries, the balance of trade is the largest single component of the BALANCE OF PAYMENTS (*q.v.*).

BALANCE ON CURRENT ACCOUNT. A component of a nation's BALANCE OF PAYMENTS (*q.v.*) (*see* figure).

BALANCE ON GOODS AND SERVICES. A component of a nation's BALANCE OF PAYMENTS (*q.v.*).

BALE CARGO. Cargo bound in burlap or similar material for international shipment.

BALESPACE. The internal cargo-carrying capacity of a vessel, including hatchways, expressed in cubic feet.

Component Factors of a Nation's Balance of Payments*

Total receipts	*minus*	*Total payments*	*equals*	*Balance of payments*
Merchandise exports		Merchandise imports		Balance of trade
Service exports		Service imports		Balance of goods & services
Transfer payments		Transfer payments		Balance on current account
Capital inflows, e.g., Investment Government borrowing Long-term private borrowing		Capital outflows, e.g., Investment Government borrowing Long-term private borrowing		Basic balance
Sales of reserves		Purchases of reserves		Official settlements balance

*Each balance shown in this table is the *cumulative sum of the balances above it*. For example, the balance on current account includes the sum of the balance of goods & services, which itself includes the balance of trade.

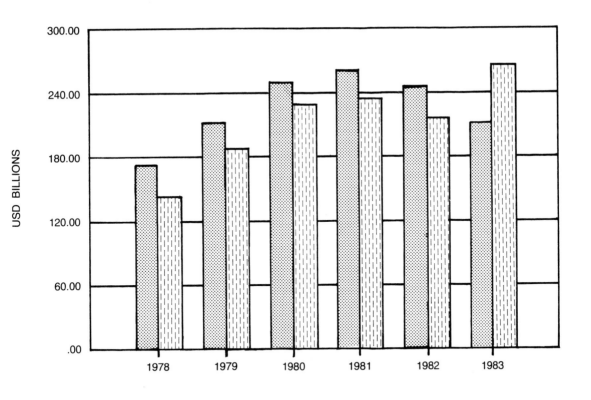

United States Merchandise Exports/Imports

1978-1983

EXPORTS
IMPORTS

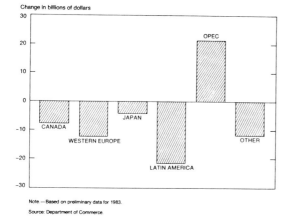

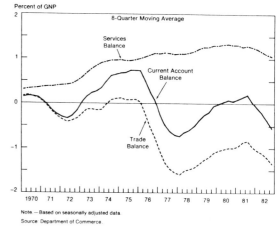

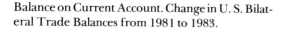

Balance on Current Account. Change in U. S. Bilateral Trade Balances from 1981 to 1983.

Balance on Goods and Services. Balances on Current Account, Trade, and Services as Percent of GNP.

BALLAST. Weighty material carried by a ship when partially or completely empty so as to stabilize the vessel in the water.

BALLAST BONUS. Additional compensation paid by charterers to a vessel's owners to position the ship close to or at the port of loading. The bonus is designed to defray the cost of running the ship empty or at less than capacity to a distant port to pick up cargo.

BALLOON CARGO. A cargo of low density, especially one that fully occupies the internal cubic capacity of a conveyance without approaching the vehicle's weight limitations.

BALLOON PAYMENTS. One or more payments toward the end of a loan that are significantly larger than the payments earlier in the life of the loan. *See* BULLET PAYMENT.

BANANA REPUBLIC. Term for any of several Central American republics that have been largely dependent upon banana exports as a source of foreign exchange. The term is used generally, in a disparaging sense, to refer to underdeveloped Latin American countries.

BANCOR. A proposed exchange to be issued by the INTERNATIONAL CLEARING UNION *(q.v.)* operating essentially as a world central bank. The original plan was significantly modified and some of its provisions adapted at the Bretton Woods Conference. *See* BRETTON WOODS AGREEMENT.

BANKABLE BILL. A bill of exchange or similar instrument that may be readily discounted at a bank.

BANKABLE CHARTER. A charter party in which the shipper is of such credit worthiness or financial standing that the vessel owner may use the charter contract as collateral for loans. In some cases, long-term charter agreements with major firms may serve as the basis for the building of ships for future use to fulfill the terms of the charter contract.

BANKABLE PAPER. Debt obligations issued or endorsed by persons or firms of sufficiently high credit standing so as to render the instruments acceptable for discount or as collateral by commercial banks.

BANKER'S ACCEPTANCE. *See* BILL OF EXCHANGE.

BANKER'S BILL. A bill of exchange drawn by a bank upon a foreign bank. Usually, these bills are drawn upon credit balances with foreign banks so as to make exchange available locally, and are *clean* bills of exchange. *See* BILL OF EXCHANGE.

BANK EXPORT SERVICES ACT. A 1982 act of Congress that amends Federal banking laws to permit banks to acquire equity, up to 100 percent, in Export Trading Companies. The act forms Title II of the Export Trading Company Act. *See* EXPORT TRADING COMPANY ACT.

BANK FOR INTERNATIONAL SETTLEMENTS. An international bank owned and controlled by the central banks of twenty-four European and five non-European central banks. The BIS was formed at the Hague Conference of 1930 in response to pressures for the restructuring of German war debts. In addition to the German reparations problem, the advent of the Great Depression and demise of the gold standard enhanced the need for international monetary cooperation and improved facilities for monetary operations. The bank commenced operations in Basel, Switzerland, on May 17, 1930, as an international institution, exempt from Swiss banking laws.

The principal function of the bank is to hold deposits and make loans to member central banks. Funds not currently required for central banking operations are invested in short-term liquid instruments. The bank's unit of account is the *gold franc,* consisting of .2903 grams of fine gold.

In addition to actual banking activities, the BIS serves as an important forum for central bankers and international banking experts.

The member states in 1984 were: Australia, Austria, Belgium, Bulgaria, Canada, Czechoslovakia, Denmark, Finland, France, Federal Republic of Germany, Greece, Hungary, Iceland, Ireland, Italy, Japan, Netherlands, Norway, Poland, Portugal, Romania, Spain, South Africa, Sweden, Switzerland, Turkey, United Kingdom, United States, Yugoslavia.

A general meeting of representatives of the central banks holding stock in the BIS is held annually. Voting is proportional to the number of shares held in each country. The Board of Governors consists of the heads of the central banks of Belgium, France, Germany, Italy, and the United Kingdom as ex officio members, plus up to five other representatives of business and industry, selected one each by the ex officio members. The United States is entitled to two ex officio seats on the board but does not occupy them. The board meets monthly to establish policy. Since the Second World War, the chairman of the board also has acted as president of the BIS. The United States is represented in bank affairs by the Federal Reserve Bank of New York.

The BIS operates with a staff of three hundred, all based in Basel, Switzerland.

BANKING AND FINANCING CONTROLLED FOREIGN CORPORATION. A controlled foreign corporation within the meaning of the Internal Revenue Code, that derives more than 50 percent of its gross income from retail or commercial banking, negotiable paper transactions, or investment banking.

BANKING EDGE. *See* EDGE ACT CORPORATION.

BANK PAPER. A bill of exchange or other negotiable that has been accepted or endorsed by a bank.

BANK-POST REMITTANCE. A settlement of a matured bill of exchange sent by a commercial bank to the foreign maker of the bill. A bank check is the customary form of remittance.

BANK RATE. The rate at which the Bank of England and the Bank of Canada lend to commercial banks.

BAR DRAFT. The distance between the water's surface and an underlying bar. This figure is important in determining whether a given ship may pass over the bar.

BAREBOAT CHARTER. A time charter under which the charterer assumes full operational control of the chartered vessel, to include providing officers, crew, and supplies. A bareboat charter is also known as a *demise charter.*

BAREBOAT COMPONENT. A vessel that is hired out on a bareboat charter. *See* CHARTER PARTY.

BARGAIN PURCHASE OPTION. A provision of a lease agreement that permits the lessee to purchase the leased asset at a price expected to be below fair market value.

BARGE. A shallow draft, walled-in marine conveyance used to haul cargo, usually in bulk. A barge may be self-propelled, although it is more commonly pulled or pushed by a tug or other vessel. Barges are used principally on inland waterways, although some oceangoing vessels are specially equipped to carry barges. *See* LIGHTER ABOARD SHIP.

BARGE-ABOARD-CATAMARAN. A method for the transport of ocean cargo by use of a small barge, which is filled at a waterfront facility and towed to a twin-hulled (catamaran) mother ship for transport abroad. The catamaran may also carry larger LASH (LIGHTER ABOARD SHIP, *q.v.*) barges between the twin hulls. This service was inaugurated in Denmark in 1973, for use between Scandinavian destinations.

BARGE-ON-BOARD. A method for the carriage of ocean cargo employing a large capacity barge that is loaded at river, lake, or harbor points and towed to an ocean port where the barge is lifted aboard an oceangoing vessel for transport abroad. Upon arrival at the port of destination, the barge is discharged into the harbor to be towed to destination, often many miles upriver or along the coast. This type of service, which began in 1969, includes BARGE-ABOARD-CATAMARAN, FLASH, LASH, and SEABEE *(qq.v.)* systems.

BARRATRY. An act committed by a master or mariners contrary to their duties to the ship, including, inter alia, mutiny, sabotage, and theft of cargo.

BARREL BARK. A unit of cargo measurement equal to five cubic feet.

BARRÉ PLAN. A scheme to enhance the European economy through monetary unification. Articulated in February 1969 by Raymond Barré, then vice-president of the European Community Commission, and later premier of France, essentially the plan provided that each member state of the European Community would set aside a portion of its monetary reserves to aid, as the need arose, other members suffering balance of payments difficulties. Through consultations between borrower and lender, efforts would be undertaken to restore financial equilibrium. The loan would mature after three months, unless arrangements between the parties involved resulted in a longer repayment schedule.

In addition, the plan advocated greater overall alignment of European economies and urged that central banks, rather than governments, be the focus for negotiations on economic matters.

The Barré Plan was adopted by the EEC Council of Ministers in July 1969.

BARTER. A direct exchange of products without cash. In some cases, a third party is brought into the transaction to dispose of some or all of the goods in a third country; this practice is known as *switch trading. See* COUNTERTRADE.

BASEL AGREEMENT. An agreement, concluded April 24, 1972, among members of the European Economic Community for the purpose of narrowing the margins of fluctuation among community currencies. Participants in the agreement were Belgium, Germany, France, Luxembourg, Italy, and the Netherlands. The agreement served as the basis for the European currency SNAKE *(q.v.).*

BASEL CLUB. A reference to the central bankers of the industrialized nations, so called because of their regular meetings in Basel, Switzerland, at the Bank for International Settlements.

BASEL CONCORDAT. An informal, voluntary agreement among the banks of major trading nations relative to bank oversight and international banking practices.

Following the collapse of the Herstatt Bank in 1974, the Bank for International Settlements formed a Committee on Banking Regulations and Supervisory Practices; commonly known as the Cooke Committee, this group draws its membership from bankers in the GROUP OF TEN *(q.v.)* countries, including Switzerland. The principal functions of the committee, which began meeting in 1975, are to coordinate regulatory supervision of banks operating outside their home country, and to provide a forum within which international bankers may discuss issues of wide interest in the international banking community.

The Basel Concordat is the principal published work of the Cooke Committee; it was adopted, with the concurrence of the central banks of the Group of Ten countries and Switzerland, in December 1975. The concordat embraces five precepts:

1. Banks operating outside their home country are responsible to the regulatory authorities of both the home and host countries, and both countries share responsibility for the adequacy of such supervision.

2. All banking institutions must be subject to supervision.

3. The host country should assume primary responsibility for ensuring that adequate liquidity is maintained; a major exception arises relative to Eurocurrency liquidity, which may be exempt from local oversight, in recognition of "local practices and regulations."

4. Supervision of solvency is assigned to the home country in the case of branches; where a foreign bank forms a local subsidiary, however, the primary responsibility for solvency shifts to the host country. This provision of the concordat is modified by a 1978 pronouncement of the Cooke Committee that solvency oversight lies in the domain of the home country, which should consolidate overseas operations into the parent for supervisory purposes.

5. Regulatory authorities in the home and host countries should seek to establish a dialogue permitting the exchange of information, and home country officials should be permitted to inspect the operations of foreign branches and subsidiaries.

The divergent banking systems of the participating nations have impeded total implementation of the principles of the concordat; for example, there is lack of uniformity on what constitutes a *bank.* In addition, local bank secrecy laws often thwart thorough supervision.

After several years' experience with the concordat in its current form, the Cooke Committee is considering several revisions, given impetus in part by the Banco Ambrosiano affair. In any case, the agreement has no legal effect outside the Group of Ten countries and Switzerland; nevertheless, it serves as a useful focus for the growth of international bank supervision, and its principles, refined over the years, may be adopted by the bankers of other nations as well.

The Basel Concordat, although adopted in 1975, was not released to the public until March 1981.

BASEL CREDITS. International credit facilities created on an ad hoc basis at meetings of the BANK FOR INTERNATIONAL SETTLEMENTS *(q.v.).*

BASE PERIOD. A given period of time, usually one year, that is used as the standard against which to measure activities in other years. For example, if the purchasing power of the dollar in various years is to be compared, we may use a year, say 1970, as the base period and may speak of purchases in 1975 in terms of 1970 dollars.

BASE PRICE. As used in conjunction with the Common Agricultural Policy of the European Economic Community, a trigger price for specific commodities at which member states will intervene to support the market price of a commodity. Member states may respond to a decline in market prices below the base price by large-scale purchases to increase prices, or may impose levies upon commodities from foreign producers to prevent disruptive competition from abroad.

BASE RATE. The specific commodity or general class rate applicable to a product in a common carrier's tariff. Various surcharges, fuel adjustments, currency adjustment factors, et cetera, may be imposed on top of the base rate; they are often expressed as a percentage of the base rate.

BASIC BALANCE. In balance of payments accounting, the sum of the *current account* plus net *long-term capital transactions,* public and private. *See* BALANCE OF PAYMENTS.

BASIC NEEDS. A code word for OFFICIAL DEVELOPMENT ASSISTANCE *(q.v.)* programs aimed toward the improvement of health care, education, nutrition, and like fundamental services in poorer nations. The basic needs concept has been criticized by some nations as a purely stop-gap welfare approach. These nations confuse *basic* with *immediate* needs of survival, while ignoring the capital and productive base necessary for the poorer nation to rise out of poverty and sustain its own national well-being.

BASING POINT SYSTEM. A system wherein freight is charged from a nominal shipping point (i.e., the basing point), irrespective of the point from which the goods are shipped. For example, if the basing point is New York, a customer in Chicago will be charged freight from New York, even if the goods are actually shipped from Minneapolis.

BASIS. As used in commodities trading, either: 1) the difference between the spot price and the futures price, or 2) the difference between the cash market price at a given geographic point and the cash market price at a current delivery point, i.e., a point where there is active trading in the tangible commodity.

BASIS POINT. A unit of measure equal to one-hundredth of a percent, used in expressing rates of interest on loans, usually where significant sums are involved.

BATTLE ACT. Known officially as the *Mutual Defense Assistance Control Act of 1951,* an act of Congress designed to discourage foreign nations from exporting strategic materials to the Soviet bloc. The act requires that an officer of the State Department be assigned the duties of administrator to compile and maintain listings of strategic items, divided into two parts: List 1 contains armaments and nuclear materials; List 2 includes petroleum and derivatives, certain transportation equipment, and implements for weapons production. Any nations found to be exporting List 1 items to the Soviet camp are denied all U.S. military and economic assisstance; nations exporting items on List 2 also may be denied American aid at the discretion of the president.

The Battle Act has been recodified in the Arms Export Control Act of 1976.

BEARER INSTRUMENT. A negotiable instrument made payable to *bearer* or any negotiable instrument endorsed in blank. As a practical matter, an instrument in bearer form is owned by the person possessing it and may be transferred by mere delivery.

BEAUFORT SCALE. A scale of wind force at sea, adjusted for the angle between the direction of the wind and the ship's course and speed. The figure shows how wind force is expressed.

Beaufort Scale

Beaufort Number	Sea Conditions	Knots
0	Calm	less than 1
1	Light air	1 - 3
2	Light breeze	4 - 6
3	Gentle breeze	7 - 10
4	Moderate breeze	11 - 16
5	Fresh breeze	17 - 21
6	Strong breeze	22 - 27
7	Moderate Gale	28 - 33
8	Fresh gale	34 - 40
9	Strong gale	41 - 47
10	Whole gale	48 - 55
11	Storm	56 - 65
12	Hurricane	over 65

BEGGAR-MY-NEIGHBOR TACTICS. The policy of expanding one nation's exports at the expense of other countries. Common vehicles for implementing such policies include currency depreciations designed to make export prices more attractive to foreigners, and significant tariff increases. Usually such practices are of limited value as they generally induce retaliation on the part of nations whose trade has been injured. *See* EXPORT UNEMPLOYMENT.

BELLY PIT. A cargo storage compartment located below the cabin of an aircraft.

BELT LINE. A short-line railway operating in and around a city; its function is to transfer cargo between long-haul railroads, and to and from piers to railroads for import/export movements.

BENEFICIARY. The party named in a letter of credit as authorized to draw bills of exchange for acceptance by the issuing bank.

BENEFICIARY DEVELOPING COUNTRY. As provided in Section 501 of the Trade Act of 1974, any nation or possession of a nation authorized by the president to be accorded duty-free entry of merchandise into the United States under the GENERALIZED SYSTEM OF PREFERENCES *(q.v.).* The act specifically excludes some countries from designation eligibility, and some products, irrespective of country of origin. The act also provides criteria under which the president is obliged to withdraw or suspend eligibility for GSP treatment.

BENEFIT OF INSURANCE CLAUSE. A provision contained in some ocean bills of lading providing that the ocean carrier is not liable for cargo losses where the merchandise is covered by insurance. This provision has been upheld by the courts (Phoenix Insurance Company vs. Erie & Western Transport Company, 117 U.S. 312, 6 S.Ct. 750 1886) but has been circumvented by insurance companies; the insurers, having been denied an opportunity to subrogate against the shipowner to recover sums paid on cargo losses, devised the *loan receipt*. Most marine policies now provide that the insurer does not *settle* with the insured in the conventional sense, but rather loans the insured the amount of the settlement, pending completion of litigation against the vessel; the amount is advanced by the insurer in the name of the insured.

The benefit of insurance clause has been disallowed by the Carriage of Goods by Sea Act on bills of lading subject to that act, although the provision may be used in trade not subject to the act.

BENELUX. An acronym for Belgium-Netherlands-Luxembourg. Following World War II, the three nations formed a customs union with long-range objectives of establishing a single monetary and fiscal system. The localized objectives of the three Benelux countries were redirected into the larger scheme for European unity with the advent of the European Communities.

BENEVOLENT NEUTRALITY. The condition in which a nation does not actively participate in warfare but supports the efforts of a belligerent through economic or political support, or by similar means.

BERNE UNION. An association of public and private financial institutions engaged in issuing export credit insurance. Known officially as the *International Union of Credit and Investment Insurers,* the group was founded at Berne, Switzerland, in 1934 to establish uniform criteria and standards for export credit insurance so as to diminish distortions of trade that might otherwise occur if some nations were granting such credit more liberally than others.

For many years, the association was headquartered in Paris but moved to London in 1976.

BERTH. A stipulation in a vessel CHARTER PARTY *(q.v.)* that LAYTIME *(q.v.)* will commence when the ship has taken up its berth, irrespective of when it arrived in port.

The term *berth clause* is synonymous with *in regular turn* or *term clause 2* and may be modified by the stipulation that laytime may commence after a specified period of time in the port waiting for a berth, whether or not a berth is actually available.

BERTH NO BERTH. A stipulation that may be included in a vessel CHARTER PARTY *(q.v.)* providing that if the point of loading or discharge is a berth, and if the berth is not immediately available upon the arrival of the vessel in port, the vessel owner may give NOTICE OF READINESS *(q.v.)*, after which LAYTIME *(q.v.)* will begin to run.

In some charter parties, this stipulation is expressed by the statement "Whether in berth or not."

BIG EIGHT. The eight currencies in which the preponderance of the world's trade is transacted: U.S. dollar, French franc, pound sterling, Swiss franc, Deutschmark, Canadian dollar, Japanese yen, and Italian lira.

The seven non-U.S. currencies cited, in the aggregate, routinely account for 90 percent of all foreign exchange transactions in New York.

BILATERAL AGREEMENT. In general, any treaty, protocol, or understanding between two nations.

The term has particular application in the area of commercial air transportation, where a *bilateral agreement* is an understanding between two countries permitting the commercial aircraft of one nation to land in and carry cargo and/or passengers into and out of the territory of another, usually in return for similar privileges.

BILATERAL CENTRAL RATES. *See* EUROPEAN MONETARY SYSTEM.

BILATERAL EXCHANGE RATES. *See* EUROPEAN MONETARY SYSTEM.

BILATERAL PARITIES. *See* EUROPEAN MONETARY SYSTEM.

BILATERAL RESTRAINT AGREEMENT. Any agreement, understanding, or program involving governmental authorities, producers, trade associations, or labor unions in one country and their counterparts in another country to control or limit trade in specified products. Generally, such agreements arise where one nation finds that domestic producers of a given product have lost substantial market share in their home market to producers concentrated in one or a few foreign countries. The importing country, confronted with the loss of jobs at home due to foreign competition, will urge the foreign exporters to reduce or halt exports for a period of time so that the injured domestic industry will have an opportunity to recover. The foreign producer is threatened with economic reprisals (such as increased duties or quotas) should there be a failure to comply with the request for 'voluntary' controls on exports.

Depending upon the circumstances, bilateral restraints may take any of several forms:

Orderly Marketing Agreement—a restraint agreement concluded between the United States and the government of the foreign producer. The authority to negotiate such agreements is vested in the president in section 203 of the Trade Act of 1974. Negotiations are conducted for the president by the United States trade representative. Orderly marketing agreements are limited initially to a period of five years from the date of the presidential proclamation, and the relief accorded must be phased down after three years unless it is found by the president that to do so would be inimical to the national interests. Should such a finding be made, import relief granted under the agreement could be extended for three more years. U.S. law permits the conclusion of agreements limiting exports to the United States only with foreign governments.

Voluntary Export Restraint—a restraint agreement, between governments, within the context of the Multifiber Agreement.

Voluntary Restraint Agreement—an agreement between a government and a nonofficial body (such as a supplier, labor union, or trade association), or between two nonofficial bodies, to limit exports. The legality of such agreements has been challenged in U.S. courts. A 1972 agreement between the U.S. government and foreign steel producers was challenged in the case of Consumers Union of the United States vs. Kissinger (506 F. 2d, D.C. Cir., 1974). Consumers Union asserted that the State Department lacked legal authority to conclude a restraint agreement with any party other than a government and in so doing illegally impeded competition in steel to the detriment of American consumers. The conflict was resolved when Congress passed a special act to retroactively authorize the steel pact.

To clarify the legal position of any future agreement between the U.S. government and nonofficial bodies, the attorney general of the United States in a letter to the U.S. trade representative, dated February 18, 1981, issued the following opinion: "In summary, this Department believes that although the President has inherent legal authority to negotiate directly with foreign governments to seek import restraints, where such negotiations are implemented through voluntary private behavior serious antitrust risks arise. Foreign or United States governmental 'approval', 'urging', or 'guidance' of such behavior cannot safely be relied on as a defense; if the foreign government does not provide adequate protection by mandating the restraints in a legally binding manner, private antitrust suits could jeopardize the effective implementation of any agreements that are negotiated."

Products covered by binding orderly marketing agreements are listed in Appendix 9, part 2.A. of the Tariff Schedules of the United States.

BILL OF CREDIT. A document requesting or directing the addressee to extend credit to a party stipulated in the letter. The person issuing the letter serves as a guarantor for any credit so extended.

BILL OF EXCHANGE. An instrument used extensively in the settlement of international transactions, it is a written, unconditional, and negotiable demand for payment of a specific sum of money, in terms of a given currency, at a prescribed date.

The term *bill of exchange* is commonly used interchangeably with *draft* even by experienced international merchants and bankers. Technically, the terms are not interchangeable, however. A bill of exchange is always negotiable, whereas a draft may or may not be negotiable. In addition, a bill of exchange requires a currency conversion (i.e., exchange transaction) at some point, while a draft does not. Hence, it might be said that bills of exchange arise from international transactions, whereas drafts are used in domestic commerce.

Bills of exchange generated by the sale of goods are known as *commercial bills;* when bills are drawn to settle accounts between financial institutions or to obtain foreign exchange, the instruments so generated are called *financial* or *banker's bills.*

Mechanically, bills are drawn by a *maker* (or *drawer*) and transmitted to the party from whom payment is demanded (the *drawee*) by a third party, usually a bank representing the maker. Upon presentation of the bill, the drawee may *accept* the instrument, thereby creating a lawful obligation to pay the face amount of the bill upon maturity. Acceptance is effected by writing "Accepted" across the face of the bill and signing underneath. Customarily, the presenting bank will prestamp the bill, requiring only the drawee's signature to create the acceptance. In the event the drawee declines to accept the bill, the instrument is said to be *dishonored*, and the bank will refer to the maker for instructions.

Bills accepted by a bank are known as *banker's acceptances*, while bills accepted by commercial firms are known as *trade acceptances*. As a rule, banker's acceptances are preferable to trade acceptances, as there is a ready market in which banker's acceptances may be sold or discounted; such facilities exist for trade acceptances only when the accepting firm is well known and enjoys a high credit standing.

A bill which is due and payable immediately upon presentation is said to be drawn *at sight*. A bill may be due at a specified period of time after presentation, e.g., thirty or sixty days; such a bill would be drawn at *thirty* or *sixty days' sight.* For example, a bill drawn at thirty days' sight would mature (i.e., become payable) thirty days after presentation to and acceptance by the drawee. It is assumed that the acts of presentation and acceptance will be almost simultaneous; if the instrument is not accepted shortly after presentation, it will be presumed dishonored. The only exception to the rule requiring acceptance immediately upon presentation is to be found in those jurisdictions allowing *days of grace.*

In many cases a bill may be drawn a number of days after *date*, which is to say the instrument matures the specified number of days after the date on the face of the bill, irrespective of the date it is presented to the drawee. For example, a bill drawn at thirty days date on June 1 matures on June 30, even if it is accepted on June 25.

Any bill of exchange that provides for a maturity later than *sight* (i.e., immediately upon presentation to the drawee) is said to be a *time bill.*

$150,000.00

December 24   19 84

At ***120*** days sight pay

One Hundred Fifty Thousand U.S.   Dollars

Value received, and charge the same to account of

ACCEPTED
Authorized Signature
BANK OF EUROPE
January 1, 1985

...h Export Company

John Smith

To   Bank of Europe
      For the account of Jones Import Company
No.   transaction 12345   Smith Export Company – Authorized Rep.

Francis d'Argent

Bill of Exchange

The preponderance of bills of exchange are drawn in conjunction with the sale of goods and are, therefore, commercial bills. Very often, the bills so drawn are submitted by the maker's bank to the drawee accompanied by negotiable bills of lading or other documents conveying title to the merchandise. Usually, the bank is instructed to release the title documents only upon acceptance of the bill by the drawee. This mechanism effectively denies the drawee access to the bills of lading or other documents necessary to secure possession of the goods until the bill of exchange has been accepted. Any bill of exchange accompanied by bills of lading, invoices, or other documents is a *documentary bill of exchange* (or, more commonly, a *documentary draft*); bills of exchange not so accompanied are *clean bills*. In most cases, documentary bills are sent by the maker to the presenting bank attached to a *direct collection letter*, which is a preprinted form listing instructions such as what to do with the bill in the event of dishonor, whether the acceptance, when created, should be held to maturity or discounted, and whether the proceeds should be remitted by check or cable.

Upon acceptance, a bill of exchange becomes an unconditional obligation of the accepting party; the obligation so created is listed on the financial statement of the obligee under the heading "Bills Payable." The accepted bill (or *acceptance*, as it is now known) may be held to maturity by the maker or his bank, at which time it will be presented to the acceptor with a demand for payment. The holder of the bill has the option, however, of *discounting* the instrument, in which case the bill is endorsed by the holder and sold in the money market for the face amount, less a sum reflecting the prevailing interest rate for the time to maturity of the instrument. As a practical matter, the discounting party remains responsible for the bill to any future holder in the event of default on the part of the acceptor.

In some cases, bills of exchange are drawn in multiple copies, any of which may be accepted by the drawee; the issuance of multiple copies reflects the old practice of sending out more than one set of documents in hope at least one would arrive intact. In cases where the bills are said to be issued in a *set*, i.e., multiple copies, each copy will bear a notation on the face as *first of exchange*, *second of exchange*, et cetera; where the bill is issued in one copy only, the instrument so raised is known as a *sole of exchange*, a *sola*, or *solus*.

BILL OF LADING. A document issued by a carrier to a shipper acknowledging receipt of the goods, and stating the points of pick-up and delivery, as well as other information relative to value declared for carriage, terms and conditions of transport, freight charges, et cetera. The bill of lading is the most fundamental of all documents in the transport of goods, although the form of the bill varies substantially among different modes of transport (such as rail and water) and from carrier to carrier. All bills of lading have two features in common: (1) they serve as a receipt from the carrier for the merchandise; and (2) they are contracts of carriage between the carrier and shipper. Commonly, *short form* bills are used; these do not include full terms of the contract of carrige but incorporate them by reference. Bills that include the full text of the contract of carriage are *long form* bills.

Bills of lading may be negotiable or nonnegotiable. Bills that are consigned *to order* of a named party may be transferred by endorsement and delivery in the same manner as a check. The endorsement and delivery of a bill of lading serve to transfer title to the goods named in the bill. Although the law provides for the use of negotiable bills of lading on domestic rail and motor shipments, the use of such instruments is rare; virtually all domestic shipments move under nonnegotiable, or *straight*, bills of lading. Negotiable bills of lading are widely used in connection with international shipments by water. Bills of lading for air shipments (generally known as *air waybills*) are never negotiable.

As a practical matter, it is the shipper of the goods who actually prepares the bill of lading, presenting it to the carrier for validation or signature when the goods are taken up for shipment. If the carrier signs off on the bill without any notation that the count is incorrect or that the merchandise is damaged or distressed, the bill is said to be *clean*; any bill bearing notations of damage or incorrect count is *unclean* or *foul*.

In the case of merchandise that is dangerous, fragile, or peculiar in size or shape, the carrier may be obliged to stow the goods or handle them in a manner more apt to cause loss or damage; bills of lading covering such shipments are often *claused* with statements relieving the carrier of responsibility for loss or damage in transit. For example, shipments of flammables by sea are stowed on deck to permit ready access and discharge overboard in the event of fire; any bill covering such a shipment will bear the clause "On Deck at Shipper's Risk" or words of like import. Claused bills of lading are unclean bills and are not acceptable for shipments where payment is expected under a letter of credit unless the credit expressly authorizes the use of such bills (*see* figures, next pages).

BILL OF SUFFERANCE. A document given by customs authorities to coastal vessels authorizies the movement of goods in bond.

BILLS IN A SET. Negotiable instruments issued in duplicate or triplicate; for example, ocean bills of lading are usually issued in triplicate, while bills of exchange are often issued in duplicate. This practice arises from earlier days when documents were apt to be lost in transit, necessitating multiple mailings to ensure that at lease one would arrive.

Any part of the set is sufficient to the accomplishment of its purpose, and after any part of the set (e.g., any third of the bill of lading) has been used, the remaining parts are rendered invalid.

BILLS PAYABLE. In conventional commercial usage, the sum of trade acceptances and notes outstanding and payable upon maturity.

BIMETALLISM. A system in which a nation defines its monetary unit in terms of a specified quantity of gold and silver, in a specific ratio of one metal to the other (*mint ratio*). Both metals are minted in unlimited quantities and each enjoys legal tender status.

BIND (TARIFF). An act whereby a nation withholds a proposed tariff rate increase on one or more products.

BINDER. A temporary, often abbreviated document evidencing that insurance coverage has been effected. A binder is an interim measure until the full policy is prepared.

BLADING. A contraction of *bill of lading*, used commonly in writing and speech.

BLANK ENDORSEMENT. An endorsement on a bill of lading, check, draft, or other negotiable instrument that does not specify to whom the instrument is endorsed. An instrument beomes bearer paper as the result of a blank endorsement, and may be negotiated thereafter by delivery alone.

BLANKET INVENTORY LIEN. A financing arrangement whereby a lending institution receives a lien on all the inventories of a borrower. Inasmuch as the lien does not distinguish between goods covered, the borrower may be able to dispose of all or part of its inventory, thus reducing the value of the lender's collateral.

BLOCKADE. An interdiction of maritime traffic to and/or from a given port or nation by the naval forces of another nation. Blockades usually arise out of declared war or other belligerent condition between the country whose area is blockaded and the country whose forces have imposed the blockade.

To be legally valid, any nation seeking to impose a blockade must proclaim its intention to do so. In addition, the Declaration of Paris of 1856 requires that the blockade be effective and maintained by sufficient force in order to be recognized.

BLOCKED ACCOUNT. Currency held in a bank account in an exchange control country by nonresidents. Such currency cannot be transferred out of the country in which it is held without permission from the government.

BLOCKED EXCHANGE. An exchange restriction, imposed by governmental authority, that forbids the unlicensed purchase of bills of exchange, currency, or negotiable instruments denominated in a foreign currency. The object of this measure is to prevent transmission of foreign currency reserves out of the country. The blocking mechanism impedes trade inasmuch as local merchants are unable to secure the foreign funds necessary to pay for imports.

In some cases, import obligations are satisfied by depositing local currency in a domestic bank for the account of the foreign seller, who must then await relaxation of the exchange restriction, or use the funds locally, perhaps to purchase local goods for export.

BLOCK RATE. A reduced rail freight rate levied on movements of ten or more cars at one time from one shipper to a simple consignor.

THE GREAT REPUBLIC LINE

BILL OF LADING

Shipper/Exporter Johnson International Corp. One World Trade Center New York, 10048	**Document No.** **Export references** Sales order No. 123456
Consignee Smith Manufacturing Company, Ltd. 21 Vicarage Lane Bexhill-on-Sea, Sussex England	**Forwarding agent — references** FMC No. 1A Reliable Forwarder, Inc. 26 Rector Street New York
	Point and country of origin / **Place of receipt** Bridgeport, Connecticut
Notify party Brown & Company 10 Newgate Street London, E.C. 1, England	**Domestic routing/Export instructions**
Pier Howland Hook Marine Terminal	
Exporting carrier (vessel) Santa Maria / **Port of loading** New York	**Onward inland routing** / **Place of delivery**
Port of discharge Felixstowe / **For transhipment to** London	

PARTICULARS FURNISHED BY SHIPPER

Marks and numbers	No. of pkgs.	Description of packages and goods	Gross weight	Measurement
JIC Smith Co. 1-up	40	Printing Machinery and accessories	16,845 lb.	1867 cu.ft

FREIGHT COLLECT

THESE COMMODITIES LICENSED BY U.S. FOR ULTIMATE
DESTINATION UNITED KINGDOM DIVERSION CONTRARY
TO U.S. LAW PROHIBITED.—

Freight and charges

	Prepaid	Collect	
1867 cu. ft. @ $120/40 cu. ft.		5601. --	
Fuel surcharge $25. as freighted		1166. 67	
CAF, 3% as freighted		168. 03	
Due: USD		6935. 70	

☐ PREPAID   ☒ COLLECT

RECEIVED the goods in apparent good order and condition and, as far as ascertained by reasonable means of checking, as specified above unless otherwise stated.
The Carrier, in accordance with the provisions contained in this document.
a) undertakes to perform or to procure the performance of the entire transport from the place of receipt to the place of delivery stated above, and
b) assumes liability as prescribed in this document for such transport.
One of the Bs/L must be surrendered duly endorsed in exchange for the goods or delivery order. IN WITNESS where of THREE (3) original Bs/L have been signed, if not otherwise stated, one of which being accomplished the other to be void.

Signed for

THE GREAT REPUBLIC MARITIME SHIPPING COMPANY, LTD.

d/b/a GREAT REPUBLIC LINE

Dated at *New York*

MO **3**   DAY **10**   YEAR **85**   BL No **1078-A**

(To be Printed on "Yellow" Paper)

UNIFORM ORDER BILL OF LADING

Original—Domestic

Shipper's No. 0123

Agent's No.

XYZ Trucking .... Carrier. .... (SCAC)

RECEIVED, subject to the classifications and tariffs in effect on the date of the issue of this Bill of Lading.

From CBA Supplies .... , Date June 30 , 19 82

At 1100 25th St. Street, Chicago .... City, ... County, IL State Zip 60601

the property described below, in apparent good order, except as noted (contents and condition of contents of packages unknown) marked, consigned, and destined as shown below, which said company (the word company being understood throughout this contract as meaning any person or corporation in possession of the property under the contract) agrees to carry to its usual place of delivery at said destination, if on its own railroad, water line, highway route or routes, or within the territory of its highway operations, otherwise to deliver to another carrier on the route to said destination. It is mutually agreed, as to each carrier of all or any of said property over all or any portion of said route to destination, and as to each party at any time interested in all or any of said property, that every service to be performed hereunder shall be subject to all the conditions not prohibited by law, whether printed or written, herein contained, including the conditions on the back hereof, which are hereby agreed to by the shipper and accepted for himself and his assigns.

The surrender of this Original ORDER Bill of Lading properly indorsed shall be required before the delivery of the property. Inspection of property conveyed by this bill of lading will not be permitted unless provided by law or unless permission is indorsed on this original bill of lading or given in writing by the shipper.

Consigned to Order of ABC Manufacturing ....

Destination 123 Main Street, Columbus ...... City, ... County, OH State Zip 43204

Notify ....

At .... Street, ... City, ... County, ... State .... Zip

Routing XYZ Trucking direct ....

Delivering Carrier .... Vehicle or Car Initial YZ No. 0102

No. Pack-ages	O HM	Kind of Package, Description of Articles, Special Marks, and Exceptions	*Weight (Subject to Correction)	Class or Rate	Check Column	Subject to Section 7 of conditions, if this shipment is to be delivered to the consignee without recourse on the consignor, the consignor shall sign the following statement:
1		Crate, Mine or Quarry Drilling Machines, NOI NMFC Item 125120 sub 4 cl 85	500 lbs.			The carrier shall not make delivery of this shipment without payment of freight and all other lawful charges.
3		Boxes, Drilling Machine Bit Shanks NMFC Item 125150 cl 70	75 lbs.			(Signature of consignor)
1		Box, Drilling Machine Parts NOI NMFC Item 125180 sub 2 cl 85	50 lbs.			If charges are to be prepaid write or stamp here "To be Prepaid." To be Prepaid
						Received $ to apply in prepayment of the charges on the property described hereon. Agent or Cashier Per (The signature here acknowledges only the amount prepaid)

* If the shipment moves between two ports by a carrier by water, the law requires that the bill of lading shall state whether it is "carrier's or shipper's weight."

Note—Where the rate is dependent on value, shippers are required to state specifically in writing the agreed or declared value of the property.

The agreed or declared value of the property is hereby specifically stated by the shipper to be not exceeding .... per ....

Charges advanced:

$

CBA Supplies .... Shipper .... Agent.

Per J. Doe .... Per ....

Permanent address of Shipper: Street, 1100 25th Street City, Chicago State IL Zip 60601

O **Mark with "X"** to designate Hazardous Materials as defined in the Department of Transportation Regulations governing the transportation of hazardous materials. The use of this column is an optional method for identifying hazardous materials on bills of lading per Section 172.201(a)(1)(iii) of Title 49, Code of Federal Regulations. Also, when shipping hazardous materials, the shipper's certification statement prescribed in Section 172.204(a) of the Federal Regulations must be indicated on the bill of lading, unless a specific exception from this requirement is provided in the Regulations for a particular material.

Uniform Order Bill of Lading for use by Motor Carrier

(To be Printed on White Paper)
UNIFORM STRAIGHT BILL OF LADING

Shipper's No. 0123

ORIGINAL—NOT NEGOTIABLE—Domestic
Agent's No.

XYZ Trucking .... Carrier. .... (SCAC)

RECEIVED, subject to the classifications and tariffs in effect on the date of the issue of this Bill of Lading.

From CBA Supplies , Date June 30 , 19 83

Street, 1100 25th ST   City, Chicago   County,   State IL   Zip 60601

the property described below, in apparent good order, except as noted (contents and condition of contents of packages unknown) marked, consigned, and destined as shown below, which said company (the word company being understood throughout this contract as meaning any person or corporation in possession of the property under the contract) agrees to carry to its usual place of delivery at said destination, if on its own railroad, water line, highway route or routes, or within the territory of its highway operations, otherwise to deliver to another carrier on the route to said destination. It is mutually agreed, as to each carrier of all or any of said property over all or any portion of said route to destination, and as to each party at any time interested in all or any of said property, that every service to be performed hereunder shall be subject to all the conditions not prohibited by law, whether printed or written, herein contained, including the conditions on the back hereof, which are hereby agreed to by the shipper and accepted for himself and his assigns.

Consigned to ABC Manufacturing

On Collect on Delivery Shipments, the letters "COD" must appear before consignee's name or as otherwise provided in Item 430, Sec. 1

Street, 123 Main ST

City, Columbus   County,   State OH   Zip 43204

Routing XYZ Trucking   direct

Delivering Carrier .... Vehicle or Car Initial   YZ   No. 0102

Collect On Delivery $ .... and remit to:

.... Street .... City .... State

C. O. D. charge } Shipper ☐
to be paid by } Consignee ☐

No. Pack- ages	O HM	Kind of Package, Description of Articles, Special Marks, and Exceptions	*Weight (Subject to Correction)	Class or Rate	Check Column	
1		Crate, Mine or Quarry Drilling Machines, NOI				Subject to Section 7 of conditions, if this shipment is to be delivered to the consignee without recourse on the consignor, the consignor shall sign the following statement:
		NMFC Item 125120 sub 4 cl 85	500 lbs			The carrier shall not make delivery of this shipment without payment of freight and all other lawful charges.
3		Boxes, Drilling Machine Bit Shanks NMFC Item 125150 cl 70	75 lbs			
1		Box, Drilling Machine Parts NOI NMFC Item 125180 sub 2				(Signature of consignor)
		cl 85	50 lbs			If charges are to be prepaid write or stamp here "To be Prepaid."
						To be Prepaid
						Received $ .... to apply in prepayment of the charges on the property described hereon.
						Agent or Cashier
						Per ....
						(The signature here acknowledges only the amount prepaid)

* If the shipment moves between two ports by a carrier by water, the law requires that the bill of lading shall state whether it is "carrier's or shipper's weight."

Note—Where the rate is dependent on value, shippers are required to state specifically in writing the agreed or declared value of the property.

The agreed or declared value of the property is hereby specifically stated by the shipper to be not exceeding .... per ....

Charges advanced:

$

CBA Supplies .... Shipper .... Agent.

Per J. Doe .... Per ....

Permanent address of Shipper: Street, 1100 25 th ST   City, Chicago,   State IL

** Recommended C. O. D. Section to be Printed in Red.

O Mark with "X" to designate Hazardous Materials as defined in the Department of Transportation Regulations governing the transportation of hazardous materials. The use of this column is an optional method for identifying hazardous materials on bills of lading per Section 172.201(a)(1)(iii) of Title 49, Code of Federal Regulations. Also, when shipping hazardous materials, the shipper's certification statement prescribed in Section 172.204(a) of the Federal Regulations must be indicated on the bill of lading, unless a specific exception from this requirement is provided in the Regulations for a particular material.

Uniform Straight Bill of Lading for use by Motor Carrier

BLOCK VOTING. A condition within some steamship conferences whereby several carriers regularly vote in unison on various issues before the conference, especially as related to pricing. By employing this approach the block may gain effective control of the conference.

BOB TAIL. The act of operating a tractor without its trailer attached.

BOGEY. A chassis for a freight container; a two-axle chassis.

BONAFIDE MOTOR VEHICLE MANUFACTURER. Within the meaning of the Automotive Products Trade Act of 1965, a firm determined by the Secretary of Commerce to have the capacity to produce at least ten motor vehicles per week, and that has actually produced at least fifteen such vehicles in the preceding twelve months.

BONDED GOODS. Goods stored in a bonded warehouse prior to release from customs jurisdiction.

BONDED WAREHOUSE. A warehouse storage area, or manufacturing facility in which imported merchandise may be stored or processed without payment of customs duties. Such premises are operated by a warehouse proprietor who holds a license from the U. S. Customs Service. Bonded warehouses are divided into eight classes:

Class 1. Facilities operated by the U.S. government for the storage or examination of merchandise that has been seized or is undergoing examination.

Class 2. Private bonded warehouses, used exclusively for the storage of merchandise belonging to the warehouse owner.

Class 3. Public bonded warehouses, used solely for storage.

Class 4. Yards or sheds, usually enclosed, for the storage of oversized equipment or goods.

Class 5. Grain elevators.

Class 6. Manufacturing warehouses, limited to goods for export made, at least in part, from imported components or ingredients, and warehouses for the manufacture of cigars from imported tobacco.

Class 7. Smelting and refining warehouses employing imported ores.

Class 8. Manipulation warehouses, where imported merchandise can be cleaned, graded, repacked, or otherwise prepared for sale or re-exportation.

A bonded warehouse may be used to defer duties on goods not immediately required, or to modify the character of merchandise so as to mitigate duty obligations (e.g., to repack so as to reduce weight on an item subject to a specific duty).

Bonded warehouses should not be confused with FOREIGN TRADE ZONES (q.v.).

BOOK. The portfolio of insurance coverage written by an underwriter.

BOOKING. The reservation of cargo space aboard a vessel. In the case of container shipments, a booking number issued at the time the space is reserved is generally required to pick up an empty container from the ocean carrier.

BORDEREAUX. A printed form used to report several transactions; used especially in conjunction with marine insurance policies. The bordereaux lists many individual shipments under an OPEN POLICY (q.v.), all of which are reported periodically to the insurer.

BORDER TAX ADJUSTMENTS. A refund or rebate of indirect taxes on merchandise, such as sales or value added taxes, when the goods are exported. Such rebates are authorized under the GENERAL AGREEMENT ON TARIFFS AND TRADE (q.v.); rebate of direct taxes, however, is not permitted under the Agreement.

BOTH-TO-BLAME CLAUSE. A provision in an ocean bill of lading that addresses the responsibilities of the vessel to the cargo interests in the event of a collision at sea. The clause arises from an anomaly of maritime law whereby a vessel involved in a collision is exempted from liability to its own cargo (as provided in the Harter Act and Carriage of Goods by Sea Act) but enjoys no such immunity from liability for losses suffered by cargo aboard the other colliding ship.

When collision is attributable to mutual fault, damages are divided equally between the vessels. For example, if Vessel A suffers $1 million in losses (including cargo), and Vessel B suffers $500,000, then Vessel B will pay Vessel A $250,000 so that each ship will bear one-half of the aggregate loss arising from collision. It must be remembered that Vessel A is exempt from legal obligation for any loss suffered by the cargo it carried; Vessel B is not exempt for losses suffered by Vessel A's cargo and will throw this liability into the pot to be shared with Vessel A, thereby forcing Vessel A to subsidize Vessel B's obligation to the cargo on A, even though A is not liable for the loss to the cargo it carried.

In response to this apparent contradiction, ocean carriers have included in their bills of lading a clause whereby the cargo indemnifies the carrying vessel for any loss or expense arising from its contribution to the other vessel in satisfaction of that ship's liability for cargo damage. Such both-to-blame clauses vary from carrier to carrier, but the following is representative:

If the vessel comes into collision with another vessel as a result of the negligence of the other vessel and any act, negligence, or default of the Master, mariners, pilots, or servants of the carrier in the navigation or in the management of the vessel, the Merchant will indemnify the carrier against all loss or liability to the other non-carrying vessel or her owner insofar as such loss or liability represents the loss or damage to or any claim whatsoever of the owner of the said goods paid or payable by the other non-carrying vessel or her owner to the owner of said cargo and set-off or recouped or recovered by the other or non-carrying vessel or her owner as part of his claim against the carrying vessel or carrier. The foregoing provisions shall also apply where the owner, operator or those in charge of any vessels or objects other than, or in addition to, the colliding vessels or objects are at fault in respect of a collision or contact.

The effects of a both-to-blame clause in a bill of lading are: cargo would sue the vessel with which its own ship collided, collecting full damage; the non-carrying vessel would insert the cargo settlement so obtained into its bill of damages and costs, thereby deriving a 50 percent reimbursement from the colliding vessel; and the carrying vessel would sue the cargo for one-half its recovery from the noncarrying ship.

In 1952, in the case of the United States vs. Atlantic Mutual Insurance Company, the Supreme Court held that in the absence of specific statutory authority, a carrier might not relieve himself of responsibility for damages. There being no such specific authority granted to ocean carriers under the Harter Act nor under the Carriage of Goods by Sea Act, nor under other legislation, the both-to-blame provisions were declared invalid for use in the foreign and domestic waterborne commerce of the United States.

It should be noted that the both-to-blame clause continues to be included in bills of lading, despite the nullifying effect of the Atlantic Mutual case, largely on the contingency that a carrier might be able to invoke the clause in a receptive foreign jurisdiction.

BOTTLENECK INFLATION. A sharp increase in general price levels due to a dramatic, often unexpected increase in demand or decrease in supply. The *bottleneck* so created is usually overcome by an increase in supply over time.

BOTTOM. *Synonymous with* vessel; e.g., foreign flag ships may be called *foreign bottoms.*

BOTTOMRY. A contract whereby the owner or master of ship borrows for the use of the vessel, pledging the ship (or *bottom*) as collateral. It is stipulated that the loan shall be forgiven if the vessel is lost during the tenor of the loan or another stipulated period.

BOUND DUTY. A rate of duty that a nation agrees it will not raise without the concurrence of its trading partners.

BOUNTY OR GRANT. As provided in the Countervailing Duty Law (19 U.S.C. 1303), an economic inducement by a foreign government or association to a manufacturer in its country to encourage exports. These inducements include, but are not limited to loans and loan guarantees, at rates lower than those commercially available; grants of capital, or sale of goods, services, or raw materials at less than market prices; operating subsidies or forgiveness of debt; and absorption of production or distribution costs.

A finding by the International Trade Commission that bounties or grants have been provided to the foreign manufacturer may result in the imposition of COUNTERVAILING DUTIES *(q.v.).*

BOURGEOISIE. Middle- to upper-income commercial and professional classes. The term relates to the renewal of commerce at the end of the Middle Ages, when trade supported the growth of towns and cities, or *bourgs.*

BOURSE. A continental European term for a commodity or stock exchange.

BOYCOTT. A conspiracy or coalition for the purpose of impeding the commerce of another. Boycotts are often attempts to advance political objectives by economic means and fall into two categories: the *primary boycott,* in which a party to the boycott refrains from trading with the boycotted nation; and the *secondary boycott,* in which a party to the boycott attempts to induce others outside the conflict to adhere to the boycott, often as a condition of continued trade with the party making the request.

U.S. law prohibits any American person or firm from "taking or knowingly agreeing to take . . . actions with intent to comply with, further, or support any boycott fostered or imposed by any foreign country against a country which is friendly to the United States and which itself is not the object of any form of boycott pursuant to United States laws or regulations." The antiboycott law is administered by the Department of Commerce.

BOYCOTTAGE D'AGGRESSION. A boycott directed by a trade combination against a nonmember firm. If the boycott is animated by a legitimate commercial interest (rather than the mere elimination of a competitor), it may be regarded as legal.

BOYCOTTAGE SANCTION. In Europe, a boycott directed against a member of a trade combination as a penalty for departing from the combination's rules or otherwise failing to perform; it is regarded as lawful.

BRANCH RULE. A provision of the Internal Revenue Code that holds that where a controlled foreign corporation operates outside its country of incorporation through a branch, the branch will be treated as a separate corporation in determining foreign base company income, when the branch's activities have "substantially the same effect as operating as a wholly owned subsidiary." *See* SUBPART F.

BRANDT COMMISSION. A group of eighteen prominent individuals from five continents, formed to explore economic relationships between industrial and developing nations and to recommend changes in those relationships with the object of accelerating development in poorer countries.

Established as an unofficial working party, called the *Independent Commission on International Development Issues,* the group, under the chairmanship of former German chancellor Willy Brandt, issued a report of its finding in March 1980. The report, entitled *North-South: A Program for Survival,* stressed the interdependence of industrial and developing nations, particularly the reliance of the industrial nations upon the raw materials produced in Third World countries, and the role of developing countries in the recycling of excess funds. The report urged immediate actions: massive transfer of technological and financial resources to developing countries, both on market and on concessional terms; a global program to relieve hunger; and an energy strategy that would reduce demand on the part of industrial nations and help developing states bear the burden of increased energy costs. The Brandt Commission and its report served to lay the groundwork for United Nations efforts to devise a global energy strategy.

See NEW INTERNATIONAL ECONOMIC ORDER.

BRASSAGE. The charge imposed by a mint to cover the cost of converting bullion into coins.

BRASS PLATE COMPANY. *See* SHELL COMPANY.

BREACH DATE. A doctrine in law that holds that, in disputes involving sums denominated in a foreign currency, a court shall require settlement in local currency at the rate of exchange in effect at the time the contract was abrogated.

BREAK-BULK. Cargo shipped in cartons, drums, bales, or other such units and stowed directly into a ship's hold, without being loaded into an intermodal container.

BREAKING BULK. The commencement of discharge operations aboard a vessel.

BRETTON WOODS AGREEMENT. The product of an international conference on monetary and economic affairs held at the end of World War II, from which resulted the International Monetary Fund and the World Bank; the term is used most commonly in reference to a program for world monetary affairs that emerged from the conference and remained in effect until 1971.

In the summer of 1944, a conference of monetary and economic experts of the Allied powers was held at Bretton Woods, New Hampshire, to devise a plan for postwar reconstruction and economic stability. At this conference it was agreed that the U.S. dollar would serve as the principal trading and clearing currency, with a value equal to 1/35 ounce of gold; nations adhering to the agreement were obliged to establish a par value for their currencies in terms of dollars or gold. The International Monetary Fund was established to ensure exchange rate stability and facilitate resolution of payment imbalances among members. Each member of the fund pledged to maintain the relationship of its currency to the dollar within 1 percent of the established par; hence, if the market value of the local currency rose more than 1 percent over its par relationship to the dollar, the central bank of the affected nation would sell dollars and buy the local currency. Under this arrangement, any national currency might fluctuate within a range of 2 percent (1 percent either way) against its predetermined dollar value without central bank intervention.

The system, under International Monetary Fund supervision, provided that chronic exchange rate aberrations against the dollar would be accommodated by a change in the par value of affected currency against the dollar, i.e., *devaluation* (for those currencies persistently weak against the dollar) or *revaluation* (where the national currency has been undervalued against the dollar); such changes in par values were to be made only after consultation with the IMF.

In those cases where the par rate was to be revised by more than 10 percent, advance IMF approval was required, although this rule was ignored by some members.

Inasmuch as the U.S. dollar was the standard against which other currencies were valued, disturbances in the American economy profoundly affected the world monetary system. Expansionary monetary policies in the United States, caused by deficit spending to finance the Vietnam War and social programs, coupled with significant balance of payment deficits, generated concern about America's capacity to redeem dollars for gold at the prescribed rate of thirty-five dollars per ounce. This concern animated massive conversions of dollars into gold by foreign central banks, threatening U.S. gold reserves. In order to avoid depletion of American official gold stocks, President Richard Nixon suspended redemption of dollars for gold on August 15, 1971.

The act of suspending official conversion of dollars into gold upon demand served to break the link between the dollar and gold; in so doing, the value of the dollar was undefined. The absence of a precise value for the dollar, which was the standard for all other trading currencies, resulted in widespread disorder in exchange markets, with attendant fluctuation of currency values.

An effort was made to resurrect the Bretton Woods system in a conference held by the International Monetary Fund at the Smithsonian Institution in Washington in December 1971. At this meeting it was decided to widen the bank around the dollar from 1 percent to 2.25 percent in either direction, thereby permitting any currency to fluctuate as much as 4.5 percent from its par value against the dollar without central bank intervention. In addition, the dollar was devalued by 8.5 percent against gold.

The expanding monetary crisis was not deflected by the so-called Smithsonian Agreement. By the winter of 1973 the situation had deteriorated to the point where a further devaluation of the dollar, this time by an additional 11.5 percent, was deemed essential.

The February 1973 devaluation of the dollar did not provide the relief anticipated by monetary experts, and most nations abandoned efforts to maintain the fixed exchange rate scheme fundamental to the Bretton Woods agreement, preferring instead to permit their currencies to float freely in the market.

BRIDGE. *See* LANDBRIDGE.

BRIDGE CARRIER. A railroad that neither originates nor delivers a given lot of cargo; an intermediate carrier.

BRITISH DEPENDENT TERRITORIES. Those overseas possessions of Great Britain that have been associated with the European Communities as part of Britain's entry into the communities. Basically, the term applies to all overseas possessions of Britain other than Gibraltar and Hong Kong.

BROAD CAPTIVE. *See* CAPTIVE INSURANCE COMPANY.

BROAD MONEY. For purposes of calculating a nation's money supply, the sum of *narrow money* (i.e., currency in circulation plus private sector demand deposits) and *quasimoney*, including time and savings deposits and foreign currency deposits of residents.

BROKEN STOWAGE. Wasted space within the cargo holds of a ship. The amount of such space on any particular vessel or voyage may vary according to the configuration of the cargoes carried; e.g., rolls of paper will permit a greater loss of useful space than small cartons.

BROKERAGE. A commission paid to a licensed foreign freight forwarder by an ocean carrier as an inducement to route cargo aboard the carrier's vessels. This commission usually runs between 1.25 and 2.5 percent of the freight paid to the carrier, although higher commission rates are not uncommon, depending upon the trade route and the volume of cargo available. Brokerage is paid in addition to any fees paid by the exporter to the forwarder, and constitutes a prime source of the forwarder's income.

BRUSSELS DEFINITION OF VALUE. A system for the valuation of imports for the application of ad valorem duties, adopted in 1953 following attempts to establish a European customs union.

The European Customs Union Study Group submitted to the contracting states the Convention on the Valuation of Goods for Customs Purposes, along with conventions to adopt uniform tariff nomenclature and to establish the Customs Cooperation Council. All three proposals were signed in Brussels on December 15, 1950; the valuation agreement came into force on July 28, 1953.

The Brussels definition embraces the *notional* concept of value: that is, goods should be valued at the price at which such goods would sell under specified conditions, irrespective of the actual selling price of the given transaction. For duty purposes, adherents to the convention assess duties upon the *normal price* of the goods, which is determined according to the following assumptions: that goods are delivered to the buyer at the port or place of introduction into the country of importation; that the seller bears all costs, charges, and expenses incidental to the sale and to the delivery of the goods at the sale and to the port or place of introduction, which are hence included in the normal price; and that the buyer bears any duties or taxes applicable in the country of importation, which are hence not included in the normal price. The *normal price* itself is defined as the price that the goods would "fetch at the time the duty becomes payable on a sale in the open market between a buyer and a seller independent of each other."

The following states have acceded to the valuation agreement: Algeria, Cyprus, Haiti, Ivory Coast, Kenya, Korea, Nigeria, Pakistan, Portugal, Rwanda, Senegal, Spain, Tanzania, Tunisia, Turkey, Uganda, Yugoslavia, Zaire.

In addition to those nations that formally adopted the Brussels convention, many trading nations, with the notable exception of the United States, employed the Brussels definition as the basis of valuing imports for duty purposes. The adoption by most nations of the Customs Valuation Agreement that emerged from the Tokyo Round of multilateral trade negotiations has served to supplant the role of the Brussels definition; however, the Brussels definition may continue to be used as an alternative valuation scheme, even in those nations that have adopted the CUSTOMS VALUATION CODE (*q.v.*) agreement.

BRUSSELS PROTOCOL OF 1968. *See* VISBY AMENDMENT.

BRUSSELS TARIFF NOMENCLATURE. *See* STANDARD INTERNATIONAL TRADE CLASSIFICATION.

BUFFER STOCK. A commodity stockpile controlled by one or more nations for the purpose of stabilizing world prices of that particular commodity. The commodity is released into the market as world prices increase and is purchased for the stockpile as prices decline. The establishment of such a stockpile is normally the product of an INTERNATIONAL COMMODITY AGREEMENT (*q.v.*), with administration of the stockpile performed by a secretariat established for that purpose.

BUILDING. Used as a noun, a vessel. The term is used in conjunction with vessels under construction or already afloat; a newly launched vessel is said to be a *new building*.

BULK STOWAGE. The transport of a commodity loose, without packaging, inside a conveyance.

BULLDOG BONDS. Sterling-denominated debt obligations issued by entities outside the United Kingdom.

BULLET PAYMENT. Also known as a *balloon payment*, a large payment made at the end of an installment loan. In many cases, a bullet payment represents the repayment of principal at the end of an interest-only loan.

BULLION VALUE. The market value of the metal in a coin, as contrasted with the denominational value of the coin as money.

BULL RINGS. Metal rings recessed into the floor of a container or trailer to permit lashing of cargo.

BUNCHING. The condition that arises when the number of cars supplied by a railroad exceeds track capacity.

BUNDLED PRICING. An arrangement between buyer and seller in which the purchase price for certain goods also includes other goods or services, such as the right to use patents, technical assistance, replacement parts under a warranty, et cetera.

BUNKER. The fuel oil burned by a ship.

BUNKER CLAUSE. A provision common to certain charter parties stipulating that the charterer shall pay to the vessel owner the value of coal or fuel oil aboard the ship at the commencement of the charter, and the owner shall pay the charterer the value of all coal or fuel oil aboard the vessel upon the termination of the charter. The prices in effect at the respective ports at the time of commencement or termination shall be used.

It is common for minimum and maximum quantities to be stated in the charter agreement.

BUNKER SURCHARGE. A charge imposed by a steamship carrier, in addition to the basic freight, to offset the impact of sudden and transitory increases in the costs of fuel. Surcharges are usually expressed as a percentage of the basic freight.

BUREAU OF EXPLOSIVES. A component of the Association of American Railroads created to promote the safe handling of dangerous cargoes. The bureau was established in 1907 and was, for many years, the authoritative source of information on the transportation of dangerous goods.

In 1910 the bureau published a listing of dangerous, questionable, and exempted articles, and prescribed packaging and handling techniques for each hazardous item. In 1918 the Bureau of Explosives standards were incorporated into Federal law, and subsequent pronouncements of the bureau were adopted as Federal requirements.

The regulatory powers of the Bureau of Explosives have been effectively preempted by the De-partment of Transportation, which promulgates standards for the handling of hazardous substances by all modes of transport.

BUREAU VERITAS. One of the major international ship classification societies, established in France in 1826. Bureau Veritas establishes standards for, oversees the construction of, and classifies vessels and marine equipment, including cargo containers.

As of January 1, 1983, tonnage classified by the society amounted to 35,026,210 gross register tons, embracing 8,083 vessels; this constitutes 8.25 percent of the world's tonnage, and 11 percent of the world's fleet.

BUSINESS CYCLE. A pattern of business activity in which, over time, the economy reaches a high, declines, enters a low point, and expands upward, reaching a high and repeating the cycle.

Within the cycle, four phases can be identified: prosperity, recession, depression, and recovery.

While economists generally agree that a business cycle possesses each of the four phases, they disagree over the period of time required to make a complete circuit. Among the most significant cycles identified are the Kitchen Cycle (forty months), Juglar Cycle (nine to ten years), and Kondratieff Cycle (fifty-four to sixty years).

Various theories have been advanced to explain why business cycles occur. Among the better-known theories are the *psychological theory*, which holds that optimism and pessimism about the future are manifested in economic behavior, and the *monetary theory*, which attributes cycles to expansion and contraction in credit (*see* figure).

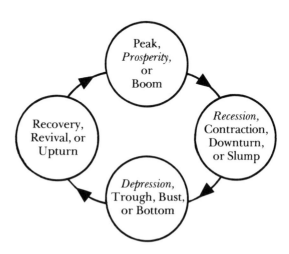

Business Cycle

BUY AMERICAN ACT. A 1933 act of Congress which provides that Federal agencies and certain contractors to the Federal government are obliged to buy articles of American manufacture unless American goods cannot be procured at reasonable cost in relation to foreign equivalents. The act has been challenged in multilateral trade negotiations as a nontariff barrier to trade. Many other nations have similar national purchasing arrangements.

The act has been largely supplanted as the result of U.S. adoption of the GOVERNMENT PROCURE-MENT CODE *(q.v.)*.

BUY-BACK. An arrangement in which the seller of capital equipment agrees either to accept a certain portion of the output of his customer as payment (in part or in full) for the original equipment, or to buy a certain portion of that output, as a condition of the sale. *See* COUNTERTRADE.

BUYER'S PREMIUM. A subsidy offered by a member state of the European Economic Community to domestic tobacco processors to encourage the use of EEC, rather than imported, tobaccos. The program, which is a feature of the COMMON AGRICULTURAL POLICY *(q.v.)* of the EEC, is designed at least to equalize the price of European tobaccos with imports, notably those of Turkey and the United States.

BYRD AMENDMENT. A 1971 amendment to the Military Procurement Authorization Act, which precludes the president from prohibiting "importation into the United States of any material determined to be strategic or critical . . . from any free world country so long as like articles could be imported from communist countries." The purpose of the amendment was to permit continued importations of chrome from Rhodesia in spite of the U.N. economic sanctions imposed on that country. As a result of the amendment, approximately seventy strategic items other than chrome were authorized entry from Rhodesia during the sanctions period.

The demise of the Rhodesian government, and U.S. recognition of the successor Zimbabwe government, have rendered the law irrelevant.

C

CABLE RATE. The exchange rate quoted for a given currency transferred by cable. The cable rate is higher than the rate for checks or bills of exchange denominated in the same currency because cable transfers are virtually instantaneous, thereby denying the bank or broker use of the funds during the collection period associated with checks or bills.

CABOTAGE. Literally, coastwise navigation, generally used to denote the proscription of foreign flag vessels in a nation's coastwise trade. Since an act of Congress in 1817 (2 Stat. 351), the coastwise trade of the United States has been reserved exclusively to American vessels.

CALL MONEY. Demand deposits in a British bank.

CALVO DOCTRINE. So named for the Argentine jurist Carlos Calvo, holds that a nation is obliged to extend to foreign business in its domain only nondiscriminatory treatment; by entering a country, a foreign firm implicitly accepts local jurisdiction and will be treated as a national. This doctrine is particularly evident in Latin America, where Calvo provisions have been enacted into law. Various bilateral agreements on foreign investments have diluted somewhat the significance of the Calvo provisions.

CAMBIST. A person engaged in the purchase and sale of bills of exchange or foreign currencies.

CAN. Slang for a container.

CANCELING DATE. The date specified in a charter party by which the vessel must be ready to load; if the vessel is not ready at the specified time, the charterer may exercise his option of rescinding the agreement.

CAP. The maximum rate of interest that may be charged on a variable or floating rate loan, irrespective of how high the money market index may fluctuate.

CAPITAL. Goods employed in the pursuit of commercial profit. Capital is one of the traditional factors of production, along with land and labor; some neofactor theorists also include entrepreneurship as a fourth factor, although traditional thought would regard entrepreneurial efforts as a form of labor. In the formal sense, capital consists of *real capital*, such as building machinery and tools, used to produce other goods, as contrasted with *finance capital*, which is the money or credit used to acquire such capital goods.

CAPITAL ACCOUNT. Entries in a nation's balance of payment accounts reflecting long- or short-term loans made to other countries, or by other countries to the recording nation. *See* BALANCE OF PAYMENTS.

CAPITAL CONSUMPTION ALLOWANCE. The entry, in national income accounting, that represents the aggregate consumption of capital equipment and facilities, i.e., depreciation incurred by the nation's business sector, as well as the aggregate of business casualty losses to plant and equipment during the reporting period.

CAPITAL FLIGHT. The movement of significant capital resources from a country in response to unstable economic or political conditions.

CAPITAL FORMATION. The aggregate value, expressed in monetary terms, of private sector investment in productive assets (e.g., physical plant and machinery) plus the sum of changes in private sector merchandise inventories, adjusted for the consumption of existing capital assets through depreciation.

CAPITAL LEASE. A leasehold extending substantially over the life of a capital asset.

CAPTAIN'S PROTEST. *See* MASTER'S PROTEST.

CAPTIVE INSURANCE COMPANY. A subsidiary formed to insure the risks of its noninsurance parent or affiliated companies. The captive may also reinsure risks that have been placed with third-party insurers, all or a portion of which have been transferred subsequently to the captive; in this arrangement, the unrelated insurer is said to *front* for the captive.

Captive insurers are normally formed in jurisdictions affording minimal capitalization requirements and limited oversight by regulatory bodies.

For many years, Bermuda has been the primary base for captive insurance companies, although many captives have been formed in the Cayman Islands, Channel Islands, and more recently, certain U.S. jurisdictions, including Colorado and Vermont. The offshore jurisdictions are usually favored because the captive's income may be sheltered from U.S. income taxes.

Captive insurers are usually organized along one of three lines: *pure* (or *limited*) *captive*, which insures or reinsures only the risks of its parent or affiliates; *partial captive* (also known as *open market, broad,* or *senior captive*), which insures or reinsures risks of third parties as well as its parent or affiliates; *association* (or *industry*) *captive*, which is controlled by several firms having common insurance needs and in which each of the member firms has an equity position.

The Internal Revenue Service has attempted to bring offshore captive income within the grasp of U.S. taxes by attributing the offshore income to the parent under SUBPART F *(q.v.)* of the Internal Revenue Code. In addition, the IRS has attempted to disallow deductions for premiums paid to a captive by its parent or affiliates, on the grounds that there has been no transfer of risk beyond the "economic family" of the parent; this proposition was advanced in REVENUE RULING 77-316 *(q.v.)*. The issue is under challenge in the courts.

CAREY STREET. British colloquialism for bankruptcy.

CARFLOAT. A barge that transports railcars about a harbor. The barge has rails on deck, and cars are shunted on at the rail terminals to be floated to a pier for off-loading onto a ship, or for continuation of the rail journey.

CARGO. Merchandise in the process of being transported; not to be confused with *freight*, which, in maritime usage, is the sum earned by a carrier for transporting goods. *General cargo* consists of various commodities comprising the property of many shippers or consignees; *special cargo* consists of a single commodity, often in bulk, in the hold of a ship.

CARGO BROKER. A broker representing the charterer in finding a vessel for hire.

CARGO-CARRYING CAPACITY. *Synonymous with* DEADWEIGHT TONNAGE *(q.v.)*.

CARGO DEADWEIGHT. The cargo-carrying capacity, expressed in long tons, of a vessel when fully loaded excepting water, stores, bunkers, and supplies.

CARGO DEADWEIGHT TONNAGE. The cargo-carrying capacity of a vessel, expressed in long tons, derived by substracting the weight of stores, fuel, water, and other necessary provisions from the vessel's deadweight tonnage.

CARGO PREFERENCE ACT. A 1954 amendment to the Merchant Marine Act of 1936 which mandates that at least 50 percent of all government-generated cargoes move on U.S. flag ships. Included in the category of such cargoes are Department of Defense movements, Department of Agriculture surplus commodities, goods financed by the Export-Import Bank, and Agency for International Development cargoes.

Since World War II, approximately five percent of all goods shipped in U.S. foreign trade were preference cargoes. Attempts to expand the cargo preference to cover a percentage of U.S. oil imports were unsuccessful before Congress or were vetoed by the president in 1974, 1977, and 1978.

CARGO RICE. A cargo of rice in bulk, of which 25 percent is *clean* (or husked) and 25 percent *paddy* (or unhusked) rice. This mixture is used during waterborne transport so as to prevent cargo sweating, i.e., the condensation of water vapor as the cargo moves from a tropical to a cooler latitude.

CARIBBEAN BASIN INITIATIVE. An economic development plan for the Caribbean area advanced by the Reagan administration. The principal features of the program include: establishment of a one-way free trade area in which most Caribbean-area products enter the United States free of duty; a reduction of the Caribbean content requirement for duty-free entry into the United States from 35 percent to 25 percent. Virtually all products, other than garments, footwear, and a very few other import-sensitive items, may now enter duty-free from most Caribbean nations. The program was enacted in 1983.

CARRIBEAN COMMUNITY AND COMMON MARKET. Commonly known as CARICOM, the successor organization to the defunct Caribbean Free Trade Association (CARIFTA). The object of CARICOM was to stimulate regional development through the adoption of a common external tariff and uniform protectionist measures, harmonization of fiscal affairs, and concerted industrialization efforts.

During the period between the inception of CARICOM (1973) and 1978, the region suffered a decline in trade in absolute terms, which resulted in the adoption of intragroup protectionist controls by Jamaica and Guyana. These and other unilateral actions by CARICOM members have impeded Caribbean economic development as a whole, although a dialogue among the members continues.

The member states of CARICOM in 1984 were: Antigua, Barbados, Belize, Dominica, Grenada, Guyana, Jamaica, Montserrat, Saint Kitts-Nevis and Anguilla, Saint Lucia, Saint Vincent, Trinidad and Tobago.

CARIBBEAN FREE TRADE AREA. *See* CARIBBEAN COMMUNITY AND COMMON MARKET.

CARICOM. *See* CARIBBEAN COMMUNITY AND COMMON MARKET.

CARIFTA. *See* CARIBBEAN COMMUNITY AND COMMON MARKET.

CARMACK AMENDMENT. The common name for the carrier liability provisions of the Hepburn Act of 1906 (49 U.S.C. Sec. 20[11]) by which the Interstate Commerce Act was amended to restrict efforts by certain common carriers to limit their liability for loss and damage of merchandise in transit.

The amendment provides that a carrier in interstate commerce shall be liable to the consignee or to another party entitled to recover:

> for the full actual loss, damage or injury to such property caused by it or any such common carrier, railroad, or transportation company to which such property shall be delivered or over whose line or lines such property may pass within the United States or within an adjacent foreign country when transported on a through bill of lading, notwithstanding any limitation of liability or limitation of amount of recovery or representation or agreement as to value in any such contract, rule, regulation, or in any tariff filed with the Interstate Commerce Commission.

At the time of the enactment of the Carmack Amendment only rail carriers were subject to regulation by the Interstate Commerce Commission. With the subsequent extension of ICC authority to cover motor carriers and domestic freight forwarders, the provisions of the Carmack Amendment were expanded to embrace these carriers as well. The amendment has not, however, been statutorily extended to cover common carriers by air or water.

The Interstate Commerce Commission is empowered to authorize *release valuation rates* under which a shipper may elect to accept a lower freight rate for a given shipment in exchange for limited carrier liability.

Due to deregulation of motor and rail transportation, argument has arisen whether the Carmack Amendment is still valid.

CARNATION CASE. A suit in which the U.S. Tax Court denied, for income tax purposes, the deduction of sums paid by the Carnation Company to its wholly owned CAPTIVE INSURANCE COMPANY *(q.v.)* as premiums for insurance coverage.

The Internal Revenue Service asserted that the premiums paid by Carnation to its subsidiary, Three Flowers Insurance Company, a Bermuda corporation, did not result in a genuine transfer of risk from the parent to the captive, but were in fact contributions to a self-insurance fund and as such were not deductible. Carnation's position was diminished by the fact that Three Flowers was thinly capitalized ($120,000), and the presence of an agreement between Carnation and American Home Insurance (an unrelated party) that American Home would reinsure 90 percent of its Carnation policy risks for Three Flowers' additional capital as required to respond for Three Flowers' obligations to American Home under the reinsurance arrangement.

The Tax Court held that insurance requires a transfer of risk from the insured to the insurer, which was absent in this case. Because Carnation remained directly responsible for any losses sustained by Three Flowers, no risk had been shifted to the captive. The decision of the Tax Court was upheld by the Court of Appeals and denied further review by the U.S. Supreme Court.

The effect of the Carnation case has been to clarify the respective relationships between a captive insurance company and its parent and affiliated companies. Among the points established are:

1. A captive must be adequately capitalized to bear the risks it has undertaken, and this capitalization must be in the form of true assets, rather than guarantees on the part of the parent to provide resources in the event of significant losses.

2. The captive must operate at arm's length from the parent, and the premiums charged to the parent or affiliated companies must be reasonable.

3. The captive must be structured as an ongoing business directed toward the generation of profit from the issuance of contracts of insurance. As a practical matter, this means that the captive must derive a sufficient volume of its premiums from unrelated third parties so as to establish its status as a bona fide insurer.

On this last point, it is unclear what percentage of total premium income must be derived from unrelated sources in order to satify the definition of an *insurer,* although various experts recommend that third-party premiums be not less than 25 to 50 percent of total premium income.

See SUBPART F.

CARNET. *See* ATA CARNET.

CARRIAGE OF GOODS BY SEA ACT. Known commonly by the acronym COGSA, the principal U.S. statute governing carrier liabilities and immunities for loss and damage arising during the transport of goods by water in the foreign commerce of the United States. Enacted in 1936, the act largely eclipses, but does not repeal, the earlier Harter Act. Unlike the Harter Act, which applies to both foreign and domestic waterborne shipments, COGSA applies only to foreign shipments, although it may be incorporated by concurrence of the parties to the transaction into bills of lading covering domestic waterborne shipments.

COGSA applies only from *tackle to tackle,* i.e., from the point on the pier where the goods are loaded onto the vessel until they are discharged from the vessel, whereas the earlier Harter Act covered goods under the care, custody, and control of the carrier, wherever situated. In addition to this limitation, COGSA stipulates a number of circumstances under which the carrier is relieved of all responsibility for loss and damage of cargo. Among the exemptions from liability are losses attributable to fire, sinking, standing, and errors in navigation and management of the vessel. In any case, the carrier's liability is limited to $500 per package or, in the absence of a package, $500 per *customary freight unit.* The shipper of valuable merchandise is permitted under the act to declare a value for shipment in excess of $500 per package, and the carrier shall be liable to the shipper for this higher value upon payment by the shipper of an increased freight charge as provided in the carrier's tariff.

The act provides that each bill of lading covering merchandise shipped subject to the act shall incorporate COGSA by reference.

The full text of the Carriage of Goods by Sea Act is to be found in Appendix A3.

CARRIER. A firm engaged in the business of transporting persons or goods for profit. Railroads, trucking companies, airlines, and steamship operators are examples of carriers. Carriers can be divided into three categories: the *private carrier* moves only its own goods or those of its affiliates; the *contract carrier* transports the goods of an unrelated firm under a written contract covering many shipments at an agreed rate over a period of time; the *common carrier* transports goods for the general public at rates published in a tariff.

Recent Federal legislation has largely exempted most carriers from economic regulation, particularly as relates to rate levels, although carriers are still subject to local regulation on purely intrastate commerce.

CARRIER'S CERTIFICATE. A document issued by a steamship line, an airline, or other transportation company carrying imported merchandise certifying to the customs authorities that the party named is the legitimate recipient of the goods and is authorized to effect clearance through customs (*see* figure). The party so named by the carrier may be the consignee shown on the bill of lading, the holder of a properly endorsed order bill of lading, or their authorized representatives, such as a licensed customs broker. *See* ENTRY (CUSTOMS).

CARTAGE. The transfer of merchandise locally, e.g., from a pier to a nearby warehouse; also, the charge for cartage services.

CARTAGENA AGREEMENT. *See* ANDEAN GROUP.

CARTEL. An alliance among firms in the same line of business aimed at controlling or dominating their field on an international basis.

CASH COMMODITY. A tangible, physical commodity or financial instrument, the delivery of which to a purchaser could be effected immediately or nearly so.

CASHIER'S CHECK. A bank check, i.e., a check drawn by the bank on itself. It constitutes a primary bank obligation and is almost universally acceptable in business transactions.

CASH MARKET. *See* SPOT MARKET.

CASH PRICE. The same as SPOT PRICE (*q.v.*), as used in grain transactions.

CEDULE. A continental European form of a negotiable warehouse receipt.

CELLULARIZED VESSEL. A vessel, also known as a *slot ship,* equipped with internal ribbing so as to accommodate rows of containers stacked one on top of the other. Modern container ships are at least partially cellularized.

CENTAL. A unit of one hundred pounds; *synonymous with* a U.S. hundredweight.

CENTER OF GRAVITY THEORY. A principle in law which contends that whenever a contract involves parties in several legal jurisdictions and the document fails to prescribe which law shall govern, a court may apply the system of law having the most significant relationship to the contract. Factors to be considered by a court in determining which law to apply may include the places where the parties are situated, the place where the contract was negotiated or signed or where performance is to take place, the currency used in the contract, and the citizenship of the parties. Local courts may apply varying weights to the various factors.

Some legal systems (including those of England, Sweden, France, and some American states) employ the principle of *validation,* i.e., if more than one legal system might apply to a given contract, the court will apply the system that validates the contract if the law of another potential jurisdiction would invalidate it.

CENTRAL AMERICAN COMMON MARKET. A free trade area among the nations of Central America, established in 1960 by a treaty between El Salvador, Guatemala, Honduras, and Nicaragua. The common market began operations in 1961, and Costa Rica joined the group in 1962. Honduras dropped out of the group in 1969 during its brief war with El Salvador; it has since maintained bilateral trade agreements with Costa Rica, Nicaragua, and Guatemala.

Economic integration within the region has been impeded by political unrest and the failure of Honduras and El Salvador to reconcile differences. Real dollar intragroup trade has declined significantly in recent years. In 1976 a treaty was advanced calling for replacement of the common market with an Economic and Social Community of Central America, but by 1984 no potential member state had ratified the instrument.

CENTRAL BANK. The principal monetary authority of a nation. In most commercially developed nations the central bank issues the currency and acts

Customs Form 7529
DEPARTMENT OF THE TREASURY
10.101, 141.11, 141.111 C.R.
(12-21-77)

CARRIER'S CERTIFICATE AND RELEASE ORDER

Form approved
O.M.B. No. 48-R0429

UNITED STATES CUSTOMS SERVICE

This space for use of Customs only.

Entry No. ....

Date ....

CARRIER'S CERTIFICATE

To The District Director of Customs,

_____ (Port of entry)   _____ (Date)

The undersigned carrier, to whom or upon whose order the articles described below or in the attached document must

be released, hereby certifies that _____ (Name) of _____ (Address)

is the owner or consignee of such articles within the purview of section 484(h), Tariff Act of 1930.

Marks and Numbers of Packages	Description and Quantity of Merchandise Number and Kind of Packages	Gross Weight in Pounds (See Note 1)	Foreign Port of Lading and Date of Sailing (See Note 2)	Bill of Lading No.

Steamship ....

Voyage No. ....

Arrived ....
(Date)

_____
(Name of carrier)

_____
(Agent)

RELEASE ORDER

To The District Director of Customs,

_____ (Port of entry)   _____ (Date)

In accordance with the provisions of section 484(j), Tariff Act of 1930, authority is hereby given to release the articles

covered by the above carrier's certificate to (See Note 3) _____

_____

_____

_____
(Name of carrier)

_____
(Agent)

SEE REVERSE SIDE FOR NOTES AND INSTRUCTIONS

Carrier's Certificate and Release Order

as banker for the government and the nation's commercial banks. By setting the rate at which it will lend money to commercial banks, the central bank effectively regulates the availability of credit. An important central bank function is to engage in transfers of gold and foreign exchange with foreign central banks. Central banking functions in the United States are performed by the Federal Reserve system, with special responsibility for foreign transactions vested in the Federal Reserve Bank of New York.

CENTRAL BOYCOTT OFFICE. An agency of the Arab League established in 1951 to orchestrate the ARAB BOYCOTT *(q.v.)* of Israeli industry. The CBO has its headquarters in Damascus, Syria, with offices throughout the Arab world, and maintains a blacklist of firms engaged in economic transactions with Israel. By 1984, more than 150,000 firms had been blacklisted, thereby effectively denying them access to the markets of the Arab world.

CENTRALLY PLANNED ECONOMY. An economy in which basic economic decisions are made by a central planning commission or a similar state agency. Price mechanism does not determine the allocation of resources; instead the planning agency assesses resource availability and reports this to the level of government that determines priorities. Once these priorities have been determined, the planning agency sets goals for each industry or factory and allocates resources as required to accomplish the stated objectives. Central planning is usually associated with communist forms of government, although it is employed in varying degrees by some socialist-oriented noncommunist states as well.

CENTRAL MARKET. A spot commodity market that serves as a national or regional center of trading activity, and often large-scale distribution of the products as well. Transactions are usually performed by dealers who serve as intermediary brokers between buyers and sellers.

CENTRAL MONETARY INSTITUTIONS. The principal agencies of government responsible for a nation's international financial affairs, particularly in exchange rate or balance of payments matters. The central monetary institutions usually consist of the ministry of finance and the central bank, or another exchange control agency.

CENTRAL RATE. Each currency affiliated with the EUROPEAN MONETARY SYSTEM *(q.v.)* is assigned a value in terms of the *European currency unit* (ECU). The central rate is the range within which any participating currency is permitted to deviate from its ECU value, after which member central banks are obliged to intervene to restore equilibrium.

CERTIFICATE OF ADMEASUREMENT. A document issued in conjunction with the construction or major overhaul of a ship for purposes of certifying the tonnage of the vessel and its cargo-carrying capacity. The certificate is used to ensure compliance with load-line regulations and serves as the basis for assessment of taxes and fees levied on tonnage.

CERTIFICATE OF ANALYSIS. A document, often required by an importer or governmental authorities, attesting to the quality or purity of commodities purchased abroad. The certification may be prepared by a chemist or other authority, or by an inspection firm retained by the exporter or importer. In some cases the document may be prepared by the manufacturer certifying that the merchandise shipped has been tested in his facility and found to conform with the specifications promised.

CERTIFICATE OF FREE SALE. A document issued by an agency of government, usually the health authority, certifying that a given product is in compliance with all local regulations and may be offered freely for sale within the country of origin.

Normally, such certificates are issued to cover food products which are being exported. The U.S. government does not issue certificates of free sale, per se; however, the Food and Drug Administration does issue a "letter of comment" within which they state U.S. standards for a given product and give observations concerning the compliance, or lack thereof, on the part of the producer with such standards.

CERTIFICATE OF MANUFACTURE. A document issued by a manufacturer attesting that the named item has been manufactured and is available for shipment. This document is used commonly with sales under letters of credit providing for full or partial payment upon manufacture of the goods.

In 1942 the Bankers' Association for Foreign Trade adopted the following as a concise format for certificates of manufacture:

We hereby certify that the attached invoice dated ———, our number ———, covers material which has been manufactured and set apart for your account and risk at ———.

This uniform certificate of manufacture is usually prepared on the manufacturer's letterhead or on a preprinted form.

CERTIFICATE OF ORIGIN. A document presented to customs authorities at the time of importation to authenticate the national origin of merchandise. The certificate is customarily issued by a recognized chamber of commerce or governmental authority in the country of origin.

CERTIFICATE OF PROTEST. The document issued by a notary public or other official confirming that a bill of exchange or other instrument has been presented for acceptance or payment and has been dishonored.

CERTIFICATE OF ORIGIN

SHIPPER/EXPORTER	DOCUMENT NO.
	EXPORT REFERENCES
CONSIGNEE	FORWARDING AGENT - REFERENCES
	POINT AND COUNTRY OF ORIGIN
NOTIFY PARTY	DOMESTIC ROUTING/EXPORT INSTRUCTIONS

PIER OR AIRPORT	
EXPORTING CARRIER (Vessel/Airline)	PORT OF LOADING	ONWARD INLAND ROUTING
AIR/SEA PORT OF DISCHARGE	FOR TRANSSHIPMENT TO	

PARTICULARS FURNISHED BY SHIPPER

MARKS AND NUMBERS	NO. OF PKGS.	DESCRIPTION OF PACKAGES AND GOODS	GROSS WEIGHT	MEASUREMENT

The undersigned .... (Owner or Agent), does hereby declare for the above named shipper, the goods as described above were shipped on the above date and consigned as indicated and are products of the United States of America

Dated at .... on the .... day of .... 19 ....

Sworn to before me this .... day of .... 19 ....

....

.... SIGNATURE OF OWNER OR AGENT

The ...., a recognized Chamber of Commerce under the laws of the State of ...., has examined the manufacturer's invoice or shipper's affidavit concerning the origin of the merchandise, and, according to the best of its knowledge and belief, finds that the products named originated in the United States of North America.

Secretary ....

X-501-AH REV. 1/71
WHSE. NO. 0941

Certificate of Origin

CERTIFICATE OF PUBLIC CONVENIENCE AND NECESSITY. The document issued to a common carrier by the appropriate regulatory agency authorizing the carrier to haul specified cargoes between designated points under established rates.

CERTIFICATE OF RECEIPT. *Synonymous with* FORWARDER'S RECEIPT *(q.v.).*

CERTIFICATE OF WEIGHT AND INSPECTION. A document prepared by a trade association or recognized inspection firm attesting to the particulars of a given shipment, e.g., number and contents of packages, markings, and weights. This document is often required by importers and is frequently stipulated in letters of credit.

CERTIFICATED AIRLINE CARRIER. An airline which has been issued a CERTIFICATE OF PUBLIC CONVENIENCE AND NECESSITY *(q.v.)* by competent governmental authority to operate airline service over prescribed routes.

CERTIFIED CHECK. A check that bears a stamp from the bank on which it is drawn certifying that the funds have been reserved for the drawee in a special account; in effect, the bank guarantees the availability of funds upon presentation of the check.

CETERUS PARIBUS. A Latin expression, commonly seen in its abbreviated form *cet. par.,* meaning "all things being equal." It is used commonly in conjunction with economic and financial analyses to reflect that some factors remain unchanged within different scenarios.

CHANNEL LENGTH. The length of a channel of distribution, as evidenced by the number of distributors, dealers, or other intermediaries involved in moving the product from the manufacturer to the final user or consumer. Typically, the channel length will be shorter for heavy industrial goods than for low-priced or consumer items.

CHARTERER'S LIABILITY. The legal liability assumed by the charterer of a vessel. By law, the charterer may be construed as *owner* of the ship and as such may be liable for damage or injury caused by the chartered vessel. The charterer of a vessel usually offsets this exposure through the purchase of a charterer's liability insurance policy.

CHARTER HIRE. The freight paid by the charterer of a vessel to the vessel owner.

CHARTER PARTY. A maritime contract for the lease of all or part of a ship for a period of time or for a voyage or voyages. The expression is derived from the Latin *carta partida*, meaning "divided document," because the charter agreement was written twice on one sheet of paper, which was then cut or torn in two halves so that each party to the transaction would have a complete copy of the terms of the charter.

Charter parties can be divided into three categories:

1. *Voyage charter*: the vessel is hired to make a single journey between two prescribed points; the shipowner provides crew, fuel, and supplies.

2. *Time charter*: the vessel is hired for a fixed period of time to make multiple journeys over defined routes, or to carry cargo for the charterer wherever he may reasonably designate; the shipowner provides crew, fuel, and supplies.

3. *Bareboat charter* (or *demise*): the vessel is hired, usually for a fixed period of time, and all operating expenses (crew, fuel, supplies, et cetera) are provided by the charterer.

Each trade employs standard form charter parties.

CHASSIS. A wheeled carriage onto which an ocean container is mounted for inland conveyance.

CHECKER. An employee of a steamship line or stevedoring firm responsible for the examination of cargo delivered to the pier for onward transport. Routinely, the checker ascertains the count and condition of the goods so delivered and issues a receipt for same, noting the date and time of delivery.

CHECK RATE. The rate of exchange applicable to bankers' checks. This rate is lower than the cable rate but higher than the rate applicable to time bills of exchange, owing to the time value of money.

CHICKEN WAR. A protracted dispute between the United States and the European Economic Community arising from the adoption of Europe's COMMON AGRICULTURAL POLICY *(q.v.)* on chicken in 1962. Prior to that year, American chicken had entered many European countries at a preferential rate. Adoption of the CAP, however, imposed minimum import pricing upon all imported chicken, increasing the levy on U.S. imports from 4.5 cents to 13.5 cents and resulting in a first-year loss of market of $26 million for U.S. chicken farmers. In response, the United States imposed punitive levies on European trucks, brandy, and other items.

The dispute is significant in reflecting the impact on American agriculture arising from implementation of the CAP.

CHINA TRADE ACT CORPORATION. A corporation formed under the China Trade Act of 1922, which provided special tax incentives to firms engaged in trade with China. Following the collapse of the Nationalist government on mainland China in 1949, the act was amended to cover only Taiwan and Hong Kong.

In its final form, the act provided for a deduction for U.S. income tax purposes computed by deriving a fraction for the par values of shares of the corporation held by persons resident in Taiwan, Hong Kong, and the United States and its possessions versus the whole number of shares outstanding. The fraction so derived would be applied to the proportional part of the corporation's income earned in Taiwan and Hong Kong.

For taxable years beginning in 1976, the deduction was reduced by one-third; commencing in 1977, the deduction was reduced by two-thirds. The deduction was eliminated entirely effective January 1, 1978, pursuant to P.L. 94-455, Section 1053 (c).

CIRCULATING MEDIUM. Any item or commodity routinely and generally accepted as a means of exchange. Currency (paper money and coins) is a circulating medium. At various times bars of copper, salt, and other items have been used.

CITES. *See* CONVENTION ON INTERNATIONAL TRADE IN ENDANGERED SPECIES OF FLORA AND FAUNA.

CIVIL EMBARGO. *See* EMBARGO.

CLASSIFICATION. The process of determining which product category of the tariff schedules applies to a given imported item. There are more than 7,300 categories in the TARIFF SCHEDULES OF THE UNITED STATES *(q.v.)* and, with very few exceptions, every imported item must be *classified* into one of them for duty and other purposes.

CLASSIFICATION SOCIETY. An organization that establishes standards for the construction of vessels and certifies vessels as having met the requirements of a given class.

The principal classification societies and the cities in which they are based are as follows: American Bureau of Shipping, New York; Det Norske Veritas, Høvik, Norway; Lloyd's Register, London; Bureau Veritas, Paris; Germanisher Lloyd, Hamburg; Nippon Kaiji Kyokai, Tokyo; Polski Registr Statkow, Gdansk, Poland; Registro Italiano Navale, Genoa; USSR Register of Shipping, Leningrad; DDR-Schiffs-Revision und Klassifikation, East Berlin; Jugoslavenski Register Brodova, Split, Yugoslavia; Korean Register of Shipping, Seoul.

CLAUSE PARAMOUNT. A provision in an ocean bill of lading that incorporates by reference laws or international agreements into the bill. The term is most commonly used with reference to the enacting clause of the CARRIAGE OF GOODS BY SEA ACT *(q.v.)* of 1936, which stipulates "that every bill of lading or similar document of title which is evidence of a contract for the carriage of goods by sea to or from ports of the United States, in foreign trade, shall have effect subject to the provisions of this Act."

CLAUSED BILL OF LADING. *See* BILL OF LADING.

CLAUSING. The insertion of a notation on the face of a bill of exchange to describe the transaction that gives rise to the bill, e.g., "export of five cases welding equipment to Argentina aboard the SS Atlantic Mariner."

The purpose of clausing a bill of exchange is to identify those bills that may be eligible for discount at the Federal Reserve, whose regulations specify the circumstances under which a bill may be discounted.

See REGULATION A.

CLAYTON ACT. An act of Congress, passed in 1914, that expands upon the ANTITRUST *(q.v.)* provisions of the Sherman Act by making it illegal for firms to engage in price discrimination and exclusive dealing arrangements, and forbidding interlocking directorates. The Clayton Act was reinforced in 1936 by the Robinson-Patman Act, and in 1950 by a further amendment to regulate certain acquisitions of assets and stock purchases.

CLEAN ACCEPTANCE. A formal acknowledgment by a principal in negotiations for the charter of a vessel that he accepts the offer submitted to him, without further modification, and that he binds himself to execute the CHARTER PARTY *(q.v.)*.

CLEAN BILL OF EXCHANGE. Any BILL OF EXCHANGE *(q.v.)* not accompanied by documents, such as invoices, bills of lading, et cetera. *See* DIRECT COLLECTION.

CLEAN BILL OF LADING. *See* BILL OF LADING.

CLEAN CREDIT. A LETTER OF CREDIT *(q.v.)* against which the beneficiary may draw without supplying documents.

CLEAN CHARTER. An imprecise expression used to describe a CHARTER PARTY *(q.v.)* that does not include onerous or unusual provisions.

CLEAN FLOAT. The condition in which the values of national currencies vis-à-vis each other are determined by market forces without government intervention to maintain prearranged rates of exchange.

CLEAN LETTER OF CREDIT. *Synonymous with* CLEAN CREDIT.

CLEAN PRODUCT CARRIER. A tank vessel that transports only refined petroleum products, such as gasoline or kerosene, as contrasted with a ship which carries crude petroleum.

CLEAN REPORT OF FINDINGS. A document issued by a recognized inspection agency certifying that certain merchandise has been examined and found to be in order. This document may be required by a letter of credit or stipulated by the exchange control authorities of certain governments. The object of the report is to ensure that the merchandise has been inspected prior to shipment by an independent third party who is satisfied that the goods conform to the buyer's specifications.

CLEAN RICE. A cargo of rice from which the husks have been removed.

CLEAN SHIP. A tanker that carries refined petroleum products, as contrasted with crude or fuel oils.

CLEARANCE. The completion of customs formalities including, but not limited to, the physical examination of imported merchandise, and the submission of documents necessary to permit the release of merchandise from customs control to the importer.

CLEARANCE PAPERS. A document issued to a ship's captain stating that the vessel is in compliance with local regulations (e.g., payment of harbor fees and compliance with health regulations) and is permitted to *clear*, i.e., leave, the port.

CLEAR DAY. Any day on which the foreign exchange markets are open for business.

CLEAR DAYS. The number of days that a vessel under charter must give to the shipper in advance of arrival in order to prepare the cargo for shipment. The day upon which the notification is received and the day on which the vessel actually arrives are excluded from the clear days. If the charter party specifies a number of *clear working days*, the notification requirement is extended to exempt Sundays and holidays as well.

CLEARING. An arrangement by which two firms in different countries agree to purchase goods from each other over a specific period of time, thereby balancing out obligations to each other. Clearing is not synonymous with *barter*, which implies a simultaneous or near simultaneous transfer of prescribed quantities of predetermined merchandise. Clearing is less rigid in that the object is for each participant to buy from its trading partner a specified value, in money terms, within the prescribed time period. In most cases, however, clearing arrangements will define the types of merchandise to be offered and in what quantities.

As in all COUNTERTRADE *(q.v.)* transactions, cash settlement is totally or virtually eliminated.

CLEARINGHOUSE FUNDS. Funds transferred among New York banks with availability at the commencement of the next business day.

CLEAR WORKING DAYS. *See* CLEAR DAYS.

CLOSED CONFERENCE. An ocean freight CONFERENCE *(q.v.)* with restrictions on the admission of nonmember lines into membership. Closed conferences are common on many trade routes but are forbidden in U.S. export or import commerce.

CLOSED ECONOMY. The economy of an isolated area that engages in virtually no trade beyond its own borders. This condition is usually the product of geographic remoteness rather than design. *See also* AUTARCHY.

CLOSING DATE. The latest date for delivery of cargo to a vessel for a particular voyage.

COASTWISE OPTION. A provision of the CARRIAGE OF GOODS BY SEA ACT *(q.v.)* (COGSA) which permits COGSA to be incorporated into bills of lading covering shipments in the domestic maritime commerce of the United States. Most shipments in the foreign waterborne commerce of the United States are automatically subject to COGSA. Excepted from the purview of the act are shipments in bulk without mark or count, on-deck shipments at shipper's risk, and shipments of live animals.

In the case of domestic waterborne shipments, COGSA will apply only if the act is incorporated by reference into the bill of lading. Where the coastwise option has not been exercised on domestic shipments, questions of carrier liability will be governed by the HARTER ACT *(q.v.)*, and other relevant legislation.

COCOM. An informal working group comprised of Western governments, established for the purpose of preventing exports of certain strategic products to potentially hostile countries. The COCOM proscribed countries are: the USSR, its WARSAW PACT *(q.v.)* allies, Albania, Vietnam, North Korea, Kampuchea, and Mongolia. Lesser controls apply on exports to the People's Republic of China. Following adoption of the Export Control Act of 1949, the United States joined with Great Britain, France, the Netherlands, Belgium, Luxembourg, and Italy to form the Consultative Group. Subsequently, the original parties were joined by West Germany, Norway, Denmark, Canada, Portugal, Greece, Turkey, and Japan. The group established a permanent Coordinating Committee (i.e., COCOM) in Paris to develop and update a list of products to be denied exportation to the Soviet bloc; the products so identified are contained in the *COCOM List*, which incorporates three individual listings of products: the International Atomic Energy List, the International Munitions List, and the International List, which includes articles having both military and nonmilitary applications. COCOM member countries may also restrict exports of other products, on a unilateral basis. A uniform control procedure, known as the INTERNATIONAL IMPORT CERTIFICATE–DELIVERY VERIFICATION SYSTEM *(q.v.)*, was devised and implemented among the member countries to ensure that restricted products were not diverted to the East.

During Fiscal Year 1983, 260 applications for export licenses for Eastern bloc destinations were denied by the Department of Commerce; of these, 228 applications involved COCOM items.

CODE OF LINER CONDUCT. *See* UNCTAD CODE.

CODETERMINATION. The corporate management process employed in some countries whereby labor representatives sit on the company's board of directors. This practice arose in Germany following World War I, gaining wide acceptance in that country following World War II. Worker participation, or *Mitbestimmung*, is mandatory in most German firms having 500 or more employees. Acceptance has grown in France and several other countries to a lesser extent. *See* VREDLING DIRECTIVE.

CODEX ALIMENTARIUS. A document published by the Codex Alimentarius Commission establishing international standards for raw and processed food products. The commission was established in 1963 by the Food and Agriculture Organization in conjunction with the World Health Organization. Member states of either the FAO or the WHO may participate in the work of the commission, and commission pronouncements are circulated to all participating governments. The Codex Alimentarius Commission establishes minimum grades or standards of raw and processed food products. Upon adherence by a government, all *codex standards* become minimum standards within that country.

COFINANCING. An arrangement whereby commercial banks and official lending institutions participate in World Bank financing of development projects in Third World countries. The World Bank acts as lead manager for the loan and provides partial funding from its own resources; commercial banks and official lenders provide the balance of the funding.

By means of this scheme the World Bank effectively expands its resources available for development. During Fiscal Years 1982-84 cofinancing added over five billion dollars to World Bank funding of development projects.

World Bank Cofinancing Operations
Fiscal 1980-84 (in millions U.S. dollars)

Period	Official	Export Credit	Private	Total
1980-82	2,140	1,431	1,510	5,081
1981-83	1,846	1,770	1,376	4,991
1982-84	1,967	1,961	1,373	5,302

COGSA. *See* CARRIAGE OF GOODS BY SEA ACT.

COINSURANCE CLAUSE. A provision in some contracts of insurance under which the insurer will restrict recovery under the policy unless the insured party maintains coverage equal to a given percentage of the value of the property covered. For example, a policy might provide that the insurer will pay the full actual value of a loss when the property involved is insured for at least 80 percent of its value. If the insured has the property covered for only 60 percent of its current value, the insurer will pay only 60 percent of the value of the loss; the insured becomes a *coinsurer* responsible for the difference.

COLLECTIVE FARM. A communal farm on which the land and heavy machinery are owned by the state, but the other means of production are owned by the participating farmers. Often the member families cultivate a private plot on the farm in addition to the communal plot. Management of the farm is ostensibly controlled by the farmers, usually under a state-defined plan or quota objective. Collective farms are common in the Soviet Union and account for 90 percent of the agricultural output of that country. Collective farming is applied widely in most socialist countries, and in Israel.

COLLECTIVE RESERVE UNIT. An artificial currency unit proposed in 1965 by Valéry Giscard d'Estaing of France. The *cru*, as it was known, was to have been linked to gold to create international reserves. The GROUP OF TEN *(q.v.)* was to have allocated the reserves so created.

The movement for creation of gold-linked collective reserve units was thwarted by the issuance of SPECIAL DRAWING RIGHTS *(q.v.)* by the INTERNATIONAL MONETARY FUND *(q.v.)*.

COLLIERY TURN. A provision in some bulk coal charter parties stipulating that loading will commence upon availability of the specified coal from the mine.

COLONIAL CLAUSE. *See* INTEREST-BEARING DRAFT.

COLUMN 1 RATE. The rate of duty applied by U.S. Customs to imports from nations enjoying MOST FAVORED NATION *(q.v.)* status. *See* TARIFF (CUSTOMS); TARIFF SCHEDULES OF THE UNITED STATES.

COLUMN 2 RATE. The rate of duty applied by U.S. Customs to imports from nations not enjoying MOST FAVORED NATION *(q.v.)* status. The Column 2 rate is the statutory rate of duty provided in the SMOOT-HAWLEY ACT *(q.v.)*, enacted in 1930, which imposes rates often several times higher than those contained in Column 1. The statutory rates are applied only to imports from a limited number of communist countries. *See* TARIFF (CUSTOMS); TARIFF SCHEDULES OF THE UNITED STATES.

COMBINATION AIRCRAFT. An aircraft equipped to carry both passengers and cargo on the same flight.

COMBINATION EXPORT MANAGER. A service organization that acts as the export department of a manufacturing or trading firm. The CEM undertakes to find overseas buyers, negotiates contracts on behalf of its principal, and is often operationally indistinguishable from a branch of the manufacturer.

COMBINATION RATE. An inland freight rate from point of origin to destination derived by adding two or more intermediate rates.

COMBINATION VESSEL. Usually used in reference to a vessel that is partially cellularized to accommodate containers, with the remainder of its cargo-carrying space dedicated to break-bulk stowage.

COMBINED TRANSPORT BILL OF LADING. A bill of lading covering movement of goods through more than one carrier, and perhaps through several modes of transport (water, air, rail, motor). The issuer of a combined transport bill of lading assumes responsibility for the goods throughout the journey until final destination, but his legal liability for the cargo, in monetary terms, may be governed by the laws or bill of lading conditions of the underlying carriers hired to perform transport services.

COMBINED TRANSPORT DOCUMENT. A bill of lading issued by a COMBINED TRANSPORT OPERATOR *(q.v.)* covering shipment of goods by more than one mode of transport. The document specifies the point at which the goods are taken up for carriage and the place of delivery.

COMBINED TRANSPORT OPERATOR. A common carrier providing multimodal transport services. These services may involve movement of the goods by several modes (e.g., rail, water, motor), with one portion of the shipment actually performed by the carrier issuing the bill of lading and other portions subcontracted out.

COMMAND DIRECTED ECONOMY. An economy in which the questions of which goods are to be produced, how they will be produced, and who will receive them are established by governmental fiat. *See* CENTRALLY PLANNED ECONOMY.

COMMERCIAL BANK GUARANTEE PROGRAM. *See* EXPORT-IMPORT BANK.

COMMERCIAL BAR. A bar of precious metal formed for use by jewelers, artists, or industry, rather than for monetary purposes.

COMMERCIAL BILL. A BILL OF EXCHANGE *(q.v.)* that arises out of a transaction involving the sale of goods.

COMMERCIAL PAPER. Unsecured debt obligations of large, credit-worthy firms, issued for periods of one year or less.

COMMERCIAL RISK. The risk borne by an exporter that his foreign customer may be unable to pay for merchandise imported under open account terms. Commercial risk is contrasted with *political risks*, which arise from governmental actions and are unrelated to the financial condition or credit-worthiness of the foreign customer.

In the case of U.S. exports, insurance against commercial and political risks can be obtained through the FOREIGN CREDIT INSURANCE ASSOCIATION *(q.v.)*.

COMMINGLED MERCHANDISE. Merchandise that is packed together so that a customs inspector cannot readily determine the value or quantity of the individual items. A provision of customs regulations stipulates that under these conditions, duty on the entire shipment will be imposed upon whichever of the commingled items bears the highest rate. Exemptions from the rule are permitted if the importer can provide evidence of the content of each of the items in the mix.

COMMISSIONAIRE. A distributor retained by a manufacturer to sell the producer's products in return for a fee.

COMMISSION ON INTERNATIONAL COMMODITY TRADE. An agency of the United Nations established in 1954 to monitor activities of primary commodities markets. The basic function of the commission is to compile statistics on commodities trading, observe the impact of the markets upon developing countries, and make reports and recommendations to the General Assembly of the U.N.

COMMITMENT FEE. The charge imposed by a bank for reserving a line of credit to be used by a customer at a future date.

COMMITTEE ON BANKING REGULATIONS AND SUPERVISORY PRACTICES. Known commonly as the *Cooke Committee*, a working party established under the auspices of the BANK FOR INTERNATIONAL SETTLEMENTS *(q.v.)* in 1975 to seek to remedy inadequacies in the supervision of banks operating outside their home countries. Because of differences in national banking laws, a bank might be able to operate overseas, beyond the scrutiny of bank regulators, in a jurisdiction where its operations were not considered "banking" under local laws; in such cases, a bank might operate without any regulatory oversight. In addition, local bank regulations often did not address transactions undertaken in Eurocurrencies.

The committee derives its membership from the GROUP OF TEN *(q.v.)* countries. The committee seeks not to harmonize local banking laws but to operate within existing laws to ensure that solvency and liquidity are maintained. To this end, the committee issued the BASEL CONCORDAT *(q.v.)* in December 1975, with the concurrence of the central banks of the Group of Ten countries.

The work of the committee is ongoing, and in 1984 the Basel Concordat was under revision.

COMMITTEE ON REFORM OF THE INTERNATIONAL MONETARY SYSTEM. *See* GROUP OF TWENTY.

COMMODITY. A nondifferentiated product produced with commonly available technology.

COMMODITY CONTROL LIST. A listing of products subject to U.S. export controls administered by the Department of Commerce. The list inclues items under controls imposed by COCOM *(q.v.)* as well as those subject to unilateral U.S. controls. *See* EXPORT CONTROL ACT.

COMMODITY CREDIT CORPORATION. A Federally chartered corporation controlled by the U.S. government and administered as a part of the Department of Agriculture. In addition to various domestic agricultural stabilization efforts, the CCC administers three foreign sales promotion programs.

COMMODITY PAPER. Drafts or bills of exchange arising from transactions involving the sale of commodities. The draft is usually accompanied by negotiable bills of lading, warehouse receipts, or similar documents of title permitting the holder of the draft to dispose of the commodities in the event the drawee defaults.

COMMODITY PRICE INDEX. An index of prices for a stipulated list of commodities. Prices may be on a spot or futures basis. Customarily, major commodities are traded on exchanges (although there are some exceptions), and price fluctuations can be monitored accordingly. The U.S. Department of Labor maintains an index of twenty-two basic commodities as a component of the Wholesale Price Index.

COMMODITY TERMS OF TRADE. *See* TERMS OF TRADE.

COMMON AGRICULTURAL POLICY. The fundamental mechanism for the integration of agriculture within the EUROPEAN ECONOMIC COMMUNITY *(q.v.)*.

The 1957 Treaty of Rome, by which the EEC was established, articulated the need to increase and stabilize agricultural productivity, improve living standards in agricultural areas, and assure adequate supplies at reasonable prices. To accomplish this objective, certain primary agricultural products were enumerated in Annex II of the treaty; these so-called *Annex II products* would be subject to community controls and supports. At the 1968 Stresa Conference, the operational elements of the CAP were devised by the (then) six members of the EEC.

In 1961, the CAP came into effect. Since that time, three principles have been the foundation of the CAP:

1. *Single market* (also referred to as *common pricing*), under which all agricultural products must be free to move within the community without duties, taxes, or other impediments; health and veterinary regulations must be harmonized, and administrative procedures made uniform. Under such conditions, free movement of agricultural products is induced with the object of uniform pricing throughout the community. For certain products (notably wheat), a *target price* is established by the EEC at the beginning of each year; it is the price determined by the EEC to be desirable from a producer standpoint. In the event the target price falls below a predetermined *intervention price*, the community will purchase the product and either store it or sell it outside the EEC.

2. *Community preference.* To ensure that imports or exports do not distort community pricing, a *sluicegate price* system is applied to products entering or leaving the EEC. Under this scheme, a *threshold price* is set by the community; if foreign prices are lower than those in the EEC, a levy will be placed on the import to bring it up to the level of comparable community products. To encourage exports of EEC agricultural products, which tend to exceed the world price for like commodities, EEC exporters are refunded the difference between the market price in the community (including costs of transportation to the port of export) and the selling price in the world market.

Most agricultural products imported into the EEC from third countries are subject to a two-tiered duty, the *fixed component* of which is the ad valorem duty prescribed in the common external tariff. In addition, a special *variable component,* computed in EUROPEAN CURRENCY UNITS *(q.v.)* (ECU), is imposed per 100 kilograms. The variable component is revised for each product four times per year (February 1, May 1, August 1, and November 1), and reflects the difference between the community's threshold price for the commodity and the world market price for the quarter. It is computed on the basis of the prices during the first two months and the first ten days of the third month of the preceding quarter. For a few commodities a maximum levy (fixed plus variable) is prescribed; in those cases, the maximum levy is published in the common external tariff and is reviewed every three months.

3. *Financial solidarity* (also known as *common financing*), whereby the costs of maintaining the CAP are borne by all the members of the EEC. Contributions by member states are made into the European Agricultural Guidance and Guarantee Fund, which finances the price support programs and related activities.

Several significant problems have arisen in administering the CAP, not the least of which has resulted from the fluctuation of the currencies of EEC member nations. Threshold prices, supports, and variable levies, inter alia, are expressed in terms of the ECU. The rate of exchange between every EEC national currency and the ECU is published. This so-called *green rate* consists of a fixed rate of exchange between national currencies and the ECU. Since 1969, it has been necessary to adjust the green rate to offset the effects of currency fluctuations within the community. Each member state is assigned a *monetary compensation amount* (mca) to maintain the position of its national currency relative to the ECU; the mca is based upon the difference between the green rate and market rate for a particular EEC currency. In the case of France, German Federal Republic, Belgium, Luxembourg, Ireland, and Denmark the mca is fully variable; for the United Kingdom, Italy, and Greece, the rates are adjusted in response to changes over a five-day reference period. This exchange rate device is further complicated by a system of *franchises* (also known as *neutral margins*) which are adjustments to the mca, and the application of *multiple green rates* in some EEC member states.

After several years of operation, it became evident that the objects of the CAP were being partially frustrated when Annex II products, which are subject to controls, were manufactured into secondary, or processed, products. Since the CAP assured all EEC members essentially the same costs for raw materials (i.e., Annex II items) those members having lower production costs enjoyed an advantage in marketing secondary products. In response to this condition, the EEC adopted price controls over *non-Annex II processed products*. Between 1969 and 1980, the *processed product regulations* were revised significantly; EEC Commission Directive 3033/80 is the basis of the current system, which covers products not listed in Annex II manufactured from one of the following:

Tariff No.	Description
04.02	skimmed milk powder
04.02	whole milk powder
04.03	butter
chapter 10	cereals: common wheat, durum wheat, rye, barley, maize [corn], rice
17.01	sugar
17.03	molasses

Processed product regulations also encompass *first stage products* which are substitutes for processed products. The first stage products, and the primary products to which they are linked, are:

Tariff No.	First Stage Product	Basis Product
11.08A IV	potato starch	maize
11.08 V	other starches (excluding rice or wheat starch) produced from roots or tubers under 07.06	maize
	goods made from fresh milk, not concentrated or sweetened, with milk fat content not exceeding 0.1%	skim powdered milk
	goods made from fresh milk or cream, not concentrated or sweetened, with milk fat content exceeding 0.1%	whole powdered milk
17.02D1	isoglucose	sugar

Processed products imported into the EEC are subject to the same scheme of fixed and variable levies applicable to primary, i.e., Annex II products. The levies are imposed on the processed products proportional to their content of Annex II products.

The CAP has been the subject of criticism both within and outside the EEC. Foreign producers, especially the United States, contend that the CAP is a major barrier to free trade; within the community, the cost of funding the CAP (11.5 billion ECU for Fiscal Year 1982) has been challenged as burdensome and excessive. Agricultural considerations have been the major impediments to the admission of Spain and Portugal to the EEC, and it is likely that there will be significant adjustment in the CAP to accommodate the entry of those largely agricultural countries into the community before 1987.

The products regulated under Annex II of the Treaty of Rome are as follows:

CCCN No.	Description
1	Live animals
2	Meat and edible offals
3	Fish, crustaceans, and mollusks
4	Dairy produce; birds' eggs; natural honey
5 (05.04)	Guts, bladders, and stomachs of animals (other than fish) whole and pieces thereof
(05.15)	Animal products not especially classified or included; dead animals of Chapter 1 or Chapter 3, unfit for human consumption
6	Live trees and other plants; bulbs, roots, and the like; cut flowers and ornamental foliage
7	Edible vegetables and certain roots and tubers
8	Edible fruits and nuts; peels of melons and citrus fruit
9	Coffee, tea and spices, excluding maté (heading no. 09.03)
10	Cereals
11	Products of the milling industry; malt and starches; gluten; inulin
12	Oils seeds and oleaginous fruits; miscellaneous grains, seeds, and fruits; industrial and medicinal plants; straw and fodder
13 (except 13.03)	Pectin
15 (15.01)	Lard and other rendered pig fat; rendered poultry fat
(15.02)	Unrendered fats of bovine cattle, sheep or goats; tallow (including "premier jus") produced from those fats
(15.03)	Lard stearin, oleo stearin and tallow stearin; lard oil; oleo-oil and tallow oil, not emulsified or mixed or prepared in any way
(15.04)	Fats and oils, of fish and marine mammals, whether or not refined
(15.07)	Fixed vegetable oils, fluid or solid, crude, refined, or purified
(15.12)	Animal and vegetable fats and oils, hydrogenated, whether or not refined, but not further prepared
(15.13)	Margarine, imitation lard, and other prepared edible fats
(15.17)	Residues resulting from the treatment of fatty substances or animal or vegetable waxes
16	Preparations of meat, of fish, of crustaceans or mollusks
17 (17.01)	Beet sugar and cane sugar, solid

(17.02)	Other sugars; sugar syrups; artificial honey (whether or not mixed with natural honey); caramel
(17.03)	Molasses, whether or not de-colourised
(17.05)	Flavoured or coloured sugars, syrups, and molasses, but not including fruit juices containing added sugar in any proportion
18 (18.01)	Cocoa beans, whole or broken, raw or roasted
(18.02)	Cocoa shells, husks, skins, and waste
20	Preparations of vegetables, fruits, or other parts of plants
22 (22.04)	Grape must in fermentation or with fermentation arrested other than by addition of alcohol
(22.05)	Wine of fresh grapes; grape must with fermentation arrested by addition of alcohol
(22.07)	Other fermented beverages (for example, cider, perry, and mead)
(22.08)	Ethyl alcohol or neutral spirits, whether or not denatured, of any strength, obtained from agricultural products listed in Annex II to the Treaty (excluding liqueurs and other spiritous beverages and compound alcoholic preparations (known as "concentrated extracts") for the manufacture of beverages
(22.10)	Vinegar and substitutes for vinegar
23	Residues and waste from the food industries; prepared animal fodder
24 (24.01)	Unmanufactured tobacco; tobacco refuse
45 (45.01)	Natural cork, unworked, crushed, granulated or ground; waste cork
54 (54.01)	Flax, raw or processed but not spun; flax tow and waste (including pulled or garretted rags)
57 (57.01)	True hemp (Cannabis sativa), raw or processed but not spun; tow and waste of true hemp (including pulled or garretted rags or rape)

COMMON CARRIER. See CARRIER.

COMMON EXTERNAL TARIFF. The uniform customs tariff applied by all the member states of a customs union or common market to imports from nonmember nations.

COMMON FINANCING. A feature of the COMMON AGRICULTURAL POLICY (q.v.) of the European Economic Community.

COMMON MARGINS ARRANGEMENT. A mechanism employed by the European Economic Community to stabilize the values of EEC member currencies relative to one another. See SNAKE.

COMMON MARKET. A supranational organization of trading nations, created to promote economic collaboration and minimize constraints on the free movement of goods among the member states. Features of a common market include elimination of tariffs on goods moving between member states; adoption of a common external tariff; and free flow of capital and labor among members. In addition, a common market is apt to possess common monetary and fiscal policies, regional plans for industrial and agricultural development, and uniform rules for social services; it may exhibit movement toward political unification. See CUSTOMS UNION and FREE TRADE AREA.

COMMON MARKET (EUROPEAN). See EUROPEAN ECONOMIC COMMUNITY.

COMMON PRICING. A feature of the COMMON AGRICULTURAL POLICY (q.v.) of the European Economic Community.

COMMONWEALTH (BRITISH). An association of sovereign states formerly comprising territories within the British Empire. The association was formed at an imperial conference in London in 1931 and implemented by the Statute of Westminster of the same year. The purpose of the Commonwealth is to foster a sense of common identity among the member states, all of which are politically equal.

In 1965, a Commonwealth secretariat was established in London to further the association's programs, including the enhancement of education and economic development in member states.

The following states were members of the Commonwealth in 1984:

United Kingdom	Guyana
Canada*	Botswana
Australia*	Lesotho
New Zealand*	Barbados*
India	Nauru†
Sri Lanka	Mauritius*
Ghana	Swaziland
Malaysia	Maldives†
Cyprus	Tonga
Nigeria	Fiji*
Sierra Leone	Bangladesh
Tanzania	Bahamas*
Western Samoa	Grenada*
Jamaica*	Papua New Guinea*
Trinidad and Tobago	Seychelles
Uganda	Solomon Islands*
Kenya	Tuvalu*†
Malawi	Dominica
Malta	Saint Lucia*
The Gambia	Kiribati
Singapore	Saint Vincent

Grenadines*†   Antigua and Barbuda*
Zimbabwe   Belize*
Vanuatu

* States recognizing the Queen as head of state.
† Associate members of the Commonwealth.

COMMONWEALTH PREFERENCE. Special preferential rates of duty applied by member states of the British Commonwealth on merchandise imported from other Commonwealth countries. In many cases, duties among Commonwealth members were totally abolished.

The accession of Britain into the European Communities, coupled with the adoption of generalized preferences by industrialized Commonwealth countries, has diminished or eliminated Commonwealth preferences as a feature of the customs tariffs of nations previously extending them.

Great Britain continues to offer trade concessions to former colonial possessions under special arrangements formulated by the European Economic Community and articulated in the LOMÉ CONVENTIONS *(q.v.)*.

COMMUNITY PREFERENCE. A component principle of the COMMON AGRICULTURAL POLICY *(q.v.)* of the European Economic Community.

COMPARABLE UNCONTROLLED PRICE. *See* ARM'S LENGTH PRICE.

COMPENSATED DOLLAR. A monetary system in which the value of the dollar against gold is adjusted periodically so that purchasing power of money remains constant against a prescribed commodity index.

COMPENSATING BALANCE. A non-interest-bearing deposit that a commercial borrower is obliged to maintain as condition of receiving a bank loan. The effect of this balance is to increase the net cost of the loan; while the amount to be held as a compensating balance is negotiable between the borrower and the bank, a balance of 20 percent of the loan is common.

COMPENSATING PRODUCTS. Locally obtained products used by a manufacturer to replace or augment imported products in the manufacture of a finished product intended for export.

COMPENSATION. Trade concessions granted by one nation to another in recompense for other trade concessions that have been withdrawn or suspended.

COMPENSATION DEAL. A semibarter arrangement in which goods are purchased partially in cash and partially with other goods.

COMPENSATORY DUTY. *See* DUTY.

COMPENSATORY FINANCING FACILITY. A special lending facility of the International Monetary Fund designed to aid developing nations confronted with temporary payment imbalances. The facility was established in 1963 to provide short-term financing to nations dependent upon primary products for export income, and where that income had declined temporarily as a result of a falloff in market prices for the export commodity. In those cases where the payments imbalance is attributable to factors other than a decline in the price paid for the export commodity, e.g., excessive imports, the IMF may require that corrective financial policies be adopted as a condition of compensatory financing.

COMPENSATORY SUSPENSION. The suspension of trade concessions by a nation in retaliation for the suspension of concessions by a trading partner.

COMPENSATORY TAX. A special import levy imposed by the European Economic Community upon certain agricultural imports when the entry price of such products falls below a *reference*, or minimum target, price and the import is priced so as to reflect an export subsidy. Compensatory taxes are institutionalized in the COMMON AGRICULTURAL POLICY *(q.v.)* of the European Economic Community.

COMPENSATORY WITHDRAWAL. The cancellation of a trade concession by a nation in retaliation for the withdrawal of a concession by a trading partner.

COMPETITIVE NEED LIMITATIONS. *See* GENERALIZED SYSTEM OF PREFERENCES.

COMPLEMENTARY EXPORTING. An arrangement in which a manufacturer markets his products internationally through the distribution channel of another firm, usually a manufacturer of similar but noncompetitive products.

COMPLEMENTARY GOODS. Products so related that a change in the demand for one similarly affects demand for the other; e.g., increased consumption of automobiles will normally increase consumption for gasoline, all things being equal.

COMPLEMENTATION AGREEMENT. An agreement between a commercial entity and two or more governments to reduce or eliminate duties among themselves on specific products produced by the firm in one or more of the signatory states. The object of such an arrangement is to induce a manufacturer to establish a plant in one of the signatory countries to supply that country and others with the output of the factory.

COMPOUND DUTY. *See* DUTY.

COMPRADOR. A marketing agent firm that enjoys a particularly intimate knowledge of the local market and its peculiarities.

COMPREHENSIVE EXPORT SCHEDULE. *See* EXPORT CONTROL ACT.

COMPULSORY CARTEL. A cartel formed by or under governmental sanction, adherence to which is required by all firms in the affected industry.

COMPUTED VALUE METHOD. An alternative method of valuing imports for the imposition of ad valorem duties, as provided in the CUSTOMS VALUATION AGREEMENT *(q.v.)*.

CONCESSION. An undertaking by one nation to reduce a tariff rate, increase a quota, or otherwise relieve an economic impediment to trade, usually in response to like concessions from trading partners.

In addition to such *reciprocal concessions,* a nation may offer special duty relief and other non-reciprocal concessions to needy and developing countries. The most comprehensive scheme of non-reciprocal concessions is the GENERAL SYSTEM OF PREFERENCES *(q.v.)*.

CONCESSIONAL SALE. A sale that allows the buyer terms less stringent than normal commercial conditions would otherwise dictate. Such sales are often made in conjunction with official aid programs and may include reduced sales price, special low-interest rates or extended payment terms, or acceptance of a "soft" currency in settlement of the transaction.

CONCURRENCE. An agreement among common carriers permitting the through movement of transportation equipment, e.g., containers, railcars, and trailers, through each carrier's system so as to permit an uninterrupted movement of goods.

CONDITIONAL CONTRABAND. *See* CONTRABAND OF WAR.

CONDITIONALLY FREE. Merchandise that is permitted duty-free entry, providing certain conditions can be met, usually the submission of evidence that the goods are the product of a given country or will be used for an approved purpose. If the prescribed conditions are not met, the goods will be assessed the prevailing duties.

CONEX CONTAINER. An ocean container somewhat smaller than standard containers, owned by the U.S. government and used primarily for transporting military cargoes. These containers measure 6'3" wide, and 6'10½" deep, and either 4'3" or 8'6" high.

CONFERENCE. An association of steamship lines operating over a specific trade route, formed for the purpose of setting freight rates and service standards to be applied uniformly by all the member carriers. The Shipping Act of 1916 empowers the Federal Maritime Commission to oversee the activities of conferences to ensure compliance with the law, but conference rate making is, in most cases, exempt from regulation. The approval of a conference by the commission exempts the carriers involved from the penalties of the antitrust laws.

The rationale for conferences is based on the international character of ocean shipping, which effectively precludes regulation of the industry by any nation. As supranational authorities, the conferences provide self-policing of the industry and, presumably, stability of rates and service.

Each conference operates through a secretariat, headed by a chairman elected by the member lines. Major policy questions or significant rate issues are addressed in executive session, attended by senior executives of the member lines. Routine requests from shippers for rate reductions are normally accommodated by the Rate Committee, which meets regularly; rate matters that are of far-reaching significance may be referred to executive session.

Although a conference issues one common tariff to which all the member lines adhere, the tariff may contain two rates for the same commodity. A *dual rate conference* offers a special discount rate to shippers who pledge to ship all their goods aboard the vessels of member lines; a higher rate is available to shippers who have not executed such a pledge, or *loyalty agreement.* A dual rate conference must give ninety days' notice in advance of any rate increase so as to permit shippers to cancel their loyalty agreements. A *single rate conference* offers only one rate, without discounts or loyalty agreements, and may increase its rates upon thirty days' notice.

Only one conference operates over a given trade route; it normally includes the major carriers involved in that trade. Carriers that elect not to join the conference are said to be *independent.* As a rule, separate conferences direct the export and import trade between two points, although the same carriers are often members of both the import and export groups.

In the United States, all conferences are *open conferences,* which is to say that any carrier can join the cartel upon application. Conferences operating between points outside the United States are often *closed,* and membership is restricted.

CONFERENCE CARRIER. A steamship line that is a member of a CONFERENCE *(q.v.)*.

CONFERENCE SIGNATORY. A merchant that has signed a contract, called a *loyalty agreement,* pledging to ship all its products to certain destinations aboard vessels of steamship lines adhering to a CONFERENCE *(q.v.)*. The agreement is executed in return for a discount on the ocean freight payable on such shipments.

CONFIRMATION. *See* LETTER OF CREDIT.

CONFIRMATION NOTE. A document prepared by a shipbroker specifying the terms and conditions agreed upon by the principals to a charter transaction. The note will be circulated to the principals for review, after which it will serve as the model for the formal charter party.

CONFIRMING HOUSE. A commercial institution engaged in nonrecourse financing of foreign trade. The confirming house may *confirm* a foreign buyer's order, acting as guarantor of payment to the seller; in some cases, the confirming house may actually take title to the goods as agent for the foreign purchaser, arranging shipment of the goods.

Confirming houses are particularly active in London, but they are growing in significance in New York and other major trading cities as well.

CONFISCATION. The takeover of foreign-owned property by a government without offer of compensation. *See* EXPROPRIATION.

CONFRONTATION AND JUSTIFICATION. A mechanism employed during multinational trade negotiations to define the positions of the various national delegations. Typically, each participating nation submits to its trading partners a statement of views, proposed tariff cuts, et cetera. During a series of meetings each nation is *confronted* by the other delegations with questions concerning the degree of tariff cuts proposed, the absence of specific products from consideration, and like matters. The delegation so confronted is obliged to justify its stand on the points raised.

CONGESTION SURCHARGE. *See* PORT CONGESTION SURCHARGE.

CONGLOMERATE. A firm engaged in diverse business activities simultaneously. Usually, a conglomerate arises over many years as the result of the acquisition of subsidiaries in different industries.

CONNECTING CONVEYANCE. Any barge, truck, or other means of transport used to carry goods to a pier or airport for onward carriage aboard the principal conveyance.

CONSIGN. The act of ordering a carrier to deliver a lot of merchandise from a given point to a given destination. The order is given via the medium of a BILL OF LADING (*q.v.*).

CONSIGNEE. The person or firm to whom goods are shipped under a BILL OF LADING (*q.v.*) and so named in the bill.

CONSIGNEE MARKS. *See* MARKS AND NUMBERS.

CONSIGNMENT. Goods in transit under a BILL OF LADING (*q.v.*)

CONSIGNOR. The person or firm shown as shipper on the BILL OF LADING (*q.v.*).

CONSOLIDATION. The combination of various small shipments into one large shipment so as to achieve a lower overall freight rate.

CONSOLIDATION POINT. A warehouse or terminal where many small shipments are combined to be shipped as a unit.

CONSORTIUM. A multiparty commercial undertaking, differing from a joint venture by virtue of the comparatively large number of participants.

CONSORTIUM BANK. A bank owned by a group of other banks, usually including foreign banks, with no one member of the group controlling more than 50 percent of the outstanding shares.

CONSTRUCTED PRICE. A value for customs purposes that ignores the invoice price of the merchandise but is derived by computing the cost inputs of the product (materials plus reasonable manufacturing expenses in the country of origin plus a profit factor), to which are added the normal costs associated with preparig the goods for export.

Constructed prices are used by customs authorities when there is reason to believe that the invoice price does not reflect the true value of the goods. As a practical matter, most trading nations have adopted the *transaction value* method of applying duties, i.e., the invoice value, as provided in the CUSTOMS VALUATION AGREEMENT (*q.v.*); however, the constructed price method may be used when the transaction value method is inappropriate or cannot be applied.

CONSTRUCTION DIFFERENTIAL SUBSIDY. An economic subsidy offered by the U.S. government to vessel operators to encourage the building of ships in American shipyards. Recognizing that American labor and material costs are generally higher than those in many other countries, Title XI of the Merchant Marine Act of 1936 empowers the Maritime Administration to subsidize U.S. shipbuilding costs up to 50 percent.

CONSTRUCTIVE TOTAL LOSS. In marine insurance, a loss where cost of repair or recovery would exceed the value of the property were it to be saved or repaired. In British usage, an insured cannot claim a constructive total loss unless the costs of rehabilitation exceed 100 percent of the value; in the United States, however, a claim for constructive total loss can be advanced, in most cases, if the costs of saving or repair exceed 50 percent of the value.

CONSUL. A government official sent abroad to a permanent station for the purpose of sustaining trade relations between his home country and the one to which he is accredited.

A consul's duties revolve around the day-to-day administration of trade-related activities, including validation of shipping documents, issuance of visas, and aiding citizens of his country who are in distress. In many cases, a consul serves as a source of information to foreign businessmen seeking commercial contracts in his country. As a rule, consuls do not normally become involved in the negotiation of trade or political relationships with the host country.

Consular officers are not diplomats, and usually do not enjoy diplomatic immunity; a rather less comprehensive form of *consular immunity* applies to consuls while stationed abroad, including exemption from local taxes in the country to which they are assigned.

In some cases, usually in smaller cities or outlying areas, a country may appoint as its consul a national of the host country. Persons so appointed usually have commercial or other ties to the country they represent. These individuals are commonly known as *consular agents* or *honorary consuls*.

CONSULAR INVOICE. *See* INVOICE.

CONSUMER PRICE INDEX. An index of the retail price of four hundred consumer products and services, computed monthly by the Bureau of Labor Statistics. Formerly known as the Cost of Living Index, the compilation includes retail price inputs of given items from many cities across the United States.

CONSUMPTION ENTRY. *See* ENTRY (CUSTOMS).

CONTAINER FREIGHT STATION. A warehouse or terminal licensed by U.S. Customs to receive in-bond consolidations of containerized cargo. The containers delivered to this station carry imported merchandise in small lots destined to many consignees; the goods will be removed from the containers under customs supervision and shipped onward in less than container lots. Customs clearance may be effected at the terminal, or the goods may be shipped in bond to another point for clearance.

In addition, exporters of small shipments may send their merchandise to the container freight station, where several small lots will be combined in a single container for shipment aboard the vessel.

CONTAINER YARD. A facility at which a steamship operator makes full container loads of merchandise available for pick-up by the consignee following discharge from the vessel.

CONTEMPORANEOUS RESERVE ACCOUNTING. *See* RESERVE ACCOUNTING.

CONTINENTAL BILL. A bill of exchange drawn on a European bank, other than a British or Irish bank.

CONTRABAND. Goods that are deemed unsuitable for entry into a country and that are subject to interdiction by customs authorities. Persons attempting to enter contraband through customs may be subject to civil and/or criminal penalties, in addition to forfeiture of the merchandise.

CONTRABAND OF WAR. Goods that may be used to advance the war-making potential of a belligerent and are subject to seizure by an enemy. Generally, neutral nations are under no obligation to prevent their citizens from dealing in articles that might be considered contraband by a warring state. Accordingly, belligerents are compelled to use their own resources to inhibit the flow of contraband goods to the enemy.

Contraband is customarily divided into two categories: (1) *absolute contraband*—munitions, military vehicles, communications equipment, or other apparatus clearly destined for military use; and (2) *conditional contraband*—articles that may be used for military purposes but not clearly destined for use by armed forces and may have nonmilitary application, e.g., chemicals and metals.

A belligerent is permitted to stop neutral vessels on the high seas to inspect for contraband. Any neutral ship found to carry contraband is subject to seizure.

CONTRACT CARRIAGE. *See* CARRIER.

CONTRACT DEMURRAGE. Liquidated damages payable by a charterer to a vessel owner for holding up the ship beyond the time allocated in the charter party. The rate of demurrage is stipulated in the charter party, and is calculated on a per day or per hour basis.

CONTRACT OF AFFREIGHTMENT. A contract, between the shipper of goods and a transport company, specifying the terms and conditions under which a given lot of merchandise is to be moved. The contract is usually evidenced by a bill of lading containing the terms of carriage, including the carrier's liability for loss and damage in transit, as well as a description of the merchandise, destination, consignee, and other relevant details of the shipment.

In some cases, the bill of lading will carry the full particulars of the contract; in other cases, particularly when a *short form* bill of lading is used, the document will summarize the terms of the contract, referring the holder of the bill to a separate source (usually the carrier's tariff or a charter party),which is incorporated by references, for the full terms and conditions of the agreement.

CONTRACT RATE. In the steamship industry, the freight rate applicable to goods shipped by a firm that has executed an EXCLUSIVE PATRONAGE CONTRACT *(q.v.)* with a CONFERENCE *(q.v.)*. In return for executing such a contract, whereby the shipper agrees to transport his goods only on the vessels of a given conference, the carriers extend to the shipper a preferential freight rate.

CONTRACT SHIPPER. A merchant that has executed an EXCLUSIVE PATRONAGE CONTRACT *(q.v.)* with a shipping conference, thereby agreeing to ship all its goods aboard vessels of steamship lines that are members of the conference, in return for specified preferential freight rates. *See* LOYALTY AGREEMENT (CONFERENCE).

CONTROLLED CARRIER ACT. *See* OCEAN SHIPPING ACT OF 1978.

CONTROLLED FOREIGN CORPORATION. *See* SUBPART F.

CONVENTIONAL DUTY. A customs duty, or rate of duty, arising out of a treaty or other international agreement, as contrasted with an *autonomous* duty unilaterally imposed by a government absent of any international agreement.

CONVENTIONAL INTERNATIONAL LAW. International law that has arisen as the product of treaties or formal agreements among nations, as compared with international law that has developed through custom and usage over time.

CONVENTION OF PARIS FOR THE PROTEC-TION OF INDUSTRIAL PROPERTY. *See* PARIS CONVENTION.

CONVENTION ON INTERNATIONAL TRADE IN ENDANGERED SPECIES OF FLORA AND FAUNA. Known commonly by the acronym CITES, a multilateral agreement to suppress international trade in endangered species of wildlife and plants. The convention was signed at Washington in 1973; in 1984, sixty-nine nations were signatories.

Adherents to the convention pledge to interdict the exportation or importation of species listed in the agreement, with limited exceptions. Endangered species are categorized into three appendixes: (1) species that are in grave danger of extinction (these are banned from all commercial trade); (2) species that are threatened but are not in danger of imminent extinction (trade in these species is permitted if licensed by the country of exportation); and (3) species that are not threatened globally but may be threatened on a local or regional scale (a signatory state may place a locally threatened species on the protected list, thereby invoking the aid of other governments in prohibiting unlicensed trade in that species).

Any adhering state is empowered to claim for itself a *reservation*, or exemption, from control for any species, irrespective of how threatened that species may be.

In the United States enforcement of the convention is entrusted to the U.S. Customs Service in conjunction with the Fish and Wildlife Service of the Department of Interior.

CONVENTION ON NOMENCLATURE FOR THE CLASSIFICATION OF GOODS IN CUS-TOMS TARIFFS. *See* BRUSSELS TARIFF NOMENCLATURE.

CONVENTION ON THE SETTLEMENT OF IN-VESTMENT DISPUTES BETWEEN STATES AND NATIONALS OF OTHER STATES. *See* INTERNATIONAL CENTRE FOR SETTLEMENT OF INVESTMENT DISPUTES.

CONVENTION ON THE VALUATION OF GOODS FOR CUSTOMS PURPOSES. *See* BRUSSELS DEFINITION OF VALUE.

CONVERGENCE HYPOTHESIS. A view held by certain economic and political thinkers that the world can be divided into three economic camps—the industrialized, capitalist world; the communist nations; and the so-called Third World developing nations—and that the capitalists and communists are losing their ideological identities, each group adopting some of the characteristics of the other (i.e., the Western nations are becoming more "socialist" through enhanced social welfare programs and government regulation of commerce,

while the communist are becoming "capitalist," as manifested by the use of productivity inducements for workers). The hypothesis holds that the Third World is drawing parallels with both camps, with the result that the developing nations are becoming an ideological *synthesis*, or admixture, of the capitalist/specialist models.

CONVERTIBILITY. The ability of a currency to be exchanged for other currencies in settlement of current account transactions. Currencies are convertible in varying degrees, although the ability of nonresidents freely to purchase and sell a given currency, without governmental restriction, indicates a high degree of convertibility. Conversely, a currency that cannot be freely purchased or sold by nonresidents is said to be *inconvertible*.

COOKE COMMITTEE. *See* COMMITTEE ON BANKING REGULATIONS AND SUPERVISORY PRACTICES.

COOLEY LOANS. Foreign-currency-denominated loans by the U.S. government to foreign nations to permit the purchase of American agricultural commodities. The loans are authorized by an amendment to the AGRICULTURAL TRADE DEVELOPMENT AND ASSISTANCE ACT *(q.v.)* of 1954 (P.L. 480). The Cooley Amendment permits such loans to be made up to 25 percent of the value of any given foreign currency derived from the sale of surplus American agricultural commodities.

COOPERAGE. Originally, wooden packaging used for the transport of merchandise; the term embraced barrels, casks, and crates. Today the term is used in the shipping industry to include outer packages generally, whether of wood or not.

COOPERATIVE FINANCING FACILITY. *See* EXPORT-IMPORT BANK.

COOPERATIVE INTERNATIONAL LAW. A general term applicable to that international law arising from multinational agreements, such as the Charter of the United Nations and the Treaty of Rome, especially when the agreement is directed toward the attainment of goals common to the signatories, and the agreement is widely accepted among those nations sharing a common problem.

COORDINATING COMMITTEE. *See* COCOM.

CORRESPONDENT BANK. A bank that acts as the representative of another bank in a given transaction. As a rule, correspondents have sums on deposit with each other for the purpose of settling the transactions of the other bank.

COSTING AGREEMENT. An arrangement among firms in a given line of business to exchange information on production costs or to employ uniform methods of accounting. The object of the arrangement is to standardize costing practices within the industry, thereby eliminating or minimizing price competition.

Agreements to exchange cost information may be viewed as collusion under the antitrust laws and, as such, constitute a criminal offense.

COST OF LIVING INDEX. *See* CONSUMER PRICE INDEX.

COUNCIL OF EUROPE. An association of twenty-one European states formed to identify and collectively pursue areas of common interest, and to provide a forum for the articulation of European unity.

The council was formed by treaty in London on May 5, 1949; permanent headquarters were established in Strasbourg, France, the same year. The council is governed through three bodies:

1. The Committee of Ministers is the executive organ of the group, consisting of the foreign ministers of the member countries. The committee considers and acts upon the recommendations of the deliberative Parliamentary Assembly, and serves as a forum for the formulation of international agreements among the member states. The work of the committee is augmented by the efforts of various committees of experts.

2. The Parliamentary Assembly is a consultative body of 170 representatives chosen by the national parliaments of the member states; each state is accorded from two to eighteen representatives, depending upon population. The assembly discusses topics of general interest, referring resolutions to the Committee of Ministers for incorporation into binding international agreements, or for other treatment.

3. The Secretariat is an international bureaucracy of 800 persons operating within eight directorates. The Secretariat reports to the secretary-general, who is elected for five years by the Parliamentary Assembly from a list of candidates submitted by the Committee of Ministers.

In addition to the three principal organs, the Council of Europe embraces the European Commission of Human Rights, the European Court of Human Rights, the European Youth Center, and the European Youth Foundation.

Among the significant achievements of the Council of Europe are the European Social Charter, which addresses labor conditions; European Code of Social Security, which establishes uniform standards for social security and old age benefits, as well as survivor's and unemployment compensation; European Convention on the Status of Migrant Workers; and European Convention on Human Rights, known officially as the Convention for the Protection of Human Rights and Fundamental Freedoms, which establishes a commission and a court to review alleged violations of human rights within member states (many council members have submitted human rights disputes to the binding judgment of the court).

In 1984, the Council of Europe was considering the adoption of conventions on pension standards and an international medical credit card for use by travelers.

The working languages of the organization are French and English.

COUNCIL FOR MUTUAL ECONOMIC COOPERATION. Known commonly as COMECON, was organized by the Soviet Union in 1949, in response to the Marshall Plan. COMECON'S objective is to facilitate trade among its members: consisting of the Soviet Union, the communist states of Eastern Europe (excepting Albania), Mongolia, and Cuba; Yugoslavia has been an associate member since 1965. A multinational trade plan among the members has not emerged, although some joint plans, including an East European electric power grid, have been accomplished. Trade among COMECON members is undertaken on a bilateral basis between the foreign trade organizations of the two nations. Settlements among the trading partners are normally resolved by the foreign trade banks on a bilateral basis. *See also* INTERNATIONAL INVESTMENT BANK.

COUNT CERTIFICATE. A document confirming the count of merchandise at time of shipment or delivery. The document is often issued by an independent third party, such as an inspection bureau.

COUNTERPURCHASE. A form of COUNTERTRADE *(q.v.)* in which two parties agree to purchase specified quantities of merchandise from each other at a fixed price. The effect is that each party simultaneously purchases and sells approximately equivalent values of merchandise with the other party. Counterpurchase differs from barter only in that the contracts of purchase and sale are independent of one another (although they are usually executed at the same time), and the sales and purchases are denominated in terms of money, rather than goods.

The counterpurchase option is used frequently in transactions with communist nations or developing countries short of foreign exchange.

COUNTERTRADE. A commercial arrangement in which the buyer pays for his purchases, wholly or partly, with something other than money. Very often countertrade deals include some cash, but a significant portion of the transaction is settled with commodities or services.

Countertrade has been employed heavily and successfully in trade arrangements with communist nations and countries of the Third World, where shortage of foreign exchange might otherwise preclude trade.

Countertrade arrangements are structured in many forms, each known by a specific name. For details on the various countertrade options, *see* BARTER, BUY-BACK, CLEARING, COMPENSATION DEAL, COUNTERPURCHASE, SWAPPING, SWITCHING.

COUNTERVAILING DUTIES. Special duties, over and above ordinary duties, imposed upon imported merchandise to counteract the economic advantage provided to the foreign supplier by his government in the form of export subsidies. The object of countervailing duties is to protect manufacturers in the importing country by neutralizing the effect of the *bounties and grants* provided to their foreign competitor. Such bounties and grants include direct payments to the foreign manufacturer as a stimulus to export, tax relief for export sales, low-cost financing directed toward export projects, or any such material assistance.

To invoke countervailing duties, a petition is filed with the International Trade Administration (ITA) of the Department of Commerce by an *interested party;* in most cases, this is an American manufacturer of a product similar to the subsidized import, but might be a labor union or trade association involved in a like product. The petition would normally include the name and address of the applicant, the name and address of any foreign firms known or believed to be producing merchandise imported to the United States under subsidy, and evidence of such subsidy.

In its investigation of any complaint, the ITA is obliged to discount subsidies provided by the foreign country to local producers for the purpose of domestic economic stimulation, and not for export promotion.

In those cases where it is necessary to demonstrate *material injury* to American firms, the application must be submitted to the International Trade Commission (ITC) as well as the ITA. A finding of material injury is necessary when the product enters the United States free of duty, or when the product derives from a country that adheres to the Agreement on Subsidies and Countervailing Measures (Subsidies Code).

If a finding of subsidy is pronounced by the ITA (and, where required, material injury is concluded by the ITC), the Department of Commerce will direct the Customs Service to assess additional, i.e., countervailing, duties at such a rate so as to offset the economic effects of the subsidies. Customs officers will require a deposit of estimated duties pending final settlement of the subsidy findings.

The findings of the ITA and ITC or the refusal of those agencies to pursue complaints may be brought before the U.S. Court of International Trade, which is empowered to rule on all questions of law or fact arising out of a countervailing duty action.

The ITA is obliged to review annually all findings of subsidy that have resulted in the imposition of countervailing duties (see figure).

COUNTRY CONTROLLED BUYING AGENT. A governmental agency or quasi-official corporation that is the sole or primary entity authorized to trade with foreign countries for the purchase of certain goods. Very often the buying agent is also the state monopoly for the sale of such goods within the country.

Country controlled buying agents are common in centrally planned economies but are used to a lesser extent in market economy countries to regulate imports of liquor, tobacco, and similar luxury or highly taxed products.

COUNTRY GROUPS. A classification scheme provided in U.S. export control regulations. The countries of the world are divided into seven groups, plus Canada; each group is designated by a letter of the alphabet. Export licensing requirements vary from group to group. An individual seeking to learn the export licensing regulations for a specific commodity to a particular country would look up the Schedule B number for the product on the Commodity Control List; a notice next to each commodity on the list stipulates whether a validated export license is required, and if so, for which countries, by country group.

The country groups are as follows:
Group Q—Romania
Group S—Libya
Group T—All countries and territories of the Western Hemisphere, excepting Cuba and Canada
Group V—All countries not included in any other group, except Canada
Group W—Hungary and Poland
Group Y—Albania, Bulgaria, Czechoslovakia, Estonia, German Democratic Republic, Laos, Latvia, Lithuania, Mongolian People's Republic, USSR
Group Z—Cuba, Kampuchea, North Korea, Vietnam
Canada is not included in any country group inasmuch as exports to that country are not normally subject to controls.

See COCOM; EXPORT CONTROL ACT.

COUNTRY OF ORIGIN. For customs tariff purposes, the country in which an imported product

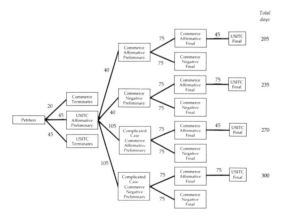

Statutory Timetable for Countervailing Duty Investigations (in days). Courtesy of U. S. International Trade Commission.

was manufactured, grown, or produced. When goods pass through more than one country in the process of manufacture, the country of origin does not change unless the product has been transformed substantially; minor manipulations of the product are not normally adequate to alter the country of origin.

As a practical matter, a product is regarded as having originated in the country in which at least 50 percent of its final value was derived, although higher percentage tests are often employed. In the case of goods entering the United States under the CARIBBEAN BASIN INITIATIVE *(q.v.)* or the GENERALIZED SYSTEM OF PREFERENCES *(q.v.),* lower levels of local content are usually permitted.

COUP D'ETAT. The overthrow of an established government by an insurgent group of forces within the government itself. A coup differs from a revolution in that a revolution implies a general uprising of the population, or at least widespread support through the nation for the insurgent forces.

COURTESY NOTICE. *See* LIQUIDATION.

COVERED TRANSACTION. A transaction denominated in terms of a foreign currency, payable at a future date, in which protection against loss on exchange has been procured, usually in the form of a FORWARD EXCHANGE CONTRACT *(q.v.).*

CRAFT AND LIGHTER. A clause in marine insurance contracts that holds the goods covered while in transit to and from the mother ship by lighters, rafts, and similar conveyances.

CRAWLING PEG. A middle ground between fixed and freely floating exchange rates. Unlike the free-floating system in which exchange rates are determined by market forces alone, and a system of fixed exchange rates (i.e., the defunct Bretton Woods system), the crawling peg scheme envisions that various trading currencies would have par values in terms of each other, usually the average over time of daily spot rates. When the spot or current market rate deviated significantly from the floating par, or *crawling* rate, central banks would intervene to restore equilibrium. *See* BRETTON WOODS AGREEMENT.

CREDIT CURRENCY. *Synonymous with* FIDUCIARY CURRENCY *(q.v.).*

CREDIT D'IMPÔT. A tax credit permitted in Belgium to recipients of certain dividend income in recognition that the corporation paying the dividend has been previously taxed upon the income.

CREDIT METHOD. *See* DOUBLE TAXATION.

CREDITOR NATION. Any nation with total foreign obligations owed to it greater than its aggregate obligations to other nations.

CREDIT TRANCHE. A lending facility at the International Monetary Fund for nations suffering balance of payments difficulties. Before borrowing in the credit tranche, a nation must have exhausted its *gold tranche* facility. The gold tranche is equivalent to the amount of gold that a nation has deposited with the IMF, usually 25 percent of its total subscription in the fund. A nation can usually borrow up to the gold tranche at its option; beyond this, it must activate the credit tranche, which requires IMF approval. When such credit is approved, the borrowing nation is obliged to deposit with the IMF a specified amount of its national currency in return for foreign currencies loaned by the IMF. Repayment is in such currencies and under such a schedule as the IMF may specify. In addition, the IMF may oblige the borrowing country to adopt corrective fiscal or monetary policies as conditions of permitting access to the credit tranche.

CROSS BILL. *Synonymous with* RE-DRAFT *(q.v.).*

CROSS-CURRENCY EXPOSURE. Obligations denominated in terms of a given currency that are not matched by equivalent revenues in terms of that currency. For example, a firm with obligations of 10 million Japanese yen but revenues of only 8 million yen are *exposed* to the degree that they must purchase, in the foreign exchange markets, 2 million yen. The exposure lies in the fact that the firm cannot predict what it will cost, in terms of dollars, to purchase the required two million yen when they are required at a point in the future. If the exposure can be predicted in terms of currency units and timing, the exposure can be mitigated or eliminated by means of a currency *hedge*. *See* HEDGING.

CROSS LICENSING. An arrangement in which one firm grants to another licenses to exploit proprietary rights in its patents or trademarks, secret processes, et cetera, in return for similar licensure to use the rights or processes of the recipient firm.

CROSS RATE. The ratio between the exchange rate of two currencies in relation to a third currency.

CROSS TRADER. A steamship line operating over a trade route not including its home country.

CUBAN ASSETS CONTROL REGULATIONS. U.S. government regulations, promulgated under authority of Section 5 (b) of the Trading with the Enemy Act, that forbid unlicensed importation of any product manufactured in Cuba, or manufactured in whole or in part of Cuban components irrespective of place of manufacture, or any product, irrespective of origin, transported from or through Cuba. Likewise, exports to Cuba (excepting licensed shipments of certain medicines and special foods for humanitarian reasons) are prohibited. The secretary of the treasury may grant exemption to the regulations by issuance of a validated import or export license.

Persons or firms found to be in violation of the regulations are subject to civil and criminal penalties.

CULTURAL ADIAPHORA. Cultural patterns and business behavior in which a foreigner may, but need not, participate at his option without giving offense to the norms of the country in which he is visiting. For example, a Western businessman in Japan may elect to bow upon greeting a Japanese associate, rather than to shake hands. The use of the local custom by the Westerner does not offend the Japanese, nor is it expected of him.

CULTURAL EXCLUSIVE. Patterns of local cultural behavior in which it would be inappropriate for a foreigner to participate. For example, a Western businessman in Saudi Arabia would be well advised not to wear traditional Arab garb in public.

CULTURAL IMPERATIVE. Business customs and behavior patterns to which all members of the business community, including foreigners, are expected to adhere. For example, business meetings in Switzerland begin on schedule, and all participants are expected to be punctual, irrespective of the habits a foreign businessman has brought with him from his native country.

CULTURALLY CONGRUENT STRATEGY. A plan for penetrating a foreign market that incorporates an offering of products similar to those already available and accepted in the target country, or that attempts to identify the product culturally with the country.

CUMULATIVE LETTER OF CREDIT. *See* RE-VOLVING LETTER OF CREDIT.

CURE AND MAINTENANCE. An ancient principle of maritime law that holds a vessel owner responsible to care for sick and injured seamen in his employ. The principle can be traced back to the sea codes of the Middle Ages and was affirmed in American law in 1823 in the case of Harden vs. Gordon.

The rules covering compensation for job-related sickness and injury were formalized in the Jones Act of 1920.

CURRENCY ADJUSTMENT FACTOR. A surcharge imposed on ocean freight by a carrier to offset or mitigate the impact of exchange rate fluctuations upon his freight revenue.

CURRENCY CONVERTIBLE IN FACT. A national currency that can be used for the settlement of private transactions, as contrasted with an ARTIFI-CIAL CURRENCY UNIT *(q.v.)*, such as *special drawing rights*, which are used only by governments for the settlement of official transactions or for reserve purposes.

CURRENCY RISK. The economic risk assumed by a lender or seller who is to be paid in units of a foreign currency that, when translated at some future date into his own currency, he will have sustained a loss (in terms of his own currency) because the foreign currency has depreciated in value prior to settlement of the obligation.

CURRENCY SWAP. *See* SWAP ARRANGEMENT.

CURRENT ACCOUNT. An entry in a nation's balance of payments accounts reflecting the purchase of goods or services for consumption immediately or in the near future. *See* BALANCE OF PAYMENTS.

CURRENT ACCOUNT PURCHASES. The value of *intermediate products* in the national production process. An intermediate product is a manufacturing input that has not been converted into a finished product; for example, steel is an intermediate product in the manufacture of an automobile.

The value of current account purchases is important as a component in measuring GROSS NA-TIONAL PRODUCT *(q.v.)*, which is a tabulation, in terms of dollars, of the national output of goods and useful services during a given time span. The distinction between finished products (inventories) and current account purchases is essential in avoiding an artificial inflation of the gross national product.

CUSTOMARY BUSINESS PRACTICES. Practices and patterns of behavior that are of long standing and generally well known throughout an industry, and that are accepted without governmental mandate. In the case of disputes, a court or other body may incorporate customary business practices into the context of the agreement, and may thereby infer the intent of the parties where that intent is not specifically defined.

CUSTOMARY FREIGHT UNIT. As used within the context of the Carriage of Goods by Sea Act, the unit upon which freight is assessed on bulk or unpackaged cargoes. The act provides that a carrier's liability for loss or damage to cargo shall be limited to $500 per package, or "other customary freight unit." Where cargo is not in packages, the customary freight unit may be the shipping ton or another customary standard recognized in the trade.

CUSTOMARY INTERNATIONAL LAW. International law that has arisen, over many years, from custom and usage and that is generally understood and accepted as binding although not codified.

CUSTOMARY QUICK DESPATCH. A provision in a vessel charter agreement that the ship will be loaded or unloaded with all reasonable speed. By including a customary quick despatch (or CQD) clause in the contract, the parties need not specify LAYTIME *(q.v.)* permitted, and neither DEMURRAGE nor DESPATCH MONEY *(qq.v.)* will be paid, except in the case of inordinate delays.

CUSTOMHOUSE BROKER. A firm licensed by the U.S. Customs Service to act as the importer's agent in facilitating the clearance of goods through customs. In this capacity, the customhouse broker files all necessary documents with customs to ensure that the merchandise is expeditiously inspected by customs and that proper tariff classification is applied to the goods and correct duties and taxes are levied; the broker also makes payment for such levies on behalf of the importer.

In order for a customhouse broker to perform for a client, the principal must invest the broker with a power of attorney, which is filed with the Customs Service.

There are more than three thousand persons licensed as customhouse brokers in the United States. Many of these individuals are employed by brokerage firms operating in major port cities.

CUSTOMS COOPERATION COUNCIL. An international organization established for the purpose of harmonizing the customs procedures and techniques of member countries. The agency is concerned with the mechanics of customs administration and is not involved in matters relating to tariff levels or similar substantive economic policy questions.

The council is the product of various post–World War II efforts to address the problems of international trade. It is the direct descendant of a study group formed in 1947 to examine the possibility of a European customs union. Efforts toward the establishment of a customs union were impeded by numerous economic and political problems; nevertheless, the study group successfully advanced three international agreements: the Convention on Nomenclature for the Classification of Goods in Customs Tariffs (BRUSSELS TARIFF NOMENCLATURE [q.v.]); the Convention on the Valuation of Goods for Customs Purposes (BRUSSELS DEFINITION OF VALUE [q.v.]); and a convention establishing a permanent Customs Cooperation Council, to be based in Brussels, to aid in the integration of customs procedures. All three conventions were signed at Brussels on December 15, 1950; the first meeting of the council took place on January 26, 1953. The council meets annually and consists of representatives of each member state.

While the Brussels definition of value has been largely supplanted by the CUSTOMS VALUATION AGREEMENT (q.v.) arising from the Tokyo Round of trade agreements, the council provides a technical committee to the GENERAL AGREEMENT ON TARIFFS AND TRADE (q.v.), or GATT, to ensure uniformity in the application of GATT valuation rules. In addition, the council provides secretariat services for implementation of the 1972 Customs Convention on Containers, and orchestrates training programs for customs officials from developing nations.

CUSTOMS COOPERATION COUNCIL NOMENCLATURE. *See* BRUSSELS TARIFF NOMENCLATURE.

CUSTOMS ENFORCEMENT AREA. An area not to extend more than fifty miles seaward, beyond the CUSTOMS WATERS (q.v.). Within this zone customs officers are authorized to enforce U.S. laws if the president finds that vessels are hovering offshore for the purpose of violating U.S. laws governing the importation or exportation of goods.

CUSTOMS ENTRY. *See* ENTRY (CUSTOMS).

CUSTOMS INVOICE. *See* INVOICE.

CUSTOMS OF THE PORT. Local usages and practices relative to the handling or discharge of cargo, or the treatment of documents relating thereto. When ambiguities exist in contracts covering the handling of cargo or cargo-related documents, a court or other competent body may apply the customs of the port in interpreting the contract.

CUSTOMS RATE. The rate of exchange employed by U.S. Customs in converting foreign currency invoices for the purpose of arriving at a value, in U.S. dollars, for imported merchandise. Ad valorem duties are applied on the dollar value.

In accordance with the Customs Simplification Act of 1956, the secretary of the treasury proclaims, on a quarterly basis, the rates of exchange to be used by the Customs Service. As a matter of procedure, the secretary proclaims the rate used in the first market transaction of each quarter, as certified by the Federal Reserve Bank of New York. The rate so proclaimed is used throughout the quarter, unless the rate for any day varies by more than 5 percent from the certified rate.

CUSTOMS SERVICE. *See* UNITED STATES CUSTOMS SERVICE.

CUSTOMS TERRITORY. The geographical area of a country, its possessions, and surrounding waters within which the customs authority is empowered to impose duties and controls upon foreign merchandise entering therein.

The customs territory need not necessarily incorporate all the territory over which a nation asserts sovereignty. For example, the customs territory of the United States does not embrace the Virgin Islands, American Samoa, nor the various FOREIGN TRADE ZONES (q.v.) established within the United States proper.

CUSTOMS TRANSIT. The condition of merchandise that is transiting the customs territory of a nation without having been released from customs jurisdiction. Goods in customs transit are processed under an *in transit* entry at the time they enter the United States; the in transit, or *I.T.*, entry is effected by filing with U.S. Customs a permit application specifying the destination and character of the goods, a declaration of value, and other information, as well as a bond or other evidence of financial security for duty and tax obligations. Goods in such status are said to travel *in bond.*

Customs transit is routinely used for goods in through transit between the port of arrival and an interior point at which customs clearance and release will be effected. For example, goods traveling between Japan and Denver, Colorado, might land at Oakland, California, but travel *in bond* on to Denver for actual inspection and release. Likewise, it is not uncommon for goods to travel over the territory of the United States from country of origin to some third country, as in the case of Canadian goods traveling to New York to board a ship for Nigeria. In this case, the bond posted for the merchandise upon entry into U.S. territory would be released by documentation evidencing export of the goods.

See ENTRY (CUSTOMS).

CUSTOMS UNION. An arrangement among participating countries whereby tariffs are eliminated or virtually eliminated on products moving between members, and a COMMON EXTERNAL TARIFF *(q.v.)* is adopted to provide uniform treatment to goods of third countries entering any customs union member.

A customs union is a level of economic integration greater than that of a FREE TRADE AREA *(q.v.)* and less encompassing than a COMMON MARKET *(q.v.).*

CUSTOMS VALUATION. The process whereby customs authorities assign a value for duty purposes to imported merchandise. Normally, the purchase price of the goods, as evidenced by the supplier's invoice, is adequate for the determination of value. In those cases where the invoice is not available or is believed to be fraudulent or otherwise unsuitable, the customs authorities may employ other methods of determining value, including appraisement, construction of value by assigning a value to each of the components and production processes, or comparison with like merchandise from the same country of origin.

Effective with the implementation of the Trade Agreements Act of 1979, the United States employs the *transaction value method* to value imports. Prior to this act, several alternative valuation schemes were applied, including export value, U.S. value, constructed value, and American selling price. These alternative valuation methods, authorized in Section 402 and 402(a) of the Tariff Act of 1930 have been effectively supplanted by the transaction value method, except in a limited number of cases when the transaction value cannot be determined or is inapplicable for whatever reason.

See CUSTOMS VALUATION CODE.

CUSTOMS VALUATION CODE. A uniform system for valuing imports for the application of customs duties. The agreement is a product of the Tokyo Round of multilateral trade negotiations. It provides for five methods of valuing imported merchandise.

Transaction value is the price actually paid or payable for the goods, with adjustments allowable for packing costs, buying and selling commissions, and certain costs borne by the buyer and not included in the sale price.

Transaction value is the primary mode of valuation under the agreement, and it is expected that it will be used in most cases. A notable exception to this rule is the valuation of sales between related parties. In those cases where it can be determined that the relationship between buyer and seller affects the price, the value for customs purposes may be adjusted to reflect this factor. In those cases where the relationship between buyer and seller does not distort the price of the merchandise, the transaction value would be employed.

In those cases where the transaction value cannot be used to ascertain value for customs purposes, alternative valuation methods may be employed. The *transaction value of identical merchandise* is the primary alternative method. For a given shipment of merchandise, the transaction value of identical merchandise shipped from the same country of origin is employed. When the previously cited methods cannot be used, the *transaction value of similar goods sold* from the same country of origin is used. The *deductive value method* is used if all previous methods are inappropriate. Under this method, value for customs is determined by using the first sale price of the goods in the country of importation, and deducting from that price certain costs incurred after importation. This method is not normally used on goods that have been further manufactured after importation. It is employed on such reprocessed merchandise only when the importer so requests; in such cases, an allowance is made for the value added during such processing. Finally, in the *computed value method,* a value is constructed based upon costs of production and imputed profit and overhead. The computed method is employed normally only when all other methods are deemed unsuitable; however, the importer may request that the computed value method be employed by customs authorities in lieu of the deductive value method being applied to the transaction.

In the event that all the foregoing methods prove unsuitable, the customs authorities may use any reasonable method of valuation consistent with Article VII of the General Agreement on Tariffs and Trade.

Under the terms of the Customs Valuation Agreement, any adhering nation may apply duties on either the C.I.F. or F.O.B. value of the imported merchandise. The United States applies duties on the F.O.B. basis, and it appears that other adherents will continue to employ the C.I.F. basis. U.S. adoption of the agreement was effected by the Trade Agreements Act of 1979.

See Appendix D8.

CUSTOMS WATERS. That portion of the high seas, not to exceed twelve miles from shore, within which law enforcement personnel of the United States are authorized to board foreign craft to enforce American laws. In those cases where a treaty between the United States and another state authorizes boarding in an area other than the twelve-mile zone, the area so specified constitutes customs waters for the vessels of the treaty partner. *See* CUSTOMS ENFORCEMENT AREA.

CUTTHROAT COMPETITION. A discriminatory pricing practice whereby one vendor deliberately reduces prices to a low level with the object of driving out competition, thereby creating a monopoly or dominant market share. In the United States such practices are banned, although they are often employed in foreign countries.

D

DAILY HIRE. The fee paid by a charterer to a vessel owner for each day that the ship is under charter.

DAMAGE FREE CAR. A railcar equipped with a cushioned underframe, adjustable bulkheads, and other special gear to afford added protection to the cargo during transit. This type of car is normally used by shippers of consumer or delicate products.

DANUBE COMMISSION. A multinational organization responsible for maintaining free navigation of the Danube from Ulm, Germany, to the Black Sea. Formed by the Belgrade Convention of 1948, it replaced an earlier body established in 1856.

The commission is composed of one representative from each country bordering the Danube: Austria, Romania, Czechoslovakia, Bulgaria, Hungary, Yugoslavia, and the USSR. Since 1957, the German Federal Republic has attended commission meetings as an observer.

The commission regulates the buoying system on the river, coordinates customs and sanitation controls, and oversees navigability. Official languages of the commission are French and Russian. The group is based in Budapest, Hungary.

DATAFREIGHT RECEIPT. A document issued by some steamship operators in lieu of a BILL OF LADING *(q.v.)* on straight consignment shipments. Rather than issue a formal bill of lading, the carrier transmits to his agent at the port of destination, by telex or other telecommunication hookup, details of the shipment and the name of the party authorized to receive the goods.

Inasmuch as no bill of lading is issued, the datafreight system cannot be used in transactions where an *order* bill of lading is called for.

DATA TAPE SERVICE. One of several export promotion services of the U.S. Department of Commerce. *See* FOREIGN TRADERS INDEX.

DATA PLATE. A metal plate attached to the door of an intermodal container giving the name and address of the manufacturer and details of the container's construction.

DATE DRAFT. *See* DRAFT.

DATE FOR VALUE DETERMINATION. The date on which imported merchandise was exported from its country of origin. The value of the merchandise in effect on that date will be applied in applying duties.

DEAD FREIGHT. A payment made by a charterer to the owner of a vessel as compensation for stowing the ship to less than its capacity. The charterer is bound to ship a "full and complete cargo"; since freight is payable only on the cargo actually shipped, failure to deliver a full load deprives the vessel owner of revenue.

Dead freight is calculated by ascertaining the freight that would have been payable had additional cargo been shipped to fill out the vessel, less any expenses the shipowner would have borne if the additional cargo had been shipped.

DEADWEIGHT TONNAGE. The capacity of a vessel to carry cargo, water, passengers, and stores when loaded to her maximum draft, expressed in long tons.

DEALS, BOARDS, BATTENS, AND SCANTLINGS. Gradings of light timber, according to dimension. The figure shows the dimensions used in the Baltic–United Kingdom trade; these measurements serve as a standard.

A provision is usually made in charter parties for *ends*, or short lengths, to travel at reduced rates.

Unit	Thickness (in inches)	Breadth (in inches)
Boards	½ to 1¾	3 to 9
Scantlings	2 to 3	3 to 5½
Battens	2 to 4	6 to 8
Deals	2 to 4	6 to 11

DEBASEMENT. The reduction, by governmental authority, of the amount of precious metal in the coinage below the conventional level. Debasement results in diluting the precious metal content of the coinage, usually to increase the supply of money for government purposes. The effect of such dilution is often a loss of faith in the money in circulation, with resulting inflation or hyperinflation.

DEBT MONETIZATION. The expansion of the national money supply through the issuance of public debt instruments. In the United States debt is monetized whenever the treasury issues bonds or bills; these instruments are purchased by the Federal Reserve system with a check. The check, once deposited, constitutes reserves of the bank holding the check; these reserves may be used for lending purposes. The borrowing capacity so generated constitutes "money" in the form of purchasing power.

The creation of money is accelerated because a bank is authorized to create demand deposits in multiples of its reserves.

DEBTOR NATION. A nation with financial obligations to foreigners greater than obligations owed to it by foreigners.

DEBT SERVICE RATIO. The percentage of a nation's export earnings that are devoted to paying interest on obligations owed to foreigners.

DECLARATION FOR THE ESTABLISHMENT OF A NEW INTERNATIONAL ECONOMIC ORDER. *See* NEW INTERNATIONAL ECONOMIC ORDER.

DECLINE. The rejection of a firm order proposal by a principal in vessel charter negotiations.

DEDICATED SERVICE. The commitment on the part of a transportation company of a vessel, rail cars, or other conveyances to the sole and exclusive use of a particular shipper for a given period of time.

DEDICATED TO SINGLE-USE TEST. A principle applied in customs law that the tariff item applicable to a finished product will be applied to a work-in-process item if the unfinished item is so far advanced in the process of manufacture as to be incapable of being used for any purpose other than completion into the finished article.

DEDUCTIVE VALUE METHOD. An alternative method of valuing goods for customs purposes under the CUSTOMS VALUATION CODE *(q.v.)*.

DEEP TANK. A tank within the hold of a vessel (other than a tanker) to accommodate liquid or semiliquid cargoes in bulk.

DEFENSIVE INVESTMENT. An investment undertaken to protect larger commercial interests rather than for the return that the investment itself generates.

DEFERRAL. The avoidance of taxes on the income of foreign subsidiaries until that income is distributed to the parent.

DEFERRED PAYMENT CREDIT. Any LETTER OF CREDIT *(q.v.)* that provides for payment to the beneficiary at any point in time later than *sight*.

DEFERRED REBATE. *See* REBATE (FREIGHT).

DEFICIENCY GUARANTEE. A common provision in lending agreements collateralized by tangible assets which provides that if the lender, as the result of default on the loan obligation by the borrower, is obliged to sell the collateral and the proceeds of the sale are not adequate to satisfy the balance due on the loan, the borrower will be responsible for the shortfall.

DEFICIENCY PAYMENT. A payment to agricultural producers reflecting the difference between the actual market price for a commodity and the higher, governmentally guaranteed price.

DEFLATION. A decline in the general level of prices, attributable to excessive savings or other factors that have reduced consumption relative to the supply of goods available. Very often, deflation is reflected during the decline phase of the business cycle.

There has been no deflation in the United States since the Great Depression, although declines have occurred in the prices of selected commodities.

DEFLATIONARY GAP. The spread between national savings and the amount of savings required to sustain full employment. Over time, the lack of consumption caused by less than full employment will cause a general decline in price levels, resulting in lower profit; likewise, the decline in price levels will stimulate consumption, increasing profits (and therefore savings), which will restore equilibrium.

DELAYED PAYMENT CREDIT. A LETTER OF CREDIT *(q.v.)* under which the beneficiary submits his draft after having supplied shipping papers or other documents. This form of letter of credit usually provides that a sight draft will be presented a stipulated number of days after submission of the shipping papers.

This type of instrument is commonly used only in conjunction with sales where the seller provides financing of nine months or more.

DEL CREDERE AGENT. A sales agent who grants credit terms to buyers of the products offered by his principal but, in the process of giving such credit, indemnifies his principal agent against credit default by the customer.

DELIVERY. The act whereby the owner of a vessel gives operational control over to the charterer.

DELIVERY ORDER. Written instructions issued by the owner of goods or his authorized agent to the holder of such goods directing that the merchandise be released or shipped to a specified party.

DELIVERY VERIFICATION CERTIFICATE.
See INTERNATIONAL IMPORT CERTIFICATE/DELIVERY
VERIFICATION SYSTEM.

DEMAND BILL. A draft or bill of exchange payable at *sight.*

DEMISE. A *bareboat* charter, i.e., a vessel charter arrangement in which the owner provides only the ship, and the charterer arranges for his own crew, fuel, and stores and otherwise operates the ship.

DEMONETIZATION. An act by governmental authority that deprives one kind of circulating currency of legal tender status, e.g., the recall of gold or silver coins.

DEMURRAGE. Charges payable by a shipper or consignee to a carrier for failing to unload, release, or otherwise return to service the carrier's equipment within a prescribed period of time. The amount of *freetime* allowed to load, unload, or return the equipment and the rate of charges are specified in the carrier's tariff or the contract of carriage.

In the vessel charter agreements, *demurrage* is a penalty payable to the owner of the ship by the charterer for failing to complete loading or unloading within the time specified in the charter party.

DEPRECIATION (MONETARY). A fall in the value of money. This fall may be reflected as (1) *internal depreciation,* a decline in the domestic buying power of money, as measured by standard indices—if it now costs $110 to buy what $100 would have bought a year ago, the dollar has depreciated by 9 percent (100 divided by 110) during that period—or (2) *external depreciation,* the decline of a nation's currency measured in terms of another currency.

DERELICT. A vessel that has been abandoned at sea.

DERIVED TARGET PRICE. *See* TARGET PRICE.

DESIGNATED STATE. A nation from which an inventor seeks patent protection under the PATENT COOPERATION TREATY *(q.v.)*

DESPATCH MONEY. The sum paid by a vessel owner to the charterer as an incentive for completing loading or unloading operations in less than the time permitted under the charter party. When there is agreement that despatch money will be paid, the conditions and rates are stipulated in the charter agreement. *See* LAYTIME.

DESTINATION CLAUSE. A provision in a contract for the purchase of a commodity specifying the countries to which the product may be shipped, thereby preventing sale in the world market which would affect the spot price. This type of arrangement is common in the petroleum industry.

DEVALUATION. The official reduction of the value of a nation's money in relation to a standard (usually gold), special drawing rights, or the U.S. dollar. Inasmuch as all currencies are ultimately valued in terms of some standard, devaluation results in the conscious increase of the number of units of the affected currency required to equal a given unit of the standard.

Until the demise of the Bretton Woods system of fixed exchange rates in 1971, most nations effectively denominated their currencies in terms of the U.S. dollar, which was itself tied to gold. More recently, efforts have been made to value individual national currencies to SPECIAL DRAWING RIGHTS *(q.v.)* as a neutral standard.

Under the articles of the INTERNATIONAL MONETARY FUND *(q.v.),* no nation is supposed to officially devalue its currency until the IMF has addressed the problem; as a practical matter, there has been widespread deviation from this principle.

The term *devaluation* should not be confused with *depreciation,* which is a decline in the purchasing power of a currency.

See BRETTON WOODS AGREEMENT.

DEVANNING. *Synonymous with* stripping or unloading a container or trailer.

DEVELOPED COUNTRIES. A generalized grouping of the industrialized nations. Customarily, the term is applied to those nations that are members of the ORGANIZATION FOR ECONOMIC CO-OPERATION AND DEVELOPMENT *(q.v.)* plus the industrialized nations of Eastern Europe.

DEVELOPING COUNTRIES. Also known as *less developed countries* (LDC), a loose reference to those nations that are neither industrialized nor members of the Organization of Petroleum Exporting Countries. The developing countries are characterized by an insufficient industrial base and, in varying degrees, by inadequate transport infrastructure, educational resources, and public health resources.

As a guideline, the term *developing country* is used for those nations with a per capita income of less than U.S. $3,000 per annum.

DEVIATION. The departure by a vessel from the scope or route of the planned voyage. An unreasonable departure from the normal course of the voyage is generally considered improper and, in those cases where cargo interests suffer losses as a result of such a departure, a finding by a court that the vessel *deviated* may vitiate the carrier's legal defenses under the Carriage of Goods by Sea Act or similar national legislation.

A deviation may occur when a vessel significantly departs from the announced course of the voyage, or when the vessel engages in acts substantially beyond those that might be reasonably contemplated; for example, a cargo ship that, during the course of routine commercial operations, gives aid willingly to belligerents, may be said to have deviated from the scope of its voyage.

The Carriage of Goods by Sea Act states:
Any deviation in saving or attempting to save life or property at sea, or any reasonable deviation shall not be an infringement of this Act or of the contract of carriage, and the carrier shall not be liable for any loss or damage arising therefrom; Provided, however, that if the deviation is for the purpose of loading or unloading cargo or passengers it shall, prima facie, be regarded as unreasonable.

The effect of having a deviation declared "unreasonable" is to deny the carrier his statutory defenses against claims for loss and damage.

DEVISEN. A word of French origin used in international banking to mean foreign bills of exchange, checks, and similar short-term negotiable instruments.

DFC CURRENCY BASKET SCHEME. A mechanism of the World Bank and related agencies whereby loans to development finance companies (DFCs) would be made in a basket of currencies so as to mitigate the effects of exchange rate fluctuations. From 1980, the World Bank has made certain development loans in a mixture of U.S. dollars (usually one-half the basket) and either deutsche marks, Swiss francs, or Japanese yen.

D.I.A.N.E. *See* EURONET.

DIFFERENCE IN CONDITIONS. A provision found in some insurance policies that provides coverage for risks omitted in other policies. Difference in conditions coverage is commonly used in relation to marine cargo risks where a buyer is purchasing goods on C.I.F. basis and the insurance coverage provided by the seller is less comprehensive than that of the buyer's policy. In this case, the buyer would not have to insure again, under his own policy, for the shipment, but could employ the difference in conditions clause, which permits him to insure against those perils not covered in the supplier's policy. In the event of a loss covered by the supplier's policy, that policy would respond; where the loss would not have been covered by the supplier's insurance but is within the scope of the (broader) purchaser's policy, that policy would address the claim.

DIFFERENTIAL DUTY. A rate of duty on a given commodity that varies according to the country of origin.

DIFFERENTIAL EXCHANGE RATES. A scheme in which a government prescribes different rates of exchange for the local currency, depending upon the transaction involved. The government may assign its currency a given value in terms of gold for capital transfers, for example, but provide for a less favorable rate of exchange for imports of luxury items, thereby increasing the price of such items with the object of discouraging their import and attendant drain upon foreign currency reserves.

The use of differential (or *multiple*) rates of exchange is officially discouraged by the International Monetary Fund, but it is recognized that such mechanisms may have limited value in those cases where a nation suffers pronounced and chronic trade imbalances.

A schedule of the differential exchange of the International Monetary Fund may be found in Appendix E.

DIFFERENTIAL RATE. A freight rate derived by compiling existing intermediate rates; this process is used where no through rate exists between the points of origin and destination.

DIFFERENTIATED PRODUCT. A product sold in a modified form in different countries with the object of accommodating perceived variations in taste or responding to differing local requirements.

DILLON ROUND. A series of multinational trade discussions conducted during 1960–1962 under the sponsorship of the GENERAL AGREEMENT OF TARIFFS AND TRADE (*q.v.*). The principal result of the discussions was the adoption of a common external tariff by the European Economic Community. In response to this action by the EEC, the United States granted to the EEC significant concessions on agricultural exports.

DIMENSIONAL WEIGHT. *See* VOLUMETRIC WEIGHT.

DIMINISHING MARGINAL PRODUCTIVITY. An economic principle that states that the production process reaches a point at which the infusion of additional units of capital and labor does not increase output commensurately to the inputs. For example, if the ten men working on an assembly line produce x units in a given time period, the addition of ten more men to the assembly line may not result in $2x$ of output. If, in this case, the doubling of labor inputs does not result in a doubling of output, all things being equal, a condition of diminishing marginal productivity for labor occurs.

DIPLOMATIC IMMUNITY. An immunity from local laws and regulations accorded by host states to accredited foreign diplomats. It is recognized in international law that diplomatic officers are the personal representatives of sovereign states and, as such, are themselves inviolable on the same basis as the states they represent. Under this principle, diplomats are exempt from arrest or prosecution and local taxes; they are usually immune from civil legal process. The immunity so accorded extends to the diplomat's offices, residence, papers, and effects; in addition, the immunity is conveyed upon members of the diplomat's family residing with him and, in some cases, to members of his staff so long as they are not nationals of the host state. In most cases the diplomat's immunity remains in effect even outside the country to which they are accredited while they travel on the official business of their government.

As a practical matter, diplomatic officers are answerable only to the laws of their own country; accordingly, they enjoy no immunity within the jurisdiction of their own country.

A definitive statement on the extent of diplomatic immunity is to be found in the Vienna Convention on Diplomatic Relations, signed April 18, 1961 (500 U.S.T.S. 95). It should be noted that diplomatic immunity does not extend to consular officers, for whom a more limited *consular immunity* applies.

DIRECT COLLECTION. A draft, bill of exchange, or similar instrument presented by a bank, acting as agent of the maker or holder, to the drawee for acceptance or payment. The most common form of such collection involves the presentation of a draft to a drawee, with or without accompanying documents such as bills of lading or negotiable warehouse receipts. A draft to which such documents are attached is a *documentary draft*, and it is understood that the documents will be released by the bank to the drawee only upon acceptance or payment of the instrument, as the case may be. A draft not accompanied by documents is said to be *clean*.

As a practical matter, the maker or holder of a draft for presentation will use a direct collection form supplied by his bank; this form contains instructions such as what the bank should do if the draft is refused, when to collect interest, and at what rate. This form, as well as any accompanying documents, will be sent to a correspondent of the maker's bank in the drawee's city; this local (i.e., *presenting*) bank will contact the drawee and endeavor to secure acceptance or payment. Depending upon the instructions given in the direct collection form, the acceptance may be held by the presenting bank until maturity, or returned to the maker. If the instructions call for the actual collection of funds, the presenting bank will obtain such funds from the drawee, remitting them to the maker's bank for credit to his account.

DIRECT ENDORSEMENT. *Synonymous with* special endorsement. See ENDORSEMENT.

DIRECT FOREIGN INVESTMENT. The acquisition abroad of specific productive resources such as mines, factories, or transport facilities. For an investment to be considered *direct*, it must be of such magnitude as to give the investor actual control or significant influence over the foreign operation. The U.S. government regards control of 10 percent or more of the voting stock of a foreign operation indicative of such influence or control.

Investments in foreign operations where influence is limited are said to be *portfolio* rather than *direct* investments since the investor does not take an active part in management of the foreign entity.

DIRECT INVESTOR. Under U.S. Department of Commerce regulations, an American firm, person, or entity that acquires or controls 10 percent or more of a foreign business, as evidenced by voting stock or capital in the foreign venture.

DIRECTIONAL RATE. A freight rate reduced for cargo moving in a direction where cargo is light, for the purpose of stimulating movements. Under such circumstances, it is quite possible that the rate for the same product moving in the other direction (where tonnage is heavy) may be significantly higher.

DIRTY FLOAT. Also known as *managed float*, the process whereby national monetary authorities intercede in the foreign exchange markets to prevent significant fluctuations in the values of their own or other currencies. The process is accomplished by selling reserves of currencies rising in value, or the purchase of declining currencies. In most cases there is a pre-existing agreement among major trading nations as to the appropriate value for any given currency in terms of another, and a definition of the *spread*, or range of values within which each currency will be permitted to float without governmental intervention.

DIRTY SHIP. A tanker that carries crude or fuel oils, as contrasted with refined petroleum products.

DISAPPEARANCE. The reduction of a nation's store of a given commodity either through consumption or exportation.

DISC. *See* DOMESTIC INTERNATIONAL SALES CORPORATION.

DISCOUNT CORPORATION. A firm engaged in the discounting and trading of bills of exchange and acceptances. In the United States these functions are usually performed by commercial banks, although there are entities other than commercial banks specializing in this area.

DISCOUNTING. The process of selling or transferring a bill or note at an amount less than the face value. A bill that matures at a future date is normally discounted by multiplying the number of days to maturity by the interest rate in effect at the time the face amount of the instrument was obtained, and deducting this sum from the face value. As a practical matter, the interest rate will correspond to the quality of the drawee and/or endorsers of the bill.

In some cases it may be possible to sell the instrument *without recourse*; under this arrangement the buyer of the bill relieves the discounting party of any responsibility for future payment of the face amount of the instrument at maturity. In many cases, however, the person requesting the discount must endorse the bill, thereby making himself secondarily liable for the payment should the drawee or prior endorsers default.

DISCOUNT LOAN PROGRAM. *See* EXPORT-IMPORT BANK.

DISCOUNT RATE. Also known as the *re-discount rate*, the rate of interest charged by the Federal Reserve to member banks for advances. The rates are set every fourteen days by the regional Federal

Reserve banks upon approval of the Board of Governors of the Federal Reserve system.

The discount rate is a prime factor in determining the amount of credit available and serves as an index upon which commercial banks base their lending rates to customers.

DISCOUNT WINDOW. The counter at a Federal Reserve bank or branch at which a member bank may present eligible instruments, such as banker's acceptances, for discount or re-discount; the acceptance of such instruments by the Federal Reserve increases lending power of the commercial bank that has offered the instruments. The discount process results in a loan by the Federal Reserve to the member bank against the collateral of the instruments offered.

DISCREPANCY PRESENTATION. *See* LETTER OF CREDIT.

DISCRETIONARY CARGO. Cargo exempt from the controls of cargo preference legislation that require certain goods be shipped only aboard vessels of the home country or of other countries with which special arrangements have been concluded. Discretionary cargoes may be shipped aboard the vessels of any country.

DISCRIMINATING DUTY. *Synonymous with* DIFFERENTIAL DUTY *(q.v.)*.

DISCRIMINATION. Unequal treatment in the duties, quotas, or administrative controls accorded to the products of one or more nations. Generally speaking, any nation which does not enjoy MOST FAVORED NATION *(q.v.)* status is the subject of trade discrimination.

DISHOARDING. The reduction of a nation's stockpiles of a given commodity, through either consumption or exportation, where those stockpiles have increased beyond normal levels.

DISHONOR. The refusal of a drawee to accept a DRAFT or BILL OF EXCHANGE *(qq.v.)* upon presentation, or, having accepted the instrument upon presentation, refusal to pay the face amount of the instrument upon maturity.

DISINFLATION. A decline in the prices of some commodities within a given economy, while the prices of other commodities remain stable or rise.

DISINVESTMENT. A reduction in the total quantity of capital goods available in an economy, either by normal depreciation not compensated by replacement, or by a conscious decline in inventories of such goods, usually as the result of excessive consumption.

DISPATCH MONEY. *See* DESPATCH MONEY.

DISPLACEMENT. The weight of the water displaced by a vessel at rest in the water, expressed in long tons. The *light* displacement is the weight of the water displaced by the vessel alone, while the weight of the water displaced by the vessel and its cargo is said to be the *loaded* displacement of the ship.

DISPONENT OWNER. The party having operational control of a vessel without actual legal title. For example, a person taking a ship under a bareboat charter is responsible for the operation of the vessel, and as such is regarded as the disponent owner.

DISTANCE FREIGHT. Additional freight monies due to a vessel owner by the charterer when, in the opinion of the ship's captain, ice conditions preclude discharge at the intended port and the vessel must divert to an alternative, more distant port. As a practical matter, such additional freight is not charged unless the diversion adds at least one hundred miles to the voyage, in which case the additional freight shall be proportional to the freight payable from port of origin to the port orginally intended.

DISTRESS DUMPING. *See* DUMPING.

DISTRESS FREIGHT. Cargo carried by a ship at a depressed freight rate because, in the absence of that cargo, the vessel would be obliged to sail empty or nearly so to its next port. The term is used most commonly in connection with tramp vessels.

DISTRICT DIRECTOR OF CUSTOMS. *See* UNITED STATES CUSTOMS SERVICE.

DIVERGENCE THRESHOLD. Within the EUROPEAN MONETARY SYSTEM *(q.v.)*, each participating currency is assigned a value in terms of the *European currency unit* (ECU). The participating currency is permitted to fluctuate as much as 2.25 percent, in either direction, against the assigned value; if the currency should fluctuate beyond this band, the member governments are obligated to intervene in the exchange markets to restore the prescribed value of the affected currency. The divergence threshold itself is reached when a currency deviates 75 percent from its assigned value within the 2.25 percent limit; it serves as an indicator of instability for that currency, thereby permitting the issuing country to take its own corrective measures prior to invoking the official intervention of other EMS member countries.

DIVERSITY OF CITIZENSHIP. A principle of American law that provides that where the parties to a civil action are located in different states, the parties shall have access to the Federal courts as the forum for trial of the case. This option may be used in lieu of suing in the state courts. Normally, the Federal court trying the case will use the procedural law of the state in which the court sits.

The Federal courts will not hear cases arising out of diversity of citizenship where the amount in controversy is less than $10,000. The U.S. Constitution forbids the Federal courts to apply diversity of citizenship as a vehicle to the trial by Federal courts of cases in which a state of the United States is a defendant.

DIVISIONS. The pro rata sharing of freight revenue of a given shipment interchanged between two or more railroads. Since there is no national rail monopoly in the United States, and there are hundreds of rail carriers operating within the country, cargo moving over long distances is apt to travel over the lines of more than one carrier. In such cases the freight earned for the entire rail move will be divided among the carriers, usually in relation to the number of miles traveled in each carrier's system.

The term *division* is also used in those cases where freight revenue is divided between a railroad and another carrier, as in the case of a division of freight with an ocean carrier on a land-bridge movement.

DOCK. The space in the water at which a ship comes to rest. A dock is not a PIER or WHARF *(qq.v.)*, each of which has its own specific meaning. It would be appropriate, however, to say that a vessel docked at a pier.

Also, used as a verb, *to dock* means to reduce the price of a product or commodity because of a quality deficiency.

DOCKAGE. The amount deducted from an invoice to offset a defect or quality deficiency in merchandise supplied.

DOCK RECEIPT. A document used at some ports to acknowledge delivery of cargo to a pier for shipment aboard a given vessel. The format of a dock receipt often resembles that of a bill of lading and contains substantially the same information concerning the cargo; it is signed and/or stamped by the stevedore when the goods are off-loaded from the truck or other delivering conveyance. At this time, any error in count or product damage will be noted on the dock receipt. Normally the exporter or his agent will be obliged to surrender the dock receipt to the carrier at the time he submits the ocean bill of lading for validation (*see* figure, next page).

DOCK WARRANT. A term often used to mean a WAREHOUSE RECEIPT *(q.v.)* issued by the proprietor of a waterfront warehouse.

DOCUMENTARY DRAFT. A draft to which there are attached bills of lading, commercial invoices, warehouse receipts, or other papers relating to the transaction that give rise to the draft. Normally the drawee must accept the draft in order to receive the attachments. *See* DIRECT COLLECTION.

DOCUMENTS AGAINST ACCEPTANCE. *See* BILL OF EXCHANGE, DIRECT COLLECTION.

DOLLAR AREA. Those countries that fix the value of their own currencies in relation to the U.S. dollar and that maintain the bulk of their reserves in dollars.

DOLLAR BILL OF EXCHANGE. *Synonymous with* DOLLAR EXCHANGE *(q.v.)*.

DOLLAR DEFICIT. The amount by which dollar outflows to a given country exceed dollar inflows from that same country over a given period of time. These *flows* may be the result of sales of actual merchandise, service transactions, or capital transfers.

DOLLAR EXCHANGE. A draft or bill of exchange, wherever drawn, payable in U.S. dollars.

DOLLAR GAP. *Synonymous with* DOLLAR DEFICIT *(q.v.)*.

DOLLAR GLUT. An excess of dollars in circulation outside the United States, over and above the quantity required for trade and normal financial transactions. This condition arose during the late 1950s and persisted through the early 1970s, largely as the result of persistent American payment deficits and foreign aid progams that exported dollars in large volumes. In 1971 President Richard Nixon suspended the automatic conversion of dollars into gold at the official level; the attendant devaluation of the dollar, plus a surcharge on imports, aided in overcoming the excessive dollar holdings abroad.

DOLLAR OUTFLOW. Payments, in terms of dollars, made to foreigners in settlement of current transactions, as investments in foreign enterprises or for any other reason. Optimally, the outflows would be offset by inflows arising from the purchase of American goods or services or investment in the United States.

DOLLAR SHORTAGE. *Synonymous with* DOLLAR DEFICIT *(q.v.)*.

DOMESTICATION. The process whereby foreign investors are forced, by governmental sanction, to relinquish their control or interest in local enterprises to local nationals. The term can be applied to an EXPROPRIATION *(q.v.)* of foreign property without adequate compensation but is used primarily in those cases where compensation is offered to the displaced foreign investors. *See* CONFISCATION.

DOMESTIC CORPORATION. A corporation operating in the jurisdiction in which it was formed; hence, a New York corporation is a domestic corporation in New York, but a *foreign* corporation everywhere else.

DOMESTIC INTERNATIONAL SALES CORPORATION. Commonly known by the acronym DISC, a U.S.-chartered corporation, qualified with the Internal Revenue Service, that derives virtually all of its income from export sales and export-related activities. A properly qualified DISC is permitted to defer indefinitely tax on a portion of its income. The DISC program was authorized by the Revenue Act of 1971 (P.L. 92-178) as a stimulus to export sales.

DOCK RECEIPT

SHIPPER/EXPORTER	DOCUMENT NO.
STU Auto Parts Hamburg, West Germany	Booking # 666666
	EXPORT REFERENCES

CONSIGNEE	FORWARDING AGENT - REFERENCES
XYZ Imports Company North Main Street Anywhere 11111	EFG Forwarders, Hamburg
	POINT AND COUNTRY OF ORIGIN

NOTIFY PARTY	DOMESTIC ROUTING/EXPORT INSTRUCTIONS
Same as above	

PIER OR AIRPORT

EXPORTING CARRIER (Vessel/Airline)	PORT OF LOADING	ONWARD INLAND ROUTING
S/S Vessel	Hamburg	
AIR/SEA PORT OF DISCHARGE	FOR TRANSSHIPMENT TO	
New York		

PARTICULARS FURNISHED BY SHIPPER

MARKS AND NUMBERS	NO. OF PKGS.	DESCRIPTION OF PACKAGES AND GOODS	GROSS WEIGHT	MEASUREMENT
XYZ New York #1/8	8	Cartons Auto Parts	480 #	60 c.f.t.

DELIVERED BY:

LIGHTER {_____
TRUCK {_____

ARRIVED— DATE _____ TIME_____

UNLOADED— DATE _____ TIME_____

CHECKED BY_____

PLACED IN SHIP / ON DOCK LOCATION _____

RECEIVED THE ABOVE DESCRIBED GOODS OR PACKAGES SUBJECT TO ALL THE TERMS OF THE UNDERSIGNED'S REGULAR FORM OF DOCK RECEIPT AND BILL OF LADING WHICH SHALL CONSTITUTE THE CONTRACT UNDER WHICH THE GOODS ARE RECEIVED? COPIES OF WHICH ARE AVAILABLE FROM THE CARRIER ON REQUEST AND MAY BE INSPECTED AT ANY OF ITS OFFICES.

FOR THE MASTER

BY _____
RECEIVING CLERK

DATE _____

Dock Receipt

In order to qualify for DISC status, the corporation must (1) be incorporated under the laws of a state or the District of Columbia; (2) derive 95 percent of its gross receipts from "qualified export receipts"; (3) have an adjusted basis of "qualified export assets equivalent to at least 95 percent of the sum of the adjusted basis of all assets at the close of the taxable year"; (4) issue only one class of stock, the par or stated value of which must be at least $2,500 on each day of the taxable year; and (5) have made a valid election, which must remain in effect. In addition, administrative regulations of the Internal Revenue Service require that a DISC must maintain continuously its own bank account and have separate books and records.

For purposes of the Act, *qualified export receipts* are defined as gross receipts derived from (1) the sale, exchange, or other transfer of "export property"; (2) lease or rental, outside the United States, of "export property"; (3) the performance of services incidental to the sale, lease, or other disposition of "export property"; (4) engineering or architectural services performed outside the United States; and (5) managerial services provided in conjunction with the production of qualified export receipts.

To qualify as *export property*, the exported merchandise must be the product of American industry or agriculture, not more than 50 percent of the fair market value of which is attributable to foreign components, and it must be held in the normal course of trade for sale, rental, or use outside the United States. Specifically excluded from the definition of export property are goods sold or leased between or among DISCs as well as sales or leases to a (now defunct) WESTERN HEMISPHERE TRADING CORPORATION (*q.v*).

Qualified export assets are defined as (1) "export property," as defined above; (2) "business assets" used primarily in the sale or handling of export property, to include manufacturing facilities, farmlands, or other qualified export receipts—general means of production employed extensively for domestic consumption do not qualify; (3) trade receivables arising from transactions that produced qualified export receipts; (4) temporary investments of working capital; (5) producer's loans; (6) securities of related foreign sales corporations; (7) certain obligations of the *Export-Import Bank of the U.S.* or the *Foreign Credit Insurance Association,* the *Private Export Funding Corporation,* or a domestic corporation formed for the purpose of financing sales of export property under an agreement with the Export-Import Bank; and (8) funds awaiting investment, and export-related interest.

Certain exclusions apply to DISCs on exports of copyrighted material, property that incurs depletion allowances, and "property in short supply," as defined in Section 933(c) of the Internal Revenue Code.

A DISC does not pay income tax on its earnings, unless the earnings are distributed or deemed to be distributed; however, the stockholders of a DISC are treated, for tax purposes, as though they had received a dividend equal to 50 percent of the earnings of the DISC.

Most DISCs are formed as wholly owned subsidiaries of manufacturers with significant export sales.

In 1984, the law was amended to replace DISCs with FOREIGN SALES CORPORATION (*q.v.*). Taxes deferred under the DISC arrangement will be permanently forgiven.

DOMESTIC OFFSHORE TRADE. Areas subject to the jurisdiction of the United States, outside the contiguous forty-eight states, over which economic regulation of ocean shipping is exercised by the Federal Maritime Commission. Apart from movements by water involving these noncontiguous areas (Hawaii, Puerto Rico, Guam, et cetera), domestic water transportation is subject to economic regulation by the Interstate Commerce Commission.

In addition to economic regulation by the Federal Maritime Commission, the Jones Act of 1920 mandates that the domestic offshore trade (as well as the domestic coastal trade) be reserved exclusively for American flag vessels; the Jones Act, however, does not apply to the U.S. Virgin Islands.

DOMESTIC SUBSIDY. An economic grant provided by a governmental authority to a domestic manufacturer, grower, or producer to increase industrial activity or stimulate output of desired products. Economic incentives may come in the form of direct payments, tax relief, low-interest financing, wage subsidies, or in many other forms.

A domestic subsidy is designed as an impetus to the local economy, whereas an *export subsidy* is oriented toward the production and sale of goods for foreign consumption. Most nations feel that export subsidies serve to cheapen foreign products, giving them an unfair price advantage over domestic merchandise, and most nations seek to impede the effectiveness of such subsidies by imposing COUNTERVAILING DUTIES (*q.v*).

See SUBSIDIES CODE.

DOOMSDAY TAX. The tax obligation incurred by a U.S. firm upon the liquidation of a tax-haven subsidiary. Under SUBPART F (*q.v.*) of the Internal Revenue Code, the proceeds of such liquidation may be deemed dividends to the parent and may be taxed as such.

DOUBLES. Two trailers, each usually twenty-eight feet in length, hauled behind a single tractor. Despite recent Federal legislation permitting the use of such equipment nationwide, many states and localities have objected to their use, resulting in conflict between the Federal and local governments. In 1984, in a case involving restrictions imposed on the operation of doubles by Connecticut, the U.S. Supreme Court effectively struck down local restrictions on the movement of such equipment in interstate commerce.

DOUBLE STANDARD. A program of precious metal coinage in which the nation employs two standards of value, usually gold and silver, each having a fixed ratio of value (the *mint ratio*). Under this system, either metal, in coined form, stands as legal tender.

The double standard differs from *bimetallism*, with which it is often confused. The double standard, while having a fixed ratio of value between the metals, permits only one to be freely coined; the other metal is coined only at the direction of the government. Under bimetallism, both metals are freely coined.

DOUBLE TAXATION. The condition that arises when a multinational firm is taxed on overseas income in both the source country and the country of the corporation's domicile. This problem arises because nations use varying systems of taxation.

Recognizing that double taxation is inimical to trade, many nations have entered into tax treaties under which the signatory states eliminate or modify income taxes on each other's enterprises with the understanding that the income will be taxed in one country alone.

One method used in addressing foreign income is the *tax credit method*, in which the home country permits the firm to apply against its tax obligations on foreign earnings a credit for all or part of the taxes paid in the country where the income was earned. In some cases, a nation permits a *full tax credit*, which is a dollar-for-dollar credit against what was paid abroad; in other instances, the home country permits an *ordinary tax credit*, which is equal to the tax the company would otherwise have paid had the income been earned in the home country. Under this process, the firm loses the difference between the taxes actually paid abroad and what it would have had to pay to its own govenment, presuming the foreign tax rate is higher. In most cases, the United States employs the ordinary tax credit method.

Another solution is the *exemption method*, in which income taxed abroad is fully exempt from taxation in the home country (the *full exemption* method) or is omitted from home country taxation but is taken into account in determining gross income when progressive methods of taxation are employed (the *exemption with progression* method).

For provisions of specific U. S. tax treaties, see Appendix F.

DOWN BY THE HEAD. The condition of a vessel where draft at the bow exceeds draft at the stern. This state usually has an adverse effect upon steering and speed.

DOWN BY THE STERN. The condition of a vessel where draft at the stern is greater than draft at the bow. It is common to find a ship operated slightly *down by the stern* for greater ease of handling than would be the case if the vessel were *in trim*, i.e., where bow and stern drafts are exactly the same.

DOWN TO HER MARKS. The condition of a vessel that has been loaded to the point in the water where she reaches her maximum permissible draft, as expressed by her load-lines. It is not necessary that all internal space be fully occupied cubicly.

DRAFT. A written, unconditional demand upon a named party to pay a specified sum of money at a prescribed date. The person who makes the demand for payment, i.e., the person who prepares the draft, is known as the *drawer* or *maker* of the instrument; the party of whom payment is demanded is the *drawee*.

Drafts are commonly used in international trade inasmuch as drafts calling for future payment, once *accepted* by the drawee, become debt obligations not dissimilar to promissory notes which may be held to maturity or discounted at a rate reflective of the credit worthiness of the drawee and prevailing interest rates. Drafts may be drawn *at sight*, that is, calling for payment immediately upon presentation, or may be *time drafts* drawn at *thirty days sight*, for example. The mere presentation of a draft to the drawee imposes no obligation upon that party; however, should the drawee *accept* the draft upon presentation, he is obliged to pay the exact amount upon maturity. A draft accepted by a bank is called a *banker's acceptance*, while the acceptance on the part of anyone other than a bank is a *trade acceptance*.

A common use of drafts is in connection with *letters of credit (q.v.)*. A letter of credit is a document issued by a bank guaranteeing that drafts will be accepted by the bank within a specified period of time if the maker demonstrates the performance of certain stipulated actions, usually the shipment of goods, as evidenced by the submission of shipping documents, such as bills of lading.

It is important to note that, while the terms *draft* and BILL OF EXCHANGE *(q.v.)* are used interchangeably even by experienced persons accustomed to these instruments, they are not, in fact, the same. A draft is redeemed in the same currency in which it was drawn (which is to say that the maker and drawee use the same currency; as a practical matter, this means they are probably in the same country); a bill of exchange involves an exchange conversion at some point. In addition, bills of exchange are always drawn *to order* and are, therefore, always negotiable; drafts may be, but not need be, negotiable.

See DIRECT COLLECTION.

DRAGO DOCTRINE. A principle enunciated in 1902 by Luis Drago, foreign minister of Argentina, that it is repugnant to international law for a foreign power to intervene forcibly in the affairs of another nation to secure the repayment of public debt obligations owed to citizens of the aggressor nation. This view has been incorporated into several treaties but has not necessarily evolved into normative international law.

DRAUGHT. An archaic form of *draft*, still used occasionally by British banks.

DRAWBACK. A feature of U.S. customs law that permits an American exporter to recover duties paid on foreign components or raw materials later fabricated into American products and exported. Upon exportation of the manufactured article a recovery or *drawback*, equal to 99 percent of the duties paid on the foreign raw materials is permitted. In addition to recovery of ordinary duties, the exporter is permitted to drawback countervailing duties, marking duties, antidumping duties, and certain Internal Revenue taxes. A domestic manufacturer may also apply for drawback when U.S.-origin components are used on the exported product to the extent that the American raw materials replace like foreign materials used elsewhere or destroyed. This latitude to substitute American for foreign components is authorized so that American manufacturers will not be burdened with the necessity of segregating domestic and foreign parts or raw materials for accounting purposes.

Any firm wishing to employ components of foreign manufacture in an American product that is to be exported is obliged to request from the district director of customs a *drawback rate*, which is an authorization to apply for recovery of duties. Normally, any firm contemplating such action is well advised to consult in advance with the district director to ensure that there is agreement among the parties concerning record keeping and documentary evidence of exportation of the finished product. Drawback is not normally allowed prior to the submission of the American manufacturer's application for a drawback rate.

In 1980, as a provision of the Omnibus Trade Act of that year, *drawback* was extended to permit recovery of duties paid on imported merchandise that was subsequently re-exported or destroyed without further processing. This new category of drawback, known as *same condition drawback*, is applicable when the imported merchandise was neither used in the United States nor advanced in value; and the foreign goods were exported, or destroyed under customs supervision, within three years of original importation.

Under current rules, the owner of the foreign merchandise is obliged to inform the customs authorities twelve working days in advance of exportation or destruction if *same condition drawback* is to be invoked.

DRAWDOWN. A release of funds against a previously approved line of credit.

DRAWING UNIT RESERVE ASSET. More commonly known by the acronym DURA, a proposed artificial currency unit to be used as an international reserve asset. The DURA was an evolutionary step toward the creation of the SPECIAL DRAWING RIGHTS (*q.v.*).

DRAYAGE. The charge imposed by a trucking company for the pick-up or delivery of an ocean container or rail trailer.

DRESSED LUMBER. Lumber that has been planed on at least one face or edge.

DRILL. The movement of rail cars from a shipper's siding to a switching yard, or vice versa.

DROP-FRAME TRAILER. A trailer with a floor bed lower to the ground than that of a conventional trailer. In the United States the standard over-the-road trailer has a floor bed that is approximately four feet off the ground; a drop-frame trailer may have a bed barely one foot off the ground. This type of equipment is used to transport goods of high bulk but low density.

DRY BULK. The shipment, without exterior packaging, of a commodity that is not, and is not likely to become, liquid during transit. The term is most commonly applied to shipments by vessel of grain, coal, cement, and other such commodities which are transported in large quantity within the holds of specially designed ships.

DRY-DOCKING CLAUSE. A provision common to many time charter contracts that stipulates that the vessel shall be docked and its bottom cleaned and painted at such times as the master and charterer shall deem appropriate, but in no case less frequently than every nine months. During the period when the vessel is in dry-dock for such work, payment of hire on the vessel ceases.

DUAL EXCHANGE MARKET. A governmentally mandated system for the handling of foreign exchange transactions under which officially sanctioned imports or other approved transactions are accommodated at a given, prescribed rate of exchange while other transactions employ the market rate of exchange.

For a listing of countries employing dual exchange rates, *see* Appendix E.

DUAL PRICING. The sale of an identical product at different prices in different markets.

DUAL RATE. *See* CONFERENCE.

DUAL RECOGNITION. The recognition of two rival governments within a country by a third power. This condition normally occurs when one government is recognized as the de jure government, and a competing regime is recognized as the de facto government of at least a portion of the country. For example, during the years 1949–79, the United States recognized the Nationalist regime in Taiwan as the lawful government of mainland China but reluctantly accepted the fact that the Communist regime in Peking was the actual governmental authority for the mainland.

DUE BILL. An invoice for freight charges issued by a steamship operator to the party paying the freight.

DUE DATE. The date on which a note, draft, bill of exchange, or similar instrument matures, i.e., becomes payable.

DUMPING. The sale of a product abroad at a price below that which it would fetch in the country of origin. Dumping is widely denounced by trading nations on the grounds that dumped merchandise does not compete fairly and is injurious to local producers. For these reasons most nations apply sanctions to dumped goods, usually in the form of *antidumping duties*, over and above ordinary duties, to offset any price advantage enjoyed by the offending imports.

Under the terms of the General Agreement on Tariffs and Trade (specifically, Article VI) a nation may legitimately impose antidumping duties where it has been found that the imported goods have been sold "at less than fair value" and where such sales result in "material injury" to an industry in the importing country.

Dumping is most commonly manifested in one of three forms:

(1) *Sporadic (or distress) dumping*, the disposal abroad of an unexpected surplus of a given product or commodity. This form of dumping is erratic.

(2) *Predatory dumping*, a conscious and willful effort to export goods at prices lower than they would derive at home with the intent of underselling foreign producers in their own market. The purpose of this approach is to drive out competition in the foreign market, thereby creating a monopoly.

(3) *Persistent dumping*, a determined, ongoing dumping effort continuing over a long period of time, usually a result of a need to compete in a foreign market that is more price elastic than the home market.

In order to impose antidumping duties upon any imported product, an aggrieved party, usually an American manufacturer, labor union, or trade association, files petitions for relief simultaneously with the International Trade Administration of the U.S. Department of Commerce (ITA) and the U.S. International Trade Commission (ITC). The ITA will ascertain whether the imports were sold at less than fair value; the ITC will adjudge whether material injury to American industry has occurred as a result of the dumping. Upon positive finding that imports have been sold at less than fair value and that such sales have caused material injury, the ITA will issue an antidumping order, directing the U.S. Customs Service to impose and collect antidumping duties at a rate determined by the ITA sufficient to offset the disparity between the sale price and fair market value.

All antidumping orders are reviewed on an annual basis. Any party to an antidumping action who feels that an injustice has occurred, including any complainant whose application for relief has been denied by either the ITA or the ITC, may appeal to the U.S. Court of International Trade for relief.

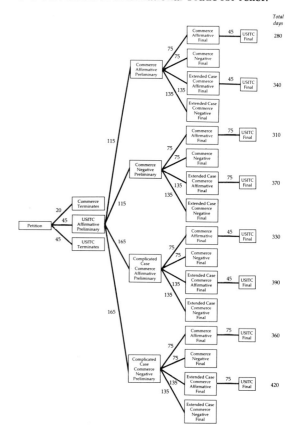

Statutory Timetable for Antidumping Investigations (in days). Courtesy of International Trade Commission.

DUMPING MARGIN. In those instances where a product has been *dumped*, that is, sold abroad at a price below the fair market value in the country of origin, the dumping margin is the difference between the home market price and the price at which the goods are sold abroad less incidental charges, such as export packing, peculiar to foreign sales.

The purpose of antidumping duties is to offset the dumping margin. *See* DUMPING.

DUNNAGE. Lumber or other materials used to brace or otherwise stabilize cargo within containers, rail cars, or ships.

DURABLE GOOD. A manufactured article, intended for either industrial or consumer use, having an anticipated useful life of at least three years.

DURATION CLAUSE. The provision in a contract of marine insurance that specifies the period of validity of coverage. As a rule, marine policies are issued for a period of one year and may be extended indefinitely.

DUTIABLE LIST. The section of a nation's tariff law that specifies those products subject to duty and the applicable rate.

DUTIABLE STATUS. A determination made by customs authorities, in accordance with the laws of the importing nation, as to whether a given imported article is subject to duty, and if so, at what rate. The dutiable status is determined by *classifying* the merchandise, i.e., determining into which category the product falls under the tariff schedules.

DUTY. A tax imposed by governmental authority on goods imported. The amount of the duty imposed on any given article is prescribed in the nation's 'customs tariff'.

There are several types of duties, the most common of which is the *ordinary duty*. Ordinary duties may be imposed in any of three forms: (1) *ad valorem duties*, which are assessed as a percentage of the value of the goods, e.g., 5 percent ad valorem; (2) *specific duties*, which are imposed on a per unit basis, e.g., ten cents per pound, one dollar per barrel; and (3) *compound duties*, those that incorporate features of both ad valorem and specific duties, e.g., fifty cents per gallon and 3 percent ad valorem. Most duties, particularly those on manufactured goods, are assessed on the ad valorem basis.

Duties are imposed for a variety of reasons. In the case of industrial countries, duties serve as a source of government revenue, albeit a small percentage; as a practical matter, the purpose of customs duties is to control imports through the price mechanism. For example, industrialized nations frequently use compound duties on manufactured goods containing raw materials that would themselves be dutiable; in such cases, the ad valorem portion of the compound duty protects the domestic finished goods industry, while the specific duty portion protects the domestic raw materials industry.

Each nation, individually or in conjunction with other nations, publishes a *tariff* containing voluminous listings of products and prescribing a rate of duty for each product. Normally, the content of the tariff is prescribed by statute, and the duties so prescribed are said to be *statutory* duties. It should be recognized that nations will "retaliate" for the imposition of duties upon their products by imposing or increasing duties upon the products of the nation that seeks to protect itself behind a tariff wall. Over time, it becomes apparent to most nations that *protectionism* impedes their own export trade and breeds inefficiency into domestic industry not challenged by import competition. As a result, over the past fifty years, and particularly since the end of World War II, many nations have sought to remove barriers to trade, consistent with the protection of essential national industries and compelling internal political circumstances. Most nations have empowered their executive authority to engage in multinational trade agreements whereby tariff reductions are offered in return for reciprocal *concessions* from other trading nations. For this reason, most

nations have at least two rates of duty: the statutory rate, and a lower *concessional* rate offered to those who have granted concessions in their own tariffs. In the case of the United States, the statutory rates are found in Column 1 of the tariff schedules. A uniform, lower rate is granted to nations with which the United States has negotiated reciprocal concessions; such nations are classed as *most favored nations*, and the duties applicable to imports from these countries are embraced in Column 2 of the tariff schedules. In addition to the most favored nation rates, most advanced countries have offered special, nonreciprocal concessions to developing nations as an impetus to their economic growth. The most comprehensive program of nonreciprocal concessions is duties are eliminated or reduced in accordance with the GENERALIZED SYSTEM OF PREFERENCES *(q.v.)*, as advanced under the auspices of the GENERAL AGREEMENT ON TARIFFS AND TRADE *(q.v.)*.

In addition to ordinary duties imposed on all merchandise of a particular type or class, special additional duties may be imposed upon certain imports under specified condition. The most common forms of such duties are *antidumping duties*, imposed to correct the distorting effects of DUMPING *(q.v.)*, i.e., sales at less than fair market value; COUNTERVAILING DUTIES *(q.v.)*, levied to compensate for subsidies provided to the foreign supplier by his government as an incentive to export; and *marking duties*, an additional duty at the rate of 10 percent ad valorem imposed on merchandise that is not properly marked as to country of origin.

In addition to customs duties, some products are subject to excise taxes, collected by the Customs Service on behalf of the Internal Revenue Service. The excise taxes so imposed are not unique to imports but are also collected on domestic products of the same type or class, such as liquor.

In some countries, duties are imposed upon some exports as well as imports. Export duties are employed only by developing countries on certain commodities in which they are a dominant supplier. The purpose of these duties is to raise revenue for the government. The U.S. Constitution prohibits the collection of export duties.

See RECIPROCAL TRADE AGREEMENTS PROGRAM, SMOOT-HAWLEY ACT, TARIFF (CUSTOMS). A table of U.S. excise taxes can be found in Appendix F1.

DUTY LIABILITY. The obligation to the government that arises from the importation of dutiable merchandise. Unpaid duties constitute a personal obligation to the government and may be satisfied from any assets of the importer or his estate. The government retains a lien upon the imported merchandise pending satisfaction of the debt.

The duty liability arises when the merchandise arrives within the *customs territory* of the United States. Normally it is not necessary to effect physical discharge of the goods off the importing conveyance to incur liability; it is sufficient that the vessel arrive in port with intent to discharge.

E

EARMARKED GOLD. Bullion or coin gold held by a nation, within its monetary reserves, in trust for another government.

EAST-WEST TRADE. A general reference to trade between the industrial nations of the West, particularly those nations that are members of the ORGANIZATION FOR ECONOMIC COOPERATION AND DEVELOPMENT *(q.v.)*, and the Soviet Union and its European satellites.

ECONOMIC AGRESSION. *See* AGGRESSION.

ECONOMIC AND SOCIAL COMMUNITY OF CENTRAL AMERICA. *See* CENTRAL AMERICAN COMMON MARKET.

ECONOMIC COMMUNITY OF WEST AFRICAN STATES. An organization of sixteen West African states committed to the elimination of trade barriers among the member states and the promotion of economic development in the region. Formed at Lagos, Nigeria, in 1975, the group, known commonly by the acronym ECOWAS, has identified the following areas as targets for action: immediate elimination of tariffs and barriers to trade in locally produced raw materials, with elimination of barriers on industrial products by 1989; elimination of nontariff barriers by 1985; establishment of a special fund to promote internal telecommunications; and formation of a common defense organization.

The following states were members of ECOWAS in 1984: Benin, Cape Verde, Gambia, Ghana, Guinea, Guinea-Bissau, Ivory Coast, Liberia, Mali, Mauritania, Niger, Nigeria, Senegal, Sierra Leone, Togo, Upper Volta.

ECONOMIC FRICTION. Cultural, religious, or ideological perspectives that interfere with and distort opportunities for trade or economic advancement.

ECONOMIC INTEGRATION. The process of unifying two or more national economies through conscious coordination of trade, fiscal, and monetary activities. Economic integration is normally preceded by the reduction or abolition of tariffs, quotas, and similar constraints upon trade among the integrating nations. Following liberalization of trade, the participating governments usually minimize impediments to the flow of labor and capital, coordinate taxation and public spending, and perhaps establish a uniform currency, or at least institutionalize cooperation among central banks so as to assure stability of member countries' currencies relative to one another.

The highest form of economic integration is manifested in an *economic community*, in which a central government or supranational authority oversees trade policy with nonmember states and coordinates other significant economic activity. The economic community serves as the precursor to full political integration. Lesser forms of economic integration are the FREE TRADE AREA, COMMON MARKET, and CUSTOMS UNION *(qq.v.)*.

ECONOMIC MOBILIZATION. The orchestration and direction of a nation's economic resources under governmental auspices, toward the attainment of a clear national goal, such as the prosecution of a war. Mobilization may involve the allocation of labor and raw materials to essential projects on a priority basis, rationing of consumer items, price controls and tax increases to finance the goal and reduce inflation, and possible temporary takeover of certain resources by the government.

ECONOMIC NATIONALISM. A conscious, articulated national drive toward economic self-sufficiency. Economic nationalism is comparable to AUTARCHY *(q.v.)* but does not mandate the economic isolation inherent in the autarchical form.

ECONOMIC UNION. Also known as an *economic community,* an advanced form of economic integration on the part of several states. The economic union incorporates the features of a COMMON MARKET *(q.v.)*—unrestricted free trade among the members, absence of duties or quantitative restrictions on intramarket commerce, and a common external tariff—but is expanded to embrace a centralized internal economic policy including taxation, interest rates, money supply, uniform social programs, and perhaps a common currency.

The formation of an economic union is a precursor to full political union of the members.

ECONOMIC WARFARE. *See* AGGRESSION.

ECU. *See* EUROPEAN MONETARY SYSTEM.

EDGE ACT CORPORATION. A federally chartered bank formed under authority of the Edge Act of 1919 (Section 25 A of the Federal Reserve Act) exclusively for the purpose of engaging in international transactions. The Edge Act permits a commercial bank, through the formation of a subsidiary under Section 25(A), to overcome the usual impediments to the conduct of banking activity outside its home state. An Edge Act bank may be established in a state other than the base state of its parent, so long as it restricts activity to international-trade-related activities.

As originally enacted, the Edge Act provided for two types of international subsidiaries: *banking Edge*, formed to engage in the issuance of letters of credit and to deal in foreign exchange; and *investment Edge*, structured to invest in foreign securities and foreign commercial paper. The act has been amended to eliminate the distinction between banking and investment Edges; all Edge Act banks may now participate in both banking and investment activities.

EFFECTIVE INTEREST RATE. Also known as the *real interest rate*, the return to capital derived by adjusting the *nominal rate* of interest for inflation. For example, a bond may bear a nominal rate of interest (the rate that the instrument pays) of 10 percent; by deducting the rate of inflation—say, 4 percent—we derive the effective rate, which is 6 percent.

EFFECTIVE LENDING RATE. The actual cost of a loan when such factors as commitment fees and compensating balances are computed on top of the interest rate.

EFFECTIVE RATE OF EXCHANGE. The true cost of acquiring a unit of a given currency in terms of another currency. The effective rate includes taxes and other costs that are factored into the price of the currency converted.

EFFECTIVE RATE OF PROTECTION. The net protection afforded by a nation's tariff system to any given domestic product. For example, the higher the rate of duty, the greater the protection against foreign imports; conversely, as rates are increased on raw materials or production inputs, the costs of domestic production are increased, thereby reducing the competitiveness of domestic manufacturers.

The effective rate of protection is calculated by deriving the difference between the duties that would be imposed on a given import and the aggregate of the duties that would be imposed on the raw materials required to manufacture locally the same product.

EFFECTIVE TARIFF RATE. *See* EFFECTIVE RATE OF PROTECTION.

EFFECTIVE UNITED STATES CONTROL. The condition attributed to vessels owned by U.S. citizens but registered in friendly *flag of convenience* countries (primarily Panama, Liberia, and Honduras) and presumed to be available for use by the United States in time of war or national emergency (*see* figure).

Operators of U.S.-registered vessels, American maritime unions, and others have raised concerns that foreign-registered vessels, although owned by Americans, cannot be counted on to augment the U.S. merchant fleet if needed.

In 1945 the Joint Chiefs of Staff, considering the role of the American merchant fleet in future conflicts, observed:

> The term "effective United States control" as applied to shipping is considered to include all shipping which can be expected to be available for requisition by the United States Government in time of national emergency even though such shipping may not be under the United States flag. (J.C.S. 1454/1)

This statement was clarified in 1947 by direct references to U.S.-owned vessels registered in foreign countries:

> Except through agreement there are no legal means by which the United States can regain control of a United States merchant vessel the registry of which has been transferred to another country. From a legal standpoint therefore it can be considered that the only time vessel is under absolute "effective United States control" is when it flies the United States flag. (J.C.S. 1454/11)

The second pronouncement, however, goes on to recognize that there are nations that will permit vessels under their registry to be employed by the U.S. government to advance war-making or other compelling needs; the Joint Chiefs conclude that several factors must be considered in determining whether a U.S.-owned vessel registered abroad is under "effective U.S. control": (1) past practices relative to transfer of vessels to foreign registry by U.S. owners; (2) the character of diplomatic relations between the United States and the foreign country concerned; (3) the relationship of the foreign country to other nations hostile to the United States; (4) geographic proximity of the foreign country of registry to the United States; and (5) stability of the government in the foreign country of registry.

Recently, additional consideration has been given to the nationalities of crews in determining the degree of control exercised by the United States over American-owned, foreign-registered ships. Recognizing that the preponderance of the affected vessels are registered in the PANLIBHON countries

As of July 1, 1984
SUMMARY

	Total			Bahamas			Honduras			Liberia			Panama	
No.	Gross Tons	Dwt. Tons	No.	Gross Tons	Dwt. Tons	No.	Gross Tons	Dwt. Tons	No.	Gross Tons	Dwt. Tons	No.	Gross Tons	Dwt. Tons
Total All Ships	399	21,135,069	42,984,829	21	2,110,166	4,027,021	7	47,301	50,714	296	16,219,259	33,376,490	75	2,758,343	5,530,604
Freighters	67	401,056	522,066	1	10,461	17,153	7	47,301	50,714	38	263,203	368,486	21	80,091	85,713
General Cargo	24	155,109	224,823	1	10,461	17,153	-	-	-	16	125,854	182,068	7	18,794	25,602
Refrigerator	29	154,492	161,990	-	-	-	7	47,301	50,714	8	45,894	51,165	14	61,297	60,111
Full Container	2	6,278	5,810	-	-	-	-	-	-	2	6,278	5,810	-	-	-
Partial Container	7	11,071	17,730	-	-	-	-	-	-	7	11,071	17,730	-	-	-
Roll-On/Roll-Off	-	-	-	-	-	-	-	-	-	-	-	-	-	-	-
Barge Carriers	5	74,106	111,713	-	-	-	-	-	-	5	74,106	111,713	-	-	-
Bulk Carriers	86	2,668,653	5,217,139	1	71,719	130,370	-	-	-	72	2,326,846	4,595,734	13	270,088	491,035
General Bulk	62	1,463,182	2,755,078	-	-	-	-	-	-	49	1,193,094	2,264,043	13	270,088	491,035
Bulk/Oil	3	120,440	231,700	-	-	-	-	-	-	3	120,440	231,700	-	-	-
Ore Carriers	-	-	-	-	-	-	-	-	-	-	-	-	-	-	-
Ore/Oil	8	442,187	969,228	-	-	-	-	-	-	8	442,187	969,228	-	-	-
OBO	13	642,844	1,261,133	1	71,719	130,370	-	-	-	12	571,125	1,130,763	-	-	-
Passenger Combination	-	-	-	-	-	-	-	-	-	-	-	-	-	-	-
Passengers	-	-	-	-	-	-	-	-	-	-	-	-	-	-	-
Tankers	246	18,065,360	37,245,624	19	2,027,986	3,879,498	-	-	-	186	13,629,210	28,412,270	41	2,408,164	4,953,856
General Tankers	224	17,388,214	36,488,734	18	1,964,491	3,811,658	-	-	-	169	13,112,139	27,846,222	37	2,311,584	4,830,854
Chemical Tankers	4	60,319	106,864	-	-	-	-	-	-	4	60,319	106,864	-	-	-
LNG	5	288,602	260,002	-	-	-	-	-	-	5	288,602	260,002	-	-	-
LPG	13	328,225	390,024	1	63,495	67,840	-	-	-	8	168,150	199,182	4	96,580	123,002

Inventory of Effective U. S. Controlled (EUSC) Merchant Ships

(Panama, Liberia, and Honduras), Secretary of Defense Caspar Weinberger, in a letter to the National Maritime Council, noted:

These ships, owned or controlled by U.S. citizens, are considered in contingency plans for sealift requirements primarily as a source of ships to move essential oil and bulk cargoes in support of the national economy. . . . The EUSC [effective U.S. control] countries of registry have stated that they will assert no control over the employment of ships on their registries, and that they will not interfere with the exercise of emergency authority by the governments of shipowners. They have indicated, with varying degrees of formality, that they would not impose any objections to the exercise of U.S. requisitioning authority over U.S. owned ships. (June 8, 1983)

American operators of foreign-registered shipping have organized the FEDERATION OF AMERICAN CONTROLLED SHIPPING (q.v.) to represent their interests.

ELIGIBLE BANKER'S ACCEPTANCE. *See* REGULATION A.

ELIGIBLE PAPER. Drafts, bills of exchange, and other instruments that satisfy requirements for discount or re-discount at the counters of a Federal Reserve bank. In addition to being *eligible*, i.e., arising from an approved transaction, the paper must be *acceptable*, i.e., drawn, accepted, or endorsed by a credit-worthy party. Rules governing the discount of bills and notes at the Federal Reserve are contained in REGULATION A (q.v.).

EMBARGO. A suspension of trade between nations, usually for political reasons. The term *embargo* is also applied to a governmental edict prohibiting entry or departure from the nation's ports of vessels flying the flag of a particular country. In those cases where ports are closed only to the commercial vessels of the other nation, a *civil embargo* exists; when ports are closed to naval or public vessels as well, the condition is a *hostile embargo*.

EMBASSY. The highest level of political mission that one nation may accredit to another. An embassy is a permanent mission charged with maintaining direct political liaison with the government of the host country. The chief officer of an embassy is the *ambassador*, who is regarded as the personal representative of the head of state of the country he represents. The ambassador is assisted in the performance of his duties by one or more *counselors*, several *secretaries*, who are diplomatic officials concerned with political and economic affairs, and various *attachés*, who are experts in fields of interest to the home government and who are charged with collecting data on those areas for use by their government. In the absence of the ambassador, an embassy official is appointed *chargé d'affaires*, or head of the mission.

In some cases, the term *chancery* has been used interchangeably with *embassy*; in current usage, however, *chancery* is applied to the main embassy building, while embassy includes all structures assigned to the diplomatic mission, including satellite facilities, such as trade missions, away from the main site. All embassy buildings, wherever situated, as well as vehicles and personal property of the embassy, are *extraterritorial*, that is, beyond the jurisdiction of the state in which they are physically located, and are subject to the jurisdiction of the home country.

In some cases, particularly in the case of smaller countries, diplomatic missions inferior to embassies are exchanged; these missions are called *legations* and are headed by a *minister* rather than an ambassador. In all other respects, legations are the effective equivalent of embassies, although they rank below embassies in order of diplomatic precedence. In recent years the trend has been to accredit all missions as embassies; relatively few states exchange legations.

See DIPLOMATIC IMMUNITY.

EMERGENCY OIL ALLOCATION SYSTEM. *See* INTERNATIONAL ENERGY AGENCY.

EMERGING NATION. A nation that is not sufficiently industrialized to provide for its own needs in manufactured goods, and that is dependent upon agriculture and/or commodity production as the principal source of foreign exchange to buy such goods. The term is often used interchangeably with *less developed country* and is used particularly for those nations having a recent history of colonial domination.

ENDORSEMENT. A signature, whether or not accompanied by other writings, on the back of a negotiable instrument. By effecting endorsement, the endorsing party usually undertakes to guarantee performance of the instrument, commonly the payment of a specified sum of money at a date prescribed in the instrument.

The endorsement of an instrument plus delivery to the new *holder* constitute *negotiation*, i.e., transfer of ownership in the paper, plus goods or money represented by the paper. Most commonly, negotiable paper takes the form of drafts, bills of exchange, checks, bills of lading, warehouse receipts, and such debt obligations as notes and bonds. The characteristic of *negotiability*, i.e., that the instrument may be endorsed and transferred to another party, is often revealed by the words *to order* in conjunction with the name of the payee or owner of the instrument; by drawing a document "to order," the parties to the original agreement that gives rise to the instrument are stating that the named payee may *order* that another be paid in his stead, and the person so designated as the new payee reserves the right to endorse and deliver the instrument to yet another party in his order or direction.

The Uniform Commercial Code, as adopted in the United States, recognizes five types of endorsements:

1. *Blank endorsement* (also known as *general endorsement*) consists merely of a signature. This form of endorsement makes the instrument into *bearer paper*, negotiable by delivery alone; ownership of the instrument is vested in whoever possesses it.

2. *Special endorsement* (also known as *endorsement in full* and *direct endorsement*) specifies a particular party to whom the instrument is payable; the endorsement of that party is essential to subsequent negotiation.

3. *Conditional endorsement* imposes stipulated conditions upon the party to whom the instrument is endorsed, e.g., that a bill of exchange be paid to the order of John Smith upon transfer of title to certain merchandise. John Smith, upon subsequent negotiation of the bill, would warrant to all subsequent holders that the prescribed conditions had been fulfilled. This form of endorsement is not employed frequently.

4. *Without recourse endorsement* is a qualified endorsement that limits the warranties of the endorser. By endorsing an instrument with the words *without recourse* above the signature, the instrument is negotiated with the express understanding on the part of the new holder that he may not look to the prior holder for relief in the event the instrument is subsequently dishonored by the drawee or maker.

5. *Restrictive endorsement* is a qualified endorsement that prohibits further negotiation of the instrument, makes the endorsee agent for the endorser, and transfers the instrument to the endorsee in trust for a third party. Under a restrictive endorsement, all subsequent endorsers acquire only the rights of the first endorser.

An endorser adds his name and credit to the integrity of the instrument, and subsequent holders may look to prior endorsers (excepting those who have endorsed "without recourse" or under restrictive endorsements) for settlement of the obligation that the instrument represents.

Endorsement may take the form of a manual signature, printed or stamped impressions, or any other form regarded as a legal signature; there is no limit to the number of endorsements that may appear on a negotiable instrument, unless the instrument or a restrictive endorsement provides otherwise. In those cases where the number of endorsements exceeds the capacity of the instrument to accommodate them all legibly, an attachment, known as an *allonge*, may be permanently affixed to the instrument.

ENGLISH WATER TON. A unit of measure, equal to 224 imperial gallons, used principally in Great Britain to express statistics relative to petroleum products.

ENLARGEMENT. The expansion of the EUROPEAN COMMUNITIES *(q.v.)* through the admission of new member states.

ENTENTE. Literally, "an agreement." In political usage, an understanding among governments as represented by accords on important areas. Commercially, the term is used on the Continent as a synonym for a *cartel*.

ENTERPRISE ZONE. *See* EXPORT PROCESSING ZONE.

ENTIRETIES DOCTRINE. A principle of customs law under which components may, in some cases, be entered for duty purposes under the tariff item applicable to the finished product. Normally, three conditions are required for the principle to be implemented: (1) the parts must be suitable for assembly into the finished item; (2) the parts must not be commingled, i.e., packed in the same shipment; and (3) the imported parts, were they to be assembled, would result in a product suitable for entry as a finished product. The absence of an essential component would defeat entry as a finished product.

ENTREPÔT. A warehouse or storage facility where foreign merchandise may be deposited and withdrawn for re-export without incurring customs duties.

ENTRY (CUSTOMS). The administrative processing associated with foreign merchandise that has landed in the United States for consumption, warehousing, or other reasons. The act of *entry* involves the submission to U.S. Customs of documents that identify the owner of the goods, the type and character of the merchandise, value for duty purposes, and other relevant information upon which the customs authorities may rely in deciding whether the merchandise is permitted admission into the United States, which permits or licenses, if any, apply to the importation, and what rate of duty is to be assessed.

All imports must be *entered* within five working days of arrival at a U.S. port of entry, unless an extension of time is permitted by the district or area director of customs. Failure to make entry within the prescribed time period will cause the goods to fall into the condition of GENERAL ORDER *(q.v.)* under which the unentered merchandise will be transported into a customs BONDED WAREHOUSE *(q.v.)*; the goods will remain there, at the owner's expense, until entry is effected. If entry is not made within one year from transfer into general order, the goods will be considered abandoned and sold or destroyed by customs authorities. In case of perishable or dangerous merchandise, customs may effect disposal immediately.

Customarily, entry is made by the owner of the goods or his authorized agent, usually a licensed customhouse broker. The common carrier that transported the merchandise into the United States will provide U.S. Customs with a CARRIER'S CERTIFICATE *(q.v.)* naming the owner of the goods; customs will rely upon this document in permitting a party to make entry. In the event a carrier's certificate is not available, is lost, or cannot be provided for any reason, ownership of the goods may be established by presentation of a bill of lading or air waybill. In those cases where the goods do not arrive by common carrier, possession alone is normally sufficient to establish right to make entry.

The owner of the merchandise or his customhouse broker will supply to customs officers at the port of entry the following: carrier's certificate or other evidence of right to make entry; entry manifest (Customs Form 7533) or application and special permit for immediate delivery; invoices or other documents establishing value; such other documentation as may be required by virtue of the nature of the shipment (e.g., certificate of origin if exemption from duty is requested on the basis of country of manufacture); and evidence that a cash deposit or a surety bond has been lodged with customs to cover any duties, taxes, or penalties applicable to the given shipment.

Following submission of the required documentation, customs will examine the merchandise and, provided that there are no violations or restrictions, release it. Estimated duties must be deposited at the designated customhouse within ten working days of the release of the goods.

There are many different types of entries possible, depending upon the purpose for which the merchandise enters the United States or the character of the goods themselves.

The following are common types of entries, each illustrated on the following pages.

1. *Consumption entry* is used when the imported merchandise is to be introduced directly into commerce, either as a finished product or an intermediate good, to be used in the United States.

2. *Warehouse entry* is used in those cases where the imported merchandise is not required for immediate use; duties and taxes may be deferred until the goods are required by placing them in a special customs-licensed warehouse. Goods may remain in the bonded warehouse up to five years from the date of importation, during which period the merchandise may be re-exported without duty obligation. In some cases, the imported product may be manufactured, sorted, packed, or otherwise manipulated within the warehouse. Upon withdrawal, duties will be levied upon the goods in their new form. Goods are withdrawn from a bonded warehouse by filing a consumption entry.

3. *Transportation and exportation entry* is used when goods of foreign origin are being transported across the territory of the United States while en route to another foreign destination, e.g., when Canadian merchandise transits the United States to meet a ship in New York for export to France. Such transportation across the United States is usually performed by common carriers specially licensed by U.S. Customs. *See* DUTY; TARIFF (CUSTOMS); TARIFF SCHEDULES OF THE UNITED STATES.

ENTRY PRICE. Under the COMMON AGRICULTURE POLICY *(q.v.)* of the European Economic Community, the price at which certain imported agricultural products enter EEC commerce. If the entry price for those commodities falls below the EEC standard (the *intervention* or *reference price*), the com-

CONSUMPTION ENTRY
UNITED STATES CUSTOMS SERVICE

RECORD COPY ☐

CASHIER'S COPY ☐

This Space For Census Use Only		Form approved.	This Space For Customs Use Only		
BLOCK AND FILE NO.	**M.O.T.**	O.M.B. No. 48-R0217.	**ENTRY NO. AND DATE**		
	MANIFEST NO.		83-856070-9 12-10-82		

FOREIGN PORT OF LADING	U.S. PORT OF UNLADING	Dist. and Port Code 10-01	Port of Entry Name New York	Term Bond No. GTB 7-30-83

Importer of Record (Name and Address)
Acme Importing Co.   123 Main St., Small Town, CT 06757

For Account of (Name and Address)
-- Same --

Importing Vessel (Name) or Carrier Always Afloat 5880	B/L or AWB No. 031-331122	Port of Lading Kobe	I.T. No. and Date
Country of Exportation Japan 588.0	Date of Exportation 11-20-82	Type and Date of Invoice FSI 11-18-82	I.T. From (Port)
U.S. Port of Unlading New York	Date of Importation 12-07-82	Location of Goods—G.O. No. 16-865087	I.T. Carrier (Delivering)

MARKS & NUMBERS OF PACKAGES COUNTRY OF ORIGIN OF MERCHANDISE (1)	DESCRIPTION OF MERCHANDISE IN TERMS OF T.S.U.S. ANNO., NUMBER AND KIND OF PACKAGES (2)		ENTERED VALUE IN U.S. DOLLARS (3)	T.S.U.S. ANNO. REPORTING NO. (4)	TARIFF OR I.R.C. RATE (5)	DUTY AND I.R. TAX (6)	
	GROSS WEIGHT IN POUNDS (2a)	NET QUANTITY IN T.S. U.S. ANNO. UNITS (2b)				DOLLARS	CENTS
C/O 5880	1104 CTNS		NOT-RELATED				
	OTHER HEATING APPARATUS UNITS						
	33248 LBS	1104 NO	66626	653.5234	4.20%	2798	29
			PEXT	66626			
			CHGS	11510			
	I.V.	66625.85					
	E.V.	66626.00 AS	66626				
	US$						
	33248 LBS	1104 PCS TOTAL	66626		TOTAL	2798.	29
	HARTFORD INDEMITY & ACCIDENT CO., HARTFORD, CT. SURETY -#163						

MISSING DOCUMENTS
NONE

THIS SPACE FOR CUSTOMS USE ONLY

I declare that I am the ☐ nominal consignee and that the actual owner for customs purposes is as shown above, or ☒ consignee or agent of the consignee. I further declare that the merchandise ☒ was or ☐ was not obtained in pursuance of a purchase or agreement to purchase. I also include in my declaration all the statements in the declaration on the back of this entry.

ACME IMPORTING CO.   10-DEC-82 _____DATE
ABC Customhouse Brokers, Inc. _____.(Signature)
123 Main St. Small Town, CT _____(Address)

{ ☐ Principal.
☐ Member of the firm.
☐ ATTY IN FACT of the corporation.
                    (Title)
☐ Authorized agent

CUSTOMS FORM **7501**
9 12 73

Consumption Entry

WAREHOUSE OR REWAREHOUSE ENTRY
UNITED STATES CUSTOMS SERVICE

RECORD COPY ☐

This Space For Census Use Only				This Space For Customs Use Only	
BLOCK AND FILE NO.	M.O.T.	Form approved. Budget Bureau No. 48-R210.6.		ENTRY NO. AND DATE	
	MANIFEST NO.				

FOREIGN PORT OF LADING	U.S. PORT OF UNLADING	Dist. and Port Code	Port of Entry Name	Term Bond No.
		10 01	New York	GTB 444555

Importer of Record (Name and Address)
XYZ Imports Company, North Main Street, Anywhere 11111

For Account of (Name and Address)
Same as Above

Importing Vessel (Name) or Carrier	B/L or AWB No.	Port of Lading	I.T. No. and Date
S/S Vessel (AW)	1000	Hamburg	

Country of Exportation	Date of Exportation	Type and Date of Invoice	I.T. From (Port)
W. Germany	xx/xx/xx	S.C.I. xx/xx/xx	

U.S. Port of Unlading	Date of Importation	Location of Goods—G.O. No.	I.T. Carrier (Delivering)
New York	xx/xx/xx	Port 4, New York	

MARKS & NUMBERS OF PACKAGES COUNTRY OF ORIGIN OF MERCHANDISE (1)	DESCRIPTION OF MERCHANDISE IN TERMS OF T.S.U.S. ANNO NUMBER AND KIND OF PACKAGES (2)		ENTERED VALUE IN U.S. DOLLARS (3)	T.S.U.S. ANNO. REPORTING NO. (4)	TARIFF OR I.R.C. RATE (5)	DUTY AND I.R. TAX (6)	
	GROSS WEIGHT IN POUNDS (2a)	NET QUANTITY IN T.S. U.S. ANNO. UNITS (2b)				DOLLARS	CENTS
XYZ NEW YORK #1/8	0/0 CONTAINER ISCU-567890 8 Cases containing Automobile parts		$500	NOT RELATED 554.8888	5.6%	28	00
			PEXT 455 CHGS 45				
c/o W. Germany							

Warehouse LMN Bonded Warehouse Co., New York, NY

MISSING DOCUMENTS	THIS SPACE FOR CUSTOMS USE ONLY
NONE	

I declare that I am the ☐ nominal consignee and that the actual owner for customs purposes is as shown above, or ☐ consignee or agent of the consignee. I further declare that the merchandise ☐ was or ☐ was not obtained in pur-

suance of a purchase or agreement to purchase. I also include in my declaration all the statements in the declaration on the back of this entry.

xx/xx/xx _____DATE

XYZ Imports Company   CUSTOM HOUSE, ATTY
_____by   North Main Street, Anywhere
(Signature)
(Address)

{ ☐ Principal.
☐ Member of the firm.
☐ _____of the corporation.
(Title)
☒ Authorized agent

CUSTOMS FORM NOV 66 7502

Warehouse/Rewarehouse

CUSTOMS FORM 7512
10-2-73

TRANSPORTATION ENTRY AND MANIFEST OF
GOODS SUBJECT TO CUSTOMS INSPECTION
AND PERMIT

UNITED STATES CUSTOMS SERVICE

Form Approved
O.M.B. No. 48-R0212

Entry No. ....Entry No...........

Port ....

Date ....

Entry No. 12345678

Class of Entry I.T.
(I.T.)(Wd.T.)(Wd.Ex.)(T.E.)(Drawback, etc.)

Dist. No. 28   Port Code No. 09   First U. S. Port of Unlading OAKLAND, CALIFORNIA

Port of SAN FRANCISCO/OAKLAND CA   Date DEC. 8,1982

Entered or imported by ALWAYS AFLOAT LINES,INC. 10 Harbor St.,Oakland, CA ....to be shipped

in bond via WESTERN PACIFIC .... consigned to
District Director of Customs CHICAGO,IL 3901 ...Final foreign destination....................
(C.H.L. number)   (Vessel or carrier)   (Car number and initial)   (Pier or station)   (For exportations only)

Consignee ACME IMPORTING CO.,123 MAIN ST.,SMALL TOWN, CONNECTICUT
(At customs port of exit or destination)

Foreign port of lading KOBE ....B/L No. 12-5432 ...Date of sailing Nov 18,1982
(Above information to be furnished only when merchandise is imported by vessel)

Imported on the SNAFU MARU V.12E   Flag Amer on DEC 8,1982 via YOKOHAMA
(Name of vessel or carrier and motive power)   (Date imported)   (Last foreign port)

Exported from JAPAN on NOV 18,1982 Goods now at BERTH X,OAKLAND,CA
(Country)   (Date)   (Name of warehouse, station, pier, etc.)

Marks and Numbers of Packages	DESCRIPTION AND QUANTITY OF MERCHANDISE NUMBER AND KIND OF PACKAGES (Describe fully as per shipping papers)	GROSS WEIGHT IN POUNDS	VALUE (Dollars only)	RATE	DUTY
SNFU12893 SNFU34256 SNFU84568 SNFU84721 SNFU84339	FIVE CONTAINERS CONTAINING: 2040 CARTONS PORTABLE KEROSENE HEATERS	80952#	$50480.00		
	I.T.T. BOND NO. 300 BLANKET CARRIERS RELEASE ON FILE	VAN COMPLY WITH SECTION 10.41a OF CUSTOMS REGULATIONS			

G. O. No. ....

CERTIFICATE OF LADING FOR TRANSPORTATION IN BOND AND/OR LADING FOR EXPORTATION FOR

CHICAGO, IL
(Port)

WITH THE EXCEPTIONS NOTED ABOVE, THE WITHIN-DESCRIBED GOODS WERE:
Delivered to the Carrier named above, for delivery to the District Director of Customs at destination sealed with Customs seals

Nos. ....
or the packages (were) (were not) labeled, or corded and sealed.

....
(Inspector or warehouse officer)

....
(Date)

Laden on the—

....
(Vessel, vehicle, or aircraft)
which cleared for —

on...........................
(Date)

as verified by export records.

....
(Inspector)

....
(Date)

I truly declare that the statements contained herein are true and correct to the best of my knowledge and belief.

Entered or withdrawn by ALWAYS AFLOAT LINES,INC .

JOHN JONES

To the Inspector or Warehouse Officer: The above-described goods shall be disposed of as specified herein.

....
For the District Director of Customs.

Received from the district director of customs of above district the merchandise described in this manifest for transportation and delivery into the custody of the customs officers at the port named above, all packages in apparent good order except as noted hereon.

....
Attorney or Agent of Carrier

Transportation Entry and Manifest of Goods

munity may impose additional duties on the imported agricultural products to offset the price advantage of the foreign product.

EO NOMINE. One of three methods for the classification of merchandise for duty purposes. The eo nomine method relies upon finding the common name of the product within the tariff schedules. In the event that the product is not described by name within the tariff schedules, the customs examiner may classify the product according to its intended use, or the materials of which it is composed.

E.P.R.G. FRAMEWORK. A system for categorizing the international marketing strategy of a given firm based upon that firm's degree of corporate commitment to supranational perceptions and objectives. The strategies can be grouped into four main categories:

1. *Ethnocentric orientation*—foreign operations are regarded as secondary to home country markets and production; overseas markets are supplied primarily by exports from the home country; and the home country operation articulates pricing, promotional, and distribution strategies.

2. *Polycentric orientation*—overseas markets have some detachment from the home country; subsidiaries are established overseas, and each subsidiary is permitted to devise its own marketing objectives and pricing policies; the sales force is composed of local nationals and local patterns of distribution are employed.

3. *Regiocentric orientation*—marketing objectives are defined on a regional (e.g., European, Latin American), rather than national, basis; local and third country nationals represent a significant portion of the management; uniform regional or worldwide image of the product is achieved or defined as an important objective.

4. *Geocentric orientation*—a truly international attitude emerges among management; national boundaries are irrelevant in defining larger corporate objectives.

EQUIDISTANCE. Geopolitical strategy, employed in varying degrees by politically nonaligned countries, involving a middle path between the superpowers.

EQUILIBRIUM RELATIVE PRICE OF CURRENCIES. *Synonymous with rate of exchange,* i.e., the price, in terms of one national currency, at which another currency can be purchased under market conditions.

EQUIPMENT INTERCHANGE RECEIPT. A document prepared by a carrier or lessor company or other firm having control over containers or trailers to be executed by a lessee, carrier, or other person taking delivery of those containers or trailers for use in the transport of goods. The interchange receipt serves as an acknowledgment that physical custody of the containers has changed

hands, and it usually contains standard clauses relating to return of the equipment, provisions for repairs, et cetera (*see* figure, next page).

EQUITY PLUS FIXED-RATE DEBT. A purchase arrangement in which the borrower contributes a portion of the purchase price (his equity) and takes a loan for the rest at a fixed rate of interest.

EQUITY PLUS VARIABLE-RATE DEBT. A purchase arrangement in which the borrower contributes a portion of the purchase price (his equity) and takes a loan for the rest at a rate of interest that fluctuates periodically in response to some specified money market index.

ERRORS AND OMISSIONS. A clause in an *open* insurance policy that permits the insured to secure cover retroactively for property inadequately insured through the clerical or adminstrative error of the insured, and where it is clear from the pattern or character of the insured's business that he would have provided coverage for the affected property except for inadvertent omission.

An errors and omissions clause is common to most marine cargo policies under which multiple shipments are declared periodically on a *bordereaux*, or listing of the particulars of the voyage and values of the property. Marine policies usually provide a given basis for insured valuation, e.g., invoice value plus 10 percent. Hence, if an insured suffered a covered loss but discovered that, through clerical error, the goods were declared for invoice value only, or that the shipment was not declared at all, the insured could invoke the errors and omissions provision of his cargo policy by declaring the shipment for its correct value and paying the premium thereon.

ESCAPE CLAUSE. A provision common to most international trade agreements under which an adhering nation is permitted to withdraw trade concessions under prescribed conditions, normally in those cases where such concessions are found to result in material injury to the domestic economy. Most major trading nations subscribe to the conditions contained in Article XIX of the General Agreement on Tariffs and Trade, as follows:

If, as a result of unforeseen developments and of the effect of the obligations incurred by a contracting party under this Agreement, including tariff concessions, any product is being imported into the territory of that contracting party in such increased quantities and under such conditions as to cause or threaten serious injury to domestic producers in that territory of like or directly competitive products, the contracting party shall be free, in respect of such product, and to the extent and for such time as may be necessary to prevent or remedy injury, to suspend the obligation in whole or in part or to withdraw or modify the concession.

EQUIPMENT INTERCHANGE RECEIPT AND SAFETY INSPECTION REPORT

No. 392956

(This form may not be reproduced without the written permission of the Equipment Interchange Association, 1616 P St., N.W., Washington, D. C.)

POINT OF INTERCHANGE	DATE	O'CLOCK A.M. ☐ P.M. ☐	CROSS REF. RECEIPT NO.

ACQUIRING CARRIER	PROVIDING CARRIER	☐ EVEN EXCHANGE
		☐ RENTAL

OWNER	TRAILER/CONTAINER UNIT NO.	CHASSIS UNIT NO.	BOGIE/DOLLY UNIT NO.

TYPE	LENGTH	IN EXCESS OF 12' 6"	LICENSE NO. AND STATE	TMT PLATE NO.	SEAL NO.

Unless otherwise checked as subject to the paragraph immediately below, this interchange is made subject to the terms and conditions of the currently effective interchange contractual provisions as contained in Equipment Interchange Schedule, and supplements thereto, the official copies of which are on file at the office of the Equipment Interchange Association, 1616 P Street, Northwest, Washington, D. C. 20036, and copies of which have been supplied to the signatories hereto. ☐ The carriers making this interchange have signed a different and presently effective written interchange contract; that contract in all its terms shall constitute the contract between them.

MARK CLEARLY ALL DAMAGE OR DEFICIENCY FOUND BY INSPECTION SYMBOL 'B' BRUISE - 'C' CUT 'H' HOLE

INITIAL RECEIPT AND INSPECTION	RETURN RECEIPT AND INSPECTION

LEFT SIDE | FRONT | FRONT | FRONT | LEFT SIDE | FRONT | FRONT

FRONT / TOP / REAR | FLOOR | REAR | FRONT / TOP / REAR | FLOOR | REAR

RIGHT SIDE | REAR | BEGINNING HUB READING | RIGHT SIDE | REAR | ENDING HUB READING

DEPARTMENT OF TRANSPORTATION SAFETY REGULATIONS REQUIRE EACH PART LISTED TO BE INSPECTED
If not defective, use check mark. If defective, describe defect.

CLEARANCE LIGHTS:	Front	Rear	Stop Lights	CLEARANCE LIGHTS:	Front	Rear	Stop Lights
SIDE MARKERS:	Left	Right	Tail Lights	SIDE MARKERS:	Left	Right	Tail Lights
REFLECTORS:	Left Side / Right Side	Rear	Turn Signals	REFLECTORS:	Left Side / Right Side	Rear	Turn Signals
FLAPS	Rear End Protection / Springs		Ident. Lights	Flaps	Rear End Protection / Springs		Ident. Lights
Container/Chassis Clamps	Wiring		SAE-ATA 7-Way Plug	Container/Chassis Clamps	Wiring		SAE-ATA 7-Way Plug
ACCESSORIES:	Tarps	Cross Bows	Chains/ Binders	ACCESSORIES:	Tarps	Cross Bows	Chains/ Binders
OTHER:				OTHER:			

B R A K E S	Air or Vacuum Loss	Hose	Connections	Tubing	B R A K E S	Air or Vacuum Loss	Hose	Connections	Tubing
	Relay Emergency Valve	Linings	Other Defects			Relay Emergency Valve	Linings	Other Defects	

POSITION	BRAND NO.	CONDITION	POSITION	BRAND NO.	CONDITION	POSITION	BRAND NO.	CONDITION	POSITION	BRAND NO.	CONDITION
L. O. FRONT			R. O. FRONT			L. O. FRONT			R. O. FRONT		
L. I. FRONT			R. I. FRONT			L. I. FRONT			R. I. FRONT		
L. O. REAR			R. O. REAR			L. O. REAR			R. O. REAR		
L. I. REAR			R. I. REAR			L. I. REAR			R. I. REAR		
SPARE			SPARE			SPARE			SPARE		

(T I R E S on left blocks and right blocks)

REMARKS: | REMARKS:

PROVIDING CARRIER	DATE	PROVIDING CARRIER	DATE
BY	TIME	BY	TIME
ACQUIRING CARRIER	PLACE	ACQUIRING CARRIER	PLACE

I hereby certify that on the date stated first above, I carefully inspected the equipment described above; that this is a true and correct report of the results of such inspection; and that possession of such equipment was taken on behalf of the acquiring carrier at the time, date and place indicated next above.

BY

I hereby certify that on the date stated above the person who made the inspection covered by this report was competent and qualified to make such inspection and was duly authorized to make such inspection and take possession of such equipment as a representative of the acquiring carrier.

BY

Signature of Owner, Partner or Officer of Acquiring Carrier

I hereby certify that on the date stated first above, I carefully inspected the equipment described above; that this is a true and correct report of the results of such inspection; and that possession of such equipment was taken on behalf of the acquiring carrier at the place, date and time first indicated above.

BY

I hereby certify that on the date stated above the person who made the inspection covered by this report was competent and qualified to make such inspection and was duly authorized to make such inspection and take possession of such equipment as a representative of the acquiring carrier.

BY

Signature of Owner, Partner or Officer of Acquiring Carrier

ACCOUNTING RECORD. TO BE USED UPON RETURN OF EQUIPMENT TO COMPUTE CHARGES FOR RENTAL. (Repairs, if any, will be billed separately.)

PER DIEM CHARGE (	DAYS AT	) $	
		Computed by	

Reorder from Equipment Interchange Association

1

LESSOR'S CONTROL COPY (Carrier Furnishing Trailer)

Equipment Interchange Receipt and Safety Inspection. Courtesy of Equipment Interchange Association

The Trade Act of 1974 liberalized the conditions under which the United States might implement the escape clause, as provided in the Tariff Act of 1930.

In order to invoke the escape clause for any particular product, current U.S. law requires that an application for relief be submitted to the U.S. International Trade Commission (ITC); the petitioner may be the president, the U.S. trade representative, the Senate Finance Committee, the Ways and Means Committee of the House of Representatives, or an American firm, labor union, or trade association affected by the foreign import. The ITC will investigate the submission and determine whether imports of the item in question have increased; whether such imports have injured, or threaten to injure, domestic industry; and whether the target imports are a substantial or only a peripheral cause of injury. If the ITC finds that imports have increased and that such imports are a substantial cause of injury, or threaten to cause substantial injury, the ITC will recommend such corrective measures as it deems appropriate, including, inter alia, increased tariff rates, quotas, or compensatory assistance to affected American firms or workers.

The president is not bound to adopt the recommendations of the ITC. As a practical matter, the escape clause is infrequently used; most trade disputes are resolved through negotiations with the nation from which the offending import originates. In those cases where the escape clause is invoked, it limits protective measures to a period of five years, which may be extended for a period up to three years more.

ETHNOCENTRIC COMPANY. *See* E.P.R.G. FRAMEWORK.

ETHNOCENTRIC PRICING. The policy of a firm to offer its products at the same price abroad as in the home market, irrespective of price sensitivity or other factors of the foreign market.

EURATOM. *See* EUROPEAN ATOMIC ENERGY COMMUNITY.

EURCO. A commercial version of the *European Currency Unit (q.v.).* In order to stimulate interest in the European currency unit (ECU), in 1973 the European Investment Bank introduced eurco as the commercial equivalent of the ECU, which was limited to use by governmental holders only.

The eurco is composed of the following national currencies:

.9	Deutschemarks
1.2	French francs
.35	Netherlands guilder
.075	Pounds sterling
.005	Irish pounds
80.	Italian lira
4.5	Belgian francs
.2	Danish kroner
.5	Luxembourg francs

The market value of the eurco fluctuates daily in response to the market values of its component currencies.

See ARTIFICIAL CURRENCY UNIT.

EUROBILL OF EXCHANGE. A BILL OF EXCHANGE *(q.v.)* drawn in a currency other than that used in the country of the maker.

EUROBOND. A bond or similar debt instrument issued by a government or a firm, denominated in the currency of the country of issue and paying interest in that currency but sold abroad.

EUROCRATS. Employees of the secretariat of the European Communities or its agencies.

EUROCURRENCY. Funds held on deposit outside their country of issue, e.g., Italian lira on deposit in Great Britain.

EURODOLLARS. U.S. dollars on deposit outside the United States. The term applies to dollars on deposit at foreign branches of American banks as well as deposits with foreign banks.

EUROEQUITIES. Shares of stock and other equity instruments denominated in a currency other than that of the country in which they are traded.

EUROMART. Any market in which monetary instruments denominated in foreign currencies are traded.

EURONATIONALISM. A geopolitical viewpoint that holds that the interests of Europeans are substantially interrelated and transcend the national boundaries that separate Europeans into different states. This viewpoint emerged strongly after World War II and is the product of a greater awareness of pan-European goals, particularly in response to Soviet aggression in Eastern Europe and what is often felt to be excessive influence over European affairs by the United States.

EURONET. An international, computer-based network founded by the European Communities to foster the movement of information among member states. Euronet consists of five *nodes*, or distribution points, located in London, Paris, Frankfurt, Rome, and Zurich; five additional access points have been established in Dublin, Brussels, Amsterdam, Copenhagen, and Luxembourg.

Information suppliers to Euronet consist of 192 data banks coordinated into the Direct Information Access Network for Europe (D.I.A.N.E.). The participating data banks provide information on commercial, scientific, legal, engineering, and social science topics, to be used by researchers from all member countries, including business entities.

Euronet was sanctioned by the Council of the European Communities on June 24, 1971; the system was inaugurated on February 13, 1980, and came into commercial operation on April 1 of that year.

Organized under an agreement among European telecommunications authorities, EURONET has been effectively replaced as an access mode by national data links.

EUROPEAN AGRICULTURAL GUIDANCE AND GUARANTEE FUND. *See* COMMON AGRICULTURAL POLICY.

EUROPEAN ATOMIC ENERGY COMMUNITY.
One of the three components of the European Communities, established by the Treaty of Rome in 1957. The entity, known commonly as *Euratom*, was created by member states of the European Coal and Steel Community (at that time, France, Italy, Federal Republic of Germany, and the Benelux countries), to harness atomic energy for peaceful purposes, particularly as a source of energy. Since its formation, Great Britain, Ireland, Denmark, and Greece have acceded to the Euratom convention. Spain and Portugal will become participants Jan. 1, 1986.

Effective July 1, 1967, the organs of Euratom were merged with those of the European Economic Community and the European Coal and Steel Community to create the European Communities.

EUROPEAN COAL AND STEEL COMMUNITY.
One of three component entities within the European Communities, the coal and steel organization was formed following World War II to permit member states to equalize their access to iron and steel resources. The ECSC was proposed by Robert Schuman of France to encourage European economic rehabilitation following the war and to enhance prospects for eventual political unification among European states.

The ECSC was established at Paris in 1951, among France, German Federal Republic, Italy, Belgium, Netherlands, and Luxembourg; the treaty became effective July 25, 1952. Great Britain, Ireland, Denmark, and Greece have joined the ECSC. Spain and Portugal will enter Jan. 1, 1986.

Principal features of the treaty include establishment of a common market among the members in coal, iron ore, and scrap (to begin February 1, 1953), steel (May 1, 1953), and specialty steel (August 1, 1954); harmonization of external tariffs on coal, iron, and steel products; joint research and development projects; and low-cost loans for financing housing of miners and steel workers.

In 1967, the council and organs of the ECSC were merged with those of the European Economic Community and the European Atomic Energy Community to form the unified European Communities.

EUROPEAN COMMON MARKET. *See* EUROPEAN ECONOMIC COMMUNITY.

EUROPEAN COMMUNITIES. The name for the collective institution that embraces the EUROPEAN ECONOMIC COMMUNITY, the EUROPEAN ATOMIC ENERGY COMMUNITY, and the EUROPEAN COAL AND STEEL COMMUNITY (*qq.v.*). Each of the three entities was established by separate convention, the earliest of which was the Treaty of Paris of 1951 forming the European Coal and Steel Community.

Initially, each community possessed its own council and organs of government. A 1965 treaty among the members of the three institutions established that, effective July 1, 1967, the three communities, while continuing to possess separate legal identities, would share common organs of adminstration and would be known as the European Communities.

EUROPEAN CURRENCY UNIT. *See* EUROPEAN MONETARY SYSTEM.

EUROPEAN DEPOSITORY RECEIPT. *See* INTERNATIONAL DEPOSITORY RECEIPT.

EUROPEAN ECONOMIC COMMUNITY. One of the three components of the European Communities. In March 1957, the members of the European Coal and Steel Community (France, Federal Republic of Germany, Italy, and the Benelux countries) expanded the sphere of economic cooperation through the Treaty of Rome, forming the European Economic Community (EEC) and the European Atomic Energy Community. It has been the object of the EEC, as expressed in the treaty creating it, to promote "a harmonious development of economic activities, a continuous and balanced expansion, an increased stability, an accelerated raising of the standard of living and closer relations between its Member States."

The EEC has succeeded in abolishing tariffs and quotas among members; creating a common external tariff; concluding agreements with former overseas possessions of the members (the so-called ACP COUNTRIES *[q.v.]*) permitting nonreciprocal duty-free importation of all industrial and most agricultural products into the EEC; developing a COMMON AGRICULTURAL POLICY (*q.v.*); establishing the virtually uninhibited movement of capital and labor among the member states; and moving toward a common European currency.

Since its foundation, the EEC has been expanded to include Great Britain, Ireland, Denmark, and Greece. Spain and Portugal will enter Jan. 1, 1986.

In 1967, the organs of the EEC were merged with those of the European Coal and Steel Community and the European Atomic Energy Community to form the European Communities.

See EUROPEAN MONETARY SYSTEM.

EUROPEAN FREE TRADE ASSOCIATION. A free trade area consisting of seven European countries among which tariffs and quantitative restrictions on industrial imports have been eliminated. Established in 1960 by the Stockholm Convention, EFTA originally included Austria, Denmark, Norway, Portugal, Sweden, Switzerland, and the United Kingdom; in 1973, Denmark and the United Kingdom left EFTA. Iceland has since joined EFTA, and Finland has become an associate member.

EFTA operates through a secretariat based in Geneva; a semiannual meeting of the EFTA Council, in which all members are represented, oversees the affairs of the association and promulgates policies (*see* figure).

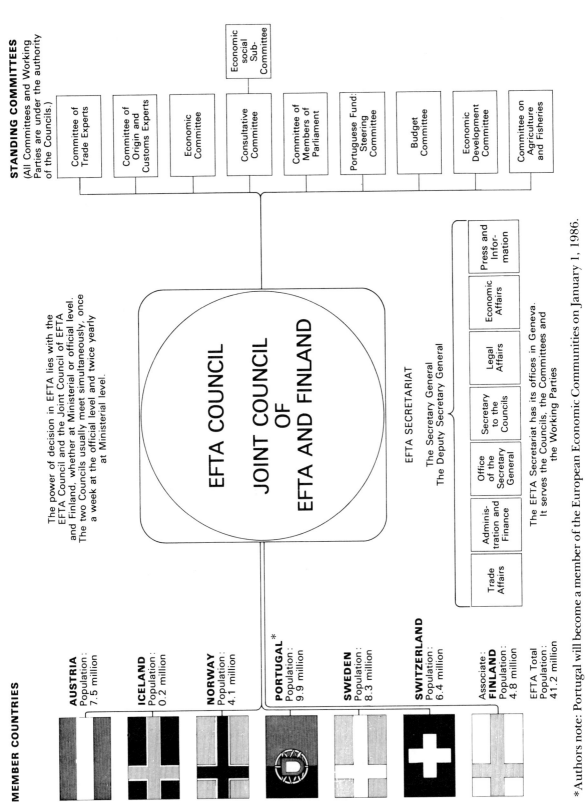

STANDING COMMITTEES

(All Committees and Working Parties are under the authority of the Councils.)

- Committee of Trade Experts
- Committee of Origin and Customs Experts
- Economic Committee
- Consultative Committee
  - Economic social Sub-Committee
- Committee of Members of Parliament
- Portuguese Fund Steering Committee
- Budget Committee
- Economic Development Committee
- Committee on Agriculture and Fisheries

The power of decision in EFTA lies with the EFTA Council and the Joint Council of EFTA and Finland, whether at Ministerial or official level. The two Councils usually meet simultaneously, once a week at the official level and twice yearly at Ministerial level.

EFTA COUNCIL

JOINT COUNCIL OF EFTA AND FINLAND

EFTA SECRETARIAT

The Secretary General
The Deputy Secretary General

- Trade Affairs
- Administration and Finance
- Office of the Secretary General
- Secretary to the Councils
- Legal Affairs
- Economic Affairs
- Press and Information

The EFTA Secretariat has its offices in Geneva. It serves the Councils, the Committees and the Working Parties.

MEMBER COUNTRIES

AUSTRIA
Population: 7.5 million

ICELAND
Population: 0.2 million

NORWAY
Population: 4.1 million

PORTUGAL *
Population: 9.9 million

SWEDEN
Population: 8.3 million

SWITZERLAND
Population: 6.4 million

Associate:
FINLAND
Population: 4.8 million

EFTA Total Population: 41.2 million

*Authors note: Portugal will become a member of the European Economic Communities on January 1, 1986.

European Free Trade Association Organization Chart

EUROPEAN INVESTMENT BANK. A multilateral development bank established in 1958 by the Treaty of Rome for the purpose of assisting in the balanced growth of the EUROPEAN ECONOMIC COMMUNITY *(q.v.)* (EEC). The bank grants long-term loans from its own resources, and provides financial guarantees to private enterprises, banks, and public institutions for the purposes of expanding the economic base of underdeveloped regions within the EEC, energy independence, and other projects of interest to the community.

In addition to providing funding from its own resources, the EIB also acts as agent for loans from the EEC's *New Community Instrument;* the NCI was established in 1979 [NCI I] with credit of 500 million European currency units (ECU), to which 1 billion ECU were added [NCI II], followed in 1983 by an additional 1.5 billion ECU [NCI III]. The Council of the European Communities directed that the NCI be used to fund projects including, inter alia:

the rational use of energy, the replacement of oil . . . and infrastructure projects facilitating such replacement . . . the development of productive activities . . . such as telecommunications, including information technology, and transport, including the transmission of energy . . . investment projects, mainly those of small and medium-sized undertakings . . . designed in particular to promote the dissemination of innovation and new techniques and the implementation of which contributes directly or indirectly to the creation of jobs.

NCI resources have also been used to support reconstruction projects, such as those following major earthquakes in Italy in 1980.

In the twelve-month period ending December 31, 1983, EIB funding for projects within the EEC totalled 4,255,700,000 ECU, in addition to NCI lending of 1,211,800,000 ECU. The bulk of funds required for project funding is derived in the capital markets. EIB support for a given project is normally limited to fifty percent of the total requirements, and averages terms of ten to fourteen years depending upon the sector of the economy.

Statement of Subscriptions to Capital
as of December 31, 1983 (in 000s ECU)

Member State	Subscribed	Paid-In
German Federal Republic	3,150,000	202,500
France	3,150,000	202,500
United Kingdom	3,150,000	202,500
Italy	2,520,000	162,000
Belgium	829,500	53,325
Netherlands	829,500	53,325
Denmark	420,000	27,000
Greece	225,000	14,465
Ireland	105,000	6,750
Luxembourg	21,000	1,350

The headquarters of the European Investment Bank are in Luxembourg. *See also* LOMÉ CONVENTIONS.

EUROPEAN MONETARY COOPERATION FUND. The successor to the EUROPEAN PAYMENTS UNION *(q.v.)*, the EMCF was established by the European Monetary Agreement of 1958 as a vehicle to enhance monetary cooperation among members of the European Communities. The agreement permitted borrowings from a European fund by members suffering balance of payment deficits. Credits were in gold for a period up to three years, with a possible extension of two more years.

The fund was capitalized at U.S. $607.5 million (predicated upon an official rate of $35 per ounce of gold); of this sum, $271.6 million was derived from the defunct European Payments Union.

See EUROPEAN MONETARY SYSTEM.

EUROPEAN MONETARY SYSTEM. A mechanism established by the European Communities to mitigate exchange rate fluctuations among the members and establish a zone of "monetary stability in Europe." The EMS is, in part, a fulfillment of the 1970 WERNER REPORT *(q.v.)*, which suggested adoption of a common European currency as a vehicle for full economic and political integration of the European Communities. More immediately, the EMS arose in response to the inadequacies of the European monetary SNAKE *(q.v.)*, which it superseded.

The EMS was established by a resolution of the European Council on December 5, 1978, and came into being on March 13, 1979. All members of the European Communities are members of the EMS, although the United Kingdom elected not to participate in exchange rate and intervention arrangements at the outset, reserving the right to participate fully at a later date.

The EMS created the *European currency unit* (ECU) as the common denominator for exchange rate transactions. The ECU was established as equal to the *European unit of account,* which is composed of a basket of European Communities (EC) member currencies (including the "nonparticipating" pound sterling) in fixed proportion. The composition of the basket was examined six months after commencement of EMS operations and left unchanged; the mix is to be reviewed automatically every five years thereafter, or more frequently if the fluctuations in exchange rates alter the value of any component currency's share by 25 percent and review is requested (*see* figure).

Each participant's currency has a central rate established for it in terms of the ECU; this results in a series of *bilateral ratios* among all participating currencies. The ratios are also known as *bilateral central rates, bilateral parities,* or *bilateral exchange rates.* Initially, currencies are permitted to float within a margin of 2.25 percent above or below the parity; when this margin is penetrated, i.e., when a cur-

Share of Individual National Currencies in the Composition of the ECU

National Currency	Units per ECU	Central Rate Feb. 85
Deutsche mark	0.719	2.242
French franc	1.31	6.875
Pound sterling	0.0878	.586
Netherlands guilder	0.256	2.526
Belgian franc	3.71	44.901
Luxembourg franc	0.14	44.901
Danish krone	0.219	8.141
Irish pound	0.00871	.726
Italian lira	140.0	1403.490
Greek drachma	1.15	87.481

rency gains or loses 2.25 percent in relation to any participating currency, participating governments are obliged to intervene, buying or selling the troubled currencies, to whatever degree necessary, to restore equilibrium. It is an object of the EMS to narrow the margins to less than 2.25 percent over time. The central rates were the same as those under the Snake for those currencies that participated in that arrangement (Belgian franc, Luxembourg franc, Danish krone, Netherlands guilder, and deutsche mark). For EMS participants that were not involved with the Snake, central rates were equated with market rates against the former Snake as of March 12, 1979. Central rates, in terms of the ECU, can be adjusted by the EMS "by mutual arrangement." A change in the central rate of any currency results in a countervailing adjustment of all participating currencies.

The purchase or sale of an EC currency by an EC member central bank results in a debit or credit on the accounts of the EUROPEAN MONETARY COOPERATION FUND (q.v.), which serves as a clearing center for intracommunity settlements. As financial settlements come due, and member central banks have automatically offset obligations, a debtor central bank will accommodate balances due by (1) employing assets denominated in the currency of the creditor nation; (2) payment in ECUs (although no member is obliged to accept ECUs for more than 50 percent of sums due); or (3) using central bank reserves, other than gold.

ECUs are created by the EMCF collateralized by 20 percent of a member central bank's gold holding, and 20 percent of its gross dollar reserves. Quarterly adjustments are made to ensure that each member's contribution reflects 20 percent of its gold and dollar reserves. On September 30, 1984, one ECU consisted of currencies in the following proportions: .719 Deutschemark; 1.31 French franc; .078 pound sterling; 140 Italian lira; .256

Netherlands guilder; 3.71 Belgian franc; .219 Danish kroner; 1.15 Greek drachma; .00871 Irish pound; .14 Luxembourg franc. For purposes of valuing reserves, gold is valued at the average of the twice daily fixings over the past six months on the London market; dollars are valued at the market rate two days prior to the value date.

The EMS also provides three credit mechanisms to member central banks:

1. *Very short-term financing*: ECU-denominated loans, unlimited as to amount, for periods up to 45 days (which may be extended up to three months), to permit intervention on behalf of EC currencies. The interest rate is the current rate applicable to ECU assets.

2. *Short-term monetary support*: to meet temporary balance of payment problems; a quota is established for each EC central bank.

3. *Medium-term financial assistance*: ECU-denominated loans for a period of two to five years to accommodate significant economic problems. In return for such financing, the recipient nation may be obliged to adopt corrective economic policies.

The percentage values of each member currency will be revised not later than December 31, 1985, at which time the Greek drachma will be included in the mix.

It is contemplated that, over time, the EMS may evolve into a true central bank, issuing a uniform currency for use in private as well as governmental transactions.

EUROPEAN PATENT CONVENTION. *See* EUROPEAN PATENT SYSTEM.

EUROPEAN PATENT SYSTEM. A series of agreements among European states, the object of which is harmonized patent laws and regulations. The system includes the following agreements:

European Patent Convention, also known as the Munich Patent Convention, and the Convention on Granting of European Patents, provides patent protection to a wide array of discoveries, including microbiological processes and, by implication, microorganisms. Although *invention*, per se, is not defined, the agreement does exclude protection for scientific theories, mathematical methods, aesthetic creations, and nontechnical mental process, including computer programs. The convention, which was adopted at Munich in 1973, came into force October 7, 1977; under the terms of the agreement, the European Patent Office (EPO) was established at Munich with a satellite office in Berlin. On January 1, 1978, the International Patent Institute, based in the Hague, was integrated into the EPO. States adhering to the convention are Austria, Liechtenstein, Sweden, Switzerland, and the members of the EUROPEAN COMMUNITIES (q.v.), with the exception of Demark.

Community Patent Convention, also known as the Luxembourg Patent Convention, provides for a common *euro-patent* with effect among the members of the EC. The object of this agreement is to supplant national patents issued by member states with community patents. This process has been impeded by constitutional problems in Denmark and Ireland.

Strasbourg Patent Convention. Originally concluded in 1963, this agreement came into force August 1, 1980, among France, German Federal Republic, United Kingdom, Ireland, Liechtenstein, Luxembourg, Sweden, and Switzerland. The convention requires common standards of patentability and interpretation in the national laws of the adhering states, particularly with respect to the novelty of the inventions, and emphasizes the special protection requirements of chemicals, foodstuffs, and pharmaceuticals.

EUROPEAN PAYMENTS UNION. An intra-European mechanism for the periodic settlement of trade balances. The EPU was established July 1, 1950, among the members of the ORGANIZATION FOR EUROPEAN ECONOMIC COOPERATION *(q.v.)* (OEEC) to promote trade equilibrium; to accomplish this, the OEEC nations made a quota contribution equal to 15 percent of all visible and invisible transactions between members and the sterling area during 1949. The United States made an initial contribution of $350 million. Transactions of the EPU were in a unit of account equal to the U.S. dollar.

In 1958 the European Payments Union was supplanted by the European Monetary Cooperation Fund.

EUROPEAN RECOVERY PROGRAM. Commonly known as the *Marshall Plan*, a post–World War II program to assist the reconstruction of Europe. The plan was proposed by U.S. Secretary of State George Marshall in 1947 and implemented by the Economic Cooperation Act of 1948. During the course of the program, U.S. $13.6 billion in assistance was provided to Western Europe.

EUROPEAN TERMS. An expression of the value of any foreign currency in terms of how many units equal one dollar; effective September 1, 1979, most New York banks have employed this foreign currency method for transactions.

EURO-SDR. Synthetic SPECIAL DRAWING RIGHTS *(q.v.),* created for use in commercial transactions. *Official SDRs* are international reserve assets created by the International Monetary Fund (IMF) solely for use in transactions involving the fund, national monetary authorities, and a limited number of international institutions. The official SDR consists of a *basket* of five national currencies (U.S. dollar, pound sterling, French franc, deutsche mark, and Japanese yen) in fixed proportions; the effect of this composite of the five trading currencies is an artificial currency that tends to be more stable against any one of the five component currencies than the

components would be to each other. Firms seeking to avoid the debilitating effects of currency fluctuation are looking increasingly to the SDR as a medium for international transactions. Inasmuch as official SDRs are not available for commercial purposes, merchants and bankers have concocted an artificial SDR by pooling the component currencies in the same ratios as found in the official SDR in debt obligations, settlements, and other transactions.

It should be noted that the mix of currencies and their respective ratios within the SDR are apt to change over time. Accordingly, it must be clarified in SDR-denominated transactions whether the values expressed are those of the SDR at the time of inception of the contract *(frozen* SDR), or whether they represent the value of the SDR (in terms of units of the component national currencies) at a future point in time *(floating* SDR).

In 1984, the following banks in the United States offered Euro-SDR facilities: Morgan Guaranty Trust Company, New York; First National Bank of Chicago, Chicago; Citibank, N.A., New York; and Kredietbank, New York.

EVEN KEEL. The condition of a vessel where the draft at the stern equals the draft at the bow.

EVER-NORMAL GRANARY. An agricultural price stabilization scheme predicated upon the principle that excess output in years of plenty should be taken off the market, to keep farm prices high and to avoid scarcities during periods of agricultural shortfalls.

EX. Literally, "from"; in transportation usage, it is the point from which the product is shipped, not necessarily its point of origin; for example, a machine made in Kentucky and exported through the port of Norfolk is said to have been shipped "ex Norfolk."

In price quotes, *ex* indicates that the pricing is predicated upon making the goods available at that point for pickup by the purchaser, who will bear all charges beyond the named point.

EXCEPTION RATINGS. An additional or special freight rate, above the general commodity rates, applied to commodities which require special handling, such as items of extraordinary dimensions or weight, live animals, or dangerous articles.

EXCEPTIONS. Products specifically exempted from trade liberalization, such as duty reductions; usually, exceptions are made to protect domestic industries that would suffer serious harm from increased imports.

EXCESS FOREIGN CURRENCIES. Foreign currency, derived from the sale of U.S. agricultural commodities under P.L. 480, in excess of current U.S. requirements. Periodically, the U.S. Treasury reviews the foreign currency position of the U.S. government. Upon finding that holdings of any given currency exceed requirements for that currency, various agencies of the government are instructed to use the excess foreign currency, rather than dollars, in satisfying U.S. obligations abroad.

EXCESS OF LOSS TREATY. A contract of reinsurance under which the primary policy issuer agrees to pay in full any loss up to a prearranged sum, with everything in excess of that amount borne by the reinsurer.

EXCESS RETURN. The positive difference between the return earned on a capital asset and the riskless rate of return (i.e., the rate paid by government securities).

EXCHANGE CONTROL. The system by which a government regulates possession of and dealings in foreign exchange. The principal objective of exchange control is to allocate foreign exchange to necessary imports and expenditures. Normally, the finance ministry or central bank is invested with the authority to issue licenses for dealings in foreign exchange.

EXCHEQUER. The British ministry of finance.

EXCISE TAX. Taxes, also commonly known as *internal revenue taxes*, imposed by the United States on certain classes of manufactures and services and on the performance of some transactions. Unlike customs duties, which are applied to imports only, excise taxes are applied equally to imports and domestic manufactures of a given class; the process of importation is viewed, for taxing purposes, as the equivalent of "manufacturing" since both processes have the common effect of introducing an article into the commerce of the United States.

Responsibility for collecting excise taxes lies with the Internal Revenue Service. Persons involved in the manufacture or importation of certain articles (alcoholic beverages, weapons subject to the special occupational and transfer taxes under the National Firearms Act) must register with the Internal Revenue Service and pay special occupational taxes prior to engaging in transactions in those articles.

U.S. manufacturers producing merchandise subject to excise taxes make quarterly filings and remittances to the Internal Revenue Service. Importers may be obliged to pay the tax when goods are released from customs custody, unless a *tax deferment bond* has been filed with the Customs Service. Generally the payment of excise taxes (as well as customs duties) may be deferred by entering the imported merchandise into a bonded warehouse or foreign trade zone.

In addition to excise taxes collected by the Federal government, the states and some localities impose excise-type taxes on various articles; the articles on which such state and local taxes are levied may or may not correspond to the articles subject to the Federal tax. Such state and local taxes, where they exist, are not collected by Federal officers and are additional to any duties and/or taxes imposed at the Federal level.

The excise tax on manufactures and imports is levied on the sale price of the article, including costs of packaging, coverings, or other preparations required for shipment. The value of the product for tax purposes does *not* include excise taxes; transportation from country of origin to the United States; insurance against loss or damage in transit; discounts and rebates actually paid; billings for local advertising billed at the time of sale, and identifiable on the invoice as such, subject to limitations prescribed in the Internal Revenue Code; and charges for warranty, if purchased voluntarily (this exemption is not applicable where the warranty charge is imposed by the seller as a requirement of purchasing the goods).

In those cases where the seller provides *bonus* or *free goods* to a buyer who purchases certain quantities of other merchandise, the tax is imposed only on the value attributable to the taxable articles, after discounting the taxable articles to reflect the value of the bonus goods. For example, the seller may give his customer a bonus of free goods equivalent to 10 percent of the sale. The bonus goods are of a class not subject to excise tax. Since the bonus goods have the effect of reducing the purchaser's cost of the goods he bought by 10 percent, the excise tax will be imposed on the purchased product at 90 percent of the invoice value. This *value apportionment process* is applied also in those instances where the bonus merchandise is subject to excise tax, but at a rate different from that imposed on the purchased product.

A general exemption from excise taxes is permitted for goods sold to the U.S. government, state and local governments, the United Nations, and diplomatic missions and personnel. In addition, exported merchandise is exempted from excise taxes, provided that exportation is effected by the manufacturer or a single intermediary; in such cases, the merchandise must be exported within six months of the date when the tax would otherwise have been due, and proof of such exportation must be available for examination by the Internal Revenue Service. For the period October 1, 1983, through June 30, 1984, excise taxes totalled $28,195,700,000.

The U.S. Tax Court lacks jurisdiction in matters affecting excise taxes. Any person having a dispute with the Internal Revenue Service over excise taxes must seek recourse in the U.S. District Court or the U.S. Court of Claims. (*See* Appendix F1 for a listing of products subject to Federal excise tax.

EXCLUSIVE DEALING AGREEMENTS. An agreement by which the manufacturer or supplier of a product permits a second party to act as sole distributor of the product within a specified geographic area.

EXCLUSIVE PATRONAGE CONTRACT. Also known as a *merchant's contract* or *shipper's rate agreement*, an agreement whereby a shipper of goods by water agrees to ship all his cargo over a given trade route aboard carriers that are member lines of the steamship CONFERENCE *(q.v.)*. In return for this commitment, the shipper receives a rate (usually 15 percent) lower than that available to those who have not executed a pledge.

A firm so pledged to ship its goods aboard conference vessels is a contract shipper; the lower rate accorded the contract shipper is the contract rate. Conversely, firms that have not signed an exclusive patronage agreement are noncontract shippers and receive the (higher) noncontract rate. A contract shipper who deviates from the terms of the agreement by shipping goods aboard nonconference vessels is subject to economic penalties, which are enforceable.

Exclusive patronage contracts are authorized by the Shipping Act of 1916. The exclusive patronage contract is a form of *loyalty agreement*, differing in that a loyalty agreement does not necessarily commit the signatory merchant to give 100 percent of its business to the conference. As a practical matter, the terms are virtually synonymous since loyalty agreements in the United States do not provide for a commitment of less than 100 percent of a merchant's cargo.

EXCLUSIVE PATRONAGE SYSTEM. A business practice by which a firm promises all its business to a supplier in return for certain concessions not otherwise available. This practice is most visible in the steamship industry; through the vehicle of the Merchant's Freight Agreement, a shipper commits his business to a CONFERENCE *(q.v.)* in return for rate concessions.

EXCLUSIVE USE. The use of a trailer, container, or similar transport equipment solely by one shipper to one consignee. The carrier is denied the option of stowing other cargo in the trailer, although space permits. Normally the shipper must request the exclusive use in advance of the actual movement and must note the bill of lading accordingly; in most tariffs, certain minimum revenues or premiums extend to this service.

EXEMPT CARRIAGE. The transport of commodities exempted from economic regulation by the Interstate Commerce Commission. The largest single group of products so exempted is agricultural commodities.

EXEMPTED COMPANY. A company exempted from income taxes of the jurisdiction in which it is organized in return for a stipulation by the company that it will not trade in that country.

EXEMPTION SYSTEM. A system to avoid double taxation of income whereby the domiciliary country exempts corporate income taxation, income earned and taxed abroad, up to the amount of tax paid in the country that was the source of income.

EXEMPTION WITH PROGRESSION. *See* DOUBLE TAXATION.

EXERCISE PRICE. The price at which the holder of an option contract may buy or sell a specified quantity of a given commodity, security, or currency.

EXIMBANK. *See* EXPORT-IMPORT BANK.

EXONERATED CARGO. Otherwise dutiable merchandise permitted duty-free entry into certain countries in furtherance of a defined governmental policy. Usually such imports are raw materials or unfinished articles not locally available but deemed essential to local industry. The exonerations are, effectively, licenses given to approved importers to import specified quantities of the desired articles. Imports in excess of the quantities authorized in the exoneration may not be permitted or may be permitted only at high rates of duty. It is often required that exonerated cargo travel on the steamship lines of the importing country or an approved alternate carrier.

EXOTIC CURRENCY. A national currency for which there is not normally a strong demand in the foreign exchange markets. Examples of such currencies are: Eyptian pound, Guyana dollar, and the Nigerian naira.

EXPLOSIONS CLAUSE. A provision in a marine insurance policy establishing coverage for losses to cargo caused by explosion, except where the explosion is the result of acts of war, strikes, rioting, or civil unrest.

EXPORT ADMINISTRATION ACT. *See* EXPORT CONTROL ACT.

EXPORT BAR. A bar of pure gold, used principally in settling balances between central banks or other official financial institutions.

EXPORT CONTROL ACT. An act of Congress passed in 1949 requiring that all commercial exports from the United States be licensed. Authority was granted to the president to devise specific regulations to control exports; this authority has been delegated to the Secretary of Commerce. The regulations subsequently developed constitute the Export Control Program administered by the Department of Commerce. Exports are divided into two categories: those requiring *general license* and those requiring a *validated license*.

Exports subject to general license cover a wide range of nonstrategic products destined for friendly countries. An actual license per se is not required; authority for anyone to export such products to nonproscribed countries is granted in a blanket notice published in the Comprehensive Export Schedules, issued by the Commerce Department.

A validated license is a written authorization from the appropriate government agency to conduct an export transaction not covered by the general license granted in the Comprehensive Export Schedules. In the case of some products (e.g., arms, narcotics) a validated license is required for any exportation, irrespective of destination. In other cases, it is not the product but the destination that is regulated (e.g., all shipments to Cuba); in a few instances, both the product and destination are controlled.

The act was originally designed as a temporary measure but was extended in 1951, 1953, 1956, 1958, 1960, 1962, and 1965. In 1969, it was superseded by the Export Administration Act, which continued substantially the form and practices of the earlier act; this legislation was extended in 1972, in 1974, and again in 1984. (*See* figure, next page).

EXPORT CONTROL PROGRAM. *See* EXPORT CONTROL ACT.

EXPORT CONTROL STATEMENT. A notation required to be entered upon the shipping documents of virtually all commercial exports leaving the United States. A statement for certain licensed commodities, for example, reads: "These commodities licensed by the United States for ultimate destination (name of country). Diversion contrary to U.S. law prohibited."

Other statements, in lieu of the foregoing, may be required, depending upon the commodity and country of destination. The use of such statements is mandatory and is prescribed in Section 386.6 of the Export Administration Regulations.

EXPORT DECLARATION. *See* SHIPPER'S EXPORT DECLARATION.

EXPORT DIVERSIFICATION. The movement of a nation away from the export of a single or limited number of products as the principal source of foreign exchange earnings. Export diversification programs are usually the priority objectives of small or underdeveloped nations, particularly those exporting primary products, which are subject to a much higher degree of market fluctuation than are manufactured goods.

The lack of sufficient export diversification may serve as an impediment to securing borrowing facilities abroad.

EXPORT DROP SHIPPER. *See* EXPORT JOBBER.

EXPORT DUTY. A tax imposed on exports. This mechanism serves as a source of government revenue and is imposed by some countries on a limited number of products. Export duties are expressly forbidden by the U.S. Constitution.

EXPORT-IMPORT BANK OF THE UNITED STATES. Commonly known as EXIMBANK, an independent, self-funding agency of the U.S. government created to facilitate exports of American products. Originally chartered under the laws of the District of Columbia in 1934, EXIMBANK was rechartered by an act of Congress in 1945. The bank provides short-, medium-, and long-term loans for U.S. export sales and TURNKEY PROJECTS *(q.v.)*. In addition, EXIMBANK collaborates with the PRIVATE EXPORT FUNDING CORPORATION *(q.v.)* to provide financing of capital projects at fixed rates. EXIMBANK programs include:

1. Direct loans at fixed rates at long terms (more than five years) for capital equipment, and capital-intensive projects.

2. Supplier credit for less costly projects with terms up to five years.

3. Export credit insurance against commercial and political risks; this insurance is offered in conjunction with the FOREIGN CREDIT INSURANCE ASSOCIATION *(q.v.)* and covers short- and medium-term financial obligations.

4. A discount loan program, through which export-oriented American financial institutions may collateralize and/or discount commercial paper or obligations arising from exports of American goods or services.

5. The Cooperative Financing Facility, whereby EXIMBANK makes funds available to foreign financial institutions to be re-lent to foreign purchasers of American products. This program operates primarily in less developed countries. It is a medium-term, direct credit program by which EXIMBANK loans one-half of the purchase price of an American purchase to the foreign bank to finance the purchase.

EXIMBANK financing is based upon a reasonable likelihood of repayment and the need to permit American firms to compete with foreign suppliers who are subsidized by their governments. Special programs are offered to support agricultural exports, lease guarantees, and small businesses. EXIMBANK is capitalized at one billion dollars, subscribed by the U.S. Treasury, and has reserves of 1.8 billion. In addition, it can borrow up to six billion dollars from the U.S. Treasury.

EXPORT-IMPORT PRICE RATIO. *See* TERMS OF TRADE.

EXPORT JOBBER. A company that purchases and exports merchandise only against a firm order from abroad. Typically the jobber does not take physical possession of the goods.

EXPORT MAILING LIST SERVICE. An export promotion service of the U.S. Department of Commerce. *See* FOREIGN TRADERS INDEX.

EXPORT MANAGEMENT COMPANY. A private company that serves as the export department of other firms, usually small- and medium-size manufacturers. An EMC will provide a variety of services for its clients, to include locating customers abroad, arranging transportation and financing for

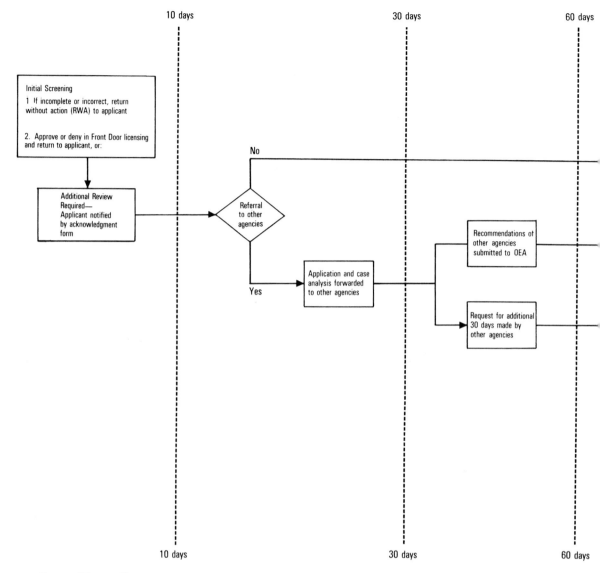

Export License Process

the merchandise, developing foreign advertising, et cetera. An EMC may derive its compensation through a direct purchase and resale of the merchandise or through a commission, ranging from 7.5 to 20 percent, depending on the product.

EXPORT MERCHANT. A firm that purchases goods from various domestic manufacturers, ships them abroad, and markets through other middlemen or their own organization. The export merchant tends to specialize in a given product category.

EXPORT PRIVILEGES. The opportunity afforded by the U.S. government to engage in export transactions. The Export Control Act and its successor Export Administration Act have provided that

all exports are under authority of license (including the *general license* requiring no prior approval); hence, exporting is a privilege subject to withdrawal by the government. Persons and firms (including freight forwarders, common carriers, and end-users abroad) found to have violated export control laws may be denied export privileges. The Department of Commerce maintains a list of firms so blacklisted.

EXPORT PROCESSING ZONE. A special type of FOREIGN TRADE ZONE *(q.v.)* within which certain exemptions from duties, taxes, and regulations are granted as an inducement to export-oriented manufacturing. Customarily a manufacturer within the zone may import equipment and raw materials

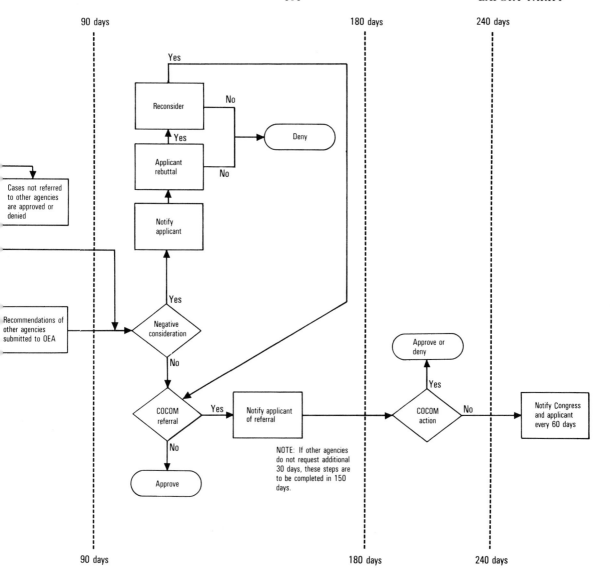

duty-free for goods that are ultimately exported as finished products. Other governmental concessions may include abatement of taxes on profits derived from export sales or relaxation of minimum wage scales.

Export processing zones are also known as *special economic zones, enterprise zones,* and *industrial free zones.*

EXPORT PROPERTY. *See* DOMESTIC INTERNATIONAL SALES CORPORATION.

EXPORT QUOTA AGREEMENT. An arrangement arising under an international commodity agreement whereby each participating exporting nation is allocated a portion of the market. Participating importing nations agree to limit imports from nonmember nations. The object of the system is to maintain price stability, thus ensuring producer income.

EXPORT REVENUE AND STABILIZATION PLAN (EEC). *See* LOMÉ CONVENTION.

EXPORT SUBSIDY. A direct payment, tax relief, or other incentive provided by a government to encourage export sales. The use of such devices is apt to be regarded as undesirable by the importing nation and may result in the imposition of COUNTERVAILING DUTIES *(q.v.)* to negate the effect of the subsidy.

EXPORT TARIFF. A tax or duty levied by a governmental authority upon the exportation of a product. Such taxes upon exports have been abolished by all major trading nations but are still retained by some developing nations, particularly on exports of mineral or agricultural commodities, as a source of state revenue.

EXPORT TRADE CERTIFICATE OF REVIEW. *See* EXPORT TRADING COMPANY ACT.

EXPORT TRADING COMPANY ACT. A 1982 act of Congress designed to promote American exports by modifying the application of antitrust laws and reducing restrictions on export financing on certain export transactions. The legislation is divided into four parts.

Title I directs the Department of Commerce to encourage the formation of export trading companies (ETCs) and to aid ETCs in finding customers abroad.

Title II (Bank Export Services Act) amends Federal banking laws to permit equity participation (up to 100 percent) by bank holding companies as well as Edge Act and Agreement Act corporations that are subsidiaries of bank holding companies and "bankers' banks." Banking entities are forbidden to invest more than 5 percent of consolidated capital and surplus in an ETC and to loan more than 10 percent of such capital and surplus to an ETC. Approval of the Federal Reserve Board is required for any proposed investment in an ETC by a banking entity; such approval can be withheld only for good reason.

In order to provide external financing to ETCs, the act directs the EXPORT-IMPORT BANK *(q.v.)* to develop a loan guarantee program for ETCs; loans are to be secured by export receivables or inventories. Federally regulated banks are also permitted to expand issuance of bankers' acceptances to finance export trade.

Title III permits the Department of Commerce, with Justice Department concurrence, to issue *export trade certificates of review*, giving antitrust preclearance on transactions involving the export of goods or services. To obtain the certificate, the applicant must not materially restrain the trade of American firms, either in domestic U.S. or export trade; not substantially affect prices in the United States; not use the export activity for which the certificate is sought as a vehicle for unfair competition against American firms; and not reasonably anticipate sale or resale in the United States of the exported products.

The act permits any "person" to apply for a certificate; "person" is defined to include any individual resident in the United States, any partnership or corporation formed under U.S. law, governmental entities, or combinations of the above.

Once issued, a certificate protects the holder from civil and criminal antitrust actions. Persons alleging injury as the result of the certified conduct may sue for injunctive relief and actual damages where the certificate holder exceeds the authority of the certificate. Also, the Justice Department may enjoin activities threatening "clear and irreparable" harm to the national interest.

Private antitrust suits are discouraged in four ways: (1) the plaintiff may recover only actual damages, as compared with trade damages authorized in conventional antitrust suits; (2) private suits claiming abuse of the certificate immunity must be brought within two years of the discovery, and four years from the occurrence, of the offending act; (3) the certificate affords the holder prima facie evidence of compliance with law; and (4) a certificate holder who wins an antitrust suit against him is entitled to recover his costs, including reasonable legal fees.

Title IV amends the Sherman Act and the Federal Trade Commission Act to exclude their application to export transactions, except where such activities have an anticompetitive impact on trade in the United States or the export trade of an American resident.

EXPORT UNEMPLOYMENT. A conscious program to relieve domestic unemployment or economic stagnation through the stimulation of export sales. The term is used generally in relation to improper export promotion vehicles such as DUMPING *(q.v.)* or the extensive use of export subsidies.

In those cases where a nation feels that it has been subject to unemployment exporting schemes, the offended nation may undertake retaliatory measures, to include the imposition of antidumping or countervailing duties, quotas, or other traderestraining devices.

EXPORT VALUE. The price at which a foreign manufacturer customarily freely offers for sale a given product for export to the United States in the usual wholesale quantities, less export discounts, packing, and costs of preparing the goods for export. The use of this value principle has been negated by the Trade Agreement Act of 1979. *See* CUSTOMS VALUATION AGREEMENT.

EXPROPRIATION. The seizure of private property by the state. Most countries have legal provisions empowering state agencies to take private property for public purpose, usually upon payment of suitable compensation. In Anglo-American usage, this practice is known as *eminent domain.* Expropriation differs from eminent domain, in international usage, as an arbitrary act, often motivated by political objectives, and rarely providing for compensation reflective of the property seized. *See* ACT OF STATE DOCTRINE.

EXTENDING THE PROTEST. *See* MASTER'S PROTEST.

EXTERNAL DEPRECIATION. *See* DEPRECIATION (MONETARY).

EXTRACTION RATE. The proportion, on a weight basis, between a finished or processed product and the raw materials from which it was manufactured.

EXTRATERRITORIAL. An exemption from the laws or jurisdiction of the state in which situated. For example, an embassy enjoys extraterritorial status because it is not subject to the laws of the country in which it is located.

F

FACTORING. A method of financing trade whereby the factor purchases the seller's accounts receivable, usually advancing a portion of the receivables, with the balance paid upon maturity of the accounts.

In most cases, the factor assumes all commercial risks associated with the receivables purchased, including nonpayment. This arrangement is known as *old-line factoring*. In recent years, *recourse factoring* has arisen. Under this method the factor advances sums against the collateral of the receivables pledged; in the event of nonpayment, the factor seek recovery from its client.

FACTOR MOBILITY. The capacity of the factors of production to move freely among nations in search of maximum economic return.

FACTOR REVERSIBILITY. The act of intensifying the input of a given production factor and reducing the input of another contrary to traditional behavior. For example, a formerly labor-intensive pursuit such as farming may undergo factor reversibility when an infusion of capital machinery eliminates significant labor involvement.

FACTOR SERVICES. Payments remitted abroad for the local use of foreign-origin factors of production, e.g., payments sent home by foreign workers or interest paid to foreign lenders.

FAIR MARKET VALUE. The value an imported product would fetch, under similar circumstances of sale, were the goods sold in the country of origin. Customs authorities are usually interested in the fair market value of imported merchandise inasmuch as sales below such value may serve as the basis of a DUMPING *(q.v.)* investigation.

FAK RATE. *See* FREIGHT, ALL KINDS RATE.

FAMILIAR DRAWING TECHNIQUES. A process within the INTERNATIONAL MONETARY FUND *(q.v.)* whereby a member nation suffering balance of payments problems may obtain foreign currencies from the IMF in exchange for its own.

Basically, a nation will move first into a *gold tranche* position, i.e., will borrow foreign currencies up to the value of gold it has on deposit with the IMF, using the gold as collateral for the drawing. Should drawings be required beyond the value of its gold deposits, it will go into a *credit tranche*, or loan, supported by deposits of its own currency with the IMF.

FASB 8. *See* FINANCIAL ACCOUNTING STANDARDS BOARD STATEMENT NO. 8.

FASB 52. *See* FINANCIAL ACCOUNTING STANDARDS BOARD STATEMENT NO. 52.

FECOM. The French acronym for the EUROPEAN MONETARY COOPERATION FUND. *(q.v.)*.

FEDERAL ARBITRATION ACT. *See* UNITED STATES ARBITRATION ACT.

FEDERAL BILLS OF LADING ACT. Known commonly as the *Pomerane Act*, the principal Federal statute on the subject of bills of lading covering transportation of goods in interstate and foreign commerce. Passed in 1915, the act deals with substantive issues of form, endorsement, and delivery of bills of lading. The act also provides criminal penalties for forgeries and frauds relating to bills covered by the act. (The act is reproduced in full in Appendix A4.) *See* BILL OF LADING.

FEDERAL FUNDS. Commercial bank reserves in excess of legally required reserves that are offered to other banks that are suffering temporary reserve deficiencies. These loans are for very short periods, usually overnight. Banks with funds in excess of requirements offer them to banks with deficiencies through a few large banks and several nonbank firms that serve as Federal funds dealers.

The rate a borrowing bank pays for these funds is the *Federal fund rate*; it represents the rate at which banks lend funds to one another.

FEDERAL MARITIME COMMISSION. An independent agency within the U.S. government charged with oversight and regulation of the steamship industry in foreign and domestic offshore commerce. The FMC was established as the Federal Maritime Board by the Shipping Act of 1916.

Principal areas of commission responsibility include acceptance or rejection of tariffs tendered by common carriers (the commission has the authority to set maximum and minimum rates in the domestic offshore trade and to suspend such rates); approval of intercarrier agreements under authority of Section 15 of the Shipping Act, thereby extending antitrust immunity to carriers engaged in collective ratemaking or rulemaking; licensing of ocean freight forwarders; administration of the vessel certification provisions of the Federal Water Pollution Control Act; rulemaking under the Shipping Act, various merchant marine acts, and related legislation; and adjudication of complaints and disputes arising within the scope of commission jurisdiction.

The commission consists of five members, including a chairman, all of whom are appointed by the president, subject to Senate confirmation. The commission is supported by a headquarters staff and six regional offices (*see* figure).

FEDERAL OPEN MARKET COMMITTEE. *See* OPEN MARKET OPERATIONS.

FEDERATION OF AMERICAN CONTROLLED SHIPPING. An association of American firms that operate Liberian- and Panamanian-registered tankers, bulk carriers, and specialized vessels. Currently, federation member firms control over forty-three million deadweight tons of foreign shipping. In addition, federation members control approximately one-half the tanker tonnage registered under the American flag, and assert that 85 percent of the foreign flag tonnage is under EFFECTIVE UNITED STATES CONTROL *(q.v.)*, thereby making the foreign

flag vessels available to the United States in the event of war or other emergency. Only American companies, controlled by U.S. citizens, are eligible for membership.

The association was formed in 1958 "to counterbalance U.S. maritime union efforts to discredit the economic and strategic value of American-controlled Liberian and Panamanian shipping." The association asserts that American construction and operating costs for vessels are not competitive with those available elsewhere in the world.

The organization is based in New York and maintains a Washington office. Membership in 1984 consisted of:

Alcoa Steamship Company, Inc.
Amoco Marine Transportation Company
Arco Marine, Inc.
Bethlehem Steel Corporation
Catle and Cooke, Inc.
Charter Shipping Agents, Inc.
Chevron Shipping Company
Conoco Division/DuPont
Cosmopolitan Shipping Company, Inc.
Dow Chemical Company
Exxon Corporation
Getty Oil Company
Grand Bassa Tankers, Inc.
Gulf Oil Corporation
Lubrizol Corporation
Marathon Oil Company
Marine Transport Lines, Inc.
Navios Ship Management Services, Inc.

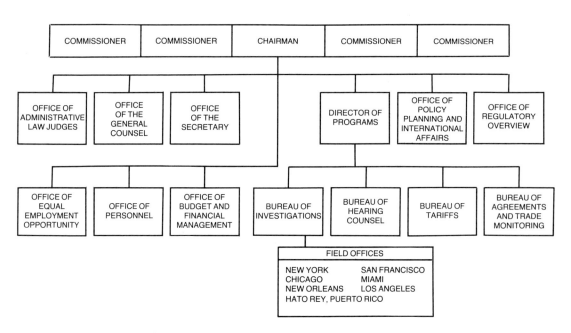

Federal Maritime Commission

Phillips Petroleum Company
Reomar, Inc.
Reynolds Metals Company
Skaarup Shipping Corporation
States Marine Corporation
Sun Transport, Inc.
Texaco, Inc.
Union Oil Company of California
Utah International, Inc.

FEEDER-LASH. *See* FLASH.

FEEDER VESSEL. A small vessel or barge that carries goods from a principal port to outlying ports not served directly by the mother ship.

FIAT MONEY. Currency that has value only because the state that issues it declares it to be legal tender; money that has no intrinsic value beyond the faith of the government that issues it. Paper money not freely exchangeable for gold or silver is fiat money.

The term is often associated with regimes which have permitted money creation to get out of control, resulting in debasement of the currency and HYPERINFLATION *(q.v.)*.

FIAT STANDARD. A monetary system in which the money in circulation is not redeemable in any other form of money (e.g., gold) but has value simply by virtue of its issuance by governmental authority.

FIBER CONSTRAINTS. The United States is party to various multilateral and bilateral agreements concerning the importation of certain textile products. In order to monitor compliance with these agreements, and to identify products subject to specific quantitative or other controls, it is necessary that certain products containing cotton, wool, or man-made fibers, or combinations thereof, be specially identified.

Most articles having their whole or chief value of cotton, wool, or man-made fibers are adequately identified for monitoring purposes in the Tariff Schedules. However, where the tariff classification does not clearly identify the whole or chief value of the item as being of cotton, wool, or man-made fibers, the imported article must be classified under the applicable "constraint" classifications if it fills the definition of such a classification.

Where the designation *"subject to cotton constraints," "subject to wool constraints,"* or *"subject to man-made fiber constraints"* is used, such designation shall have the following meaning, as provided in Statistical headnote 3, Schedule 3, Tariff Schedules of the United States (TSUS):

A. *Subject to Cotton Constraints.* (1) Articles in which the cotton component equals or exceeds 50 percent by weight of all component fibers thereof; or (2) Articles in which the cotton with wool and/or man-made fibers in the aggregate equal or exceed 50 percent by weight of the component fibers thereof

and the cotton component equals or exceeds the weight of each of the total wool and/or man-made fiber components.

B. *Subject to Wool Constraints.* Articles in which the wool content exceeds 17 percent by weight of all component fibers, and which are not provided for as "articles subject to cotton constraints."

C. *Subject to Man-Made Fiber Constraints.* Articles not meeting the requirements of (A) or (B) above, but those in which: (1) The man-made fiber components equal or exceed 50 percent by weight of all component fibers thereof; or (2) The man-made fibers in combination with cotton and/or wool in the aggregate equal or exceed 50 percent by weight of the component fibers thereof and the man-made fiber component exceeds the weight of the total wool and/or total cotton component.

FIDUCIARY CURRENCY. A currency backed solely by the faith of the government that issues it. The term does not carry the negative import often associated with FIAT MONEY *(q.v.). See also* MONEY.

FIDUCIARY STANDARD. *Synonymous with* FIDUCIARY CURRENCY *(q.v.)*.

FIELD WAREHOUSING. An inventory financing arrangement characterized by the act of storing goods at or near the user's premises, but under effective control of a public warehouseman. The warehouseman issues a negotiable warehouse receipt that is used as collateral to procure the merchandise. As merchandise is needed for use or sale, the customer redeems the warehouse receipt and secures release of the goods.

FIFTH INTERNATIONAL TIN AGREEMENT. An international commodity agreement among major tin-producing and consuming nations. Principal features of the agreement are (1) establishment of the International Tin Council in which votes are divided equally among producing and consuming nations; the council establishes agreed ceiling and floor prices for the metal; (2) maintenance of a reserve stock of at least 20,000 metric tons of tin that may be sold off as prices approach the ceiling, or added to as prices approach the floor, to ensure stable prices; (3) imposition of export controls by producers after a threshold of falling prices has been reached; and (4) requirement that members consult with the council before selling from national stocks.

The United States is a signatory to this agreement.

FIFTY-MILE RULE. An arrangement between the International Longshoremen's Association and steamship operators designed to eliminate waterfront labor unrest arising from the use of ocean containers.

Essentially, the agreement provides that work for longshoremen will be preserved by permitting ILA labor to load and/or unload ocean containers bound from or to points within fifty miles of an ocean port. An exception is made for a *qualified shipper* or *qualified consignee*, which means a shipper/importer located with fifty miles of the port who has an actual proprietary interest in the goods. A qualified shipper or importer may employ his own or other non-ILA labor to handle the goods. The object of the measure is to ensure that less-than-containerload shipments would be routed to the piers to be handled by ILA labor, rather than to non-ILA warehouses operated by consolidators.

A steamship operator allowing cargo to be released in violation of the accord is subject to liquidated damages of $1,000 per container.

The pact has been challenged through the Federal courts but continues to function.

FIGHTING SHIP. A vessel employed by a steamship line, conference, or group on a given trade route at less than competitive rates for the purpose of driving out competition, thereby gaining control or preeminence over the route. The use of ships for such purpose is prohibited under the laws of the United States and many other countries.

FILING COMPANY. An insurance company that issues a front policy, i.e., issues a policy but retains little or none of the risk exposure, reinsuring it with another carrier.

FINAL LIST. A listing of products upon which a unique standard of valuation was applied for duty purposes. Prior to 1958 duties were applicable on virtually all imports on the basis of *foreign value* or *export value*, whichever was higher. The foreign value was the price at which goods were freely offered for consumption in the country of origin, whereas export value was the price at which those goods were freely offered for export to the United States. Owing to export discounts or quantity purchases, it was possible that the export price might be lower than the foreign value. In 1958 the export value standard was adopted except for certain products where it was felt that the assessment of duties on the export value alone would constitute a de facto tariff reduction on those products. The Secretary of the Treasury was instructed to ascertain those items that would be afforded optional assessment of duties on either foreign value or export value, with the result of a reduction of up to 5 percent in duty rates on those items. The items so identified were placed on the Final List, and duties were assessed under the old system. The Final List was abolished by the Trade Agreements Act of 1979.

FINAL INVOICE. *See* INVOICE.

FINAL SAILING. The passage by a vessel out of the commonly recognized commercial boundaries of the port on the contemplated voyage without intentions of returning.

FINANCE CAPITAL. *See* CAPITAL.

FINANCIAL ACCOUNTING STANDARDS BOARD. A private, non-profit organization concerned with formulating standards for financial accounting and reporting by U.S. industry. The FASB is independent of the American Institute of Certified Public Accountants (AICPA) and other professional bodies.

In 1973 the FASB succeeded the Accounting Principles Board of the AICPA, which had been the author of financial accounting standards. In the same year, the Securities and Exchange Commission (SEC) issued Accounting Series Release 150 (now codified in SEC Financial Reporting Release No. 1, section 101) recognized FASB pronouncements as authoritative. The Securities and Exchange Act of 1933 empowers the SEC to devise accounting standards to ensure compliance with Federal securities statutes. In one instance, the SEC rejected an FASB standard; in all other cases, however, U.S. financial accounting must conform to FASB pronouncements.

The FASB is assisted by an advisory council of approximately forty individuals drawn from public accounting, government, the academic community, and others concerned with financial accounting; the Comptroller General of the United States is included among the members.

The FASB has issued two pronouncements dealing with the problems of currency fluctuation, FINANCIAL ACCOUNTING STANDARDS BOARD STATEMENT NO. 8, which was succeeded by FINANCIAL ACCOUNTING STANDARDS BOARD STATEMENT NO. 52 (*qq.v.*). The FASB maintains its headquarters in Stamford, Connecticut.

FINANCIAL ACCOUNTING STANDARDS BOARD STATEMENT NO. 8. A far-reaching and controversial pronouncement by the Financial Accounting Standards Board governing accounting practices used by American firms in transactions involving foreign currencies. The pronouncement, known commonly as FASB 8, came into effect for fiscal years beginning January 1, 1976.

Among other important features, FASB 8 requires (1) that foreign subsidiaries of U.S. firms employ U.S. generally accepted accounting principles in measuring assets and liabilities; (2) that fixed assets, inventories, goodwill, and deferred income be valued, in terms of dollars, at the *historical rate*, i.e, the exchange rate for the foreign currency in effect at the time of the transaction; and (3) that most liquid assets and current liabilities be valued at the *current rate*, i.e., the rate of exchange in effect at the time of statement preparation irrespective of the rate in effect at the time the transaction occurred.

The statement was adopted in response to problems of valuing foreign transactions, a condition exacerbated by the high degree of fluctuation among major currencies following the collapse of the system established by the BRETTON WOODS

AGREEMENT *(q.v.)* in 1971. FASB 8 has been an object of criticism before and since its adoption; in 1981, the Financial Accounting Standards Board published FINANCIAL ACCOUNTING STANDARDS BOARD STATEMENT NO. 52 *(q.v.)*, replacing FASB 8 effective not later than December 15, 1984.

FINANCIAL ACCOUNTING STANDARDS BOARD STATEMENT NO. 52. A set of accounting rules governing offshore and multicurrency transactions, adopted in 1981 and mandatory for use by December 15, 1984. FASB 52 replaces FINANCIAL ACCOUNTING STANDARDS BOARD STATEMENT NO. 8 *(q.v.)*, with which there had been much dissatisfaction.

Significant features of FASB 52 include: (1) gains or losses arising from exchange transactions will be reflected in the firm's capital account rather than in current income (there had been significant criticism of FASB 8 in that its treatment of gains and losses on exchange in current income was distortive and at variance with economic reality); (2) all vehicles for mitigating the effects of exchange fluctuation, e.g., any contract, transaction, or balance, would be treated as a hedge, irrespective of form; and (3) the functional currency of an entity in a "highly inflationary economy" (i.e., experiencing an inflation rate of 100 percent or more) shall be the U.S. dollar. The board felt that a national currency under such inflationary pressures is unsuitable as a reporting medium.

FINANCIAL GUARANTEE PROGRAM. *See* EXPORT-IMPORT BANK.

FINANCIAL PAPER. Short-term, unsecured promissory notes issued by finance companies. The funds raised by the sale of financial paper are loaned out to commercial firms to finance inventories and current receivables.

FINANCIAL RISK. The risk borne by an exporter that his foreign customer may be unable or unwilling to pay for the merchandise purchased; the financial risk relates purely to commercial considerations and not to such "political" risks as expropriation or inconvertibility of currency.

FINANCIAL SOLIDARITY. A component principle of the COMMON AGRICULTURAL POLICY *(q.v.)* of the European Economic Community.

FINDLEY AMENDMENT. An amendment to the AGRICULTURAL TRADE DEVELOPMENT AND ASSISTANCE ACT *(q.v.)* of 1954 (P.L. 480) that precludes sales of agricultural produce under Title I of the act to any country engaged in trade with Cuba or Vietnam.

The amendment, sponsored by Congressman Paul Findley of New Jersey, specifies that nations trading with Cuba or Vietnam do not fulfill the statutory definition of "friendly" to the United States. Only "friendly" countries are eligible for Title I sales.

FINENESS (METAL). The relative purity of a precious metal. Fineness may be expressed as a percentage, e.g., .999 fine, or, in the case of gold, in karats.

FIRE STATUTE. An act of Congress (46 USCA Sec. 182) passed in 1851 to relieve carriers of obligations to shippers for fire losses aboard ship, "unless such fire is caused by the design or neglect of the owner"; this provision has been effectively supplanted by Section 4(2)(b) of the CARRIAGE OF GOODS BY SEA ACT *(q.v.)*.

FIRKIN. A unit of measure equal to nine gallons or, when used in conjunction with butter or cheese, to fifty-six pounds avoirdupois.

FIRM INDICATION. An emphatic form of INDICATION *(q.v.)* in vessel charter transactions.

FIRM OFFER. A formal offer by a principal in a vessel charter transaction stipulating the precise terms under which he will enter the charter.

FIRST ENGLARGEMENT. The addition of Great Britain, Ireland, and Denmark in 1972 to the original six members (France, Federal Republic of Germany, Italy, Belgium, Netherlands, Luxembourg) of the EUROPEAN ECONOMIC COMMUNITY *(q.v.)*.

FIRST FLAG CARRIAGE. The shipment of goods aboard a vessel flying the flag of the exporting country.

FIRST WORLD. A general reference to the industrialized nations of the West, primarily the members of the ORGANIZATION FOR ECONOMIC COOPERATION AND DEVELOPMENT *(q.v.)*, but often including other prosperous nations as well. *See* SECOND WORLD, THIRD WORLD.

FIXED EXCHANGE RATES. A condition in which the official rates of exchange for most currencies, particularly those of major trading nations, are in an established ratio to one another; generally, this is the result of each currency having an established rate to gold from which a series of bilateral exchange ratios can be established.

Under the Bretton Woods system, all trading currencies had values *fixed*, or denominated in terms of U.S. dollars; in turn, the dollar had an established value of $35 per ounce of gold. A growing disparity between the official and market prices of gold in dollars, as well as mounting American inflation and balance of payments deficits, resulted in wholesale redemption of dollars for gold during the 1960s. On August 15, 1971, President Richard Nixon halted conversion of dollars for gold; this act marked the demise of the Bretton Woods system, and with it, fixed exchange rates.

FIXING A CHARTER. The conclusion of a contract (charter party) for the charter of a vessel.

FIXING LETTER. A summary of the agreement between a vessel owner and charterer pending signing of the actual charter party. This document is usually prepared by a joint effort of the owners and charterer's brokers.

FIXTURE. The act whereby a contract for the charter of a vessel is *fixed*, or concluded.

FLAG. The country of registration of a vessel or aircraft. *See* Appendix B2 for flag abbreviations.

FLAG DISCRIMINATION. Actions taken by a government to favor or discourage movement of cargoes aboard vessels flying certain flags; for example, a nation may require that certain cargoes or percentages of overall cargo tonnage move aboard its own vessels.

FLAGGING OUT. The act of transferring a vessel's registry to a lower-cost jurisdiction.

FLAG OF CONVENIENCE. Registration of a vessel in a country other than that of the ship's owners, because the registering nation affords the owners tax or other benefits not available in the home country.

FLASH. A feeder-LASH (LIGHTER ABOARD SHIP, *q.v.*) system used in Malaysia and Indonesia in which a LASH barge is positioned on top of a semisubmersible barge; the barge is pumped out, and the LASH barge towed to the pier or wharf for loading.

FLATION. A period of generally stable prices, absent of both inflation and deflation.

FLEXIBLE SDR. *See* SPECIAL DRAWING RIGHTS.

FLEXIBLE SPECIAL DRAWING RIGHTS. *See* SPECIAL DRAWING RIGHTS.

FLEXIBLE TARIFF. A customs tariff in which rates of duty can be raised or lowered by administrative action. In the United States the Reciprocal Trade Agreements Act of 1934 and other legislation have authorized the President to adjust duty rates downward in response to concessions from other nations, or to push rates upward in reprisal for discrimination against U.S. goods.

FLIGHT FROM THE DOLLAR. The large-scale divestiture of dollars and dollar-denominated securities by speculators and capital markets in 1970–1971 in anticipation of a dollar devaluation. Pessimism concerning the dollar arose in response to growing balance of trade deficits and capital outflows attributable to low U.S. interest rates. The conversion of U.S. dollars into gold by foreign governments exacerbated concerns.

In August 1971 President Richard Nixon suspended official conversions of dollars for gold; this act was followed by two devaluations of the dollar.

FLIGHT OF CAPITAL. A significant movement of capital, usually in liquid form, from one jurisdiction to another. This capital movement usually occurs in response to troubled economic or political conditions that might result in confiscation, excessive tax-

ation, or loss in value. However, this term may be applied as well to instances where capital moves to another county in search of a higher return.

FLOATING EXCHANGE RATES. A condition in which parities among foreign currencies are absent; a currency's worth in relation to other currencies is determined largely by market forces, with only occasional government intervention to prevent disruptive swings in the value of an important currency.

FLOATING POLICY. A contract of marine insurance that remains in force until canceled. Within the geographic, dollar, or product limitations stipulated, the policy is designed to cover all the shipments of the assured, who reports them to the underwriter on a regular basis.

FLOATING RATE LOAN. *See* VARIABLE RATE LOAN.

FLOATING SUPPLY. Commodities and securities held outside the normal channels of consumption or investment solely for speculative purposes.

FLOOR. In the case of a VARIABLE RATE LOAN *(q.v.)*, a prearranged minimum rate of interest that will be imposed, irrespective of how low the money market index falls.

FLOTSAM. Wreckage of a ship or its cargo found floating upon the sea.

FOOD BALANCE. A nation's supply of food relative to its population.

FOOD RESERVES. A nation's stockpile of food in excess of current requirements; used primarily in relation to measurement of the shortfall or excess of food production by developing nations.

FOOTLOOSE INDUSTRY. A manufacturing operation in which the cost of transportation, either of raw materials or the finished product, is not significant, thereby eliminating the requirement that the factory be located near either raw materials or the market.

FORCED TAX SYSTEM. A practice applied in some countries (most notably in Europe) in which corporate income taxes are computed by a governmental agency. Unlike the American system, under which the firm prepares its own return and computes its tax liability (subject to subsequent review by the government), the forced tax system involves the government in the actual preparation of the return.

FORCE MAJEURE. A superior or irresistible force, the impact of which is to discharge parties to a contract from their obligations to perform. Examples of such conditions are acts of war, governmental edicts, or natural disasters.

FOREIGN ASSETS CONTROL REGULATIONS. A pronouncement issued under authority of Section 5(b) of the TRADING WITH THE ENEMY ACT *(q.v.)* that prohibits importation of products manufactured in, or containing components originating in, countries proscribed by the president. Exports to proscribed countries are forbidden also. The Secretary of the Treasury, however, may license specific transactions with listed countries. Violations of the regulations carry civil and criminal penalties.

FOREIGN BANKING CORPORATIONS. An Edge Act bank. *See* EDGE ACT CORPORATION.

FOREIGN BASE COMPANY SALES INCOME. *See* SUBPART F.

FOREIGN BASE COMPANY SERVICE INCOME. *See* SUBPART F.

FOREIGN BASE FINANCE COMPANY. A financing operation organized abroad (usually in a tax haven) that has as its main purpose the arranging of loans abroad in eurocurrencies, almost always on behalf of its parent or affiliates.

FOREIGN BILL OF EXCHANGE. A BILL OF EXCHANGE *(q.v.)* drawn in one state or country and payable in another.

FOREIGN CORPORATION. A corporation operating in a jurisdiction other than the one in which it was chartered. For example, a corporation chartered in France and one chartered in Connecticut would be equally foreign in New York. Occasionally the term *alien corporation* is applied to distinguish corporations chartered in non-U.S. jurisdictions.

FOREIGN CORRUPT PRACTICES ACT. A Federal law, adopted in 1977, that forbids any U.S. company, its officers, employees, directors, agents, or major stockholders to make payments to any foreign official, candidate for office, or political party as an inducement to obtain, retain, or expand business. Violation of the act authorizes fines up to one million dollars on corporate violators, as well as fines up to ten thousand dollars and/or five years in prison for individual violators.

The act has been criticized for restricting opportunities for American firms to compete in countries where payments to officials are part of doing business, and such payments are made routinely by foreign competitors. Some modification of the act is anticipated.

FOREIGN CREDIT INSURANCE ASSOCIATION. An association of fifty U.S. insurance companies that operates in conjunction with the EXPORT-IMPORT BANK *(q.v.)*, or EXIMBANK, to insure commercial risks associated with export transactions.

The FCIA provides credit insurance on foreign receivables arising from export sales; EXIMBANK normally insures the receivables against political risks and excess commercial risks. Coverage is provided in the following forms:

1. The *master policy* covers all, or virtually all, of an exporter's sales during a one-year period; both short-term (up to 180 days) and medium-term (180 days to five years) are covered. The master policy is subject to an aggregate credit limit; however, special increased limits for a particular buyer can be arranged. Under this plan, FCIA covers 90 percent of commercial risks and 100 percent of political risks. Medium-term sales normally require a 15 percent down payment by the borrower.

2. The *short-term policy* has features similar to the master policy, except receivables must mature in 180 days or less, with the exception of agricultural sales, which may be extended to one year. Products must contain at least 50 percent U.S. content to be eligible for coverage.

3. The *medium-term policy* covers capital and quasi-capital goods with terms up to five years and longer. Each policy is written on a case-by-case basis. Agricultural exports may be insured under this plan.

4. The *combination policy* is designed primarily to cover dealers and distributors. This plan embraces coverage of up to 180 days on parts and accessories, 270 days on inventory financing, and three years on receivable financing.

The FCIA offers special programs for small businesses and extends discretionary lines to participating U.S. banks. Export commitments during fiscal 1984 totalled $5.8 million supporting exports of $6.8 billion.

FOREIGN CURRENCY STATEMENT. A financial statement prepared using a functional currency other than that in which the firm customarily reports.

FOREIGN CURRENCY TRANSACTION. For accounting purposes, a transaction stated in terms of a currency other than the firm's functional currency. The purchase or sale of goods priced in terms of a foreign currency and the lending or borrowing of foreign funds represent such transactions.

FOREIGN CURRENCY TRANSLATION. The accounting process employed in expressing, in terms of a firm's reporting currency, those transactions that are denominated in a different currency.

FOREIGN ENTITY. Within the meaning of FINANCIAL ACCOUNTING STANDARDS BOARD STATEMENT NO. 8 *(q.v.)* relative to accounting for foreign currency transactions, a *foreign entity* is an affiliated firm whose financial statements are prepared in a functional currency other than that used by the reporting enterprise. An example would be the case of a Belgian subsidiary (foreign entity) that maintains its accounts in Belgian francs (functional currency) rather than in the U.S. dollars employed by the reporting enterprise, i.e., the parent U.S. corporation.

FOREIGN FREIGHT FORWARDER. A firm, licensed by the Federal Maritime Commission, that serves as the agent of a merchant in arranging the shipment of goods by water. Among other services, the forwarder obtains vessel space, prepares documents, and arranges delivery of merchandise to the pier.

The forwarder is paid a handling fee, which is commercially negotiable, by the merchant. In addition, the forwarder usually receives a "brokerage" commission from the steamship line.

FOREIGN HOLDING COMPANY INCOME. *See* SUBPART F.

FOREIGN INTERNATIONAL SALES CORPORATION. A foreign corporation controlled by a DOMESTIC INTERNATIONAL SALES CORPORATION *(q.v.)* (DISC) that satisfies the requirements of Section 993 of the Internal Revenue Code as follows:

1. The DISC must own directly, on each day of the taxable year, more than 50 percent of the rating stock of the foreign corporation.

2. Of the foreign corporation's gross receipts 95 percent must be derived from "qualified export receipts" and interest on working capital and qualified accounts receivable.

3. "Qualified export assets" must account for 95 percent or more of the adjusted basis of all assets held by the foreign corporation.

The Foreign International Sales Corporation should not be confused with the Foreign Sales Corporation which was authorized by law in 1984 as successor to DISCs.

See FOREIGN SALES CORPORATION ACT.

FOREIGN INVESTMENT. *See* DIRECT FOREIGN INVESTMENT.

FOREIGN INVESTMENT REVIEW ACT. An act of the Canadian Parliament directed toward protection of Canada's economy from domination by foreign direct and portfolio investment. The act is concerned with the establishment or takeover of Canadian businesses only; the acquisition of shares in Canadian firms, where such acquisition does not constitute control, is not subject to the act.

The act provides that "non-eligible" persons (anyone other than a resident Canadian or landed immigrant) must apply to the Foreign Investment Review Agency (FIRA) to establish or acquire a business or businesses in Canada, or to expand an existing business. In considering an application by such persons (including firms controlled by them), FIRA will address numerous factors including, inter alia: the effect of the investment on the Canadian economy, including employment, resource processing, and export potential; the degree of participation by Canadians in the enterprise, and the industry as a whole; the effect the proposed venture would have on advancing Canadian technology and industry; the competitive effect on established Canadian businesses; and compatibility with Canadian economic policies.

With the exception of small businesses (defined as having gross assets under two million dollars and fewer than one hundred employees), the act applies to investments in every sector of Canada's economy.

The Foreign Investment Review Act has been strongly criticized by many foreign governments, especially the United States, as arbitrary and protectionist, and was, in 1984, the object of formal enquiry before the General Agreement on Tariffs and Trade.

In December 1984, the newly elected Conservative government introduced the Investment Canada Act, which would abolish FIRA and encourage foreign investment. Under the proposed law, a new agency, Investment Canada, would be established; this agency would be limited to reviewing: (1) direct takeovers of Canadian firms having gross assets of more than five million dollars; (2) indirect takeovers (i.e., the acquisition of a Canadian firm by reason of the purchase of its foreign parent) where the acquired Canadian company has gross assets of more than fifty million dollars; (3) acquisition by foreigners of certain "culturally sensitive" enterprises.

The Investment Canada Act was approved by the House of Commons in June 1985, and awaits Senate approval and the Royal Assent, which are assured. It is contemplated that the new act will be fully implemented with supporting regulations by the end of 1985.

FOREIGN LICENSING AGREEMENT. *See* LICENSING.

FOREIGN MARKET PRICE. For purposes of customs valuation comparisons, generally the price of like merchandise sold for consumption in the country of origin.

FOREIGN SALES CORPORATION ACT. A component of the Tax Reform Act of 1984, which permits formation of Foreign Sales Corporations (FSC, pronounced "fisk") as a tax incentive to American exporters, and revises tax treatment of income earned by DOMESTIC INTERNATIONAL SALES CORPORATIONS *(q.v.)*, DISCs, which have been criticized by many foreign governments as an unlawful export subsidy under the rules of the GENERAL AGREEMENT ON TARIFFS AND TRADE *(q.v.)*.

The Foreign Sales Corporation Act of 1984, with effect for taxable years after December 31, 1984, adds new sections 921 through 927 of the Internal Revenue Code, and amends DISC provisions 991 through 997, and section 291(a) (4) of the Code.

A FSC is a corporation, formed in a foreign country or a U. S. possession other than Puerto Rico, structured so as to derive a corporate tax exemption on a portion of the earnings from the sale of U.S. exports. To qualify for the exemption, the income must arise from the sale of "export property" within the meaning of the Code; i.e., tangible goods having at least 50 percent U. S. content, plus services ancillary to the export of such goods. This includes minerals (other than oil and gas) subject to percentage depletion allowances. Service exports, other than architectural and engineering services for foreign construction projects, and the management of unrelated FSCs, are not eligible.

FSCs can be formed by manufacturers, exporters, and groups; the FSC may have up to twenty-five shareholders, and, so long as there is a legitimate business purpose to do so, may issue different classes of stock. If the FSC buys from an arm's length purchaser, or uses arm's length pricing (as prescribed in section 482 I.R.C.), 32 percent of the FSC's income will be exempt from U. S. income taxes.

If the FSC is related to the supplier of the export property, the FSC will share the profit from the export sale on the basis of 23 percent allocated to the FSC and 77 percent allocated to the supplier. Presuming the FSC performs a required minimum of activity outside the Customs Territory of the U. S. (which includes Puerto Rico), then 16/23 of its 23 percent share of the combined profits will be exempt from U. S. corporate taxes. An alternate method of tax treatment for related party transactions permits a FSC to take 1.83 percent of gross receipts (not to exceed 46 percent of combined income) as its share of combined income, of which 1.27 percent of gross receipts (not to exceed 32 percent of combined income) would be exempt from U. S. corporate income taxes. In addition, a U. S. corporate shareholder is entitled to a 100 percent intercorporate dividend deduction.

With the exception of "small business FSCs" (those having $5 million or less in gross receipts from exports) a FSC must, outside the Customs Territory: maintain an office outside the U. S. (although not necessarily in the jurisdiction where chartered); conduct all meetings of the directors (of whom at least one must be a nonresident of the U. S. or Puerto Rico) and shareholders; effect all disbursements for dividends, officers' salaries, and professional fees; maintain one set of books of account (including invoices); and maintain the principal bank account.

Small business FSCs can be chartered and maintain their offices outside the U. S., have one nonresident of the U. S. or Puerto Rico as a director, and maintain the books of account offshore. All FSCs must make a FSC election with the IRS.

The Foreign Sales Corporation Act requires that a FSC must be based in a U. S. possession (other than Puerto Rico), or in a country which has agreed to exchange tax information with the Internal Revenue Service. At the beginning of 1985, the following foreign countries had entered into such an agreement: Australia, Austria, Barbados, Belgium, Canada, Denmark, Egypt, Finland, German Federal Republic, Iceland, Ireland, Jamaica, Korea (Republic of), Malta, Morocco, Netherlands, New Zealand, Norway, Pakistan, Philippines, South Africa, Sweden, and Trinidad and Tobago.

The act permits U. S. possessions to impose a tax on FSC income after December 31, 1986.

Under the act, a U. S. exporter may continue an existing DISC or begin a new one, with tax deferral benefits for up to 94 percent of export earnings (up to $10 million); the shareholder of a DISC must pay an interest charge, at the Treasury bills rate, on the accumulated tax-deferred income held by the DISC. The tax year of the DISC must be that of its majority shareholder, and a new election for DISC status must be made with the IRS. In addition, all tax liabilities on DISC deferrals accumulated prior to January 1, 1985, were forgiven.

FOREIGN SOVEREIGN IMMUNITIES ACT. An act of Congress passed in 1976 and having effect from January 19, 1977, clarifying the circumstances under which foreign states, their political subdivisions, and state-owned corporations may lose sovereign immunity and become subject to the jurisdiction of U.S. courts. The act reaffirms that foreign states, per se, are immune from suit in the United States, but clarifies exceptions under which U.S. jurisdiction may be exercised. The act stipulates that a foreign state is not immune where it waives immunity, expressly or by implication; where the foreign state engages in commercial activities in the United States, or undertakes actions in the United States to further commercial activity elsewhere; and where the suit is brought against a commercial entity owned or controlled by a foreign state.

Normally, the property of a foreign state is not subject to attachment, except where the state expressly waives immunity. Exception to this rule may apply in the case of funds impounded where a foreign state is in default of loan obligations; this point is unclear and relies upon opinions expressed in Congress that loans are inherently "commercial" in character.

The abrogation of state immunities authorized by the act is subordinate to any immunities granted by the United States in treaties of friendship, commerce, and navigation.

FOREIGN TAX CREDIT SYSTEM. A taxing scheme which permits a firm to offset income tax liabilities in its home country by applying sums paid to foreign tax authorities as credits against the domestic tax burden. For example, if an American firm doing business in Canada paid one million dollars in income taxes to the Canadian government, the firm might be permitted to apply an equivalent amount as a credit against its U.S. tax liability.

Normally, only income taxes are creditable; other taxes, such as payroll taxes or value added taxes, cannot be used as the basis for a tax credit, unless such taxes were levied in lieu of income taxes.

See OVERSPILL.

FOREIGN TRADE ANTITRUST IMPROVE-MENTS ACT. A 1982 act of Congress, constituting Title IV of the EXPORT TRADING COMPANY ACT *(q.v.)*, which amends the Sherman Act and Federal Trade Commission Act to clarify their inapplicability to export trade, except where such trade diminishes competitiveness in domestic U.S. commerce or injures the export commerce of a U.S. resident.

FOREIGN TRADE ORGANIZATION. An instrumentality of the Soviet government charged with controlling the importation or exportation of specified products, or with providing trade-related functions such as shipping and insurance. Most of the sixty-plus FTOs are subject to control of the Ministry of Foreign Trade and are limited to a narrow range of products. Operationally, export-import transactions are planned in advance by the State Planning Committee (GOSPLAN) with an object of maintaining a high degree of Soviet economic self-sufficiency and preserving foreign exchange. After GOSPLAN completes a basic export-import plan, the scheme is articulated through the Ministry of Foreign Trade to the various FTOs.

FOREIGN TRADERS INDEX. A database of foreign importers or potential importers of American products maintained by the International Trade Administration of the U.S. Department of Commerce as a source of business data for U.S. exporters. The file contains information on more than 140,000 potential purchasers in 143 countries. The database is updated and new firms are added continuously. Information may be retrieved in several forms:

1. *Export Mailing List Service.* Lists are prepared for selected countries by commodity classification, detailing name and address of the firm, telephone, telex, cable address, name of chief executive, relative size, year established, number of employees, and product or service cited by Standard Industrial Classification number. Information is collected by agents of the Foreign Commercial Service stationed abroad and may be obtained by American users in the form of a computer printout or on gummed labels.

2. *Data Tape Service.* Information on all firms in any or all countries in the Foreign Traders Index is available on magnetic tape at a cost, in 1984, of $177.50 per country, or $2,500 for the entire file.

3. *Trade Lists.* A printed summary of all data in the Foreign Traders Index for selected developing countries is priced at three to five dollars per list.

Access to the data contained in the Foreign Traders Index can be obtained by contacting any district office of the U.S Department of Commerce, International Trade Administration. (A full list of district offices of the Department of Commerce can be found in Appendix C2.)

FOREIGN TRADE ZONE. An enclosed area in or near a port of entry that, while located on American territory, is effectively outside the customs jurisdiction of the United States. Such zones were authorized by the Foreign Trade Zones Act of 1934 as areas where foreign products might be entered, stored, manipulated, manufactured, and exported without imposition of customs duties or similar limitations, with the exception of certain operations involving liquor, tobacco, firearms, and a very few other items. Virtually any merchandise may enter into the zones. Every port of entry is entitled to at least one zone, which must be operated by a municipal authority or a private corporation, expressly authorized by local statute. (A listing of foreign trade zones can be found in Appendix C7.)

FOREX. An acronym for *foreign exchange.*

FORFAITING. A means of financing trade based upon the transfer of debt obligations arising from the sale of goods and services, usually exports. The merchant sells to the forfaiter, without recourse, the debt obligation of the foreign purchaser, usually in the form of a trade bill of exchange or promissory note, bearing an *aval*, i.e., an unconditional and transferable guarantee of a bank or governmental agency.

FORTY FOOTER. An ocean container with an overall length of approximately forty feet. A standard forty-foot container has an external height of approximately eight feet. A standard forty-foot container constitutes two twenty-foot equivalent units in measuring a ship's container-carrying capacity.

FORTY-FORTY-TWENTY. A provision of the UNCTAD CODE OF CONDUCT FOR LINER CONFERENCES *(q.v.)* that calls for a system of cargo preference in which 40 percent of export cargoes would move on ships of the exporting country, 40 percent on ships of the importing country, and the remaining 20 percent available to ships of other nations. The agreement applies only to cargoes moving in liner conference trade; it does not govern movements aboard vessels of nonconference carriers or bulk charters. The agreement has been adopted by most maritime nations with a few notable exceptions, including the United States.

FORWARDER. A person or firm employed by a shipper of merchandise to book passage for the goods, prepare documents, and generally coordinate the shipping transaction. Ocean freight forwarders are regulated under General Order IV of the Federal Maritime Commission; domestic surface forwarders are subject to Part IV of the Interstate Commerce Act; airfreight forwarders are licensed by the Civil Aeronautics Board.

FORWARDER'S RECEIPT. A document issued by a freight forwarder acknowledging receipt of merchandise into his custody for purposes of shipment to a specified location. This receipt is not a bill of lading and does not attest to actual shipment of

FRANK P. DOW COMPANIES, INC.
333 South Flower Street, Los Angeles, California 90071

CUSTOMS BROKERS – FREIGHT FORWARDERS
FMC License No. 923

(213) 489-7630 • TWX: 910-321-3939 • TLX: 698-110 • Cable DOW Los Angeles

Date:

Subject: Forwarder's Receipt.

To Whom It May Concern:

We hereby certify that we have received _____ pieces of

_____ for the account of_____

_____. This cargo weighs _____ pounds

and is measured at approximately _____ cubic feet.

Cargo has been received at _____

to meet the vessel _____ Voyage No. _____

Booking Number _____sailing on or about _____.

Very truly yours,

Frank P. Dow Co.

Forwarder's Receipt. Courtesy of The Myers Group, Inc., Rouses Point, NY.

the goods; accordingly, it is not acceptable under letter of credit transactions unless specifically provided for (*see* figure).

FORWARD EXCHANGE. *See* HEDGING.

FORWARD EXCHANGE CONTRACT. An agreement to exchange, at a specified future date, a fixed number of units of one currency for a fixed number of units of another currency. Such contracts are often procured by merchants when they must settle future accounts in a foreign currency and wish to protect against possible losses due to fluctuations in the rate of exchange.

The rate of exchange specified in the contract is the *forward rate*.

FORWARD MARGIN. In foreign exchange transactions, the difference between the current, or "spot," price for a given currency and the price at some future date. If the "futures" price, that quoted by sellers of contracts for future purchase of that currency, is higher than the spot price, the subject currency is said to be trading at a "premium"; if the futures price is less than the spot price, however, the currency is trading at a "discount."

FORWARD RATE. *See* FORWARD EXCHANGE CONTRACT.

FORWARD VERTICAL INTEGRATION. *See* VERTICAL INTEGRATION.

FOUL BILL OF LADING. *See* BILL OF LADING.

FOURTH SEACOAST. A reference to the Great Lakes as an area of maritime activity.

FOURTH WORLD. A general reference to the poorest nations of the world, i.e., those with per capita incomes under three hundred dollars. *See* FIRST WORLD, SECOND WORLD, THIRD WORLD.

FRANCHISE. A provision in a marine cargo policy that partial losses will be adjusted if the loss exceeds a certain percentage of the total value of the shipment. A clause providing "with average if amounting to 3 percent," for example, would oblige the underwriter to settle a partial-loss claim without a deductible if the claim exceeded 3 percent of the insured value of the shipment; losses under that amount would not be covered.

As used in the COMMON AGRICULTURAL POLICY *(q.v.)* of the European Economic Community, an adjustment in the Monetary Compensation Amount. *See* GREEN RATE.

FRANCO DELIVERY. A delivery to a consignee of goods upon which all charges, including freight, have been paid.

FRAUDULENT ENTRY. The deliberate undervaluing or misclassifying of merchandise for the purpose of evading duties or customs control.

FREE ALONGSIDE. A condition in a shipping contract whereby the shipper bears all costs of delivering the goods up to a ship's tackle. This definition is modified to accommodate local customs of the port.

FREE ASTRAY. The free onward movement to the consignee by a common carrier of merchandise that has been erroneously discharged at the wrong terminal.

FREE COINAGE. The system under which any individual may take bullion to the mint and have it coined. In the United States free coinage of silver persisted from 1792 to 1873; free coinage of gold was practiced from 1792 to 1933. The government's charge for converting bullion to coin is known as *brassage*; any premium beyond the brassage is *seigniorage*. If no charge is imposed, this is called *gratuitous coinage*.

FREE DISPATCH. A provision in a charter party that precludes payment of DESPATCH MONEY *(q.v.)* for early release of a vessel.

FREE IN AND OUT. A condition in transportation under which the carrier has no responsibility to load or unload the vessel, barge, or other conveyance. The shipper is obliged to stow the cargo, and the consignee to effect unloading; loading and unloading expenses may be borne by either the shipper or the consignee or a third party, or divided among them, but in no case are they borne by the carrier under a free in-and-out (commonly known as F.I.O.) clause.

FREE LIST. A listing of all commodities on which no customs duties are imposed.

FREELY OFFERED. Goods offered in the normal course of trade to all buying on essentially the same basis, e.g., with like prices, terms, discounts, et cetera. Under prior valuation schemes, the value at which the goods were "freely offered" served as the basis for the assessment of customs duties; this concept has been largely discarded by the CUSTOMS VALUATION CODE *(q.v.)* of the GENERAL AGREEMENT ON TARIFFS AND TRADE *(q.v.)*, which relies upon the transaction value as the principal method of customs valuation.

FREE MARKET ECONOMY. The economic system of a nation in which market forces determine which goods and services are produced, and at what price they are offered. Free market economies do not contain substantial government controls on resource availability, price levels, or central planning of economic objectives.

FREE OF ADDRESS. A condition in some charter parties stipulating that no ADDRESS COMMISSION *(q.v.)* will be paid.

FREE OF CAPTURE AND SEIZURE. A clause in an ocean marine policy that deletes from the list of covered perils the WAR RISKS *(q.v.)* of capture and seizure, and losses attributable thereto. All such war-related perils are covered under a separate war-risk policy.

FREE OF PARTICULAR AVERAGE. A clause in a basic marine cargo insurance policy restricting settlements in the case of partial losses attributable to perils of the sea or incidents where the vessel has been sunk, burned, or stranded during the course of the voyage. An F.P.A. policy provides the most limited coverage. The word *free* conveys that the insurance is free of the burden of settling partial loss. An FPA clause is written under one of two conditions:

1. *FPA—English conditions*, the more liberal and more common form, provides for settlement of partial losses when the vessel has been sunk, burned, or stranded at any time during the voyage.

2. *FPA—American conditions* responds for partial losses only when directly caused by sinking, burning, or stranding. This form of limitation is used primarily in relation to special risks, e.g., cargo transported by barge or sailing craft.

The terms *English* and *American conditions* refer only to the origins of the respective clauses; today, either cover would be written in both the London and American insurance markets.

FREE OF TURN. A condition in a vessel charter party that laytime commences as soon as the ship arrives in port and notice of readiness has been given, irrespective of whether a berth is ready.

FREE PERIMETER. A free trade area similar to a free port, consisting of a defined geographical area, often in a nation's interior, where customary trade regulations, taxes, and/or duties are not imposed; the usual object in establishing such a perimeter is to stimulate local production.

FREE PORT. A type of FOREIGN TRADE ZONE (*q.v.*), encompassing an entire port area, into which goods can be shipped, stored, and exported free of duty. Customarily, only goods entered for local consumption will be subject to duties and taxes. Hong Kong, Singapore, and the Canary Islands, among others, are free ports.

FREE PRATIQUE. The condition of a vessel which is in compliance with the health and sanitation laws of the country where it is berthed at any point in time. Prior to leaving port, a vessel must normally obtain from civil health authorities a "certificate of free pratique," also known as a bill of health. The U.S. Customs Regulations state: "No clearance shall be granted to a vessel subject to the foreign quarantine regulations of the Public Health Service unless it has been issued a certificate of free pratique. . ." (19 CFR 4.70).

FREE SHIPS/FREE GOODS. A position asserted by certain authorities in international law that all cargo carried aboard a neutral vessel is exempt from seizure by belligerents in time of war. This view conflicts with a more widely held attitude that belligerents have a legal right to interdict munitions and supplies with war-making potential en route to enemies, even when carried aboard neutral ships.

FREE TRADE. Technically, a condition in which no restrictions are imposed on the movement of goods in international trade. Among the restrictions that would have to be abolished to achieve free trade would be customs duties, quotas, import licenses, exchange controls, and domestic subsidies. Under a free trade system, each country would be free to specialize in products where it enjoyed comparative advantage. The term is generally applied to an environment in which only minimum controls are imposed.

FREE TRADE AREA. An association of states that seeks to overcome impediments to trade among members by reducing or eliminating tariffs among the participants. The members of a free trade area do not maintain a common external tariff nor do they (usually) provide for the free flow of labor or capital among the members. *See* COMMON MARKET, CUSTOMS UNION.

FREIGHT. The earnings that a carrier derives from the carriage of merchandise. Freight should not be confused with *cargo*, which is the merchandise itself. Also, the term *freight* is used to represent payment made by a charterer to the vessel's owner for use of a ship under a voyage charter.

FREIGHT, ALL KINDS RATE. A fixed charge levied by a carrier to ship a container, trailer, car, et cetera, from one point to another, irrespective of the contents. A FAK rate supersedes class or commodity rates. The shipper, in effect, pays a flat charge to move the unit and may ship whatever he wishes up to the rated capacity of the unit. Very often conditions are imposed in FAK rates, e.g., prohibiting shipment of hazardous materials or requiring that the contents consist of three or more different commodities. The use of FAK rates may afford substantial cost savings over conventional commodity or class rates, depending upon the products involved and the shipping points.

FREIGHT-ALLOWED PRICING. *Synonymous with* ZONE-DELIVERED PRICING (*q.v.*).

FREIGHT BROKER. *Synonymous with* CARGO BROKER (*q.v.*), in vessel charter transactions.

FREIGHT FORWARDER. *See* FORWARDER.

FRONTING. Arrangement in which an insurance company issues a policy but transfers the risk to another insurer. This arrangement may arise when an insurer wishes to participate in a market where it is not admitted or where its policies may not be commercially acceptable. Under such circumstances, the insurer desiring to write the risk may ask an acceptable local insurer to write the policy for a fee, passing on the risk and premiums. Insurance companies are selective in issuing *front* policies, inasmuch as the issuing company stands before the world as responsible to respond for claims. As a practical matter, an insurer can be paid to have issued a front policy where it retains 10 percent or less of the face amount of the policy, reinsuring the remainder.

The fronting company may derive a fee ranging from 2½ to 30 percent out of the policy premium, depending upon the reliability of the reinsurer and the level of services (e.g., claims, salvage) to be performed.

FROZEN SDR. *See* SPECIAL DRAWING RIGHTS.

FROZEN SPECIAL DRAWING RIGHTS. *See* SPECIAL DRAWING RIGHTS.

FRUSTRATION. A condition or occurrence during the period when a vessel is under charter that precludes performance of the charter contract or has the effect of defeating the object of the charter. Where frustration occurs, the charter is terminated.

FULL AND DOWN. The condition of a vessel that is *down to marks*, i.e., loaded up to the maximum LOAD-LINE (*q.v.*) capacity as well as having all cargo-carrying space fully occupied.

FULL-BODIED COINAGE. Coins containing precious metal with a market value at least equal to the face value.

FULL BERTH TERMS. Conditions of carriage by water under which the owner of the goods is not responsible for the costs of loading or discharging his cargo to or from the vessel.

FULL INTEREST ADMITTED. A stipulation commonly included in open marine insurance policies whereby the insurer *admits* or accepts without documentary evidence the insurable interest of the policyholder in all merchandise declared and for which a premium is paid.

FULL TAX CREDIT. *See* DOUBLE TAXATION.

FULL TAX EXEMPTION. *See* DOUBLE TAXATION.

FULL TERMS. A promise in an offer to charter a vessel that the owners must accept certain allowances or reductions in addition to normal commissions.

FUNCTIONAL CURRENCY. The currency primarily employed by a multinational firm in its principal transactions. Normally this is the currency of the nation in which the firm is based. *See* FINANCIAL ACCOUNTING STANDARDS BOARD STATEMENT NO. 52.

FUNDAMENTAL DISEQUILIBRIUM. A significant and persistent disparity between the official and market exchange rates for a nation's currency.

FUNDED DEBT. Long-term debt of a firm or governmental authority evidenced by bonds or similar instruments, as compared with short-term or current debt.

FUNGIBLE GOODS. Goods of a given type or class, any unit of which is interchangeable with any other unit and would be equally acceptable in settling obligations denominated in terms of the commodity. For example, corn is fungible in that one bushel of corn of a given grade is interchangeable on an equal footing with any other bushel of corn of a like grade.

FURTHER PROCESSING METHOD. *See* SUPER-DEDUCTIVE.

FUTURES COMMISSION MERCHANT. Under rules of the Commodity Futures Trading Commission, effective June 9, 1980, the designation applicable to any person acting as an agent of foreign brokers or traders for the purpose of accepting delivery and service of communications issued to them by the commission; also any broker who has positions in accounts carried in the name of a foreign broker.

G

GALLOPING INFLATION. *See* HYPERINFLATION.

GARAGE. An overseas point to which assets are sent to await employment. The term is used most commonly with shifting of funds to offshore tax havens.

GATE PRICE. The minimum price at which pork, poultry, and eggs are permitted to enter the European Economic Community under the COMMON AGRICULTURAL POLICY *(q.v.)* without imposition of a supplementary levy in addition to the basic variable levy.

The gate price, known also as the *lock-gate price*, *sluice-gate price*, and *minimum import price*, is derived by computing the cost of feed for covered swine and poultry and all other costs of production. The feed costs are adjusted quarterly in conformity with world market prices for the relevant feed. The other factors are constructed so as to represent producer costs in non-EEC countries. From the two inputs, a theoretical C.I.F. (*See* Appendix B1.) price is derived for imports. When imported products fall below this value, levies may be imposed to negate the price advantage of the foreign producer.

GATEWAY. A city or other point at which cargo is transferred between tariff jurisdictions.

GATT. *See* GENERAL AGREEMENT ON TARIFFS AND TRADE.

GENERAL AGREEMENT ON TARIFFS AND TRADE. Commonly known as GATT, an international organization, affiliated with the United Nations, that aims to reduce tariffs and other barriers to trade. The GATT was established in 1947 as an interim agreement pending creation of a permanent International Trade Organization (ITO) as provided in the Havana Charter of 1947. The U.S. Senate declined to confirm the agreement establishing an ITO, thereby leaving GATT as a permanent entity.

For the first twenty-five years of its existence GATT devoted its efforts to reduction of duty rates, reconciliation of systems of valuation, elimination of quantitative restrictions on imports, and media-tion of trade disputes. The work of GATT has been promoted through seven rounds of multilateral trade negotiations: 1947, Geneva; 1949, Annecy (France); 1951, Torquay (United Kingdom); 1956, Geneva; 1960–61, Geneva (Dillon Round); 1964–67, Geneva (Kennedy Round); and 1973–79, Tokyo/Geneva (Tokyo Round).

Unlike prior rounds, the Tokyo Round went substantially beyond matters of tariff levels and restrictions, addressing such areas as subsidies and countervailing duties; government procurement; restrictions in the trade in bovine animals, meat, dairy products, and civil aircraft; technical barriers to trade; import licensing; and the special needs of developing countries.

Specific products of the Tokyo Round include:

1. *Tariff reductions*, to take place in installments over the years 1980–87, resulting in a 34 percent reduction of duty collections on manufactured goods.

2. *Subsidies Code* forbids governments from giving subsidies to manufacturers as a stimulus to export.

3. *Standards Code* precludes the use of technical standards as an impediment to trade.

4. *Government Procurement Code* requires governments to open to foreign firms, on the same basis as domestic firms, bids for government purchases of goods where the amount of the contract exceeds SPECIAL DRAWING RIGHTS *(q.v.)* 150,000; certain exceptions are made, particularly where national security matters are involved.

5. *Customs Valuation Code* standardizes the method of valuing imports for the purpose of applying ad valorem duties. The code provides that the *transaction value*, i.e., the arm's length sale price, shall be the basis for duties. Alternative methods of valuation are stipulated for those instances where the transaction value cannot be used.

6. *Civil Aviation Agreement* eliminates duties on all civil aircraft, parts, and repairs.

The Tokyo Round also reaffirmed the principle of nonreciprocal concessions to less developed countries, reflected in the GENERALIZED SYSTEM OF PREFERENCES *(q.v.)*.

GENERAL AGREEMENTS TO BORROW

The highest policymaking body of GATT is the Session of Contracting Parties, which is held annually. Decisions during the session are usually arrived at by consensus; when voting does take place, each nation has one vote. Majority votes are sufficient for most questions, although two-thirds votes are required to authorize a deviation from specific obligations arising under GATT. Much GATT work is performed by working parties. Panels of conciliation are formed to resolve trade disputes between members.

GATT headquarters are located in Geneva.

Countries to whose territories GATT has been applied and that now, as independent states, maintain a de facto application of GATT pending final decisions as to their future commercial policy:

Algeria	Mozambique
Angola	Papua New Guinea
Bahamas	Qatar
Bahrain	Saint Lucia
Botswana	Saint Vincent
Cape Verde	São Tomé and Príncipe
Dominica	Seychelles
Equatorial Guinea	Solomon Islands
Figi	Swaziland
Grenada	Tonga
Guinea-Bissau	Tuvalu
Kampuchea	United Arab Emirates
Kiribati	Yemen, Democratic
Lesotho	Republic of
Maldives	Zambia
Mali	

See Appendix D8.

GENERAL AGREEMENTS TO BORROW. An arrangement among the GROUP OF TEN (*q.v.*) nations to provide supplemental financing to the INTERNATIONAL MONETARY FUND (*q.v.*) "to forestall or cope with an impairment of the international monetary system."

The participating nations (United States, Great Britain, West Germany, Japan, Sweden, Netherlands, Canada, France, Italy, and Belgium) commenced the GAB in 1962 by pledging to lend up to six billion U.S. dollars in national currencies over a four-year period. The agreement has been extended several times, most recently for five years in 1980.

GENERAL ASSET CURRENCY. Bank notes secured not by specific assets, e.g., gold or foreign currency on deposit, but by the overall assets of the issuer.

GENERAL AVERAGE. An ancient principle in international maritime law requiring a contribution by the vessel and cargo interests to pay for "extraordinary expenses and sacrifices" incurred in saving the vessel and its cargo. The term *average* derives from an Arabic word meaning a loss attributable to sea water. A general average (i.e., common loss) arises when the vessel is endangered and extraordinary actions are required to save it.

The law views the vessel owner and owners of the cargo aboard it as bound in a common *adventure*; the vessel's master is vested with the responsibility for this common interest. Should the adventure become imperiled, and losses arise in order to save the enterprise, the costs of this saving will be apportioned over the vessel and cargo, proportional to the value of each party's rescued property. A general average condition is apt to arise, for example, when cargo is *jettisoned* (i.e., thrown overboard) in a conscious effort to lighten a vessel during a storm. The law regards this sacrifice as being in the common interest of all; as a result, the owners of the jettisoned cargo will be substantially reimbursed by the owners of the vessel and cargo saved.

It is recognized that three conditions must exist in order to invoke general average: (1) the adventure must be exposed to a common and imminent peril; (2) extraordinary expenses or sacrifices must be incurred to avert or mitigate the peril; and (3) the adventure (or at least part of it) must be saved. Should the vessel and cargo sink or be lost through fire or otherwise, general average would not apply.

A general average is *proclaimed* by a participant in the adventure; as a practical matter, this proclamation is usually made by the vessel owner, who is apt to hear first of any incident from which a general average condition arises. A maritime lien arises for sums owed in satisfaction of a general average claim and the vessel owner is empowered to withhold the consignee's goods until a cash deposit or bond is posted to cover the estimated contribution of each shipment to the fund used to pay for the expenses generated to save the ship. Such contributions are covered by marine cargo policies. The exact obligation of each shipper may not be known for several years, during which time an *average adjuster* will calculate each party's contribution in accordance with accepted practice. The rules of average adjusting are substantially codified in the YORK-ANTWERP RULES (*q.v.*).

The institution of general average is addressed in Justinian's Code, which refers to the practice in the lost Rhodian Sea Code, promulgated c. 900 B.C.

GENERAL AVERAGE SECURITY. A cash deposit, surety, or other guarantee posted by or on behalf of a consignee for an obligation arising under GENERAL AVERAGE (*q.v.*). The steamship operator has the right to withhold release of cargo to a consignee pending the posting of such security, and is under obligation to do so when cargo interests are entitled to recover general average allowances.

GENERAL CARGO. *See* CARGO.

GENERAL ENDORSEMENT. Within the meaning of the Uniform Negotiable Instruments Law, the unconditional ENDORSEMENT (*q.v.*) of a negotiable instrument.

GENERALIZED SYSTEM OF PREFERENCES. A nonreciprocal trade concession extended to various "beneficiary" *less developed countries* (LDCs) by the industrial nations of the West and some Eastern bloc countries.

Known commonly as the GSP, the generalized system permits duty-free entry into the industrial countries of a wide array of manufactures and agricultural products of the LDCs. Orchestrated by the United Nations Conference on Trade and Development, the object of the GSP is to expand LDC exports, thereby giving impetus to industrial and agricultural growth in the LDCs, while enhancing foreign currency earnings.

Under the American GSP program, the United States grants exemption from duty on approximately half the products listed in the TARIFF SCHEDULES OF THE UNITED STATES *(q.v.)*, when such products originate in a beneficiary country. For purposes of the exemption, a *product* is defined as any article within the five-digit product code in the Tariff Schedules. (Articles eligible for GSP treatment are identified in the Tariff Schedules by the letter *A* immediately to the left of the product code, i.e., the tariff item number.) The duty exemption granted under the GSP is in addition to those products already classified as free of duty under the MOST FAVORED NATION *(q.v.)* rates.

Under GSP the law requires, with certain exceptions permitted by the International Trade and Tariff Act of 1984 (Trade Act of 1984), denial of duty-free treatment to a given product from a particular country where the appraised value of the given product to the United States during the calendar year exceeds 50 percent of the total U.S. imports of that product, or where the appraised value of the shipments of the given product to the United States during the calendar year exceeds a fixed sum. The dollar-value competitive needs limitation is predicated upon a base of twenty-five million dollars, established in the Trade Act of 1974 and adjusted annually to reflect changes in the U.S. gross national product.

If any beneficiary country's exports of a particular product fill either of these criteria, the *competitive needs limitations* provision of the law may be invoked. In such cases, shipments of the affected product from the specific beneficiary country will be afforded the duty exemption through the remainder of the current calendar year, but the duty exemption will be rescinded within the first ninety days of the subsequent calendar year. Where competitive needs limitations provisions are invoked, they apply only to the product originating in a specific country; like products originating in other beneficiary countries are not affected; they continue to enjoy duty-free entry into the United States.

The president is permitted to waive the 50 percent limitation where the value of the item in question is *de minimis*. For purposes of the act, de minimis is defined as one million dollars for the base year 1979, adjusted annually to reflect changes in the U.S. gross national product. In addition, the 50 percent limitation is not applied on any product where a like or directly competitive product was not produced in the United States on January 3, 1975.

When a product is subject to a competive needs limitation for any beneficiary country or territory, it will be so identified in the Tariff Schedules by an asterisk accompanying the *A* designation next to the tariff item number. Where an *A** appears, the importer or other user is directed to the general headnotes of the Tariff Schedules, where the country affected by the limitation is identified.

In those cases where a nation has been denied duty-free entry of a particular product because of competitive needs limitations, the affected country *may* have the duty exemption reinstated for subsequent years if its shipments of the given product fall below the 50 percent or dollar-value thresholds. Competitive needs limitations are applied only to individual member states, not cumulatively to regional associations of countries.

To qualify for duty-free entry under the GSP, all articles must:

1. be included on the U.S. GSP list of approved items;

2. be of beneficiary country origin (in those cases where the article was produced in part with imported materials, the product will qualify for GSP treatment where the value of beneficiary country materials, plus the value of imported materials substantially transformed into new and different materials in the beneficiary country, plus the direct manufacturing or processing costs in the beneficiary country, collectively equal at least 35 percent of the appraised value of the product at the time of entry into the United States);

3. be imported into the United States "directly" from the beneficiary country (the direct shipment requirement does not preclude transshipment or storage in a foreign trade zone while en route to the United States, though apart from such incidental operations as packing, sorting, and grading, the goods must not be transformed or enter the commerce of the countries through which they pass).

In addition to the foregoing requirements, the importer is obliged to "request" GSP treatment for the goods. This is accomplished by placing the letter *A* immediately to the left of the tariff item number on the customs documentation submitted for entry purposes. The importer is also obliged to submit a certificate of origin from the beneficiary country: the special certificate Form A must be used for this purpose.

U.S. participation in the GSP was authorized by the Trade Act of 1974, and imports were first accorded duty-free entry under GSP beginning January 1, 1976. The Trade Act of 1984 extended the life of the GSP program through July 4, 1993.

Amendments to the U.S. GSP list, including additions and deletions of specific products, are implemented by executive order of the president, upon recommendation of the U.S. trade representative. Parties seeking to have particular items added to or deleted from the GSP list may file comments and applications with:

Chairman, GSP Subcommittee
Trade Policy Staff Committee
Office of the U.S. Trade Representative
1800 G Street, N.W.
Washington, D.C. 20506

Applications received by June 1 will be considered for implementation during the subsequent calendar year. Amendments to the GSP list take effect the following April.

Beneficiary countries and territories under the Generalized System of Preferences as contained in the Tariff Schedules of the United States, 1984:

Independent Countries

Angola	Ivory Coast
Antigua and Barbuda	Jamaica
Argentina	Jordan
Bahamas	Kenya
Bahrain	Kiribati
Bangladesh	Korea, South
Barbados	Lebanon
Belize	Lesotho
Benin	Liberia
Bhutan	Madagascar
Bolivia	Malawi
Botswana	Malaysia
Brazil	Maldives
Burma	Mali
Burundi	Malta
Cameroon	Mauretania
Cape Verde	Mauritius
Central African	Mexico
Republic	Morocco
Chad	Mozambique
Chile	Nauru
Colombia	Nepal
Comoros	Nicaragua
Congo	Niger
Costa Rica	Oman
Cyprus	Pakistan
Djibouti	Panama
Dominica	Papua New Guinea
Dominican Republic	Paraguay
Ecuador	Peru
Egypt	Philippines
El Salvador	Portugal
Equatorial Guinea	Romania
Fiji	Rwanda
Gambia	Saint Christopher-Nevis
Ghana	Saint Vincent and
Grenada	Grenadines
Guatemala	Saint Lucia
Guinea	Saõ Tomé and Príncipe
Guinea-Bissau	Senegal
Guyana	Seychelles
Haiti	Sierra Leone
Honduras	Singapore
India	Solomon Islands
Indonesia	Somalia
Israel	Sri Lanka

Sudan	Tuvalu
Surinam	Uganda
Swaziland	Upper Volta
Syria	Uruguay
Taiwan	Vanuatu
Tanzania	Venezuela
Thailand	Western Samoa
Togo	Yemen (Sana)
Tonga	Yugoslavia
Trinidad and Tobago	Zaire
Tunisia	Zambia
Turkey	Zimbabwe

Non-Independent Beneficiary Territories

Anguilla	Monserrat
Bermuda	Netherlands Antilles
British Indian Ocean	New Caledonia
Territory	Niue
Brunei	Norfolk Island
Cayman Islands	Pitcairn Islands
Christmas Island	Saint Helena
Cocos (Keeling) Island	Tokelau
Cook Islands	Trust Territory of the
Falkland Islands	Pacific Islands
French Polynesia	Turks and Caicos Islands
Gibraltar	Virgin Islands, British
Heard Island and	Wallis and Futuna
McDonald Island	Islands
Hong Kong	Western Sahara
Macau	

Associations of countries, treated as one country for application of GSP, except for application of the competitive needs limitation:

Association of Southeast Asian Nations

Indonesia	Singapore
Malaysia	Thailand
Philippines	

Cartagena Agreement (Andean Group)

Bolivia	Peru
Colombia	Venezuela
Ecuador	

Caribbean Common Market

Antigua and Barbuda	Monserrat
Barbados	Saint Christopher-Nevis
Belize	Saint Lucia
Dominica	Saint Vincent and the
Grenada	Grenadines
Guyana	Trinidad and Tobago
Jamaica	

In addition to extending the GSP program, the Trade Act of 1984 instituted the following changes, inter alia: deletes Hungary from the list of ineligible countries; excludes footwear, handbags, luggage, flatgoods, work gloves, and leather wearing apparel; retains current competitive needs limitations but permits the president to waive all competitive needs limitations on least developed developing countries (as defined in the Tariff Schedules of the United States) and on one-half of 15 percent of all imports under GSP for any country with more than a 10 percent share of GSP or a per capita gross national product (GNP) of $5,000; requires that countries with a per capita GNP of $8,500 be *graduated,* i.e., denied GSP treatment, phased over a two-year period (the $8,500 GNP benchmark for beneficiary countries will be adjusted annually at a rate equal to 50 percent of the change in the U. S. GNP); empowers the president (following a two-year study period, to be completed by 1987) to reduce by up to one-half the threshold for the competitive needs limitation on any product, if he determines that the product is otherwise competitive.

GENERAL LICENSE. A privilege extended by the Federal government that permits exportation of various nonstrategic materials to certain countries without the necessity of formally applying for a validated export license. The general license is a legal illusion; no application is required and no document is issued. However, by maintaining the premise that every export shipment is "licensed," the government reserves the right to withdraw a firm's export "privilege," should that become desirable.

GENERAL ORDER. A condition imposed upon merchandise that is imported into the customs territory of the United States but that is not promptly cleared through customs. General order merchandise is deposited in an approved warehouse pending disposition. Section 127 of the Customs Regulations governs the treatment of such goods. Merchandise not claimed or exported within one year of landing may be sold, destroyed, or disposed of in accordance with Treasury regulations.

GENERAL ORDER MERCHANDISE. Goods that have arrived at a U.S. port of entry but have not been claimed or entered within the prescribed period after arrival. In most cases an importer must claim and enter merchandise within five working days following arrival of the goods. District directors of customs may authorize a longer period upon application of the importer or his agent. Goods not entered within the prescribed time period enter the condition of *general order* and may be moved at the risk and expense of the consignee into the public stores or a privately operated warehouse licensed by customs to receive such merchandise.

Goods that have not been entered within one year of arrival into the customs territory may be sold at auction; any sums so derived will be used first to settle warehouse charges, duties, taxes, and administrative expenses. Remaining proceeds will be given to the owner of the goods upon application to customs authorities.

In the case of dangerous items, perishables, or goods likely to decrease in value, sale or other disposition is authorized immediately, without the one-year waiting period applied to other goods.

GENERAL ORDER 16. An order of the Federal Maritime Commission that permits the commission to hear and resolve certain disputes arising from shipping transactions under FMC jurisdiction. The order provides for a simplified procedure before a hearing officer, although a hearing before the full commission is authorized. Cases are limited to disputes involving amounts of $5,000 or less; cases involving cargo loss or damage are specifically excluded.

GENERAL SUPERINTENDENCE. A generic term applied to any one of a number of firms associated with the Société Générale de Surveillance of Geneva. The basic responsibility of these offices is to inspect cargo to ensure compliance with the terms of purchase or import regulations. Several nations, as a condition of entry of merchandise, require a preshipment physical examination of the goods. The examination of the merchandise may be performed at the piers prior to shipment, or at the supplier's warehouse or factory, depending upon the type of goods involved. Invoices and shipping documents are also examined for conformity with prices and terms of sale quoted to the foreign buyer. Upon satisfactory completion of the examination, a Clean Report of Findings will be issued to the shipper and the buyer. In some countries, this report is required before exchange control authorities will release funds to settle accounts.

GENERAL TARIFF. A tariff schedule in which a single rate of duty applies to a given commodity irrespective of the country of origin. A general tariff makes no provision for preferential duties.

GENERAL TERM BOND. A surety provided by an importer to the U.S. Customs Service to cover duty obligations arising from the importation of merchandise. These bonds are issued in amounts over $100,000 by approved bonding firms and may be used to cover all of the firm's importations in any U.S. port.

GENEVA CONVENTION ON BILLS OF EXCHANGE (1932). *See* UNIFORM LAW ON BILLS OF EXCHANGE.

GENEVA ROUND. *See* GENERAL AGREEMENT ON TARIFFS AND TRADE.

GENEVA TRADE CONFERENCE. *See* GENERAL AGREEMENT ON TARIFFS AND TRADE.

GENOSSENSCHAFT. A form of corporate organization permitted under German law. A minimum of seven natural persons are required to form the entity, and the individual liability of the members varies, depending upon how the firm is organized.

GENUINE LINK. A provision arising from the 1958 Convention on the High Seas (450 United Nations Treaty Series 82, Article V), that "there must be a genuine link between the State [that registers the vessel] and the ship"; this "link" is not clearly defined and has not served as a serious impediment to registering under a FLAG OF CONVENIENCE *(q.v.).*

GEOCENTRIC PRICING. A pricing policy within a multinational firm that permits individual foreign subsidiaries substantial latitude in pricing standardized products, within guidelines prescribed by the parent company.

GEOGRAPHIC STRUCTURE. A form of organization employed by some multinational firms in structuring their control of international markets. The firm divides the world into various contiguous geographic segments, each directed by a general manager or similar officer who reports to headquarters. Within each geographic sector, a wide variety of the firm's products is sold using substantially the same marketing apparatus and distribution channels. *See* PRODUCT STRUCTURE.

GERMINAL FRANC. A unit of value employed in some international agreements. It was established after the French Revolution by a law of March 28, 1803 (7 Germinal of the year XI of the Revolutionary calendar) with a gold content of ten thirty-firsts gram of gold, nine-tenths fine.

GESELLSCHAFT MIT BESCHRÄNKTER HAFTUNG. A common form of business organization in Germany, especially for small businesses or those with a limited number of shareholders. Identified by the letters *G.m.b.H.* in the company's name, this form of incorporation conveys limited shareholder liability. The company is formed by registration upon application of the management; a board of directors is optional.

G FORCE. The product of the acceleration of mass times the force of gravity, measured as 32 feet per second. For example, if 10 Gs of force were exerted on a five-ton load, the resultant G force would be 50 tons.

The effects of G forces exerted upon a vessel in heavy weather may be a significant factor in ship stability.

GLIDING PEG. *See* CRAWLING PEG.

GLOBAL QUOTA. *See* QUOTA.

GMA STANDARD PALLET. A widely used variety of wooden pallet adopted in the 1960s by the Grocery Manufacturers of America to overcome logistical problems associated with a lack of uniformity of pallet sizes. The GMA pallet measures forty-eight by forty inches and permits four-way entry.

G.m.b.H. *See* GESELLSCHAFT MIT BESCHRÄNKTER HAFTUNG.

GNOMES OF ZURICH. A supposedly secretive bond of bankers and financiers based in Zurich who are reported to act in concert for the purpose of manipulating, on a worldwide basis, international financial and gold transactions. The phrase is believed to have originated with British Deputy Prime Minister George Brown in 1964.

GODOWN. A waterfront storehouse; customarily, the term is limited to use in relation to Far East ports.

GOLD BULLION STANDARD. A monetary policy that permits redemption of currencies into gold, but only for significant amounts. Under a true gold standard, all currency is redeemable into gold on demand; under a gold bullion standard, gold might be redeemable only in mimimum lots of one ingot.

GOLD CERTIFICATES. Paper currency issued by the U.S. Treasury denominated in dollars and freely convertible by the bearer into gold at the fixed rate. When the United States went off the gold standard in 1933, gold certificates were removed from circulation, except for use by Federal Reserve banks.

GOLD CLAUSE. A provision in a debt instrument defining the monetary obligation in terms of gold, or a dollar of a prescribed weight and fineness of gold

GOLD CRISIS. A condition that arises when a nation exports so much gold as to draw close to the amount legally required as a reserve for currency outstanding. Often this condition is the product of a severe and protracted deficit in balance of payments.

GOLD EXCHANGE STANDARD. A condition in which a nation maintains its reserves in a currency convertible into gold rather than in the metal itself. Since August 15, 1971, the U.S. dollar has not been freely convertible into gold by foreign central banks; it therefore does not qualify as a reserve currency for a nation on a gold exchange standard.

GOLD FLOW. Also known as *gold movements,* the pattern by which monetary gold enters and leaves a country. Theoretically, an inflow of gold should expand the national monetary supply; conversely, an export of gold should contract the money supply, thus eliminating imbalances in international payments over time. As a practical matter, most nations no longer equate the supply of money in circulation to gold reserves.

GOLD FRANC. A unit of exchange employed in certain international financial transactions. The gold franc contains .2903 grams of fine gold; it is identical with the Swiss franc prior to its 1936 devaluation.

GOLD INFLATION. A condition that arises in a nation where holdings of gold are tied to money supply, and excessive stocks of monetary gold increase the creation of money, resulting in inflation. The remedy for this condition is to remove gold from the treasury, thereby reducing the quantity of money available.

GOLD MOVEMENTS. *See* GOLD FLOW.

GOLD POINTS. A variation in the value of two gold standard currencies against the value of physical gold so as to warrant the export of gold. For example, if the exchange rate for French francs rose above a certain point, it would be more profitable to export gold to France and sell it for francs than to exchange dollars directly for francs. The abandonment of the gold standard by most major trading nations and the advent of instantaneous arbitrage facilities have obviated the significance of gold points.

GOLD RESERVES. The gold held by a nation as reserves for currency issued. After U.S. abandonment of the gold standard in 1933, Congress mandated that the Federal Reserve banks would have to hold gold certificates, reflecting gold on deposit with the U.S. Treasury equivalent to at least 25 percent of currency and demand deposits outstanding. In 1968 Congress repealed the Gold Reserve Act, thus abolishing this requirement.

GOLD STANDARD. A system under which a nation's currency is freely convertible into gold. The quantity of gold per unit of currency is fixed by law. Most major trading nations, however, abandoned the gold standard because of the constraints it imposes upon liquidity, although some interest has been expressed in its revival for precisely that reason, i.e., to control expansionary monetary policies.

GOLD STERILIZATION. A governmental policy to prevent the expansion of a nation's money supply by preventing the accumulation of gold. In the case of a nation on the GOLD STANDARD *(q.v.)*, a given quantity of gold is represented by a fixed number of units of currency. Augmentation of the national gold stock would permit introduction of additional units of currency into the economy, thereby expanding the money supply.

The term *gold sterilization* is sometimes used by nations not on the gold standard to indicate an unwillingness to acquire reserve assets other than gold, such as foreign currency, for fear of expanding the money supply.

GOLD STOCK. A nation's supply of monetary gold.

GOLD TRANCHE POSITION. A drawing of foreign exchange from the INTERNATIONAL MONETARY FUND *(q.v.)*, by a member nation up to or equal with that country's gold on deposit with the IMF. In effect, the nation is using its gold deposit as collateral for the loan. Drawings in excess of gold on deposit fall into the country's CREDIT TRANCHE *(q.v.)*.

GOLD WIRE. The telegraphic transfer of gold among Federal Reserve banks to clear interbank balances. The gold is physically on deposit with the treasurer of the United States.

GOOD DELIVERY BAR. The standard gold bar used in international transactions, having a purity of at least 99.5 percent pure gold, and weighing between 350 and 430 troy ounces. The shape of the bar is immaterial, although U.S. bars are traditionally brick-shaped, whereas foreign-poured bars are trapezoidal.

GOOD SHIP. The term *good ship* or *good vessel* in a charter party or other maritime contract is an expressed or implied assurance that the ship is seaworthy.

GOODS IN FREE CIRCULATION. Merchandise not subject to customs restrictions. These goods would include locally produced (i.e., not imported) merchandise and goods that have been cleared by customs and upon which all duties and taxes have been paid.

GOOD VESSEL. *See* GOOD SHIP.

GOSPLAN. *See* STATE PLANNING COMMITTEE.

GOVERNMENT PROCUREMENT CODE. A multinational agreement among trading nations, concluded at Geneva in April 1979, opening government purchasing contracts to competitive bids from firms in other signatory nations. The code was adopted by the United States as Title III of the Trade Agreements Act of 1979 and provides that, after January 1, 1981, the president is empowered to waive any so-called Buy-American law or regulation on behalf of specified eligible products from a prescribed list of countries or instrumentalities.

The underlying principle of the code is reciprocity among signatory states, although each nation has imposed limitations upon foreign-origin tenders.

See Appendix D8.

GRADUATION. The act of recognition by the world community that formerly LESS DEVELOPED COUNTRIES *(q.v.)* have undergone sufficient economic development to be regarded as "developed" or industrialized nations. The recognition of this new status is usually accompanied by the withdrawal of trade concessions and aid programs routinely granted to less developed countries. Brazil, Korea, and Hong Kong, among others, are often regarded as having "graduated" into developed nations.

GRAIN BILLS. Bills of exchange arising from sales of grain.

GRAINSPACE. The complete cargo-carrying capacity of a ship, including hatchways, measured in cubic feet. The term is used in relation to any powder or nuggetlike cargoes, including coal, sulphur, and salt.

GRATUITOUS COINAGE. The coinage of standard metal without a minting fee, i.e., brassage or seigniorage. This act should not be confused with free coinage, which is the unrestricted minting of a standard metal, with or without minting fees.

GREEN CLAUSE. A provision in a LETTER OF CREDIT *(q.v.)* similar to a RED CLAUSE *(q.v.)*, but providing that an advanced payment will be made upon presentation of warehouse receipts evidencing the goods are available for shipment.

GREEN RATE. A special rate of exchange used in converting agricultural prices fixed in units of account into national currencies, within the framework of the COMMON AGRICULTURAL POLICY *(q.v.)* of the European Economic Community. The green rate is established periodically and does not respond to daily fluctuations in the market rates for the national currencies involved.

For the main agricultural products, the difference between the market rates for national currencies and the periodically revised green rate is resolved between countries in the form of MONETARY COMPENSATORY AMOUNTS *(q.v.)*.

GREEN REVOLUTION. A significant increase in agricultural productivity beginning in the 1960s with the development of high-yield hybrid strains of cereal grains. The movement to expand output in underdeveloped areas was further accelerated by aid programs, such as Food for Peace, designed to disperse advanced agricultural techniques.

GRESHAM'S LAW. A principle, articulated by Sir Thomas Gresham in the sixteenth century, that bad money drives good money out of circulation, i.e., when two or more varieties of money are in circulation, both with equal power as legal tender, the one having the greatest intrinsic value will be hoarded, and the less favored currency will continue to circulate.

GROSS CHARTER. Also known as *gross terms*, a vessel charter arrangement whereby all expenses, to include loading, unloading, PILOTAGE *(q.v.)*, et cetera, are for the account of the vessel.

GROSS DOMESTIC PRODUCT. The aggregate value, expressed in monetary terms, of all goods and services produced within a national economy during a given time period, usually one year.

GROSS DOMESTIC PURCHASES. An item within the National Income and Product Account Tables that represents the gross national product less exports plus imports.

GROSS LINE. The face value of all insurance policies that an insurer has in force at any point in time, irrespective of any reinsurance.

GROSS NATIONAL PRODUCT. The aggregate value, expressed in monetary terms, of all goods and services attributable to a national economy during a given period, usually one year. The final sum includes all goods and services produced within the economy, plus income earned overseas (e.g., interest, dividends, workers' remissions) less domestic earnings owed to foreigners.

GROSS PRIVATE DOMESTIC INVESTMENT. The aggregate value, expressed in monetary terms, of private expenditures, for capital goods (e.g., physical plant, equipment) adjusted by the inventory investment (the sum of the increase or decrease of merchandise in inventory during a given time period, usually one year).

GROSS REGISTER TON. Synonymous with GROSS TON *(q.v.)*.

GROSS TERMS. Synonymous with GROSS CHARTER *(q.v.)*.

GROSS TON. A unit of measurement in determining the size of a ship. In this case, the ton is a unit of cubic measure approximately equal to one hundred cubic feet. Gross tonnage, therefore, is derived by determining the entire internal cubic footage of the ship, including all enclosed spaces, and dividing by one hundred.

GROSS WEIGHT. The total weight of a package, i.e., the contents plus all packaging.

GROUNDED (CONTAINER). An ocean container, loaded or empty, that is positioned flat on the ground without a chassis underneath it. In order to be moved, such a container would have to be raised off the ground by a lifting device and loaded onto a chassis or flatbed truck.

GROUNDED (VESSEL). The condition of a vessel which has struck a submerged sandbar, rock, or similar protrusion and is incapable for a period of time (during low water, for example) of navigating free and returning to open water.

GROUP OF TEN. Also known as the *Paris Club*, the ten principal trading nations. The group, consisting of the United States, Great Britain, Federal Republic of Germany, France, Japan, Italy, Belgium, the Netherlands, Canada, and Sweden, derived the name from a 1962 General Agreement to Borrow signed to make U.S. $6.2 billion in credit available to the International Monetary Fund.

Discussions among the member nations are commonly conducted in the larger arena of the ORGANIZATION FOR ECONOMIC COOPERATION AND DEVELOPMENT *(q.v.)* in recent years. In April 1984, Switzerland formally joined the Group as a full member.

GROUP OF TWENTY. A committee established by the INTERNATIONAL MONETARY FUND *(q.v.)* to recommend reforms in the world monetary order. On July 26, 1972, the IMF adopted resolution 27-10, establishing the Committee on Reform of the International Monetary System and Related Issues (the Committee of Twenty), consisting of one member for each country or group of countries electing a member of the fund. The Committee reported that: floating exchange rates were useful in overcoming imbalances; a reformed system required stable but adjustable par values for currencies; trade controls should be avoided as a means of regulating balance of payments; and SPECIAL DRAW-ING RIGHTS *(q.v.)* must be the basis of global liquidity, with gold and reserve currencies relegated to a secondary position. The committee held its final meeting in Washington in June 1974. It was recommended that a permanent council of twenty members be established to monitor and direct IMF policies.

GROUP OF TWENTY-FOUR. A block of less developed nations that has called for the allocation of 45 percent of the voting quota at the INTERNATIONAL MONETARY FUND *(q.v.)* to Third World nations. Currently, voting quotas in the IMF are assigned to member nations in accordance with their individual economic capabilities, leaving control of the fund in the hands of the industrialized nations.

GUATEMALA PROTOCOL (1971). A modification of the WARSAW CONVENTION *(q.v.)* of 1929.

GUEST CURRENCY. The currency in which a EUROBOND *(q.v.)* or other financial obligation is is-sued. The currency is selected to be acceptable to both the foreign borrower and the lender, and may be the currency of neither party to the transaction.

GUIDE PRICE. As used in conjunction with the European Economic Community's Common Agricultural Policy on cattle and calves, it is *synonymous with* ORIENTATION PRICE *(q.v.)*.

GYOSEI-SHIDO. A Japanese term commonly translated as "administrative guidance." The term relates to official or unofficial pronouncements from the Japanese government which serve as guidelines to business concerning the application of Japanese law or regulations. The guidance provided may take the form of a written opinion, or a seemingly casual remark made by an official to a business executive.

The often informal character of these pronouncements has been criticized by foreign firms doing business in Japan on the grounds that foreigners tend to be excluded from inside information.

H

HAGUE AGREEMENT. The product of a 1924 conference on ocean carrier liability sponsored by the International Chamber of Commerce. The agreement embraced various defenses to carrier liability for loss or damage to cargo and established a limitation of liability at one hundred pounds sterling (approximately five hundred dollars at the time) per package or customary freight unit. The agreement has been adopted, with some modification, by most maritime countries, usually as a carriage of goods by sea act. The United States substantially adhered to the agreement by enactment of the U.S. CARRIAGE OF GOODS BY SEA ACT *(q.v.)* of 1936, providing a carrier liability of five hundred dollars per package or customary freight unit.

In 1967 a conference was convened in Belgium to update the Hague Agreement, including an increase in the carrier's liability per package; the product of this conference, known as the VISBY AMENDMENT *(q.v.)*, has not entered into force.

See HAMBURG RULES.

HAGUE AGREEMENT CONCERNING THE INTERNATIONAL DEPOSIT OF INDUSTRIAL DESIGNS. An international agreement that provides protection for industrial designs in all contracting states, usually by means of a single application.

In the case of registrations affecting Egypt, France, German Democratic Republic, German Federal Republic, Holy See, Indonesia, Liechtenstein, Monaco, Morocco, Spain, Surinam, Switzerland, Tunisia, and Vietnam, nationals or residents of any of those countries (including persons having bona fide places of business in any of them) file a single application for protection with the WORLD INTELLECTUAL PROPERTY ORGANIZATION *(q.v.)* (WIPO). No application need be made to the national industrial property office. A person filing a design is deemed, prima facie, to be the owner in all states adhering to the agreement.

Designs may be submitted under *open cover,* i.e., available for inspection, or *sealed cover,* at the option of the party making application. Protection is afforded for fifteen years; after the first five years, designs are placed under open cover.

In transactions between Belgium, Liechtenstein, Luxembourg, Netherlands, Surinam, and Switzerland, special procedures apply. The applicant applies either to WIPO directly, or through his national industrial property office, as the laws of his country stipulate. Applications cannot be made under sealed cover, and the term of protection varies; in no case may it be less than five years, or ten years if renewed during the first five years. Protection may be afforded for longer periods, as specified in national laws.

The Hague Agreement was adopted in 1925, and was revised at London (1934) and The Hague (1960), and by an Additional Act at Monaco (1961); in addition, a Complementary Act was appended at Stockholm (1967) and a Protocol was added at Geneva (1975).

The agreement is administered by WIPO and is open to all states adhering to the PARIS CONVENTION FOR THE PROTECTION OF INDUSTRIAL PROPERTY *(q.v.)*. On March 15, 1983, the following states were adherents to The Hague Agreement:

Belgium	Luxembourg
Egypt	Monaco
France	Morocco
German Democratic	Netherlands
Republic	Spain
German Federal Republic	Surinam
Holy See	Switzerland
Indonesia	Tunisia
Liechtenstein	Vietnam

HAGUE CLUB. A loose association of European countries engaged in trade with Brazil from the mid-1950s, acting in concert in response to Brazilian economic and exchange rate instability.

HAGUE PROTOCOL (1955). A modification of the WARSAW CONVENTION *(q.v.)* of 1929.

HAGUE VISBY RULES. *See* VISBY AMENDMENT.

HAMBURG RULES. A proposed international convention dealing with carrier liability for loss or damage to cargo transported by sea. Known formally as the *United Nations Convention on the Carriage of Goods by Sea—1978,* the convention was the product of a conference held at Hamburg, Federal Republic of Germany, March 6-31, 1978. The convention was designed to correct deficiences in the earlier (1924) HAGUE AGREEMENT *(q.v.)* and to accommodate such technological innovations as containerization.

The Hamburg Rules provide that the convention shall be applicable to a shipment if the bill of lading is issued in any state adhering to the convention or if the port of loading, port of discharge, or optional ports are in a contracting state; or in any case where the contract of carriage provides for their incorporation. The convention does not apply to charter parties, except where a bill of lading is issued and shipments under bills of lading are otherwise subject to the convention.

The responsibility of the ocean carrier continues from the time he takes delivery of the goods until he relinquishes control; for purposes of the convention, the ocean carrier is responsible for the actions of his agents and servants. The carrier is also responsible for losses due to fires that result from his "fault or neglect."

Liability is limited to 835 *units of account* (UA) or 2.5 UA per kilogram, whichever is higher. One UA equals one *special drawing right* (approximately U.S. $1.25) of the International Monetary Fund. Carrier liability for delay would be limited to 2.5 times the freight on the goods delayed, not to exceed the total freight payable on the shipment.

A container would be deemed a *package*, unless the shipper listed the number of shipping units or cartons on the bill of lading, in which case each carton or shipping unit would constitute a package.

Limitations of carrier liability would be vitiated if it could be proved that the loss was the result of "an act or omission of the carrier done with the intent to cause such loss, damage, or delay, or recklessly and with knowledge that such loss, damage, or delay would probably result." Judicial or arbitral proceedings against a carrier must be commenced within two years.

The convention will take effect upon ratification by twenty states. As of March 1983, twenty-seven states had signed the agreement, but only eight (Barbados, Chile, Egypt, Morocco, Rumania, Tanzania, Tunisia, and Uganda) had deposited instruments of ratification.

HAND STACKING. The practice of loading a trailer, boxcar, or ocean container by hand, rather than by means of mechanical devices. Hand stacking usually involves stowage of the cargo directly upon the floor of the vehicle so as to utilize most fully its cargo-carrying capacity.

HARBOR DUES. Charges levied by a local port authority upon vessels entering a harbor; their purpose is to maintain channels, buoys, and similar facilities. Normally these charges are absorbed by the vessel, but they may be passed on to shippers in the form of a freight surcharge.

HARD CURRENCY. A national currency freely exchangeable into gold or the currencies of other nations.

HARMONIZED SYSTEM. Known formally as the *Harmonized Commodity Description and Coding System*, a product statistical classification system based upon the Customs Cooperation Council Nomenclature (CCCN) and designed to replace various statistical classification schemes now employed by various trading nations.

Currently several important statistical classification systems are in use globally. The absence of a uniformly applied system impedes comparison of trade data among nations. In some cases the statistical systems used by a given nation for capturing data on import and export transactions are not compatible with the system employed to monitor domestic output. (In the United States, for example, export data are captured under one classification, import data under another, and domestic production under yet a third.) To remedy these deficiencies, the Customs Cooperation Council has proposed that the harmonized system be used as the single product classification structure in international trade, and that all customs tariffs, tariffs of shipping lines, and similar classifications be based upon the harmonized system.

Although based upon the CCCN, the harmonized system is more detailed, embracing many new subdivisions reflective of changes in trading patterns, technological advancements, and user needs. The system is designed to permit further product subdivision by user nations to accommodate special customs or statistical requirements.

As proposed, the harmonized system identifies approximately five thousand articles, which appear as *headings* or *subheadings*. Articles are organized into ninety-six chapters grouped in twenty sections. Each heading is assigned a four-digit number: the first two digits represent the chapter within which the article is classified; the second two digits reflect the position of the article within the chapter. A subheading bears an additional two digits. Further subdivision beyond six digits is at the option of the user nation.

In considering the applicability of the harmonized system to U.S. statistical requirements, the president directed the U.S. International Trade Commission (USITC) to prepare a conversion from the U.S. Tariff Schedules into the harmonized system. The commission was directed to avoid, where practicable, changes in tariff rates and "to simplify the tariff where possible without rate changes significant for U.S. industry, workers, or trade." The converted tariff was submitted by the USITC to the president on June 30, 1983. An act of Congress would be required to adopt the harmonized system in place of the current Tariff Schedules.

As an additional complication, section 484(e) of the Tariff Act of 1930 requires, inter alia, that statistical systems used for imports and exports shall comprehend "all merchandise imported into the United States and exported from the United States, and shall seek, in conjunction with statistical programs for domestic production and programs for international harmonization of statistics, to establish the comparability thereof." The USITC interprets this section of the law to mean that should the United States adopt the harmonized system as the statistical classification system for imports,

> it will be necessary to convert the Statistical Classification of Domestic and Foreign Commodities Exported from the United States (Schedule B) into the format of the Harmonized System. Similarly, the commodity classification codes used for domestic production must be revised to improve their comparability with the domestic and international programs for imports and exports which are now being converted into the structure of the Harmonized System. (USITC Publication 1400, June 1983)

The president has not recommended legislation to adopt the harmonized system.

HARTER ACT. An act of Congress (27 Stat. 445) passed in 1893 to define more clearly carrier liabilities in cases of loss and damage at sea. Originally maritime law left the carrier responsible for virtually any loss or damage that might occur while the goods were in his custody. Carriers sought to repudiate this responsibility by adding various disclaimers to their bills of lading. The act largely compromised between these divergent interests and served as a basis for subsequent international agreements on ocean carrier responsibility. The full text of the Harter Act may be found in Appendix A2. *See* CARRIAGE OF GOODS BY SEA ACT, HAGUE RULES.

HAT MONEY. *See* PRIMAGE.

HAVANA CHARTER. *See* GENERAL AGREEMENT ON TARIFFS AND TRADE.

HAZARDOUS CARGO. Cargo having dangerous properties requiring special stowage or handling in transit. Precise regulations defining what is hazardous and prescribing how such materials shall be packed, labeled, and documented are to be found in Title 49 of the Code of Federal Regulations. In addition, goods going abroad may be obliged to comply with foreign regulations as well, commonly the INTERNATIONAL MARITIME DANGEROUS GOODS CODE *(q.v.)*.

For purposes of transport, the word *hazardous* is used to embrace items not necessarily dangerous by their nature. For example, the transport of magnetized substances by air is regulated to ensure that the aircraft's compass is not affected.
See HAZARDOUS MATERIALS TRANSPORTATION ACT.

HAZARDOUS CARGO REGULATIONS. *See* HAZARDOUS MATERIALS TRANSPORTATION ACT.

HAZARDOUS MATERIALS TRANSPORTATION ACT. A component of the Transportation Safety Act of 1974 aimed at controlling the packaging, labeling, documenting, and handling of hazardous substances moving in the interstate and foreign commerce of the United States, by all modes of transportation. The act authorizes the secretary of transportation to promulgate regulations for the transportation of hazardous materials, which include, inter alia, explosives, flammables, combustibles, poisons, radioactive substances, corrosives, compressed gases, and etiologic agents. A comprehensive compendium of regulations, on a commodity-by-commodity basis, addressing standards of packaging and prescribing the form of documentation for hazardous shipments, was published in Title 49 of the Code of Federal Regulations (CFR 49), with effect from July 1, 1976.

CFR 49 contains the definitive Federal statement on hazardous materials shipments, preempting earlier Federal regulations and transportation industry practices such as those devised by the International Air Transport Association (IATA). Moreover, CFR 49 generally requires that imported and exported merchandise comply with its requirements, which presents difficulties to shippers inasmuch as most nations subscribe to the Dangerous Goods Code of the International Maritime Organization. This means exporters must comply not only with CFR 49 but also with international regulations; the two sets are not always entirely compatible.

Exemption is made in CFR 49 for limited quantities of consumer products containing hazardous substances (e.g., cosmetics containing alcohol) if the products are properly marked. International regulations, however, grant no such exemption.

HEADQUARTERS COMPANY. A company organized in a foreign country for the purpose of providing administrative support to affiliate companies. It does not normally take title to products or provide financing.

HEAVY CARGO. A load of cargo that settles a vessel down to its marks in the water but does not fully occupy the cubic capacity of the ship.

HEAVY GRAIN. Grain having a density of forty-eight to fifty cubic feet per ton and including wheat, rye, and corn.

HEAVY WEATHER. *See* STRESS OF WEATHER.

HEDGING. The act of avoiding price fluctuations over time of commodities or foreign currencies by buying or selling "forward." By hedging, a merchant fixes the future price of a commodity or currency. For example, an American who has purchased ten thousand yards of cloth at one pound per yard from a British supplier on ninety-day terms must be prepared to settle a ten-thousand-pound obligation ninety days hence. The American merchant may buy pounds now and hold them for ninety days; if he waits until the obligation matures, there is a chance that the pound sterling will appreciate (i.e., rise in value) against the dollar, thereby increasing the dollar price of the fabric. In response to these two undesirable alternatives, the American merchant may buy a contract in the futures market; this contract will specify that the merchant will buy ten thousand pounds at a specified rate ninety days in the future. The merchant is thereby assured of the price in dollars he will pay for the sterling exchange, without having to purchase it now. The seller of the contract is speculating that sterling will depreciate against the dollar, thereby permitting the ten thousand pounds to be supplied at reduced dollar cost.

HELL-OR-HIGH-WATER CHARTER. A long-term charter in which the charterer agrees to pay the vessel hire without the customary deductions, such as off-hire time.

HICKENLOOPER AMENDMENT. A provision of the Foreign Assistance Act of 1964 sponsored by Senator Burke Hickenlooper to permit U.S. courts jurisdiction over litigation arising from expropriations of U.S. property abroad by foreign governments.

Also known as the *Rule of Law Amendment*, or the *Sabbatino Amendment* after the famous case of Banco Nacional de Cuba v. Sabbatino, the Hickenlooper Amendment was largely directed at Cuban confiscations of U.S. property. Enacted on October 7, 1964, as Section 301(d)(4) of the act, it provided: (1) that no foreign state might assert immunity from U.S. courts on the basis of the ACT OF STATE DOCTRINE *(q.v.)* when it acted contrary to international law, in particular, when it averted "the principles of compensation"; (2) that the president of the United States might permit Federal courts to invoke Act of State immunities when U.S. foreign policy interests so required; and (3) that the act applied to cases arising after January 1, 1959, and for which litigation was begun by January 1, 1966.

The amendment was reenacted and made permanent, with minor modification, by the Foreign Assistance Act of 1965.

HIDDEN TAX. Tax not paid directly by the consumer but included in the price to him, often without his knowledge. Customs duties exemplify this type of tax.

HIGH CUBE CONTAINER. An ocean container of the same length and width as a standard container but higher, permitting expanded cargo-carrying capacity.

HIGHEST ORIGINAL STATUTORY RATE. A provision contained in General Headnote 10(d) of the Tariff Schedules that stipulates that in any case where two or more tariff classifications could be applied equally to an imported product, the classification having the highest original statutory rate

(Column 2) shall be imposed, even though a lower concessional rate (Column 1) would be applied otherwise. *See* STATUTORY RATE OF DUTY.

HIGH SEAS. The open ocean outside the boundary of any country as distinguished from other international waters that may be enclosed between headwaters or promontories.

HIMILAYA CLAUSE. A provision in an ocean bill of lading that extends to stevedores or other employees of a carrier the carrier defenses against claims for loss and damage of cargo provided in the CARRIAGE OF GOODS BY SEA ACT *(q.v.)*; so named for the case of Adler v. Dickson (1955) I Q.B. 158 concerning the vessel *Himilaya*.

HIRE. The revenue earned by a vessel under charter.

HIRE-PURCHASE. In British usage, an installment purchase.

HISTORICAL RATE. *See* FINANCIAL ACCOUNTING STANDARDS BOARD STATEMENT NO. 8.

HOGSHEAD. A wooden cask used principally for the storage of tobacco, generally with a capacity of 600 to 1,200 pounds.

HOLD ON DOCK. An accommodation sometimes provided by a port authority or steamship line to a shipper who wants to release merchandise from his warehouse but may not be able to put it to sea. This condition is common in the case of an exporter who sells on an FAS or FOB pier basis; by delivering goods to the pier for future shipment, he can book sales while not actually dispatching the goods to his customer prematurely.

This practice has been challenged as an improper inducement and is not as common as in the past.

HOLIDAY. As used in vessel charter parties, any time period during which loading or discharging of cargo that might otherwise take place is suspended because of local law or practice in the port.

HOME OFFICE EXPENSE. A tax deduction accorded to a local subsidiary of a foreign firm for certain administrative expenses incurred by a parent; such an allowance is permitted in some countries on the grounds that the services would probably have been provided locally, perhaps at greater expense, had they not been undertaken by the parent company.

HOOK AND HAUL. In motor carrier usage, an arrangement in which the shipper loads the trailer and the consignee unloads; the carrier does not handle the merchandise, other than to hook up his tractor to a loaded trailer and haul it away.

HORIZONTAL INTEGRATION. Also known as *horizontal expansion*, the expansion of a firm through the acquisition of additional production capacity in its primary field. For example, a shipping company may expand horizontally by acquiring other vessels on the same trade route.

HOSTILE EMBARGO. *See* EMBARGO.

HOT MONEY. Short-term capital movements animated by speculation (as in response to an expected significant change in exchange rates) or to take advantage of interest rate differentials. The term is particularly relevant to funds placed overseas in accounts that may be rapidly liquidated if exchange or interest rates are seen as taking a downward turn.

HOUSE AIR WAYBILL. *See* AIR WAYBILL.

HOUSE BILL. A bill of exchange drawn by a bank upon its branch or subsidiary abroad.

HUMAN CAPITAL. An enrichment of the productive capacity of labor by means of specialized training and education.

HUNDREDWEIGHT. In American usage, one-twentieth of a short ton, or 100 pounds. In Britain, one-twentieth of a long ton, or 112 pounds.

HUSBANDING AGENT. A firm retained by a steamship line in a given port to care for the needs of vessels calling at that port. The husbanding agent may be responsible for providing pilots, refueling, provisions and crew stores, and routine repairs.

HYPERINFLATION. A rate of inflation that exceeds 50 percent per month. Hyperinflation usually occurs during a war or its immediate aftermath when governments are in urgent need of revenue. Hyperinflation accelerates when the public concludes that the government cannot control, or actually abets, the rise in prices, thereby causing an "inflation mentality." The most commonly cited case of hyperinflation is Germany following World War I, at which time prices rose 322 percent per month. Following World War II, Hungary suffered an even worse case of hyperinflation: prices rose at the rate of 19,800 percent per month.

HYPOTHEC. A claim upon property that the claimant neither owns nor possesses. Of Roman origin, the term is used occasionally in referring to a MARITIME LIEN *(q.v.)*, which is a true hypothec.

HYPOTHECATION. The pledge of acceptances, bills of lading, warehouse receipts, or other negotiable instruments as collateral for a loan. The instruments are usually deposited with the lender until the obligation is satisfied.

HYPOTHECATION CERTIFICATE. Also known as a *letter of hypothecation*, a document attached to a BILL OF EXCHANGE *(q.v.)* that arises from a shipment of merchandise. The hypothecation certificate empowers the bank presenting the bill or any subsequent holder of the accepted bill, to sell the specified merchandise in the event the bill is dishonored.

I

IATA. *See* INTERNATIONAL AIR TRANSPORT ASSOCIATION.

IMITATION LAG. The period between achievement of a technological advantage in one country and its successful imitation by another. Initially, a *demand lag* occurs until a desire for the new product is fully articulated; this stage is followed by a *reaction lag*, during which time local potential producers of the new product sense the demand, realize that the innovating country enjoys an export monopoly, and respond by imitating the product. *See* TECHNOLOGY GAP.

IMPERFECT COMPETITION. *See* MONOPOLISTIC COMPETITION.

IMPERIAL PREFERENCE. A synonym occasionally used for COMMONWEALTH PREFERENCE *(q.v.)*.

IMPORT CERTIFICATE/DELIVERY VERIFICATION. *See* INTERNATIONAL IMPORT CERTIFICATE/DELIVERY VERIFICATION SYSTEM.

IMPORT STATEMENT. *See* MANUFACTURING CLAUSE.

IMPORT SUBSTITUTION. The act of eliminating imports of a given product by commencing production locally, often accompanied by controls such as increased duties, quotas, or outright bans to discourage or prevent continued foreign imports. This approach is fairly common on the part of developing countries in the process of industrializing, and rather less employed by developed nations seeking to protect import industries.

IMPOST. A general term covering various duties, taxes, excises, or fees imposed by the state to raise revenue or regulate trade.

IMPREVISION. A doctrine of contract law applied in some legal systems that recognizes a fundamental disturbance of the economics of a contractual relationship attributable to forces that were unforeseeable at the time the parties entered into the contract. The concept of *unforeseeable* disturbance is essential to the doctrine, which may be asserted in law to restore the original economic equilibrium of the contract. This doctrine is often asserted in cases where abnormal fluctuations in exchange rates have negatively affected one or more parties to a contract.

IMPROPER INDUCEMENT. A payment or remission in violation of law, tariffs, or industry practice, provided by a transportation company to a shipper in order to obtain business. Inducements may take the form of bribes, unauthorized rebates of freight paid, absorption of demurrage charges, or excessive entertainment of company officials. In some cases such inducements may be illegal, bringing penalties upon the shipper and/or carrier.

IN BOND. The condition of goods that have been temporarily exempted from customs clearance and duties, in lieu of which the importer or custodian of the goods has posted a surety with customs authorities to ensure that the goods will not be released or consumed until formal examination and clearance have taken place. Normally, in-bond merchandise must remain under the supervision of customs personnel or of firms specially licensed by customs, e.g., bonded warehousemen.

IN-BOND TRANSIT. The movement of goods, without completion of customs formalities, from a point of arrival in the customs territory to a point of exportation or another point for customs examination and release. For example, goods arriving off a ship in Los Angeles might travel in bond to Phoenix for actual customs clearance. The intervening transportation would be performed by a carrier approved and bonded for such purposes.

INCHMAREE CLAUSE. A customary provision in marine cargo policies for coverage from losses sustained because of bursting of boilers, breakage of shafts, latent defects in the hull or machinery of the ship, or errors in the navigation or management of the vessel.

INCOME ELASTICITY OF IMPORT DEMAND. *See* PROPENSITY TO IMPORT.

INCOME EXPLOSION. A dramatic increase in per capita income, especially where the income increases are well dispersed throughout the population. Such income increases will stimulate consumer demand, usually reflected in an increase of imports.

INCOME VELOCITY. *See* VELOCITY OF MONEY.

INCONVERTIBILITY. *See* CONVERTIBILITY.

INCOTERMS. A codification of terms used in foreign trade contracts. Local customs and usage imported variations in meaning for such common terms as F.A.S., C.I.F., et cetera, often resulting in disputes between buyer and seller as to the respective obligations of each.

In 1936 the Paris-based International Chamber of Commerce published the first Incoterms; the terminology was amended and updated in 1953, 1967, 1976, and 1980. The International Chamber of Commerce urges that merchants incorporate by reference the Incoterms into contracts.

INDENT. An offer to purchase at prices and under such terms as are stipulated by a prospective buyer; the term is often used to apply to any foreign order.

INDENT AGENT. A sales agent abroad who markets the products of a foreign supplier on a commission basis.

INDEPENDENT ACTION. The reserved right of a carrier participating in a CONFERENCE *(q.v.)* or rate agreement to deviate unilaterally from the common tariff and publish its own rate for a given commodity. In those tariffs that permit independent action, the common practice is for the group of carriers collectively to consider the rate proposal; if agreement cannot be reached, or if the party applying for the rate remains unsatisfied, a member line may negotiate directly with the shipper and may publish its own rate for the cargo.

INDEPENDENT CARRIER. A steamship line that is not a member of the CONFERENCE *(q.v.)* over a given trade route.

INDEPENDENT COMMISSION ON INTERNATIONAL DEVELOPMENT ISSUES. *See* BRANDT COMMISSION.

INDEX CLAUSE. *See* MAINTENANCE-OF-VALUE CLAUSE.

INDEXING. A practice employed in some countries of adjusting wages, rents, taxes, et cetera, to reflect changes in general or consumer prices. This device usually reflects a high level of domestic inflation.

INDICATION. A nonbinding statement by a principal stipulating generally the terms and conditions under which he would be prepared to conclude a contract to charter a ship. This statement is used in charter transactions as a basis for negotiations.

INDICATIVE PRICE. Also known as the *norm price*, the TARGET PRICE *(q.v.)* for producers of olive oil under the COMMON AGRICULTURAL POLICY *(q.v.)* of the European Economic Community. The indic-

ative price is established at a level substantially below the market target price for olive oil; the object of the disparity between the indicative price and the target price is to reflect the competition between olive oil and its substitutes.

INDICATIVE WORLD PLAN. A comprehensive investigation of world agricultural production and trade begun in 1946 by the Food and Agricultural Organization. The object of the investigation was to assess (then) current conditions in agriculture, identify future needs and opportunities, and recommend strategies. Significant objectives of the plan included stabilization of world food supplies through increased cereal output; diet diversification and increased protein consumption; improved marketing strategies designed to enhance opportunities among developing countries to earn foreign exchange, or to minimize foreign currency outflows by increasing domestic productivity of staples; identification of employment opportunities in agriculture-related industries; and improved land use, to increase yields and relieve unemployment. The program was published in 1969 as *The Provisional Indicative World Plan for Agricultural Development.*

INDORSEMENT. *See* ENDORSEMENT.

INDUCEMENT. In maritime shipping, the tender by a shipper to a carrier of a sufficient amount of cargo so as to warrant a vessel calling at a port not ordinarily scheduled during the voyage.

INDUSTRIAL COMPETITIVENESS INDEX. A measure of the relative competitiveness of various nations' industrial exports, derived by adjusting the effective exchange rate for a given nation's currency against that of a competitor nation after adjusting for the inflation of wholesale prices of non-food manufacturers.

INDUSTRIAL FREE ZONE. *See* EXPORT PROCESSING ZONE.

INDUSTRIAL PROPERTY. Intangible property such as patents and trademarks.

INDUSTRIAL WEST. A group of seventeen industrialized democracies whose levels of trade with communist nations are monitored by the U.S. Department of Commerce as a measure of East-West trade.

The nations comprising the group are:

Austria	Japan
Belgium	Luxembourg
Canada	Netherlands
Denmark	Norway
Finland	Sweden
France	Switzerland
Germany	United Kingdom
Ireland	United States
Italy	

INDUSTRY CAPTIVE. *See* CAPTIVE INSURANCE COMPANY.

INELIGIBLE BANKERS ACCEPTANCE. *See* REGULATION A.

INFANT INDUSTRY. An industry that is not fully developed in a given country, resulting in a high susceptibility to foreign competition. This condition is often particularly acute in the case of basic industries, such as steel, where the expansion of the industry locally is important to economic development, but economies of scale and other efficiencies cannot be achieved because imports reduce the market share of the local producer.

The customary response is to "protect" infant industries through the adoption of higher tariffs, quotas, or similar restrictions on imports.

INFORMAL ENTRY. An abbreviated entry procedure permitted by U.S. Customs for shipments of merchandise under $250 and certain household effects. Unless the district director of customs provides otherwise on a given shipment, entry may be made on Customs Form 5119-A; at time of entry, estimated duties and taxes must be deposited with customs (*see* figure, next page).

INFORMATION LETTER. A pronouncement by the headquarters of the U.S. Customs Service drawing attention to or illuminating already established interpretations of customs law, without addressing a particular set of facts.

INHERENT VICE. A latent defect in a product that causes damage to it, renders it useless, or otherwise inflicts an economic loss that is limited to the item itself. Insurance policies do not respond for losses attributable to inherent vice.

INLAND BILL OF EXCHANGE. A bill drawn and payable in the same state.

INLAND SHIPPING DOCUMENT. A bill of lading for land transportation that covers only a portion of the journey. An inland shipping document often underlies a *through* bill of lading issued by a carrier providing point-to-point service.

INNOCENT PASSAGE. The right of a ship of one state to transit the territorial sea of another state, so long as the voyage does not disturb the peace or well-being of the coastal state. This right is subject to limitations, such as the right of the coastal state to prescribe reasonable rules governing navigation and pollution. A vessel in contravention of such regulations may be subject to seizure, excepting warships or public vessels, which enjoy sovereign immunity. Additional restrictions may apply to warships; for example, submarines must transit on the surface. Violations by public vessels are normally treated through diplomatic channels.

IN REGULAR TURN. *Synonymous with* BERTH CLAUSE *(q.v.).*

IN REM. *See* ACTION IN REM.

INSCRUTABLE FAULT. A condition in which the cause of collision between vessels cannot be attributed to either vessel.

INSTRUMENTS OF INTERNATIONAL TRAFFIC. Transportation equipment, used to transport goods in international commerce. Such equipment is permitted duty-free entry and exemption from local property taxes. Such equipment must itself move in international commerce in order to qualify for the exemption. Hence, a container would normally qualify, whereas a container chassis (which does not leave the country) normally would not qualify.

INSULAR POSSESSIONS. Certain offshore possessions of the United States that are considered to be beyond the CUSTOMS TERRITORY *(q.v.).* The insular possessions are the Virgin Islands, Guam, American Samoa, Wake Island, Kingman Reef, Johnson Island, and Midway Islands. Manufactures of the insular possessions are accorded duty-free entry into the United States so long as they do not contain foreign materials in excess of 50 percent of the value of the finished article. Components of U.S. manufacture, as well as items that could be imported into the United States duty free (except items of Cuban or Philippine manufacture) are not counted in the 50 percent limitation. Puerto Rico is not considered an insular possession inasmuch as it is within the customs territory of the United States.

INSURABLE INTEREST. An interest such that, should an insured peril occur, the insured party would suffer an economic loss.

INTEGRATED TUG/BARGE. A self-propelled barge consisting of two increments: a barge and a separate propulsion unit. The barge and propulsion unit are joined in the water upon completion and may be separated at a later date.

INTELLECTUAL PROPERTY. A general term covering industrial property such as patents, trademarks, and trade names, as well as literary and artistic property, including copyrights.

INTER-AMERICAN DEVELOPMENT BANK. A multinational development bank established in 1959 to promote economic and social development in Latin American member countries.

The bank is owned by its forty-three member countries, of which twenty-seven are *regional*, i.e., Western Hemisphere nations; the sixteen nonregional members were admitted in 1976. The bank's charter provides that the Latin American nations shall as a group be preserved as majority shareholders.

During the 1961–80 period, the bank channeled $66 billion to aid development projects. The principal vehicles used by the bank to aid Latin American development are direct loans to specific development projects; the financing of industrial and ag-

6.7, 10.71, 141.68, 142.13, 143.23 -
143.26, 145.4, 145.12, C.R.

DEPARTMENT OF THE TREASURY
UNITED STATES CUSTOMS SERVICE

Form approved
O.M.B. No. 48-R0236

ORIGINAL

INFORMAL ENTRY

#555555

IMPORTER	PORT
XYZ Imports Company	New York

ADDRESS OF IMPORTER (Show Zip Code)
North Main Street, Anywhere 11111

MARKS & NOS.; AWB OR B/L NO.	DESCRIPTION OF MERCHANDISE AND/OR T.S.U.S. ANNO. REPORTING NUMBER	VALUE	RATE	DUTY	
XYZ NEW YORK #1/8	Eight (8) Carton QUANTITY 8				
	Automobile parts 554.8888	240.00	5.6%	13	44
B/L 1000	Inv. Val: $500.00				
c/o West Germany					
		07	TOTAL DUTY	13	44
			TOTAL I.R. TAX		
			TOTAL COLLECTION	$ 13	44

I.T. NO. I.T. FROM PORT OF:	DATE OF IMPORTATION xx/xx/xx	COUNTRY OF EXPORTATION West Germany	IMPORTING CARRIER S/S Vessel	G.O. NO.

I declare that the information above set forth is accurate to the best of my knowledge and belief and that I have not received and do not know of any other invoice than that attached.

SIGNATURE OF IMPORTER OR AGENT
XXXXX

Validation shows location, date and amount of payment.

Customs Form 5119-A (10-27-77)

Informal Receipt

ricultural credit programs; and equity financing through loans to permit capital participation in Latin American enterprises.

In addition to conventional financing activities, the bank operates the Fund for Special Operations which makes long-term, concessional loans to needier countries for such fundamental needs as potable water, sanitation, and rural health projects. As of 1980, this fund had extended loans for $7.2 billion.

In 1961 the Social Progress Trust Fund was established to administer $525 million advanced by the United States to promote low-cost housing, land use, and sewage treatment. In 1975 the Venezuelan Trust Fund was established to administer $500 million advanced by Venezuela to promote development of nonrenewable natural resources and hydroelectric energy. Similar special-purpose trusts have been administered over the years.

Bank financing is available to member states in Latin America, political subdivisions of such states, and private enterprise; where a private entity receives financing, a governmental entity must serve as guarantor.

The bank is governed by a board of governors; one governor and an alternate are chosen by each member state. The board elects a president, who administers the affairs of the bank.

The bank was capitalized originally with $1 billion; this capital was augmented, or *replenished*, in 1964, 1967, 1970, 1976, and 1980; a sixth replenishment, covering the years 1983–86, totalling $15.7 billion, was adopted in 1983.

The bank's regional members are:

Argentina	Haiti
Bahamas	Honduras
Barbados	Jamaica
Bolivia	Mexico
Brazil	Nicaragua
Canada	Panama
Chile	Paraguay
Colombia	Peru
Costa Rica	Surinam
Dominican Republic	Trinidad and Tobago
Ecuador	United States
El Salvador	Uruguay
Guatemala	Venezuela
Guyana	

The nonregional members are:

Austria	Japan
Belgium	Netherlands
Denmark	Portugal
Finland	Spain
France	Sweden
Germany	Switzerland
Israel	United Kingdom
Italy	Yugoslavia

INTERBANK MARKET. A market for the purchase and sale in the spot and forward markets for foreign exchange among major commercial banks. Very often, these banks will offer to purchase or sell exchange through brokers, thereby initially protecting the identity of the market participants in a given currency at a point in time. Customarily, a bank or broker will approach a potential transaction partner looking to *make a market*, i.e., stand ready to buy or sell a given currency. Quotes are usually given as a two-way price, the rate at which the bank is prepared to buy and sell a given currency. The difference between the *bid* (the price at which the bank would buy) and the *offer* (the price at which it would sell) is the *spread*.

INTERCHANGE AGREEMENT. An agreement among carriers permitting transport equipment (e.g., containers, rail trailers) to move freely between their respective systems. *See* EQUIPMENT INTERCHANGE RECEIPT.

INTERCITY CARRIER. A motor carrier subject to Interstate Commerce Commission authority with a majority of revenues derived from nonlocal cartage.

INTEREST ARBITRAGE. The shift of short term funds from one country to another to exploit higher interest rates.

INTEREST-BEARING DRAFTS. A draft or bill of exchange containing a clause requiring the drawee to pay interest at a prescribed rate from the date the instrument was drawn until settlement at maturity. A common form of the clause reads: "With interest added thereto at _____ percent per annum from the date hereof to the approximate due date of remittance in _____." For many years, the interest clause was used largely in conjunction with exports to Africa and Asia, and so came to be known as the *colonial clause*.

INTEREST RATE RISK. The risk borne by the holder of fixed rate securities that interest rates will rise above those paid by his holdings, thereby depriving him of interest that might otherwise have been earned.

INTERGOVERNMENTAL COUNCIL OF COPPER EXPORTING COUNTRIES. *See* INTERNATIONAL COMMODITY ORGANIZATION.

INTER-GOVERNMENTAL MARITIME CONSULTATIVE ORGANIZATION. *See* INTERNATIONAL MARITIME ORGANIZATION.

INTERLINE. The act of passing cargo from one carrier to another to continue the transit; this term is common among motor carriers and railroads and, to a lesser degree, among airlines. The analogous term among ocean carriers is *transship*.

INTERMEDIATE CONSIGNEE. A person named in a bill of lading or other shipping paper as authorized to receive cargo for the purpose of effecting delivery to the ultimate consignee.

INTERMEDIATE GOODS. Synonymous with INTERMEDIATE PRODUCTS *(q.v.)*.

INTERMEDIATE PRODUCTS. Goods that constitute inputs to the manufacture of other goods; for example, flour is an intermediate product in the manufacture of bread. The oven in which the bread was baked is not an intermediate product, however; instead, it is a *capital good*. Capital goods, such as buildings and equipment, used to make goods are not included in the category of intermediate goods.

Intermediate products are sometimes known as *current account purchases*, inasmuch as they are "current" inputs (in the sense that they are sold to be consumed by the manufacturing process in the manufacture of inventory).

INTERMODAL. Shipments that pass from one mode of transport (air, water, rail, or motor) to another in the same conveyance without unloading or rehandling of the merchandise.

The most common application of the term is in conjunction with containers used aboard ships. Containers can be loaded at the shipper's warehouse and railed and/or trucked to the vessel. Barring examination of the contents by customs or other authorities, it is possible for the goods to remain undisturbed within the container until delivery to the final consignee.

Intermodal conveyances are also carried aboard cargo aircraft; intermodal movements of trailers aboard rail flatcars (piggyback) have been in use for thirty years.

INTERNAL DEPRECIATION. *See* DEPRECIATION (MONETARY).

INTERNATIONAL AIR TRANSPORT ASSOCIATION. A nongovernmental industry organization of the world's scheduled airlines. Commonly known as IATA, the group effectively sets standards and, in many cases, fares for international airline services. Among the many airline activities in which IATA plays a leading role are conferences to establish procedures for cargo and baggage handling, passenger accommodations, reservations, and ticketing; tariff coordination conferences, at which fares and rates are set; and technical areas, including interline reservations and ticketing, finance, air law, training, and antihijack measures.

IATA was established in 1945 by an act of the Canadian Parliament; the organization succeeded a previous International Air Transport Association, which was founded at the Hague in 1919.

Each member airline is entitled to one vote at the annual general meeting; during the year, management is vested in the Executive Committee of elected airline chief executives. Day-to-day administration is performed by the nine-member Executive Board, headed by an executive director. IATA has two main offices, one each in Geneva and Montreal; other offices are located at Singapore, Buenos Aires, Washington, Bangkok, London, Nairobi, and Rio de Janeiro. Membership in the organization is open to any scheduled air carrier; intranational carriers are associate members.

Members of the International Air Transport Association (including associate members designated by an asterisk [*]) in 1984 were as follows:

Aer Lingus Teoranta
Aerolíneas Argentinas
Aeronaves de México (AEROMEXICO)
Aerovias Nacionales de Colombia (AVIANCA)
Air Afrique
Air Algérie
Air Botswana
Air Gurundi
Air Canada
Air France
Air Gabon
Air Guinée
Air India
*Air Liberia
Air Malawi
Air Mali
Air Malta
Air Mauritius
Air New Zealand
Air Niugini
Air Pacific
*Air Queensland
Air Tanzania
Air Tungaru
Air UK
Air Vanuatu
Air Zaire
Air Zimbabwe
ALIA Royal Jordanian Airlines
ALITALIA
American Airlines
*Ansett Airlines
Ariana Afghan Airlines
Austrian Airlines
*Aviacion y Comercio (AVIACO))
British Airways
British Caledonian Airways
Cameroon Airlines
Caribbean Air Cargo Company
*Commercial Airways
Companía Mexicana de Aviación
Continental Air Lines
CP Air
Cruzeiro do Sul
CSA Czechoslovakian Airlines
Cubana (Empresa Consolidada Cubana de Aviacion)
Cyprus Airways
Deutsche Lufthansa
*Douglas Airways
Eastern Air Lines
*Eastern Provincial Airways
*East-West Airlines
Ecuatoriana
Eqyptair
El Al Israel Airlines
Ethiopian Air Lines
Finnair
Flying Tiger Line
Garuda Indonesian Airways
Ghana Airways

Gulf Air
IBERIA
Icelandair
Indian Airlines
*IPEC Aviation
Iran Air
Iraqi Airways
Jamahiriya Libyan Airlines
Japan Air Lines
Jugoslovenski Aerotransport
*Kendall Airlines
Kenya Airways
KLM Royal Dutch Airlines
Kuwait Airways
Lesotho Airways
LAM - Linhas Aéreas de Moçambique
Linea Aérea del Cobre
LAN Chilean Airways
Líneas Aéreas Costarricenses (LACSA)
Lloyd Aéreo Boliviano
LOT Polish Airlines
MALEV Hungarian Airlines
*Mid Pacific Airlines
Middle East Airlines - Air Lebanon
*Mount Cook Airlines
*Namib Air
Nigeria Airways
Olympic Airways
Pakistan International Airlines
Pan American
Philippine Airlines
Polynesian Airlines
Primeras Lineas Uruguayas de Navegacion Aerea
Qantas Airways
*Quebecair
Royal Air Maroc
Royal Swazi National Airways
SABENA Belgirlines
Saudi Arabian Airlines
Scandinavian Airlines System (SAS)
Sierra Leone Airlines
Solomon Islands Airways
Somali Airlines
South African Airways
*South American and Far East Air Transport
Sudan Airways
SWISSAIR
Syrian Arab Airlines
TAAG Angola Airlines
*TALAIR
TAP Portuguese Airlines
Tower Air
*Trans-Australia Airlines
*Trans-Brasil Airlines
*Trans-Jamaican Airlines
Trans-Mediterranean Airways
Trans World Airways
Trinidad and Tobago Airways (BWIA)
Tunis Air
Turkish Airlines
Union des Transports Aériens (UTA)

United Airlines
VARIG Brazilian Airlines
*Vayudoot
*Viaçao Aérea Sao Paulo (VASP)
VIASA Venezuelan Airlines
Yemenia Airways
Zambia Airways

INTERNATIONAL BANK FOR ECONOMIC COOPERATION. A clearinghouse for international settlements among COMECON members established at Moscow in 1963. The object of the bank was to eliminate the need for strict bilateral settlement of trade balances among members by use of accounts in "transferable rubles." The tranferable ruble, however, has not yet been established as a convertible currency, which has impeded the goals of the bank and left settlements largely at the bilateral level.

INTERNATIONAL BANK FOR RECONSTRUCTION AND DEVELOPMENT. *See* WORLD BANK GROUP.

INTERNATIONAL BANKING FACILITIES. Expanded powers granted to U. S. banks to participate in offshore financing, largely beyond domestic U. S. banking regulation. Recognizing that American reserve requirements and other regulatory factors were inhibiting the competitiveness of U. S. banks in international transactions, the Federal Reserve amended their regulations in June 1981 to permit American banks to establish separate domestic facilities for international transactions; these international banking facilities (IBFs) would be exempt from reserve requirements and interest rate ceilings. The Federal Reserve regulations permit an IBF to acccept deposits or extend credit only on the customer's "operations outside the United States"; offer foreign nonbank customers time deposits with minimum maturity or notice of withdrawal of two business days, and minimum deposits and withdrawals of $100,000; offer time deposits to other IBFs, their parents, or foreign offices of U. S. banks, with minimum overnight maturities; and accept deposits or extend credit in U. S. dollars or other currencies.

Regulations permit a domestic (U. S.) depository institution to offer international banking facilities upon notice to the Federal Reserve system, with operations to commence on or after December 3, 1981. At the beginning of 1984, more than two hundred fifty U.S. banks were offering international banking facilities.

INTERNATIONAL BAUXITE ASSOCIATION. *See* INTERNATIONAL COMMODITY ORGANIZATION.

INTERNATIONAL BOYCOTT FACTOR. An element of Section 999 of the Internal Revenue Code dealing with income derived in support of an international boycott. U.S. policy generally opposes international economic boycotts against friendly nations, and income derived by U.S. firms in furtherance of such boycotts receives adverse tax treatment. In accordance with SUBPART F *(q.v.)* of the code, certain income is subject to taxation based upon the sum derived upon multiplication by the *international boycott factor.* This factor is a fraction: the numerator reflects the operations of a firm in countries carrying out an international boycott, and the denominator reflects worldwide operations of the firm. The secretary of the treasury prescribes regulations for the computation of the fraction.

INTERNATIONAL CENTRE FOR SETTLEMENT OF INVESTMENT DISPUTES. An international agency affiliated with the World Bank and serving as a forum for the resolution of international investment disputes.

List of contracting states and signatories to the Convention on the Settlement of Investment Disputes between States and Nationals of Other States
(as of June 4, 1984)

State	Signature	Deposit of Ratification	Entry into Force of Convention	State	Signature	Deposit of Ratification	Entry into Force of Convention
Afghanistan	Sep 30, 1966	Jun 25, 1968	Jul 25, 1968	Madagascar	Jun 1, 1966	Sep 6, 1966	Oct 14, 1966
Australia	Mar 24, 1975			Malawi	Jun 9, 1966	Aug 23, 1966	Oct 14, 1966
Austria	May 17, 1966	May 25, 1971	Jun 24, 1971	Malaysia	Oct 22, 1965	Aug 8, 1966	Oct 14, 1966
Bangladesh	Nov 20, 1979	Mar 27, 1980	Apr 26, 1980	Mali	Apr 9, 1976	Jan 3, 1978	Feb 2, 1978
Barbados	May 13, 1981	Nov 1, 1983	Dec 1, 1983	Mauritania	Jul 30, 1965	Jan 11, 1966	Oct 14, 1966
Belgium	Dec 15, 1965	Aug 27, 1970	Sep 26, 1970	Mauritius	Jun 2, 1969	Jun 2, 1969	Jul 2, 1969
Benin	Sep 10, 1965	Sep 6, 1966	Oct 14, 1966	Morocco	Oct 11, 1965	May 11, 1967	Jun 10, 1967
Botswana	Jan 15, 1970	Jan 15, 1970	Feb 14, 1970	Nepal	Sep 28, 1965	Jan 7, 1969	Feb 6, 1969
Burkina Fasso	Sep 16, 1965	Aug 29, 1966	Oct 14, 1966	Netherlands	May 25, 1966	Sep 14, 1966	Oct 14, 1966
Burundi	Feb 17, 1967	Nov 5, 1969	Dec 5, 1969	New Zealand	Sep 2, 1970	Apr 2, 1980	May 2, 1980
Cameroon	Sep 23, 1965	Jan 3, 1967	Feb 2, 1967	Niger	Aug 23, 1965	Nov 14, 1966	Dec 14, 1966
Central African Rep.	Aug 26, 1965	Feb 23, 1966	Oct 14, 1966	Nigeria	Jul 13, 1965	Aug 23, 1965	Oct 14, 1966
Chad	May 12, 1966	Aug 29, 1966	Oct 14, 1966	Norway	Jun 24, 1966	Aug 16, 1967	Sep 15, 1967
Comoros	Sep 26, 1978	Nov 7, 1978	Dec 7, 1978	Pakistan	Jul 6, 1965	Sep 15, 1966	Oct 15, 1966
Congo	Dec 27, 1965	Jun 23, 1966	Oct 14, 1966	Papua New Guinea	Oct 20, 1978	Oct 20, 1978	Nov 19, 1978
Costa Rica	Sep 29, 1981			Paraguay	Jul 27, 1981	Jan 7, 1983	Feb 6, 1983
Cyprus	Mar 9, 1966	Nov 25, 1966	Dec 25, 1966	Philippines	Sep 26, 1978	Nov 17, 1978	Dec 17, 1978
Denmark	Oct 11, 1965	Apr 24, 1968	May 24, 1968	Portugal	Aug 4, 1983		
Egypt	Feb 11, 1972	May 3, 1972	Jun 2, 1972	Romania	Sep 6, 1974	Sep 12, 1975	Oct 12, 1975
El Salvador	Jun 9, 1982	Mar 6, 1984	Apr 5, 1984	Rwanda	Apr 21, 1978	Oct 15, 1979	Nov 14, 1979
Ethiopia	Sep 21, 1965			Saudi Arabia	Sep 28, 1979	May 8, 1980	Jun 7, 1980
Fiji	Jul 1, 1977	Aug 11, 1977	Sep 10, 1977	Senegal	Sep 26, 1966	Apr 21, 1967	May 21, 1967
Finland	Jul 14, 1967	Jan 9, 1969	Feb 8, 1969	Seychelles	Feb 16, 1978	Mar 20, 1978	Apr 19, 1978
France	Dec 22, 1965	Aug 21, 1967	Sep 20, 1967	Sierra Leone	Sep 27, 1965	Aug 2, 1966	Oct 14, 1966
Gabon	Sep 21, 1965	Apr 4, 1966	Oct 14, 1966	Singapore	Feb 2, 1968	Oct 14, 1968	Nov 13, 1968
Gambia	Oct 1, 1974	Dec 27, 1974	Jan 26, 1975	Solomon Islands	Nov 12, 1979	Sep 8, 1981	Oct 8, 1981
German Fed. Rep.	Jan 27, 1966	Apr 18, 1969	May 18, 1969	Somalia	Sep 27, 1965	Feb 29, 1968	Mar 30, 1968
Ghana	Nov 26, 1965	Jul 13, 1966	Oct 14, 1966	Sri Lanka	Aug 30, 1967	Oct 12, 1967	Nov 11, 1967
Greece	Mar 16. 1966	Apr 21, 1969	May 21, 1969	St. Lucia	Jun 4, 1984	Jun 4, 1984	Jul 4, 1984
Guinea	Aug 27, 1968	Nov 4, 1968	Dec 4, 1968	Sudan	Mar 15, 1967	Apr 9, 1973	May 9, 1973
Guyana	Jul 3, 1969	Jul 11, 1969	Aug 10, 1969	Swaziland	Nov 3, 1970	Jun 14, 1971	Jul 14, 1971
Iceland	Jul 25, 1966	Jul 25, 1966	Oct 14, 1966	Sweden	Sep 25, 1965	Dec 29, 1966	Jan 28, 1967
Indonesia	Feb 16, 1968	Sep 28, 1968	Oct 28, 1968	Switzerland	Sep 22, 1967	May 15, 1968	Jun 14, 1968
Ireland	Aug 30, 1966	Apr 7, 1981	May 7, 1981	Togo	Jan 24, 1966	Aug 11, 1967	Sep 10, 1967
Israel	Jun 16, 1980	Jun 22, 1983	Jul 22, 1983	Trinidad & Tobago	Oct 5, 1966	Jan 3, 1967	Feb 2, 1967
Italy	Nov 18, 1965	Mar 29, 1971	Apr 28, 1971	Tunisia	May 5, 1965	Jun 22, 1966	Oct 14, 1966
Ivory Coast	Jun 30, 1965	Feb 16, 1966	Oct 14, 1966	Uganda	Jun 7, 1966	Jun 7, 1966	Oct 14, 1966
Jamaica	Jun 23, 1965	Sep 9, 1966	Oct 14, 1966	United Arab			
Japan	Sep 23, 1965	Aug 17, 1967	Sep 16, 1967	Emirates	Dec 23, 1981	Dec 23, 1981	Jan 22, 1982
Jordan	Jul 14, 1972	Oct 30, 1972	Nov 29, 1972	United Kingdom	May 26, 1965	Dec 19, 1966	Jan 18, 1967
Kenya	May 24, 1966	Jan 3, 1967	Feb 2, 1967	United States	Aug 27, 1965	Jun 10, 1966	Oct 14, 1966
Korea	Apr 18, 1966	Feb 21, 1967	Mar 23, 1967	Western Samoa	Feb 3, 1978	Apr 25, 1978	May 25, 1978
Kuwait	Feb 9, 1978	Feb 2, 1979	Mar 4, 1979	Yugoslavia	Mar 21, 1967	Mar 21, 1967	Apr 20, 1967
Lesotho	Sep 19, 1968	Jul 8, 1969	Aug 7, 1969	Zaire	Oct 29, 1968	Apr 29, 1970	May 29, 1970
Liberia	Sep 3, 1965	Jun 16, 1970	Jul 16, 1970	Zambia	Jun 17, 1970	Jun 17, 1970	Jul 17, 1970
Luxembourg	Sep 28, 1965	Jul 30, 1970	Aug 29, 1970				

The center was established by the Convention on the Settlement of Investment Disputes between States and Nationals of Other States, which was opened for signature on March 18, 1965; the convention came into being on October 14, 1966. As of June 30, 1984, ninety-one states had ratified the convention.

The center is governed by an administrative council, which is composed of one representative from each nation that has adhered to the convention. The president of the World Bank is ex officio nonvoting chairman of the council.

The center provides an impartial panel for the settlement of disputes. Panels of conciliators and of arbitrators are available to assist parties in reconciling differences. Failing such conciliation, binding arbitration may be enforced. Each adhering state is obliged to recognize as binding any arbitral award and must designate a court or other authority that will enforce awards.

Any state that is a member of the World Bank may adhere to the convention and participate in the affairs of the center.

INTERNATIONAL CLEARING UNION. An international credit-creating institution proposed by John Maynard Keynes as a prime vehicle for reestablishing postwar liquidity. During World War II, Keynes proposed the clearing union, suggesting it would extend overdraft rights to member nations suffering payment deficits. It was anticipated that the sum total of such overdraft rights would be twenty-six billion U.S. dollars. The clearing union would issue credit in the form of *bancors*, a new international currency unit. Nations with international payment surpluses would be credited in bancors, which would extend overdraft facilities to nations in deficit.

The plan for the international clearing unit did not win strong support by the United States, which, as the only nation capable of sustaining a postwar trade surplus, was expected to be the prime contributor to the fund.

At the Bretton Woods Conference of July 1944, the International Clearing Union/bancor plan was abandoned in favor of establishing the International Monetary Fund and the World Bank.

See BRETTON WOODS AGREEMENT.

INTERNATIONAL COFFEE ORGANIZATION. *See* INTERNATIONAL COMMODITY ORGANIZATION.

INTERNATIONAL COMMODITY AGREEMENT. A multilateral trade agreement aimed at promoting price and supply stability as related to the production of a particular commodity. Such agreements are characterized by the adherence of the principal producing and consuming nations, and the establishment of a commission to ensure the orderly implementation and maintenance of the control features customarily incorporated in the treaty. These controls usually extend to the building

of reserve stocks, export and import controls, long-term purchase arrangements, and the fixing of prices. These measures are designed to mitigate major price fluctuations or supply gluts or shortages.

INTERNATIONAL COMMODITY ORGANIZATION. An organization of the producing nations of a particular commodity. The principal motive for the organization is to foster price collaboration among the producers; the organization may establish buffer stocks to prevent wide swings in the market price of the commodity.

The principal international commodity organizations are listed below.

1. *Association of Natural Rubber Producing Countries* was conceived in Kuala Lumpur, Malaysia, in 1967 and formally organized in 1970 by Sri Lanka, Thailand, India, Malaysia, Indonesia, Singapore, and Papua New Guinea. In 1979 the members and Vietnam agreed to enter into an international commodity agreement beween producing and consuming nations with a buffer stock of 550,000 tons to be established.

2. *Intergovernmental Council of Copper Exporting Countries,* organized in Paris in 1967, includes Chile, Indonesia, Peru, Zaire, and Zambia as full members; Australia, Papua New Guinea, and Yugoslavia are associate members. Spurred by the successes of OPEC in controlling prices, the copper producers attempted to increase prices by withholding supply; the efforts were unsuccessful. An attempt was made in 1979 to establish a commodity agreement with consuming nations, but the agreement did not proceed because of U.S. insistence upon a three million ton buffer stock to stabilize prices.

3. *International Bauxite Association* commenced activities in 1975. It embraces Australia, Dominican Republic, Ghana, Guinea, Guyana, Haiti, Indonesia, Jamaica, Sierra Leone, Surinam, and Yugoslavia. The principal efforts of the organization are directed toward supporting the market price of alumina. In 1979 the association agreed to begin a dialogue with consuming nations.

4. *International Coffee Organization* is the administrator of the International Coffee Agreement of 1976, an international commodity agreement among the principal coffee-producing and consuming nations designed to control the amount of coffee produced and sold internationally. The agreement establishes production objectives and quotas; administration is performed by the International Coffee Council. The agreement expires September 30, 1986, unless renewed by the signatory states.

Exporting members of the agreement are:

Angola	Cameroon
Benin	Central African Republic
Bolivia	Colombia
Brazil	Congo
Burundi	Costa Rica

Dominican Republic	Malawi
Ecuador	Mexico
El Salvador	Nigeria
Ethiopia	Panama
Gabon	Papua New Guinea
Ghana	Paraguay
Guatemala	Peru
Haiti	Rwanda
Honduras	Sierra Leone
India	Tanzania
Indonesia	Togo
Ivory Coast	Trinidad
Kenya	Uganda
Liberia	Venezuela
Malagasy Republic	Zaire

Importing members are:

Australia	Israel
Austria	Italy
Belgium (and Luxem-	Japan
bourg)	Netherlands
Canada	New Zealand
Cyprus	Norway
Denmark	Portugal
Finland	Spain
France	Sweden
German Federal	Switzerland
Republic	United Kingdom
Hungary	United States
Ireland	Yugoslavia

5. *International Cotton Advisory Committee* originated at a 1939 meeting of ten producing nations. In 1945 the group was opened to all interested nations. Its principal efforts are directed to improvements in technology and market promotion of cotton. Current members are:

Argentina	Ivory Coast
Australia	Japan
Austria	Korea
Belgium	Mexico
Brazil	Netherlands
Cameroon	Nicaragua
Chad	Nigeria
Colombia	Norway
Denmark	Pakistan
Egypt	Peru
El Salvador	Philippines
Finland	Portugal
France	Spain
German Federal	Sudan
Republic	Sweden
Greece	Switzerland
Guatemala	Syria
Honduras	Tanzania
Hungary	Turkey
India	Uganda
Iran	USSR
Iraq	United Kingdom
Israel	United States
Italy	Yugoslavia

6. *International Lead and Zinc Study Group* was formed in 1959. The group devotes most of its efforts to statistical and technical matters. Members are:

Algeria	Mexico
Australia	Morocco
Austria	Netherlands
Belgium	Norway
Bulgaria	Peru
Canada	Poland
Czechoslovakia	South Africa
Denmark	Spain
Finland	Sweden
German Federal	Tunisia
Republic	United Kingdom
Hungary	United States
India	USSR
Ireland	Yugoslavia
Italy	Zambia
Japan	

7. *International Olive Oil Council* administers the International Olive Oil Agreement, the third of which was implemented in 1980; previous accords had been adopted in 1956 and 1963. The organization is concerned with balancing supply and demand, product standardization, and technical cooperation. The producing members are Algeria, Greece, Morocco, Portugal, Spain, Turkey, Tunisia, and Yugoslavia. The importing members are Egypt, the European Economic Community, Libya, and Panama.

8. *International Sugar Organization* was formed to implement the International Sugar Agreement of 1977, designed to establish upper and lower price limits within which sugar prices would respond to market forces. The price range established is 11¢ to 21¢ per pound. Reserve stocks would be built over a three-year period, and the reserves would be released and export quotas imposed as the prices approach the lower limit. Similarly as prices approach the upper limit, the manufacturing quotas of the producing states would be increased. Interest-free loans of 1.5¢ per pound would be provided to nations obliged to hold reserve stocks; this fund would be financed by a 2.8¢ per pound tax on all free-market sugar sales.

Exporting members are:

Argentina	Guyana
Australia	Haiti
Austria	Honduras
Bangladesh	India
Barbados	Indonesia
Bolivia	Ivory Coast
Brazil	Jamaica
Colombia	Kenya
Costa Rica	Malawi
Cuba	Mauritius
Dominican Republic	Mexico
Ecuador	Mozambique
El Salvador	Nicaragua
Fiji	Panama
Guatemala	Paraguay

Pakistan
Peru
Philippines
South Africa
Swaziland
Thailand
Trinidad

Uganda
United Kingdom (for
  Anguilla, Belize, Saint
  Kitts)
Venezuela
Yugoslavia

Importing members are:

Bulgaria
Canada
Peru
Philippines
South Africa
Swaziland
Thailand

Trinidad
Uganda
Norway
Singapore
Sweden
United States
USSR

9. *International Tin Council* implements the fifth International Tin Agreement, which came into force in 1977. Agreements are adopted for periods of five years and cannot be extended. The principal objective of the group is to foster price equilibrium. Plans were advanced to establish a seventy-thousand-ton buffer stock.

Producing members are:

Australia
Bolivia
Indonesia
Malaysia

Nigeria
Thailand
Zaire

Consuming members are:

Austria
Belgium (and Luxem-
  bourg)
Bulgaria
Canada
Czechoslovakia
Denmark
France
German Federal
  Republic
Hungary
India

Ireland
Italy
Japan
Netherlands
Norway
Poland
Romania
Spain
Turkey
United Kingdom
USSR
Yugoslavia

10. *International Wheat Organization* was established in 1949 to promote trade in wheat and flour and to stabilize the trade. Various wheat agreements of 1949, 1953, 1956, 1967, and 1971 have been implemented by the organization; the group provides food aid to developing nations.

Exporting members are:

Argentina
Australia
Canada
Greece
Kenya

Spain
Sweden
United States
USSR

Importing members are:

Algeria
Austria
Barbados
Bolivia
Brazil
Costa Rica

Cuba
Dominican Republic
Ecuador
Egypt
El Salvador
Finland

Guatemala
India
Iran
Iraq
Israel
Japan
Korea
Lebanon
Libya
Malta
Mauritius
Morocco
Nigeria
Norway
Pakistan

Panama
Peru
Portugal
Saudi Arabia
South Africa
Switzerland
Syria
Trinidad
Tunisia
Turkey
United Kingdom (for
  certain overseas
  territories)
Vatican
Venezuela

INTERNATIONAL CONVENTION ON THE SIMPLIFICATION AND HARMONIZATION OF CUSTOMS PROCEDURES. *See* KYOTO CONVENTION.

INTERNATIONAL COTTON ADVISORY COMMITTEE. *See* INTERNATIONAL COMMODITY ORGANIZATION.

INTERNATIONAL DEPOSITORY RECEIPT. A document issued by a bank or other trustee evidencing that it holds on behalf of a named party a given number of shares of stock in a foreign firm. The IDR is issued in lieu of actual share certificates for various reasons: to circumvent Securities and Exchange Commission requirements concerning registration of stock issues (because many foreign issues are in bearer form, whereas IDRs can be registered) or to facilitate local purchase and sale of shares. In the United States the term *American depository receipt* applies; similarly, *European depository receipt* is the applicable term in Western Europe.

INTERNATIONAL DEVELOPMENT ASSOCIATION. *See* WORLD BANK GROUP.

INTERNATIONAL ENERGY AGENCY. An autonomous group within the ORGANIZATION FOR ECONOMIC COOPERATION AND DEVELOPMENT *(q.v.)* established in 1974 to coordinate the responses of the developed, oil-importing countries to the 1973 oil embargo and subsequent price escalations.

With the commencement of IEA operations in 1976, the group has directed its efforts to the following projects: agreed limitations on oil imports, a system of emergency sharing within the Emergency Oil Allocation System, enhanced conservation efforts, and the development of alternative energy sources.

Membership in the IEA consists of:

Australia
Austria
Belgium
Canada
Denmark
German Federal
  Republic
Greece
Ireland
Italy
Japan

Luxembourg
Netherlands
New Zealand
Norway
Spain
Sweden
Switzerland
Turkey
United Kingdom
United States

INTERNATIONAL FINANCE CORPORATION.
See WORLD BANK GROUP.

INTERNATIONAL GOLD BULLION STANDARD.
A GOLD BULLION STANDARD *(q.v.)* that permits redemption of currency into gold only for purposes of export.

INTERNATIONAL IMPORT CERTIFICATE/ DELIVERY VERIFICATION SYSTEM.
A control mechanism established by certain Western countries to prevent diversion of strategic commodities to communist-bloc countries. The system was devised by COCOM *(q.v.)*, an informal working group of the United States, Great Britain, France, Italy, and the Benelux countries established in 1949 to control strategic exports to communist states; the original group has been expanded to include Canada, Federal Republic of Germany, Greece, Turkey, Norway, Denmark, Portugal, and Japan.

The system is based upon an agreement among the adhering states that they will monitor the importation and disposition of strategic commodities exported under license by any other signatory state. The principal documentary controls are the *international import certificate*, issued by the importing country upon request, confirming that that government will exercise control over the named commodities and will undertake to prevent unlawful diversions; and the *delivery verification certificate*, issued after actual importation of the restricted merchandise, certifying that the goods have actually been accounted for or disposed of as specified in the issuing country's export license. The second document is required on a selective basis by the U.S. Department of Commerce Office of Export Administration.

See EXPORT CONTROL ACT, EXPORT CONTROL STATEMENT. (*See* figure.)

INTERNATIONAL INVESTMENT BANK.
A multinational development bank, membership of which is comprised of the Soviet Union and its allies. The bank was formed in 1970 to foster "economic efficiency and intensification" in the member states. The authorized capital of the bank is 1,071,300,000 *transferable rubles*, of which 374,480,000 is paid in.

The preponderance of projects funded are in the areas of heavy manufacturing and infrastructure development, high technology research and development, and agricultural productivity.

The bank may grant credits to (1) banks, economic organizations, and enterprises in member countries, (2) international economic organizations, and (3) bank and economic organizations of third world countries. Since its founding, the bank has supported 83 projects to a value of ten billion transferable rubles. It is estimated that during the period 1972-82, bank-funded projects have resulted in fifteen billion rubles' worth of exports among the member countries.

Headquarters of the bank is in Moscow. In 1984, the following states were members of the bank:

Bulgaria	Mongolia
Cuba	Poland
Czechoslovakia	Romania
German Democratic	USSR
Republic	Vietnam
Hungary	

INTERNATIONAL LEAD AND ZINC STUDY GROUP.
See INTERNATIONAL COMMODITY ORGANIZATION.

INTERNATIONAL MARITIME ORGANIZATION.
A specialized agency of the United Nations concerned with maritime safety and protection of the marine environment. The IMO was created as the result of the United Nations Maritime Conference of 1948; the convention creating the IMO did not, however, come into force until 1958. Prior to 1982, the organization was known as the Inter-Governmental Maritime Consultative Organization.

The organization is governed by an assembly, which meets every two years, and in which every member state (121 members and 1 associate as of 1981) enjoys one vote. Between assembly sessions, a council of twenty-four members, elected by the assembly, directs the affairs of the organization.

Since its inception, the IMO has promoted conventions and has adopted numerous codes relating to maritime affairs. Details of IMO agreements in force can be found in Appendix D7.

In 1984, the membership of the International Maritime Organization was as follows:

Algeria	Equatorial Guinea
Angola	Ethiopia
Argentina	Fiji
Australia	Finland
Austria	France
Bahamas	Gabon
Bahrain	Gambia
Bangladesh	German Democratic
Barbados	Republic
Belgium	German Federal
Benin	Republic
Brazil	Ghana
Bulgaria	Greece
Burma	Guatemala
Cameroon	Guinea
Canada	Guinea-Bissau
Cape Verde	Guyana
Chile	Haiti
China	Honduras
Colombia	Hungary
Congo	Iceland
Costa Rica	India
Cuba	Indonesia
Cyprus	Iran
Czechoslovakia	Iraq
Denmark	Ireland
Djibouti	Israel
Dominica	Italy
Dominican Republic	Ivory Coast
Ecuador	Jamaica
Egypt	Japan
El Salvador	Jordan

FORM ITA-645P/ATF-4522/DSP-53 (REV. 5-84)   Form Approved: OMB No. 0625-0064 - Modele approuve: OMB No. 0625-0064

U.S. DEPARTMENT OF COMMERCE INTERNATIONAL TRADE ADMINISTRATION U.S. DEPARTMENT OF THE TREASURY BUREAU OF ALCOHOL, TOBACCO AND FIREARMS U.S. DEPARTMENT OF STATE OFFICE OF MUNITIONS CONTROL	INTERNATIONAL IMPORT CERTIFICATE (CERTIFICAT INTERNATIONAL D'IMPORTATION)

NOTE: Read instructions on the reverse side before completing and submitting this form. (Lire les instructions au verso avant de remplir et de présenter la présente formule.)

Certificate Number

1. U.S. Importer/Importateur (Name and address—Nom et adresse)

FOR U.S. GOVERNMENT USE (Réservé pour le Gouvernement des Etats-Unis)

2. Exporter/Exportateur (Name and address—Nom et adresse)

If this form has been approved by the Department of Commerce or the Department of State, it is not valid unless the official seal of the Department of Commerce, or the Department of State, appears in this space. If this form is approved by the Treasury Department, a seal is not required. (Ci cette forme été approuvée par le Ministère du Commerce, ou le Ministère d'Etat elle n'est pas valide à moins qu'un sceau officiel du Ministère du Commerce ou le Ministère d'Etat soit apposé dans cette espace. Ci cette forme est approuvée par le Ministère du Trésor, un sceau official n'est pas nécessaire.

3.

Description of goods (Désignation de la Marchandise)	TSUS Anno. No. (Numéro de la liste)	Quantity (Quantité)	Value (Valeur) (FOB, CIF, etc.)

4. Representation and undertaking of U.S. importer or principal

The undersigned hereby represents that he has undertaken to import into the United States of America under a U.S. Consumption Entry or U.S. Warehouse Entry the commodities in quantities described above, or, if the commodities are not so imported into the United States of America, that he will not divert, transship, or reexport them to another destination except with explicit approval of the Department of Commerce, the Department of State, or of the Department of the Treasury, as appropriate. The undersigned also undertakes to notify the appropriate U.S. Department immediately of any changes of fact or intention set forth herein. If a delivery verification is required, the undersigned also undertakes to obtain such verification and make disposition of it in accordance with such requirement. **Any false statement willfully made in this declaration is punishable by fine and imprisonment.** (See excerpts from U.S. Code on reverse side.)

Déclaration et engagement de l'importateur ou du commettant des Etats-Unis

Le soussigné déclare par les présentes qu'il a pris l'engagement d'importer aux Etats-Unis d'Amerique, en vertu d'une Déclaration américaine de Mise en Consommation, ou d'une Déclaration américaine d'Entrée en entrepôt, la quantité de produits ci-dessus, et que, dans le cas où ces produits ne seraient pas ainsi importés aux Etats-Unis d'Amerique, il ne les détournera, ne les transbordera, ni les réexportera à destination d'un autre lieu, si ce n'est avec l'approbation formelle du Ministère du Comerce, du Ministère d'Etat ou Ministère du Tresor, comme requise. Le soussigné prend également l'engagement d'aviser le Ministère intéresse des Etats-Unis de tous changements survenus quant aux faits ou à l'intention énoncés dans la présente déclaration. Si demande est faite d'une confirmation de la livraison, le soussigné prend également l'engagement d'obtenir cette confirmation et d'en disposer de la manière prescrite par cette demande. **Toute fousse declaration faite intentionnellement expose l'auteur aux pénalités prévues par la loi.** (Voir l'extrait du Code des Etats-Unis au verso.)

Type or Print
(Prière d'écrire
à la machine ou
en caractères
d imprimerie)

Type or Print
(Prière d'écrire
a la machine ou
en caractères
d'imprimerie)

Name of Firm or Corporation
(Nom de la Firme ou de la Société)

Name and Title of Authorized Official
(Nom et titre de l'agent ou employé autorisé)

Signature of Authorized Official
(Signature de l'agent ou employé autorisé)

Date of Signature
(Date de la signature)

This document ceases to be valid unless presented to the competent foreign authorities within six months from its date of issue. (Le présent document perd sa validité s'il n'est pas remis aux autorités étrangères compétentes dans un délai de six mois à compter de sa délivrance.)

No import certification may be obtained unless this International Import Certificate has been completed and filed with the appropriate U.S. Government agency (Department of Commerce: 50 U.S.C. app. §2411, E.O. 12214, 15 C.F.R. §368; Department of the Treasury; 22 U.S.C. §2778, E.O. 11959, 27 C.F.R. §47; Department of State: 22 U.S.C. 2778, 2779, E.O. 11958, 22 C.F.R. §123). Information furnished herewith is subject to the provisions of Section 12(c) of the Export Administration Act of 1979, 50 U.S.C. app. 2411(c), and its unauthorized disclosure is prohibited by law.

FOR U.S. GOVERNMENT USE (Réservé pour le Gouvernement des Etats-Unis)

Certification: This is to certify that the above declaration was made to the U.S. Department of Commerce, State, or Treasury through the undersigned designated official thereof and that a copy of this certificate is placed in the official files.

Certification: Il est certifié par les présentes que la déclaration ci-dessus a été faite au Ministère du Commerce, d'Etat, ou du Trésor des Etats-Unis par l'intermédiaire du fonctionnaire compétent soussigné et qu'une copie de ce certificat a été placée dans les archives officielles.

Designated Commerce, State, or Treasury Official (Fonctionnaire competent du Ministère du Commerce, d'Etat, ou du Trésor)   Date

International Import Certificate

Kampuchea
Korea (Republic of)
Kenya
Kuwait
Lebanon
Liberia
Libya
Madagascar
Malaysia
Maldives
Malta
Mauritania
Mauritius
Mexico
Morocco
Mozambique
Nepal
Netherlands
New Zealand
Nicaragua
Nigeria
Norway
Oman
Pakistan
Panama
Papua New Guinea
Peru
Philippines
Poland
Portugal
Qatar
Romania
St. Lucia

St. Vincent and
   Grenadines
Saudi Arabia
Senegal
Seychelles
Sierra Leone
Singapore
Somalia
Spain
Sri Lanka
Sudan
Surinam
Sweden
Switzerland
Syria
Tanzania
Thailand
Togo
Trinidad and Tobago
Tunisia
Turkey
USSR
United Arab Emirates
United Kingdom
United States
Uruguay
Venezuela
Yemen (Arab Republic)
Yemen (Democratic
   Republic)
Yugoslavia
Zaire

INTERNATIONAL MONETARY FUND. An international financial institution established by the BRETTON WOODS AGREEMENT *(q.v.)* in 1944 to preserve world monetary stability and foster the expansion of international trade. The IMF commenced operations on March 1, 1947, and became a specialized agency of the United Nations in November of that year.

The principal efforts of the IMF are directed toward maintaining exchange rate stability and aiding member states in overcoming balance of payments difficulties. To accomplish these objectives, each member establishes a par value for its currency, in terms of gold or an acceptable currency redeemable in gold; a nation may not change its par value without consulation and/or permission of the fund. Each member is assigned a quota, or *subscription,* in the fund according to the respective size of the nation's economy; the quota share (25 percent in gold, 75 percent in national currency) must be deposited with the IMF.

Nations requiring financing to accommodate balance of payments shortfalls, or for other reasons, may borrow up to 25 percent of their subscription; borrowings beyond this *gold tranche* require special permission. Chronic balance of payment deficits in the late 1950s and early 1960s resulted in increased pressure on the resources of the IMF. In response to these pressures, the ten principal creditor nations (commonly known as the Paris Club, or Group of Ten) agreed to lend up to six billion U.S. dollars in national currencies to augment IMF resources; these "General Agreements to Borrow" have been renewed several times since their inception in 1962.

Recognizing that international liquidity required further augmentation, in 1969 the fund created SPECIAL DRAWING RIGHTS *(q.v.)* or SDRs, as unconditional reserve assets. The SDR was established on par with the U.S. dollar, with one SDR equal to 1/35 ounce of gold. The dollar has since been devalued in terms of gold, but the SDR has retained its original relationship to gold; at the beginning of January 1985, 1 SDR = U.S. $1.28.

In the first allocation, 3.4 billion SDRs were issued to IMF members, in proportion to their respective allocations within the fund. A nation in need of financing may assign its SDRs to another member in return for hard currency; each member is obliged to accept SDRs up to three times its allocation.

The IMF was confronted with a crisis in 1971 when the United States unilaterally devalued the dollar in terms of gold. This act, plus U.S. suspension of redemption of dollars for gold, resulted in an international monetary crisis. The dollar had been the basis of the world economy; the suspension of convertibility into gold left nations without a measure of value for the dollar or their own currency, with the result that exchange rates fluctuated widely. In response to this condition, the IMF convened an international monetary conference at Washington in December 1971. From these discussions emerged the so-called Smithsonian Agreements, whereby the devaluation of the dollar was formalized, par values were adjusted, and currencies were permitted to *float* within a band on either side of the par value before intervention was undertaken to stabilize the rates. In 1972 further adjustments were made to the dollar; the *band* scheme broke down in favor of a wider float of major currencies.

In 1974 the IMF established the Oil Facility in response to balance of payment shortfalls resulting from significant oil price increases; before its elimination in 1976, fifty-five nations received assistance through this special fund. Over the past several years, other specialized lending programs have been established, including the Buffer Stock Facility (1969), Compensatory Financing Facility (1963), Extended Facility (1974), and Trust Fund for Less Developed Countries (1976). The Trust Fund has been financed with sales of IMF gold; apart from serving to raise cash for the trust fund, the gold sales are aimed at reducing the impact of gold in international monetary affairs.

The IMF is managed by a board of governors, with one governor and an alternate from each member. Because voting power is a function of a member's quota, which is determined by the size of a nation's economy, control of the IMF resides with the industrial states. Effective management of the fund's affairs is vested in a board of executive directors; the twenty executive directors sit in continuous session. Headquarters of the IMF are in Washington.

Members of the International Monetary Fund and their respective quota shares in millions SDR as of November 15, 1984, were:

Afghanistan	86.7
Algeria	623.1
Antigua and Barbuda	5.0
Argentina	1113.0
Australia	1619.2
Austria	775.6
Bahamas	66.4
Bahrain	48.5
Bangladesh	287.5
Barbados	34.1
Belgium	2080.4
Belize	9.5
Benin	31.3
Bhutan	2.5
Bolivia	90.7
Botswana	22.1
Brazil	1461.3
Burkina Fasso	31.6
Burma	137.0
Burundi	42.7
Cameroon	92.7
Canada	2941.0
Cape Verde	4.5
Central African Republic	30.4
Chad	30.6
Chile	440.5
China	2390.9
Colombia	394.2
Comoros	4.5
Congo	37.3
Costa Rica	84.1
Cyprus	69.7
Denmark	711.0
Djibouti	8.0
Dominica	4.0
Dominican Republic	112.1
Ecuador	150.7
Egypt	463.4
El Salvador	89.0
Equatorial Guinea	18.4
Ethiopia	70.6
Fiji	36.5
Finland	574.9
France	4482.8
Gabon	73.1
Gambia, The	17.1
German Federal Republic	5403.7
Ghana	204.5
Greece	277.5
Grenada	6.0
Guatemala	108.0
Guinea	57.9
Guinea-Bissau	7.5
Guyana	49.2
Haiti	44.1
Honduras	67.8
Hungary	530.7
Iceland	59.6
India	2207.7
Indonesia	1009.7
Iran	660.0
Iraq	504.0
Ireland	343.4
Israel	446.6
Italy	2909.1
Ivory Coast	165.5
Jamaica	145.5
Japan	4223.3
Jordan	73.9
Kampuchea	25.0
Kenya	142.0
Korea, Rep. of	462.8
Kuwait	635.3
Laos	29.3
Lebanon	78.7
Lesotho	15.1
Liberia	71.3
Libya	515.7
Luxembourg	77.0
Madagascar	66.4
Malawi	37.2
Malaysia	550.6
Maldives	2.0
Mali	50.8
Malta	45.1
Mauritania	33.9
Mauritius	53.6
Mexico	1165.5
Morocco	306.6
Mozambique	63.0
Nepal	37.3
Netherlands	2264.8
New Zealand	461.6
Nicaragua	68.2
Niger	33.7
Nigeria	849.5
Norway	699.0
Oman	63.1
Pakistan	546.3
Panama	102.2
Papua New Guinea	65.9
Paraguay	48.4
Peru	330.9
Philippines	440.4
Portugal	376.6
Qatar	114.9
Romania	523.4
Rwanda	43.8
St. Christopher and Nevis	4.5
St. Lucia	7.5
St. Vincent	4.0
Sao Tome and Principe	4.0
Saudi Arabia	3202.4
Senegal	85.1
Seychelles	3.0
Sierra Leone	57.9
Singapore	92.4
Solomon Islands	5.0
Somalia	44.2
South Africa	915.7
Spain	1286.0
Sri Lanka	223.1
Sudan	169.7
Surinam	49.3
Swaziland	24.7
Sweden	1064.3

Syrian Arab Rep.	139.1
Tanzania	107.1
Thailand	386.6
Togo	38.4
Trinidad and Tobago	170.1
Tunisia	138.2
Turkey	429.1
Uganda	99.6
United Arab Emirates	202.6
United Kingdom	6194.0
United States	17918.3
Uruguay	163.8
Vanuatu	9.0
Venezuela	1371.5
Vietnam	176.8
Western Samoa	6.0
Yemen Arab Rep.	43.3
Yemen, People's Dem. Rep. of	77.2
Yugoslavia	613.0
Zaire	291.0
Zambia	270.3
Zimbabwe	191.0

INTERNATIONAL OLIVE OIL COUNCIL. *See* INTERNATIONAL COMMODITY ORGANIZATION.

INTERNATIONAL PATENT CLASSIFICATION AGREEMENT. A system for the classification of patents, created to promote uniformity in classifying technological innovations.

The International Patent Classification System segments technology into eight categories, with a total of 52,000 subdivisions, each of which consists of Roman letters and Arabic numerals. The system is essential to searches involving the novelty of an invention, and to international patent filings.

The agreement was adopted in 1971; it is administered by the WORLD INTELLECTUAL PROPERTY ORGANIZATION *(q.v.)* and is open to any state adhering to the PARIS CONVENTION FOR THE PROTECTION OF INDUSTRIAL PROPERTY *(q.v.)*. On March 15, 1983, the following states were party to the agreement:

Australia	Italy
Austria	Japan
Belgium	Luxembourg
Brazil	Monaco
Czechoslovakia	Netherlands
Denmark	Norway
Egypt	Portugal
Finland	Spain
France	Surinam
German Democratic	Sweden
Republic	Switzerland
German Federal Republic	United Kingdom
Ireland	United States
Israel	

INTERNATIONAL PRICE INDEX. A price index that serves as a standard to measure inflation in industrialized countries. The index consists of the C.I.F. value (in U.S. dollars) of exports of industrial country manufactures to developing countries.

INTERNATIONAL RESERVES. Gold, hard currencies, and SPECIAL DRAWING RIGHTS *(q.v.)* issued by the INTERNATIONAL MONETARY FUND *(q.v.)* which can be used to settle a nation's international obligations.

INTERNATIONAL SOCIAL SECURITY AGREEMENTS. Governmental agreements to address the problems that arise when a person who has worked in more than one country during the course of a career pays taxes into, and claims benefits under, the social security scheme of more than one nation. The primary objectives of international social security agreements are to avoid double social security taxes and coverage for the same work and to assure that social security credits will be accumulated for work performed in other countries.

In 1984 the United States had three social security agreements in force: with Italy (1978), Federal Republic of Germany (1979), and Switzerland (1980). Agreements have been concluded with Norway, Belgium, and Canada but await Congressional action. An agreement with Great Britain has been negotiated but not yet signed.

INTERNATIONAL SUGAR ORGANIZATION. *See* INTERNATIONAL COMMODITY ORGANIZATION.

INTERNATIONAL TANKER NOMINAL FREIGHT SCALE. A schedule of nominal rates for movements of tankers between world ports. Publication was ceased in 1969; it has been succeeded by WORLDSCALE *(q.v.)*.

INTERNATIONAL TIN COUNCIL. *See* INTERNATIONAL COMMODITY ORGANIZATION.

INTERNATIONAL TRADE COMMISSION. *See* UNITED STATES INTERNATIONAL TRADE COMMISSION.

INTERNATIONAL TRAFFIC IN ARMS REGULATIONS. Known commonly by the acronym ITAR, a body of Federal regulations designed to restrain, regulate, and control the manufacture, exportation, and importation of military equipment and weapons. The regulations which derive their authority primarily from which the Arms Export Control Act of 1976 (22 U.S.C. 2778) provide that:

The President is authorized to control, in furtherance of world peace and the security and foreign policy of the United States, the export and import of arms, including technical data relating thereto [and] to designate those articles which shall be considered as arms, ammunition, and implements of war, including technical data relating thereto.

By virtue of several executive orders, the president has delegated his authority under the law to the secretaries of state and the treasury; both of these officials are obliged to seek the concurrence of the secretary of defense in all modifications of the list of articles to be controlled.

The articles subject to controls are enumerated in the U.S. Munitions List. U.S. manufacturers and exporters of articles on the Munitions List are obliged to register with the Office of Munitions Control, Department of State, by filing Form DSP-

UNITED STATES OF AMERICA	DEPARTMENT OF STATE	DEPARTMENT USE ONLY

APPLICATION FOR REGISTRATION

PM/MC DATE REC'D.　　ESC/C DATE REC'D.

NEW PM''

1. Applicant's name, address & tel. no.

ABC Manufacturing Company
1111 15th Street, NW
Foggybottom, Florida   32999

Telephone no.: 104/567-8910

2. Current PM/MC applicant code: 576-6978

3. $ 500.00 enclosed for 5 years' registration

4. Applicant is: ☐ individual ☐ partnership ☒ company ☐ corporation

5. Applicant is: ☒ manufacturer and/or ☐ exporter of Munitions List articles

6. Incorporation or commencement of business: date 7/16/41 city & state Foggybottom, Florida

7. Principal executive officers, partners, owners:

Name	Home address	Position	Citizenship
Ronald H. Smith	132 Hunt Lane Foggybottom,Florida 32999	President	U.S.
Robert A. Fish	2964 Chinook Trail Foggybottom,Florida 32999	Vice-President	U.S.
Max P. Simcox	45 Parrot Court Foggybottom,Florida 32999	Secretary/ Treasurer	U.S.

8. Munitions List articles manufactured and/or exported

Category	Commodity	Purchasing U.S. Gov't. Agency
I	disintegrator ray guns	Army
XI	radar	Army
XII	laser equipment	Army

9. Names & addresses of applicant's wholly- and partially-owned U.S. subsidiaries

Acme Products Co., 17 Knox St., San Francisco, CA 96469

10. Names & addresses of applicant's wholly-and partially-owned foreign subsidiaries

ABC Products, Ltd., 69 Bassin Court, London, England

11. Name, address & tel. no. of applicant's Washington, DC representative
John A. Jones
1799 North Ft.Myer Dr.
Arlington, VA   22209

12. Name, address & tel. no. of applicant's parent company

None

13. Does applicant submit separate Federal income tax forms? ☒ yes ☐ no

14. Applicant's statement:

Max P. Simcox
(typed name)

Under penalty according to Federal law, I, warrant the truth of all statements made herein.

(See 22 CFR 127)

Max P. Simcox
(signature)

Secretary/Treasurer
(title)

6/7/76
(date)

15. Corporate seal:

FORM DSP-9
3-76 (DESTROY PREVIOUS EDITIONS)　　　**1—APPLICATION**　　　FORM APPROVED OMB NO. 47-R0020

Department of State Application for Registration

9. Importers register with the Bureau of Alcohol, Tobacco, and Firearms, Department of the Treasury, by filing Form 4587. Registration fees for manufacturers, exporters, and importers are: one year, $125; two years, $250; three years, $350; four years, $425; five years, $500.

In addition to registration, U.S. manufacturers and importers are required to obtain occupational licenses from the Bureau of Alcohol, Tobacco, and Firearms. Exporters do not require an occupational license, but must obtain a transaction license from the Office of Munitions Control for each export shipment.

The Gun Control Act of 1968 directs the secretary of the treasury to prepare a listing of weapons suitable for importation into the United States; this authority has been delegated to the director, Bureau of Alcohol, Tobacco, and Firearms. The listing so prepared constitutes the U.S. Munitions Import List, which is a sublisting within the U.S. Munitions List.

(The U.S. Munitions List and U.S. Munitions Import List can be found in Appendix D3.)

INTERNATIONAL UNION OF CREDIT AND INVESTMENT INSURERS. *See* BERNE UNION.

INTERNATIONAL WHEAT ORGANIZATION. *See* INTERNATIONAL COMMODITY ORGANIZATION.

INTERVENTION. A process within the framework of the COMMON AGRICULTURAL POLICY *(q.v.)* of the European Economic Community whereby the EEC will purchase certain commodities currently selling below a stipulated *target price*. The price actually paid is the *intervention price*. Intervention is employed to ensure that EEC farmers receive a fair income, thereby discouraging the conversion of land from agricultural to other uses.

INTERVENTION PRICE. The price at which the European Economic Community, in accordance with the COMMON AGRICULTURAL POLICY *(q.v.)*, will intervene in the market to buy excess agricultural produce, thereby protecting EEC farmers.

INVENTORY CHANGE. *See* INVENTORY INVESTMENT.

INVENTORY INVESTMENT. The aggregate national increases or decreases, expressed in monetary terms, of inventories held by the private sector. Also known as *inventory change*, an increase or decrease in private sector inventories not offset by current consumption is viewed as an investment in the economy.

INVESTMENT BILL. A bill of exchange purchased at a discount and held to maturity.

INVESTMENT EDGE. *See* EDGE ACT CORPORATION.

INVISIBLES. *Synonymous with* INVISIBLE EXPORTS AND IMPORTS *(q.v.)*.

INVISIBLE EXPORTS AND IMPORTS. Nontangible services (e.g., shipping, insurance, tourism) that are provided on behalf of foreigners and through which foreign exchange is earned or spent.

INVISIBLE HAND DOCTRINE. A concept articulated by Adam Smith in *The Wealth of Nations*, holding that all individuals are motivated by self-interest, which, in the absence of government controls on individual economic pursuits, will produce a condition of competitiveness ultimately beneficial to all.

INVOICE. A statement of charges, usually on a preprinted form, given by a seller to a buyer covering a specific transaction. Invoices commonly contain the following data: name and address of purchaser; description of merchandise, including prices; place at which goods were delivered or point to which they were shipped; date of the transaction; and terms of sale.

Some invoices, particularly those arising from international transactions, may be highly detailed, including specifics of the currency used for billing, shipping arrangements, special markings on the goods or packaging, as well as statements of correctness, purity, or other stipulations required by governmental and/or customs authorities.

Several types of invoices are common in international trade.

1. *Commercial invoice* is issued by the seller, on his standard invoice form, to the buyer. Depending upon the importing country and the type of transaction involved, this invoice may not be acceptable to the authorities of the importing country.

2. *Preliminary (or provisional) invoice* is issued when final details of the transaction are not known at the time of shipment, or when the goods are subject to rejection by the purchaser.

3. *Final invoice* is issued to finalize a transaction in cases where preliminary invoices were previously issued.

4. *Memorandum invoice* is a brief statement of charges, perhaps in letter form, not intended by the seller as a formal billing, but used as such by the purchaser.

5. *Customs invoice* is a special invoice, in addition to a commercial invoice, required by the customs authorities of the importing nation. This invoice is prepared on a prescribed form, which may be obtained from commercial stationers. The purpose of this type of invoice is to obtain data in addition to that normally contained in commercial invoices (*see* figure).

6. *Consular invoice* is a special type of customs invoice. In addition to the invoice required by the importing country, the consular form requires special validation, or *legalization* by the importer's counsel. The purposes of the consular invoice are to ensure compliance with import licensing, to ensure an orderly system of import declaration for the ease

REVENUE CANADA
CUSTOMS AND EXCISE
RC-CE 46.1-2/79

REVENU CANADA
DOUANES ET ACCISE

CANADA CUSTOMS INVOICE

PAGE   PAGES
OF

1. VENDOR (NAME & ADDRESS)	2. DATE OF DIRECT SHIPMENT TO CANADA	3. INVOICE NO. AND DATE
ACME EXPORTING CO. 123 Main Street Small Town, CT.	12-15-82	15236, dated 12-14-82

4. OTHER REFERENCES (INCLUDE PURCHASER'S ORDER NO.)

AEO# 014/12/82

5. CONSIGNEE (NAME & ADDRESS)	6. PURCHASER (IF OTHER THAN CONSIGNEE AND/OR IMPORTER)
IMPORT, LTD. 1001 Meyerside Drive Missisauga, Ontario Canada	SAME

8. IMPORTER (NAME & ADDRESS)

Same

7. COUNTRY OF ORIGIN OF GOODS

JAPAN

IF SHIPMENT INCLUDES GOODS OF DIFFERENT ORIGINS ENTER ORIGINS AGAINST ITEMS IN 16

10. TRANSPORTATION: GIVE MODE AND PLACE OF DIRECT SHIPMENT TO CANADA

MAISLIN TRUCK to Missisauga, Ontario

9. CONDITIONS OF SALE & TERMS OF PAYMENT

Net 30 Days

11. CURRENCY OF SETTLEMENT

U.S. Dollars

12. MARKS & NUMBERS	13. NO. & KIND OF PACKAGES	14. GENERAL DESCRIPTION OF CONTENTS	15. TOTAL WEIGHT	
			NET	GROSS
Addr	9 skids	Battery powered syphon pumps	4845 lbs	5115 lbs

16. SPECIFICATION OF COMMODITIES (CHARACTERISTICS, E.G. GRADE, QUALITY, SIZE, ETC.)	17. QUANTITY (STATE UNIT)	18. FAIR MARKET VALUE / AMOUNT	SELLING PRICE TO PURCHASER IN CANADA (IF ANY)	
			19. UNIT PRICE	20. AMOUNT
Battery powered syphon pumps	5010	USD30,060	USD 6 00	USD30,060

21. WE CERTIFY THIS INVOICE TO BE TRUE AND CORRECT AND TO THE BEST OF OUR KNOWLEDGE IN CONFORMITY WITH CANADIAN CUSTOMS LAWS	CHARGES	SPECIFY CURRENCY	STATE IF INCLUDED IN 18	STATE IF INCLUDED IN 20	AMOUNT
NAME OF SIGNATORY (PRINT) M.L. Smith	22. Export Packing		No	No	
TITLE Export Manager	23. Freight from place of direct shipment to Canada		No	No	
PLACE AND DATE OF ISSUE Small Town, CT, USA 12-14-82	24. Freight and insurance to place of direct shipment to Canada		No	No	
SIGNATURE	25. Insurance from place of direct shipment to Canada		No	No	
	26. Royalties		NO	No	
27. EXPORTER'S NAME AND ADDRESS (IF OTHER THAN VENDOR)	Commissions and similar charges		No	No	
	Other charges (specify)		No	No	
	28. VALUATION RULING — DEPARTMENTAL FILE REFERENCE AND DATE (IF APPLICABLE)				
	29. IF CONTINUATION SHEETS ARE USED ENTER TOTAL FIGURES HERE ⟶		FAIR MARKET VALUE	SELLING PRICE	

SEE REVERSE SIDE FOR GENERAL INFORMATION ON RULES OF ORIGIN AND FAIR MARKET VALUE. FOR MORE DETAILED INSTRUCTIONS FOR COMPLETING THIS INVOICE REFER TO CANADA CUSTOMS MEMORANDUM D13

Printed and Sold by Unz & Co., Division of Scott Printing Corp.
190 Baldwin Ave., Jersey City, N.J. 07306 — N.J. (201) 795-5400/N.Y. (212) 344-2270
Toll Free (800) 631-3098

Form 10-135

Customs Invoice

of customs, and to generate fees to maintain local consulates. The failure to supply a legalized consular invoice to importers in countries requiring it may prevent clearance of the goods by customs or may result in heavy fines for the importer. The use of consular invoicing is largely restricted to Latin America.

IRREVOCABLE LETTER OF CREDIT. *See* LETTER OF CREDIT.

ISLAMIC DEVELOPMENT BANK. A multinational development bank formed by Muslim countries to provide economic development assistance to member states, and to foster economic progress in Muslim communities in nonmember states. The financing practices of the bank are conducted in conformity with the principles and laws of Islam.

The bank was formed in 1975 with an authorized capital of two billion Islamic dinars; an Islamic dinar is the equivalent of one *special drawing right* of the International Monetary Fund. Two hundred thousand shares, each with a par value of ten thousand Islamic dinars, were authorized. Subscribed capital of the bank equals 790 million Islamic dinars, payable in the convertible currencies.

Bank membership as of the end of 1981 embraced forty countries. Headquarters of the bank are in Jedda, Saudi Arabia.

ISLAMIC DINAR. The unit of account of the Islamic Investment Bank, equal to one SPECIAL DRAWING RIGHT *(q.v.)*.

ITEM 807. *See* AMERICAN COMPONENTS ASSEMBLED ABROAD.

ITEMS OF TRADE. Goods or services that a nation buys or sells in the world markets. The items fall into three categories: *commodities* (goods, agricultural produce, or other tangibles), *services* (shipping, insurance, et cetera), and *credit* (loans and other interest-earning transactions). Commodity transactions are regarded as *visible* items of trade, whereas service and credit transactions are known as *invisible* items.

IUS VOLUNTARIUM. The body of international law that is the product of treaties, conventions, and other express engagements among nations, as contrasted with normative international law which has arisen through custom and usage.

IZMIR GROUP. A loosely connected group of eighteen Third World cotton-producing nations founded after the April 1981 publication of a report by the UN Commission for Trade and Development (UNCTAD) that documented that 90 percent of the world's cotton trade is controlled by fifteen multinational corporations, and that barely 2 to 15 percent of the value of a cotton product is paid to the producer, whereas approximately 40 percent goes to the retailer.

Inasmuch as 80 percent of the world's cotton is produced in developing nations, the Izmir Group countries have called for the formation of an international cotton organization to regulate the flow of cotton into world markets, thereby stabilizing prices and improving producer income.

See INTERNATIONAL COMMODITY AGREEMENT.

J

J-LIST. A list issued by the secretary of treasury under the authority of 19 U.S.C. 1304 (a)(3)(J) excepting certain classes of articles from country of origin marking requirements. The list is modified from time to time. See Appendix D6 for a complete listing.

JACKSON-VANIK AMENDMENT. An amendment to the Trade Reform Act of 1973 attached by Senator Henry Jackson and Congressman Charles Vanik, designed to preclude the granting of MOST FAVORED NATION *(q.v.)* status to the Soviet Union in the absence of a Soviet commitment to permit emigration of dissidents and Soviet Jews. The amendment was denounced by the Soviet government as an unacceptable intrusion into its internal affairs. Nevertheless, the act, including the amendment, passed Congress on December 20, 1974, and was signed into law on January 3, 1975.

JAPAN–UNITED STATES ECONOMIC RELATIONS GROUP. *See* WISEMEN'S GROUP.

JASON CLAUSE. *See* NEW JASON CLAUSE.

JAVA TOBACCO SURVEY CLAUSE. A condition in marine insurance contracts that obliges exporters of bulk tobacco from Java, Sumatra, and certain other areas in Southeast Asia to have the goods surveyed in advance of shipment. Inability to provide a report from an independent surveyor serves as a barrier to claims of damage or deterioration in transit. This clause is not in common use.

JERQUER. A customs official assigned to examine vessels to ensure that all cargo has been off-loaded for examination.

JERQUER NOTE. A document issued by customs authorities attesting that a named vessel has been examined and that all cargo has been off-loaded for inspection.

JETSAM. Goods voluntarily cast overboard in an emergency to lighten a ship.

JETTISON. The act of throwing cargo overboard to lighten the vessel in a storm, suppress fires, or otherwise avert disaster. Such losses are recoverable in GENERAL AVERAGE *(q.v.)*.

JETTY. A structure built more or less perpendicular to the coast against which vessels may lie, but lacking the T-formation characteristic of a pier.

JOHNSON ACT. An act of Congress that prohibits private persons from extending credit to any foreign government in default on financial obligations to the United States. Two amendments in 1945 exempted all members of the International Monetary Fund from the prohibition, as well as any transaction to which the Export-Import Bank is a participant. As a result, the act effectively applies only to certain communist countries.

JOINT RATE. A single factor rate applicable to the movement of goods through two or more carriers.

JOINT VENTURE. A business enterprise with more than one equity participant; for example, an agreement between a German firm and a U.S. firm to capitalize jointly a new factory in Venezuela. Many countries impose restrictions on joint ventures; these restrictions may take the form of limitations on foreign equity participation, majority, local control and management, and repatriation of dividends.

JONES ACT. A provision of the Merchant Marine Act of 1920 designed to clarify the law by which a seaman could recover for injuries sustained in the course of employment. An earlier act (38 Stat. 1164 [1915]) had permitted seamen to recover more than cure and maintenance for injuries attributable to negligence of the vessel owner or the ship's commanders. Previously, such recoveries in excess of cure and maintenance were recoverable only in demonstrated unseaworthiness.

The Jones Act was added as Section 33 of the Merchant Marine Act of 1920; it amended the 1915 act to read:

> Any seaman who shall suffer personal injury in the course of his employment may, at his election, maintain an action for damages at law, with the right of trial by jury, and in such action, all statutes of the United States modifying or extending the common-law right or remedy in cases of personal injury to railway employees shall apply.

Suits under the act must be commenced in the Federal District Court having jurisdiction over the home office of the vessel owner.

JUDGMENT CURRENCY CLAUSE. An indemnification provision commonly included in Eurocurrency loan agreements. The clause specifies that in the event the lender obtains a court award or judgement against the borrower by reason of default or otherwise, and the award is granted in a currency other than that in which the loan is to be repaid, the borrower will assume the burden for any resultant loss on exchange. For example, were a British borrower to obtain a loan of $1,000,000 from an American bank and subsequently default, the American bank might sue the borrower in a British court and receive a judgment in pounds sterling. The borrower, under a judgment currency clause, would be responsible for any exchange loss sustained by the bank in converting the pounds into dollars.

JUMBOIZING. The process of increasing a vessel's cargo-carrying capacity, usually by cutting a vessel in two halves amidships and inserting additional hold sections.

K

KABUSHIKI KAISHA. A limited stock form of business organization common in Japan. Signified by the letters *KK,* a *kabushiki kaisha* usually has at least three directors, of whom one must participate in the management of the company; there are no nationality or residence requirements. Incorporators, or *founders,* must number at least seven natural or juridical persons. No minimums or maximums for capital are prescribed, but at least 25 percent of authorized capital must be subscribed. Shares may be of virtually any type, but nonvoting preferred shares are limited to 25 percent of all shares issued; directors may disallow share transfers. Incorporation fees are .07 percent of capital.

Foreigners are generally permitted to acquire stock of Japanese firms without restriction, although limitations on foreign equity participation may be imposed for strategic or essential industries.

KARAT. A measure of the fineness, i.e., purity, of gold. Pure gold is twenty-four karats; hence, an object that is an alloy of 50 percent gold and 50 percent other metals would be twelve-karat gold.

KEELAGE. A charge levied upon a vessel for the privilege of entering into, or anchoring in, a harbor.

KEIRETSU. A loose coalition of Japanese businesses, usually with equity holdings in one another. The group of companies may span several industries, and strict parent-subsidiary relationships are not usually evident. Mitsubishi, Mitsui, and Yasuda are representative of Japanese *keiretsu.*

The *keiretsu* coalitions emerged in the 1950s in a reformed industrial policy following the post–World War II unbundling of the highly structured ZAIBATSU *(q.v.)* cartels.

KENNEDY ROUND. A series of international trade discussions commencing in Geneva in May 1964, under the auspices of the GENERAL AGREEMENT ON TARIFFS AND TRADE *(q.v.).* The discussions were prompted by the U.S. government in the wake of the Trade Agreements Act of 1962. The Kennedy Round did not fully attain its announced objectives, but several important benefits were achieved, including an average 35 percent reduction in duties on approximately sixty thousand industrial products, the adoption of an antidumping code, and the acknowledgment that tariff reductions accorded to developing nations did not require reciprocal concessions.

The Kennedy Round ended officially on June 30, 1976, with the official adoption of the agreement by fifty-three countries.

KEY CURRENCY. The currency of a major trading nation widely accepted in settlement of international accounts. At present, eight currencies are regarded as key currencies and are known as the BIG EIGHT *(q.v.).*

KEY INDUSTRY. An industry that, because of its size, export earnings, or other economic reasons, is viewed as essential to the economic well-being of the nation. The condition of a key industry is often viewed as a reflection of the economy as a whole.

KNOCK-OFF. An unauthorized copy of trademarked, copyrighted, or brand-identifiable merchandise. Imports of such counterfeits constitute a significant nuisance to brand name producers. U.S. customs authorities are empowered to seize knock-offs in those cases where trademark or copyright owners or authorized users have registered the trademark or copyright with customs, as specified in Section 133 of the Customs Regulations. In addition, offended firms may bring an action under Section 301 of the Trade Act of 1974, which authorizes retaliation against unfair trade practices.

KNOT. The unit for measuring a vessel's speed, equaling one nautical mile per hour.

KNOW HOW. Technical expertise that a firm has acquired through its operations and to which it has proprietary rights, whether the knowledge is patented or not. This expertise may consist of blueprints, plans, and manuals, as well as technical assistance.

KONDRATIEFF CYCLE. *See* BUSINESS CYCLE.

KONZERN. A group of companies bound together through ownership or control by a common parent company. The term is of German origin but is applied to corporate families in Scandinavia and elsewhere.

KYOTO CONVENTION. An international agreement, sponsored by the CUSTOMS COOPERATION COUNCIL *(q.v.)*, the object of which is to harmonize the methods and procedures of national customs authorities. The agreement, known formally as the International Convention on the Simplification and Harmonization of Customs Procedures, was adopted at Kyoto, Japan, in May 1973.

The convention is divided into two parts, (1) a body of principles which applies to all contracting states, and (2) thirty individual annexes dealing with specific problems or procedures. A contracting state may accept or reject any of the annexes, but most adopt at least one of the thirty.

The convention includes a review procedure whereby a state must examine, every three years, its national legislation relative to any of the standards or recommended practices against which it has lodged an objection. It is an object of the convention that adhering states seek to implement all of the annexes as soon as feasible.

List of the Annexes to the Kyoto Convention which have been adopted by the Customs Cooperation Council

A.1. Formalities prior to the lodgement of the goods declaration
A.2. Temporary storage of goods
A.3. Formalities applicable to commercial means of transport
A.4. Customs treatment of stores
B.1. Clearance for home use
B.2. Relief from import duties and taxes in respect of goods declared for home use
B.3. Reimportation in the same state
C.1. Outright exportation
D.1. Rules of origin
D.2. Documentary evidence of origin
D.3. Control of documentary evidence of origin
E.1. Customs transit
E.2. Transshipment
E.3. Customs warehouse
E.4. Drawback
E.5. Temporary admission subject to re-exportation in the same state
E.6. Temporary admission for inward processing
E.7. Duty-free replacement of goods
E.8. Temporary exportation for outward processing
F.1. Free zones
F.2. Processing of goods for home use
F.3. Customs facilities applicable to travellers
F.4. Customs formalities in respect of postal traffic
F.5. Urgent consignments
F.6. Repayment of import duties and taxes
F.7. Carriage of goods coastwise
G.1. Information supplied by the customs authorities
G.2. Relationship between customs authorities and third parties
H.1. Appeals in customs matters
H.2. Customs offences

L

LABOR INTENSIVE. A product or manufacturing process that requires a significant infusion of labor in relation to other factor inputs.

LACHES. A delay in the execution of a MARITIME LIEN *(q.v.)*. Inasmuch as maritime liens have priority by inverse order, i.e., the last lien has priority over preceding liens, a failure to execute against a lien may prejudice the lienor in a subsequent action.

LAFTA. *See* LATIN AMERICAN FREE TRADE ASSOCIATION.

LAGAN. Goods cast into the sea attached to a buoy to mark the owner's intent to retrieve them. *See* FLOTSAM, JETSAM, JETTISON.

LAGGED RESERVE ACOUNTING. *See* RESERVE ACCOUNTING.

LAISSEZ FAIRE. A doctrine that government should refrain from any form of trade regulation, leaving productivity and distribution of wealth purely to market forces and individual industry. The concept arose around the beginning of the eighteenth century in France, which was then highly commercially regulated. Various eighteenth- and early nineteenth-century economic thinkers asserted that the absence of governmental regulation would permit a pure market allocation of resources, economic growth, and enhanced individual freedom. The doctrine lost momentum toward the end of the nineteenth century because of social abuses arising out of free market industrial society, as well as the mitigation of free market competition caused by the emergence of monopolies and similar trade restraints.

LAKER. A vessel engaged in commerce solely on the Great Lakes.

LANDBRIDGE. A method of transporting goods partially by land and partially by water as a substitute for all-water movements. Originated in the mid 1960s as a means of moving European–Far East cargoes across the United States during the interruption of Suez Canal service, the concept of landbridge has been expanded to include a variety of transoceanic movements encompassing an inland leg. Landbridge movements can be categorized as follows:

1. *Pure landbridge*, a transcontinental land movement with prior and subsequent movement by water (e.g., Yokohama to Oakland, thence by rail to Baltimore, then by vessel to Rotterdam).

2. *Mini-landbridge*, a transcontinental movement with prior *or* subsequent movement by water (e.g., Yokohama to Oakland, thence by rail to New York); this service is a substitute for running a ship through the Panama Canal from Japan to New York.

3. *Micro-landbridge*, a movement from or to an interior point with prior or subsequent movement by water (e.g., Yokohama to Oakland, thence by rail to Saint Louis).

In all "bridge" movements, the ocean carrier issues a through bill of lading to final destination, making all arrangements for land transportation; the cost of such land transportation is included in the ocean carrier's rate (*see* figure).

Containers loaded aboard flatcars for landbridge shipment

LARGEST HATCH PRINCIPLE. In charter parties covering movement of dry cargoes it is not uncommon to fix laytime in terms of a quantity of

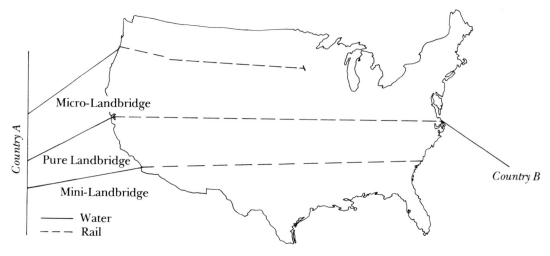

Micro-Landbridge

Pure Landbridge

Mini-Landbridge

Country A

Country B

——— Water
- - - Rail

Landbridge

cargo to be loaded (or discharged) "per workable hatch per day." Recognizing that any given vessel is apt to have hatches of varying sizes, and that the size of the hatch affects the amount of cargo which can be loaded or unloaded during a given time period, some courts have held that it may be unreasonable to compute laytime as a function of the number of holds times the days specified in the contract. The principle asserts that once they have been fully 'worked,' i.e., stowed or stripped of cargo, the smaller holds should be disregarded in computing the ship's ability to be worked.

The largest hatch principle is supported in English case law by *The Sandgate* (1929) Ll.L. Rep 151 (C.A.) and the *Corfu Island* (1953) 2 Lloyd's Rep 472 (Q.B.).

LASH. *See* LIGHTER ABOARD SHIP.

LATENT DEFECT. Deficiency in goods offered for shipment not discernible by diligent inspection.

LATENT DEFECT, NEGLIGENCE AND ADDITIONAL PERILS CLAUSE. Commonly known as the INCHMAREE CLAUSE (*q.v.*).

LATIN AMERICAN FREE TRADE ASSOCIATION. A now defunct association of various Latin American states formed to orchestrate the elimination of tariffs among members within twelve years of its formation (at the rate of eight percent). LAFTA was created by the treaty of Montevideo on February 18, 1960, and commenced activities on June 1, 1961. The association consisted originally of Brazil, Argentina, Uruguay, Mexico, Chile, Paraguay, and Peru. Colombia and Ecuador joined in 1962, Venezuela in 1966, and Bolivia in 1967.

LAFTA members gravitated toward regional organizations, and the association was disbanded in 1981 in favor of a new organization, the Latin American Integration Association.

LATINDOLLARS. U.S. dollars on deposit with banks in Latin America.

LAW MERCHANT. A body of customary law arising from mercantile practices and usages over centuries. Many of the practices have origins in Roman, or even pre-Roman, times. During the Middle Ages merchants, courts, or guilds employed locally recognized commercial rules to resolve disputes. Significant variations in local practice were not uncommon, but underlying principles were observed widely.

The law merchant was never a uniform body of laws as such. Nevertheless, its various local forms have been embraced widely in municipal law. Today the term refers to widely accepted international commercial practices, rather than a body of laws.

LAW OF NATIONS. An outdated term for what is now known as PUBLIC INTERNATIONAL LAW (*q.v.*).

LAYDAY. *See* LAYTIME.

LAYTIME. The amount of time permitted the charterer of a vessel to perform loading and unloading without incurring additional charges. Charter parties normally provide for *demurrage* charges to accrue for time used beyond that allocated; similarly, the contract may provide for *despatch* money to be paid to the charterer for releasing the vessel ahead of schedule.

Lay days may be in the form of *running days* (every calendar day applies toward the laytime), *working days* (excludes from laytime calculations Sundays and holidays observed in the port of loading or discharge, as the case may be), or *weather working days* (excludes not only Sundays and holidays, but also any days on which work is prohibited by weather conditions).

LEAD MANAGER. An international bank that organizes other banks into a syndicate for the purpose of funding a major financial project, often extending to hundreds of millions or even billions of dollars.

LEAST DEVELOPED COUNTRIES. Those nations suffering the most severe economic and development problems, and requiring substantial and ongoing economic assistance. As a general rule, they are nations with a literacy rate of less than 20 percent and per capita income below two hundred dollars per year.

LEGAL TENDER. A medium of exchange issued by a lawful authority that may be used to satisfy public and private obligations.

LEGAL WEIGHT. The total weight of a product and its immediate packaging, but not including any outer packaging. For example, the legal weight of canned fruit would include the fruit itself, plus the cans, but not the cartons in which the cans were packed.

The legal weight is used in some countries for purposes of computing specific duties.

LEONTIEF PARADOX. Derived from a study by Wassily Leontief of U.S. trade statistics, commencing in 1947 and spanning twenty-five years, which revealed that capital/labor ratios of U.S. exports were lower than those of imports during the same time span. This empirical analysis contradicts conventional views that a nation exports products in which it enjoys a relative factor advantage.

LESS DEVELOPED COUNTRIES. *See* DEVELOPING COUNTRIES.

LESS DEVELOPED COUNTRY CORPORATION. As provided in U.S. tax laws, a firm that derives at least 80 percent of its income in less developed countries (LDCs) and has at least 80 percent of its assets in LDCs. Dividend and interest income from such corporations is excluded from foreign-base company income to the extent it is reinvested in an LDC. Sheltering of income on trading in the stock of LDC corporations ended with the Tax Reform Act of 1976.

LESS THAN CONTAINER LOAD. A quantity of product less than that which fills a container. In some ocean tariffs, certain minimum utilizations of space are required; if this minimum is not filled, the shipper will be billed for the space not used, up to the minimum required utilization, usually at the rate applied to the highest rated commodity in the container. In other tariffs, the minimum utilization

is accomplished if the container generates a specified dollar revenue for the carrier, irrespective of content usage.

LESS THAN FAIR VALUE. An export sale price below that charged on like sales in the country of origin. Such sales are usually regarded as DUMPING *(q.v.)*, which may result in the imposition by the importing country of additional duties on the offending product, or other retaliatory trade measures.

LESS THAN TRAILERLOAD. In motor freight usage, a quantity of cargo less than that for which the truckload rate is applicable for the given product. Often this term applies to a shipment of less than twenty-two to twenty-four thousand pounds for many products, ten thousand for products of low density.

LETTER OF COMFORT. A statement, usually in letter form, issued by a bank or other commercial entity attesting to the stature, credit worthiness, or reputation of another. The writer of the letter will, however, expressly disclaim any responsibilty for the obligations of the subject party.

Letters of comfort are commonly issued by parents on behalf of subsidiaries and by banks for good clients, usually in conjunction with credit or capital raising transactions.

LETTER OF COMMENT. *See* CERTIFICATE OF FREE SALE.

LETTER OF CONDITIONAL REIMBURSEMENT. A commitment in writing by the U.S. Department of Agriculture to a nation qualified to receive U.S. agricultural aid under P.L. 480, but with which a formal aid agreement has not been signed. The letter guarantees that the U.S. government will reimburse the importer for payments made, in its local currency, to American sellers, once the actual agreement is in place. The letter customarily limits the guarantee to the percentage of the purchase price specified in the financing agreement.

LETTER OF CREDIT. A document issued by a commercial bank committing itself to honor drafts drawn in accordance with the terms of the credit. The party to whom the credit is issued is the *beneficiary*; the party on behalf of whom the bank issues the credit is the *applicant*. Letters of credit may be issued as either *revocable*, subject to recall or amendment at the option of the applicant, or *irrevocable*, not subject to recall or amendment during the specified life of the credit, except with the agreement of the beneficiary (*see* figure, next page).

In addition, a letter of credit may be *confirmed* or *unconfirmed*. A confirmed letter of credit is one for which a bank, other than the issuing bank, has made itself responsible for honoring properly presented drafts; an unconfirmed letter of credit relies solely upon the good name of the issuing bank. Customarily, a bank will charge the applicant or beneficiary for adding its confirmation.

StateStreet

TRANSFERABLE
IRREVOCABLE COMMERCIAL
LETTER OF CREDIT NO. 10000

ADVISED BY: AIRMAIL
THRU ADVISING BANK:
STATE STREET ASIA, LTD.
ROOM 2109
CONNAUGHT CENTRE
CONNAUGHT ROAD
CENTRAL, HONG KONG

ACCOUNTEE (APPLICANT):
BOSTON IMPORT COMPANY
225 FRANKLIN STREET
BOSTON, MA

BENEFICIARY:
HONG KONG EXPORT CO.
HONG KONG, B.C.C.

ISSUANCE DATE:
DECEMBER 10, 1982

MAXIMUM/AGGREGATE
CREDIT AMOUNT:
USD 124,800.00

LATEST SHIPMENT DATE:
MARCH 10, 1983

EXPIRATION/NEGOTIATION DATE:
MARCH 25, 1983

GENTLEMEN:

WE HEREBY ESTABLISH OUR IRREVOCABLE LETTER OF CREDIT IN YOUR FAVOR FOR ACCOUNT OF THE APPLICANT UP TO AN AGGREGATE AMOUNT NOT TO EXCEED ONE HUNDRED TWENTY FOUR THOUSAND EIGHT HUNDRED AND 00/100 US DOLLARS AVAILABLE BY YOUR DRAFTS DRAWN ON OURSELVES AT 90 DAYS SIGHT FOR 100 PERCENT FULL INVOICE VALUE ACCOMPANIED BY THE FOLLOWING DOCUMENTS:

- SIGNED INVOICES IN QUADRUPLICATE,
- SPECIAL CUSTOMS INVOICE FORM 5515 IN TRIPLICATE,
- PACKING LISTS IN DUPLICATE,
- CERTIFICATE OF INSPECTION SIGNED BY PO SALLY AN OFFICIAL OF YOUR FIRM CERTIFYING THAT THE RELATIVE MERCHANDISE CONFORMS TO ALL SPECIFICATIONS OF THE PURCHASE ORDER.
- FULL SET PLUS ONE NON-NEGOTIABLE COPY CLEAN ON BOARD OCEAN BILLS OF LADING TO THE ORDER OF STATE STREET BANK AND TRUST COMPANY MARKED FREIGHT COLLECT AND NOTIFY BOSTON FREIGHT FORWARDER, 177 MILK STREET, BOSTON, MA.

EVIDENCING SHIPMENT OF LADIES WEARING APPAREL AS FOLLOWS:
QUANTITY/DOZEN	STYLE NO.	UNIT PRICE/DOZEN
200	9001	USD 150.00
300	9002	USD 126.00
500	9003	USD 114.00

FOR CARRIER FROM HONG KONG TO BOSTON, MASSACHUSETTS.

INSURANCE TO BE COVERED BY BUYER.

PARTIAL SHIPMENTS ARE PERMITTED.

TRANSHIPMENTS ARE PROHIBITED.

DOCUMENTS MUST BE NEGOTIATED WITHIN 15 CALENDAR DAYS FROM DATE OF SHIPMENT.

ALL BANKING CHARGES OUTSIDE USA ARE FOR ACCOUNT OF BENEFICIARY.

DRAFTS DRAWN BY A TRANSFEREE MUST BE ACCOMPANIED BY YOUR LETTER OF TRANSFER, IN ADDITION TO THE OTHER REQUIRED DOCUMENTS. THE VALIDITY OF YOUR SIGNATURE ON THE LETTER OF TRANSFER MUST BE VERIFIED BY YOUR BANK, WHO MUST ALSO CERTIFY THAT THE AMOUNT OF THE TRANSFER HAS BEEN ENTERED ON THE LETTER OF CREDIT INSTRUMENT.

DRAFTS MUST STATE "DRAWN AGAINST STATE STREET BANK AND TRUST COMPANY LETTER OF CREDIT NO. 10000".

THE AMOUNT OF EACH DRAFT NEGOTIATED TOGETHER WITH DATE NEGOTIATED MUST BE ENDORSED ON THE REVERSE HEREOF.

ALL DOCUMENTS MUST BE FORWARDED BY AIRMAIL.

EXCEPT AS OTHERWISE EXPRESSLY STATED HEREIN, THIS CREDIT IS SUBJECT TO THE "UNIFORM CUSTOMS AND PRACTICE FOR DOCUMENTARY CREDITS (1974 REVISION), INTERNATIONAL CHAMBER OF COMMERCE, PUBLICATION NO. 290."

WE HEREBY AGREE WITH THE DRAWERS, ENDORSERS AND BONA FIDE HOLDERS OF DRAFTS DRAWN UNDER AND IN COMPLIANCE WITH THE TERMS OF THIS LETTER OF CREDIT THAT SUCH DRAFTS WILL BE DULY HONORED UPON PRESENTATION TO THE DRAWEE.

VERY TRULY YOURS,

STATE STREET BANK AND TRUST COMPANY

AUTHORIZED SIGNATURE   AUTHORIZED SIGNATURE

Letter of Credit. Courtesy of State Street Bank and Trust Co., Boston, MA.

Upon performance of the actions specified in the credit, usually the shipment of goods as evidenced by the submission of shipping documents, the bank will accept the beneficiary's draft. A draft accepted by a bank is a *banker's acceptance.* If the letter of credit provides for drafts at *sight,* the acceptance will be redeemed for cash; if the credit provides for time drafts, e.g., drafts at thirty days' sight, the beneficiary may hold the draft to maturity or may discount it at the accepting bank or another financial institution; in most cases, the draft must be ac-companied by bills of lading, invoices, and other documents.

In those cases where drafts or documents submitted are not in complete conformity with the conditions stipulated in the credit, the documents are said to suffer *discrepancies,* and the bank is under no obligation to accept the draft or make payment without the applicant's approval. Any presentation, other than one in which all documents submitted conform precisely to the requirements stipulated in the credit, is a *discrepancy presentation.*

Recognizing the international character of letters of credit and the necessity for standardized terminology in their use, the international business community has developed a common code of usages for applying credits. These rules are embraced within the UNIFORM CUSTOMS AND PRACTICES *(q.v.),* issued by the International Chamber of Commerce.

See BACK-TO-BACK LETTER OF CREDIT, DELAYED PAYMENT CREDIT, RED CLAUSE, REVOLVING LETTER OF CREDIT, TRANSFERABLE LETTER OF CREDIT.

LETTER OF CREDIT CLAUSE. A clause in a marine cargo insurance policy designed to protect an exporter until such time as he is paid under a letter of credit. An exporter selling on an F.O.B. or F.A.S. basis, for example, does not provide marine insurance; this obligation is undertaken by the importer. If the purchaser's insurance fails to respond for marine losses (which have not been covered by the exporter), the letter of credit provision of the exporter's policy will ensure that he is paid.

LETTER OF EXCHANGE. An infrequently used synonym for BILL OF EXCHANGE *(q.v.).*

LETTER OF HYPOTHECATION. *See* HYPOTHECATION CERTIFICATE.

LETTER OF INDEMNITY. A document issued by a shipper of merchandise to a steamship line as an inducement for the carrier to issue a clean BILL OF LADING *(q.v.)* where it might not otherwise do so. A letter of indemnity is normally issued where the goods are short or damaged and the carrier would provide only a *foul* bill of lading; the issuance of a foul bill would preclude the shipper from collecting under a letter of credit.

The letter of indemnity acts as a form of guarantee whereby the shipper agrees to settle a claim against the steamship line by a holder of the bill of lading arising from issuance of a clean bill.

LETTERS PATENT. A document, issued under governmental authority, conveying to one or more individuals exclusive rights or privileges. Letters patent are instruments used to bestow titles of nobility and to grant lands for service to the crown or state. In modern usage, the term commonly refers to the protection afforded by the state to an inventor, granting him or his assigns the sole right to manufacture and sell his invention for a specified period of time.

LEVELING CHARGE. A charge for leveling cargoes of sulphur in bulk, which is normally borne by the vessel owner. This charge is in addition to any normal loading fee.

LEX MERCATORIA. *See* LAW MERCHANT.

LIBEL. A lawsuit in admiralty jurisdiction.

LIBELANT. The complainant in an admiralty suit, or *libel*; corresponds to a plaintiff.

LIBOR. *See* LONDON INTERBANK OFFERED RATE.

LICENSING. A process whereby a firm (the licensor) permits another firm abroad to use its trademarks, manufacturing processes, patents, or other inputs to manufacture or assemble the product locally, for which the licensee remits royalties to the firm granting the license.

Licensing is often a vehicle for deriving income from a foreign source where exporting or direct entry is prohibited or not desirable.

LIFT-ON/LIFT-OFF. A type of vessel that is loaded by lifting break-bulk or containerized cargo aboard by cranes or similar gear.

LIGHT CARGO. A cargo that fully occupies the cubic capacity of a ship but does not bring the vessel down to its marks in the water.

LIGHT DISPLACEMENT. *See* DISPLACEMENT.

LIGHTER. A shallow-draft barge used to transfer cargo from an oceangoing vessel to a wharf that could not accommodate the ship itself; the practice of lightering is common in ports with severe congestion or primitive conditions.

LIGHTER ABOARD SHIP. A marine cargo system incorporating a barge that is lifted aboard a specially constructed vessel by means of a crane. This system permits the barge to be loaded at almost any waterfront facility, from which it is towed to the mother vessel and stowed aboard intact. The process is reversed at the port of destination (*see* figures).

LIGHTERAGE. A charge imposed for the transfer of cargo from vessel to shore and vice versa by means of lighters.

LIGHT GRAIN. Grains, including barley and oats, having a density of fifty-six to seventy cubic feet per ton.

Lighter Aboard Ship (LASH)

LIGHT MONEY AND TONNAGE TAXES. Special duties applied to commercial vessels entering U.S. ports. The charges are collected as follows:

Regular tonnage tax: imposed on all vessels, irrespective of nationality, at the rate of 2 cents per net ton (not to exceed 10 cents in any one year) for vessels entering the United States from any port in North America, the Caribbean, or the Caribbean coast of South America, including the mouth of the Orinoco River; the rate for vessels entering from ports elsewhere is 6 cents per ton (not to exceed 30 cents per year). The maximum any vessel may be assessed in any one year is 40 cents, i.e., five payments at 2 cents and five payments at 6 cents. The manner by which the port of origin is determined for application of the rate is specified in 19 CFR 4.20 (1), et seq.

Special tonnage tax: collected in addition to the regular tonnage tax on vessels not documented in the United States at the rate of 30 cents per ton on vessels built in the United States but owned wholly or in part by foreign citizens or interests; foreign vessels not built in U.S. yards, and any vessel having one or more foreign officers are subject to tax at the rate of 50 cents per ton. Where a foreign vessel "entered in the United States from any foreign port or place, to and with which vessels of the United States are not ordinarily permitted to enter and trade," the rate is two dollars per ton, as specified in 46 U.S.C. 121.

Light money: assessed, in addition to tonnage taxes, at the rate of 50 cents per ton on vessels not documented in the United States.

Taxes are assessed on the net tonnage stated in the vessel's marine document. Whenever a maximum tax is payable in any year, the year runs 365 days from the date of the first tax payment. Exemptions from the tax are permitted, inter alia, for vessels in distress, bunkering, and scientific vessels not carrying cargo.

Vessels of the following states, as the result of treaties, presidential proclamations, or orders of the secretary of the treasury, are exempted from payment of light money, as well as tonnage duties higher than those imposed on U.S. ships:

Algeria	Costa Rica
Argentina	Cuba
Australia	Cyprus
Austria	Denmark (including the
Bahamas	Faeroe Islands)
Bangladesh	Dominica
Barbados	Dominican Republic
Belgium	Ecuador
Bermuda	Egypt
Bolivia	El Salvador
Brazil	Estonia
Bulgaria	Ethiopia
Burma	Figi
Canada	Finland
Cayman Islands	France
Chile	Gambia
Colombia	German Democratic
	Republic

German Federal Republic	Nigeria
Ghana	Norway
Greece	Oman
Greenland	Pakistan
Guatemala	Panama
Guinea	Papua New Guinea
Guyana	Paraguay
Haiti	Peru
Honduras	Philippines
Iceland	Poland
India	Portugal
Indonesia	Qatar
Iran	Romania
Iraq	Saudi Arabia
Ireland	Singapore
Israel	Somalia
Italy	Spain
Ivory Coast	Sri Lanka
Jamaica	St. Vincent & the
Japan	Grenadines
Kenya	South Africa
Korea	Surinam
Kuwait	Sweden
Latvia	Switzerland
Lebanon	Syria
Liberia	Taiwan
Libya	Thailand
Malaysia	Togo
Malta	Tunisia
Mauritius	Turkey
Mexico	U.S.S.R.
Monaco	United Arab Emirates
Morocco	United Kingdom
Nauru	Uruguay
Netherlands	Vanuatu
Netherlands Antilles	Venezuela
New Zealand	Yugoslavia
Nicaragua	Zaire

LIKE PERILS. A provision of the perils clause of a marine policy wherein the covered perils are enumerated. "Like perils" does not mean that all conceivable perils are covered; rather, it applies to perils that are of nature similar to those already specified in the policy.

LIMITED CAPTIVE. *See* CAPTIVE INSURANCE COMPANY.

LIMITED COINAGE. A government policy limiting the right of individuals to bring bullion to the mint and have it coined. *See* FREE COINAGE.

LINEAR TARIFF CUT. A reduction in customs tariffs, on an across-the-board basis, by a given percentage.

LINE BREADTH. The number of products or variations carried in a manufacturer's or marketer's product line.

LINER. A cargo-carrying vessel that offers regularly scheduled service over an established route.

LINER CONFERENCE. *See* CONFERENCE.

LINER NEGLIGENCE CLAUSE. A provision commonly incorporated into marine hull insurance policies that states that the insurer will pay for damage to the vessel when an accident has occurred without the necessity of identifying a specific peril, less "the cost of repairing, replacing, or renewing any port condemned solely as a result of a latent defect, wear and tear, gradual deterioration or fault or error in design or construction." The clause was first offered by the American Hull Insurance Syndicate in 1964.

LINER TERMS. A provision in some ship charter contracts in which the vessel pays loading or discharging costs, or both.

LIQUIDITY. The quality of being convertible into monetary wealth; as relates to a given nation's economic condition, *liquidity* consists of that country's supply of gold, foreign exchange holdings, and SPECIAL DRAWING RIGHTS (q.v.), and its line of available credit with the International Monetary Fund.

LIQUIDITY BALANCE. In national balance of payments accounting, the sum of the basic balance (i.e., current account plus long-term capital transactions), short-term capital transactions, net changes in holdings of special drawing rights, plus errors and omissions.

LIQUIDITY RATIONING. The regulation of a nation's money supply by central banking authorities. A central bank is able to control the money supply and the availability of funds to different sectors of the economy by freezing reserves, intervening in the money market, and similar devices.

LISBON AGREEMENT FOR THE PROTECTION OF APPELLATIONS OF ORIGIN AND THEIR INTERNATIONAL REGISTRATION. An international agreement to protect appellations of origin that are defined as the "geographical name of a country, region, or locality, which serves to designate a product originating therein, the quality and characteristics of which are due exclusively or essentially to the geographical environment, including natural and human factors." Examples of such appellations of origin include *champagne* and *madeira* (wine), *limoges* (ceramics), and *Havana* (cigars).

A contracting state submits to the WORLD INTELLECTUAL PROPERTY ORGANIZATION *(q.v.)* (WIPO) a listing of the names for which it seeks protection; WIPO transmits these names to the other contracting states. Each state adhering to the convention is permitted one year within which it may declare its inability to protect the appellation transmitted by WIPO. In the absence of a formal declaration within the one-year period, or upon expiry of that period, each adhering state is obliged to protect the internationally registered name so long as it is protected in the country of origin.

The agreement was adopted in 1958 and was amended at Stockholm in 1967. On March 15, 1983, the following states were adherents to the Lisbon Agreement: Algeria, Bulgaria, Congo, Cuba, Czechoslovakia, France, Gabon, Haiti, Hungary, Israel, Italy, Mexico, Portugal, Togo, Tunisia, Upper Volta.

LIST. The measure of a vessel's tilt from the vertical plane, in degrees.

LLOYD'S OF LONDON. A major world insurance market, which arose to provide coverage of marine risks but which now insures against virtually any loss or calamity. Contrary to popular belief, Lloyd's is not an insurance company; it has no shareholders and assumes no liability for insurance contracts written by its members. Lloyd's is an association of underwriters, each of whom accepts risks for his own private account.

Risks may be accepted at Lloyd's only by an *underwriting member,* of which there are more than nineteen thousand; underwriting members pledge their personal fortunes to respond for risks they have accepted, and they retain the premium income derived, less reinsurance and other expenses.

To protect underwriting members from catastrophe losses, members often form syndicates in which risks are assumed collectively. At present, there are more than four hundred syndicates operating at Lloyd's; some have only a few members while others may have more than a thousand. This pooling of resources also permits the members to hire professional underwriters to assume risks for the group.

With the exception of long-term life insurance and financial guarantees, virtually every form of insurance is written at Lloyd's.

The institution of Lloyd's rose around 1680, when merchants, ships, captains, and others involved in maritime enterprises congregated at the coffeehouse of Edward Lloyd to receive shipping news. There is no evidence to support the belief that Edward Lloyd himself ever wrote a contract of insurance.

As a response to excessive speculation in various offshore investment schemes on the part of the British propertied classes, culminating in the collapse of the South Sea Company, Parliament enacted a law (1729) limiting marine insurance to the Royal Exchange Assurance and the London Assurance Company. The act, however, did not prohibit private individuals from underwriting contracts of marine insurance. The passage of the 1729 act and the competition imposed by the Royal Exchange and London Assurance forced the loose federation of private underwriters to regularize their affairs into an ongoing society. In 1811 the underwriting members subscribed to a *trust deed,* which served as the legal basis of Lloyd's. In 1871, the association was chartered by act of Parliament.

The act of 1871 formed the Corporation of Lloyd's, the affairs of which are directed by the Committee of Lloyd's, comprising sixteen underwriting members. Except in a very few instances, thresources also permits the members to hire professional underwriters to assume risks for the group.

LLOYD'S REGISTER. A publication containing details of the characteristics and construction of various oceangoing vessels. The publication is not produced by LLOYD'S OF LONDON *(q.v.)*, which is a separate organization, although both bodies have common origins in the maritime community that congregated at the coffeehouse of Edward Lloyd.

A liaison with Lloyd's of London is maintained through the participation of members of the Committee of Lloyd's in the register's committee.

LLOYD'S STANDARD POLICY. A form of marine policy adopted by Lloyd's in 1779 and recognized in Britain by the Marine Insurance Bill of 1899 and the Marine Insurance Act of 1906 as the standard policy for Britain; policy forms used in the United States vary from the Lloyd's policy, but significant portions are retained.

LOADCENTER. A geographical point at which cargo from outlying points is routinely collected for onward carriage. For example, cargo moving from Philadelphia and Norfolk to Europe may be transported by barge or other means to Baltimore where it is loaded upon a Europe-bound vessel.

The purpose of operating a loadcenter is to eliminate a call by a ship at a port which does not, of itself, generate sufficient cargo.

LOADED DISPLACEMENT. *See* DISPLACEMENT.

LOADING. A risk premium in addition to interest charges and acceptance fees deducted by a bank or discount house from the face value of a BILL OF EXCHANGE *(q.v.)* presented for discounting. This additional margin will vary, depending upon the quality of the drawee and endorsers on the bill and perhaps on the type of transaction that gave rise to the bill.

LOAD-LINE. A marking painted on the bow of merchant vessels, denoting how much cargo may be loaded aboard, as determined by how low in the water the ship may ride. The object of the mark is to prevent the overloading of a ship, with attendant risk to its safety. The load-line marks are sometimes known as the *Plimsoll line,* in deference to Samuel Plimsoll, M.P., who was instrumental in passage of the first load-line statute, in Great Britain. The current international load-line standard is the International Convention on Loadlines (1966), 18 U.S.T. 1857, enforced by the Coast Guard in the United States.

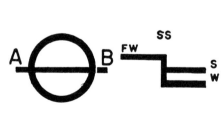

Loadline

LOAN PRICING. The process used by a financial institution to derive the effective rate of interest on a prospective loan; the process includes calculating the income derived from commitment fees, and compensating balances on top of the nominal rate of interest.

LOAN PURCHASE PROGRAM. *See* PRIVATE EXPORT FUNDING CORPORATION.

LOAN RECEIPT. *See* BENEFIT OF INSURANCE CLAUSE.

LOCAL CARRIER. A motor carrier that operates wholly within a single or contiguous commercial zone but is still subject to Interstate Commerce Commission authority because of other motor carriage business, for example, because it handles interstate interline business or hauls certain regulated commodities.

LOCAL MARKET. *See* PRIMARY MARKET.

LOCATION THEORY. A theory that, all things being equal, a firm will locate its manufacturing and distribution facilities wherever transportation charges will be lowest on the production inputs and the outbound movement of finished products.

LOCK-GATE PRICE. *See* GATE PRICE.

LOCO. A term used in commodity markets to designate a geographic point for delivery of a given commodity, e.g., "wheat loco Chicago."

LOLO. *See* LIFT-ON/LIFT-OFF.

LOMBARD LOANS. Short-term loans in Britain and some European countries secured by bonds or corporate securities; the rate of such loans is slightly higher than the commercial loan rate.

LOMBARD RATE. The interest rate charged West German commercial banks on loans from the central bank using securities as collateral.

LOMÉ CONVENTIONS. A series of trade and economic assistance agreements between the EUROPEAN ECONOMIC COMMUNITY *(q.v.)* and various developing nations, former colonies of EEC members.

The TREATY OF ROME *(q.v.)* which established the EEC provided for a special relationship between the Community and former colonies. In 1964, the (then) six members of the EEC concluded the first Yaoundé Convention with eighteen African states and Madagascar; the agreement provided for commercial, financial, and technical assistance. A second Yaoundé Convention was signed in 1969.

The entry of Great Britain into the EEC in 1973 required a reexamination of the relationship between the Community and former colonial possessions, now independent. A series of discussions between the EEC and the forty-six African-Caribbean-Pacific states (known collectively as the ACP countries) resulted in the first Lomé Convention (Lomé I) in 1975. A second agreement (Lomé II) was concluded between the EEC and 58 ACP countries in 1979, to run through February 1985.

The current agreement (Lomé III) was executed December 8, 1984, among representatives of the EEC and 64 developing nations. During the five-year life of Lomé III, the ACP countries will receive financial aid of 8.5 billion ECU (EUROPEAN CURRENCY UNITS [*q.v.*]); at time of signing, the ECU was valued at approximately .75 U. S. dollars.

Lomé III incorporates several innovations over prior agreements, including a statement of human rights and denunciation of apartheid; conditions for private investment in the ACP countries; and new rules which permit funding of distressed industries and imports. Recognizing that many ACP countries remain dependent upon agricultural and mineral commodities for export earnings, Lomé III continues and expands the Stabex and Sysmin programs. Stabex is a fund from which a participating developing country may receive financial assistance when the world price for certain agricultural commodities falls below prescribed levels. Sysmin provides support to countries dependent upon mineral exports.

EEC financial support of Lomé III for the period 1985–89 is as follows:

Project	Resources (millions of ECUs)
Grants	4,860
Stabex	925
Sysmin	415
Special Loans	600
Risk Capital	600
European Investment Bank Loans	1,100
	8,500

It is expected that Angola and Mozambique will join the 64 nations already participating in Lomé III. Those nations are:

Antigua & Barbuda	Jamaica
Bahamas	Kenya
Barbados	Kiribati
Belize	Lesotho
Benin	Liberia
Botswana	Madagascar
Burkina Fasso	Malawi
Burundi	Mali
Cameroon	Mauritania
Cape Verde	Mauritius
Central African Republic	Niger
Chad	Nigeria
Comoros	Papua New Guinea
Congo	Rwanda
Djibouti	St. Christopher and Nevis
Dominica	St. Lucia
Equatorial Guinea	St. Vincent and
Ethiopia	Grenadines
Fiji	Sao Tome and Principe
Gabon	Senegal
Gambia	Seychelles
Ghana	Sierra Leone
Grenada	Solomon Islands
Guinea	Somalia
Guinea-Bissau	Sudan
Guyana	Surinam
Ivory Coast	Swaziland
Tanzania	Western Samoa
Togo	Vanuatu
Tonga	Zaire
Trinidad and Tobago	Zambia
Tuvalu	Zimbabwe
Uganda	

LONDON DISCOUNT MARKET. The group of London discount houses that make a market for short-term government and commercial paper. The discount market is financed by secured loans from the London clearing banks.

LONDON GOLD POOL. An arrangement among certain European central banks and the Federal Reserve Bank of New York designed to maintain stability in the market price of gold in private transactions. The United States had been committed to buy and sell gold in official transactions at thirty-five dollars per ounce; a private market in gold arose in London during 1954, and the price of gold in this market rose significantly over the official price. In response, the New York Federal Reserve Bank, the Bank of England, and certain European central banks formed the Gold Pool in the fall of 1961; the pool was committed to selling gold as required to offset market forces, thereby maintaining a close relationship between the official and market prices.

Various economic and political pressures, partly attributable to U.S. involvement in Vietnam, continued upward pressure in the gold market, thereby draining official gold reserves. In March 1968 President Lyndon Johnson announced termination of U.S. participation in the London Gold Pool, effectively terminating official intervention in the private gold market. Gold continued to be available to foreign central banks and treasuries at the official price after the end of the gold pool. Official conversion of gold was ended by President Richard Nixon on August 15, 1971.

LONDON INTERBANK OFFERED RATE. Often abbreviated as LIBOR, the rate at which major London banks will lend funds to each other. It is used as a money market index, and loans are often expressed in terms of LIBOR plus a percentage. LIBOR is used, in Eurodollar loans, as an equivalent to prime rate in the United States.

LONG AND SHORT HAUL CLAUSE. A provision in Section 4 of the Interstate Commerce Act that a rail carrier may not charge more to haul a product a shorter distance than a longer distance over the same route under substantially the same conditions.

LONG BILL. A bill of exchange having a tenor of at least thirty days' sight, although the term is customarily used in connection with bills having tenors of sixty to ninety days' sight.

LONG RATE. The rate paid by a bank or foreign exchange broker for long bills of exchange (i.e., those having a tenor of more than thirty days) payable abroad.

LONGSHOREMAN. A person employed in the loading and unloading of a vessel and the handling of cargo in and about the harbor area. The term *longshoreman* is often confused with *stevedore;* the latter is a firm contracted by the vessel to provide loading and unloading services, and employing longshoremen.

LONG STERLING. A bill of exchange drawn on London with tenor of more than thirty days' sight.

LONG-TERM CAPITAL TRANSACTIONS. A component in a nation's balance of payment accounting, long-term capital transactions represent loans with a maturity of more than one year granted to or obtained from foreigners, including direct and portfolio investments.

LORO ACCOUNT. An account on a bank's ledger referring to sums due from or payable to a second bank on behalf of a third bank. This term is not common in American usage but is employed widely in foreign exchange transactions outside North America.

LOSS OF SPECIE. In marine insurance usage, a transformation of merchandise as the result of external physical forces so as to deprive the goods of their original fundamental characteristics. For example, when a cargo of copper pipe is melted down as the result of a shipboard fire, the copper may still have value as scrap, but it has "lost specie," i.e., lost its identity as pipe.

LOSS PAYEE. A person or firm named in an insurance policy to receive the proceeds of a claim settlement. Very often the loss payee is a bank or other financial institution with a financial interest in the goods insured.

LOYALTY AGREEMENT. A contract between a shipper and a CONFERENCE *(q.v.),* whereby the shipper pledges to move all or a specified portion of his cargo aboard conference vessels in return for certain economic inducements. In the United States the inducement is limited to a discount of up to 15 percent of the freight levied by the carrier; in other countries, the inducement may provide for rebates as well. (For a representative loyalty agreement *see* Appendix D2.)

LUMPING. The use of casual laborers, employees of neither the carrier nor the shipper, to load or unload trucks.

LUMP SUM CHARTER. A flat fee payable by charterer to a vessel owner, irrespective of whether the stipulated cargo, or any portion thereof, is actually shipped.

M

MADRID AGREEMENT CONCERNING THE INTERNATIONAL REGISTRATION OF MARKS.
An international agreement under which the owner of a trademark or service mark can secure protection for his mark in all the states adhering to the convention by means of a single application.

To enjoy protection under the convention, the applicant must be a national or resident of, or have a place of business in, one of the contracting states. After registering the mark in the national trademark office of that state, the applicant will apply through that office to the WORLD INTELLECTUAL PROPERTY ORGANIZATION *(q.v.)* (WIPO) for an international registration. The applicant must submit all materials in French. WIPO will transmit the international application to the trademark offices of the various contracting states. Each state may reject the application, citing the reasons for such rejection, within one year of submission. In the event an application is rejected, the applicant is entitled to access to the courts, or to any remedies which would have been available had application been submitted for a national registration. In the absence of a formal rejection within one year, the mark is afforded protection by each state on the same basis as a local registration.

The registration must be renewed every twenty years. In addition, the cancellation of registration in the country where the mark was initially filed, within five years of such original filing, may serve to cancel the international filing as well.

The agreement was concluded at Madrid in 1891, and has been revised at Brussels (1900), Washington (1911), The Hague (1925), London (1934), Nice (1957), and Stockholm (1967). Participation is open to all states party to the PARIS CONVENTION FOR THE PROTECTION OF INDUSTRIAL PROPERTY *(q.v.)*. In 1984, the following states were party to the agreement:

Algeria	Italy
Austria	· Hungary
Belgium	Korea (North)
Czechoslovakia	Liechtenstein
Egypt	Luxembourg
France	Monaco
German Democratic	Morocco
Republic	Netherlands
German Federal Republic	Portugal
Romania	Tunisia
San Marino	U.S.S.R.
Spain	Vietnam
Switzerland	Yugoslavia

See also TRADEMARK REGISTRATION TREATY.

MADRID AGREEMENT FOR THE REPRESSION OF FALSE OR DECEPTIVE INDICATIONS OF SOURCE ON GOODS. An international agreement, commonly known as the Madrid Union, concluded for the purpose of suppressing false or misleading origin markings on goods sold in international commerce. Adhering states are obligated to seize and deny importation to merchandise bearing false markings indicating origin in any other adhering state.

The Madrid Union was established in 1891, and was revised at Washington (1911), The Hague (1925), London (1934), Lisbon (1958), and Stockholm (1967). The agreement is administered by the WORLD INTELLECTUAL PROPERTY ORGANIZATION *(q.v.)* and is open to all states adhering to the PARIS UNION *(q.v.)*. In 1984, the following states were party to the Madrid Union:

Algeria	Lebanon
Brazil	Liechtenstein
Bulgaria	Monaco
Cuba	Morocco
Czechoslovakia	New Zealand
Dominican Republic	Poland
Egypt	Portugal
France	San Marino
German Democratic	Spain
Republic	Sri Lanka
German Federal	Sweden
Republic	Switzerland
Hungary	Syria
Ireland	Tunisia
Israel	Turkey
Italy	United Kingdom
Japan	Vietnam

MADRID UNION. *See* MADRID AGREEMENT FOR THE REPRESSION OF FALSE OR DECEPTIVE INDICATIONS OF SOURCE ON GOODS.

MAINTENANCE AND CURE. *See* CURE AND MAINTENANCE.

MAINTENANCE-OF-VALUE CLAUSE. Also known as an *index clause*. A provision in a contract for adjustment in prices or values in the contract in response to exchange rate fluctuations under specified conditions.

MAKE A MARKET. *See* INTERBANK MARKET.

MALTA AGREEMENT. Adoption by certain governments of air carrier liability limitations as expressed in the Montreal Intercarrier Agreement. *See* WARSAW CONVENTION.

MANAGED FLOAT. *Synonymous with* DIRTY FLOAT *(q.v.).*

MANAGEMENT CONTRACT. An arrangement whereby a firm manages or operates a foreign plant on behalf of its local owners in return for a stipulated fee or percentage of the profits.

MANAGING AGENT. A firm that serves as a resident exclusive agent on behalf of a foreign manufacturer. The MA often invests in the local venture and exercises considerable latitude in its operation. Compensation is usually derived on the basis of costs plus a share of the profits.

MANDATE OF CARTAGENA. *See* ANDEAN GROUP.

MANIFEST. A document listing all the cargo stowed aboard a vessel, usually broken down by port of unloading. The manifest is an abstract of the individual bills of lading issued for each consignment and is customarily provided to customs authorities for inspection upon landing.

MANIPULATION WAREHOUSE. *See* BONDED WAREHOUSE.

MANNING AND SUBSISTENCE. The expenses associated with paying and feeding a ship's crew, including allied fringe benefits.

MANSHOLT PLAN. A series of programs, originally articulated by European Economic Community Commissioner Sicco Mansholt in 1968, for the development and harmonization of European agriculture. The objects of the programs were to ensure farmers' levels of income comparable to their counterparts in industry, as required by the Treaty of Rome; to halt the migration of agricultural labor to the cities; to reallocate farmlands from small family farms to larger, more efficient tracts; and to provide occupational skills to farmers to enhance productivity.

Mansholt's proposals were adopted by the EEC Council of Ministers in several directives: 72/159/EEC, farm modernization; 72/160/EEC, land reallocation; 72/161/EEC, skills training; 75/268/EEC, subsidies to enhance the continuation of farming in mountainous and other unfavorable areas; and 77/355/EEC, streamlining the processing and marketing of agricultural products.

In addition, special pronouncements were adopted to accommodate conditions peculiar to certain regions, such as the Mediterranean.

MANUFACTURED OR PROCESSED. In determining DRAWBACK *(q.v.)* eligibility, an article must have been manufactured or processed in the United States; a simple change is not enough to permit recovery in drawback. The article must be transformed into a new item having a distinctive name, character, or use. An exception to this criterion is permitted where a product is unfit for the use for which it was intended; in such cases, rehabilitation of the unfit product into suitable merchandise will normally qualify as a "manufacture."

This requirement does not apply to articles subject to export under *same condition drawback.*

MANUFACTURER'S EXPORT AGENT. Middleman who, on behalf of a domestic manufacturer or trading firm, promotes export sales. The MEA operates under its own name, rather than as a component of the manufacturer's marketing department.

MANUFACTURER'S PARTICULARS. Details of the construction of an intermodal container, as specified in the container's DATA PLATE *(q.v.)*.

MANUFACTURING CLAUSE. A provision of U.S. copyright law which restricts importation of certain printed materials not manufactured in the United States.

The manufacturing clause was incorporated into U.S. copyright law in 1891 as a means of preserving employment in the American printing industry; since that time, the law has been liberalized by several amendments. The current law (17 U.S.C. 601) stipulates that "a work consisting preponderantly of nondramatic literary material in the English language" created by a U.S. citizen or resident may not be imported unless the work was physically manufactured in the United States or Canada. This requirement is satisfied if typesetting, platemaking, or other substantial manufacturing processes are undertaken in the U.S. or Canada.

The manufacturing clause does not apply to a work if the author was not a U.S. citizen or resident at the time the work was first published, or if the work was first published in a country adhering to the UNIVERSAL COPYRIGHT CONVENTION *(q.v.)*.

A limited exemption permitting entry of up to 2,000 copies of a nonconforming work may be obtained by the holder of the U.S. copyright upon application to the Copyright Office, Library of Congress. The *import statement* provided to the applicant by the Copyright Office must be presented to U.S. Customs to effect release of the merchandise.

The manufacturing clause will expire on July 1, 1986.

MANUFACTURING WAREHOUSE. *See* BONDED WAREHOUSE.

MAQUILADORA. Export-oriented industries operating in Mexico in a narrow zone along the U.S. border. The zone was established by the Mexican government in response to high unemployment in the region. Foreign firms locating within the zone (mostly U.S. manufacturers) are generally exempt from Mexico's strict foreign investment code. The manufacturers are permitted to import raw and semiprocessed materials duty free, to employ Mexican workers, and to re-export the finished product paying duty only on the value of labor and foreign materials added in Mexico.

Attracted by low wage rates and an improved transportation network, more than seven hundred U.S. firms now operate *maquiladoras* in the zone.

MARAD. *See* MARITIME ADMINISTRATION.

MARGIN. A cost calculation performed in association with vessel operations that allows for potential cost overruns, e.g., lost days due to adverse weather. A margin of 5 percent is common per voyage.

MARGINAL PROPENSITY TO IMPORT. *See* PROPENSITY TO IMPORT.

MARGIN FEE. In marine insurance, an excise tax imposed upon insurance premiums remitted to foreign insurers.

MARINE BELT. Coastal waters subject to the municipal jurisdiction of the states which they border. By custom and tradition, a nation enjoys dominion over the sea to a distance of three nautical miles from the shore. This rule has been modified by various conventions and unilateral actions by some states to expand their jurisdiction over coastal waters to much greater distances. For example, the United States exerts "customs jurisdiction" up to twelve miles from the shore, and many states claim authority up to two hundred miles from shore or to the edge of the continental shelf as exclusive preserves for fishing, mining, or oil drilling.

A careful distinction should be made, in American usage, between "marine belt" and "maritime belt." In most other countries, the two terms would be interchangeable. However, inasmuch as the United States is a confederation of states, the latter term is used to describe the authority of coastal states of the U. S. over their coastal waters, as distinguished from the broader jurisdiction of the federal government over maritime affairs.

MARINE EXTENSION CLAUSE. A provision in an ocean marine cargo policy for coverage of the merchandise in cases where: (1) there is a deviation by the vessel, transshipment, forced discharge, or the exercise of any liberty granted to the vessel operator under the contract of affreightment; or (2) the goods are landed at a port for sale and remain at the port, up to fifteen days from time of discharge, pending sale and/or commencement of transit to a point other than that covered by the policy. Marine extension clauses are customary in virtually all ocean marine cargo policies.

MARINE INTEREST. The rate of interest applicable to bonds for BOTTOMRY and RESPONDENTIA

(*qq.v.*). Customarily, such rates were far in excess of those charged on commercial transactions generally.

MARITIME BELT. *See* MARINE BELT.

MARITIME ADMINISTRATION. An agency of the U.S. Department of Transportation assigned the task of promoting the American Merchant Marine. MARAD was established in 1950 and pursues its objective through various programs, including ports and intermodal systems development, research and development in vessel and equipment design, and extensive market promotion efforts to encourage the use of American vessels.

The agency also administers *operating differential subsidies* and *construction differential subsidies* to overcome higher costs of building ships under the American flag, and the Cargo Preference Act, which requires that at least 50 percent of government-generated cargoes travel on U.S. flag ships. It operates the U.S. Merchant Marine Academy and provides financial assistance to the state maritime academies to produce qualified officers to staff U.S. vessels.

In addition, during national emergencies, MARAD directs the National Shipping Authority, which coordinates the mobilization of the merchant marine in furtherance of national objectives. Similarly, MARAD administers a war-risk insurance program to provide cover for U.S. flag vessels when war or other conflict makes such insurance commercially unavailable.

MARAD should not be confused with the FEDERAL MARITIME COMMISSION (*q.v.*), an unrelated regulatory agency.

MARITIME LIEN. A claim upon a vessel arising from a maritime operation. Apart from certain statutory "liens" that arise under ship mortgages and governmental guarantees to finance ship construction, a maritime lien must arise from actions involving the vessel itself, its cargo, maritime tort, or other peculiarly maritime occurrences.

Maritime liens traditionally arise from the following obligations: seamen's claims for wages; salvage; torts, involving collisions and personal injuries (excepting seamen's injury claims covered by the Jones Act); general average; preferred ship mortgages (the Federal Ship Mortgage Act statutorily provides a maritime lien against vessels covered; prior to the advent of the statute, the bottomry bank fulfilled a like purpose); supplies and repairs; piloting, wharfage, stevedoring; claims against cargo for unpaid freight; obligations for damage to cargo; breach of charter parties; and bottomry and respondentia bonds. As a practical matter, a maritime lien will not normally arise except in conjunction with one of these conditions.

In 1910 Congress enacted the Federal Maritime Lien Act to supersede various state lien laws so far as maritime claims are concerned, and to clarify obscurities in the customary and Federal case law on the subject. Maritime liens attach in inverse order; that is, the latest lien must be satisfied before prior liens.

Because a maritime lien attaches in reverse order, and there is no statute of limitations per se on the exercise of the lien, it is in the interest of the lienor to execute under his lien as soon as feasible, lest it be superseded by a subsequent lien or become occluded through LACHES *(q.v.)*, that is, an unreasonable delay in execution.

The vehicle for execution of a maritime lien is a *libel in rem*, that is, an in rem action before an admiralty court. Upon commencement of the action, the court may order the marshal to arrest (seize) the ship pending final judgment. Upon a finding for the libelant (lien holder), the vessel will be sold and the lien satisfied. It should be noted that judgments so rendered are (customarily) universally recognized, and that the new owner of the ship is bound by any prior liens not resolved by the court action.

MARITIME PASSPORT. Also known as a sea-brief, sea-letter, and sea-pass, a special document issued to the merchant vessels of a neutral country by their government, describing the vessel and her cargo, and asserting the right to pass upon the seas without interference from belligerent states. Maritime passports are no longer issued by U.S. authorities.

MARITIME SUBSIDY BOARD. A body collateral to the MARITIME ADMINISTRATION *(q.v.)* responsible for reviewing applications for subsidies to U.S. merchant vessel operators to permit competition with lower-cost foreign vessel operators. The board is responsible to the assistant secretary of transportation for maritime affairs.

MARKET ACCESS. The degree of participation in the domestic market that a nation allows to foreign suppliers. Tariffs, quotas, and similar protective devices are devices imposed to limit market access.

MARKET DISRUPTION. A condition in which foreign imports of a given product increase in quantity so rapidly as to cause, or threaten to cause, material injury to a competing domestic industry. A finding of market disruption before the International Trade Commission may result in retaliatory actions against the offending products or the countries from which they are imported.

MARKETING ORIENTATION. The act of locating a manufacturing facility near its principal markets. It usually occurs in cases where the cost of transporting the finished product significantly exceeds the cost of transporting the raw materials. *See* RESOURCE ORIENTATION, WEIGHT GAINING, WEIGHT LOSING.

MARKETING RELATIVISM. A principle that marketing strategies are based upon the seller's personal experiences, which are, in part, culturally prescribed.

MARKET-ORIENTED DISTRIBUTION CENTER. A product distribution center located close to the point of consumption rather than the point of manufacture. For example, an American manufacturer of a product sold in Europe might supply European customers from a (market-oriented) distribution center in Rotterdam, rather than directly from the U.S. warehouse. Such an arrangement would permit a faster response to customer orders, and might permit reduced freight charges arising from large-volume shipments to stock the warehouse, as compared with a large number of small orders sent directly to customers.

MARKING DUTIES. A special duty, in addition to ordinary duties, imposed upon merchandise not properly marked so as to indicate to the ultimate purchaser the country of origin. Section 304 of the Tariff Act of 1930, as amended, requires that the country-of-origin marking be legible, indelible, and permanent. Imported articles may be exempted from the marking requirements in those cases where the country of origin is obvious or marking is not feasible. A listing of imports specifically exempted from marking can be found in 19 U.S.C. 1304 (a) (3) (J), the so-called J-LIST *(q.v.)*.

Marking duties are levied at the rate of 10 percent, ad valorem, in addition to other duties; such marking duties are not construed to be penal and as such are not eligible for remission or mitigation as customs penalties. Marking duties do qualify for recovery through DRAWBACK *(q.v.)* should the foreign article be re-exported.

Payment of marking duties does not relieve the importer from the obligation to mark the goods retroactively as to country of origin.

MARKS AND NUMBERS. The use of identifying symbols and numbers on BREAK-BULK *(q.v.)* cargoes to differentiate among shipments. The practice, still widely followed, originated as a response to the illiteracy common among dock workers in some ports. A shipper assigns a given mark to cargo traveling to a common point and numbers the packages sequentially. The marks ordinarily include the port of destination and may also include the consignee's name, although this name is often omitted for security reasons. The marks and numbers so used are customarily shown on the ocean bill of lading.

MARQUE AND REPRISAL. *See* MART AND COUNTERMART.

MARSHALL PLAN. *See* EUROPEAN RECOVERY PROGRAM.

MART AND COUNTERMART. LETTERS PATENT *(q.v.)* issued by governmental authority to vessel owners authorizing them to wage war upon national enemies and to derive profit from vessels or goods acquired from such enemies.

The U.S. constitution authorizes Congress to commission such privateers through "letters of marque and reprisal." In 1851 most maritime nations (excepting the United States) signed the Treaty of London, prohibiting issuance of letters of mart and countermart.

MASTER. The captain of a merchant vessel.

MASTER AIR WAYBILL. *See* AIR WAYBILL.

MASTER POLICY. A casualty insurance policy that provides a multinational firm with uniform protection for all, or substantially all, its operations worldwide; it usually supplements insurance purchased locally against common perils, e.g., fire.

MASTER'S HAT MONEY. *See* PRIMAGE.

MASTER'S PROTEST. Also known as a *captain's protest,* a document issued by a vessel's master upon reaching port in which he details unusual occurrences during the voyage, such as heavy seas or damage to the ship or cargo. This document may be used in legal proceedings, such as claims for loss or damage in transit, or to support the carrier's defenses against such claims.

MATCHED SALE-PURCHASE TRANSACTIONS. An arrangement whereby Treasury bills are sold by the Federal Reserve system, through the Federal Reserve Bank of New York, for periods of one to seven days, with subsequent repurchase by the Federal Reserve. Such transactions, also known as *reverse repurchase agreements,* serve initially to reduce bank reserves, with a reverse effect at the time the securities are repurchased by the Federal Reserve.

MATE'S RECEIPT. A document issued by a ship's officer acknowledging receipt of a specific quantity of cargo. A mate's receipt is usually issued only in conjunction with a vessel charter.

MATURE ECONOMY. A developed economy in which population growth is declining and new capital investment is slowing. Mature economies tend to be highly urban and industrial. Many economists hold that limited new investment in productive capital will, over time, result in economic stagnation and high unemployment.

MEASUREMENT TON. An expression of cubic measurement equal to forty cubic feet, used either to define the interior of a vessel or as a basis for assessing freight on cargo.

With virtually worldwide conversion to metric measurement, a measurement/stow ton may be defined as the equal of a cubic meter, depending upon the ocean carrier's tariff.

MEMBER BANK. A bank that holds membership in the Federal Reserve system. Membership is mandatory for banks with Federal charters. State-chartered banks may join if qualified. Member banks are obliged to subscribe a fixed portion of their capital and surplus to stock of their regional banks, must maintain prescribed reserves, and submit to periodic examinations.

MEMBER LINE. A steamship line that is a member of a CONFERENCE *(q.v.).*

MEMORANDUM INVOICE. *See* INVOICE.

MEMORANDUM TARIFF. An abstract of a freight tariff. This document, usually published by carriers in a given trade, contains selected rates and other information extracted from the official tariff. The purpose of a memorandum tariff is to highlight information of wide interest.

MERCANTILE AGENCY. A firm that specializes in commercial credit reporting.

MERCANTILE PAPER. Acceptances, short-term notes, and similar short-term obligations of firms engaged in the merchandising, but not the production, of commodities.

MERCHANDISE BALANCE. *See* BALANCE OF TRADE.

MERCHANT BANK. A bank that provides a variety of financial services to commercial entities, including investment banking, acceptance of bills of exchange, insurance portfolio management, as well as business financing. Merchant banks are a Western European institution and do not customarily accept retail banking business.

MERCHANTMAN. A vessel engaged in the business of carrying goods.

MERCHANT MARINE. A nation's fleet of ocean-going commercial cargo and passenger vessels. In some nations these vessels may be owned and operated by instrumentalities of the government. For most of the major maritime nations, however, the vessels are privately owned and operated, although government subsidies are often provided (*see* figure, next page). A vessel is part of the merchant marine of the country in which it is registered; it may be impressed into naval service of that country in time of war or other national emergency.

MINEX. *See* LOMÉ CONVENTION.
usage of most Commonwealth nations, *synonymous with* MERCHANT MARINE *(q.v.).*

MERCHANT'S CONTRACT. In steamship usage, a LOYALTY AGREEMENT *(q.v.).*

METALLIC BASIS. A system in which a national currency is supported by a base of precious metal.

MICRO-BRIDGE. *See* LANDBRIDGE.

MINEX. *See* LOMÉ CONVENTION.

MINI-BRIDGE. *See* LANDBRIDGE.

MINIMUM BILL OF LADING. An ocean bill of lading that incurs the minimum charge provided in the carrier's tariff. The minimum charge, usually forty to seventy-five dollars, depending upon the conference or carrier, is imposed to prevent inundation with small, unprofitable shipments.

UNITED STATES OCEANGOING MERCHANT MARINE
September 1, 1984
(Tonnage in Thousands)

	Total			Privately Owned			Maritime Administration Owned		
	Number Ships	Gross Tons	Deadweight Tons	Number Ships	Gross Tons	Deadweight Tons	Number Ships	Gross Tons	Deadweight Tons
Active Fleet:									
Passenger/Pass. Cargo	9	119	75	5	75	43	4	44	32
General Cargo	49	585	702	45	559	673	4	26	29
Intermodal	114	2,377	2,549	114	2,377	2,549	–	–	–
Bulk Carriers (Incl. TB)	22	615	1,056	22	615	1,056	–	–	–
Tankers (Incl. TKB & LNG)	205	6,212	11,198	203	6,198	11,177	2	14	21
Total	399	9,908	15,580	389	9,824	15,498	10[1/]	84	82
Inactive Fleet:									
Passenger/Pass. Cargo	28	369	213	1	14	6	27	355	207
General Cargo	217	1,863	2,461	24	255	309	193	1,608	2,152
Intermodal	36	614	662	29	498	545	7	116	117
Bulk Carriers (Incl. TB)	3	42	65	3	42	65	–	–	–
Tankers (Incl. TKB & LNG)	69	2,665	4,944	55	2,474	4,629	14	191	315
Total	353	5,553	8,345	112	3,283	5,554	241	2,270	2,791
Passenger/Pass. Cargo	37	488	288	6	89	49	31	399	239
General Cargo	266	2,448	3,163	69	814	982	197	1,634	2,181
Intermodal	150	2,991	3,211	143	2,875	3,094	7	116	117
Bulk Carriers (Incl. TB)	25	657	1,121	25	657	1,121	–	–	–
Tankers (Incl. TKB & LNG)	274	8,877	16,142	258	8,672	15,806	16	205	336
Total American Flag	752	15,461	23,925	501	13,107	21,052	251[2/]	2,354	2,873

1/ - Includes 6 Vessels in Custody of Other Agencies.
2/ - Includes National Defense Reserve Fleet which consist of 231 Ships of which 8 are Scrap Candidates.
      7 Vessels in Bareboat Charter.

United States Oceangoing Merchant Marine

MINIMUM IMPORT PRICE. As used in conjunction with the Common Agricultural Policy of the European Economic Community, GATE PRICE (q.v.).

MINIMUM LENDING RATE. The rate at which the Bank of England lends to members of the discount market against the security of treasury bills or other government paper with less than five years to mature.

MINIMUM LIST. A statistical classification system for foreign trade advanced by the League of Nations. The report entitled *Minimum List of Commodities for International Trade Statistics* was published in 1938. Following World War II, it was superseded by the United Nations STANDARD INTERNATIONAL TRADE CLASSIFICATION (q.v.).

MINTAGE. The charge imposed by a mint for converting bullion into coin money.

MINT FINE BARS. Bars of gold or silver having a fineness of .992 (i.e., 99.2 percent purity) or greater. In American usage, the standard size of such bars is 400 ounces for silver.

MINT PAR OF EXCHANGE. The relationship, in terms of precious metal value, of two nations' currencies, derived by dividing the gold or silver content, by weight, of one nation's currency unit by the comparable metal content of another nation's currency unit.

MINT RATIO. The ration of the amount of gold in a nation's monetary unit to the amount of silver in the same unit, when the nation is on a bimetallic standard. *See* BIMETALLISM.

MISSIONARY RATE. A freight rate established at a particularly low level as an impetus to an infant industry.

MITBESTIMMUNG. The West German version of *codetermination*, i.e., the participation of labor in directing the company. Labor codetermination in Germany arose following World War I and was mandated in the coal and steel industries after World War II. The law provides for a board of twenty-one members: ten representing the shareholders, ten representing labor, and one neutral member selected jointly. In 1976 the act was expanded to embrace a great many industries, and businesses employing more than five hundred workers. *See* VREDLING DIRECTIVE.

MIXED ECONOMY. An economy that possesses the elements of both public and private ownership of the means of production.

MIXED REGULATIONS. Regulations that require that certain imported raw or processed products be mixed with a specified portion of equivalent domestic products as a condition of sale.

MONETARY APPROACH. A view held by one school of economics, that the rate of exchange between two currencies is determined by the relative supply and demand for those currencies.

MONETARY BLOC. A group of countries that have in common the use of a particular reserve asset. Traditionally, the U.S. dollar and the pound sterling have served as primary reserve assets for many nations, resulting in monetary blocs arising around the dollar or the pound.

MONETARY COMPENSATORY AMOUNTS. Settlements between member states of the European Economic Community to reflect the market rate of currencies used in agricultural transactions and the periodically revised GREEN RATE *(q.v.)* used to stabilize commodity prices within the community.

MONETARY RESERVES. Precious metal, or foreign currencies convertible into metal, held by a national treasury or central bank as security for money in circulation.

MONETARY UNIT. The unit of account established by law in terms of which transactions are expressed. In the United States the monetary unit is the dollar, which, although no longer officially converted into gold, is tied to gold at the rate of $42.22 per fine ounce.

MONEY. Any unit or instrument generally accepted as having value to effect the purchase of goods or services, or to settle debts. All money enjoys three characteristics: (1) it is a unit of account in which values can be measured; (2) it is a medium of exchange; and (3) it is a store of value (i.e., a seller of goods can take money in exchange for the property he gives up, and can hold the money until a future time when it may be exchanged in satisfaction of a purchase). Over the centuries, various commodities have been used as money including, inter alia, metals, stones, shells, salt, cattle, and tobacco.

The most recent (1980) pronouncement of the Federal Reserve Board embraces the following definitions of money:

1. *M-1A* is coin and currency in circulation, plus demand deposits at commercial banks, excluding demand deposits of foreign banks, and official institutions.

2. *M-1B* is M-1A plus all other demand deposits at any depository institution, including negotiable order of withdrawl (NOW) acounts, credit union share drafts, automotive transfers, et cetera.

3. *M-2* is M-1B plus savings accounts and small-denomination time deposits, money market mutual funds shares, overnight repurchase agreements at commercial banks, and overnight Eurodollar deposits held by U.S. residents (other than deposits at Caribbean branches of Federal Reserve system member banks);

4. *M-3* is M-2 plus large-denomination time deposits, and term repurchase agreements at commercial banks and savings and loans.

MONEY AT CALL. Also known as *call money*, a demand deposit in a British bank.

MONEY CAPITAL. *See* CAPITAL.

MONEY OF ACCOUNT. The currency unit used in a particular country to record governmental and private transactions. In the United States the money of account is the dollar; in Britain it is the pound sterling.

MONEY VALUE. The value of a good or service expressed in units of the currency in use.

MONOBANK. A bank created when the banks of a nation are consolidated into a single institution. This consolidation occurred in the Soviet Union following the Revolution, and in certain other countries with centrally planned economies.

MONOMETALLISM. *See* SINGLE STANDARD.

MONOPOLISTIC COMPETITION. A condition in the marketplace wherein there are several producers of a product of a given class, but purchasers perceive differences in quality or value among the products of the various manufacturers, thereby according a unique character to each manufacturer's products. For example, there are multiple producers of bourbon whiskey, yet the market segments the various products according to tastes and perceived quality. As a result, a given producer enjoys a *monopoly* in his particular product, although there are like products offered by other producers.

MONOPOLY. The condition in which a given product or service can be obtained only from a single supplier that is free to use its market position to exact excessive prices for the product or service it controls.

The Sherman Act of 1890 makes monopolies and attempts to monopolize illegal in the United States.

MONOPOLY PROFITS. An excess profit achieved by the monopolist as a result of monopolistic behavior. The effect is to make the marginal cost of production higher than necessary, thereby disrupting the allocation of resources through market forces.

MONOPSONY. The condition in which there is a single buyer for a given product or service, although there may be many suppliers.

MONTANT FORFAITAIRE. Also known as *abattement forfaitaire*, the amount by which members of the European Economic Community reduce levies on products imported from other EEC members, thereby ensuring a price advantage to Community products over imports from the outside.

MONTANT DE SOUTIEN. A plan devised by the European Economic Community in 1963 as the basis of agricultural trade negotiations during the Kennedy round. The plan is predicated upon a *reference price* for a given agricultural commodity; any imports below the reference price would incur a levy equal to the spread between the market and reference prices, thereby effectively eliminating import price competition with domestic EEC produce.

The MDS scheme was proposed by Sicco Mansholt and became known as *Mansholt II*.

MONTREAL INTERCARRIER AGREEMENT. *See* WARSAW CONVENTION.

MONTREAL PROTOCOLS. *See* WARSAW CONVENTION.

MOORSOM TON. A unit of measurement consisting of one hundred cubic feet, used principally in connection with measuring vessels.

MORATORIUM. An official suspension of foreign remittances, including commercial settlements, usually as a result of a chronic negative balance of payments.

MORDIDA. Latin American usage for a gratuitous payment to a business associate or government official to stimulate a desired result.

MOST FAVORED NATION. A privilege granted to a nation to have customs duties levied upon its products at the lowest rate offered to any other nation. Customarily, the extension of most favored nation status is reciprocal. *See* TARIFF (CUSTOMS).

MOST SERIOUSLY AFFECTED. A description applied by the United Nations Special Fund to less developed countries whose balances of payments have been "most seriously affected" by the significant increase in the price of oil since 1973. The purpose of the fund is to provide financial assistance to the developing countries affected to permit their economies to restabilize.

MOTHER EDGE. *See* REGULATION K.

MOTHER SHIP. A long-haul vessel that serves only selected major ports directly, turning over its cargo for output to barges or smaller conveyances for delivery.

MOTOR SHIP. A vessel that employs a marine diesel engine as its propulsion method. The fuel efficiency of diesel engines causes them to operate more cost effectively than steam turbine plants, which were used in earlier vessel designs.

MTN VALUATION CODE. An agreement on valuation for customs purposes, more commonly known as the CUSTOMS VALUATION AGREEMENT *(q.v.)*.

MULTIFIBER ARRANGEMENT. An international agreement among textile-producing and consuming nations to provide a framework for orderly trade in textiles and apparel. For many years, the textile manufacturing industries of the developed nations have been beset by intense competition from lower-cost imports, resulting in unemployment and economic disruption in the importing countries. In most developed industrial nations, textile manufacturing represents a major industry. In the United States, the textile and apparel industry is the nation's largest manufacturing employer, representing 2.1 million manufacturing jobs (or one out of every nine).

In response to sharply rising imports, with attendant loss of jobs in the United States, Congress authorized the president in Section 204 of the Agricultural Act of 1956 to negotiate textile restraint agreements with foreign governments. In 1962 Congress authorized unilateral restraints on disruptive imports from countries not participating in an international textiles agreement.

Various international agreements undertaken between 1962 and 1971 did not fully resolve the problems of textile imports. To address the problem on a broader basis, the General Agreement on Tariffs and Trade in 1973 called a meeting of producing and importing nations to consider a comprehensive plan for trade in all fibers, natural and man-made. Fifty nations participated in the meeting, from which emerged the Multifiber Arrangement Regarding International Trade in Textiles (MFA). The MFA took effect January 1, 1974, for a four-year period; it was renewed through December 31, 1981, and again through July 31, 1986.

Operating under authority of the MFA is the Textile Surveillance Body (TSB), which seeks to implement the agreement and which reviews disputes among participating countries. The United States, Japan, and the European Communities are permanent members of the TSB; other TSB members are selected annually by the states adhering to the MFA.

Under the umbrella of the MFA, the United States has concluded bilateral textile agreements with twenty-five MFA states, and eight agreements with non-MFA. In the aggregate, these bilateral agreements cover almost 90 percent of the textiles and apparel entering the United States from foreign sources.

The various bilateral agreements set total limits, on a per-country basis, for exports to the United States of various fibers, specific textile or apparel products, or groups of products; in addition, all agreements concluded by the United States assure undisturbed access to the American market, provide for reasonable growth, and stipulate consultative processes to resolve disputes.

In November 1984, *MFA Signatory States* were:

Argentina	Colombia
Austria	Czechoslovakia
Bangladesh	Dominican Republic
Bolivia	European
Brazil	Economic Community
Canada	Egypt

El Salvador
Finland
Ghana
Guatemala
Haiti
Hungary
India
Indonesia
Israel
Jamaica
Japan
Korea, Republic of
Malaysia
Maldives
Mexico

Peru
Philippines
Portugal (for Macao)
Romania
Singapore
Sri Lanka
Sweden
Switzerland
Thailand
Turkey
United Kingdom
(for Hong Kong)
United States
Uruguay
Yugoslavia

The United States has *Bilateral Textile Agreements* with specific restraints with the following nations:

	Expiration date
Brazil	12/31/87
China	12/31/87
Colombia	6/30/86
Costa Rica	12/31/87
Dominican Republic	5/31/88
Egypt	12/31/87
Haiti	12/31/86
Hong Kong	12/31/87
Hungary	12/31/86
India	12/31/87
Indonesia	6/30/85
Jamaica	no expiration date
Japan	12/31/85
Korea	12/31/87
Macao	12/31/88
Malaysia	12/31/89
Maldives	9/28/85
Mauritius	12/31/87
Mexico	12/31/85
Pakistan	12/31/86
Panama	11/30/85
Peru	4/30/89
Philippines	12/31/86
Poland	12/31/89
Romania	12/31/87
Singapore	12/31/85
Sri Lanka	5/31/88
Taiwan	12/31/87
Thailand	12/31/87
Uruguay	6/30/87
Yugoslavia	12/31/85

The United States has agreements without specific restraints and without expiration dates with: Costa Rica, Greece, Jamaica, Malta, Mauritius, Nicaragua, and Peru.

MULTILATERAL DEVELOPMENT BANK. Any of several banks owned or controlled by governments or public international institutions and created to stimulate economic development in less developed countries. It is characteristic for such banks to be capitalized and supported by more affluent nations, and to fund large-scale development programs and infrastructure in poorer member countries.

The World Bank is the largest multilateral development bank, although there are several others, including the Inter-American Development Bank, the African Development Bank, and the Asian Development Bank.

MULTILATERAL TRADE NEGOTIATIONS. Negotiations among many nations acting in concert for the purpose of reducing trade barriers. Since the inception of the GENERAL AGREEMENT ON TARIFFS AND TRADE *(q.v.)*. in 1947, the most significant multilateral negotiations have occurred under GATT auspices. The first five rounds of GATT-sponsored negotiations involved series of simultaneous bilateral negotiations with tariff reductions pursued on an item-by-item basis. With the Kennedy Round (1964–67) products were grouped for tariff reduction by the application of a single formula. The Tokyo Round (1973–79) employed a single reduction formula and addressed various nontariff barriers.

MULTIMODAL BILL OF LADING. A bill of lading that provides for carriage of goods by more than one mode of transport (i.e., water, air, rail, motor), unlike a *combined transport bill of lading*, in which the issuer of the bill assumes responsibility for the goods through to destination. The multimodal bill may leave each carrier responsible for loss or damage during its respective segment of the journey.

MULTIMODAL TRANSPORT. The movement of goods by more than one mode, or type, of transport, for example, a movement by truck to a pier, then by ship to a foreign port, and finally by rail to the customer.

MULTIPLE CHANNEL. A marketing strategy that recognizes and employs various types of channels of distribution to penetrate different markets, depending upon local conditions.

MULTIPLE COLUMN TARIFF. *See* TARIFF (CUSTOMS).

MULTIPLE CURRENCY SYSTEM. *Synonymous with* DIFFERENTIAL EXCHANGE RATES *(q.v.)*.

MULTIPLE EXCHANGE RATES. *Synonymous with* DIFFERENTIAL EXCHANGE RATES *(q.v.)*.

MULTIPLE GREEN RATES. *See* GREEN RATE.

MULTITANK CONTAINER. An intermodal container which is internally segmented to allow carriage of different liquids. Such containers may be equipped with heating coils to accommodate substances normally solid or semisolid but which liquefy when heated.

MUNICIPAL LAW. In international affairs, the internal, domestic law of a particular country.

N

NAIROBI TREATY ON THE PROTECTION OF THE OLYMPIC SYMBOL. An international agreement to protect the Olympic symbol against commercial use without the approval of the International Olympic Committee (IOC).

The treaty specifies that adhering states will prohibit use of the Olympic symbol on goods or advertising or as a trademark except under license from the IOC. In those instances where the IOC imposes a license fee for use of the symbol, a portion of the revenue must be allocated to the relevant national Olympic committee.

The agreement is administered by the WORLD INTELLECTUAL PROPERTY ORGANIZATION *(q.v.)* and is open to any state which is a member of that organization, the United Nations or any of its specialized agencies, or the PARIS CONVENTION *(q.v.)*. In 1984 the following states had adopted the Nairobi Treaty: Congo, Egypt, Equatorial Guinea, Ethiopia, Guatemala, and Kenya.

NAMUCAR. The Spanish acronym for the Caribbean Multinational Shipping Company, a joint venture established in 1976 by Costa Rica, Cuba, Venezuela, Trinidad and Tobago, Jamaica, Nicaragua, and Mexico. The purpose of the corporation is to build a merchant fleet beyond the capabilities of the members individually.

NARROW SEAS. Open seas between two coasts not widely separated, e.g., the English Channel, Persian Gulf.

NATIONAL CARGO BUREAU. A nonprofit, membership corporation concerned with the safe loading, stowage, transport, and unloading of cargoes aboard vessels. The NCB provides on-site inspection services to ensure that cargoes are stowed correctly and that incompatible materials are not stowed together. In the case of shipments aboard bulk vessels, the NCB may provide draft or deadweight surveys; such surveys can be used as a render of the amount of cargo laden or discharged in ports where shoreside scales are not available.

In addition, the NCB performs equipment inspections to satisfy compliance with government regulations. The Coast Guard and Department of Labor accept NCB certification of compliance for ship's gear. NCB certificates are accepted by the major maritime nations as evidence of compliance with the requirements of International Labor Organization Convention No. 32 concerning safety at sea. Also, the NCB has been appointed as vessel inspection agent in the United States for Liberian and Panamanian flag ships.

The National Cargo Bureau was formed in 1952 by the merger and expansion of the Board of Underwriters of New York (formed 1820) and the Board of Marine Underwriters of San Francisco (founded 1886).

The NCB maintains its headquarters in New York and operates through ninety-two offices in the United States and the Panama Canal Zone.

NATIONAL EXPORTS. Exports consisting of goods domestically produced or goods produced within customs-bonded facilities.

NATIONAL FLAG CARRIER. A COMMON CARRIER *(q.v.)*—usually a steamship line or an airline—that bears its country's flag and is viewed in the trading community as representing the commercial interests of the home country.

NATIONALIZED EXPORTS. Goods previously imported and cleared through customs that are exported without having been changed in form or substance.

NATIONAL LINE. *Synonymous with* NATIONAL FLAG CARRIER *(q.v.)*.

NATIONAL TREATMENT PRINCIPLE. A view of international economic transactions that asserts that a nation should accord the same treatment to foreign merchandise, investments, shipping, and entrepreneurs as it does to domestic counterparts under like commercial conditions. Apart from international practice on the part of the European Economic Community and the Central American Common Market, this approach has not been widely adopted.

NAVICERT. *See* NAVIGATION CERTIFICATE.

NAVIGABLE WATERS. Bodies of water, including the sea, rivers, and some lakes, over which the public has a right to sail and anchor. This right of passage conveys no claim upon the lands underlying the water; title to such lands remains with the owner or the state (except in the case of open seas), although the title holder may not impede innocent passage over the waterway.

Various pronouncements of the United Nations have declared the lands beneath the open seas to be the "common heritage of mankind."

NAVIGATION CERTIFICATE. A document issued by a belligerent, in time of war, certifying that a ship and its cargo have been searched and permission has been given for the vessel to proceed on to a neutral port.

NEGATIVE INVESTMENT. *See* DISINVESTMENT.

NEGOTIATION. The act whereby title to, and rights in, a negotiable instrument are transferred from one party to another. Instruments payable to "bearer" or endorsed in blank are negotiated by mere delivery; instruments payable "to order" of a specific party are negotiated by ENDORSEMENT *(q.v.)* and delivery.

NEOFACTOR. A revisionist definition of the means of production to include factors other than land, labor, and capital, or to expand the meaning of a given factor substantially beyond its conventional usage.

NET AVAILS. The proceeds of an acceptance, note, or like obligation after discount charges are deducted.

NET CAPACITY. *Synonymous with* DEADWEIGHT TONNAGE *(q.v.)*.

NET CHARTER. A peculiarly American usage, under which all charges beyond delivery of a vessel to the first port of call are for the account of the charterer.

NET LINE. The face value of all insurance policies that an insurer has in force, less any amounts reinsured.

NET NATIONAL PRODUCT. The sum total, expressed in monetary terms, of all goods and services produced in a country during a given period (usually one year), less the value of capital consumed (depreciation).

NET REGISTER TON. *Synonymous with* NET TON *(q.v.)*.

NET TON. A unit of measurement in determining the cargo-carrying capacity of a vessel. It is computed in the same manner as the GROSS TON *(q.v.)* but includes only revenue-producing (i.e., cargo storage) capacity, less engine and fuel space, crew quarters, et cetera.

NET TRANSFER OF CAPITAL. Funds available for investment after deducting principal and interest payments.

NEUTRAL MARGINS. *See* GREEN RATE.

NEW DELHI DECLARATION. A pronouncement, incorporating an action plan, articulated by developing nations at a 1980 New Delhi conference of the United Nations Industrial Development Organization (UNIDO). The 1980 declaration reiterated the goal defined in the 1975 Lima Declaration, i.e., that developing countries would control 25 percent of world industrial production by the year 2000; in addition, the New Delhi Declaration proposed a North-South Global Fund, financed by the industrialized nations, to provide three hundred billion dollars in concessional aid to developing countries by A.D. 2000. The declaration also proposed that UNIDO be used to negotiate commitments by the industrialized countries.

The declaration was prepared by the GROUP OF SEVENTY-SEVEN *(q.v.)* but repudiated by the advanced nations.

NEW ECONOMIC MECHANISM. A technique applied in certain socialist economies, most notably Hungary, in which the management of productive facilities is entrusted to professional managers, rather than the bureaucracy or state planning apparatus. The concept is viewed as a movement toward the use of incentive-oriented stimulus to increase productivity.

NEW INTERNATIONAL ECONOMIC ORDER. A scheme for the restructuring of the world's economy to permit greater participation by and benefit to developing nations. The "new order" is not a specific program, per se, but a declaration of principles and an agenda of topics for discussions between industrialized and developing nations; these discussions are known as the *North-South Dialogue*.

The articulation of principles arose in response to the general deterioration of economic conditions in the early 1970s. The formal "Declaration for the Establishment of a New International Economic Order" emerged from the United Nations General Assembly in 1974.

Among basic elements to be resolved in creating the new order are reaffirmation of the international monetary system; assured and affordable supplies of food to underdeveloped nations; debt relief and concessionary aid; commodity agreements and relaxation of tariffs; long-range development questions, including exploitation of the seas.

The declaration calling for a new economic order has stimulated specific aid measures on behalf of developing nations, including debt restructuring and reduction or elimination of tariffs on some developing country exports.

See GENERALIZED SYSTEM OF PREFERENCES, RETROACTIVE TERMS ADJUSTMENT.

NEW JASON CLAUSE. A stipulation in ocean bills of lading subject to the U.S. CARRIAGE OF GOODS BY SEA ACT *(q.v.)*.

Prior to the adoption of the Harter Act of 1893, American law recognized no right of participation in general average for losses sustained by the vessel through whose fault the averageable expenses and sacrifices had been sustained. Because the Harter Act provided shipowners with broad relief from responsibility for loss or damage of cargo, it was presumed by some that the act also relieved the proscription on contributions in general average to a negligent vessel. In the *Irrawaddy* case, however, the United States Supreme Court rejected a claim of general average by a vessel that had contributed to the marine peril.

To establish a basis by which a negligent vessel could recover in general average, shipowners inserted into their bills of lading a condition that permitted recovery whenever the ship would have been exonerated from claims to cargo under the Harter Act and the shipowner exercised due diligence to make the ship seaworthy. In the case of the ship *Jason*, the Supreme Court held the clause valid in 1912.

The carrier immunities incorporated in the original Jason clause were refined by the Carriage of Goods by Sea Act of 1936. The following constitutes the "new" Jason clause:

> In the event of accident, danger, damage, or disaster, before or after commencement of the voyage resulting from any cause whatsoever, whether due to negligence or not, for which, or for the consequence of which, the Carrier is not responsible by statute, contract, or otherwise, the goods, shippers, consignees, or owners of the goods shall contribute with the Carrier in general average to the payment of any sacrifices, losses, or expenses of a general average nature that may be made or incurred, and shall pay salvage and special charges incurred in respect of the goods.

This statement is incorporated by reference into every ocean bill of lading subject to the U.S. Carriage of Goods by Sea Act of 1936.

NEWLY INDUSTRIALIZING COUNTRY.

A nation in transition between developing and developed status. Characteristic of such a change are the development of an industrial base and an increasing portion of gross national product derived from industrial, rather than agricultural, production. Mexico, Taiwan, and Brazil are examples of nations in such transition.

NEW YORK CONVENTION ON THE RECOGNITION AND ENFORCEMENT OF FOREIGN ARBITRAL AWARDS.

An international convention that emerged on June 10, 1958, at the conclusion of the United Nations Conference on International Commercial Arbitration. The convention establishes principles and procedures for the arbitration of international commercial disputes, and reinforces the position that signatory states are obliged to enforce arbitration awards granted under terms of the convention, excluding instances where irregularities are demonstrated to have affected the award. The convention is not applicable to domestic arbitration agreements. In those cases where a party to an arbitration agreement, or another party with an interest in the dispute, seeks relief through the courts of a signatory state, the courts shall stay any judicial remedies pending an outcome of the arbitration proceedings. The New York convention is not clear on which law shall be applied by the arbitrators. A presumption has arisen through usage that, in those cases where choice of law is not specified in the arbitration agreement, the law of the jurisdiction where the arbitration takes place (lex loci arbitri) shall apply.

The New York convention supersedes the Geneva Protocol on Arbitration Clauses (1923) and the Geneva Convention on the Execution of Foreign Arbitral Awards (1927) to the extent that the parties to the dispute are subject to the jurisdiction of states that have accepted the 1958 New York agreement.

The convention entered into force in the United States on February 1, 1971, and is given effect in Chapter 2 of the U.S. Arbitration Act, Title 9, U.S.C.

NEW YORK DOLLARS. Funds payable in New York. A Detroit bank opening a letter of credit on London, for example, may instruct the London bank to reimburse itself by drawing on deposits maintained by the Detroit bank in New York.

NEXUS. The relationship, for tax purposes, between an individual or firm and the jurisdiction in which they conduct their activities. For example, the sale of goods from a warehouse in Denver may constitute a nexus under which an out-of-state firm becomes subject to Colorado corporate income taxes.

NIMEXE. The statistical classification system employed in the Common Customs Tariff (CCT) of the European Economic Community. The CCT is based upon the four-digit Customs Cooperation Council Nomenclature; under Nimexe, two suffix digits are provided to permit further subdivision of statistical classifications. Each member of the EEC is permitted to have further statistical subdivisions beyond those provided in Nimexe.

The Harmonized Coal and Steel Nomenclature for Foreign Trade, in force since 1964, is fully incorporated into Nimexe.

The Nimexe system was devised in 1966 in order to meet the need of the EEC members for more refined capture of foreign trade data; the system was modified in 1969.

THE NINE. A reference to the European Communities after the so-called first enlargement in 1972, which added Great Britain, Ireland, and Denmark to the original six member states (France, Germany, Italy, Belgium, Netherlands, Luxembourg). The European Communities have since undergone a second enlargement to include Greece.

NO ARRIVAL, NO SALE. A contractual arrangement between a buyer and seller under which the buyer assumes no interest in the goods and no risk of loss or damage until actual delivery has been accomplished.

NOMINAL INTEREST RATE. The rate of interest earned by an investment, without adjustment for inflation. Deducting the inflation factor from the nominal rate yields the *effective* or *real* interest rate, which is a more accurate reflection of the return on the investment.

NOMINALISM. An economic viewpoint that asserts that MONEY *(q.v.)* consists only of legal tender issued by governmental authority, as contrasted with more widely held views that would include demand deposits, certain securities, et cetera, within the definition of *money*.

NONADMITTED. An insurance company that writes policies in a jurisdiction where it is not registered to do business.

NONCONFERENCE CARRIER. A steamship line that is not a member of the CONFERENCE *(q.v.)* over a given trade route.

NONCONTRACT RATE. The freight rate applicable to commodities shipped by a firm that has not executed an EXCLUSIVE PATRONAGE CONTRACT *(q.v.)*.

NONCONTRACT SHIPPER. A firm that has not executed an EXCLUSIVE PATRONAGE CONTRACT *(q.v.)*.

NONCUMULATIVE LETTER OF CREDIT. *See* REVOLVING LETTER OF CREDIT.

NONDUMPING CERTIFICATE. A seller's certification, either in the form of a separate document or as a notation upon the invoice, that the merchandise described is being sold at a price no lower than that applicable to like sales in the country of origin. The purpose of the certification is to allay concerns of customs authorities that imported merchandise is being dumped. *See* DUMPING.

NONDURABLE GOODS. Products, usually consumer items, that have a short useful life. In the United States the criterion is a life of three years or less. Such items are usually purchased as needed.

NONINTERVENTIONISM. A view that central banks and other governmental agencies should refrain from attempting to set or stabilize rates of exchange through purchases or sales, leaving exchange rates to market forces.

NONMARKET ECONOMY. Essentially, an economy that is centrally planned, i.e., allocation of resources is directed by a governmental authority, rather than by market forces.

For purposes of trade reporting and other reasons, the U.S. government defines the following states as nonmarket economies:

China	Bulgaria
USSR	Hungary
Yugoslavia	Albania
Poland	Mongolia
Romania	Vietnam
German Democratic	Cuba
Republic	Korea, North
Czechoslovakia	

NONPRIVILEGED DOMESTIC STATUS. The condition of merchandise of U.S. origin entered into a FOREIGN TRADE ZONE *(q.v.)*, other than goods that have been granted PRIVILEGED DOMESTIC STATUS *(q.v.)*. Nonprivileged merchandise is subject to classification, appraisal, and taxation at the time the goods leave the foreign trade zone and enter the customs territory of the United States. Imported merchandise upon which duties have already been paid prior to entry into the zone may be subject to additional levies unless the privileged status is obtained at time of entry into the zone.

NONPRIVILEGED FOREIGN STATUS. The condition of imported merchandise entered into a FOREIGN TRADE ZONE *(q.v.)*, other than goods that have been granted PRIVILEGED FOREIGN STATUS *(q.v.)*. Nonprivileged merchandise will be assessed the rates of duties and taxes applicable at the time of entry into the customs territory of the United States for consumption or bonded storage.

NONRECOURSE EXPORT FINANCING. *See* FORFAITING.

NONTARIFF BARRIER. An economic, political, legal, or administrative impediment to trade, other than the specific exclusions conveyed by quotas or the cost impact of duties. The most common nontariff barriers are found in administrative regulations a country imposes on the manufacture, sale, or use of a specific product, irrespective of whether its origin is domestic or foreign. Very often these regulations are not aimed at impeding trade. Even among highly integrated free trade areas such as the European Economic Community such barriers exist; for example, France levies a high tax on grain-based spirits, thereby impeding sales of foreign whiskey in France.

NON-VESSEL OPERATING COMMON CARRIER. A common carrier providing point-to-point international transport of goods. This type of carrier, commonly known as NVOCC, may not actually operate any transport equipment, acting instead as a coordinator among actual carriers. For example, an NVOCC might issue a bill of lading from Saint Louis to Munich, contracting with motor carriers to take the goods to the U.S. pier and from the European pier, as well as with the steamship carrier to move goods across the ocean. The NVOCC will issue its own bill of lading from origin to destination, assessing one charge for the entire movement.

The principal value of the NVOCC is in providing through transportation services, especially to smaller firms or those with a limited knowledge of transportation services.

As a practical matter, NVOCCs are not regulated and instances of poor management or unethical behavior are not unknown. The principal criticism of NVOCCs derives from the fact the NVOCC does not actually perform any transportation services, subcontracting them to conventional common carriers and thereby deriving profits without the substantial capital investments customarily associated with transport operations.

NORAZI AGENT. An export/ import middleman who trades in illicit merchandise, such as arms, untaxed liquor, or other contraband; the norazi agent also engages in trade of otherwise legitimate cargoes to countries ordinarily closed to normal commercial channels.

NORMAL PRICE. Within the scope of the BRUSSELS DEFINITION OF VALUE *(q.v.)*, the value basis upon which ad valorem duties will be assessed on imports. The normal price is the price the goods would command in an open-market sale between buyer and seller for delivery at the time and place of actual importation; it includes transportation and other costs incidental to bringing the goods to the point of importation. When the purchase price does not reflect all consideration given by the buyer to the seller (e.g., patent rights), the value of the goods will be adjusted for customs purposes.

The CUSTOMS VALUATION AGREEMENT *(q.v.)* emerging from the Tokyo Round of multilateral trade negotiations has substituted the *transaction value* for the normal price concept.

NORMAL TRADE LOSS. The amount of product in a bulk shipment that is routinely lost during the routine course of transit, for example, the amount of grain that remains in the hold of a ship after normal discharge and cannot economically be retrieved. Such losses, within defined parameters, are not usually covered by insurance.

NORM PRICE. *See* INDICATIVE PRICE.

NORTH-SOUTH DIALOGUE. Various discussions and negotiating sessions between the industrialized (North) and developing (South) countries directed toward a restructuring of the global economy. *See* NEW INTERNATIONAL ECONOMIC ORDER.

NOSTRO ACCOUNTS. Funds that a domestic bank holds abroad, denominated in local currencies, on deposit with its own branches or correspondents.

NOTICE OF READINESS. Written notification provided by a vessel owner to a charterer, shipper, or consignee that the vessel has arrived at port and is prepared to commence loading or discharging of cargo, as the case may be. Failure by the charterer, shipper, or consignee to commence loading/discharging is apt to start LAYTIME *(q.v.)* running.

NOTIONAL CONCEPT OF VALUATION. An approach to the application of ad valorem duties that holds that duties should be applied upon the price the goods "ought to fetch" under specified conditions; this view was widely held for many years and was embraced in the BRUSSELS DEFINITION OF VALUE *(q.v.)*. The notional concept is contrasted with the *positive* concept, which asserts that duties should be applied upon the value of the transaction, as defined by buyer and seller. The major trading nations have recently adopted the notional view in the CUSTOMS VALUATION AGREEMENT *(q.v.)*.

NUMERAIRE SYSTEM. A multinational currency stabilization arrangement wherein participating national currencies are assigned a central rate, or value, in terms of a given unit of account; this rate is based upon a basket of all the participating currencies, weighted according to defined criteria. A margin would be fixed within which each currency might fluctuate. Fluctuations beyond the assigned margins would require intervention by the country issuing the unstable currency so as to restore equilibrium.

NVOCC. *See* NON-VESSEL OPERATING COMMON CARRIER.

O

OCEAN FREIGHT DIFFERENTIAL. A sum representing the difference in freight costs associated with moving subsidized agricultural exports on American rather than cheaper foreign vessels. The differential is provided for shipments under the AGRICULTURAL TRADE DEVELOPMENT AND ASSISTANCE ACT *(q.v.)*, and is paid by the Commodity Credit Corporation.

OCEAN SHIPPING ACT OF 1978. P.L. 483, 46 U.S.C. 842, also known as the *Controlled Carrier Act,* is an amendment to the Shipping Act of 1916 designed to inhibit so-called predatory rate practices on the part of certain carriers controlled by foreign governments. For several years prior to the adoption of the act it had been evident that some state-owned vessels, most notably Soviet, had been successful in attracting cargo away from Western flag carriers by offering rates below those necessary to sustain profit-oriented businesses.

Under the act, all rates must be "just and reasonable," as determined by comparing the rates charged with the carrier's costs; rates at or below cost are presumed unreasonable. If no cost information is available for the controlled carrier, costs will be "constructed" by comparison with noncontrolled carriers on the same trade route.

A controlled carrier may not reduce rates on less than thirty days' notice to the Federal Maritime Commission, which may suspend or disapprove rates found to be unjust or unreasonable. Rate reductions resulting from the action of a CONFERENCE *(q.v.)* of which a controlled carrier is a member are presumed to be just and reasonable. No test of reasonableness of rates is required on commerce between the country controlling the carrier and the United States.

For purposes of the act, a controlled carrier is one owned by a foreign state or its instrumentalities, or in which a majority of the carrier's directors or its chief executive is appointed by a foreign government.

OFF-CHARTER. The termination of a vessel charter agreement, freeing the vessel to pursue other cargoes. Off-charter should not be confused with *off-hire,* in which the payment of hire is suspended for some reason, but the contract remains in force.

OFFER. In vessel charter transactions, *synonymous with* FIRM OFFER *(q.v.)*.

OFFER LIST. A list of products, usually prepared in conjunction with multilateral trade negotiations, upon which a nation is prepared to negotiate trade liberalization; the list may also identify products that are to be specifically exempted from discussion.

OFF-HIRE. A period of time when a chartered vessel is not earning income for the owner. Most charter parties provide for times when a vessel will be considered off-hire, e.g., when the vessel fails to perform properly.

OFF-HIRE CLAUSE. Also known as the *breakdown clause,* a provision in a time charter party that charter hire shall cease from the breakdown or inability of the vessel to perform until the condition is remedied. A common breakdown clause provides that hire shall abate as the result of

any detention of or loss of time due to deficiency of men or stores, fire, breakdown of or damage to hull, machinery or equipment, grounding, dry-docking, cleaning of boilers, fumigation (including deratization and extermination of vermin) and guarantee unless occasioned by the nature of the cargo carried or ports visited . . . or to any cause whatsoever rendering the vessel inefficient for duties.

In some charter parties, hire continues for a specified period, usually forty-eight hours, following breakdown.

OFFICE OF EXPORT CONTROL. A branch of the Department of Commerce charged with reviewing, approving, or denying validated export licenses.

OFFICIAL DEVELOPMENT ASSISTANCE. Financial and technical assistance provided by the governments of industrial nations to less developed nations. This assistance may be provided on a bilateral or multilateral basis, but always emanates from the governmental (i.e., official) sector, as compared with assistance provided by nongovernmental entities, e.g., Red Cross, CARE, and religious groups.

OFFICIAL SETTLEMENTS BALANCE. An element of national balance of payments accounting that represents the transfer of reserve assets to, or borrowing from, foreign governments in order to offset a balance of payments deficit.

OFFICIAL VALUE. A value for duty purposes officially assigned by a nation to certain imported goods. Usually the official value is compared with the invoice value, and ad valorem duties are levied upon the higher value.

OFFSET TRADES. *See* COUNTERTRADE.

OFFSHORE CENTER. A locale with many foreign banks in residence.

OFFSHORE FINANCE COMPANY. *Synonymous with* FOREIGN BASE FINANCE COMPANY *(q.v.).*

OFFSHORE HOLDING COMPANY. *Synonymous with foreign base holding company. See* SUBPART F.

OFFSHORE TRADING COMPANY. *Synonymous with foreign base trading company. See* SUBPART F.

OIL FACILITY. A borrowing facility established by the International Monetary Fund in June 1974 to provide member nations with financial resources to accommodate balance of payments deficits due to increased petroleum prices. The facility was eliminated in 1976.

OLD-LINE FACTORING. *See* FACTORING.

OLIGOPOLY. Literally, a market in which there are only a few sellers of a given product or service. Under oligopolistic conditions, no one seller can establish market prices, except in concert with the other suppliers; if such concerted action develops, the suppliers are operating as a *cartel.*

While limited competition may occur among the sellers, a single large supplier may assume a leadership position that the others will follow in establishing prices and terms of sale.

OLIGOPSONY. A market condition in which there are a limited number of buyers of a given product or service.

ON BOARD BILL OF LADING. An ocean BILL OF LADING *(q.v.)* bearing the carrier's endorsement "on board" or words of like import stipulating that the cargo covered by the bill of lading has been physically loaded aboard the vessel for transit. Customarily, bills of lading requiring the "on board" endorsement are not released by the carrier to the shipper until the vessel has actually sailed.

ON DECK BILL OF LADING. An ocean BILL OF LADING *(q.v.)* bearing the specific endorsement "on deck," "on deck at shipper's risk," or words of like import. Such bills of lading are properly issued for cargo that must be stowed on deck because size does

not permit stowage below decks, or where the hazardous character of the goods obliges they be kept on deck for easy jettison in the event of danger. The issuance of an "on deck" bill of lading mitigates the carrier's liability for the cargo, and most ocean marine insurance policies specifically limit the underwriter's exposure on such shipments. ("On deck" bills are not acceptable for presentation under a LETTER OF CREDIT *[q.v.],* except where the credit expressly authorizes them.) Nonhazardous goods may also be shipped on the deck of the vessel but do not constitute *on deck cargo* unless an on deck bill is issued.

ON DECK CARGO. Cargo, normally of a hazardous nature, that is stowed on the deck of the vessel for easy discharge overboard in the event of fire or other danger. The bill of lading for cargo stowed on deck for reasons of safety will bear a special "on deck" notation which conveys that the goods are carried at the shipper's risk, thereby imposing a reduced liability upon the carrier.

ON HER BEAM ENDS. The condition of a ship that lists to such a degree that her decks are awash on one side, and the vessel cannot be righted by her own means.

OPEN ACCOUNT SALES. A form of trade credit in which the seller allows the buyer to postpone payment for a stipulated period, usually thirty to ninety days, without payment of interest. Payment of the account ahead of schedule may earn the buyer a cash discount.

OPEN CHARTER. A charter party that specifies neither the port(s) of destination nor the cargo to be carried.

OPEN CONFERENCE. *See* CONFERENCE.

OPEN MARKET CAPTIVE. *See* CAPTIVE INSURANCE COMPANY.

OPEN MARKET OPERATIONS. A principal vehicle of the Federal Reserve system in expanding or contracting bank reserves. The Federal Open Market Committee, consisting of the entire Board of Governors of the Federal Reserve system, plus representatives of five of the twelve regional Federal Reserve banks (the New York Federal Reserve is permanently represented; the other four memberships rotate), engages the purchase and sale of U.S. government and Federal agency obligations and, to a lesser extent, bankers acceptance. The sale by the Federal Reserve of such obligations removes money from circulation; conversely, by purchasing such obligations, the Federal Reserve pays out money, which becomes bank deposits and reserves, available for creation of credit and monetary expansion.

OPEN POLICY. Marine insurance policy issued to cover various unspecified voyages over the life of the policy. An open policy is issued to a firm engaged in extensive shipping transactions, the details of which are probably unknown at the time the policy is issued; usually, the policyholder declares his transactions on a regular basis (e.g., monthly) and is held covered for all transactions declared at the last reporting date, as well as those undertaken since that time but not yet due to be reported. *See* BORDEREAUX.

OPEN POSITION. The economic exposure created when a bank buys or sells a quantity of foreign currency. Until the bank reserves, or *covers*, the transaction by an equivalent purchase or sale, it is considered open.

OPEN RATE. A freight rate that is not set by a CONFERENCE *(q.v.)* and is therefore negotiable. An open rate may result from the absence of a conference rate agreement, or similar rate-setting scheme over a given trade route, or the failure of conference members to agree on a rate for a specific commodity, leaving the matter to the individual member carriers to decide on a case-by-case basis.

OPEN REGISTRY SHIPPING. An arrangement under which a nation permits vessels owned by foreigners to be registered under its flag. The United Nations Conference on Trade and Development (UNCTAD) estimates that one-third of the world's fleet is operated under open registries. UNCTAD has criticized open registry and urges a stronger link between the nationality of the vessel's owner and the flag flown by the ship.

OPERATING DIFFERENTIAL SUBSIDY. A grant provided by the Federal government to U.S. firms that operate American-built vessels over certain prescribed trade routes deemed essential to American commerce. The object of the subsidy is to reduce the net operating costs to American shipping firms so as to permit them to compete against lower-cost foreign operators.

The trade routes on which subsidies are offered are essentially those that were laid out in 1981 by the Maritime Administration. During Fiscal Year 1983, operating subsidies amounted to $368.2 million.

OPERATIVE INSTRUMENT. A LETTER OF CREDIT *(q.v.)* transmitted by cable rather than on bank stationery. Customarily a bank may send a telex notification to the beneficiary of the letter of credit to inform that the actual instrument is being sent. This cable communication, known as an *advice* or *preadvice*, does not normally contain extensive details of the transaction being financed and offers no security to the intended beneficiary. When the cable contains full particulars of the transaction and does not contain a clause such as "mail confirmation to follow" or words of like import, the cable is the actual letter of credit, and drafts may be drawn and presented under it. A telex letter of credit would usually include the statement "this is the operative instrument" or a similar definitive statement, al-

though this affirmation is not required under the UNIFORM CUSTOMS AND PRACTICES *(q.v.)*, which governs most letter of credit transactions.

OPERATOR. The person or firm responsible for putting a vessel in condition to trade; this person may be the owner, agent, or a charterer.

OPTIMUM CUBE. The maximum achievable utilization of the interior cargo-carrying space of a container or trailer, irrespective of weight limitations.

OPTIONAL BILL OF LADING. An ocean BILL OF LADING *(q.v.)* that gives the carrier the prerogative of stowing the cargo anywhere aboard the vessel at his convenience; the effect is to permit cargoes suitable to travel under an "under deck" bill of lading to travel on deck. For legal and insurance reasons, cargo is regarded as having been stowed under deck, irrespective of its actual location, unless the bill of lading is endorsed "on deck."

ORDER BILL OF LADING. *See* BILL OF LADING.

ORDERLY MARKETING AGREEMENT. *See* BILATERAL RESTRAINT AGREEMENT.

ORDINARY COURSE OF TRADE. A concept routinely applied in customs valuation that holds that the dutiable value of goods is the price at which they would normally sell if customary channels of distribution were observed. For example, where it was industry practice for a product to be sold directly by a manufacturer to an end user, customs would apply duty upon the manufacturer's selling price, even where an intervening broker had added a markup, thereby increasing the price to the importer. Under the CUSTOMS VALUATION AGREEMENT *(q.v.)* of the General Agreement on Tariffs and Trade, the principle of applying the price used in the "ordinary course of the trade" has been largely supplanted by the transaction value method.

ORDINARY TAX CREDIT. *See* DOUBLE TAXATION.

ORDRE PUBLIC. A term used in international law and agreements, meaning public policy.

ORGANIZATION FOR ECONOMIC COOPERATION AND DEVELOPMENT. An association of industrial countries formed in 1961 to promote the economic well-being of its member countries while contributing to the development of the world economy. The OECD is the successor to the Organization for European Economic Cooperation, which was established in 1948 to implement the Marshall Plan.

The OECD undertakes research on economic conditions, recommends policy actions to its membership, and orchestrates aid programs for developing countries.

Membership in the OECD consists of twenty-four nations:

Austria	Canada
Australia	Denmark
Belgium	Finland

France
Germany
Greece
Iceland
Ireland
Italy
Japan
Luxembourg
Netherlands

New Zealand
Norway
Portugal
Spain
Sweden
Switzerland
Turkey
United Kingdom
United States

Yugoslavia enjoys a special associate status and participates in cetain OECD activities.

ORGANIZATION FOR EUROPEAN ECO-NOMIC COOPERATION. A post–World War II organization established to coordinate the reconstruction of Europe. The OEEC arose in response to an Anglo-French declaration in 1947 calling for European cooperation to advance the Marshall Plan. Sixteen European nations responded to the call by forming the Commitee of European Economic Cooperation, which devised a program to rehabilitate the European economy by the end of 1951. In 1948 the committee was restructured as a permanent organization; Canada and the United States became associate members of the OEEC in 1950.

The two main purposes of the OEEC were to collaborate in carrying out the U.S. aid program in Europe (the Marshall Plan), and to advance trade liberalization and financial stability in Europe. In 1950 the European Payments Union (EPU), under OEEC auspices, supplanted the Intra-European Payments Agreement. The EPU provided an automatic clearing system for settling trade balances between members and for the granting of short-term credits.

In 1961, the OEEC was succeeded by the ORGANIZATION FOR ECONOMIC COOPERATION AND DEVELOPMENT (*q.v.*).

ORGANIZATION OF PETROLEUM EXPORT-ING COUNTRIES. A cartel of oil-producing nations founded at Baghdad in 1960 by Iran, Iraq, Kuwait, Libya, Saudi Arabia, and Venezuela. The cartel was joined subsequently by Qatar (1961), Indonesia (1962), United Arab Emirates (Abu Dhabi in 1967, with the other emirates admitted in 1974), Algeria (1969), Nigeria (1971), Ecuador (1973), and Gabon (1973 as an associate, becoming a full member in 1975).

In 1973 OPEC members participated in a politically motivated oil embargo of the industrialized nations; since 1973 oil prices have risen tenfold. In response to the escalation of oil prices, OPEC established a fund to assist less developed countries; in 1979, OPEC adopted a second replenishment of the fund in the amount of eight hundred million dollars.

ORIENTATION PRICE. As used in conjunction with the Common Agricultural Policy of the European Economic Community it is the TARGET PRICE (*q.v.*) for cattle and calves, i.e., the equilibrium price for a commodity that the EEC wishes to see maintained. Theoretically, this price will permit an acceptable return for producers within the EEC without imposing a burden upon consumers.

The orientation price is also known as the *guide price.*

ORIGINAL BILL. *Synonymous with first of exchange. See* BILL OF EXCHANGE.

ORIGINAL SITC. *See* STANDARD INTERNATIONAL TRADE CLASSIFICATION.

OS & D. *See* OVER, SHORT, AND DAMAGED.

OTHER HOLDERS. Institutions other than central banks, national treasuries, and the International Monetary Fund itself that are approved by the IMF to hold SPECIAL DRAWING RIGHTS (*q.v.*). Other holders are limited currently to the following organizations:

Andean Reserve Fund, Bogotá
Arab Monetary Fund, Abu Dhabi
Bank of International Settlement, Basel
East Caribbean Currency Authority, Saint Kitts
International Bank for Reconstruction and Development, Washington, D.C.
International Development Association, Washington, D.C.
International Fund for Agricultural Development, Rome
Nordic Investment Bank, Helsinki
Swiss National Bank, Zurich
Islamic Development Bank, Jedda
West African Development Bank, Yaoundé
Central Bank for West African States, Dakar
East African Development Bank, Kampala
Bank of Central African States, Yaoundé.

OTTAWA AGREEMENT. A 1932 agreement among members of the British Commonwealth to extend preferential duty rates to one another and to British dependencies.

As a condition of entry into the European Economic Community, Great Britain was obliged to depart substantially from the agreement; this departure, coupled with the independence of most British colonies and possessions, has led to a rapid decline of the preferences granted at Ottawa.

OUTSIDER. In steamship usage, a carrier that is not a member of a given steamship CONFERENCE (*q.v.*).

OUT TURN REPORT. A document issued by a vessel upon arrival at a given port detailing the cargo off-loaded. The report is used as evidence in cases where it is alleged that goods were not off-loaded, or were discharged in bad order.

OVERBOOKED. The condition in which too much cargo has been accepted for a given vessel sailing. It is not necessary that all the cargo be delivered to the pier, merely that too many bookings, or space allocations, have been issued. The customary carrier response is to hold some of the cargo, usually the late arrivals, for a subsequent sailing.

OVERCARRIED CARGO. Goods not discharged at their port of destination, but left aboard the vessel for discharge at a subsequent port.

OVERLAND COMMON POINT. A geographic point in the nation's interior to which shipments (usually ocean containers) can be made over more than one coast. For example, St. Louis is an overland common point for shipments from Asia inasmuch as it can be reached by shipping containers via the Pacific coast, or through the Panama Canal and then via the Gulf or Atlantic coasts.

OVERLAP. In vessel charters, the period of time that the charterer holds the vessel beyond the appointed time for its return to the owner at the appointed place.

OVERSEAS PRIVATE INVESTMENT CORPORATION. An independent agency of the U.S. government formed in 1971 to stimulate private investment in overseas projects, usually in developing countries. In furthering this objective, OPIC provides: (1) cost assistance, up to 75 percent, in the establishment of the foreign venture; (2) direct loans ranging from fifty thousand to four million dollars to firms smaller than the Forture 1000 for equity participation in offshore programs, with loan guarantees for larger sums; and (3) insurance for losses sustained by U.S. investors in foreign equity ventures as the result of political risks. OPIC services are available only to U.S. citizens and U.S.-controlled corporations.

OVER, SHORT, AND DAMAGED. A report prepared by a vessel's port agent listing goods landed in excess of those shown on the manifest (over), quantities less than those manifested (short), or merchandise that arrived in bad condition (damaged). A carrier normally consults this report in the course of reviewing a shipper's claim for loss or damage in transit.

OVERSIDE DELIVERY CLAUSE. A provision in some charter parties permitting the consignee to take delivery in his own lighters, providing that the parcels to be discharged reach a specified minimum quantity. The provision is also known as a *tackle clause.*

OVERSPILL. Taxes paid by a firm to a foreign government beyond the amount which can be offset in the home country by means of foreign tax credits or other double taxation relief. For example, if a firm paid one million dollars in taxes to country A, but was able to receive a tax credit of only $700,000 in its home country because of a limitation on the amount of foreign tax credits which can be applied, then an *overspill* of $300,000 would occur.

OVERTONNAGED. A condition in which a given trade route is served by more vessels than warranted by the volume of cargo being shipped. The usual outgrowth of an overtonnaged route is increased carrier competition for available cargoes and declining rates.

OWNER'S ACCOUNT. An expense, during the course of a vessel charter, that is borne by the ship's owner.

OWNER'S BROKER. A broker representing the vessel owner in ship chartering.

OWNER'S CHARTER PARTY. A contract covering the hire of a vessel with provisions particularly favorable to the vessel's owner. *See* CHARTER PARTY.

OWNER'S ITEM. *Synonymous with* OWNER'S ACCOUNT *(q.v.).*

P

PACKAGE. Generally, a unit of cargo tendered by a shipper to a common carrier for onward transportation. The term is not explicitly defined. It attains its greatest significance within the meaning of the Carriage of Goods by Sea Act. The act (46 U.S.C.A. Sec. 181) stipulates:

Neither the carrier nor the ship shall in any event be or become liable for any loss or damage to or in connection with the transportation of goods in an amount exceeding $500 per package lawful money of the United States, or in case of goods not shipped in packages, per customary freight unit, or the equivalent of that sum in other currency, unless the nature and value of such goods have been declared by the shipper before shipment and inserted in the bill of lading. . . . By agreement between the carrier, master, or agent of the carrier, and the shipper another maximum amount than that mentioned in this paragraph may be fixed: Provided, that such maximum shall not be less than the figure above named.

Through the period of BREAK-BULK *(q.v.)* shipping, when it was necessary to encase goods fully for transit, the courts were not greatly burdened with conflicting definitions of *package*. The advent of containerization, however, has generated significant definitional problems. Steamship lines have attempted to mitigate liability by construing a container as a package, thereby limiting themselves to $500 for the entire contents of the container. The carrier position has been largely repudiated in the case of Mormaclynx v. Leather's Best (451 F. 2d 800, C.C.A. 2d, 1971), in which the bill of lading described the goods as "one container S.T.C. [said to contain] 99 bales of leather." The court held that each bale was a package, stating that the purpose of the Carriage of Goods by Sea Act "was to set a reasonable figure below which the carrier should not be permitted to limit his liability and . . . 'package' is thus more sensibly related to the unit in which the shipper packed the goods and described them than to a large metal object, functionally part of the ship."

Although subsequent cases have tended to reinforce the position that a container is not a package, the matter is not fully resolved. It is in the shipper's interest to describe the merchandise in terms of the number of packages covered by the bill of lading. For example, a bill of lading on which the goods are described as "one pallet containing 30 cartons glassware" might be construed as extending the $500-per-package limitation to each carton within the pallet unit, whereas "one pallet glassware" would seem to identify the entire pallet load as the package.

PACTA SUNT SERVANDA. A principle of international law that treaties and other international engagements are binding upon the nations that accede to them, and obligations accepted under such engagements must be performed, or reparations made in the event of a breach.

PADDY RICE. Rice, shipped in bags or bulk, without the husks removed.

PALLET ALLOWANCE. A provision in some ocean tariffs that the cubic measurement of pallets used in unitized cargoes will be deducted from total cubic measurement for computation of freight. This allowance reflects the carrier's ease of handling palletized cargo. Normally, pallet dimensions must be shown on the bill of lading to accrue the deduction.

PANCAFE. Trading arm of the International Coffee Organization. *See* INTERNATIONAL COMMODITY ORGANIZATION.

P & I CLUB. A mutual property and indemnity insurance association established by shipowners to provide coverage against various perils, including: injury to crewmen, collision liability, cargo damage, damage caused by the vessel's wake, costs arising from removal of a wreck, fines and penalties, uncollectible contributions by cargo interests in general average, and legal expenses arising from liability claims.

Most P & I clubs are oriented toward vessels of common nationality, although many clubs accept foreign members. The directors of the club are usually drawn from the management of the participating carriers, although day-to-day management is often performed by an outside organization for a fee.

PANLIBHON GROUP. An acronym for a group of countries where foreign vessels are registered under flags of convenience, derived from the first letters of Panama, Liberia, and Honduras, where many such vessels are registered. *See* FLAG OF CONVENIENCE.

PAPER BASIS. A system in which the national currency is not based upon precious metal.

PAPER GOLD. A common reference to SPECIAL DRAWING RIGHTS *(q.v.)* issued by the International Monetary Fund.

PAPER PIRACY. *See* PIRACY.

PAPER RATE. A rate in a tariff under which no cargo moves.

PARALLEL FINANCING. An arrangement whereby two lenders participate in financing in different parts of a given project without having legal ties between the loan contracts. Each lender evaluates the project independently and administers its own loan.

PARALLEL STANDARD. A system under which a nation coins at least two metals, usually gold and silver, without establishing an exchange ratio between the metals. *See* BIMETALLISM, MINT PAR OF EXCHANGE.

PARALLEL TRADE. *See* COUNTERTRADE.

PARCEL TANKER. A liquid bulk tanker containing several (perhaps as many as fifty) individual tanks, thereby permitting the vessel to carry a variety of liquid cargoes during a given voyage.

PAR EXCHANGE RATE. *See* PAR OF EXCHANGE.

PARI PASSU. Literally, "with equal progress." In economics, the term indicates an equal and simultaneous charge. In commercial lending, the phrase means a clause in a borrowing agreement designed to prevent the borrower from giving to any party security in property to a degree higher than given to the lender.

PARIS CLUB. Also known as the *Group of Ten*, an infomal association of creditor nations which since 1956 has held informal meetings among senior financial officers of the member states to discuss international financial and trade conditions. Participating nations are:

Belgium	Italy
Canada	Japan
France	Netherlands
Germany, West	Sweden
Great Britain	United States

Switzerland originally participated in the group as an associate; it has since become a full member.

Since Argentina first approached the club in 1956 to restructure its foreign debts, the group has been involved in fifty-six different negotiations involving twenty debtor countries to reschedule payments.

PARIS CONVENTION. Known formally as the *Paris Convention for the Protection of Industrial Property,* an international agreement formulated to protect rights to industrial property including inventions, trademarks, service marks, trade names, and appellations of origin. The substantive provisions of the convention can be grouped into two main categories:

National treatment, also known as assimilation, by which an adhering state must grant to citizens of other adhering states all rights and protection it provides to its own citizens. Citizens of states which have not adhered to the convention will be afforded the same protection if they are domiciled or have a bona fide industrial presence in an adhering state;

Right of priority, by which an owner of industrial property who makes application for protection in any state adhering to the convention is permitted, within a prescribed period of time (twelve months for patents, six months for industrial designs and trademarks) to apply for protection in any other adhering state and have that application treated as though it were filed on the same day as the first application. For example, an inventor who files for a patent in country A has twelve months within which to file for protection in any other adhering state; if he files for protection in country B within this period, B will regard his protection within that country as having taken place on the same day as filed in country A. In this sense, the inventor from A enjoys retroactive protection in any convention member state, but he must apply for it on a state-by-state basis.

The convention specifies that conditions for filing shall be prescribed by local law, and enumerates circumstances under which it is appropriate for a state to decline to register or revoke protection previously afforded.

The convention was concluded in 1883, was modified at Brussels (1900), Washington (1911), The Hague (1925), London (1934), Lisbon (1958), and Stockholm (1967), and is administered by the WORLD INTELLECTUAL PROPERTY ORGANIZATION *(q.v.).* In 1984 the following states had acceded to the convention:

Algeria	Canada
Argentina	Central African Republic
Australia	Chad
Austria	Congo
Bahamas	Cuba
Belgium	Cyprus
Benin	Czechoslovakia
Brazil	Denmark
Bulgaria	Dominican Republic
Burundi	Egypt
Cameroon	Finland

France
Gabon
German Democratic
   Republic
German Federal Republic
Ghana
Greece
Guinea
Haiti
Holy See
Hungary
Iceland
Indonesia
Iran
Iraq
Ireland
Israel
Italy
Ivory Coast
Japan
Jordan
Kenya
Korea (North)
Korea (South)
Lebanon
Libya
Liechtenstein
Luxembourg
Madagascar
Malawi
Mali
Malta
Mauritania
Mauritius
Mexico
Monaco

Morocco
Netherlands
New Zealand
Niger
Nigeria
Norway
Philippines
Poland
Portugal
Romania
San Marino
Senegal
South Africa
Spain
Sri Lanka
Surinam
Sweden
Switzerland
Syria
Tanzania
Togo
Trinidad and Tobago
Tunisia
Turkey
U.S.S.R.
Uganda
United Kingdom
United States
Upper Volta
Uruguay
Vietnam
Yugoslavia
Zaire
Zambia
Zimbabwe

PARIS UNION. *See* PARIS CONVENTION.

PAR ITEM. A collection or other transaction in which a paying bank remits to another bank without assessing a fee.

PARITY. In arbitrage usage, an equivalent value for two currencies; for example, the Bermuda dollar enjoys parity with the U.S. dollar (B$1 = U.S.$1).

PAR OF EXCHANGE. The value, in gold, of a unit of a nation's currency in relation to the gold value of a unit of another nation's currency.

PARTIAL CAPTIVE. *See* CAPTIVE INSURANCE COMPANY.

PARTICIPATION LOAN. A financing scheme in which two or more banks "participate" in a loan. On large loans, a syndicate of banks may be orchestrated by a major bank, which serves as the LEAD MANAGER *(q.v.)*. Other banks contribute to the loan and receive a portion of the profits.

PARTICULAR AVERAGE. A partial loss of the value of cargo shipped by sea attributable to a marine peril. *See* FREE OF PARTICULAR AVERAGE.

PAR VALUE. The nominal value assigned to a currency by its issuing authority. Normally, this value is expressed as a quantity of gold, or another currency convertible into gold.

When the market value of a currency, expressed in terms of other convertible currencies, deviates significantly from its par value over a protracted period, it may be necessary to set a new par value, i.e., to revalue the currency. Normally, revaluation occurs after consultation with the International Monetary Fund.

PATENT. A grant issued by a governmental authority to an inventor permitting, for a fixed number of years, an exclusive right to the invention. The grant includes the prerogative of preventing others from making, using, or selling the invention covered.

Through various international arrangements, a patent granted in one country may protect the inventor's rights in certain other countries as well.

PATENT COOPERATION TREATY. An international agreement which permits nationals and residents of any adhering state to seek patent protection in any or all of the adhering states by means of a single patent application.

The applicant files his application with the national patent office of the country of which he is a citizen or resident, specifying the "designated states" where he seeks patent protection. If the applicant is a national or resident of a state which is an adherent to the EUROPEAN PATENT CONVENTION *(q.v.)*, the application may be filed with European Patent Office. Nationals or residents of countries which are members of the African Intellectual Property Organization may file with WIPO, the WORLD INTELLECTUAL PROPERTY ORGANIZATION *(q.v.)*. Each designated state regards the international patent application as a direct application to its national patent office. If a designated state is an adherent to the European Patent Convention the applicant may request a *European,* rather than a national, patent. Persons listing Belgium or France as designated states will be obliged to request a European patent.

The application is processed by one of the major national patent offices or the European Patent Office, resulting in an "international search" of patents already on file in the countries listed in the application. An "international search report" will be sent to the applicant and the patent offices of the countries which he has designated; in addition, the report will be published by WIPO.

Twenty months after filing the initial application, the applicant must furnish to the patent office of each nation he has selected a translation of his application into its official language and pay the appropriate fees. This period may be extended an additional five months under certain circumstances.

By filing the international patent application, the applicant reserves the right to obtain a patent in any state adhering to the treaty, and have that patent take effect from the date of his original "international" filing. In addition, the work of the national patent offices is greatly reduced since an international search has been performed to determine the novelty of the invention.

The agreement was adopted in 1970, and is open to states that are party to the PARIS CONVENTION *(q.v.)*. The following states were party to the treaty in 1984:

Australia	Luxembourg
Austria	Madagascar
Belgium	Malawi
Brazil	Mauritania
Cameroon	Monaco
Central African Republic	Netherlands
Chad	Norway
Congo	Romania
Denmark	Senegal
Finland	Sri Lanka
France	Sweden
Gabon	Switzerland
German Federal Republic	Togo
Hungary	U.S.S.R.
Japan	United Kingdom
Korea (North)	United States
Liechtenstein	

PAYABLE WITH EXCHANGE. A condition that may be written on a bill of exchange or check, the effect of which is to stipulate that exchange conversion or collection costs shall be borne by the payee in the case of a bill, or the maker in the case of a check.

PAYMENT FOR HONOR. *See* ACCEPTANCE SUPRA PROTEST.

PEAGE DUES. A special form of harbor dues imposed by some North African ports upon cargoes of phosphates in bulk.

PECUNIARY EXCHANGE. The settlement of obligations by payment of money, rather than by goods or services.

PER DIEM. A daily charge levied by the owner of transport equipment for its use.

PERILS OF THE SEA. Extraordinary influence of wind, waves, and other violent marine forces serving to endanger a maritime adventure; to be distinguished from the normal, undisturbed forces of the sea that a vessel might reasonably be expected to encounter during the course of the voyage.

PERIOD AND TRADING LIMITS. A provision in a charter party that specifies limitations on the use of a chartered vessel, e.g., restrictions on the carriage of certain cargoes.

PERIOD CHARTER. A time charter. *See* CHARTER PARTY.

PERIODIC REQUIREMENTS LICENSE. A special validated license authorizing the exportation, during a one-year period, of articles covered in the COMMODITY CONTROL LIST *(q.v.)* to one or more specified consignees in a named ultimate destination.

PERMANENT ESTABLISHMENT. For international tax purposes, defined in the model tax convention of the Organization of Economic Coopera-

tion and Development as "a fixed place of business in which the business of the enterprise is wholly or partly carried on." It can include an office, factory, or similar facilities. The presence of a permanent establishment in a country may expose the business to local taxation.

PER PROCURATION. A signature or endorsement on a bill of exchange, check, or other document performed by an agent under a limited authority granted by the principal. An endorsement per procuration (indicated as "per proc.," "per pro.," or "P.P.") gives notice that the agent's authority is limited, and the recipient of a document so signed should ascertain the agent's authority, which must be given by the agent.

PERSISTENT DUMPING. *See* DUMPING.

PERSONAL EFFECTS. In customs usage, those articles that a traveler might reasonably require during the course of his journey, excluding goods carried for commercial purposes (e.g., trade samples) or contraband.

PETROCURRENCY. Currency remitted to petroleum-producing countries in satisfaction of oil purchase transactions.

PETRODOLLAR. Dollars remitted to oil-producing countries in settlement of petroleum purchase accounts. As a practical matter, purchases of petroleum from members of the Organization of Petroleum Exporting Countries are usually settled in U.S. dollars because of the immense volumes of currency required for these transactions.

PHYSICAL DISTRIBUTION. A branch of business management concerned with past product logistics, i.e., those functions that relate to the movement of goods from one place to another. Among those areas generally ascribed to physical distribution are transportation, material handling, warehousing, inventory control, packaging, and order processing.

PHYSICAL INVENTORY. An actual count of inventory merchandise that is subsequently reconciled with the books inventory, i.e., the asset value shown on the books of the firm. Physical inventories are normally taken periodically as a routine part of a firm's audit procedure.

PHYTOSANITARY CERTIFICATE. Also known as a *sanitary certificate,* a document issued by an appropriate governmental authority in the country of export certifying that a given shipment of plants or agricultural products has been inspected and is free from disease or pests. This document is customarily obtained by the exporter and provided to the importer so as to effect customs clearance.

In the United States, phytosanitary certificates are issued by the Animal and Plant Health Inspection Service of the Department of Agriculture (*see* figure).

UNITED STATES DEPARTMENT OF AGRICULTURE
ANIMAL AND PLANT HEALTH INSPECTION SERVICE
PLANT PROTECTION AND QUARANTINE PROGRAMS

PHYTOSANITARY CERTIFICATE

UNITED STATES DEPARTMENT OF AGRICULTURE
ANIMAL AND PLANT HEALTH INSPECTION SERVICE
PLANT PROTECTION AND QUARANTINE PROGRAMS

TO: THE PLANT PROTECTION SERVICE OF:

FOR OFFICIAL USE ONLY

Place

Date
and No.

852044

Date Inspected

This is to certify that the plants, parts of plants or plant products described below or representative samples of them were thoroughly examined on the date shown above by an authorized representative of the Plant Protection and Quarantine Programs, Animal and Plant Health Inspection Service, United States Department of Agriculture, and were found, to the best of his knowledge, to be substantially free from injurious diseases and pests; and that the consignment is believed to conform to the current phytosanitary regulations of the importing country both as stated in the additional declaration hereon and otherwise.

FUMIGATION OR DISINFECTION TREATMENT

Date: .... Duration of exposure and temperature: ....

Treatment: .... Chemical and concentration: ....

DESCRIPTION OF THE CONSIGNMENT

Name and address of the exporter: ....

Name and address of the consignee: ....

Quantity and name of produce and botanical name: ....

....

....

Number and description of packages: ....

Distinguishing marks: ....

Origin: ....

Means of conveyance: .... Point of entry: ....

ADDITIONAL DECLARATION

....
(Signature)

Inspector
....
(Title)

No liability shall attach to the United States Department of Agriculture or to any officer or representative of the Department with respect to this certificate.

PPQ FORM 577
(JUL 76)

SHIPPER'S ORIGINAL

Phytosanitary Certificate

PIER. A man-made structure perpendicular to the coast, against which vessels may lie; normally has a T form to seaward.

PIG. A railway trailer designed to travel aboard a rail flatcar.

PIGGYBACK. A service offered by railroads to compete with pure trucking. A trailer (*pig*) is detached from the power unit in a railyard and placed aboard a flatcar for transport to the destination city, where a power unit is again attached to the trailer for final delivery to the consignee.

PIGGYBACKING. *See* COMPLEMENTARY EXPORTING.

PIGGYBACK PLANS. Various service schemes offered by rail carriers to piggyback users. Some railroads do not offer piggyback service, or offer only some of the plans. Each plan has its own peculiar features and carries its own rates.

Plan 1: a joint rail carrier/motor carrier service wherein the motor carrier delivers its trailers to the railroad for haulage to the destination city. The motor carrier bills the shipper/consignee at the prevailing trucking rates and performs local pickup and delivery of the trailers.

Plan 2: the railroad provides the trailers and performs both pickup and delivery.

Plan 2¼: same as Plan 2, but the rail carrier provides pickup or delivery, not both.

Plan 2½: the railroad provides service only between TOFC [trailer on flatcar] ramps; pickup and delivery of trailer are performed by consignor/consignee.

Plan 2¾: same as plan 2½, except one rail-owned and one shipper-owned trailer move together on a two-trailer rate. Pickup and delivery are performed by consignor/consignee.

Plan 3: the railroad provides ramp-to-ramp service; trailers are provided by the shipper. Pickup and delivery are performed by consignor/consignee. Ocean containers moving to or from interior points may employ this plan.

Plan 4: flatcars and trailers are provided by the shipper; the railroad provides rails and power. Pickup and delivery are provided by consignor/consignee. This plan is used primarily by freight forwarders and consolidators.

Plan 5: a joint motor/rail service with through rates and routings filed by either the rail or the motor carrier. Door-to-door service is provided under this arrangement, with either carrier supplying trailers.

Plan 5¼: same as Plan 5, except the rail carrier provides only pickup or delivery, not both.

Plan 7: so-called substitute service, wherein a rail carrier, at its convenience, substitutes two or more trailers in place of a boxcar. Door-to-door service is provided.

Plan 8: ramp-to-ramp mail service provided on a contract basis.

PIGGYPACKER. A self-propelled device used in railyards to lift piggyback trailers on and off flatcars.

PILOTAGE. The charge imposed on a vessel for the services of a pilot to guide the ship into or out of a harbor. The actual costs of pilotage are computed in terms of PILOTAGE UNITS (*q.v.*).

PILOTAGE UNIT. A unit of measure used to calculate pilotage fees charged a vessel for entering or leaving a harbor. The figure is determined by multiplying the ship's length by its breadth by its depth from its lowest continuous deck, and dividing by ten thousand.

PIP. In foreign exchange markets, a term used to quote a change (up or down) of .00001 in the value of a given currency.

PIRACY. Commonly, the forcible seizure of a vessel by armed bandits for the purpose of stealing the vessel, its equipment, or its cargo. Piracy committed upon the high seas is a violation of the laws of nations, and all nations are charged with the suppression of piracy. Any nation that captures pirates may try and punish them for acts committed in international waters. Pirates captured on land or within territorial waters are normally tried under the laws of the jurisdiction where they are found. Any vessel used in piratical acts is forfeit to the state that seizes it.

Contrary to popular view, piracy continues in many areas and flourishes in some. In addition to classical piracy, the term has been expanded in modern maritime usage to encompass such actions as *rust bucket piracy*, in which an aged vessel is loaded with a valuable cargo. En route to its scheduled destination, the vessel discharges its cargo at an unscheduled port; thereafter the vessel is sunk in water too deep to permit an inspection, and an insurance claim is placed for the vessel and cargo (which has already been sold). In *paper piracy*, false bills of lading and other forged documents are presented under a letter of credit; upon release of the funds, the thieves disappear.

A *rogue shipowner*, who sells the cargo in his possession, would also be considered a pirate.

PISANI-BAUMGARTNER PLAN. An agricultural stabilization and relief plan advanced in 1961 by Edgard Pisani, French agriculture minister, and Wilfred Baumgartner, French minister of finance. The plan urged that world export prices be adjusted upward, resulting in a higher return on commercial sales; the excess profits so earned would be used to finance food aid to poorer nations. Output would be maintained through continued "controls" (i.e., aid) to farmers. The commercial excess of supply over demand thus produced would be used as aid to hungry nations.

PIVOT CHARGE. The minimum charge imposed by an air carrier for the use of a UNIT LOAD DEVICE (*q.v.*), or air container. The charge is based upon a PIVOT WEIGHT (*q.v.*) assigned to the container.

PIVOT WEIGHT. The minumum chargeable weight assigned to an air container or UNIT LOAD DEVICE *(q.v.)*. Each type of unit load device is assigned a weight (the pivot weight) for which the shipper will be charged even if he does not fill the unit. In the event the shipper loads cargo into the container in excess of the pivot weight, he will be charged at a fixed rate for the excess, in addition to the pivot charge.

P.L. 480. *See* AGRICULTURAL TRADE AND DEVELOP- MENT ACT.

PLANS, RAIL. *See* PIGGYBACK PLANS.

PLIMSOLL LINE. *See* LOAD-LINE.

POCKET. A bag of rice weighing one hundred pounds.

POINCARÉ FRANC. A unit of value, created by the Raymond Poincaré government of France in 1928, used largely in connection with international transportation conventions, equivalent to 65.5 milligrams of gold nine-tenths fine.

POINT FORECAST. An anticipated rate of exchange for a given foreign currency at a fixed point in time, e.g., July 15.

POINT FOUR PROGRAM. A program of technical assistance to underdeveloped nations incorporated in the Foreign Economic Assistance Act of 1950. The plan derived its name from its position as the fourth segment of President Harry Truman's inaugural address in 1949, during which it was first articulated.

POLICY PROOF OF INTEREST. A stipulation in an ocean marine insurance policy whereby the insurer admits the insurable interest of the policyholder.

POLITICAL RISK. An economic risk assumed by foreign creditors that political or military conditions in a debtor's country may preclude settlement of the obligation when due.

POLYCENTRIC COMPANY. *See* E.P.R.G. FRAMEWORK.

POLYCENTRIC PRICING. A pricing policy in a multinational firm that permits substantially uniform products to be priced differently in various countries, to accommodate local conditions.

POMERANE ACT. *See* FEDERAL BILLS OF LADING ACT.

PORT. An area within which vessels regularly load or discharge cargo, including such places where vessels await berthing.

PORT CHARGES. Fees incurred by a vessel upon entering or leaving a harbor including harbor dues paid to the port authority, as well as fees for pilots and tugs.

PORT CONGESTION SURCHARGE. A charge imposed by a steamship to offset the loss of revenue sustained by vessel calls at ports lacking adequate discharging facilities or sufficient labor. The surcharge is usually expressed as a percentage of the basic freight assessed on the cargo.

PORT DUES. *Synonymous with* HARBOR DUES *(q.v.)*.

PORTFOLIO INVESTMENT. A minority interest in a foreign venture from which income is derived in the form of dividends; normally such an interest does not convey any significant control over the management or operations of the foreign firm.

PORT OF ENTRY. A point designated by a nation's customs authority through which goods may be entered for examination and clearance; ports of entry may be actual ocean ports, land border points, or interior locations to which goods are carried in bond.

POSITIVE CONCEPT OF VALUATION. An approach to the application of ad valorem duties that holds that duties should be applied upon the actual value of the transaction, as defined by buyer and seller. This view has been substantially fulfilled by the recent adoption of the *transaction value* basis of valuation in the CUSTOMS VALUATION AGREE- MENT. *(q.v.)*.

This *positive* view contrasts with the *notional* view of valuation, which holds that ad valorem duties should be applied to the price the goods "ought to fetch" under specified conditions. This view was widely held for many years and was embraced in the BRUSSELS DEFINITION OF VALUE *(q.v.)*.

POSSUM BELLY. *See* DROP-FRAME TRAILER.

POULTRY WAR. *Synonymous with* CHICKEN WAR *(q.v.)*.

PRECLUSIVE BUYING. The purchase of foreign-made merchandise to prevent acquisition by other foreign entities. Most commonly a government will buy up foreign production to prevent purchase by a third (usually unfriendly) power.

PREDATORY DUMPING. *See* DUMPING.

PREDATORY RATE. An ocean freight rate set intentionally low so as to drive out competition. Soviet flag carriers, animated by motives other than commercial profit, were widely criticized for establishing predatory rates. Certain noncommunist carriers, enjoying heavy state subsidies, were also suspected of setting predatory rates.

In 1980, Congress passed the Controlled Carrier Act, requiring sixty days' advance notice of rate reduction by any carrier controlled by a foreign state; during the sixty-day period, the Federal Maritime Commission will investigate allegations of predatory rate making and will invalidate the predatory rate.

PREEMPTION. The prerogative of customs authorities to seize and sell merchandise that an importer has deliberately undervalued to avoid payment of duties.

PREEMPTIVE BUYING. *Synonymous with* PRECLUSIVE BUYING *(q.v.).*

PREFERENTIAL DUTIES. Especially low rates of duty granted by members of a political system to one another, or by a mother country to her colonial possessions.

PREFERENTIAL TARIFF. *See* TARIFF (CUSTOMS).

PRELIMINARY INVOICE. *See* INVOICE.

PREMIUM (EXCHANGE). In foreign exchange transactions, the rise in value of one currency when measured against another currrency.

PREMIUM (INSURANCE). The compensation paid to an insurance underwriter in return for the assumption of an agreed risk, as evidenced by issuance of a policy.

PRICE CARTEL. An agreement among business entities to fix prices, to establish ranges within which prices may move, or to establish methods by which prices may be determined.

PRICE SUPPORTS. A program of governmental action designed to stabilize or lift the price that producers receive for their products. These actions may include direct cash payments, goverment purchase of output to force up market prices, or special financing. Such supports are most commonly applied to agriculture.

PRIMAGE. A gratuity formerly paid to a ship's captain and (often redistributed in part among) crew by a shipper of goods to ensure safe handling of the merchandise. Primage was once a significant source of a mariner's income, but it now would be archaic, as the crew's income is paid out of freight revenues by the vessel's operator.

PRIMAGE AND AVERAGE ACCUSTOMED. An assessment by a steamship line upon the cargo, pro-rated by value, to cover such port charges as wharfage and pilotage, and unusual expenses incurred on behalf of a particular cargo. In modern practice, such charges are included in the carrier's freight rate.

PRIMARY BOYCOTT. *See* BOYCOTT.

PRIMARY MARKET. A spot commodity market dealing in a local producing area. Ordinarily such markets develop around local transportation centers.

PRIMARY PRODUCT. Any agricultural, forest, or fishery product or any mineral sold in its original form, including such processing as may be required to make the product suitable for sale in international commerce.

PRIME BANKER'S ACCEPTANCE. An ACCEPTANCE *(q.v.)* of a major, highly regarded commercial bank that is actively engaged in acceptance financing. The term *prime* is a mark of distinction over the acceptances of banks that, although sound, are not regularly or substantially traded in the money market.

PRIME BILL OF EXCHANGE. A BILL OF EXCHANGE *(q.v.)* that states on its face that it arises from the sale of goods.

PRIME MAKER. The party that originally draws a draft or bill of exchange, or that issues negotiable paper, and is ultimately responsible for payment or settlement of the instrument so created.

PRIME RATE. The rate of interest on business loans by commercial banks to their most credit-worthy customers. The maintenance of a COMPENSATING BALANCE *(q.v.)* by the borrower is customary in prime rate loans.

PRINCIPAL MARKETS. In customs usage, the chief places in the country of exportation where the goods are freely sold or offered for sale, not necessarily the place where they are manufactured or delivered.

PRINCIPAL SUPPLIER. A nation that serves as the major source of supply to another country for a specific product.

PRIOR IMPORT DEPOSIT. A sum that an importer is obliged to deposit with his nation's central bank or other governmental authority as a condition for the issuance of an import license. Most industrialized nations do not require such deposits, but they are common in many developing nations, where the deposit may equal 100 percent of the value of the imported merchandise. The deposits are almost always denominated in the importer's local currency.

PRIOR OR SUBSEQUENT MOVEMENT BY WATER. A domestic freight rate established exclusively to accommodate import and export traffic. To obtain the rate, the shipper (on export movements) must declare that the goods have traveled or will travel by vessel, usually without significant interruption of transit, during the course of their journey from point of shipment to point of delivery. On import movements, the consignee makes this declaration.

As a rule, rates stipulating a prior or subsequent movement by water are lower than those for purely domestic movements over the same routes.

PRIVATE BILL. A BILL OF EXCHANGE *(q.v.)* drawn upon and accepted by a party other than a bank; trade acceptances, for example, are private bills.

PRIVATE CARRIAGE. *See* CARRIER.

PRIVATEER. *See* MART AND COUNTERMART.

PRIVATE EXPORT FUNDING CORPORA-TION. A private corporation organized in 1970 for the purpose of providing medium- to long-term financing to foreign buyers of U.S. goods and services. PEFCO is owned by commercial banks and major industrial firms. Working capital is raised by issuance of commercial paper, guaranteed by the U.S. EXPORT-IMPORT BANK *(q.v.)*, and through a fifty million dollar revolving line of credit with EXIM-BANK. Loans made by PEFCO are designed to supplement traditional financing and most bear the guarantee of EXIMBANK.

In January 1979 PEFCO introduced the Loan Purchase Program, under which it purchases from banks nonrecourse debt obligations of foreign importers so long as these obligations have been guaranteed by EXIMBANK. The object of this program is to provide exporters with the liquidity essential to expand export sales.

PRIVATE INTERNATIONAL LAW. The branch of international law that deals with the actions of private persons or firms. Disputes rising under private international law are normally addressed in the municipal courts.

PRIVILEGED DOMESTIC STATUS. A condition that may be accorded to merchandise of U.S. origin, or to imported merchandise upon which duties have been paid, that is entered into a FOREIGN TRADE ZONE *(q.v.)*. Any eligible merchandise so entered that is subject to internal revenue tax must have taxes paid prior to application for this status. Application is made to the district director of customs. Goods granted this status may re-enter the customs territory free of duties and taxes.

PRIVILEGED FOREIGN STATUS. A condition that may be accorded to foreign merchandise entering a FOREIGN TRADE ZONE *(q.v.)*. Foreign merchandise entering a zone remains exempt from duty until withdrawn, by means of a *consumption entry*, for use. Customarily, duties and taxes are assessed and levied upon removal of the foreign merchandise from the zone. With foreign privileged status, however, duties and taxes are assessed (but not collected) at the rates applicable to the merchandise at time of application; actual payment occurs only upon withdrawal of the goods from the zone. This procedure permits the importer to fix his duties and taxes against anticipated future increases.

Privileged foreign status may be granted to imported merchandise upon application to the district director of customs. This status cannot be accorded to goods that have been manipulated so as to change their tariff classification prior to application.

PROCESSING TAX. A tax levied upon the first processing of certain raw materials and semi-processed goods. In the case of imported materials, this tax is usually collected after clearing customs, upon first manipulation of the product.

PROCTOR. Derived from the Latin *procurator,* a person who formerly served as an advocate in an ecclesiastical or admiralty court.

The title *proctor in admiralty* was applied to lawyers admitted to admiralty courts. The reorganization of the Federal court structure, and the elimination of admiralty courts, per se, have caused the title to fall into disuse. However, the Maritime Law Association of the United States does accord the title to lawyers who have been members of the association for at least four years and who have acquired additional professional training in the field of maritime law.

PRODUCT LINE CYCLE. The concept that a product undergoes three stages of development: (1) *new product* (a firm introduces a new product or significant differentiated product and for a period of time enjoys a virtual monopoly), (2) *growth product* (the product is imitated and produced by several firms; nonprice competition ensues and efforts are made toward differentiation), and (3) *mature product* (the product is widely recognized, although brand identifications become blurred; competition is based on price).

PRODUCT STRUCTURE. A technique of international marketing employed by some manufacturing firms. The firm is organized into product groups responsible for all marketing, profit and loss, and production of the product worldwide. Each product group reports directly to corporate headquarters, which provides financial, legal, and administrative support to the groups. *See* GEOGRAPHIC STRUCTURE.

PRO FORMA INVOICE. An invoice prepared in advance of actual shipment of the goods for the purpose of documenting to a customer the cost of the merchandise to be sold, and such charges as freight and insurance. This document is customarily used by the potential purchaser in applying for a letter of credit, import license, or foreign exchange allocation.

In the case of importations into the United States, an importer may file a pro forma invoice in lieu of a missing commercial or special customs invoice, providing the missing documents are provided by the exporter within 180 days.

PROHIBITIVE DUTY. A rate of duty so high as to effectively preclude entry of an item. Generally, prohibitive duties increase the selling price to such a level that the item cannot compete with domestic substitutes. Prohibitive duties are designed to protect domestic infant or ailing industries from vigorous competition or to retaliate for duty increases by other countries.

PROJECT LICENSE. A special validated license covering the exportation of controlled articles or articles to controlled destinations as specified in the COMMODITY CONTROL LIST *(q.v.)* in furtherance of an approved activity abroad. Such licenses are normally limited to a period of one year or less.

PROMISSORY WARRANTY. *See* WARRANTY.

PROMPT SHIP. A vessel prepared to load on short notice.

PRO NUMBER. The number assigned to a freight bill by a rail or motor carrier. The term derives from the *pro*gressive, i.e., sequential, numbering of bills.

PROPENSITY TO IMPORT. The relationship between income and the value of imports, expressed in monetary terms. Generally, the relationship is expressed in terms of the *average propensity* to import (imports as a percentage of national income) and the *marginal propensity* to import (changes in the average propensity to import in relation to increases and declines in national income). *Income elasticity* of demand for imports (the relationship between average propensity and marginal propensity) may be expressed as:

$$\frac{\text{Marginal propensity}}{\text{Average propensity}} = \frac{\text{Income elasticity of}}{\text{demand for imports.}}$$

The marginal propensity to import has significance to the other nations in that changes in national income of the importing country may be manifested as changes in exports for trading partners.

PROPORTIONAL RATE. A freight rate that is constructed by adding separate joint or local rates applying to a through movement. A proportional rate, unlike a COMBINATION RATE *(q.v.)*, is applicable only when the goods have been transported prior or subsequent to the journey for which the rate applies.

PROTECTION AND INDEMNITY. Insurance carried by a vessel operator to respond to third-party liabilities, e.g., cargo loss and crew injury claims. It does not cover physical loss or damage to the ship itself, or loss of income.

PROTECTIONISM. A governmental policy or attitude designed to remedy domestic economic problems attributed to excessive imports. The most common problems are a drain on exchange reserves and injury to infant domestic industries. The typical protectionist responses include import surcharges, quotas, exchange controls, and nontariff barriers.

PROTECTIVE TARIFF. *See* PROTECTIONISM, TARIFF (CUSTOMS).

PROTEST. A notice in writing, prepared before a notary public or other official authorized to administer oaths, stipulating that a draft, check, bill of exchange, or other instrument has been dis-honored, either by a refusal to accept on the part of the drawee, or by failure to pay the instrument upon maturity. The effect of a protest is to confirm repudiation of the instrument in question and to inform parties secondarily liable under the instrument (e.g., endorsers) that the bill or note has been dishonored.

PROVISIONAL INVOICE. *See* INVOICE.

PUBLIC INTERNATIONAL LAW. The body of international law that governs the conduct of a nation as a sovereign entity in its relations with other nations. It does not deal with the international activities of private individuals or firms.

PUBLIC STORES. Generally, a warehouse or other facility operated by the Federal government for the storage of contraband, seized merchandise, or goods not released from Federal custody. Under the customs regulations, these storage facilities are operated by government personnel for merchandise not released from customs control pending clearance. Goods not entered through customs within five days of arrival in the customs territory may be placed in the public stores (or a *general order warehouse*) at the discretion of the customs authorities. Goods placed in such status are held at the risk and expense of their owner.

A general order warehouse, unlike a public stores facility, is a privately owned and operated warehouse acting under license from the Customs Service.

PUPS. *Synonymous with* DOUBLES *(q.v.).*

PURCHASE PRICE. Defined in 19 U.S.C. 162 as the price at which imported merchandise has been purchased, or will be purchased, prior to exportation. It is usually based on the ex factory price excluding any export duties levied in the country of manufacture.

Within the framework of the European Economic Community's COMMON AGRICULTURAL POLICY *(q.v.)*, the purchase price is the point at which EEC governments will directly intervene in the market to buy certain agricultural commodities selling at distressed prices.

PURCHASING POWER PARITY. An equal relationship of prices between two countries. Price levels in both countries are substantially the same, considering the rate of exchange.

PURE CAPTIVE. *See* CAPTIVE INSURANCE COMPANY.

PURPOSES. *See* ALL PURPOSES.

Q

QUALIFIED EXPORT ASSETS. *See* DOMESTIC INTERNATIONAL SALES CORPORATION.

QUALIFIED EXPORT RECEIPTS. *See* DOMESTIC INTERNATIONAL SALES CORPORATION.

QUALIFIED SHIPPER'S FACILITY. *See* FIFTY-MILE RULE.

QUANTITATIVE QUOTA. *Synonymous with* absolute quota. *See* QUOTA.

QUANTITATIVE RESTRICTION. A limitation on the quantity of a given commodity that may be imported into a country during a specified period of time. A quantitative restriction is manifested as a QUOTA *(q.v.).*

QUASI MONEY. *See* BROAD MONEY.

QUAY. A wharf, usually of solid construction, parallel with the sea, allowing berthing on one side only.

QUAYAGE. *Synonymous with* QUAY DUES *(q.v.).*

QUAY DUES. The charge levied upon a vessel for berthing at a quay.

QUEEN'S WAREHOUSE. A warehouse operated by Canadian customs for the safe storage of imported merchandise that has been abandoned, seized, or left unclaimed. Goods that remain in the warehouse for two months may be sold or disposed of otherwise.

QUICK RATIO. The number of times a firm's most liquid assets (cash, marketable securities, accounts receivable) exceed current liabilities. The quick ratio differs from the current ratio in that the latter includes the value of inventories.

QUINTAL. A unit of measure in the metric system equivalent to one-tenth of a (metric) ton.

QUINTAL BAG. The standard unit of bagged coffee, equivalent to sixty kilograms.

QUOIN. A wooden wedge used to secure barrels during shipment.

QUOTA. A restriction on the amount of a given item that may be imported during a given period. Quotas can be divided into two categories. An *absolute,* or *quantitative, quota* permits a definite limit on the quantity of an item that may be imported from a given country during a specified time span. A *tariff-rate quota* does not restrict the total quantity of a specified item that may enter but limits the quantity that may be entered under a preferred rate of duty; additional quantities may be admitted at higher rates.

Quotas may be *global,* meaning the restrictions do not differentiate among the countries from which the product might come. Quotas may also be *allocated,* meaning various producing nations may be assigned a portion of the total quantity to be imported.

QUOTA CARTEL. An agreement among firms in a particular industry by which each participant is assigned a portion of market demand.

QUOTA-CLASS MERCHANDISE. Goods subject to QUOTA *(q.v.)* restrictions.

QUOTA PRIORITY. The precedence accorded one entry of QUOTA-CLASS MERCHANDISE *(q.v.)* over other quota-class merchandise.

QUOTA PRORATION. An adjustment to a consumption entry for QUOTA-CLASS MERCHANDISE *(q.v.)* when the entry calls for more merchandise than will be allowed under the quota.

QUOTA SHARE TREATY. A contract of REINSURANCE *(q.v.)* whereby the reinsurer agrees to accept a stipulated percentage of all business of a particular class.

R

RACK CAR. A railroad flatcar, usually eighty-five feet long, with several levels, used to transport automobiles. Also, a railcar with racks at either end used to transport pulpwood.

RAG TOP. A container or trailer equipped with a canvas top which can be rolled back during loading and unloading.

RAIL PLANS. *See* PIGGYBACK PLANS.

RAILROAD THROUGH BILL OF LADING. An export BILL OF LADING *(q.v.)*, issued by a railroad, covering shipment overseas of merchandise by combined rail/water service under a through rate. The bill of lading may be consigned in *to order* form and gives an itemization of rail and ocean charges and various fees.

This form of bill of lading is applicable only to shipments from certain points, usually Midwestern cities, destined for export via West Coast ports.

RALLY. An increase in stock or commodity prices following a decline.

RANGE. As used in conjunction with ship charter agreements, a group of ports within a defined geographic area. For example, a shipowner may hire out his vessel to be operated under charter between north Europe and the "New Orleans-Brownsville range," in which case the charterer may elect to load or discharge cargo at any U.S. Gulf port between New Orleans and Brownsville. A stopover at Jacksonville would not be within the stipulated range.

RATE OF DRAWBACK. *See* DRAWBACK.

RATIONALIZATION AGREEMENT. *See* SPECIALIZATION AGREEMENT.

RATIONING OF EXCHANGE. An exchange control imposed by governmental authority to regulate transactions in foreign exchange. Under a rationing of exchange scheme, only the government may issue exchange to importers, and holders of bills of exchange denominated in a foreign currency must surrender them to the government in exchange for local currency at the official rate.

REACHABLE ON ARRIVAL. *See* ALWAYS ACCESSIBLE.

REACTION. A decline in stock or commodity prices following an advance.

READILY MARKETABLE STAPLES. Merchandise suitable for warehouse financing under eligible banker's acceptances, as provided in Federal Reserve REGULATION A *(q.v.)*. To qualify as a readily marketable staple, an item must be "an article of commerce, agriculture, or industry" that is constantly traded in spot markets and is not so perishable as to be in danger of losing value through spoilage during the life of the draft drawn to finance its purchase.

REAL CAPITAL. *See* CAPITAL.

REAL INTEREST RATE. *Synonymous with* EFFECTIVE INTEREST RATE *(q.v.)*.

REAL PROPERTY HOLDING COMPANY. A foreign corporation (i.e., not chartered in the United States) in which a DOMESTIC INTERNATIONAL SALES CORPORATION *(q.v.)*, or DISC, controls more than 50 percent of the voting stock, the sole purpose of the foreign corporation being to hold title to non-U.S. real property used exclusively by the DISC. The property is not considered as being used exclusively by the DISC if it is leased to any party other than a related supplier that accounts for at least 90 percent of the *qualified export receipts* of a DISC.

REAL UPVALUATION. A rise in the value of a given currency against other currencies, accompanied by above average domestic inflation.

REASONABLE DESPATCH. The duty of a common carrier to convey goods from shipper to consignee with all reasonable speed. The carrier, however, assumes no obligation for loss of market or other losses sustained as a result of delays in transit.

REBATE (FREIGHT). A return by a steamship carrier to a shipper of a portion of freight monies paid. Rebating is specifically prohibited in trade to or from the United States by the Shipping Act of 1916.

In trade routes not involving the United States (e.g., Japan to Europe), the practice is legal and accepted. Rebating is often institutionalized in the merchant's contract with a CONFERENCE (q.v.), wherein a specified percentage of freight paid to member lines of the conference is pledged to be refunded to the shipper after a fixed period of time.

REBATE AGREEMENT. An agreement among firms in a given industry to standardize the amount or basis of rebates to be granted under specified conditions, thereby eliminating a competitive factor.

RECIPROCAL TRADE AGREEMENTS PROGRAM. An act of Congress which authorized the president to reduce tariffs in exchange for like concessions by trading partners. The Reciprocal Trade Agreements Act of 1934, enacted as an amendment to the SMOOT-HAWLEY ACT (q.v.) of 1930, authorized reductions up to 50 percent in tariff rates under bilateral agreements. The act prescribed that each agreement concluded contain an unconditional MOST FAVORED NATION (q.v.) clause, thereby providing that any reduction that either party to the agreement might grant to a third nation would automatically apply to the other signatory's trade as well. The act was diluted by post–World War II legislation animated by protectionist and defense-oriented forces. The Trade Expansion Act of 1962 largely superseded the RTA program, as did U. S. participation in the GENERAL AGREEMENT ON TARIFFS AND TRADE (q.v.).

RECIPROCITY. Bilateral reduction of trade barriers; each nation reduces its barriers in return for similar concessions by the other nation. Reciprocity is an official policy of the United States, originated by the Reciprocal Trade Agreements Act of 1934.

RECONSIGNMENT. The diversion of goods in transit from the consignee named in the bill of lading to a different party. Common carriers normally impose a charge for such diversions.

RECONSTITUTION. A regulation of the INTERNATIONAL MONETARY FUND (q.v.) relating to the use of SPECIAL DRAWING RIGHTS (q.v.), or SDRs, by member states. Specifically, the rules of reconstitution state that a member must, over a period of five years, maintain an average SDR holding equal to or greater than 30 percent of its average allocation within the same period; a member may be obliged to acquire SDRs to meet its 30 percent minimum. A member must also show "due regard to the desirability of pursuing over time a balanced relationship" between its holding of SDRs, gold, and other reserve assets.

RECOURSE FACTORING. See FACTORING.

RECYCLING. The process whereby the income of oil-producing nations is deposited with major international banks, through which the funds are loaned to oil-importing nations to finance their purchases.

RED CLAUSE. A special provision that may appear in a LETTER OF CREDIT (q.v.) that permits the beneficiary to draw advances before presentation of the documents stipulated in the credit. The amount of the advances and the circumstances under which they may be drawn are stipulated in the credit.

The term derives its name from the red ink once used to highlight the clause.

RE-DELIVERY. The point in time at which a charterer returns operational control of the vessel to the owner.

RE-DISCOUNT RATE. See DISCOUNT RATE.

RE-DRAFT. A BILL OF EXCHANGE (q.v.) drawn by a holder of a dishonored draft to recover the face amount of the original instrument, plus protest fees and any exchange loss. The substitute bill may be drawn upon either the maker or any endorser of the dishonored bill.

REEFER. Refrigerated transport equipment, such as refrigerated containers, cars, or trucks.

RE-EXPORTS. The exportation of merchandise previously imported.

REFERENCE PRICE. A mechanism of the COMMON AGRICULTURAL POLICY (q.v.) of the European Economic Community designed to prevent disruptive import competition for certain vegetables, fruits, fish, and wine. The reference price is an average of EEC market prices compiled over time. When the entry price of an import falls below the reference price, the EEC may suspend further imports of that product or impose a levy (a *compensatory tax*) to negate the price advantage of the foreign produce.

REFLATION. The recovery of price levels following a depression or deflation.

REGIOCENTRIC COMPANY. See E.P.R.G. FRAMEWORK.

REGIONAL APPELLATION CERTIFICATE. A document prepared by a recognized local authority certifying that certain referenced merchandise derives from a given defined geographic area. This document is akin to a CERTIFICATE OF ORIGIN (q.v.) but is issued on behalf of items produced within a given locale. For example, a certificate may attest that certain brandy was produced within the Cognac region of France and is entitled therefore to be sold as "Cognac."

REGISTER TON. A unit of measure, equal to one hundred cubic feet, used in defining the cubic capacity of a ship.

REGULAR TONNAGE TAX. See LIGHT MONEY AND TONNAGE TAXES.

REGULATION A. A pronouncement of the Federal Reserve Board (12 CFR 201) governing the creation of banker's acceptances. In essence, the regulation requires that an "eligible" banker's acceptance (i.e., one acceptable for discount at the Federal Reserve discount window) have a maturity of not more than 180 days, exclusive of days of grace, and

1. arise as the result of the importation or exportation of goods between the United States and another country or two foreign countries; or

2. cover a domestic shipment of goods within the United States, providing the transaction is secured by a trust receipt for the goods; or

3. cover the financing of goods in a warehouse where the goods are secured by a negotiable warehouse receipt. It is a further condition of warehouse financing that the goods be READILY MARKETABLE STAPLES (q.v.).

Banker's acceptances created outside the conditions set forth above are "ineligible" for discount at the Federal Reserve and for certain other uses, such as investments by pension funds. Effective with the repeal of Regulations B and C on April 1, 1974, certain ineligible acceptances with tenor up to 270 days from acceptance are acceptable for purchase and sale by the Federal Open Market Committee.

REGULATION K. A pronouncement of the Federal Reserve system that permits both domestic and foreign banks to establish a "mother" EDGE ACT CORPORATION (q.v.), which can establish branches in other locations, thereby circumventing interstate branching prohibitions.

REHYPOTHECATION. The act whereby a lender uses negotiable instruments or similar collateral left with him by borrowers as collateral for his own borrowings. Rehypothecation commonly occurs when a member bank pledges eligible customer collateral at the Federal Reserve for a loan. The original borrower's HYPOTHECATION (q.v.) agreement routinely conveys to the lending bank the right to repledge, i.e., rehypothecate, the collateral.

REINSURANCE. An arrangement in which an insurance underwriter contractually spreads its policy risks with other underwriters, sharing the premium with them. For example, an underwriter may issue a policy for fifty million dollars to cover the loss of a ship; being unwilling to assume the full risk of loss, the insurer may retain the first five million dollars of risk and invite other insurers to assume portions of the remaining forty-five million dollars at risk in return for an agreed share of the shipowner's premium.

In many cases, prior agreements between underwriters provide for the acceptance of reinsurance risks within a given class and dollar limit; this arrangement is a *treaty arrangement*. The acceptance of an individual risk in the absence of a treaty is known as a *facultative agreement*.

RELATED FOREIGN EXPORT CORPORATION. According to Section 933 of the Internal Revenue Code, any foreign corporation that satisfies the definition of a FOREIGN INTERNATIONAL SALES CORPORATION, a REAL PROPERTY HOLDING COMPANY, or an ASSOCIATED FOREIGN CORPORATION (qq.v.). See DOMESTIC INTERNATIONAL SALES CORPORATION.

RELATED SPECIFICITY. A rule of customs law that when two or more tariff provisions might be applied to an item, the one that most specifically describes the article shall be applied.

RELEASED VALUATION RATE. A lower tariff rate provided by a common carrier to a shipper in return for a reduced claim liability on the part of the carrier. For example, a carrier may offer a reduced rate if the shipper agrees to release the value of the product at fifty cents per pound. The Interstate Commerce Commission must approve released valuation rates.

RELIEF CONSIGNMENTS. Emergency supplies, including food, blankets, medicines, and vehicles for transport of such supplies, destined to aid victims of natural disasters, famines, or other catastrophes. Customs authorities are pledged to accelerate the release of such items.

RELIQUIDATION. An amendment of a customs entry LIQUIDATION (q.v.)

REMONETIZE. To restore the characteristic of legal tender to a medium of exchange that had been previously demonetized; for example, to reissue gold coins for circulation as money.

RENT-A-CAPTIVE. The use of an offshore CAPTIVE INSURANCE COMPANY (q.v.) owned or controlled by another firm to provide coverage not readily available commercially or to shelter income from taxation. The rent-a-captive approach may provide a firm with the benefits of owning a captive insurer without some of the difficulties. For example, the rented captive may be used in lieu of captive formation (1) to eliminate up-front capitalization of an owned captive; (2) where insurance expense is not sufficient to warrant such formation; (3) to overcome potential pitfalls associated with the CARNATION CASE and REVENUE RULING 77-316 (qq.v.), which regard payments by U.S. firms to offshore captives as "capital transfers," and as such not deductible; and (4) to provide experience in captive operation and the accumulation of a surplus upon which the insured can establish his own captive.

REPARATION. A payment made by a carrier to a shipper in satisfaction of improper charges levied. Unlike claims for an overcharge, which occurs when the rate is applied, reparation claims occur when the rate itself is unlawful. Reparations are awarded by the Interstate Commerce Commission.

REPATRIATION. The transfer of investment proceeds or the return of capital from a foreign country back to the home country of the investor.

REPLY TIME. A specified period of time during which an offer to charter a vessel remains valid. If the offering principal receives a CLEAN ACCEPTANCE *(q.v.)* from his counterpart within the prescribed time period, the party making the offer agrees to be bound to the charter; if a clean acceptance is not received in time, the offer expires.

REPORTING CURRENCY. The currency used by a multinational firm to prepare its financial statements.

REPORTING DAY. The day on which a vessel under charter advises it is available to commence loading.

REPORT TO THE COUNCIL AND COMMISSION ON ECONOMIC AND MONETARY UNION IN THE COMMUNITY (1970). *See* WERNER REPORT COMMUNITY.

REPRESENTATIVE MONEY. Currency secured by specie; paper money fully backed by gold or silver and redeemable into metal on demand.

REPURCHASE AGREEMENT. An arrangement whereby securities or foreign exchange is purchased for a short period of time with a prearranged plan for repurchase by the seller. The Federal Reserve system engages extensively in such deals, employing government securities, as a vehicle for regulating bank reserves.

RESALE PRICE METHOD. *Synonymous with* ARM'S LENGTH PRICE *(q.v.).*

RESERVE ACCOUNTING. The practice whereby a bank posts reserves against its asset balances. The percentage of reserves is prescribed by the Federal Reserve system and varies from time to time as an instrument of monetary policy. There are two schemes for reserve accounting:

1. *Lagged reserve accounting.* Reserves are posted on balances as of a date two weeks earlier. This approach, in effect since September 1968, is often criticized inasmuch as a disparity is apt to exist at any point in time between reserves and money in circulation.

2. *Contemporaneous reserve accounting.* Reserves are posted daily on current balances. This procedure was in effect prior to September 1968 but was abandoned as administratively burdensome upon banks.

RESERVE ASSETS. Gold or foreign currency held by a central bank or national treasury as backing for currency it issues.

RESERVE CURRENCY. The currency of a major trading national, widely accepted in international transactions and regarded as stable, that is held by the central banks or monetary authorities of other nations as a form of *collateral* for their own currency. The use of reserve currencies arose after World War I as a substitute for gold. From the end of World War II up to the collapse of the Bretton Woods System, the U.S. dollar was the principal reserve currency. It still remains the largest reserve currency.

RESERVES. In insurance industry usage, funds set aside to satisfy claims which have arisen but not yet paid. Such reserves fall into two categories: (1) Those arising from claims made upon the insurer but not yet actually paid; and (2) claims which have been incurred but not yet reported.

In the latter case, depending upon the type of risk insured, considerable time may pass between the occurrence of a loss and the reporting of that loss to the insurer. This span of time, known as the "tail," may run several months or even years. During that period, the insurer remains financially obligated for the loss. In order to put aside enough money to cover such eventual settlements, insurers create reserves for "incurred but not reported losses." The actual amount of such reserves is computed by actuaries and other experts, relying upon past claims experience and other factors. In most countries, the amount so projected is considered a current expense for income tax purposes.

RESOURCE ORIENTATION. The act of locating a manufacturing facility near its source of raw materials. It usually occurs in cases where the cost of transporting the raw materials significantly exceeds the cost of transporting the finished product. *See* MARKETING ORIENTATION, WEIGHT GAINING, WEIGHT LOSING.

RESPONDENT. In admiralty, one who answers to a libel, or action. The term corresponds with *defendant.*

RESPONDENTIA. The pledge of cargo by a vessel's master as collateral for a loan to permit the ship to continue on its journey or to make arrangements to forward the goods. The bond so created gives the lender a MARITIME LIEN *(q.v.)* on the goods pledged, with the provision that no repayment shall be made if the goods do not arrive at destination; if only part of the cargo arrives intact, repayment will be proportional.

RESTITUTIONS. Export and producer subsidies granted by the European Economic Community to EEC farmers and processors. The subsidies are a feature of the COMMON AGRICULTURAL POLICY *(q.v.).*

RESTRAINT OF PRINCES, RULERS, AND PEOPLE. A stipulation in the Hague Agreement by which common carriers by sea are exempt from liability for losses to cargo arising from the acts of sovereign states.

RESTRAINT OF TRADE. Combinations, contracts, agreements, or arrangements, either oral or written, designed to effect a monopoly, impede competition, fix prices, retard entry into the field, or otherwise obstruct trade that would otherwise occur if left to natural economic forces. Acts in restraint of trade are generally viewed as contrary to public policy, and many are specifically prohibited by law.

RESTRICTED ARTICLE. A hazardous or potentially hazardous item tendered for carriage; the term *restricted article* is used primarily in conjunction with air transport. Restricted articles transported into, out of, or within the United States are subject to the provisions of Title 49 of the Code of Federal Regulations; international shipments are also subject to the requirements of the INTERNATIONAL AIR TRANSPORT ASSOCIATION *(q.v.)*. See HAZARDOUS MATERIALS TRANSPORTATION ACT.

RESTRICTIVE ENDORSEMENT. *See* ENDORSEMENT.

RETALIATION. The act of erecting trade barriers or posting restrictions by a nation against a trading partner that has withdrawn a trade concession.

RETALIATORY DUTY. A customs duty imposed by one nation on the imports of another in response to actual or perceived trade discrimination against the first country. A duty so imposed would not apply to imports of the same merchandise from other countries.

RETIRING A BILL. The redemption of a BILL OF EXCHANGE *(q.v.)* for less than its face amount on or before its maturity.

RETROACTIVE TERMS ADJUSTMENT. The mitigation of debt owed by Third World countries to industrial nations as a vehicle to improve economic conditions in poorer lands. The *adjustments* arose as a result of a 1979 meeting of the United Nations Conference on Trade and Development (UNTAD), when thirteen industrial countries agreed to eliminate or restructure five billion dollars of Third World debt. The term has since expanded to encompass any debt forgiveness or amelioration to a Third World state. It may include refinancing of unpaid debt, elimination of interest, or other concessional terms in additon to outright forgiveness of debt.

RETURNED SHIPMENT RATE. A rate for the return of empty packages or drums to the original shipper to be refilled with product.

REVALUATION. The increase in value of a given currency in relation to other currencies; the opposite of DEVALUATION *(q.v.)*.

REVENUE RULING 77-316. A 1977 pronouncement of the Internal Revenue Service that contends that a firm is not entitled to business deductions for insurance premiums paid to a so-called CAPTIVE (i.e., owned or controlled) INSURANCE COMPANY *(q.v.)*. The ruling asserts that related and subsidiary firms constitute an "economic family" and that payments made by one member of the family to another on behalf of "insurance" do not constitute a genuine transfer of risk between the parties; hence, no insurance is purchased and no deduction arises for payments made.

Both the ruling and the "economic family" doctrine have been attacked and subjected to extensive court challenges.

REVENUE TARIFF. *See* TARIFF (CUSTOMS).

REVENUE TON. The unit of measure upon which freight is computed by a carrier. The unit is commonly one of weight or cubic measurement. For example, if a tariff provides for the carriage of a particular commodity at a rate of thirty dollars per cubic meter, the *revenue ton* is defined as a cubic meter. Freight may be assessed on the basis of a *measurement ton* (usually forty cubic feet, but sometimes a cubic meter, depending upon the tariff) or of various *weight tons* (e.g., the short ton [2,000 pounds], the long ton [2,240 pounds], or the metric ton [2,205 pounds]).

As a rule, the revenue ton is computed using the base rate only, not including surcharges or accessorial charges such as wharfage.

REVERSE REPURCHASE AGREEMENT. *See* MATCHED SALE-PURCHASE TRANSACTIONS.

REVERSIBLE LAYDAYS. A provision in a charter party that permits the charterer to combine the LAYTIME *(q.v.)* for loading and discharging into a single unit, applying the time as needed. If loading was effected in less than the laytime permitted in the contract, the time saved could be applied as a credit in the event of a time overrun during discharge, or vice versa.

REVISED AMERICAN FOREIGN TRADE DEFINITIONS—1941. A standardized listing of terms of sale for use by importers and exporters. The original American foreign trade definitions were published in 1919; by 1940 it was evident that significant revision was necessary, and this work was undertaken by a joint committee of the National Foreign Trade Council, the National Council of American Importers, and the Chamber of Commerce of the United States. The Revised American Foreign Trade Definitions were published in 1941.

While the definitions have no legal standing per se, they have been used extensively by foreign traders for four decades and have achieved wide adherence. Importers and exporters may incorporate them by reference into contracts of sale, thereby giving the terms legal effect.

In recent years, the INCOTERMS *(q.v.)* developed by the International Chamber of Commerce have at least partially supplanted the Revised American Foreign Trade Definitions.

The full text of the *Revised American Foreign Trade Definitions* can be found in Appendix D1.

REVOCABLE LETTER OF CREDIT. *See* LETTER OF CREDIT.

REVOLVING LETTER OF CREDIT. A LETTER OF CREDIT *(q.v.)* in which, pursuant to the terms and conditions contained therein, the dollar amount is renewed without the necessity of amending the credit.

A revolving letter of credit may revolve according to time, in which case a fixed sum becomes available at the beginning of a given time period—monthly, for example. If sums unused during one period may be carried over to the next period, the letter of credit is said to be *cumulative*; if such unused sums cannot be carried forward, the letter of credit is *noncumulative*.

A revolving letter of credit may also revolve according to value; such credits have their value reinstated after each drawing. Unless an overall value is assigned to the credit, this type of instrument permits unlimited drawings; for this reason, it is not commonly used.

RHODIAN SEA CODE. The earliest known compilation of maritime laws, believed to have been formulated c. 900 B.C. on Rhodes. The text is lost, save the provision concerning jettisons, which has been preserved in Justinian's Code. The jettison article deals with a ratable contribution to an owner whose merchandise has been cast overboard to save the ship. This practice has been absorbed into the law of all maritime nations, and is manifested in GENERAL AVERAGE *(q.v.)*.

RIDER. An endorsement or modification to a standard insurance policy to accommodate a particular need.

RIPARIAN NATIONS. In international law, nations which share opposite banks of a river or different parts of the banks of a river.

RISKLESS RATE OF RETURN. The rate of interest paid by government securities; it constitutes a base against which other rates of return may be judged in assessing the effective use of capital.

RISK MANAGEMENT. The application of management techniques to identify, quantify, and respond to threats of loss or damage to a firm's assets. Such threats may arise from random events such as fire, explosion, theft, and acts of nature, or from the conscious efforts of external forces such as acts of terrorism, expropriation, or legislative enactment.

Two elements are essential to risk management: *control*, the identification and neutralization or reduction of risks, and *risk financing*, to provide for funds at the lowest possible cost to respond for losses that could not be identified or prevented.

The management of risk financing requires that a conscious decision be made between risk retention (i.e., the amount of financial exposure the firm is prepared to retain) and risk transfer. Risk transfer can often be accomplished by the purchase of insurance from an underwriter, although insurance may not be the most economical or efficient vehicle.

RISK RETENTION. Also known as *self-insurance*, a conscious decision to retain an identified economic risk rather than purchase insurance. This decision is made after comparing the cost of insurance with the likelihood, frequency, and severity of a possible loss. Normally, the money saved by not purchasing insurance is placed in a fund against a possible loss. Unlike *no insurance*, which is generally the result of a failure to identify or quantify the risk and is, therefore, an absence of a plan to respond to a loss, self-insurance is the product of a conscious decision to forego commercial insurance.

ROADSTEAD. A point off a harbor where vessels may safely anchor while awaiting berthing.

ROBINSON-PATMAN ACT. An act of Congress, passed in 1936, as an amendment to the Clayton Act reinforcing prohibitions against discriminatory pricing practice. *See* ANTITRUST.

ROGUE SHIPOWNER. *See* PIRACY.

ROLL-ON/ROLL-OFF. A method of ocean cargo service employing a vessel with ramps astern or amidships to permit wheeled vehicles to be loaded aboard. The opportunity to run cargo on and off by ramps, without the necessity of cranes or similar equipment, permits accelerated loading and unloading of the vessel, particularly in ports where congested or substandard conditions would otherwise impede cargo movement.

ROLLOVER RATIO. A measure of a nation's liquidity, reflected in the reciprocal of the average maturity of foreign debt.

ROLL TRAILER. A low-bed trailer used to carry containers, machinery, and similar cargo, usually on a pier-to-pier basis in conjunction with ROLL-ON/ROLL-OFF *(q.v.)* vessels. These trailers are carried aboard the vessel but do not leave the pier area at port of discharge. Cargo is loaded on other trailers for overroad transport.

Roll trailers may be twenty or forty feet in length and may range in height from sixteen to twenty-nine inches off the ground. They have solid rubber tires and may be rated to carry up to two hundred tons. They are also known as MAFI trailers, after the original German manufacturer.

ROOSA BONDS. Bonds sold by the U.S. Treasury in the 1960s to foreign central banks for dollars as part of a SWAP ARRANGEMENT *(q.v.)* to relieve exchange rate instability. The bonds provided intermediate-term financing for the U.S. Treasury and were denominated in the purchaser's currency.

RO-RO. *See* ROLL-ON/ROLL-OFF.

ROUGH LUMBER. Lumber, whether or not resawn or trimmed, as it comes from the saw, without surface dressing or planing.

ROUTING ORDER. A document, usually a printed form, signed by a foreign buyer instructing his supplier to effect shipments through a named freight forwarder.

ROYALTY RATE. The return that a firm receives from granting license for the use of its processes, trademarks, et cetera, to another firm.

RULE OF LAW AMENDMENT. *See* HICKEN-LOOPER AMENDMENT.

RUNNING DAYS. *See* LAYTIME.

RUST BUCKET. A vessel in decrepit condition.

RUST BUCKET PIRACY. *See* PIRACY.

RYE TERMS. A condition of sale often included in contracts for shipment of grain in bulk whereby the seller warrants the condition of the goods on arrival, less a stipulated allowance for deterioration. This condition is most commonly applied when shipment is to be made by tanker, rather than by dry-bulk type vessels. *See also* TALE QUALE.

S

SABBATINO AMENDMENT. *See* HICKENLOOPER
AMENDMENT.

SACRIFICE. The economic loss sustained when
cargo, rigging, or other property is jettisoned or
destroyed in the course of saving an imperiled ship;
sacrifice losses are usually recoverable in GENERAL
AVERAGE *(q.v.)*.

SAFEGUARD MEASURES. Actions taken by a nation to protect its domestic industry and commerce
from what it views as unfair or improper practices
by a trading partner. For example, a trading partner's use of improper subsidies designed to artifi-
cially stimulate exports might result in such safeguard measures as the imposition of COUNTERVAIL-
ING DUTIES *(q.v.)*, a QUOTA *(q.v.)*, or other trade
restrictions.

Safeguard measures are customarily imposed under the ESCAPE CLAUSE *(q.v.)* of most trade
agreements.

SAFE PORT. A port into which a vessel may enter
and remain, and from which it may depart without
abnormal dangers that are avoidable through the
exercise of normal care and seamanship.

SALE AT LESS THAN FAIR VALUE. The sale of
merchandise to a foreign purchaser at a price below
the price that would be charged for a like sale in the
home market. Such sales may serve as the basis for
an allegation of DUMPING *(q.v.)*.

SALVAGE. In maritime law, the compensation allowed to persons through whose assistance a ship or
its cargo is saved in whole or in part. Four elements
are essential to validate a salvage claim: (1) a marine
peril must have existed; (2) the service must have
been voluntary; (3) the vessel and/or cargo, in whole
or part, must have been saved; (4) the service performed must have contributed to the saving. *See*
ADVENTURE, FLOTSAM, JETSAM, Appendix D5.

SAME CONDITION DRAWBACK. *See* DRAWBACK.

SAMURAI BONDS. Yen denominated bonds issued in Japan by foreign borrowers. In 1983, the
volume of samurai bonds issued exceeded U.S. $4.3
billion.

SANITARY CERTIFICATE. *See* PHYTOSANITARY
CERTIFICATE.

SATELLITE STATE. A country that is heavily dependent upon or strongly influenced by another
state, so that the policies of the satellite are largely
shaped by the nation it orbits. A satellite condition
may arise as a result of economic dependence, proximity to a significantly stronger power, or idealogi-
cal fealty (as in the case of certain communist states
led by Moscow).

SCHEDULE B NUMBER. A seven-digit commodity number prescribed in the U.S. Census Bureau's
Schedule B (Statistical Classification of Domestic
and Foreign Commodities Exported from the
United States). The appropriate Schedule B number applicable to a product must be shown on the
Shipper's Export Declaration at time of export
from the United States. The purpose of the number
is to identify U.S. exports by product and to regulate the exportation of controlled articles (*see* figure,
next page).

SCHEDULED TERRITORIES. *See* STERLING AREA.

SCHEDULE TARE. A tare weight specified in the
U.S. Customs Regulations that shall be deducted
from the weight of certain products for the application of specific duties. The following are the schedule tares provided for in Customs Regulations, 19
CFR 159.22(c):

Apple boxes: Eight pounds per box. This schedule tare includes paper wrappers, if any, on the
apples.

China clay in the so-called half-ton casks: Seven-
ty-two pounds per cask.

Figs in skeleton cases: Actual tare for outer containers plus 13 percent of the gross weight of
the inside wooden boxes and figs.

Fresh tomatoes: Four ounces per 100 paper
wrappings.

Lemons and oranges: Ten ounces per box and 5
ounces per half box for paper wrappings, and
actual tare for outer containers.

Ocher, dry, in casks: Eight percent of the gross
weight.

SCHEDULE 6. METALS AND METAL PRODUCTS; MACHINERY AND TRANSPORTATION EQUIPMENT

(6-4-A)   (6-4-A)

Schedule B number	Commodity description	Unit of quantity	Schedule B number	Commodity description	Unit of quantity
	Internal combustion engines and parts thereof--Con. 　Piston-type engines--Con. 　　Engines other than compression-ignition engines--Con.			Internal combustion engines and parts thereof--Con. 　Non-piston-type engines: 　　Other:	
660.4830	Automobiles, automobile trucks and buses.........	No.	660.4965	Gas turbines for mechanical drives.............	No.
660.4840	Outboard motors for marine craft...................	No.		Other:	
	Other:		660.4970	Missile and rocket engines and turbines..	No.
			660.4980	Other.................	No.
	Marine:		660.5000	Cast iron (except malleable cast-iron) parts, not alloyed and not machined beyond cleaning and machined only for the removal of fins, gates, sprues and risers to permit location in finishing machinery........	Lb.
660.4860	Inboard engines with outboard drive.....	No.			
660.4865	Inboard engines with inboard drive......	No.			
	Other gasoline engines:			Other parts: 　　Parts of piston-type engines other than compression-ignition engines:	
660.4872	Under 6 brake hp....	No.			
660.4874	6 brake hp and over but under 11 brake hp................	No.	660.5210	Parts of automobile engines, automobile truck engines and bus engines..	X
660.4876	11 brake hp and over, but not over 50 brake hp........	No.	660.5220	Parts of marine craft engines................	X
660.4878	Over 50 brake hp....	No.	■ 660.5252	Parts of aircraft engines: 　　　Designed for use in civil aircraft........	X
660.4880	Gas (natural or LP) engines, except gas turbines.............	No.	■ 660.5254	Other.................	X
660.4890	Other.................	No.	660.5260	Parts of tractor engines..	X
			660.5270	Other...................	X
	Non-piston-type engines:				
	Aircraft jet and gas turbines:			Parts of compression-ignition piston-type engines:	
	Military:		660.5410	Parts of automobile engines, automobile truck engines and bus engines..	X
660.4922	New...................	No.			
660.4925	Used..................	No.	660.5420	Parts of marine craft engines................	X
	Nonmilitary:				
660.4930	New...................	No.	660.5440	Parts of tractor engines..	X
660.4935	Used..................	No.	660.5445	Other...................	X

Schedule B

Ocher, in oil, in casks: Twelve percent of the gross weight.

Pimientos in tins imported from Spain: The following schedule drained weight shall be used as the customs dutiable weight in the liquidation of entries, the difference between the weight of the net contents of pimientos in tins and such drained weight being the allowance made in liquidation for tare for water:

Size can	Drained weight
3 kilo	30 lb.—case of 6 tins
28 oz.	36.72 lb.—case of 24 tins
15 oz.	17.72 lb.—case of 24 tins
7 oz.	8.62 lb.—case of 24 tins
4 oz.	5.33 lb.—case of 24 tins

SCHUMAN PLAN. A series of proposals for the pooling of European coal and steel resources as a vehicle for European economic recovery and integration, advanced by Robert Schuman of France in 1950. Schuman's plan was accepted by the governments of Belgium, Luxembourg, the Netherlands, Italy, and West Germany, as well as France. Negotiations among the six governments began in Paris in June 1950, resulting in the establishment of the EUROPEAN COAL AND STEEL COMMUNITY *(q.v.)* in April 1951.

SCIENTIFIC TARIFF. A concept in which duties would fluctuate and be levied on an item-by-item, shipment-by-shipment basis, so as to equalize the cost of imports and their domestic counterparts. The object of this plan is to put imported and domestic products on an equally competitive basis. To do so, however, would be to eliminate the comparative advantages that are the basis of international trade.

SEABEE. A marine cargo system that employs a barge loaded aboard a specially designed vessel. The barge, which is substantially larger than those employed in LASH-type systems, measures more than 97 feet in overall length, features double-hull construction, and accommodates a bale capacity of 39,140 cubic feet. The barges are hoisted aboard the vessel by means of winches. Each barge has hatch openings measuring 30 feet by 84 feet for ease of loading. In addition, flat deck barges are used to handle oversized machinery and similarly awkward cargoes. Seabee barges are the same width and half the length as the "jumbo" barges used on U.S. inland waterways.

The Seabee system was introduced in 1972 by Lykes Brothers Steamship Line.

SEABRIDGE. A service offered by some ocean carriers whereby cargo moving between Europe and East Asia is taken by one vessel from the exporting country to a U.S. port for relay, from the same port, to destination. The goods move under a single through bill of lading.

A seabridge movement is the effective equivalent of a LANDBRIDGE *(q.v.)* movement except that the cargo moves entirely by water, without inland carriage across America.

SEA-BRIEF. *See* MARITIME PASSPORT.

SEA-LETTER. *See* MARITIME PASSPORT.

SEA-PASS. *See* MARITIME PASSPORT.

SEA-SHED. A removable section in the hold of a container ship permitting the vessel to accommodate outside and heavy-lift loads.

SEASONAL PORTS. Ports open only during certain times of the year.

SEAVAN. A term sometimes used in nonmaritime shipping circles to describe a dry-freight ocean container.

SEAWORTHY. A vessel that is properly constructed, equipped, manned, documented, and otherwise outfitted to undertake the voyage contemplated; a vessel may be seaworthy for one purpose or voyage, and not for another.

SECONDARY BOYCOTT. *See* BOYCOTT.

SECONDARY LIABILITY. A contingent liability borne by unqualified endorsers of negotiable instruments. In the event of default or dishonor by the primary obligee, the endorsers may be held to settle the obligation to the holder of the instrument.

SECOND ENLARGEMENT. The expansion of the European Communities beyond its 1980 membership. The *first enlargement* occurred when Great Britain, Ireland, and Denmark joined the EC in 1972, raising the membership to nine (the original members were France, Federal Republic of Germany, Italy, Netherlands, Luxembourg, and Belgium).

The second enlargement added Greece, Spain, and Portugal to the community. Greece joined on January 1, 1981; Spain and Portugal are expected to be accepted into membership not later than 1987.

SECOND FLAG CARRIAGE. The shipment of goods aboard a vessel that flies the flag of the importing country.

SECOND WORLD. A general reference to those countries having centrally planned economies. *See* FIRST WORLD, THIRD WORLD.

SECTION 15. A provision of the Shipping Act of 1916 (46 U.S.C. 814) that permits ocean carriers to enter into agreements to eliminate rate and service competition between them. Approval by the Federal Maritime Commission of a Section 15 agreement extends to the carriers involved immunity from the penalties of the antitrust statutes for collaboration undertaken within the scope of the approved agreement. A CONFERENCE *(q.v.)*, for example, derives its antitrust immunity from Section 15 agreements.

SECTION 204. A provision of the Agricultural Act of 1956 authorizing the president to negotiate bilateral agreements to limit exports to the United States of "any agricultural commodity or product manufactured therefrom or textiles or textile products." The president is also empowered to take steps to limit exports to the United States of such products and to issue regulations to implement any bilateral arrangements concluded. U.S. participation in the MULTIFIBER ARRANGEMENT *(q.v.)* is a product of Section 204 authority.

SECTION 301 COMMITTEE. A component of the Office of the United States Trade Representative that investigates allegations of unfair trade practices on the part of foreign governments, practices that impede the foreign commerce of the United States. These practices fall under the broad category of *nontariff barriers* and include, inter alia, discrimination in the procurement practices of the foreign government, restrictive business practices, special border taxes, and horsepower taxes. The committee is empowered to investigate complaints of unfair practices, hold hearings, and report its findings to the president. The committee derives its name from Section 301 of the Trade Act of 1974, under which the president is authorized to retaliate against foreign states that impose unfair burdens on American trade by suspending the benefits of U.S. trade concessions previously granted and by imposing restrictions or fees on the commerce of the attending nation.

SECTION 482 TRANSACTION. *See* ARM'S LENGTH TRANSACTION.

SECTION 931 CORPORATION. A corporation operating in various U.S. possessions that, under certain circumstances, might accrue significant tax benefits. So named for Section 931 of the Internal Revenue Code, a firm might be exempt from Federal income tax on U.S. possessions income (so long as the dividends were not distributed in the United States) if (1) 80 percent or more of its gross income was derived from U.S. possessions sources during the previous three-year period; and (2) 50 percent or more of the gross income was the product of active trade within a U.S. possession.

This opportunity was effectively eliminated by the Tax Reform Act of 1976.

SEIGNIORAGE. A premium imposed by a mint, over and above actual manufacturing costs, for converting bullion metal into coin. An example of seigniorage would be the difference between the face value of the quarter-dollar coin versus its metal content and manufacturing cost.

SELECTIVE SAFEGUARDS. In European usage, a synonym for a BILATERAL RESTRAINT AGREEMENT *(q.v.)*.

SELF-HELP. A provision of Title I of the Agricultural Trade Development and Assistance Act of 1954 (commonly known as P.L. 480) that stipulates that an aid recipient nation must undertake steps to improve its own agriculture. This self-help is manifested through allocating land to food, versus nonfood, crops; developing privately owned sources of agricultural chemicals, farm implements, and related industries; training farmers in improved techniques; constructing suitable storage facilities; improving distribution and marketing systems; improving the economic climate for investment in agriculture; adopting producer-incentives programs; expanding agricultural research; committing local funds to programs of agricultural expansion; and implementing voluntary population control programs.

Failure to adopt adequate self-help measures may imperil continued aid.

SELF-LIQUIDATING LOAN. *Synonymous with* ASSET CONVERSION LOAN *(q.v.)*.

SELF-REFERENCE CRITERION. A concept in marketing that most failures to market products overseas derive from an inability on the part of the seller to adjust from his own cultural frame of reference to perceive the peculiarities of the market he is attempting to penetrate.

SELLING GROUP. An arrangement in which several manufacturers collaborate in a joint effort to sell their merchandise overseas. Two common selling group approaches are associations that fall under the WEBB-POMERANE ACT and COMPLEMENTARY EXPORTING *(qq.v.)*.

SENIOR CAPTIVE. *See* CAPTIVE INSURANCE COMPANY.

SERVICE SUPPLY LICENSE. A validated export license issued by the U.S. government to a U.S. or foreign firm authorizing the export of spare and replacement parts to controlled purchasers abroad who originally purchased American equipment under license.

SHELL COMPANY. A "paper" company, usually operated without employees. Normally an attorney or other local agent or management company performs the legal duties of the company on behalf of the stockholders.

Shell companies often operate in tax-free or low-tax jurisdictions such as Bermuda, Liechtenstein, or the Cayman Islands. The shareholders may structure their business affairs or earnings so as to shift income to the shell company, thereby avoiding higher taxes in their own countries.

Shell companies are often known as *brass plate* companies, because it is common for the shell to have a name plate on the entrance into the managing agent's office.

SHERMAN ACT. An act of Congress, passed in 1890, that makes illegal all contracts, combinations, and conspiracies in restraint of trade, as well as monopolies and attempts to monopolize. *See* ANTITRUST.

SHIPBREAKING. The act of disassembling a ship for scrap.

SHIPPER'S CREDIT AGREEMENT. An arrangement by which certain conferences grant terms usually fourteen to thirty days, for freight services performed by member carriers. Customarily the shipper provides the CONFERENCE *(q.v.)* with bank and credit references on a prescibed form and executes a pledge to settle accounts within the authorized credit period.

SHIPPER'S EXPORT DECLARATION. An official document that a U.S. exporter is obliged to submit to Federal authorities whenever merchandise is shipped from the United States to a foreign destination or certain offshore possessions. The primary authority for requiring the filing of the declaration is the Export Administration Act of 1969, as amended; failure to file the declaration or making false statements therein may subject the preparer to civil and/or criminal penalties.

The purpose of the declaration is twofold: to permit a pre-export control on shipments of sensitive commodities or general shipments to unfriendly countries, and to permit the gathering of statistical data on exports. For these purposes, the declaration requires, inter alia, a description of the merchandise (including the SCHEDULE B NUMBER *[q.v.]* for the commodity), value, country of destination, and export license number, where applicable.

A shipper's export declaration is required on all commercial shipments valued over $250 and on any shipment, irrespective of value, requiring a validated export license (except those involving shipments of technical data, even where licensed).

For shipments made to foreign destinations (other than Canada) two copies of the declaration are required; only one copy need be filed on shipments to Canada, Puerto Rico, or the U.S. Virgin Islands. Except for exports by mail, the declarations are filed with U.S. customs authorities at the port of exportation. In those cases where exportation is done by mail and a declaration is required, the filing may be made with the postmaster.

Two forms of shipper's export declaration are available for use. Form 7525-V is the older form; form 7525-V-ALT was designed for use with so-called international trade master sets, permitting the simultaneous preparation of several trade documents. Either form is acceptable (*see* figure).

Shipper's Export Declaration

SHIPPER'S LOAD AND COUNT. A notation on a bill of lading that stipulates that the goods were loaded and counted by the shipper, without verification by the carrier.

SHIPPER'S RATE AGREEMENT. *See* LOYALTY AGREEMENT.

SHIPPING ACT (OF 1916). The full text of the act can be found in Appendix A5.

SHIPPING DOCUMENTS. A general term relating to any of several documents customarily associated with the international shipment of merchandise. Among these documents are a *bill of lading* (or AIR WAYBILL), CERTIFICATE OF ORIGIN, customs or consular INVOICE, insurance certificate, DOCK RECEIPT *(qq.v.)*, and inspection certificates. Shipping documents are usually required by letters of credit and in transactions involving bills of lading.

SHORE CLAUSE. A provision in marine insurance policies providing coverage for losses to cargo arising from overturning, derailment, collision, or other accidents involving land conveyance; fire, earthquakes, and other natural catastrophes; sprinkler leakage and collapse or shifting of piers or wharves; and losses during inland transit while en route to or from the vessel.

SHORT FORM BILL OF LADING. A BILL OF LADING *(q.v.)* that, unlike the conventional, or long form, document, does not include the full terms and conditions of transport but only refers to them.

SHORT HUNDREDWEIGHT. In Britain, a U.S. hundredweight, i.e., one hundred pounds.

SHORT-TERM CAPITAL TRANSACTIONS. An element of a nation's balance of payment accounting that reflects loans with a maturity of one year or less, granted to or received from foreigners during a given period of time.

SHUNTO. Literally, the "spring offensive," representing the annual wage talks between Japanese labor unions and employers. Such meetings are often punctuated by worker demonstrations (of brief duration), hanging of banners proclaiming worker demands, and the wearing of red armbands bearing the inscription "solidarity" by the workers.

As a result of the 1984 Shunto, Japanese workers were accorded average annual wage increases of 4.4 percent; this had also been the result in 1983.

While the Shunto is a noisy and outwardly menacing demonstration of worker demands, union-employer discussions tend to be businesslike and productive, and protracted work stoppages are rare; this is manifested in the fact that over one-half of all Japanese "strikes" have a duration of less than four hours.

SHUT-OUT. The act of leaving behind certain cargoes when too much cargo arrives for a given vessel sailing. Usually the cargo is not turned away upon delivery to the pier but is accepted by the carrier and despatched aboard a subsequent vessel.

SIGHT BILL. A BILL OF EXCHANGE *(q.v.)*, payable at sight, i.e., upon presentation.

SIGHT CREDIT. A LETTER OF CREDIT *(q.v.)* under which sight drafts shall be drawn.

SIGHT DRAFT ENDORSEMENT. A provision in a contract of marine insurance designed to protect an exporter while his merchandise lies in a foreign port awaiting ACCEPTANCE *(q.v.)* of drafts by the importer. The assured may, by special arrangements with the insurer, extend coverage for a fixed or indefinite period upon payment of an additional premium.

SIGHTING. The presentation for acceptance of a BILL OF EXCHANGE *(q.v.)* payable at sight or a given number of days after sight.

SIGHT RATE. The rate of exchange used by a bank or foreign exchange dealer in purchasing a sight bill of exchange or similar instrument denominated in a foreign currency.

SIMILITUDE. A practice followed by customs authorities when an imported article does not conveniently fit into any existing classification within the customs tariff. Through the process of similitude, the article will be compared with various like articles listed in the tariff; if there are several comparable articles, the import will be classified under the heading of the article in the tariff which is most alike, in terms of component materials.

SINGLE MARKET. A component feature of the COMMON AGRICULTURAL POLICY *(q.v.)* of the European Economic Community.

SINGLE RATE TARIFF. *See* CONFERENCE.

SINGLE STANDARD. A condition in which a nation endows a single metal as the basis of the monetary stock. This system is also known as *monometallism*. As a practical matter, virtually all commercial nations use gold as the standard.

SISTER SHIP POLICY. A provision of marine hull policies that effectively permits the owner of several ships to sue himself and recover under his liability policy should two of his ships collide.

THE SIX. The member states of the European Communities (Federal Republic of Germany, France, Italy, Belgium, Netherlands, and Luxembourg) prior to the enlargement of the community to embrace Great Britain, Ireland, and Denmark (all in 1972) and Greece (1981).

SLIDING SCALE TARIFF. A customs tariff in which rates of DUTY *(q.v.)* vary according to the price of a given import. Usually, as the price of the item declines, the duty is reduced. Duties may be applied on an ad valorem or specific basis.

SLIDING PEG. *See* CRAWLING PEG.

SLOPS. Liquid or semi-liquid residues of bulk cargoes (notably crude petroleum), mixed with water, cleaning agents, or other substances to be discharged as waste from a vessel's holds.

SLOT SHIP. *Synonymous with* CELLULARIZED VESSEL *(q.v.)*.

SLUICE-GATE PRICE. *See* GATE PRICE.

SMITHSONIAN AGREEMENT. A largely unsuccessful effort to revive the fixed exchange rate system established by the BRETTON WOODS AGREEMENT *(q.v.)*.

SMOOT-HAWLEY ACT. *See* TARIFF ACT OF 1930.

SMUGGLING. The unlawful importation of contraband or dutiable merchandise by evading customs inspection.

SNAKE. A medium for the stabilization of the exchange rates of European currencies. In October 1970 the Werner Plan addressed the adoption of a common European currency as a vehicle for the full economic and political integration of Europe. The demise of the BRETTON WOODS AGREEMENT *(q.v.)* system, following the abandonment of U.S. dollar convertibility into gold on August 15, 1971, gave rise to intense fluctuation of major trading currencies. In response to this condition, and with an objective of enhancing European integration, members of the European Economic Community held a meeting at Basel in April 1972 and devised the *common margins arrangement*, which came to be known as the *snake in the tunnel*, or simply the Snake. Original participants in the arrangement were Belgium, Federal Republic of Germany, France, Netherlands, Luxembourg, and Italy. In anticipation of their accession into the European Economic Community, Britain, Ireland, and Denmark joined the agreement on May 1, 1972; however, the pound sterling and Irish pound left the Snake on June 23, followed by the Danish krone four days later.

Over the next six years, the Snake was troubled with the entry and exit of the Danish krone, French franc, Norwegian krone, Swedish krona, and various revaluations of the remaining currencies. The snake was dismembered with the advent of the EUROPEAN MONETARY SYSTEM *(q.v.)* in March 1979.

SOCIAL PROGRESS TRUST FUND. *See* INTER-AMERICAN DEVELOPMENT BANK.

SOCIETY FOR WORLDWIDE INTERBANK FINANCIAL TELECOMMUNICATIONS. An organization, commonly known as SWIFT, established in 1977 by the international banking community to facilitate transactions among member banks. The SWIFT system is a data processing network for the purpose of remitting and collecting funds among the members. Banks interface with the system through regional centers, which are connected into three operating centers, one each based in Belgium, the Netherlands, and the United States. Each operating center is connected directly with the other two. The system verifies bank codes and validates messages for onward transmission. The system consists of over 1,100 banks in 50 countries (as of June 10, 1983) and is supported by dues from member banks and user fees. SWIFT is based in Brussels.

SOFT CURRENCY. A national currency that, because of exchange controls, is not freely convertible into gold or other currencies. Such controls are usually manifest in officially set rates of exchange that do not reflect the price of the soft currency, were it permitted to trade freely.

SOFT GOODS. *See* NONDURABLE GOODS.

SOFT LOAN. A loan repayable by a foreign borrower in a SOFT CURRENCY *(q.v.)*. Such loans usually have been the product of long-term sales to countries without hard currency repayment resources. The practice of making such loans by industrial nations has largely given way to extended term repayments in hard currencies.

SOGO SHOSHA. A Japanese general trading company. Customarily, the term is used in connection with the largest of such companies.

According to the *Trade Business Statistics* report for 1981 issued by the Japanese Ministry of International Trade and Industry, there are over 8,500 trading companies operating in Japan. The nine sogo shosha, however, account in the aggregate for over 40 percent of all Japanese exports, and over 47 percent of all imports. For the twelve month period ending March 1982, the sogo shosha reported sales as follows:

Company	Sales (in trillion yen)
Mitsubishi	14.7
Mitsui	13.2
C. Itoh	12.3
Marubeni	11.5
Sumitomo	11.0
Nissho-Iwai	7.4
Tomen	3.7
Kanematsu-Gosho	3.3
Nichimen	2.9

Sales data are derived from company annual reports which, in accordance with Japanese law, must be published.

SOLA. *See* BILL OF EXCHANGE.

SOLE OF EXCHANGE. *See* BILL OF EXCHANGE.

SOLUS. *See* BILL OF EXCHANGE.

SOLVENCY. The capacity to pay one's debts. There are two states of solvency: *actual solvency* (the firm's total assets would exceed total liabilities upon liquidation) and *technical solvency* (the ability to pay current debts as they come due). It is possible, therefore, for a firm to be actually solvent but not technically solvent, and vice versa.

SOVEREIGN. The supreme political power that, within its own defined geographical boundaries, is accountable to no authority higher than its own.

SOVEREIGN IMMUNITY. A principle of international law that holds that the territory, property, and official agents of a sovereign state are exempt from seizure, suit, trial, or other submission to the jurisdiction of any other state. Normally a state may not be sued in a foreign court without its consent, nor its property seized nor its diplomatic agents arrested by a foreign power for any reason. Violation of this immunity may constitute an act of war.

Some limitations on this immunity have arisen through statute and international agreement.

See ACT OF STATE DOCTRINE, HICKENLOOPER AMENDMENT.

SPACE CHARTER. An arrangement by which a shipper or carrier commits to a vessel owner to fill a specified portion of the ship's hold, on one or more voyages.

SPECIAL AND DIFFERENTIAL TREATMENT. The concept that developing nations require special consideration in bilateral and multilateral trade negotiations, and that concessions should be granted to the developing nations without reciprocity. Although this concept has been advanced in various individual multilateral trade agreements, the Tokyo Round institutionalized the practice of giving tariff preferences to developing nations en masse, most notably embodied in the GENERALIZED SYSTEM OF PREFERENCES *(q.v.)*.

SPECIAL CARGO. *See* CARGO.

SPECIAL CARGO POLICY. A marine cargo policy issued to cover a specific shipment. A special policy may be issued when the shipper infrequently transports goods by water, or when the merchandise is so unusual or so valuable as to warrant a special policy. Frequent shippers customarily obtain an OPEN POLICY *(q.v.)*.

SPECIAL CUSTOMS INVOICE. A special form of customs invoice formerly used for importations into the United States. Prior to March 1, 1982, the special customs invoice (SCI) was required on any importation when the purchase price of the merchandise exceeded five hundred dollars and the rate of duty was in any way dependent upon value.

Purchased and nonpurchased merchandise required separate invoices. Merchandise assembled by a carrier for shipment to a single consignee could be covered by a single SCI. Installment shipments on a single SCI were permitted so long as there were only one consignor and one consignee, and all goods arrived at a single port within a period of seven days.

The SCI is no longer required for most shipments to the United States, although the exporter's commercial invoice must contain substantially the same information (*see* figure).

SPECIAL DRAWING RIGHTS. An artificial currency unit created by the INTERNATIONAL MONETARY FUND *(q.v.)*, or IMF, to augment international reserves. The expansion of world trade following World War II necessitated an expansion in reserves; prior to the creation of SDRs, the international reserve function had been performed largely by the U.S. dollar. Concerns over American fiscal policies, largely a persistent balance of payments deficit, plus massive deficit spending resulting from the Vietnam War and the expansion of Federally sponsored social programs, caused dissatisfaction with the dominant role of the dollar.

In January 1970, the IMF created 3.4 billion SDRs which were allocated to IMF members in proportion to their quotas in the fund. The SDR was valued at 1/35th of an ounce of gold, which made the value of one SDR equal to one dollar at that time. Further allocations of SDRs have raised the number of units outstanding as of January 1, 1981, to 4,052,494,000 SDR. As a result of two dollar devaluations against gold (8.5 percent in December 1971 and a further 11.5 percent in February 1973), the dollar and SDR are no longer of equal value.

A nation with a balance of payment deficit can convert its SDRs, which constitute an unconditional international reserve asset, into a convertible currency upon application to the IMF. The IMF will designate another country (one with a balance of payment surplus, or extensive foreign currency reserves) to receive the SDRs in return for cash. Each country is obliged to accept SDRs in exchange for currency upon designation by the fund, up to three times the nation's allocation. Effective May 1, 1981, SDRs held in excess of allocation earn interest at the full market rate; previously, SDRs earned interest at the rate of 1.5 percent per year. Likewise, when holdings are run below the allocation, interest is payable at the rate of 1.5 percent per year. No nation is permitted to let its holdings slip below 30 percent of its allocation, averaged over a five-year period.

By 1974 dramatic fluctuations in the value of gold disrupted the relationship between the official value of the SDR (in terms of gold) and the market value of the metal. In response to this disturbance, the IMF approved a new "interim" value for the SDR; effective July 1, 1974, the SDR would be valued on the basis of a *basket of currencies*, weighted proportionally to the exports of goods and services of the issuing countries. By this arrangement, as some currencies appreciated in value, others would depreciate, with the value of the SDR remaining stable. By 1980 it had become evident that a basket of sixteen currencies was cumbersome, particularly since many of the currencies used were not significant in terms of international transactions. Effective January 1, 1981, the number of currencies composing the SDR balance was reduced to five prime trading currencies: the U.S. dollar, French franc,

SPECIAL CUSTOMS INVOICE
(Use separate invoice for purchased and non-purchased goods.)

Form Approved.
O.M.B. No. 48-RO342

1. SELLER	2. DOCUMENT NR. *	3. INVOICE NR. AND DATE*
STU Auto Parts Hamburg, West Germany	4. REFERENCES *	

5. CONSIGNEE	6. BUYER *(if other than consignee)*
XYZ Imports Company North Main Street Anywhere 11111	
	7. ORIGIN OF GOODS West Germany

8. NOTIFY PARTY *	9. TERMS OF SALE, PAYMENT, AND DISCOUNT
Same as Above	Letter of Credit

10. ADDITIONAL TRANSPORTATION INFORMATION*			
	11. CURRENCY USED U.S. Dollar	12. EXCH. RATE *(if fixed or agreed)*	13. DATE ORDER ACCEPTED xx/xx/xx

14. MARKS AND NUMBERS ON SHIPPING PACKAGES	15. NUMBER OF PACKAGES	16. FULL DESCRIPTION OF GOODS	17. QUANTITY	UNIT PRICE		20. INVOICE TOTALS
				18. HOME MARKET	19. INVOICE	
XYZ NEW YORK #1/8	8	Cartons Automobile Parts	8		62.50	$500.00

21. ☐	If the production of these goods involved furnishing goods or services to the seller *(e.g., assists such as dies, molds, tools, engineering work)* and the value is not included in the invoice price, check box (21) and explain below.	22. PACKING COSTS	included

27. DECLARATION OF SELLER/SHIPPER (OR AGENT)

	23. OCEAN OR INTERNATIONAL FREIGHT	collect

I declare:

(A) ☐ If there are any rebates, drawbacks or bounties allowed upon the exportation of goods, I have checked box (A) and itemized separately below.

(B) ☒ If the goods were not sold or agreed to be sold, I have checked box (B) and have indicated in column 19 the price I would be willing to receive.

24. DOMESTIC FREIGHT CHARGES	included

I further declare that there is no other invoice differing from this one (unless otherwise described below) and that all statements contained in this invoice and declaration are true and correct.

(C) SIGNATURE OF SELLER/SHIPPER (OR AGENT):

▶ XXXXX

25. INSURANCE COSTS	included
26. OTHER COSTS *(Specify Below)*	none

28. THIS SPACE FOR CONTINUING ANSWERS

THIS FORM OF INVOICE REQUIRED GENERALLY IF RATE OF DUTY BASED UPON OR REGULATED BY VALUE OF GOODS AND PURCHASE PRICE OR VALUE OF SHIPMENT EXCEEDS $500. OTHERWISE USE COMMERCIAL INVOICE.

*Not necessary for U.S. Customs purposes.

Customs Form 5515 (12-20-76)

Special Customs Invoice

Deutsche mark, British pound, and Japanese yen, each weighted relative to trading importance.

Inasmuch as the SDR is a basket of currencies in which appreciation in the value of a given component currency is apt to be offset by comparable depreciations in the value of other component currencies, the SDR offers the potential for serving as a more stable standard of value than any single currency. For this reason, international firms and banks have expressed interest in valuing transactions in SDRs so as to minimize overall exchange risks. Since SDRs are international reserve assets, they may be held only by the IMF, national monetary authorities, and a limited number of other holders, all of which are intergovernmental agencies; accordingly, SDRs per se are not available for commercial transactions. In order to secure the benefits of relative rate stability, various commercial entities have duplicated the SDR, creating a so-called Euro-SDR by pooling various national currencies of proportional values in the official SDR basket.

In fixing values in terms of SDRs (official or Euro-SDRs) it is important to understand that the mix of currencies and their respective ratios in the SDR are apt to change over time. The parties to an SDR-denominated transaction must define whether in the event of a change in the makeup of the SDR, the transaction is to be valued in terms of so-called "frozen" SDRs (keeping the SDR makeup at the time the transaction was adopted) or in terms of the new (or *flexible*) SDRs.

SPECIAL ECONOMIC ZONE. *See* EXPORT PROCESSING ZONE.

SPECIAL ENDORSEMENT. *See* ENDORSEMENT.

SPECIALIZATION AGREEMENT. Also known as a *rationalization agreement*, an arrangement among competing manufacturers of like products that each will sell only certain products, thereby providing each participant in the agreement a dominant position for a given product.

SPECIAL REPRESENTATIVE FOR TRADE NEGOTIATIONS. *See* UNITED STATES TRADE REPRESENTATIVE.

SPECIAL SUMMARY STEEL INVOICE. A special form of customs invoice required by the United States for importations of steel, or for an imported product made substantially of steel where the value of the goods exceeds $10,000 ($5,000 if from a contiguous country).

The Special Invoice Form 5520 is filed in duplicate at the time of the entry summary, and the following information is required in addition to the normal commercial information: date the price terms were established; base price for each steel category; American Iron and Steel Institute category of the product(s) imported; cost and description of "extras" (i.e., any fabrication or manipulation of the product, other than cutting to width or length); and name of the producer and importer and the price paid by the first unrelated purchaser in the United States.

The products requiring submission of the special summary steel invoice are:
1. Ingots, blooms, billets, slabs, etc.
2. Wire rods.
3. Structural shapes, plain 3 inches and over.
4. Sheet piling.
5. Plates.
6. Rail and track accessories.
7. Wheels and axles.
8. Concrete reinforcing bars.
9. Bar shapes under 3 inches.
10. Bars, hot rolled, carbon.
11. Bars, hot rolled, alloy.
12. Bars, cold finished.
13. Hollow drill steel.
14. Welded pipe and tubing.
15. Other pipe and tubing.
16. Round and shaped wire.
17. Flat wire.
18. Bale ties.
19. Galvanized wire fencing.
20. Wire nails.
21. Barbed wire.
22. Black plate.
23. Tin plate.
24. Terne plate.
25. Sheets, hot rolled.
26. Sheets, coated, alloy.
27. Sheets, coated including galvanized.
28. Strip, hot rolled.
29. Strip, cold rolled.
30. Strip, hot and cold alloy, rolled.
31. Sheets, other, electric, coated.

SPECIAL TONNAGE TAX. *See* LIGHT MONEY AND TONNAGE TAXES.

SPECIAL TRADE REPRESENTATIVE. *See* UNITED STATES TRADE REPRESENTIVE.

SPECIE. Gold or silver used for monetary purposes, in either coin or bullion form.

SPECIFIC DUTY. *See* DUTY.

SPECULATION. The act of purchasing interests in land, securities, commodities, foreign currencies, or futures contracts with the object of achieving profits through short-term changes in market prices.

The speculator does not use the land, commodities, or financial interests purchased in conjunction with the processing, production, or handling of any product or other business activity.

SPLIT DELIVERY. A load of cargo that a carrier must break down into smaller quantities and deliver to multiple consignees. It is common for a carrier to impose an additional charge for this service.

SPLIT PICKUP. A shipment, usually to a single destination, that must be picked up in more than one location. A carrier normally imposes an additional charge for this service.

SPORADIC DUMPING. *See* DUMPING.

SPOT. In foreign exchange and commodities markets, the current price for a given commodity or currency; the *spot* price is contrasted with the *futures* price, which is the price that is offered for delivery at some specified time in the future.

SPOT CHARTER. A vessel that is prepared to commence loading immediately upon fixing of the charter. As a practical matter, spot charters arise only in relation to vessels already in port but not otherwise occupied.

SPOT MARKET. A market for commodities or currency in which the sale results in an immediate or nearly immediate exchange of the goods or instruments for cash, as compared with a *futures market*, which trades in contracts for the future delivery of the product.

SPOT PRICE. The price of a commodity in the SPOT MARKET *(q.v.)*, i.e., the price quoted for immediate sale and delivery.

SPREAD. Generally, the difference between the buying and selling rates for a foreign currency. Also, the difference between the spot and forward rates.

SPREADER BAR. A device with attachments at each of four corners that affixes to an ocean carrier from above. The spreader bar is suspended from a crane and lifts containers from their chassis into the hold of a ship, and vice versa.

STABEX. *See* LOMÉ CONVENTION.

STAGNATION. A lack of growth in a national economy, usually measured in terms of per capita real gross national product.

STALE DOCUMENT. A document presented after the time customarily allowed for such presentations. For example, the Uniform Customs and Practices for Documentary Credits provides that bills of lading dated more than twenty-one days prior to presentation will be unacceptable under letter of credit transactions, unless the letter of credit specifically authorizes a later presentation.

STANDARD BULLION. Gold or silver in bars of the same composition as gold or silver coins. Since gold and silver coins consist of 90 precent precious metal and 10 percent base metal (usually copper), standard bullion would consist of a like mixture of precious and base metals. In effect, the bullion is suitable for immediate coinage.

STANDARD INTERNATIONAL TRADE CLASSIFICATION. A system for capture of international trade statistics developed under the auspices of the United Nations. The original SITC was adopted by the Economic and Social Council of the United Nations in July 1950. By 1960 many nations were compiling data on a commodity basis; coincidental with the rise of the SITC, the Brussels Tariff Nomenclature (BTN) was adopted by many countries. The BTN classifies goods according to the material of which they are made. Coordination of the SITC and BTN proved difficult, resulting in efforts to reconcile both systems. The first revision (SITC, revised) was published in 1960; a second revision (SITC, revision 2) was published in 1975. Each member of the UN is requested to report trade statistics categorized according to SITC, revision 2.

The system divides commodities into groups and subgroups, each of which is correlated with a heading or subheading of the BTN, as well as the related heading of the 1960 (revised) SITC. In addition, items are classified according to a *broad economic category (see* figure, next page).

The SITC, revision 2, is published by the Statistical Office of the United Nations.

STANDARDIZED PRODUCT. A product marketed worldwide without substantial variation in the product's composition or appearance. Product standardization helps in achieving significant economies of scale. *See* DIFFERENTIATED PRODUCT.

STANDARD MONEY. Units of exchange created by lawful authority, i.e., legal tender.

STANDARD PRICE. The TARGET PRICE *(q.v.)* for tobacco under the Common Agricultural Policy of the European Economic Community.

STANDARDS AGREEMENT. Offically, the *Agreement on Technical Barriers of Trade*, an understanding among trading nations arising from the Tokyo Round of trade negotiations, signed at Geneva in April 1979, with the object of eliminating so-called technical barriers to trade. U. S. participation in the agreement is authorized by Title IV of the Trade Agreements Act of 1979. Specifically, the agreement provides that technical standards may not be used to impede trade unless the standards are required to advance a "legitimate domestic objective," such as health, safety, security, or environmental protection. The agreement envisions the establishment of an international organization to collect standards data and assist in resolving disputes. The U.S. act provides that the president may withdraw the benefits of U.S. trade concessions from any na-

Group	Subgroup	Item		Corresponding BTN heading or subheading	Related heading of SITC, Revised	BEC Category
056			Vegetables, roots and tubers, prepared or preserved, n.e.s.			
	056.1		Vegetables, dried, dehydrated or evaporated (excluding leguminous vegetables), whole, cut, sliced, broken or in powder, but not further prepared	07.04	055.1	122
	056.4		Flours, meals and flakes of potatoes, fruits and vegetables, n.e.s. (including sago and tapioca)		055.4	
		056.43	Flour, meal and flakes of potato	11.05	055.43	121
		056.45	Tapioca and sago; tapioca and sago substitutes obtained from potato or other starches	19.04	055.45	121
		056.49	Flours of the leguminous vegetables falling within heading 054.2 or of the fruits falling within any heading of group 057; flour and meal of sago and of roots and tubers falling within heading 054.81			121
		056.49[a]	Flours of the leguminous vegetables falling within heading 054.2	[11.03]⎫	055.41	
		056.49[b]	Flours of the fruits falling within group 057	[11.04]⎬ 6/	055.42	
		056.49[c]	Flour and meal of sago and of manioc, arrowroot, salep and other roots and tubers falling within heading 054.81	[11.06]⎭	055.44	
	056.5		Vegetables, prepared or preserved, n.e.s.			
		056.51	Vegetables and fruit, prepared or preserved by vinegar or acetic acid, with or without sugar, whether or not containing salt, spices or mustard	20.01	055.51	122
		056.59	Vegetables prepared or preserved otherwise than by vinegar or acetic acid, n.e.s.	20.02	(7/)	122

Standard International Trade Classification, Revision 2. Courtesy of United Nations Statistical Office.

tion using technical barriers to unlawfully impede U.S. trade.

STANDBY LETTER OF CREDIT. A guarantee issued by a bank to a firm as security for the actions of a third party; in the event the third party does not perform specified acts (usually the payment of obligations) within a prescribed period, the beneficiary of the credit may unilaterally draw upon the letter of credit in satisfaction.

STANDSTILL AGREEMENTS. An arrangement between the United States and the European Economic Community emerging at the end of the Dillon Round in 1961 concerning certain agricultural commodities. In essence, status quo was maintained on U.S. exports of wheat, corn, rice, poultry, and sorghum grain pending further negotiations with the EEC.

Failing to secure adequate access for American poultry, the United States suspended tariff concessions covering a variety of European products equal to the value of U.S. poultry trade lost.

See CHICKEN WAR.

STATE CAPITALISM. The ownership and operation of business enterprises by agencies of government. Unlike Marxism, which espouses state ownership of the means of production, state capitalism is not necessarily motivated by ideological consideration; a particular economic enterprise may be run by the state because it is unattractive to private enterprise but viewed as necessary. In many cases an enterprise may be operated as a means of generating state revenue.

In developing countries, state capitalism often reflects ownership of basic industries because private capital is inadequate to fund infant industries or does not perceive a sufficiently attractive return.

STATE-CONTROLLED TRADING COMPANY. An instrumentality of a foreign government charged with the exclusive importation or exportation of a specific group of products. Such entities are most common in communist or centrally planned economies.

STATE PLANNING COMMITTEE. Also known as GOSPLAN, as important agency of the Soviet government responsible for planning economic output. In response to objectives established by the Politburo, the SPC assesses the economic resources of the nation and establishes targets for the quantitative output of specified commodities. The output goals are articulated to the various state production enterprises, which are obliged to prepare a plan for meeting their output quota. These plans are supplied to GOSPLAN to coordinate the various elements of the production process and to ensure compliance with the stated objectives.

STATUTORY RATE OF DUTY. The rate of duty on the given product specified by the SMOOT-HAWLEY ACT *(q.v.)* of 1930. The rates established by this act are applied to Column 2 countries, i.e., those that do not enjoy most favored nation status. Lower rates of duty, as reflected in Column 1 of the Tariff Schedules, have been negotiated under the authority of various acts in response to duty reductions on American products.

STEAMSHIP. A vessel propelled by steam-driven turbines; steam is generated under pressure in boilers and is directed to a rotor shaft, causing the propeller to spin. Most steamships in current use burn fuel oil to fire the boilers. Steam generation was the favored propulsion method, owing to its reliability of performance and low maintenance, until spiraling energy costs mandated more fuel-efficient plants. *See* MOTOR SHIP.

STEAMSHIP CONFERENCE. *See* CONFERENCE.

STEMDATE. *See* SUBJECT TO STEM.

STEP-DOWN RATE. A financing agreement in which a lower rate of interest is charged later in the life of the loan than at the beginning.

STEP-UP RATE. A financing arrangement in which a higher rate of interest is charged later in the life of the loan than at the beginning.

STERLING AREA. Following the Imperial Conference at London in 1931, at which the Commonwealth was established, most Commonwealth countries (excluding Canada) agreed informally to maintain a significant portion of their official reserves in sterling and to peg their currencies in relation to the pound. At different times, certain non-Commonwealth countries (including Sweden, Thailand, and Japan) participated in this arrangement.

Exchange controls implemented by Britain during World War II formalized the agreement, resulting in *scheduled territories* (i.e., participating areas) that agreed to maintain reserves in London and to impose exchange controls compatible with those of Britain.

Following the war, with the creation of the International Monetary Fund, various governments left the scheduled territories scheme.

STERLING BALANCES. The official reserves of a national monetary authority held in pounds sterling, both in STERLING AREA *(q.v.)* countries and in others.

STERLING BILL. A BILL OF EXCHANGE *(q.v.)* denominated in pounds sterling.

STERLING BLOC. *Synonymous with* STERLING AREA *(q.v.)*.

STERLING CREDIT. A LETTER OF CREDIT *(q.v.)* against which bills of exchange are to be drawn in pounds sterling.

STEVEDORE. One who engages in the loading and unloading of vessels. The term is usually applied to the firm contracted by the shipowner to perform the loading and unloading function, rather than the individuals who perform the physical work. *See* LONGSHOREMAN.

STOCKHOLM CONVENTION. *See* EUROPEAN FREE TRADE ASSOCIATION.

STOP CHARGE. A special charge imposed by a carrier for stopping en route prior to final destination to deliver a portion of the shipment.

STOP LOSS TREATY. A contract of reinsurance under which the primary policy issuer accepts all losses up to a prearranged loss ratio (derived by applying the losses against premium income for the year), after which the reinsurer is liable up to a specified limit.

STOP-OUT. An order to a bank to buy or sell a given quantity of a foreign currency when a specified exchange rate has been reached in market transactions.

STORAGE WAREHOUSE. *See* BONDED WAREHOUSE.

STOWAGE. The act of placing cargo within the hold of a vessel for transit. The term has been extended to include the loading of cargo within containers.

STOW TON. *See* MEASUREMENT TON.

STRADDLE CARRIER. A self-propelled vehicle which lifts a container within its own framework. The device is commonly used at port facilities and container yards.

STRAIGHT CONSIGNMENT. Goods conveyed under a *straight*, i.e., nonnegotiable, BILL OF LADING *(q.v.)*.

STRATEGIC PETROLEUM RESERVE. A program established under authority of the Energy Policy and Conservation Act of 1975 that directs the U.S. Department of Energy to build a buffer stock of petroleum to insulate the United States against an interruption of foreign supplies.

The act mandates a reserve of 750 million barrels by the end of 1990. On November 1, 1984, over 434 million barrels were in storage facilities in Texas and Louisiana, which would replace more than ninety days' imports. The reserve is being expanded by 159,000 barrels per day. During fiscal 1985, the Strategic Petroleum Reserve has been authorized to spend $2.05 billion for acquisition and transportation; the cost to complete the program will be approximately $27 billion.

STRATEGIC STOCKPILE. The store of critical metals and other industrial commodities maintained by the U.S. government as a buffer against disruptions of supply in times of war or national emergency. The maintenance of such stockpiles is authorized by the Strategic and Critical Materials Stockpiling Act of 1946.

STRATEGY OF PLANNED CHANGE. A marketing strategy that seeks to overcome cultural impediments to a foreign product by modifying those aspects of the culture that offer resistance. *See* STRATEGY OF UNPLANNED CHANGE.

STRATEGY OF UNPLANNED CHANGE. A plan for the penetration of a foreign market that, while recognizing that there may be an initial cultural resistance to the product, contemplates sufficient cultural shifts already underway so as to permit a growing awareness of the product's value. *See* STRATEGY OF PLANNED CHANGE.

STRESS OF WEATHER. Also known as *heavy weather*, the extraordinary force of wind, waves, or sea conditions exerted upon a vessel and its cargo. Stress of weather is a "peril of the seas" and is routinely covered in marine cargo policies.

STRIPPING. The act of unloading an intermodal ocean container.

STRUCTURAL ADJUSTMENT LENDING. A World Bank program designed to assist developing nations with balance of payments problems resulting from correctable internal economic patterns. The program provides hard currency loans conditional upon agreement by the beneficiary country to undertake certain specified corrective measures, which may include improvements in budgeting and management of public debt; enhancement of free enterprise institutions; shift in public investment priorities from traditional to more profitable ventures; elimination of protective tariffs that have sheltered inefficient domestic industries; and tax incentives to stimulate increased production and energy efficiency.

Structural adjustment loans are normally paired with five- to ten-year programs, so as to minimize economic shock in the recipient countries.

For fiscal 1984, it was contemplated that structural adjustment lending may consume up to 10 percent of all bank lending.

STUFFING. The act of loading a container.

SUBJECT OPEN. Provision in a vessel charter offer that permits the shipowner to commit the vessel to another enterprise prior to receipt of full details of the offer. The term is *synonymous with subject ship being free.*

SUBJECT SHIP BEING FREE. *See* SUBJECT OPEN.

SUBJECT TO COTTON CONSTRAINTS. *See* FIBER CONSTRAINTS.

SUBJECT TO LICENSE BEING GRANTED. A provision in a vessel offer or charter party that makes the charter conditional upon governmental approval.

SUBJECT TO MAN-MADE FIBER CONSTRAINTS. *See* FIBER CONSTRAINTS.

SUBJECT TO STEM. A condition in charter parties covering shipments of coal, stipulating that the cargo must be delivered within the laydays provided. The *stemdate* is the date upon which such loading actually commences.

SUBJECT TO WOOL CONSTRAINTS. *See* FIBER CONSTRAINTS.

SUBPART F. A provision of the Internal Revenue Code (Sections 951–64) that imposes U.S. income taxes on the undistributed earnings of "controlled foreign corporations." Subpart F was incorporated into the Code by the Revenue Act of 1962; prior to that time, earnings by foreign subsidiaries of U.S. firms were not subject to U.S. income taxes until actually distributed to the parent. For purposes of tax treatment, a "controlled foreign corporation" is defined as a company in which "U.S. shareholders" own or control 51 percent of the voting stock of all classes. A "U.S. shareholder" is a "U.S. person" (within the meaning of Section 957(d) of the Code) who owns or controls 10 percent or more of the voting stock, of all classes, of the company.

The income of a controlled foreign corporation is taxable under Subpart F on:

1. Foreign base company income, which consists of: a. Foreign personal holding company income, Section 954(c)

b. Foreign base company sales income, Section 954(d)

c. Foreign base company service income, Section 954(e)

d. Foreign base company shipping income, Section 954(f).

2. Income on the insurance of U.S. risks.

3. The sum of illegal bribes, kickbacks, or similar payments (within the meaning of Section 162(c) Internal Revenue Code) to any foreign official.

4. Certain income as specified in Section 952(a)(3) multiplied by the INTERNATIONAL BOYCOTT FACTOR *(q.v.)*.

SUBSIDIES CODE. A multilateral agreement arising out of the Tokyo Round of trade negotiations sponsored by the GENERAL AGREEMENT ON TARIFFS AND TRADE *(q.v.)*, or GATT. The code, also known as the *Agreement on Subsidies and Countervailing Measures*, seeks to reduce the distortive effects of export subsidies on world trade.

Under the Subsidies Code bounties are given to stimulate exports, and subsidies are given, without regard to export activity, to advance purely domestic objectives; export subsidies on nonprimary products and primary mineral products are prohibited. Purely domestic subsidies are permitted, so long as they do not adversely affect the industries of other countries. Limited exemptions are permitted for developing countries.

The code established an enforcement mechanism whereby an aggrieved nation may impose countervailing measures to protect its injured industries; this vehicle may be employed after a finding by GATT that domestic industries are being materially injured by subsidized exports. The code also authorizes the use of GATT facilities for mediation of disputes by a committee of signatories, which may impose multilateral retaliation against a subsidizing nation to enforce compliance.

The code was adopted by the United States under the Trade Agreements Act of 1979.

See Appendix D8.

SUBSIDIZED TRADE ROUTES. *See* OPERATING DIFFERENTIAL SUBSIDY.

SUBSIDY. A payment or other emolument provided by a governmental authority for the purpose of advancing an economic objective defined as being in the public interest. Usually the object is to make available certain goods or services that, in the absence of a subsidy to the supplier, might be so costly as to preclude or seriously circumscribe its use or manufacture.

"SUBSTANTIAL OR ESSENTIAL PART" DOCTRINE. A principle in customs usage that an imported product that lacks a significant part or component essential to its basic function cannot be classified for tariff purposes in the same category as the finished product.

SUBSTITUTED EXPENSES. A principle employed in GENERAL AVERAGE *(q.v.)* adjusting that permits recovery for an expense arising in place of another expense that would be otherwise recoverable in general average. The expense is defined in Rule F on the York-Antwerp Rules as:

Any extra expense incurred in place of another expense which would have been allowable as general average and so allowed without regard to saving, if any, to other interests, but only up to the amount of the general average expense avoided.

SUBSTITUTE GOODS. Products related in such a way that an increased demand for one will be reflected by a decreased demand for the other.

SUBSTITUTION EFFECT. The impact on demand for a given commodity or service caused by a change in the price of that product or service relative to available substitutes. For example, improvements in technology may make a machine tool a cheaper source of output than the manual labor used previously.

SUE AND LABOR. A common provision in ocean marine cargo insurance policies that the owner of the merchandise will "sue, labor, and travel for the benefit of the goods." In essence, the owner of the goods is compelled to take all reasonable steps within his power to prevent or mitigate losses; he may be reimbursed by the underwriter for costs attendant upon loss mitigation efforts, once a loss has occurred.

SUFFERANCE WHARF. A pier where goods may be stored temporarily, exempt from taxes or duties, while awaiting transport to another destination or clearance through customs.

SUMMARY SALE. A simplified procedure for disposing of merchandise seized or forfeited for violation of the customs laws. Currently, the U.S. Customs Service may sell, without judicial proceedings, seized merchandise valued up to ten thousand dollars.

SUMPTUARY TAX. A tax imposed upon certain goods to discourage consumption.

SUPERDEDUCTIVE. A procedure authorized by U.S. Customs in ascertaining the deductive value of merchandise for assessment of ad valorem duties; deductive valuation is an alternative valuation method specified in the CUSTOMS VALUATION AGREEMENT *(q.v.)*.

Also known as the *further processing method,* the superdeductive method permits a deduction from the value of the goods for duty purposes of further processing undertaken in the United States prior to sale to the ultimate purchaser. In applying the deduction, customs will take into account normal processing costs, reasonable waste, and industry practice. The superdeductive can be applied to goods not sold within 90 days from importation but within 180 days of importation. Normally the superdeductive will not apply if the further processing destroys the identity of the goods as imported.

SUPER GOLD TRANCHE. A condition in which drawings by a member of the INTERNATIONAL MONETARY FUND *(q.v.)* cause fund holdings of the member's currency to fall below 75 percent of the member's quota.

SUPERIMPOSED CLAUSE. A notation on the face of a BILL OF LADING *(q.v.)* that indicates a defect in the cargo or its mode of transport. Such notations include "received in damaged condition" and "on deck stowage." A bill of lading bearing such clauses is said to be *foul* or *unclean* and will be unacceptable for presentation under a LETTER OF CREDIT *(q.v.)* unless that instrument specifically authorizes bills of lading bearing such clauses.

SUPERINTENDENCE COMPANY. *See* GENERAL SUPERINTENDENCE.

SUPPLEMENTARY LEVY. An additional tax that may be imposed upon imports of pork, poultry, or eggs into the European Economic Community when the purchase price of such items falls below the GATE PRICE *(q.v.)* provided in the EEC Common Agricultural Policy.

SUPPRESSED INFLATION. A condition in which inflationary pressures are impeded because of specific governmental controls in the form of price controls and/or rationing. Such steps prevent prices from escalating.

SURETY. A guarantor who undertakes, in the event a principal is unable or unwilling to perform certain acts, to pay specified amounts.

SURPLUS TREATY. A contract of reinsurance under which the reinsurer agrees to accept risks within a stipulated scale of limits, with degrees of participation varying according to a prearranged plan.

SURVEY. An examination of a vessel or cargo by an independent third party for the purpose of establishing condition. For example, a survey may be performed on damaged cargo to ascertain the circumstances surrounding the loss and potential salvage.

SUSTAINABLE GROWTH. A rate of national economic growth, as measured in per capita real growth, national product, or per capita real income, that can be expected to continue over many years.

SWAP. By agreement, the combined purchase and sale of a specified amount of foreign exchange, with different dates for sale and purchase. This arrangement permits each party to the transaction to use, for a given period of time, a currency he needs in return for one he does not need, without any exchange risk.

SWAP ARRANGEMENT. An agreement between central banks to lend each other prearranged sums of each other's currency. This arrangement is designed to permit a central bank to intervene in the foreign exchange market so as to retard speculative pressures on its currency. Such agreements are generally bilateral and usually provide for the borrowing central bank to repay loans within three months.

SWAP MARGIN. *See* FORWARD MARGIN.

SWAPPING. A form of COUNTERTRADE *(q.v.)* by which the parties trade off goods that each controls at various locations so as to eliminate or mitigate transportation costs.

SWAP RATE. *See* FORWARD MARGIN.

SWIFT. *See* SOCIETY FOR WORLDWIDE INTERBANK FINANCIAL TELECOMMUNICATIONS.

SWITCHING. Also known as *switch trading*, a COUNTERTRADE *(q.v.)* arrangement under which a purchaser in one country assigns to a seller in another country an obligation due from a third party in satisfaction of the purchase price of the goods.

SWITCH TRADING. *See* SWITCHING.

SYNDICATED LOAN. A large-scale loan (often in excess of one billion dollars) for a single project or borrower provided from the collective resources of several banks.

T

TACIT ACCEPTANCE. A mechanism employed by the INTERNATIONAL MARITIME ORGANIZATION *(q.v.)* to facilitate adoption of technical agreements among member states. Generally, international conventions come into force upon the express acceptance of a specified number of states. The IMO found this procedure cumbersome in light of rapid changes in marine technology. In some cases, important amendments could not be brought into force for want of formal acceptance by the required number of member states.

In response to the problem, the IMO adopted the posture that express acceptance would no longer be required for technical agreements. Since 1972, technical agreements come into force on a specified date, unless a prescribed number of member states expressly object.

TACKLE CLAUSE. *See* OVERSIDE DELIVERY CLAUSE.

TALE QUALE. Literally, "as it arrives"; used in contract for shipment of grain in bulk to signify that the consignor will accept the goods in whatever condition they arrive, so long as they were in good order at time of shipment, as evidenced by a certificate of quality issued by an impartial inspection agency. This condition arises most commonly when the grain is shipped in dry-cargo type vessels, rather than tankers. *See also* RYE TERMS.

T & E. *See* TRANSPORTATION AND EXPORTATION ENTRY.

TARE. The weight of packaging in which a product is encased.

TARGET PRICE. An important concept within the COMMON AGRICULTURAL POLICY *(q.v.)* of the European Economic Community. It represents an optimum wholesale price within the community for a given commodity. In devising this optimum price, the EEC must regard the income requirements of farmers, consumer needs, and world market prices.

When a commodity price falls below the target price the EEC intervenes to purchase surpluses to return the market price to the target.

Shortages of a given commodity may sometimes occur in some parts of the community while supplies are adequate elsewhere. Under such circumstances, the target price in the area of shortage will be reduced by the cost of transport from areas of plenty, to encourage adequate distribution of supplies.

TARIFF (CUSTOMS). A document issued by a nation's customs authority principally for the purpose of specifying rates of duty to be applied on various imported products. A tariff customarily also includes quantitative restrictions (quotas) upon certain imports, preferential duties on products imported from specified nations, and administrative rules concerning valuation and entry procedures.

A *protective tariff* is designed to discourage foreign imports; a *revenue tariff* is designed to raise money for the government. Most tariffs contain both protective and revenue elements.

Tariffs that apply the same rates of duty uniformly to imports of all countries are said to be *general* tariffs. Most nations, however, permit lower rates to some nations with which favorable trade agreements have been negotiated. Rates of duty on products of nations enjoying MOST FAVORED NATION *(q.v.)* status, for example, will be shown in a column apart from the higher general rates. In addition, special low rates of duty may be permitted on certain products of less developed nations. The rates on such products would be shown in yet another column within the tariff. Such tariffs are known as *multiple-column tariffs* inasmuch as several rates of duty might apply to a given product, depending upon the country of origin and other factors. Tariffs in which lower rates of duty accrue to products of some countries but not others are said to be *preferential tariffs.*

Duties within a tariff may be *statutory* (prescribed by law) or *conventional* (derived by negotiations with trading partners). The TARIFF SCHEDULES OF THE UNITED STATES *(q.v.),* for example, contain both. The rates shown in Column 1 are statutory rates, enacted in the TARIFF ACT OF 1930 *(q.v.).* The rates in Column 2 reflect concessions granted to some nations in return for reciprocal concessions (*see* figure, next page).

TARIFF SCHEDULES OF THE UNITED STATES ANNOTATED (1984)

SCHEDULE 3. - TEXTILE FIBERS AND TEXTILE PRODUCTS
Part 4. - Fabrics of Special Construction or For Special Purposes
Articles of Wadding or Felt; Fish Nets; Machine Clothing

Page 3-71

3 - 4 - C
355.45 - 356.45

G S P	Item	Stat. Suf- fix	Articles	Units of Quantity	Rates of Duty 1	LDDC	2
			Fish netting and fishing nets (including sections thereof), of textile materials (con.):				
	355.45		Other...	....	15¢ per lb. + 26.7% ad val.		82% ad val.
			Of man-made fibers:				
		20	Salmon gill netting, of nylon 1/....(669)	Lb.			
		30	Other..............................(669)	Lb.			
		90	Other..	Lb.			
			Woven or knit fabrics, in the piece or in units, coated, filled, or otherwise prepared for use as artists' canvas:				
	355.50	00	Of cotton...................................(320)	Sq. yd.v Lb.	6.2% ad val.		35% ad val.
A	355.55	00	Of vegetable fibers, except cotton.................	Sq. yd..	4.7% ad val.	3.9% ad val.	45% ad val.
	355.60	00	Of man-made fibers..........................(627)	Sq. yd.v Lb.	7¢ per lb. + 11.8% ad val.		70% ad val.
			Woven or knit fabrics (except pile or tufted fabrics), of textile materials, coated or filled with rubber or plastics material, or laminated with sheet rubber or plastics:				
	355.65		Of vegetable fibers................................	....	6.9% ad val.	5.3% ad val.	40% ad val.
		10	Of cotton....................................	Sq. yd.			
		30	Of vegetable fibers, except cotton...........	Sq. yd.			
	355.70	00	Of wool...	Sq. yd.v Lb.	26¢ per lb. + 26.6% ad val.	14% ad val.	54% ad val.
	355.75	00	Of silk...	Sq. yd..	10.2% ad val.	6.9% ad val.	65% ad val.
			Of man-made fibers:				
A*	355.81	00	Over 70 percent by weight of rubber or plastics...	Sq. yd..	5.1% ad val.	4.2% ad val.	25% ad val.
	355.82		Other.......................................	....	6¢ per lb. + 11.8% ad val.		84.5% ad val.
		10	Of strips...........................(627)	Sq. yd.v Lb.			
		20	Other..............................(627)	Sq. yd.v Lb.			
	355.85	00	Other...	Sq. yd..	6.9% ad val.	5.3% ad val.	40% ad val.
			Woven or knit fabrics (except pile or tufted fabrics), of textile materials, coated or filled, not specially provided for:				
			Oilcloths:				
	356.05	00	Of silk....................................	Sq. yd..	9.5% ad val.	5.4% ad val.	65% ad val.
	356.10	00	Other......................................	Sq. yd..	4.4% ad val.	3.7% ad val.	30% ad val.
	356.15	00	Tracing cloth..............................	Sq. yd..	9.6% ad val.	6.6% ad val.	30% ad val.
	356.20	00	Window hollands of cotton..........................	Sq. yd..	5.9% ad val.	4.7% ad val.	30% ad val.
			Other:				
A*	356.25		Of vegetable fibers...........................	....	5.9% ad val.	4.7% ad val.	35% ad val.
		10	Of cotton..................................	Sq. yd.			
		30	Of vegetable fibers, except cotton.......	Sq. yd.			
	356.30	00	Of wool......................................	Sq. yd.v Lb.	21¢ per lb. + 25.1% ad val.	16% ad val.	65% ad val.
	356.35	00	Of silk......................................	Sq. yd..	10.2% ad val.	6.9% ad val.	65% ad val.
A	356.40	00	Of man-made fibers...........................	Sq. yd.v Lb.	6¢ per lb. + 11.5% ad val.	8% ad val.	74.5% ad val.
	356.45	00	Other..	Sq. yd..	6.9% ad val.	5.3% ad val.	40% ad val.

1/ See part 4 statistical headnote 1.

Note: For explanation of the symbol "A" or "A*" in the column entitled "GSP", see general headnote 3(c).

TARIFF (FREIGHT). A document issued, usually in booklet form, by a COMMON CARRIER *(q.v.)* listing its charges for transportation services. Commonly, the *rate*, or cost of transportation, varies by commodity or product; some tariffs contain thousands of specific products. Charges are imposed by standard units of measure (e.g., ton, cubic meter, board foot). Tariffs also contain a description of the geographic areas served by a carrier, rules of carriage, and limitations upon carrier liability. Tariffs are published by the carrier or an organization such as a CONFERENCE *(q.v.)* or rate bureau representing a group of carriers. The law may require that they be filed with or approved by regulatory agencies having economic supervision over the particular mode of transport (*see* figure, next page).

TARIFF ACT OF 1930. Also known as the Smoot-Hawley Act, this established the highest rates of duty ever imposed by the United States. Its passage was essentially a response to domestic unemployment during the Depression and protectionist forces in the agricultural and certain manufacturing sectors. Other nations accompanied the United States in adopting protective tariff measures, resulting in a significant overall decline in the level of world trade. In order to revitalize trade, Congress authorized the president, under the Reciprocal Trade Agreements Act of 1934, to grant tariff reductions to trading partners in return for like concessions on American goods. The result of this arrangement, over time, was two tariff schedules: one representing the *statutory* rate embodied in the Smoot-Hawley Act, and the other reflecting the lower, *most favored nation* rates negotiated under the Reciprocal Trade Agreements Act and subsequent legislation.

The rates of duty imposed by the Smoot-Hawley Act remain in effect, as reflected in Column 2 of the Tariff Schedules of the United States, and are applied on imports from nations to which *most favored nation* status has not been granted.

The Tariff Act of 1930, although amended many times, remains the cornerstone of U. S. import control legislation.

TARIFF COMMISSION. *See* UNITED STATES INTERNATIONAL TRADE COMMISSION.

TARIFF PREFERENCES. Essentially *synonymous* with TRADE PREFERENCES *(q.v.)*.

TARIFF RATE. A rate for insurance coverage specifically prescribed by local regulation. Usually the rate is higher than might be derived through negotiations with a NONADMITTED *(q.v.)* carrier.

TARIFF SCHEDULES OF THE UNITED STATES. Commonly known by the acronym TSUSA, the Tariff Schedules constitute the enumeration of all products entering the United States, giving the rates of duty and statistical classification of each article, plus rules for the classification of

merchandise and other administrative provisions applicable to the entry of goods.

The current Tariff Schedules, which are published annually, are the product of a study begun in 1954 by the Tariff Commission (now known as the U.S. International Trade Commission) in response to a mandate contained in the Tariff Simplification Act of 1954 (PL 83-768). The commission submitted its study of the opportunities to simplify entry of goods through customs in 1960; the report, entitled *The Tariff Classification Study*, resulted in enactment of the Tariff Act of 1962. Under authority of this act, the president proclaimed the Tariff Schedules effective on articles entered or withdrawn from warehouse for consumption on or after August 31, 1963 (Proclamation 3548, August 21, 1963/ F.R. 9279).

The Tariff Schedules are divided into eight schedules plus an appendix. The first seven schedules address particular groups of products:

Schedule 1. Animal and vegetable products.
Schedule 2. Wood, paper, and printed matter.
Schedule 3. Textile fibers and textile products.
Schedule 4. Chemicals and related products.
Schedule 5. Nonmetallic minerals and products.
Schedule 6. Metals and metal products.
Schedule 7. Specified products: miscellaneous products and those not accounted for elsewhere.

Schedule 8 deals with special classification provisions of a permanent nature, including treatment of articles exported and returned, articles released under bond, personal exemptions, and exemptions applicable to government agencies and institutions.

The appendix, sometimes called *Schedule 9*, embraces temporary legislative, executive, and administrative actions and controls, temporary duty modifications, agricultural import restrictions, and quotas.

Effective January 1983 the number of classes of articles in the Tariff Schedules was expanded from 5,348 to 7,320; at the same time the number of statistical categories was expanded to about 13,700 from 7,350. These changes were taken to reflect adjustments in rates of duties, the need for more precise statistical data, and other administrative factors.

Each class of article within the tariff is assigned a five-digit number. For example, 703.65 represents "headwear, of leather." The first digit identifies the schedule within which the article is classified; the next two digits reflect the type of product; the remaining two digists establish the specific article. Within a given five-digit classification, several variations of the article may be described. For example, "headwear, of leather" might be further refined to "... of leather, with fabric lining" or "... of leather— suede," depending upon the degree of refinement required in capturing data on imports of this particular type of product. All articles within the five-digit classification are subject to the same rate of duty.

From: Ports in Japan and Korea (See Rule 1)	To: United States Atlantic Coast and Gulf Ports (See Rule 1)	Effective Date
		December 15, 1982
		Correction No. 5118

Except as otherwise provided herein, rates are stated in US Dollars and apply per ton of 1,000 kgs. (W) or 1 cubic meter (M), whichever produces the greater revenue. Commodity Description and Packing	Type	Rate Basis	Base Rate		Item No.
			Japan	Korea	
MACHINERY AND TRANSPORT EQUIPMENT DIVISION (Cont'd)					
Machinery and Parts: (Cont'd)					
Photocopying Machines, Attachments, and Parts Photocopying Machine Supplies (Non-dangerous and Non-hazardous), viz: Bag/Filter Sets Master Papers Cleaning Brushes Silicon Oil, Packed Developers Toners includes: Collators for Photocopying Machines Microfilmers, Microfilm Processors, Microfilm Readers, and Microfilm Reader-printers, and Accessories, Attachments, and Parts thereof Microfilm Reader-printer Supplies (Non-dangerous and Non-hazardous), as named above excludes: Collators, N.O.S. - See Item 4840 Ⓘ - Lenses for Photocopying Machines - See Item 5720 Photographic Systems, as named - See Item 5710 Special Rate	C		71	71	5010-00
	C		60	60	5010-01
Note: The application of this rate on such accessories (for Microfilmers, Microfilm Processors, Microfilm Readers, and Microfilm Reader-printers only), attachments, parts, and supplies is conditioned upon their being identified on commercial invoices as being shipped with or used with Photocopying Machines, Microfilmers, Microfilm Processors, Microfilm Readers, or Microfilm Reader-printers.					
Photofinishing Equipment for Commercial Applications Special Rate	C		95	95	5013-00
X-ray Film Processors Special Rate	C		116	116	5013-50
Polymerizers (Steel Tanks) Special Rate	C		106	106	5018-00
Note: Subject to all rules, but heavy-lift charges per rule 4 will be reduced by 50%.					
Portable Generators Special Rate	C		96	96	5025-00
Powered Tools (Including Electrical Hand Tools) and Non-electrical Parts thereof	C		91	91	5060-00
includes: Drill Bits for Powered Tools Rotary Brushes for Powered Tools					
Special Rate	C		90	90	5060-01

Tariff (Freight). Courtesy of Japan/Korea-Atlantic and Gulf Freight Conference.

The general headnotes and rules of interpretation at the beginning of the TSUSA include definitions of terms and abbreviations rules for the use of the tariff, and the orders of priority applicable to the classification of merchandise. The instructions contained in this section apply within the TSUSA generally, unless expressly provided otherwise. Headnotes and rules applicable to a given schedule only appear at the outset of that schedule.

Within the schedules, a product must be defined and matched to the appropriate classification number so that the rate of duty for the product, depending upon the country of origin, can be determined. The rates are set forth in three columns:

Column 1

The rate accorded to imports from countries enjoying MOST FAVORED NATION (*q.v.*) status. As a practical matter, this includes all of the noncommunist industrial world.

LDDC

The rate applicable to imports from the least developed and developing countries, which are defined as:

Bangladesh	Malawi
Benin	Maldives
Bhutan	Mali
Botswana	Nepal
Burundi	Niger
Cape Verde	Rwanda
Central African Republic	Somalia
Chad	Sudan
Comoros	Tanzania
Gambia	Uganda
Guinea	Upper Volta
Haiti	Western Samoa
Lesotho	Yemen (Sana)

Where no rate of duty is provided in the LDDC column, the rate provided in Column 1 applies.

Since the foregoing countries are all listed as beneficiary states under the GENERALIZED SYSTEM OF PREFERENCES (*q.v.*), or GSP, the rates of duty listed in the LDDC column have relevance only where the product is not eligible for duty-free entry under GSP.

Column 2

The rate imposed on imports from certain communist countries:

Albania
Bulgaria
Cuba
Czechoslovakia
Estonia
German Democratic Republic and East Berlin or control)
Korea (any part that may be under communist domination or control)
Kurile Islands
Latvia
Lithuania
Outer Mongolia (Mongolian People's Republic)
Polish People's Republic

Southern Sakhalin
Tanna Tuva
USSR and the area in East Prussia under the provisional administration of the USSR

In those rare cases where a nation is not specifically assigned to one of the three columns, the products of that nation enter under the rates provided in Column 1.

More than half the products enumerated in the TSUSA are accorded duty-free entry under the GSP if they originate in any beneficiary country, which includes all the countries eligible for LDDC rates plus many other countries and territories. *A full listing of the countries eligible for duty relief under the GSP can be found in this text under* GENERALIZED SYSTEM OF PREFERENCES.

Articles eligible for duty-free entry from beneficiary developing countries are identified by the letter *A* in the GSP column of the tariff page. Where an *A** appears, the duty exemption is permitted for some, but not all, beneficiary countries. The general headnotes reveal whether GSP treatment will be afforded to a particular import from a given country.

All rates of duty are established by Congress or by the president under authority granted by the Congress. The Column 2 rates (with certain exceptions) are those set by Congress in the Tariff Act of 1930. The Column 1 rates are largely the product of multilateral agreements whereby the participating states agree to reduce their tariff rates in return for concessions on the part of their trading partners. In most cases the Congress has delegated to the president the authority to agree on rates, within certain bounds and under specified conditions. Nonreciprocal concessions, such as those granted under the GSP, are specifically legislated, leaving to the president the option of selecting eligible products (within defined criteria).

The Tariff Schedules are prepared by the U.S. International Trade Commission, in collaboration with the secretaries of commerce and the treasury, under authority granted in Section 484(e) of the Tariff Act of 1930. Prior to adoption of the current Tariff Schedules in 1963, separate classification systems were prescribed for duty classification and statistical reporting. The incorporation of the statistical reporting system into the Tariff Schedules has resulted in an amalgamated publication, the Tariff Schedules of the United States, Annotated.

See GENERAL AGREEMENT ON TARIFFS AND TRADE, TARIFF (CUSTOMS).

TAX CREDIT METHODS. *See* DOUBLE TAXATION.

TAXE SUR VALEUR AJOUTÉE. The French translation of VALUE ADDED TAX (*q.v.*).

TAX EXEMPTION METHOD. *See* DOUBLE TAXATION.

TAX HAVEN. A legal jurisdiction that levies no, or very low, taxes on the income of firms organized under its laws or operating within its borders. Often the exemption is limited to firms organized in, but not operating in, the country.

TAX HOLIDAY. A period of time (usually several years) during which an enterprise is exempt from some or all taxes. This device is often used in conjunction with economic development programs as an inducement to attract industry.

TAX INCIDENCE. The place where a tax finally comes to rest. For example, a value added tax is passed through the marketing process to the final purchaser.

TAX SPARING. The remission, reduction, or deferral of certain taxes offered to foreign businesses as an inducement to invest locally.

TECHNICAL BARRIERS TO TRADE. A specialized form of nontariff barrier that arises when a nation adopts or retains peculiar product standards. Often, these standards reflect genuine local usages not designed to impede imports; other standards are devised for precisely such purposes. An example of such technical barriers in U.S. emission control requirements on imported (and domestic) cars.

TECHNICAL DATA. Information that can be transferred to overseas users only in accordance with export control regulations. The Office of Export Administration regulations (Part 379) define technical data as:

> Information of any kind that can be used, or adopted for use, in the design, production, manufacture, utilization, or reconstruction of articles or materials. The data may take a tangible form, such as a model, prototype, blueprint, or operating manual; or they may take an intangible form such as technical service.

Export control regulations should be consulted to ascertain licensing requirements depending upon the destination country.

TECHNICAL SOLVENCY. *See* SOLVENCY.

TECHNOLOGY GAP. A disparity in production functions among nations due to technological advancements in one country that have not been fully imitated by others. During the period of this gap, the nation possessing the advancement enjoys an export monopoly of the new product or process. *See* IMITATION LAG.

TEMPORARY IMPORTATION UNDER BOND. An arrangement whereby foreign merchandise may be entered into the United States for a limited period of time without payment of duties. Normally, duties paid on foreign merchandise are not recoverable upon re-exportation of the goods from the United States. To avoid a loss on duties paid but not recoverable, a U.S. importer may post a *temporary import bond* (T.I.B.) equivalent to twice the value of the duties and excises that would otherwise be assessed on the goods. With the exception of automobiles and certain automotive equipment, which must be re-exported after six months, items imported under T.I.B. may remain in the United States for one year; extensions are permitted up to a total of three years from original importation. Failure to re-export the goods at the end of the authorized period results in forfeiture of the bond to the government as liquidated damages.

Temporary importations under bond are commonly used to accommodate equipment sent to the United States for repair, samples for the purpose of soliciting orders, and articles for testing.

TEMPORARY IMPORT BOND. *See* TEMPORARY IMPORTATION UNDER BOND.

TEMPORARY TARIFF SURCHARGE. An increased rate of duty on imports temporarily applied, usually to aid in correcting a balance of payments deficit.

THE TEN. A reference to the European Communities.

TENOR. The dating provided in a draft or bill of exchange. A draft may provide for a tenor of, for example, sixty days' sight, which means the sum is payable sixty days from presentation. A tenor of sixty days date, on the other hand, means the instrument matures sixty days from the date of execution, irrespective of when it is presented to the drawee.

TERM BILL. *See* USANCE BILL.

TERMINAL OPERATOR. A firm furnishing wharfage, warehousing, container facilities, or similar services to oceangoing common carriers. Such firms are subject to regulation by the Federal Maritime Commission.

TERMS OF DELIVERY. A specification of the point at which title and risk of loss on merchandise are transferred from seller to buyer. The point of transfer is determined by commercial negotiations or customs of the particular trade and is stipulated by such terms as *F.O.B.* (named point), *C.I.F.* (named port), and *ex warehouse*. A full listing of terms of delivery can be found in Appendix D1.

TERMS OF TRADE. An export-import price ratio derived by dividing indices of export prices by indices of import prices. For example, when export indices are 105 percent of a base period, and import indices are 98 percent of the same base period, then the terms of trade (export-import) price ratio would be 107 percent of the base period.

When export prices received are higher than import prices paid, the terms of trade are said to be *favorable*; when the condition is reversed, the terms of trade are *unfavorable*.

TERRITORIAL SEA. A bank of sea adjacent to a nation's coastline within which the coastal state exercises sovereign control. By ancient custom, this bank ran three miles (said to be a cannonball's range offshore).

In recent years, various nations have asserted that the bank runs from twelve to two hundred miles to sea, or to the limits of the continental shelf. How far the territorial sea runs out from the shore remains an area of intense debate.

TEU. *See* TWENTY-FOOT EQUIVALENT UNIT.

THEORY Z. A concept articulated by Professor William Ouchi to identify a Japanese-style, worker-participating corporation. Theory Z is an expansion upon terminology developed by the late Douglas MacGregor, which identified a Theory X, in which workers are viewed as basically lazy and begrudgingly productive, and a Theory Y, which holds workers to be animated and zealous.

Theory Z typifies a firm that identifies long-range goals (rather than near-term income performance only), maintains worker loyalty through incentives during profitable times and avoidance of layoffs during harder times, and seeks to generate a consensus among all levels of staff.

Professor Ouchi sees this stucture most aptly displayed in Japanese firms, where lifetime employment is assumed, and salary cuts are shared at all levels during periods of reduced earnings.

THIRD WORLD. That group of less developed and developing nations not included in the political camps of either the Western industrialized states or the communist bloc. Most nations in Latin America, Africa, and Asia fall into this category. The term is commonly applied to nations with a per capita income under one thousand dollars.

A distinction is sometimes made between the Third World generally and the so-called Fourth World, defined as those nations having a per capita income under three hundred dollars.

See FIRST WORLD, SECOND WORLD.

THIRD-FLAG CARRIAGE. The shipment of goods aboard a vessel that flies the flag of neither the exporting nor the importing country.

THRESHOLD PRICE. A minimum import price for commodities established under the COMMON AGRICULTURAL POLICY *(q.v.)* of the European Economic Community, set so as not to hamper sales of EEC produce within the community.

The threshold price of grain, for example, is computed by subtracting from the TARGET PRICE *(q.v.)* the costs of inland tranportation and handling to the EEC market center evidencing the greatest shortage of the commodity. Costs would be calculated from the nearest ocean port to the market center.

THROUGH RAILROAD EXPORT BILL OF LADING. *See* RAILROAD THROUGH BILL OF LADING.

THROUGH RATE. A freight rate that is the total rate from origin to destination; in some cases, surcharges may be applicable to the basic freight, and are additional to the through rate.

THROUGH TRANSPORT CLUB. The common name for the *Through Transport Mutual Insurance Association Limited,* a mutual insurance fund of firms in the container or unit load industry. The insureds are member firms, and the membership is derived from three main groups: vessel owners and charterers, container terminal operators, and forwarders, multimodal transport operators, and others who lease, own, or transport containers.

The association is chartered and managed in Bermuda. It was founded in 1968 as a nonprofit association to insure its members against loss or damage arising from container shipments. Coverage available to members includes loss or damage to third-party property, other than cargo; death, injury, or illness of persons, other than employees; quarantine and disinfection of equipment; removal of damaged equipment; fires and penalties; misdelivery or delay in delivery of cargo; and financial losses arising from a member's breach of contract with third parties.

THROUGH TRANSPORT MUTUAL INSURANCE ASSOCIATION LIMITED. *See* THROUGH TRANSPORT CLUB.

T.I.B. *See* TEMPORARY IMPORTATION UNDER BOND.

TIED LOAN. A loan to a foreign nation or firm that requires the proceeds of the loan to be spent only in the creditor nation. Such an arrangement stimulates the economy of the country making the loan. The debtor nation, however, because it is constrained in spending the funds, may encounter higher prices for its purchases than it might have if it had been permitted to buy elsewhere.

TIED PRODUCT. *See* TIE-IN CONTRACT.

TIE-IN CONTRACT. An arrangement by which a desired product (tying product) can be purchased only upon agreement to purchase certain other products (tied products). Tie-in contracts are largely forbidden by the antitrust Clayton Act.

TIMBER TON. A unit of measure, equal to forty cubic feet, used to measure wood and wood products.

TIME BILL OF EXCHANGE. A BILL OF EXCHANGE *(q.v.)* payable other than "at sight," i.e., immediately upon presentation. Bills drawn at sixty days' sight or thirty days date, for example, are time bills.

TIME CHARTER. The charter of a vessel for a specific period of time, during which the vessel will respond to operational direction from the charterer.

TIME-CHARTERED OWNER. The party having operational control of a vessel under a time charter.

TIME CREDIT. *See* USANCE CREDIT.

TIME DRAFT. *See* DRAFT.

TIME LOST WAITING FOR BERTH. *See* AS LAYTIME.

TIME VOLUME RATE. A contract between a shipper of cargo and a steamship line or conference in which the shipper pledges to ship a specific quantity of cargo aboard the carrier's vessels between agreed ports, during a given time period for a fixed sum of money per freight unit.

TIR CONVENTION. An international agreement designed to speed international cargo movements across third countries en route to final destination. Originally established in 1949 as a means of speeding European road transportation, the convention now applies to other modes of transport as well.

Basically, each nation adhering to the convention designates an organization to handle the issuance of *carnets*, or transit documents. This organization issues carnets to approved transport firms, thereby permitting the truck or other vehicle to pass over the territory of any member state without customs inspection until arrival in the country of final destination. A nominal fee is charged for each carnet issued.

Participants in the convention include all European countries, including the USSR, its satellites, and Albania, many Near Eastern countries, Canada, and the United States.

TITLE XI FINANCING. In the Merchant Marine Act of 1936, a provision for the U.S. government to act as guarantor on debt obligations contracted by U.S. citizens for the purpose of constructing vessels to trade under the American flag.

TO AVERAGE. A condition in some vessel charter parties that provides for separate calculations to be made for loading and discharging when time saved in one operation is to be used to offset excess time consumed in the other.

TOKYO DECLARATION. The pronouncement of a 1973 gathering in Tokyo of foreign, finance, and trade ministers of the major industrial nations, meeting to discuss economic and trade problems. The joint communiqué issued by the ministers called for increased trade through the elimination of tariff and nontariff barriers and through nonreciprocal concessions to developing nations.

The objectives of the meeting were reflected in the TOKYO ROUND *(q.v.)* of multilateral trade negotiations.

TOKYO ROUND. The seventh, and latest, round of multilateral trade negotiations sponsored by the GENERAL AGREEMENT ON TARIFFS AND TRADE *(q.v.)*. Running from 1973 to 1979, the Tokyo Round resulted in a series of international agreements on significant tariff rate reductions, and also agreements on nontariff measures, such as subsidies, valuation, and technical barriers. (*See* Appendix D8.)

Specifically, the Tokyo Round produced a series of annual tariff reductions, running from January 1, 1980, through January 1, 1987, resulting in a 34 percent reduction in customs collections; the weighted average tariff on manufactured products in the world's nine largest industrial markets will decline from 7.0 to 4.7 percent ad valorem. It eliminated export subsidies on nonprimary products and primary mineral products and established standards for countervailing measures. It prohibited the use of technical standards as a barrier to trade.

The Tokyo Round made a commitment to limit import licensing and to apply licensing so as not to hamper trade unnecessarily. It produced a liberalization of most government procurement practices to permit foreign firms to bid on projects valued at more than 150,000 SPECIAL DRAWING RIGHTS *(q.v.)*. It established a uniform system of valuation for customs purposes and revised the Antidumping Code negotiated during the earlier Kennedy Round. It also eliminated all duties on civil aircraft, parts, and repairs.

The Tokyo Round firmly established the principle of nonreciprocal trade concessions to developing nations.

TOLKATSCHS. A colloquialism applied in Russia to procurement officers sent about the country to secure scarce supplies required by their employers; literally the term means "roving magician."

TON (TONNE). *See* ENGLISH WATER TON, GROSS TON, NET TON, REGISTER TON.

TON MILE. The carriage of one ton (two thousand pounds in the United States) of cargo for one mile; used to measure quantity of cargo transported by a carrier or group of carriers (usually rail or motor) within a given time span.

TONNAGE TAX. A Federal tax imposed upon commercial vessels entering the territory of the United States. *See* LIGHT MONEY AND TONNAGE TAXES.

TORQUAY ROUND. *See* GENERAL AGREEMENT ON TARIFFS AND TRADE.

TOTAL LOSS. *See* ACTUAL LOSS, CONSTRUCTIVE TOTAL LOSS.

TOUCH AND STAY. A clause in a marine insurance contract which stipulates that a vessel may call at customary ports along its route, and that such calls will not of themselves be regarded as a DEVIATION *(q.v.)* for purposes of vitiating coverage under the policy.

TRADE ACCEPTANCE. *See* ACCEPTANCE.

TRADE ACT OF 1974. An act that provided the president the negotiating authority essential to participate in the TOKYO ROUND *(q.v.)* of tariff reductions. The act empowered the president to reduce by up to 60 percent all duty rates above 5 percent ad valorem and to abolish duty rates of 5 percent ad valorem or below; such duty reductions were to be phased over ten years. In addition, the act authorized an accelerated elimination of nontariff barriers and adjustment assistance (such as unemployment compensation and job training for American workers displaced by exports), and permitted a grant of MOST FAVORED NATION *(q.v.)* status to communist countries under certain circumstances. Apart from these trade liberalizing measures, the act empowered the president to withdraw from any trade agreement and to institute higher duties.

The grounds upon which domestic industries might receive a finding by the International Trade Commission that they had been injured by foreign competition were also reinforced. Such a finding would mandate punitive tariff or quota action by the president.

TRADE AGREEMENTS ACT OF 1962. An act that authorized the president, during the period of July 1, 1962, through June 30, 1967, to reduce or eliminate certain tariffs in return for similar concessions on the part of other trading nations. The act was largely in response to the elimination of internal duties by members of the European Economic Community. The act empowered the president, inter alia, to reduce by up to 50 percent duties in effect at the commencement of the act, to eliminate duties under 5 percent, and to eliminate duties on certain agricultural products in return for the likely maintenance or expansion of U.S. exports. Any such reductions were to be implemented in at least five installments, a year apart. The act served as a basis for the KENNEDY ROUND *(q.v.)* discussions.

TRADE AGREEMENTS ACT OF 1979. An act of Congress implementing certain agreements negotiated under the TOKYO ROUND *(q.v.)*. The act replaced the Countervailing Duty Law and Antidumping Act of 1921 and abolished the FINAL LIST and AMERICAN SELLING PRICE *(qq.v.)* methods of valuation for customs, as used for certain products.

Under this act, intangible assists (e.g., design work) are not dutiable to the extent that they are the product of labor performed in the United States. The actual selling price of the merchandise will determine value for duty, irrespective of whether this price is the "freely offered" price or the price that conforms with "ordinary course of trade." This *transaction value* supersedes the export value of merchandise. "Generally accepted accounting principles" will be employed by customs where values must be determined other than by invoice.

The act opens government procurement, on a reciprocal basis, to non-U.S. suppliers and establishes a policy on technical barriers to trade. Title VIII of the act (also known as the Distilled Spirits Tax Revision Act of 1979) provided authority for new regulations governing importation of liquor.

TRADE BALANCE. *See* BALANCE OF TRADE.

TRADE BARRIER. Constraints upon the exchange of goods among nations imposed by governments; such constraints are manifested in the form of tariffs, quotas, exchange controls, and a variety of so-called nontariff barriers. Barriers usually arise to protect domestic industries, preserve foreign exchange, reduce unemployment, or retaliate for barriers established by other nations; also barriers may arise out of protracted political disputes among nations, although the object in such cases is the advancement of political rather than economic objectives. The effect of trade barriers is to reduce trade, thereby denying a more efficient use of the world's resources.

TRADE CREATION. The substitution of lower-cost foreign goods for higher-cost domestic manufactures.

TRADE CREDIT. Credit granted by nonfinancial firms, usually in the form of short-term deferral of payment of invoices by customers, e.g., account open sales. Also, trade credit represents the purchase of a firm's accounts receivable or trade acceptances.

TRADE CYCLE. The British equivalent term for the U.S. term BUSINESS CYCLE *(q.v.)*.

TRADE DEFICIT. An excess of imports over exports during a given period of time (usually a year) as measured in units of currency.

TRADE DIVERSION. The shift in purchases from sources outside a free-trade area (within which tariffs have been eliminated) to a union member, even though the cost of purchasing outside the union (before duty) is less than procuring from within. The absence of duty among members of the free-trade area more than offsets the lower unit costs available from outside suppliers.

TRADE GAP. The spread between the value of a nation's merchandise imports and a lesser value of merchandise exports during a fixed time period.

TRADE IMPACTED AREA. As provided in the Trade Act of 1974, a geographic area defined by the secretary of commerce in which significant numbers of workers have been laid off or in which the sales and/or production of firms has fallen, and where these conditions are directly attributable to increased imports of products similar to or competitive with those of the affected area. Such a finding by the secretary will make the designated area eligible for economic redevelopment under Section 401 of the Public Works and Economic Development Act of 1965, plus certain loan guarantees authorized by the Trade Act.

TRADEMARK. A device, symbol, or word used by a firm to distinguish its products from those of other manufacturers. The object of trademarks is to permit brand identification of products, which may permit a more ready market acceptance of current and new products. Trademarks are protected in the United States under the Lonham Trademark Act of 1946 and may be protected internationally under various agreements on the protection of industrial (intangible) property.

TRADEMARK REGISTRATION TREATY. An international agreement which provides for the protection of trademarks in adhering states by means of a single international filing.

The Trademark Registration Treaty (TRT) is similar in many respects to the MADRID AGREEMENT CONCERNING THE INTERNATIONAL REGISTRATION OF MARKS *(q.v.)*, but differs from that agreement in several important respects. Under the TRT, no prior filing of the mark with a national trademark office is required; a single filing is made with the WORLD INTELLECTUAL PROPERTY ORGANIZATION *(q.v.)* (WIPO). Filings must be in English or French. Also, cancellation of the basic national registration during the first five years does not negate the international registration.

Registration is effected for a period of ten years, and may be renewed for like periods in perpetuity. In addition, the TRT provides a moratorium of three years within which no contracting state may deny recognition of the mark on the grounds that it has not been in actual use in that country.

The treaty was concluded in 1973, and is administered by WIPO. The agreement is open to any state which adheres to the Paris Convention for the Protection of Industrial Property.

On March 15, 1984, the following states were adherents to the TRT: Congo, Gabon, Togo, U.S.S.R., and Upper Volta.

TRADE OPPORTUNITIES PROGRAM. An export promotion service of the U.S. Department of Commerce, International Trade Administration. U.S. firms interested in marketing abroad may list their products with the International Trade Administration; this data will be retained in ITA computers and matched with inquiries received by U.S. diplomatic posts and trade missions abroad. When a match occurs, the U.S. firm will receive a bulletin outlining the foreign firm's interests.

Participation in the Trade Opportunity Program can be undertaken by contacting any district office of the U.S. Department of Commerce. (See Appendix C2 for a full listing of district offices of the U.S. Department of Commerce, International Trade Administration.)

TRADE PREFERENCES. Certain trade concessions, usually preferential tariff treatment, granted by a nation to some countries but not others.

TRADE SURPLUS. An excess of exports over imports during a given period of time (usually a year) as measured in units of currency.

TRADING COMPANY. A firm engaged in the purchase, distribution, and marketing of products in international trade. Generally, the trading company deals with products of unrelated firms as well as the manufacturers of joint ventures in which it is involved.

TRADING WITH THE ENEMY ACT. An act of Congress, originally enacted in 1917 and amended in 1941, that grants to the president, during times of war or national emergency, the authority to prohibit or regulate trade, investments, remittances, travel, and virtually any economic transactions with any designated country or its nationals, wherever located. President Harry Truman's proclamation of national emergency in 1950, at the outbreak of the Korean War, brought the act into force again. An act of 1976 rescinding the national emergency specifically excluded the Trading with the Enemy Act, hence its provisions continue to remain in force.

TRAMP. A vessel that offers nonscheduled service between such ports as afford cargoes of opportunity. Unlike a LINER *(q.v.)*, a tramp seeks to acquire a full load from one shipper destined to a single consignee. Tramps usually operate under the terms of a VOYAGE CHARTER *(q.v.)*.

TRANSACTION VALUE. The primary method of valuing goods for customs purposes under the CUSTOMS VALUATION AGREEMENT *(q.v.)*.

TRANSACTION VALUE OF IDENTICAL MERCHANDISE. An alternative method of valuing goods for customs purposes under the CUSTOMS VALUATION AGREEMENT *(q.v.)*.

TRANSACTION VALUE OF SIMILAR GOODS SOLD. An alternative method of valuing goods for customs purposes under the CUSTOMS VALUATION AGREEMENT *(q.v.)*.

TRANSACTION VELOCITY. *See* VELOCITY OF MONEY.

TRANSBORDER DATA FLOW. The movement of information across international boundaries. Laws restricting the movement of data across borders have been enacted in some countries and contemplated in others, ostensibly to protect individual privacy. Restrictions on the movement of certain types of data (e.g., credit reports) may serve as nontariff barriers to trade.

TRANSFERABLE LETTER OF CREDIT. A LETTER OF CREDIT *(q.v.)* that is transferable from the original beneficiary to a subsequent beneficiary. This type of credit is used when the original beneficiary is a broker or other intermediary who is not actually supplying the merchandise. The original beneficiary assigns the right to receive a portion of the proceeds of the credit in return for performing some of the actions prescribed in the credit (e.g., presentation of a negotiable bill of lading evidencing shipment of the goods).

TRANSFERABLE RUBLES. *See* INTERNATIONAL BANK FOR ECONOMIC COOPERATION.

TRANSFER COSTS. Costs associated with the movement of goods from one country to another. Transfer costs may be divided into two categories:

physical transfer (i.e., transportation and handling) and governmental regulations (e.g., duties and exchange controls).

TRANSFER PAYMENTS. A payment by governments, firms, or individuals that results in no purchase of goods or services. Charitable contributions and welfare are examples. On the international level, transfer payments occur in the form of foreign aid grants, disaster relief, and similar undertakings.

TRANSFER PRICING. The pricing level at which goods are sold between related entities, subsidiary to parent. Transfer pricing has been an area of considerable interest to customs authorities, inasmuch as such sales are often suspected of being manipulated by the parties deliberately to undervalue the goods for duty purposes; conversely, the country of exportation may suspect the transaction as a vehicle to transfer funds out of the country.

Under the CUSTOMS VALUATION AGREEMENT (q.v.), sales between related parties are dutiable under the transaction value method, unless it can be determined that the relationship between the buyer and seller has affected the price.

TRANSFER RISK. The economic risk assumed by a creditor that the government of a foreign debtor will be unable or unwilling to make payment of the obligation in the agreed currency.

TRANSIT TARIFF. A duty or tax imposed by a nation on merchandise crossing its territory en route from one country to another. Transit tariffs have been abolished by all major nations but are still imposed by some developing nations as a source of revenue.

TRANSIT ZONE. An entry point established by a coastal state for the benefit of a neighboring nation that is landlocked or lacking adequate port facilities for its own trade. Generally a transit zone is cordoned off from the main port facility, and goods passing through the zone are usually exempt from the customs jurisdiction of the nation operating the zone, except as may be required to preserve local security. Goods pass to and from the zone under customs bond to the recipient country.

TRANSLOAD. The act whereby goods are transferred from one transport vehicle to another; for example, cargo may be removed from an ocean container at a port and reloaded into a rail trailer for movement to an interior point.

TRANSPORTATION AND EXPORTATION ENTRY. An entry filed with U.S. Customs permitting foreign goods temporarily to enter the United States in the course of transit across American territory en route to a foreign destination. During the course of such transit, the goods may not be altered or modified in any way.

TRANSPORT INTERNATIONALES ROUTIERS. *See* TIR CONVENTION.

TRANSSHIPMENT. The act of passing cargo from one carrier to another to continue the journey in those cases where the first carrier does not go from origin of a shipment to destination.

TREATY (INSURANCE). *See* REINSURANCE.

TREATY (INTERNATIONAL LAW). A formal, written compact entered into by sovereign nations. Customarily, an agreement provides that the treaty will not come into force until it has been *ratified*, i.e., approved by each government in accordance with its respective constitutional process.

TREATY OF ROME. The document, signed at Rome in 1957 (effective January 1, 1958), by which the six founding states established the EUROPEAN ECONOMIC COMMUNITY *(q.v.)*.

TREATY OF STOCKHOLM. *See* EUROPEAN FREE TRADE ASSOCIATION.

TRIFFIN PLAN. A proposal advanced by Professor Robert Triffin to establish a system for the settlement of international accounts. Originally articulated in *Gold and the Dollar Crisis* (1960), the Triffin Plan urged the creation of an international reserve asset to be used only for international account settlement. In some respects the plan resembled the INTERNATIONAL CLEARING UNION *(q.v.)* scheme proposed by John Maynard Keynes in the early 1940s. Triffin's proposal, however, stimulated interest on the part of the Group of Ten, which resulted in further investigation of international liquidity problems; the efforts of the Group of Ten subsequently resulted in creation of SPECIAL DRAWING RIGHTS *(q.v.)* by the International Monetary Fund.

TRIGGER PRICE MECHANISM. A program of import surveillance instituted by the U.S. government in 1977. Under this scheme, a floor price is established for designated import items; this floor is predicated upon the production cost of the most efficient foreign producer, with adjustments for freight and currency fluctuations. If recent import purchase prices fall below the current trigger price, an antidumping investigation is initiated.

TRIM. The disparity between the bow and stern drafts of a ship. A vessel that has the same draft both fore and aft is said to be *in trim*.

TRIPARTITE DECLARATION OF PRINCIPLES CONCERNING MULTINATIONAL ENTERPRISES AND SOCIAL POLICY. A pronouncement by the Governing Body of the International Labour Office concerning the obligations of multinational firms to the workers and societies within which they operate. The declaration encourages, inter alia, promotions within the local work force; equality of opportunity and treatment of all workers; employment security; wages, benefits, and working conditions at least comparable to those offered by other firms (in the case of developing nations, multinationals should set the standard for other firms); due regard to safety and health conditions in the workplace; the right of workers to organize and bargain collectively; and grievance procedures to permit due investigation of employee dissatisfaction. The declaration was adopted at Geneva on November 16, 1977.

TRIP CHARTER. The operation of a vessel, under a TIME CHARTER *(q.v.)*, for a specific voyage or voyages.

TROUGH. A low point in national economic activity. *See* BUSINESS CYCLE.

TRUST RECEIPT. An instrument in which a borrower pledges certain specific goods as collateral for a loan. The trust receipt certifies that the named goods are held in trust for the creditor or are segregated in the borrower's premises on behalf of the lender. Proceeds from the sale of the pledged goods are immediately due to the lender. One defect of trust receipts is that the instrument applies only to specific merchandise, which must be clearly identifiable (e.g., by serial number). Nevertheless, this method of financing is widely used.

TURN CLAUSE. *See* BERTH.

TURNING POINT. A change in the economy marking transition into the next phase in the BUSINESS CYCLE *(q.v.)*.

TURNKEY PROJECT. A capital construction project in which the contractor agrees to design and build the physical plant, train local personnel in its management, and leave the buyer with an operating plant.

TURNOVER. The rate at which sales occur, relative to the capital employed. For example, if sales are one million dollars, and capital employed is one hundred thousand, the capital turnover is ten.

TWENTY-FOOT EQUIVALENT UNIT. Often expressed as TEU, a measure of a vessel's cargo-carrying capacity, equivalent to one standard twenty-foot ocean container, measuring twenty feet by eight feet by eight feet. One forty-foot container constitutes two TEUs.

TWO PERCENT IN LIEU OF WEIGHING. A common provision in coal charter parties that the consignee may pay freight on the quantity actually discharged from the vessel as determined by weighing or on the amount manifested, at consignee's option. The option must be exercised prior to actual commencement of unloading.

TWO-TIER GOLD MART. A system under which gold is traded at two distinct prices. A fixed price is set for transactions among governments, while a market price (subject to the supply and demand mechanism) is established for public-sector transactions. This system was reestablished in the United States in 1968. In those cases where a significant disparity exists between the official and market prices, extensive speculation is apt to arise.

TWO-WAY PRICE. *See* INTERBANK MARKET.

TYING CONTRACT. *See* TIE-IN CONTRACT.

TYING PRODUCT. *See* TIE-IN CONTRACT.

U

UBERRIMAE FIDEI. Literally, "utmost good faith," i.e., presuming a higher degree of good faith than normally required for an ordinary contact.

ULLAGE. The shortage of contents from a cask or sack that occurs from handling or motion in transit. Evaporation, per se, does not constitute ullage.

ULTIMATE CONSIGNEE. A person specified on an export license as the party authorized by the license as the end recipient of the merchandise in the specified country of destination.

ULTIMATE PURCHASER. As used by customs officials, the last person who will receive an imported article in the form it was imported. In the event an imported article is processed or manipulated following importation, the processor is the ultimate purchaser.

ULTRALARGE CRUDE CARRIER. A tanker exceeding three hundred thousand deadweight tons.

UMBRELLA COMPANY. A local subsidiary of a multinational corporation that permits each product division to operate separately but retains at local headquarters the responsibility for cash management, advertising, and physical distribution. The object of such a company is to permit autonomy among product lines without unnecessary duplication of administrative services.

UNBUNDLING EXPENSES. The act of breaking out the component costs of a contract of insurance. In addition to pure protection against risk, an insurer must provide for costs of administration, claims processing, actuarial work, et cetera. These and other cost elements are indistinguishable in the policy rate. By unbundling, each factor is attributed its own cost. As a result, the insurer and insured may agree that some functions, such as claims handling, may be undertaken by the insured, resulting in an appropriate reduction of insurance costs.

UNCLEAN BILL OF LADING. *See* BILL OF LADING.

UNCONFIRMED LETTER OF CREDIT. *See* LETTER OF CREDIT.

UNCTAD CODE OF LINER CONDUCT. An international agreement sponsored by the UNITED NATIONS CONFERENCE ON TRADE AND DEVELOPMENT *(q.v.)*, or UNCTAD, to regularize the role and functions of shipping conferences. The code emerged in April 1974, following several months of discussion and participation by seventy-nine countries. Adoption of the code, which provides a framework within which conferences are to operate and which stipulates the bases for conference ratemaking, would supersede national regulation of conferences.

The convention permits closed conferences, but an otherwise qualified carrier must be admitted to any conference trading to its home country. Each conference must have an independent self-policing apparatus. Shipper loyalty agreements are authorized, and tariffs must be available for inspection. Mechanisms must be instituted to facilitate consultations between conference and shipper organizations. Finally, fighting ships are proscribed.

The most controversial provision of the code relates to the sharing of cargo among first, second, and third flag carriers. The so-called 40-40-20 rule stipulates that 40 percent of a nation's trade shall be carried on *first flag* vessels (i.e., vessels flying the flag of the exporting country); 40 percent of the trade shall be carried on *second flag* vessels (i.e., those flying the flag of the importing country); and 20 percent of the trade may be carried on *third flag* vessels (i.e., those of other countries).

The 40-40-20 rule has been strongly supported by the developing nations as a vehicle to expand their participation in the carriage of their national cargoes. The European Economic Community and Japan have also supported the rule. The United States has not adopted a formal position on the code.

The code took effect following ratification by states representing at least 25 percent of the world's total liner tonnage, which occurred with the ratification by the Federal Republic of Germany and the Netherlands in April 1983; the formal accession of these countries put 28.7 percent of the world's liner fleet under the code, which was operationally implemented among the adhering states in October 1983.

At the beginning of 1984, nations representing 28.68 percent of world tonnage had adhered to the convention. Those nations are:

Bangladesh	Jordan
Barbados	Kenya
Benin	Korea (Republic of)
Bulgaria	Lebanon
Cameroon	Madagscar
Cape Verde	Mali
Central African Republic	Mauritius
Chile	Mexico
China	Morocco
Congo	Netherlands
Costa Rica	Niger
Cuba	Nigeria
Czechoslovakia	Pakistan
Egypt	Peru
Ethiopia	Philippines
Gabon	Romania
Gambia	Senegal
German Democratic	Sierra Leone
Republic	Sri Lanka
German Federal Republic	Sudan
Ghana	Tanzania
Guatemala	Togo
Guinea	Trinidad and Tobago
Guyana	Tunisia
Honduras	USSR
India	Uruguay
Indonesia	Venezuela
Iraq	Yugoslavia
Ivory Coast	Zaire
Jamaica	

UNDER DECK BILL OF LADING. An ocean BILL OF LADING *(q.v.)* bearing the specific notation that the goods have been stowed below deck. Under deck stowage has been traditionally regarded as safer than stowage on deck. Under deck bills are no longer commonly issued by carriers, particularly in the case of container ship operators; so-called optional bills are issued instead, giving the carrier the option of stowing the goods at his convenience. Such bills of lading are generally accorded the status of under deck bills except where specifically endorsed "on deck."

UNDERDEVELOPMENT. A condition in which a nation's per capita real income is significantly below that enjoyed in the industrialized world, and where national income is inadequate to provide the investment capital essential to expand the economy. In addition, most underdeveloped nations have heavy dependence upon agriculture, with antiquated farming methods and low productivity; high birth rates; significant illiteracy; political instability and high levels of governmental corruption; only a few key export products, usually primary products or low-value manufactures; and limited industrial infrastructure (e.g., railroads, highways, and electrical generating and transmissions capacity).

Most underdeveloped nations have coalesced into a loose bloc in order to stimulate a redistribution of wealth from the industrialized countries. This group is known commonly as the THIRD WORLD *(q.v.)*.

See GROUP OF SEVENTY-SEVEN.

UNDERLAP. In vessel charters, the period of time by which a charterer prematurely returns a vessel to the owner's control in advance of the appointed date.

UNDERWRITER. An insurance company or syndicate that, in return for a specified premium, agrees to indemnify the assured in the event certain losses are sustained during the course of a marine venture.

UNIFIED LAW ON THE BOYCOTT OF ISRAEL. Enacted by the Council of the Arab League in 1954 and adopted by the twenty member states of the league, a law that calls upon Arab states to ban all economic transactions with Israel. In addition, foreign firms engaged in transactions with Israel are to be blacklisted, i.e., denied access to Arab markets.

UNIFORM CERTIFICATE OF MANUFACTURE. *See* CERTIFICATE OF MANUFACTURE.

UNIFORM CUSTOMS AND PRACTICES. Generally known as the UCP, a body of rules governing and guiding banking practices relative to letters of credit. The first version of the UCP was promulgated by a congress of the International Chamber of Commerce in Amsterdam in 1933 but was rejected by the banking communities of the United States and Great Britain.

In 1951, the ICC issued a revised version of the UCP, which was adopted by American, but not British, banks. A further revision of the UCP in 1962, forbidding acceptance by banks of received-for-shipment or "on-deck" bills of lading unless specifically authorized in the credit, overcame British objections.

By the early 1970s, additional revision of the UCP was needed to overcome certain problems of bank discretion and to accommodate containerized shipping. This latest revision was adopted by the Executive Committee of the ICC in December 1974, to take effect with credits issued on or after October 1, 1975.

Although the UCP is not enacted as statute, it is recognized in the courts of virtually every nation and is incorporated by reference into every credit that stipulates the instrument is governed by the UCP.

UNIFORM DELIVERED PRICE. A single delivered price that is offered to all customers within a defined geographic area, irrespective of the actual cost of delivering the merchandise.

UNIFORM LAW ON BILLS OF EXCHANGE. A product of the 1932 Geneva Convention on Bills of Exchange. The object of the act was to standardize various national laws and usages relative to bills of exchange, thereby overcoming an impediment to trade. The act specifies that a bill of exchange must contain:

1. The term *bill of exchange* inserted in the body of the instrument and expressed in the language employed in drawing up the instrument;
2. An unconditional order to pay a determinate sum of money;
3. The name of the person who is to pay (payee);
4. A statement of the time of payment;
5. A statement of the place where payment is to be made;
6. The name of the person to whose order payment is to be made;
7. A statement of the date and of the place where the bill is issued;
8. The signature of the person who issues the bill (drawer).

Adherents to the Geneva convention include:

Austria	Japan
Belgium	Luxembourg
Brazil	Monaco
Denmark	Netherlands
Finland	Norway
France	Poland
Germany*	Sweden
Greece	Switzerland
Hungary	USSR
Italy	

In addition to the full adherents, various other countries have signed the convention with reservations or have adopted provisions of the act into their national laws. [*Since the division of Germany, the Federal Republic of Germany has continued adherence to the agreement.]

UNILINEAR TARIFF. *Synonymous with* GENERAL TARIFF *(q.v.)*.

UNION D'ASSUREURS DES CREDITS INTERNATIONAUX. The full, formal name of the BERNE UNION *(q.v.)*.

UNITARY TAXATION. A form of corporate taxation adopted by some U.S. states whereby state income tax is assessed on a pro rata portion of the company's worldwide profits, rather than on locally earned profits only.

Unitary taxation emerged in the United States in 1926; at that time it was applied to interstate railroads to permit a fair apportionment of the railroad's earnings among the states in which the company operated. At least eleven states use the unitary tax system, although unitary taxation is most closely identified with California, which has applied it aggressively and has become the object of litigation to overturn the principle on constitutional and other grounds.

In 1983 the Supreme Court, by refusing to hear an appeal from a lower court, tacitly admitted the legality of applying the unitary method to the income of American firms with foreign subsidiaries. The application of the tax to foreign corporations is somewhat more complicated because of tax treaties and other international agreements. Nevertheless, the Supreme Court in December 1983 rejected an appeal from Shell Petroleum of the Netherlands (and supported by eight European governments and Japan) that challenged the authority of local tax officials to include the worldwide profits of a foreign corporation in taxing a subsidiary in their state. The Federal government has taken no official position on the issue of unitary taxation, but there is strong pressure from foreign governments to abolish it.

In computing the taxable profits of a local firm, tax officials in states employing the unitary method do not look merely to transactions performed by the local firm. Because that firm is viewed as part of a larger "global entity," the tax burden of the local firm is derived by utilizing three ratios: local sales to worldwide sales, local assets to worldwide assets, and local payroll to worldwide payroll. The average of the three reflects that portion of a multijurisdiction entity's profits subject to tax by the unitary state.

UNITED NATIONS CONFERENCE ON TRADE AND DEVELOPMENT. An agency of the United Nations General Assembly formed in 1964 to stimulate the economies of less developed countries through trade. UNCTAD has tried to reduce or abolish the tariff and nontariff barriers of developed nations on the manufactured exports to developing countries.

UNCTAD serves as a forum for developed and developing countries on trade matters. In recent years UNCTAD has addressed the creation of nonreciprocal concessions to products of developing countries; the principle of such concessions is embraced in the GENERALIZED SYSTEM OF PREFERENCES *(q.v.)*, which emerged from the Tokyo Round of multilateral trade negotiations. UNCTAD has proposed establishment of a so-called Common Fund of $470 million as the financial vehicle behind a commodities program; the fund would be used to build buffer stocks of certain commodities. It has discussed debt restructuring and relief, and the adoption of a CODE OF CONDUCT FOR LINER CONFERENCES *(q.v.)* that would guarantee the merchant fleets of Third World nations a higher portion of their import and export cargoes.

Membership in UNCTAD is open to all members of the United Nations; the agency includes several nonmembers of the UN as well. UNCTAD headquarters are located in Geneva (*see* figure, next page).

UNITED NATIONS CONVENTION ON THE CARRIAGE OF GOODS BY SEA—1978. *See* HAMBURG RULES.

UNITED NATIONS CONVENTION ON THE RECOGNITION AND ENFORCEMENT OF ARBITRAL AWARDS. *See* NEW YORK CONVENTION ON THE RECOGNITION AND ENFORCEMENT OF FOREIGN ARBITRAL AWARDS.

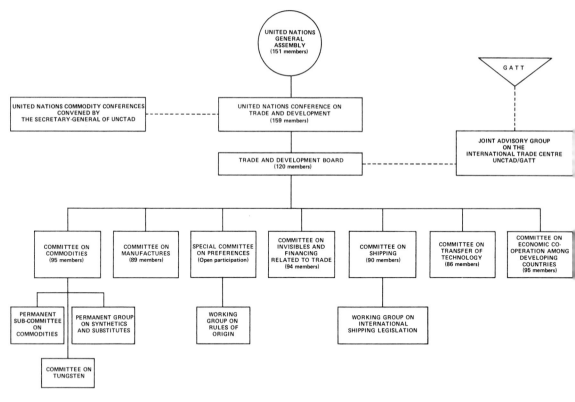

UNCTAD Structure. Courtesy of United Nations Conference on Trade and Development, Geneva, Switzerland.

UNITED NATIONS STANDARD INTERNA-TIONAL TRADE CLASSIFICATION. *See* STANDARD INTERNATIONAL TRADE CLASSIFICATION.

UNITED STATES ARBITRATION ACT. An act of Congress that prescribes the basis for arbitration of commercial disputes arising from maritime contracts and contracts involving foreign entities. The act is divided into two chapters.

Chapter I, dealing with maritime transactions, was enacted in 1947 and based upon an earlier statute. For purposes of the act, a maritime dispute is any complaint under bills of lading for carriage by water, charter parties, collisions, or any other matter involving interstate or foreign commerce that would be otherwise subject to admiralty jurisdiction. In a maritime contract a written provision for arbitration of subsequent disputes is "valid, irrevocable, and enforceable" under the act. In those cases where a participant in a dispute refuses to adhere to the arbitration provisions of the contract, the Federal courts shall compel arbitration. In addition, awards in arbitration are enforceable through the Federal courts.

Chapter II was enacted in 1970 to embrace the provisions of the NEW YORK CONVENTION ON THE RECOGNITION AND ENFORCEMENT OF FOREIGN ARBI-

TRAL AWARDS *(q.v.)*. Under this chapter, which took effect in February 1971, the act does not apply to disputes between citizens of the United States, unless the relationship involves property outside the United States or has a "reasonable relation to one or more foreign states." The Federal courts, which would have jurisdiction over the dispute if arbitration were not involved, may complete arbitration if interrupted and may remove actions from State courts if a participant to a dispute has commenced an action in a state court. Finally, the court may appoint arbitrators and enforce an award granted.

The act applies, in both maritime cases and international disputes, only where an arbitration clause has been included in the contract prior to the advent of the dispute. Arbitration may not be compelled in the absence of such agreement.

UNITED STATES CUSTOMARY SYSTEM. The system of weights and measures currently in use in the United States. In the early years of the Republic, varying standards of weights and measures were in use in different parts of the country; even such common measures as the pound, ton, and foot were not standardized. Inasmuch as most duties at the time were specific duties tied to units of measure rather than value, the collection of customs duties was erratic. In response to this condition, the U.S. Senate in 1830 called upon the forerunner of the Customs Service to adopt standard units of weight and measure to be applied universally at all ports of entry. In implementing the Senate's directive, the customs agency adopted the units in common use at the larger ports of entry (hence the origin of the name *customary* system).

The standards so adopted are substantially still in effect and are used by the Customs Service in the assessment of specific duties.

UNITED STATES CUSTOMS SERVICE. An agency within the U.S. Department of the Treasury charged with the enforcement of the tariff acts and other laws relating to the importation of goods.

The Customs Service was established by Congress in 1789. Among its duties are assessment and collection of duties, excises, and penalties on imported merchandise; seizure of contraband entering the United States; protection of domestic economic interests by enforcing the antidumping and countervailing duty laws, trademark and patent safeguards, and quota restrictions; monitoring and examining exports from the United States to ensure compliance with U.S. export control regulations; cap-

turing statistical data on U.S. international trade; and administration of U.S. health, safety, and marking laws on behalf of various governmental agencies.

The Customs Service is headed by a commissioner of customs. For administrative reasons, the service is divided into nine regions, each headed by a regional director. Regions (excepting Region II) are further subdivided into districts, each headed by a district director; Region II, covering the port of New York, does not have districts but is divided into three areas. Each district encompasses various *ports of entry* through which foreign merchandise may enter the United States and undergo customs inspection. In all, there are more than three hundred ports of entry functioning in the United States, Puerto Rico, and the Virgin Islands (*see* figures).

UNITED STATES INTERNATIONAL TRADE COMMISSION. An independent agency within the Federal government charged with the ongoing investigation of the levels of U.S. import activity. It was established as the United States Tariff Commission in 1916; the current name was adopted in 1974.

The commission inquires into the impact of laws and regulations of the United States and other countries, examines foreign competition with U.S.

U. S. Customs Service Organization (map)

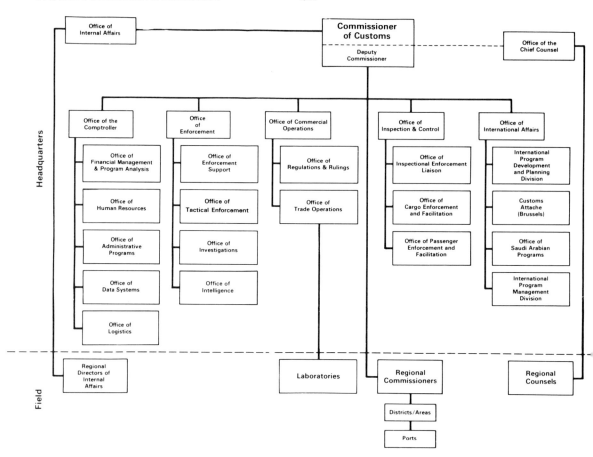

U. S. Customs Service Organization (chart)

industries, and compares importations with American manufacture and consumption of like items. It investigates injury to domestic industries caused by import competition; when a finding of domestic injury is made, the president may impose quantitative import restrictions, orderly marketing arrangements, or like constraints on offending imports.

The commission advises the president on the likely economic effects upon U.S. industry and consumers of any proposals to change tariffs or embark upon new trade agreements, and on the removal of duties under the GENERALIZED SYSTEM OF PREFERENCES *(q.v.)* accorded to developing countries. It also monitors trade with communist countries.

The commission investigates, under the Tariff Act of 1930, dumping and the resulting injury to U.S. producers, and unfair trade practices. As directed by the president, it also investigates interference with U.S. agricultural programs by imported products. It cooperates with the Departments of the Treasury and Commerce in compiling a uniform system for the capture of data relative to foreign trade, and publishes annually the Tariff Schedules of the United States, Annotated.

The commission consists of a chairman, vice-chairman, and four commissioners appointed by the president. Commissioners are appointed for nine years and may not be reappointed; the chairman and vice-chairman are designated for two-year terms.

UNITED STATES MUNITIONS LIST. *See* INTERNATIONAL TRAFFIC IN ARMS REGULATIONS.

UNITED STATES SHAREHOLDER. Within the meaning of the Internal Revenue Code, a U.S. person owning 10 percent or more of the voting stock of a *controlled foreign corporation* (i.e., one in which U.S. shareholders own 50 percent or more of the voting stock). *See* SUBPART F.

UNITED STATES TRADE REPRESENTATIVE. An office, with ambassadorial rank, created by Congress to direct U.S. trade negotiations during the Kennedy and Tokyo Rounds. Known previously as the *special trade representative* and the *special representative for trade negotiations,* the office was reorganized with expanded powers by Executive Order 12188, effective January 2, 1980. Responsibilities currently include all activities relating to the GENERAL AGREEMENT ON TARIFFS AND TRADE *(q.v.);* all trade or commodity issues involving the ORGANIZATION FOR ECONOMIC COOPERATION AND DEVELOPMENT *(q.v.);* bilateral and multilateral trade negotiations; direct investment incentives and disincentives and barriers to investment; negotiations before the UNITED NATIONS CONFERENCE ON TRADE AND DEVELOPMENT *(q.v.)* and other multilateral organizations when trade is the primary issue under consideration *(see* figure).

In addition, the trade representative serves as vice-chairman of the board of the Overseas Private Investment Corporation and a nonvoting member of the board of the Export-Import Bank. The trade representative reports directly to the president and sits as a member of the Cabinet.

UNITED STATES VALUE. A basis for assessing duties predicated upon the wholesale price of the imported product (or a like domestic product if the value of the imported product cannot be ascertained), less normal markups, transportation costs, insurance, and duties. This method of valuation has been supplanted by the CUSTOMS VALUATION CODE *(q.v.).*

UNITIZATION. The act of consolidating several smaller packages into a single unit for shipping purposes (e.g., the strapping of cartons onto a pallet). Unitization affords additonal security in transit to the merchandise and facilitates handling.

UNIT LOAD DEVICE. A container used aboard aircraft for the purpose of unitizing cargo. Unit load devices, commonly known as ULDs, come in various configurations, depending upon the type of aircraft on which they are used as well as where they are stowed aboard the aircraft. On 747 cargo freighters, aluminum (and occasionally steel) twenty- and forty-foot containers are used in conjunction with smaller ULDs. Other aircraft use special steel pallets, covered with netting, or smaller devices.

ULDs are usually stowed by airfreight forwarders and delivered to the airline intact, although large air shippers often stow and unload their own ULDs *(see* figures, next pages).

UNIT OF MEASURE. In international accounting, the currency used by a firm to measure assets, liabilities, revenues, expenses, et cetera.

UNIT TRAIN. A movement of an entire trainload of goods between one shipper and one consignee. Customarily, a shipment of fifty carloads at one time is required to justify a unit train movement.

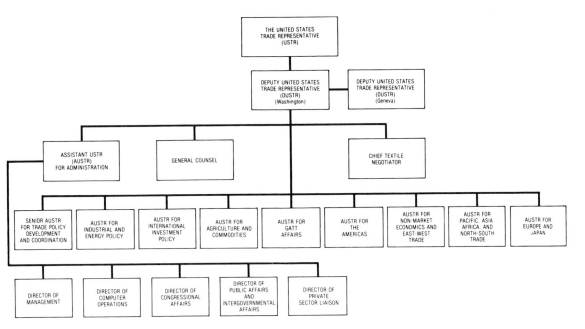

Office of the United States Trade Representative, Executive Office of the President

747F

Main-deck palletized cargo volume: 18,270 cu ft

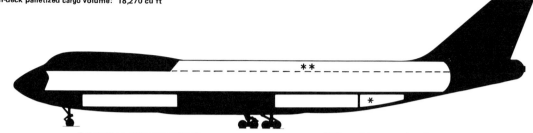

Forward lower-lobe compartment
containerized volume: 2,768 cu ft

Aft lower-lobe compartment
containerized volume: 2,422 cu ft

* Bulk volume: 800 cu ft
**Additional compartment height available
with side cargo door, approximately 2,500 cu ft

707-320C

Main-deck palletized volume: 5,693 cu ft
Freighter configuration

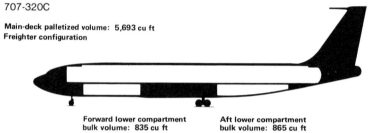

Forward lower compartment
bulk volume: 835 cu ft

Aft lower compartment
bulk volume: 865 cu ft

727-100C

Main-deck palletized volume: 3,177 cu ft
New interior

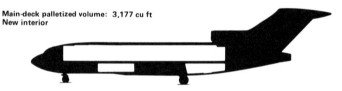

Forward lower compartment
bulk volume: 420 cu ft

Aft lower compartment
bulk volume: 470 cu ft

737-200C

Main-deck palletized volume: 2,730 cu ft
New interior

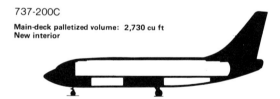

Forward lower compartment
bulk volume: 505 cu ft

Aft lower compartment
bulk volume: 370 cu ft

Unit Load Device. Courtesy of SAS, Jamaica, NY.

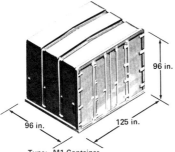

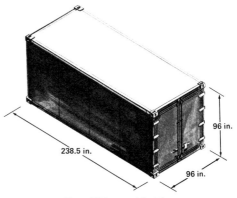

Type: M1 Container
Internal volume:
  1. Structural design: 572 to 605 cu ft
  2. Non-structural design: 609 cu ft
Tare weight:
  1. Structural design: 1,024 to 1,150 lb
  2. Non-structural design: 661 to 840 lb
Weight limitations:
  1. Structural design: 15,000 lb
  2. Non-structural design: 15,000 lb
Aircraft type: 747 main deck

(1) Type: M2 Structural Container
  Internal volume: 1,178 cu ft
  Tare weight: 2,090 lb
  Weight limitations: 25,000 lb
  Aircraft type: 747 main deck

(2) Type: M2 Structural Container
  Internal volume: 1,165 cu ft
  Tare weight: 2,115 lb
  Weight limitations: 25,000 lb
  Aircraft type: 747 main deck

(1) Without corner fittings
(2) With corner fittings

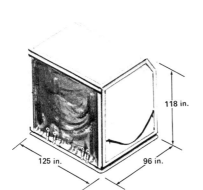

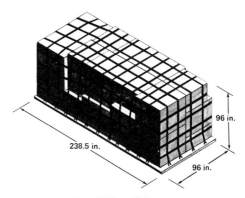

Type: M1H Structural Container
Internal volume: 760 to 773 cu ft
Tare weight: 705 lb
Weight limitations: 15,000 lb
Aircraft type: 747 main deck
Loaded through side cargo door only.

Type: M2 Netted Pallet
Internal volume: 1,183 cu ft
Tare weight pallet:
  Aluminum with balsa core: 890 lb
Tare weight net: 77 lb
Weight limitations: 25,000 lb
Aircraft type: 747 main deck

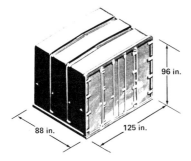

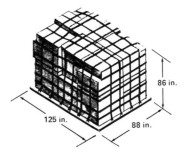

Type: M3 Structural Container
Internal volume: 560 cu ft
Tare weight: 925 lb
Weight limitations: 15,000 lb
Aircraft type: 747 main deck

Type: M4 Netted Pallet
Internal volume: 490 cu ft
Tare weight pallet:
  1. Solid aluminum sheet: 229 to 260 lb
  2. Aluminum with balsa core: 199 to 279 lb
Tare weight net: 35 lb
Weight limitations: 10,200 lb
Aircraft type: 747 main deck

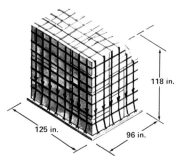

118 in.

125 in.

96 in.

Type: M5 Netted Pallet
Internal volume: 745 cu ft
* Tare weight: 254 to 270 lb (no support structure)
Tare weight net: 46 lb
Weight limitations: 15,000 lb
Aircraft type: 747 main deck
Loaded through side cargo door only.

*Pallet option—Tare weight: 610 lb with structural
aluminum support frame, aluminum
shelf, vinyl cover, and net

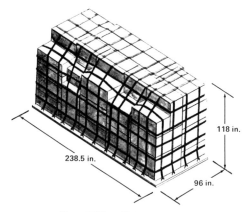

118 in.

238.5 in.

96 in.

Type: M6 Netted Pallet
Internal volume: 1,483 cu ft
Tare weight pallet:
Aluminum with balsa core: 890 lb
Tare weight net: 98 lb
Weight limitations: 25,000 lb
Aircraft type: 747 main deck
Loaded through side cargo door only.

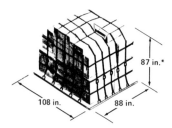

87 in.*

108 in.

88 in.

Type: "A" Netted Pallet
Internal volume: 311 to 380 cu ft
Tare weight pallet:
1. Solid aluminum sheet: 210 lb
2. Aluminum with balsa core: 176 to 216 lb
Tare weight net: 30 to 75 lb
Weight limitations: 8,000 to 10,000 lb
Aircraft type: Main deck, combination
passenger/cargo 707, 727, 737

*Height will vary from 78 to 87 in.

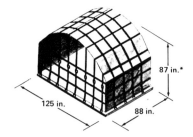

87 in.*

125 in.

88 in.

Type: A1, A2, or A3 Container
Internal volume:
1. Structural design: 390 to 458 cu ft
2. Non-structural design: 371 to 460 cu ft
Tare weight:
1. Structural design: 760 to 810 lb
2. Non-structural design: 452 to 692 lb
Weight limitations:
1. Structural design: 10,000 to 13,300 lb
2. Non-structural design: 8,000 to 13,300 lb
Aircraft type: 707, 727, 737, 747 main deck

*Height will vary from 78 to 87 in.

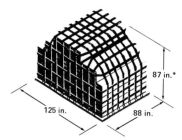

87 in.*

125 in.

88 in.

Type: A1, A2, or A3 Netted Pallet
Internal volume: 379 to 505 cu ft
Tare weight pallet:
1. Solid aluminum sheet: 229 to 260 lb
2. Aluminum with balsa core: 199 to 279 lb
Tare weight net: 33 to 80 lb
Weight limitations: 10,000 to 13,300 lb
Aircraft type: 707, 727, 737, 747 main deck

*Height will vary from 78 to 87 in.

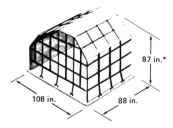

87 in.*

108 in.

88 in.

Type: A4 Container
Internal volume:
1. Structural design: 345 to 380 cu ft
2. Non-structural design: 303 to 364 cu ft
Tare weight:
1. Structural design: 470 to 570 lb
2. Non-structural design: 397 to 551 lb
Weight limitations:
1. Structural design: 8,000 lb
2. Non-structural design: 8,000 to 10,000 lb
Aircraft type: Main deck, combination
passenger/cargo 707, 727, 737

*Height will vary from 78 to 87 in.

International Container Standard			Unit Load Planforms							
			Based upon Regional Rail and ISO Containers						Based Upon International Container Standards	
			Europe		Japan		United States			
Type	Minimum Floor Dimensions (in.)	Floor Area (in.²)	40 in. x 48 in. (1000 x 1200 mm)		45 in. x 45 in. (1143 x 1143 mm)		45 in. x 54 in. (1143 x 1372 mm)		45" X 57.75" (1143 X 1467 mm)	
			No.	Eff.	No.	Eff.	No.	Eff.	No.	Eff.
8 ft x 40 ft	91.75 x 472.4 (2330 X 12 000 mm)	43340	20	87%	20	93%	16	90%	16	95%
8 ft x 20 ft	91.75 x 231 (2330 X 5867 mm)	21194	10	91%	10	96%	8	92%	8	97%
ATA/IATA 8 ft x 10 ft	91.75 x 117.5 (2330 X 2985 mm)	10781	4	71%	4	75%	4	90%	4	95%

UNIVERSAL AIR WAYBILL. A single, uniform AIR WAYBILL *(q.v.)* that can be used for either domestic or international shipments. The universal AWB was achieved through airline industry concurrence. It became available for use on an optional basis in April 1982 and mandatory after January 1984.

UNOBSTRUCTED CAPACITY. The internal, cargo-carrying capacity of a trailer, railcar, or container determined by multiplying the internal dimensions of the conveyance.

UNPARTED BULLION. A bar of precious metal containing base metal impurities.

UNREQUITED TRANSFER. A transfer payment, ie., the transfer of assets from one nation to another without expectation of recompense.

URGENT CONSIGNMENTS. Goods that, because of their character, require expeditious release by customs authorities. Among these goods are perishables and relief supplies to catastrophe victims.

USANCE. The time allowed for settlement of a BILL OF EXCHANGE *(q.v.)*, as established by custom of the particular trade or usage.

USANCE BILL. Also known as a *term bill*, a BILL OF EXCHANGE *(q.v.)* that affords a term of credit to the party accepting the bill (e.g., thirty days' sight, sixty days date). In effect, a usance bill is any bill other than one payable at sight.

USANCE CREDIT. Also known as a *time credit*, a LETTER OF CREDIT *(q.v.)* that provides that the drafts drawn under the credit will mature thirty, sixty, or more days, up to nine months, after sight or date.

A letter of crdit providing for settlement more than nine months from shipment of the goods is normally in the form of a DELAYED PAYMENT CREDIT *(q.v.)*.

USURY. A rate of interest in excess of that permitted by law. Usury may negate repayment of the excessive interest, or even the principal. In many jurisdictions usury statutes do not apply to corporate borrowings.

V

VALEUR MERCURIALE. An official value, used in the computation of ad valorem duties, assigned by governmental authority to certain classes of imported products. The term is peculiar to certain West African countries, notably Senegal and Benin.

VALIDATED LICENSE. *See* EXPORT CONTROL ACT.

VALIDATION. A concept applied in some jurisdictions relative to choice of law under contracts. *See* CENTER OF GRAVITY THEORY.

VALUATION TARIFF. A customs tariff in which ad valorem duties are applied not on the sale or commercial value of the merchandise, but on a nominal value for the product prescribed by governmental authority. For example, sheet steel might carry a duty of 5 percent ad valorem, but the tariff prescribes that the value for duty shall be $30 per ton, irrespective of the actual sale price of the goods. In this case, sheet steel will always pay a duty of 5 percent of $30, or $1.50 per ton.

Ad valorem duties in valuation tariffs are, effectively, specific duties.

VALUE ADDED TAX. A tax imposed upon the value added to a product at each stage of the production process. The tax is applicable to all goods, from primary to consumer products. Each processor in the chain of production pays the tax in the purchase price of the goods, applying the tax paid by prior handlers to its own tax obligation. Only the consumer pays the full tax.

The tax is applicable to imported merchandise (usually on top of any duties imposed) but is routinely rebated on goods that are exported.

The VAT is applied by members of the European Economic Community and a few other countries. A modified form of VAT, called the *single business tax,* is employed in Michigan.

VALUE DATE. The day on which foreign exchange will be delivered and paid for, usually two business days following the transaction.

VALUTA. A word of Italian origin, meaning literally "foreign currency," but used in international banking as a synonym for *divisen,* or short-term foreign bills.

VANNING. *Synonymous with* stowing or loading a trailer or container.

VARIABLE IMPORT LEVY. A duty applicable to imports of certain significant agricultural commodities into the European Economic Community. The COMMON AGRICULTURAL POLICY *(q.v.).* of the EEC specifies that this levy shall be equal to the difference between the THRESHOLD PRICE and the lowest ADJUSTED C.I.F. PRICE *(qq.v.).* On imports of cattle, beef, and veal, the variable import levy is in addition to normal customs duties.

The variable import levy is adjusted daily for sugar and grain; weekly for dairy products, beef, live cattle, veal, and rice; monthly for olive oil; and quarterly for pork, poultry, and eggs.

VARIABLE RATE LOAN. A loan on which the rate of interest is adjusted periodically in accordance with market rates.

VELOCITY OF MONEY. The speed at which a currency unit circulates within an economy. If money turns over at an increasing rate, this velocity indicates a speedup in the economy; conversely, a declining velocity may indicate a slowdown.

The overall velocity of money is the product of two components. (1) *Transaction velocity* is measured by the frequency with which a dollar, for example, is used in a transaction (spent). This velocity is measured by dividing total sales volume by the number of currency units in circulation. (2) *Income velocity* is measured by the number of times a currency unit is paid as income. This velocity is determined by dividing the gross national product by the money in circulation.

VENEZUELAN TRUST FUND. *See* INTER-AMERICAN DEVLOPMENT BANK.

VERTICAL EXPANSION. *See* VERTICAL INTEGRATION.

VERTICAL FOREIGN INVESTMENT. Investments made by a firm, usually an oligopolistic firm in an industrially advanced nation, in a foreign source of raw or semiprocessed materials that can be used in the manufacture of the investing firm's product.

VERTICAL INTEGRATION. Also known as *vertical expansion,* the incorporation into a business or economy of earlier or subsequent stages in the channel of production. For example, a chemical producer may undertake (backward) vertical integration by producing its own petroleum as raw material or may pursue (forward) vertical integration by converting the chemicals manufactured into finished plastics.

VERY LARGE CRUDE CARRIER. A tanker measuring between two and three hundred thousand deadweight tons.

VISA. A stamp or seal placed on invoices or other shipping documents by consular officials in connection with export shipments; also a stamp placed in a passport by a foreign official as a permit to enter the country.

VISBY AMENDMENT. A proposed revision to the HAGUE AGREEMENT *(q.v.)* of 1924 on the liability of ocean carriers for loss and damage to cargo. The Visby Amendment does not contemplate material change in carrier defenses (such as sinking, burning, and stranding), but it does seek to define more clearly what is a *package* and to raise the per package liability of a carrier from 100 pounds sterling to a maximum of 667 SPECIAL DRAWING RIGHTS *(q.v.).*

The Visby Amendment has been ratified by fifteen countries and adopted in principle by five other states; the United States has not adhered to the amendment, leaving the CARRIAGE OF GOODS BY SEA ACT *(q.v.)* of 1936 as the primary authority upon which claims involving shipment to or from the United States may be settled.

VISIBLE ITEM OF TRADE. A transaction in international trade that arises from the physical exchange of merchandise. *See* INVISIBLE EXPORTS AND IMPORTS.

VISIBLE SUPPLY. A quantity of a given commodity stored at loading centers and available for distribution.

VIS MAJOR. An overwhelming force of natural cause not involving human intervention, such as an earthquake, resulting in a loss that could not have been prevented by reasonable care.

VOLUMETRIC WEIGHT. An abstraction used in freight pricing that, for purposes of applying freight charges, equates a given unit of weight with a prescribed measure of volume. For example, the airline industry until recently usually equated one pound with 194 cubic inches; a shipment of feathers weighing one pound but measuring 970 cubic inches (5×194) would be rated as five pounds for freight purposes. Recently, air carriers revised this relationship to make 166 cubic inches equal to one pound.

VOLUNTARY EXPORT QUOTA. A quantitative restriction that a nation puts upon the export of a certain product to another country. This condition is usually in response to complaints from the importing country that its domestic industry is being injured by continuing exports of the product from its trading partner.

VOLUNTARY EXPORT RESTRAINTS. *Synonymous with* ORDERLY MARKETING AGREEMENT *(q.v.). See* BILATERAL RESTRAINTS AGREEMENT.

VOLUNTARY RESTRAINTS AGREEMENT. *See* BILATERAL RESTRAINTS AGREEMENT.

VOLUNTARY STRANDING. A grounding which results from the design and actions of the master to save the ship from imminent peril. Costs and sacrifices resulting from the voluntary act are recoverable in GENERAL AVERAGE *(q.v.).* However, recovery in general average will be barred if the stranding would have occurred without the intervention of the vessel's management.

VOSTRO ACCOUNT. Funds denominated in local currency that a foreign bank holds in a local bank.

VOYAGE CHARTER. The charter of a stipulated vessel to move specified quantities of cargo between named ports during a given time period.

VREDLING DIRECTIVE. Proposed legislation of the EUROPEAN ECONOMIC COMMUNITY *(q.v.)* (EEC) which would establish the right of workers to be informed of major policy decisions by corporate management. The directive was formulated in 1979 by Henk Vredling, who was EEC commissioner for employment and social affairs at the time.

The draft directive, which awaits final approval, would require management of firms employing at least 1,000 workers to inform employees of major changes in corporate structure, financial condition of the firm, business trends and projections, investment opportunities, and employment prospects. Such information would be provided by management each year on a prescribed day. In addition, management would be obliged to consult with employees in advance of actions which would have a major impact upon the firm. Employees would be granted 30 days to reply. Specifically included as areas for mandatory consultation are: proposed closure of plants or transfer of significant portions of the productive capacity thereof; contraction of the firm; workers' safety and health; and major organization changes.

The Vredling Directive has been accepted in principle by most EEC member states, with the notable exception of Great Britain. The measure has been attacked, within and outside the EEC, as an unwarranted infringement upon management prerogatives; additionally, concern has been expressed that the consultation process would expose trade secrets and other confidential business information. For example, management would be obliged to furnish employee representatives with data supplied to shareholders or creditors.

The directive would apply to both EEC-based companies and foreign firms doing business in the EEC.

The Vredling Directive should not be confused with CODETERMINATION *(q.v.),* or other forms of worker participation in management of the firm.

W

WALK-ON/WALK-OFF. A ship designed primarily for the transporting of livestock.

WAREHOUSE CERTIFICATE. A WAREHOUSE RECEIPT *(q.v.)*.

WAREHOUSE ENTRY. *See* ENTRY (CUSTOMS).

WAREHOUSE RECEIPT. A document issued by a public warehouseman, acknowledging receipt of and title to specific merchandise held in the warehouse. Such receipts are issued in accordance with the provisions of the Uniform Commercial Code, where applicable, or the Uniform Warehouse Receipt Act.

Warehouse receipts are issued in two types:

1. *Negotiable* warehouse receipts are issued to order of the party depositing the goods or his designee; title to the goods may be transferred by the owner by endorsement and delivery of the warehouse receipt. A negotiable warehouse receipt is a title document and must be presented to the warehouseman whenever goods are withdrawn. This type of warehouse receipt is used commonly in commodity transactions, where goods are stored in a public warehouse pending subsequent sale, which can be effected by endorsement and delivery of the warehouse receipt.

2. *Nonnegotiable* warehouse receipts are more common and cannot be used to effect title transfer. Title to the goods is vested in a named party, and merchandise will be delivered to that party or his designee only. Inasmuch as the warehouse receipt is purely a receipt and cannot be used to convey title, it is not necessary to present the document each time a withdrawal is made; any written instruction to release goods will be accepted by the warehouseman.

Warehouse receipts are common forms of collateral used in bank financing of inventories *(see* figures, next pages).

WAREHOUSE TO WAREHOUSE. A provision that can be included in marine insurance policies for coverage on merchandise from initial point of shipment until final delivery at a specified destination.

WARRANT. A WAREHOUSE RECEIPT *(q.v.)* containing TRUST RECEIPT *(q.v.)* provisions. Customarily, this document is issued in duplicate; the warehouse receipt portion is released by the lender to the merchant upon execution of the trust agreement.

WARRANTED FREE. In marine insurance policies, an exclusion of coverage for the named peril. For example, "warranted free of capture and seizure" means the underwriter will assume no responsibility for such losses.

WARRANTY. In marine insurance contracts, either an exemption from or limitation to the policy, or a *promissory* warranty whereby the insured agrees to do, or not to do, some particular act. Failure to adhere strictly to a promissory warranty may invalidate a contract of insurance, whether or not the action involved was material to the loss sustained.

WAR RISKS. The risks borne by a cargo owner or shipper that his goods will be lost or damaged owing to hostile actions at sea. Marine cargo policies exclude war risks from coverage, responding only for *marine perils* such as sinking, fire, collision, and various *perils of the sea*. War risks are covered in a separate policy, normally purchased in conjunction with the marine perils policy. The perils clause of a war risk policy reads substantially:

This coverage applies only against the risks of capture, seizure, destruction, or damage by men-of-war, piracy, takings at sea, arrests, restraints, detainments, and other warlike operations and acts of kings, princes, and people in prosecution of hostilities or in the application of sanctions under international agreements, whether before or after declaration of war and whether by a belligerent or otherwise, including factions engaged in civil war, revolution, rebellion, or insurrection, or civil strife arising therefrom, and including the risks of aerial bombardment, floating or stationary mines, stray or derelict torpedoes, and weapons of war employing nuclear fission and/or fusion or radioactive force; but excluding claims for delay, deterioration, and/or loss of market.

PORT OF SEATTLE

P.O. BOX 1209 / SEATTLE, WASHINGTON 98111

WAREHOUSE RECEIPT

WAREHOUSE RECEIPT NUMBER	999999
CUSTOMER'S OCEAN SHIPMENT NUMBER	9999999999

This is to Certify THAT WE HAVE RECEIVED IN STORAGE

AT WAREHOUSE_____ SEATTLE, WASHINGTON 98111

PAGE _____ OF _____

IN APPARENT GOOD ORDER, EXCEPT AS NOTED HEREON (CONTENTS, CONDITION AND QUALITY UNKNOWN) THE FOLLOWING DESCRIBED PROPERTY, SUBJECT TO ALL TERMS AND CONDITIONS HEREIN AND ON THE REVERSE SIDE HEREOF, SUCH PROPERTY TO BE DELIVERED TO THE CUSTOMER NAMED BELOW OR HIS ORDER UPON THE PAYMENT OF ALL STORAGE, HANDLING AND OTHER CHARGES.

CUSTOMER NUMBER 83412   CUSTOMER NAME Great American Imports, Ltd.   DATE CARGO RECEIVED INTO WAREHOUSE 2 / 13 /83

VESSEL NAME American Glory   VOYAGE NUMBER 1E   OCEAN BILL OF LADING 12345

GENERAL DESCRIPTION OF CARGO Televisions   VESSEL ARRIVAL PIER 13

VESSEL NUMBER 84567   STEAMSHIP AGENT NAME Seattle Maritime Corp.

CONTAINER NUMBER SEAU 128754   WAREHOUSE ENTRY NO. 48576   CUSTOM'S TIME 13-42   GENERAL ORDER NO. NA

PORT OF ORIGIN Yokohama   CUSTOMER REFERENCE NUMBER FOR THIS RECEIPT 777543   BILLING CODE E-14

STOCK NUMBER	QUANTITY MANIFESTED	QUANTITY RECEIVED	CARTONS EACHES	RECP'T REC. #	REMARKS
J-3487654	257	257	1/ea.	36	4 cartons water damaged
TOTAL PIECES ▶	257	257			

PORT OF SEATTLE CLAIMS A LIEN FOR ALL LAWFUL CHARGES FOR STORAGE AND PRESERVATION OF THE GOODS, ALSO FOR ALL LAWFUL CLAIMS FOR MONEY ADVANCED; INTEREST, INSURANCE, TRANSPORTATION, LABOR, WEIGHING, COOPERING AND OTHER CHARGES AND EXPENSES IN RELATION TO SUCH GOODS.

NOT NEGOTIABLE

Joe Jones
CHECKER

Mary Smith
CLERK

BY PORT OF SEATTLE

OFFICE DUP

Nonnegotiable Warehouse Receipt. Courtesy of the Port of Seattle.

AMERICAN WAREHOUSE COMPANY
A PUBLIC WAREHOUSE
2121 AMERICAN AVENUE • AMERICA

AWA Seal of Security

Date of Issue __February 15, 1983__   Consecutive No. __A-12__

THIS IS TO CERTIFY that we have received in Storage Warehouse __six ---__
situated at __1482 Main Street, Middle America, New York__

for the account of __Great American Trading Corp. or ORDER__

in apparent good order, except as noted hereon (**contents, condition and quality unknown**) the following described property, subject to all the terms and conditions contained herein and on the reverse hereof, such property to be delivered to ~~His~~ (Their) (Its) order, upon payment of all storage, handling and other charges and the surrender of this Warehouse Receipt properly endorsed,

LOT NO.	QUANTITY	SAID TO BE OR CONTAIN	STORAGE PER MONTH		HANDLING IN AND OUT	
			RATE	PER	RATE	PER
345	250ctn	Televisions, 1 per carton	.25	mo.	.30	i/o

NEGOTIABLE
Quantities subject to deliveries noted below.

Advances have been made and liability incurred on such goods, as follows:

__all "in" charges and first__
__month's storage paid; to be__
~~insured by receipt holder~~

The property covered by this receipt has NOT been insured by this company for the benefit of the depositor against fire or any other casualty.

(This clause to be omitted from forms used in those states where warehousemen are required by law to insure goods.)

American Warehouse Company claims a lien for all lawful charges for storage and preservation of the goods; also for all lawful claims for money advanced, interest, insurance, transportation, labor, weighing, coopering and other charges and expenses in relation to such goods.

AMERICAN WAREHOUSE COMPANY

By _____

This Receipt Is Valid Only When Signed by an Officer of the Company.

THE GOODS MENTIONED BELOW ARE HEREBY RELEASED FROM THIS RECEIPT FOR DELIVERY FROM WAREHOUSE. ANY UNRELEASED BALANCE OF THE GOODS IS SUBJECT TO A LIEN FOR UNPAID CHARGES AND ADVANCES ON THE RELEASED PORTION.

DELIVERIES

DATE	LOT NUMBER	QUANTITY RELEASED	SIGNATURE	QUANTITY DUE ON RECEIPT
2/15/83	345	50		50

Negotiable Warehouse Receipt. Courtesy of American Warehousemen's Association.

Premiums for war risk coverage are stated separately from premiums for marine perils coverage, even when both policies are issued by the same underwriter.

WARSAW CONVENTION. An international agreement adopted to provide uniform rules concerning liability and jurisdiction in cases of death, injury, or property damage arising from international carriage by air. It was signed at Warsaw in 1929. More than one hundred nations have adhered to the convention, which applies to virtually all international flights (*see* figure).

The basic 1929 agreement provides for a carrier liability limitation of 125,000 gold francs per passenger plus 250 gold francs for each kilogram of baggage or effects. Various amendments have modified these limits.

The 1955 Hague Protocol doubled liability for death, injury, or delay of passengers, but did not increase liability for effects. It did, however, abolish the carrier defense of errors in navigation or pilotage.

The 1966 Montreal Intercarrier Agreement (CAB 18900) was adopted in response to U.S. dissatisfaction with the levels of carrier liability for death and injury. The previous year, the United States had given notice of intent to withdraw from

CONTRACTING PARTIES TO THE WARSAW CONVENTION
AND THE HAGUE PROTOCOL

Dates shown are those upon which the Convention/Protocol
entered into force in the signatory state

STATE	WARSAW CONV.	HAUGUE PROT.
Afghanistan	May 21, 1969	May 21, 1969
Algeria	Aug 31, 1964	Aug 31, 1964
Antigua[6]		
Argentina	Jun 19, 1952	Oct 09, 1969
Australia	Oct 30, 1935	Aug 08, 1963
Austria	Dec 27, 1961	Jun 24, 1971
Bahamas[1]*		Jun 01, 1967
Bangladesh[1]	Feb 13, 1979	Feb 13, 1979
Barbados[2]		
Belgium	Nov 10, 1936	Nov 25, 1963
Belize[6]		
Botswana[3]		
Brazil	Feb 13, 1933	Sep 14, 1964
Brunei[6]		
Bulgaria	Sep 27, 1949	Mar 13, 1964
Burma[2]		
Byelorussian SSR	Dec 25, 1959	Aug 01, 1963
Cambodia[1]*		Aug 01, 1963
Canada	Sep 08, 1947	Jul 17, 1964
Chile	May 31, 1979	May 31, 1979
China (People's Rep.)	Oct 18, 1958	Nov 18, 1975
Colombia	Nov 13, 1966	Nov 13, 1966
Congo[1]*		Aug 01, 1963
Cuba	Oct 19, 1964	Nov 28, 1965
Cyprus[2]*		Oct 21, 1970
Czechoslovakia	Feb 15, 1935	Aug 01, 1963
Dahomey[1]*		Aug 01, 1963
Denmark	Oct 01, 1937	Aug 01, 1963
Dominica[6]		
Dominican Republic	May 25, 1972	May 25, 1972
Ecuador	Mar 01, 1970	Mar 01, 1970
Egypt	Sep 06, 1955	Aug 01, 1963
El Salvador	Aug 01, 1963	Aug 01, 1963
Ethiopia	Nov 12, 1950	
Fiji[1]	Oct 10, 1970	Oct 10, 1970
Finland	Oct 01, 1937	Aug 23, 1977
France	Feb 13, 1933	Aug 01, 1963
Gabon	May 16, 1969	May 16, 1969
Gambia[3]		
Germany (Demo. Rep.)[4]	Dec 29, 1933	Aug 01, 1963
Germany (Fed. Rep.)[4]	Dec 29, 1933	Aug 01, 1963
Ghana[3]		
Greece	Apr 11, 1938	Sep 21, 1965
Grenada[6]		
Guatemala	Oct 26, 1971	Oct 26, 1971
Guinea	Dec 10, 1961	
Guyana[3]		

STATE	WARSAW CONV.	HAUGUE PROT.
Hungary	Aug 27, 1936	Aug 01, 1963
India[2]*		May 15, 1973
Indonesia[2]		
Iran	Oct 06, 1975	Oct 06, 1975
Iraq	Sep 26, 1972	Sep 26, 1972
Ireland	Dec 13, 1935	Aug 01, 1963
Israel	Jan 06, 1950	Nov 03, 1964
Italy	May 15, 1933	Aug 02, 1963
Ivory Coast[1]*		Aug 01, 1963
Jamaica[3]		
Jordan[2]*		Feb 13, 1974
Kenya[2]		
Kiribati[6]		
Korea (Demo. Rep.)	May 30, 1961	
Korea (Republic of)*		Oct 11, 1967
Kuwait	Nov 09, 1975	Nov 09, 1975
Laos[2]*		Aug 01, 1963
Lebanon[2]*		Aug 08, 1978
Lesotho[2]*		Jan 15, 1976
Liberia	Jul 31, 1942	
Libya	Aug 14, 1969	Aug 14, 1969
Liechtenstein	Aug 07, 1934	Apr 03, 1966
Luxembourg	Jan 05, 1950	Aug 01, 1963
Madagascar[1]*		Aug 01, 1963
Malawi*		Sep 07, 1971
Malaysia[3]*		Dec 19, 1974
Mali	Apr 26, 1961	Mar 29, 1964
Malta[3]		
Mauritania	Nov 04, 1962	
Mauritius[3]		
Mexico	May 15, 1933	Aug 01, 1963
Monaco*		Jul 08, 1979
Mongolia	Jul 29, 1962	
Morocco	Apr 05, 1958	Feb 15, 1976
Nauru[3]		
Nepal	May 13, 1966	May 13, 1966
Netherlands	Sep 29, 1933	Aug 01, 1963
New Zealand	Jul 05, 1937	Jun 14, 1967
Niger[1]*		Aug 01, 1963
Nigeria[2]*		Sep 29, 1969
Norway	Oct 01, 1937	Aug 01, 1963
Oman	Nov 04, 1976	
Pakistan[2]*		Aug 01, 1963
Papua New Guinea[1]		
Paraguay	Nov 26, 1969	Nov 26, 1969
Philippines	Feb 07, 1951	Feb 28, 1967
Poland	Feb 13, 1933	Aug 01, 1963
Portugal	Jun 18, 1947	Dec 15, 1963
Romania	Feb 13, 1933	Aug 01, 1963
Rwanda[2]		
St. Christopher/Nevis[6]		
St. Lucia[6]		
St. Vincent[6]		
Saudi Arabia	Apr 27, 1969	Apr 27, 1969
Senegal	Sep 17, 1964	Sep 17, 1964
Seychelles[6]		
Sierra Leone[2]		
Singapore*	Dec 03, 1971	Feb 04, 1968
Somalia[3]		
South Africa	Mar 22, 1955	Dec 17, 1967
Southern Yemen[3]		
Spain	Feb 13, 1933	Mar 06, 1966
Sri Lanka[2]		
Sudan*		May 12, 1975
Swaziland[3]*		Oct 18, 1971
Sweden	Oct 01, 1937	Aug 01, 1963
Switzerland	Aug 07, 1934	Aug 01, 1963
Syria[5]		
Tanzania	Jul 06, 1965	
Tonga[6]		
Trinidad & Tobago[3]		
Tunisia	Feb 13, 1964	Feb 13, 1964
Turkey	Jun 23, 1978	Jun 23, 1978
Uganda	Oct 22, 1963	
Ukranian SSR	Nov 12, 1959	Aug 01, 1963
Union of Sov. Soc. Rep.	Nov 18, 1934	Aug 01, 1963
United Kingdom[6]	May 15, 1933	Jun 01, 1967
United States	Oct 29, 1934	
Upper Volta	Mar 09, 1962	
Uruguay	Oct 02, 1979	
Venezuela	Sep 13, 1955	Aug 01, 1963
Viet-Nam[7]	Dec 28, 1958	
Western Samoa[2]*		Jan 14, 1973
Yugoslavia	Feb 13, 1933	Aug 01, 1963
Zaire[2]		
Zambia[2]*		June 23, 1970
Zimbabwe[6]		

NOTES AND EXPLANATIONS

* According to Articles XXI and XXIII of the Protocol, adherer to the Protocol by a state which is not a party to the Conventi shall be deemed adherence to the Convention as well.

[1] the state regards itself an adherent to both the Conventi and the Protocol as the result of actions taken prior to independer by the colonial power

[2] the state regards itself an adherent to the Convention the result of actions taken prior to independence by the colonial power

[3] the state has neither affirmed nor denounced adherence the Convention/Protocol as the result of actions taken pri to independence by the colonial power

[4] both the Federal Republic of Germany and the German Democrat Republic regard themselves as adherents to the Convention the result of the commitments made by the German Reich

5 Syria regards itself an adherent to the convention as the result of the adherence of Egypt, with which Syria was once in union as the United Arab Republic

6 the United Kingdom entered into the Convention, with effect from March 3, 1935 on behalf of the following dependant territories, some of which have since become independant states: Akrotiri and Dhekelia [dependencies of Cyprus], Antigua, Bermuda, British Antarctic Territory, British Honduras, British Solomon Islands Protectorate, British Virgin Islands, Brunei, Cayman Islands, Dominica, Falkland Islands and Dependencies, Gibraltar, Gilbert and Ellice Islands [now Kiribati], Grenada, Hong Kong, Montserrat, Rhodesia St. Christopher & Nevis, St. Helena and Ascension, St. Lucia, St. Vincent, Seychelles, Tonga, Turks & Caicos Islands.

7 As a result of commitments made by France, Viet-Nam became and adherant to the Convention, with effect from November 15, 1932. The Republic of [South] Viet-Nam formally acceded to the Convention in 1958; the Socialist Republic of [North] Viet-Nam, while denying the validity of actions taken by the South Viet-Nam, did not repudiate the commitments made by France during the colonial period. The statust of this country is unclear, and id under discussion with the ggovernment of Poland, as depository of the Convention.

the Warsaw Convention if liability limits were not increased. The air carriers, independent of governmental authority, increased the limits to $75,000, inclusive of legal fees, or $58,000 plus fees. (The agreement was stated in terms of U.S. dollars.) The adoption of this plan prevented U.S. repudiation of the Warsaw Convention. Subsequently, many governments formally adopted the $58,000 standard, under a consensus generally known as the Malta Agreement.

The 1971 Guatemala Protocol proposed to increase death and injury liability to 1.5 million gold francs, with delay liability to be increased to 62,500 gold francs. Under this arrangement, liability for effects would increase to 15,000 gold francs per passenger. In 1984 this amendment had not yet come into force.

The 1975 Montreal Protocol Number 3 amends the convention to employ SPECIAL DRAWING RIGHTS *(q.v.)* as the unit of value. In 1984 this agreement had not yet come into force.

Other amendments include Montreal Protocol Number 2, which substitutes special drawing rights for the gold franc in the 1955 Hague Protocol, and Montreal Protocol Number 4 (1975), which permits a carrier defense, in the loss or damage of goods, of inherent vice on the part of the merchandise, acts of war or conflict, or actions of public authority.

The Warsaw Convention, through its amending protocols, effectively imposes upon the carrier a strict liability for the goods carried from initial receipt until final delivery.

The convention limitations of liability do not apply if the apropriate documents of carriage (e.g., air waybill) have not been delivered by the carrier or if the carrier or its employees engaged in gross deviations from sound practice in the care of passengers or cargo or in the operation of the flight.

See GOLD FRANC.

WARSAW PACT. An Eastern European military alliance formed as the Warsaw Treaty Organization by a treaty concluded in Poland in 1945. Membership consists of the USSR, Poland, Czechoslovakia,

Hungary, Romania, German Democratic Republic, and Bulgaria. Albania formally resigned from the group in 1968 after a six-year hiatus in participation. The group is effectively controlled by the Soviet Union, and headquarters are in Moscow.

The ostensible purpose of the pact is to provide for an orchestrated military response to aggression from North Atlantic Treaty Organization members. The alliance provides a legal basis for the maintenance of Soviet military forces in the six satellite nations, thereby permitting significant Soviet leverage in local affairs.

WARSAW TREATY ORGANIZATION. *See* WARSAW PACT.

WASTE CUBE. The space which is not occupied by cargo within a trailer, railcar, or container.

WEATHER PERMITTING. A condition in a vessel charter party that provides that time lost during loading or discharge because of weather conditions shall not count as LAYTIME *(q.v.)*.

WEATHER WORKING DAYS. *See* LAYTIME.

WEBB-POMERANCE ACT. An act of 1918 authorizing exemptions from the SHERMAN ACT *(q.v.)* to certain combinations of firms for the purpose of promoting exports. The combinations formed under the authority of the Webb-Pomerance Act may not engage in acts that would reduce competition in the United States but may fix prices and terms on export sales to enhance competitiveness through reductions of export costs and the achievement of favorable terms derived from combining the economic strengths of the participant firms.

WEIGHT GAINING. An increase in physical bulk or weight of a finished product over that of the component materials as a result of the manufacturing process.

WEIGHT LOSING. A decrease in physical bulk or weight of a finished product over that of the component materials as a result of the manufacturing process.

WEIGHT OR MEASUREMENT. A provision in a carrier's tariff that permits the carrier, in those cases where the tariff provides both weight and measurement rates for the same product, to use either rate at its option. Essentially, the carrier is authorized to use either rate in order to achieve the greatest revenue.

WERNER REPORT. A report on the subject of European integration, prepared by a committee under the leadership of Pierre Werner, prime minister of Luxembourg. The report, published in October 1970, urged full economic and monetary union within the European Economic Community as "a catalyst for the development of the political union which it [the European Economic Community] cannot do without in the long term."

The report suggests adoption of a common European currency as a vehicle to accelerate economic integration. This proposal has been largely implemented through the EUROPEAN MONETARY SYSTEM (q.v.).

WESTERN HEMISPHERE TRADING CORPORATION. A domestic U.S. corporation entitled to certain tax advantages under Sections 921–22 of the Internal Revenue Code. To qualify, a U.S.-chartered corporation must (1) derive at least 95 percent of its gross income for the three-year period immediately preceding the taxable year (or throughout the corporation's existence if less than three years) from sources outside the United States; (2) derive virtually all income from business activities within the Western Hemisphere (other than U.S. sources); and (3) derive at least 90 percent of its income from the active conduct of a trade or business.

Originally, a WHTC was entitled to a deduction computed by deriving the tax the corporation would otherwise pay, then multiplying this figure by a fraction whose numerator was 14 percent and whose denominator equaled the highest rate applicable in Section 115 of the Internal Revenue Code (i.e., the *normal tax,* not including the surcharge). Beginning with taxable years ending December 31, 1975, the deduction was phased out by reducing the numerator percentage as follows:

1976	11%
1977	8%
1978	5%
1979	2%

The tax deduction for WHTC was completely phased out for taxable years beginning after December 31, 1979, as a result of P.L. 94-455, Section 1052(a).

WHARF. A structure, built upon piles, against which a vessel may dock and discharge cargo.

WHARFAGE. A charge imposed by a pier operator for receiving, handling, and transferring cargo to or from a vessel. Customarily, these charges are absorbed by the vessel.

WHETHER IN BERTH OR NOT See BERTH NO BERTH.

WIRE FATE ITEM. A BILL OF EXCHANGE (q.v.) or other collection item sent with instructions to the collecting bank to wire acknowledgment of acceptance/collection or dishonor of the instrument.

WISEMEN'S GROUP. Known formally as the Japan–United States Economic Relations Group, a semi-official committee consisting of four members each from Japan and the United States which considers economic relations between the two countries and makes recommendations to their governments. The group was created by joint agreement between President Carter and the late Prime Minister Ohira in 1979.

While the pronouncements of the group are not binding, the influential character of the persons appointed to serve and the group's utility as a sounding board for topics which cannot be addressed conveniently at the official level, have permitted the group to influence Japan–United States economic issues.

WITHDRAWAL PRICE. A floor price at which European Economic Community producers of certain food products may withhold their goods from the market. The withdrawal price is generally below the *base price* (i.e., the target price set for a given commodity) and the *purchase price* at which EEC governments will intervene in the market to buy commodities selling at distressed prices.

The costs of withholding produce from the market may be borne by the EEC through the medium of the COMMON AGRICULTURAL POLICY (q.v.).

WITH EXCHANGE. See PAYABLE WITH EXCHANGE.

WITHOUT RECOURSE. See ENDORSEMENT.

WORKED LUMBER. Lumber that has been *matched* (as with tongue-and-groove joints), shiplapped, or patterned on a matching machine, sticker, or molder.

WORKING CAPITAL. A measurement of a firm's liquidity, determined by the excess of current assets over current liabilities. The ratio so derived is the *working capital ratio.*

WORKING CAPITAL RATIO. See WORKING CAPITAL.

WORKING DAYS. See LAYTIME.

WORLD BANK GROUP. A group of international financial institutions, affiliated with the United Nations, that works to fund development projects in less developed countries. The group includes the International Bank for Reconstruction and Development (known commonly as the World Bank) and its two affiliates, the International Development Association and the International Finance Corporation. The group does not include the International Centre for Settlement of Investment Disputes, which is a nonfinancial affiliate of the World Bank.

The oldest of the three institutions is the World Bank, which was established under the BRETTON WOODS AGREEMENT (q.v.) in 1944 to mobilize and orchestrate post–World War II economic reconstruction. The World Bank began operations in 1946 and became a specialized agency of the United Nations the following year. Having completed its postwar reconstruction tasks, the bank now devotes most of its efforts to funding development projects (*see* figure, next page).

The bank was originally capitalized with U.S. $6.35 billion; in fiscal 1983, its capital comprised 716,500 shares, with a par value of 100,000 SPECIAL DRAWING RIGHTS (q.v.) each (1 SDR = +/− U.S.

$1.09). Approximately 10 percent of this capital is paid, with the balance subject to call as required by the bank. The bank makes commercially sound loans for periods of fifteen to twenty years at a current interest of 9.25 percent and a commitment fee of .75 percent; grace periods of three to five years are commonly granted.

Financing of long-term projects is undertaken by the International Development Association (IDA). A sister organization of the World Bank, the IDA was established at Washington, D.C., in 1960. Only member states of the World Bank may become members of the IDA, and most have elected to do so. The president, executive directors, and governors of the bank perform like roles in the IDA, which employs no staff, using the staff of the bank instead.

The IDA was formed to address the compelling need for long-term, low-cost financing by the world's poorer countries to establish an economic infrastructure. The construction of railroads and highways, development of agriculture, and dispersal of basic literacy were viewed as essential to a nation's economic base; however, the funding for such projects was inherently long term, and conditions in the recipient countries would not permit early repayment. Inasmuch as the World Bank derives much of its financing from private capital markets, it was decided that a portfolio of "soft" long-term debt instruments from the world's poorest countries would hamper the borrowing capacity of the bank. Unlike World Bank loans, which are usually repaid within twenty years and carry an interest charge, IDA *credits* are granted for up to fifty years, without interest (although a .75 percent administrative fee is imposed); loan repayments do not usually commence for ten years. To be funded, an IDA project must demonstrate that a rate of return of at least 10 percent in real terms is achievable (*see* figure, next page).

The IDA, originally funded by subscriptions from members in proportion to their capital subscriptions in the World Bank membership, is divided into two groups. *Part I countries* consist of the advanced industrial countries, whose subscriptions are paid in convertible currencies, all of which may be used for lending. *Part II countries* are all other members, who contribute 10 percent of their commitment in convertible currencies; the balance is contributed in the member's own currency, which can be used for lending only with the contributing member's consent.

Unlike the World Bank, which provides direct, long-term financing for commercially sound projects, or the IDA, which provides long-term direct concessional financing, the International Finance Corporation (IFC) was organized to promote and channel private investment in developing countries. The IFC was established in 1956 and became a specialized agency of the United Nations in 1957. In 1961 the Articles of Agreement of the IFC were amended to permit direct equity participation in development projects. The first such equity involvement was the underwriting of an equity offering by a Mexican steel mill. While it receives administrative support from the World Bank, the IFC maintains its own operating and legal staffs.

Each of the three institutions enjoys a separate legal identity, although the governors of the World Bank also serve as governors of the IDA and IFC, wherever a nation is a member of three bodies. The institutions are managed by a board of governors, with one governor from each member nation. Routine business is delegated to a board of executive directors.

The following states were members of World Bank Group institutions at the beginning of 1985. Unless otherwise indicated, a nation is a member of all three group components—International Bank for Reconstruction and Development (IBRD); International Development Association (IDA); International Finance Corporation (IFC):

Afghanistan	France
Algeria†	Gabon
Antigua and Barbuda*	Gambia
Argentina	German Federal Republic
Australia	Ghana
Austria	Greece
Bahamas*	Grenada
Bangladesh	Guatemala
Barbados*	Guinea
Belgium	Guinea-Bissau
Belize	Guyana
Benin†	Haiti
Bhutan	Honduras
Bolivia	Hungary*
Botswana	Iceland
Brazil	India
Burkina Fasso	Indonesia
Burma	Iran
Burundi	Iraq
Cameroon	Ireland
Canada	Israel
Cape Verde	Italy
Central African Republic†	Ivory Coast
Chad†	Jamaica*
Chile	Japan
China	Jordan
Colombia	Kampuchea
Comoros†	Kenya
Congo	Korea (Republic of)
Costa Rica	Kuwait
Cyprus	Laos†
Denmark	Lebanon
Djibouti	Lesotho
Dominica	Liberia
Dominican Republic	Libya
Ecuador	Luxembourg
Egypt	Madagascar
El Salvador	Malawi
Equatorial Guinea†	Malaysia
Ethiopia	Maldives
Fiji	Mali
Finland	Malta*

Expressed in United States dollars (in millions)			IBRD loans to borrowers, by region[2]				
Purpose[1]	Eastern Africa	Western Africa	East Asia and Pacific	South Asia	Europe, Middle East, and North Africa	Latin America and the Caribbean	Total
AGRICULTURE AND RURAL DEVELOPMENT							
Agricultural credit	$ 30.0	$ 253.5	$ 326.5	$ 200.0	$ 1,358.3	$ 1,251.9	$ 3,420.2
Agriculture sector loan	5.6	9.0	54.3	26.3	99.7	325.7	520.6
Agroindustry	—	—	145.8	—	828.3	822.9	1,797.0
Area development	155.5	908.4	1,064.4	197.0	859.5	1,767.9	4,952.7
Fisheries	—	—	68.2	14.0	48.0	16.2	146.4
Forestry	70.0	66.0	8.5	—	213.5	22.0	380.0
Irrigation and drainage	78.2	32.0	2,423.0	290.5	1,760.9	1,405.3	5,989.9
Livestock	11.8	32.6	48.0	10.0	226.0	991.0	1,319.4
Perennial crops	57.4	437.5	999.4	—	108.0	89.0	1,691.3
Research and extension	13.1	—	318.1	25.0	84.9	363.0	804.1
Total	$ 421.6	$1,739.0	$ 5,456.2	$ 762.8	$ 5,587.1	$ 7,054.9	$ 21,021.6
DEVELOPMENT FINANCE COMPANIES	$ 314.9	$ 239.3	$ 2,425.5	$1,126.2	$ 3,404.3	$ 2,415.7	$ 9,925.9
EDUCATION	$ 157.1	$ 155.6	$ 1,518.5	$ —	$ 1,148.1	$ 709.7	$ 3,689.0
ENERGY							
Oil, gas, and coal	$ 30.6	$ 131.5	$ 997.0	$1,589.5	$ 848.8	$ 292.5	$ 3,889.9
Power	997.1	571.0	4,275.8	2,170.6	3,144.0	7,164.3	18,322.8
Total	$1,027.7	$ 702.5	$ 5,272.8	$3,760.1	$ 3,992.8	$ 7,456.8	$ 22,212.7
INDUSTRY							
Engineering	$ —	$ —	$ 10.0	$ —	$ 11.0	$ 9.5	$ 30.5
Fertilizer and other chemicals	—	—	193.9	723.1	481.4	583.5	1,981.9
Industry sector loan	5.1	0.6	322.4	212.0	901.7	302.8	1,744.6
Iron and steel	—	20.0	—	189.0	512.8	667.0	1,388.8
Mining, other extractive	212.5	191.0	—	—	181.2	532.5	1,117.2
Paper and pulp	30.0	12.0	5.5	104.2	204.0	20.0	375.7
Textiles	63.0	—	157.4	—	307.3	—	527.7
Total	$ 310.6	$ 223.6	$ 689.2	$1,228.3	$ 2,599.4	$ 2,115.3	$ 7,166.4
NONPROJECT	$ 412.9	$ 510.7	$ 1,879.3	$ 60.0	$ 3,075.9[3]	$ 558.6	$ 6,497.4
POPULATION, HEALTH, AND NUTRITION	$ 11.0	$ —	$ 176.5	$ —	$ 29.0	$ 164.8	$ 381.3
SMALL-SCALE ENTERPRISES	$ —	$ 140.7	$ 572.4	$ —	$ 276.0	$ 1,185.6	$ 2,174.7
TECHNICAL ASSISTANCE	$ 6.0	$ 74.0	$ 13.0	$ —	$ 8.8	$ 54.3	$ 156.1
TELECOMMUNICATIONS	$ 166.3	$ 61.8	$ 381.9	$ 267.5	$ 427.8	$ 463.3	$ 1,768.6
TOURISM	$ 17.0	$ 37.5	$ 25.0	$ —	$ 96.6	$ 187.5	$ 363.6
TRANSPORTATION							
Airlines and airports	$ 49.0	$ 10.0	$ 9.2	$ 5.6	$ 7.0	$ 218.5	$ 299.3
Highways	455.3	704.4	2,759.1	39.9	2,156.8	3,964.7	10,080.2
Pipelines	—	—	—	37.0	57.5	23.3	117.8
Ports and waterways	84.9	194.8	715.3	359.8	1,138.3	355.3	2,848.4
Railways	490.2	183.8	968.4	1,035.8	852.5	1,338.5	4,869.2
Transportation sector loan	28.0	25.0	261.2	—	137.0	47.8	499.0
Total	$1,107.4	$1,118.0	$ 4,713.2	$1,478.1	$ 4,349.1	$ 5,948.1	$ 18,713.9
URBANIZATION	$ 126.0	$ 132.8	$ 900.9	$ 49.1	$ 354.0	$ 1,133.7	$ 2,696.5
WATER SUPPLY AND SEWERAGE	$ 161.2	$ 295.5	$ 826.1	$ —	$ 1,548.8	$ 1,966.1	$ 4,797.7
GRAND TOTAL	$4,239.7	$5,431.0	$24,850.5	$8,732.1	$26,897.7	$31,414.4	$101,565.4

[1] Operations have been classified by the major purpose they finance. Many projects include activity in more than one sector or subsector.

[2] Except for the total amount shown in footnote 4. no account is taken of cancellations and refundings subsequent to original commitment. Amounts of cancellations and refundings are shown by country and purpose in the Statement of Loans and of Development Credits. IBRD loans of $1,267.7 million to IFC are excluded.

IBRD and IDA Lending, by Region

Eastern Africa	Western Africa	East Asia and Pacific	South Asia	Europe, Middle East, and North Africa	Latin America and the Caribbean	Total	IBRD and IDA total
$ 189.5	$ 42.4	$ 118.7	$ 1,717.9	$ 104.2	$ 23.5	$ 2,196.2	$ 5,616.4
28.0	4.5	77.7	150.0	—	—	260.2	780.8
293.5	—	—	404.9	63.0	10.0	771.4	2,568.4
572.2	495.2	192.3	659.0	90.7	51.1	2,060.5	7.013.2
38.5	1.3	10.0	55.7	54.1	—	159.6	306.0
119.8	54.3	—	331.2	—	4.0	509.3	889.3
429.2	130.9	271.2	3,704.5	395.7	18.5	4,950.0	10,939.9
200.7	100.0	10.6	90.6	49.5	67.5	518.9	1,838.3
150.6	156.5	266.8	126.0	15.0	3.2	718.1	2,409.4
25.5	19.5	75.5	394.6	6.0	—	521.1	1,325.2
$2,047.5	$1,004.6	$1,022.8	$ 7,634.4	$ 778.2	$177.8	$12,665.3	$ 33,686.9
$ 245.9	$ 67.0	$ 143.0	$ 364.5	$ 93.0	$ 27.2	$ 940.6	$ 10,866.5
$ 613.4	$ 289.6	$ 480.3	$ 261.6	$ 271.3	$ 57.6	$ 1,973.8	$ 5,662.8
$ 146.3	$ 90.0	$ 3.0	$ 154.2	$ 74.0	$ 18.0	$ 485.5	$ 4,375.4
259.8	130.0	126.0	2,937.3	261.4	133.8	3,848.3	22,171.1
$ 406.1	$ 220.0	$ 129.0	$ 3,091.5	$ 335.4	$151.8	$ 4,333.8	$ 26,546.5
$ 4.3	$ —	$ —	$ —	$ —	$ —	$ 4.3	$ 34.8
4.0	21.0	35.0	895.0	21.4	—	976.4	2,958.3
1.2	6.9	—	28.5	18.7	—	55.3	1,799.9
—	—	—	—	—	—	—	1,388.8
13.5	7.4	—	16.0	—	7.5	44.4	1,161.6
50.0	—	—	—	—	—	50.0	425.7
20.0	—	—	29.7	7.0	—	56.7	584.4
$ 93.0	$ 35.3	$ 35.0	$ 969.2	$ 47.1	$ 7.5	$ 1,187.1	$ 8,353.5
$ 517.5	$ 186.0	$ —	$ 2,756.6	$ 35.0	$ 22.0	$ 3,517.1	$ 10,014.5
$ 44.6	$ 31.7	$ 171.3	$ 234.2	$ 57.7	$ ---	$ 539.5	$ 920.8
$ 19.2	$ 63.5	$ 40.0	$ 226.0	$ 2.3	$ —	$ 351.0	$ 2,525.7
$ 124.2	$ 124.6	$ 35.0	$ 93.5	$ 6.9	$ —	$ 384.2	$ 540.3
$ 101.6	$ 44.6	$ 12.8	$ 804.2	$ 83.0	$ —	$ 1,046.2	$ 2,814.8
$ 14.0	$ 4.0	$ 16.0	$ 4.2	$ 48.5	$ —	$ 86.7	$ 450.3
$ 9.0	$ 5.0	$ —	$ —	$ 2.5	$ —	$ 16.5	$ 315.8
1,054.3	701.3	120.4	315.4	155.1	147.3	2,493.8	12,574.0
—	—	—	—	—	—	—	117.8
143.2	110.5	19.9	293.3	9.2	16.0	592.1	3,440.5
138.0	129.6	40.0	1.034.2	38.5	8.0	1,388.3	6.257.5
15.0	—	—	38.5	—	—	53.5	552.5
$1,359.5	$ 946.4	$ 180.3	$ 1,681.4	$ 205.3	$171.3	$ 4,544.2	$ 23,258.1
$ 132.3	$ 66.4	$ —	$ 432.0	$ 50.3	$ 75.0	$ 756.0	$ 3,452.5
$ 166.6	$ 84.3	$ 26.4	$ 833.4	$ 199.1	$ 18.6	$ 1,328.4	$ 6,126.1
$5,885.4	$3,168.0	$2,291.9	$19,386.7	$2,213.1	$708.8	$33,654.0	$135,219.4[4]

[3] Includes $497 million in European reconstruction loans made before 1952.

[4] Cancellations, terminations, and refundings amount to $3,627.3 million for the IBRD and $710.7 million for IDA, totaling $4,338.0 million. This amount includes $46.1 million of loans and $175.8 million of credits made to Pakistan in earlier years for development projects in its former eastern wing, now Bangladesh. The loans and credits were reactivated, in revised form, as commitments to Bangladesh.

IBRD Credits, by Region

Mauritania	Somalia
Mauritius	South Africa
Mexico	Spain
Morocco	Sri Lanka
Nepal	Sudan
Netherlands	Surinam*
New Zealand	Swaziland
Nicaragua	Sweden
Niger	Syria
Nigeria	Tanzania
Norway	Thailand
Oman	Togo
Pakistan	Trinidad and Tobago
Panama	Tunisia
Papua New Guinea	Turkey
Paraguay	Uganda
Peru	United Arab Emirates
Philippines	United Kingdom
Portugal*	United States
Qatar*	Uruguay*
Romania*	Vanuatu
Rwanda	Venezuela*
St. Lucia	Vietnam
St. Vincent†	Western Samoa
Sao Tome and Principe†	Yemen Arab Republic
Saudi Arabia	Yemen (People's
Senegal	Democratic Republic)†
Seychelles*	Yugoslavia
Sierra Leone	Zaire
Singapore*	Zambia
Solomon Islands	Zimbabwe

*Member of IBRD only
† Member of IBRD and IDA only

WORLD INTELLECTUAL PROPERTY OR-GANIZATION.

A specialized agency of the United Nations charged with fostering international agreements to protect rights to intellectual property, with the object of facilitating international technology transfer.

WIPO serves as the nucleus for new international agreements relating to patents, trademarks, copyrights, and related areas, and promotes wider acceptance of existing agreements. In addition, WIPO aids developing countries in establishing local laws and agencies to protect and promote intellectual property.

WIPO administers the following international agreements:

Industrial property. PARIS CONVENTION *(q.v.)* for the Protection of Industrial Property; MADRID AGREEMENT FOR THE REPRESSION OF FALSE OR DECEPTIVE INDICATIONS OF SOURCE ON GOODS *(q.v.)*; MADRID AGREEMENT CONCERNING THE INTERNATIONAL REGISTRATION OF MARKS *(q.v.)*; The HAGUE AGREEMENT *(q.v.)* Concerning the International Deposit of Industrial Designs; Nice Agreement Concerning the International Classification of Goods and Services for the Purposes of the Registration of Marks; LISBON AGREEMENT FOR THE PROTECTION OF APPELLATIONS OF ORIGIN AND THEIR INTERNATIONAL REGISTRATION *(q.v.)*; Locarno Agreement Establishing an International Classification for Industrial

Designs; PATENT COOPERATION TREATY *(q.v.)*; INTERNATIONAL PATENT CLASSIFICATION AGREEMENT *(q.v.)*; TRADEMARK REGISTRATION TREATY *(q.v.)*; Vienna Agreement Establishing an International Classification of the Figurative Elements of Marks; Vienna Agreement for the Protection of Type Faces and their International Deposit; Budapest Treaty on the International Recognition of the Deposit of Microorganisms for the Purposes of Patent Procedure; Geneva Treaty on the International Recording of Scientific Discoveries; NAIROBI TREATY ON THE PROTECTION OF THE OLYMPIC SYMBOL *(q.v.)*.

Copyrights and related rights. Berne Convention for the Protection of Literary and Artistic Works; Rome Convention for the Protection of Performers, Producers of Phonograms and Broadcasting Organizations; Geneva Convention for the Protection of Producers of Phonograms against Unauthorized Duplication of Their Phonograms; Brussels Convention Relating to the Distribution of Programme-Carrying Signals Transmitted by Satellite; Madrid Multilateral Convention for the Avoidance of Double Taxation of Copyright Royalties.

The secretariat of WIPO is located in Geneva. The following states were members on April 30, 1984:

Algeria	Honduras
Argentina	Hungary
Australia	India
Austria	Indonesia
Bahamas	Iraq
Barbados	Ireland
Belgium	Israel
Benin	Italy
Brazil	Ivory Coast
Bulgaria	Jamaica
Burundi	Japan
Byelorussian SSR	Jordan
Cameroon	Kenya
Canada	Korea (North)
Central African Republic	Korea (South)
Chad	Libya
Chile	Liechtenstein
China	Luxembourg
Colombia	Malawi
Congo	Mali
Costa Rica	Malta
Czechoslovakia	Mauritania
Denmark	Mauritius
Egypt	Mexico
El Savador	Monaco
Fiji	Mongolia
Finland	Morocco
France	Netherlands
Gabon	New Zealand
Gambia	Niger
German Democratic	Norway
Republic	Pakistan
German Federal Republic	Panama
Ghana	Peru
Greece	Philippines
Guatemala	Poland
Guinea	Portugal
Holy See	Qatar

Romania	Turkey
Rwanda	U.S.S.R.
Saudi Arabia	Uganda
Senegal	Ukrainian SSR
Somalia	United Arab Emirates
South Africa	United Kingdom
Spain	United States
Sri Lanka	Upper Volta
Sudan	Uruguay
Surinam	Vietnam
Sweden	Yemen
Switzerland	Yugoslavia
Tanzania	Zaire
Togo	Zambia
Tunisia	Zimbabwe

WORLD PRICE. The price at which a given commodity is selling internationally under market conditions in effect at the time of sale. To provide a valid comparison between prices, the world price quoted must normally include quality, location, and perhaps other factors, depending upon the commodity.

WORLDSCALE. A schedule, published semiannually on January 1 and July 1 as the *Worldwide Tanker Nominal Freight Scale,* which lists all world petroleum ports and a nominal freight rate for the movement of petroleum products between any two ports. The nominal rate listed between any two ports is known as *worldscale flat* or *worldscale 100,* and all tanker rates are quoted as a percentage of the worldscale rate. For example, the worldscale 100 rate from Kuwait to Rotterdam might be $15 per ton, and a vessel fixed (i.e., chartered) to make that run at $12 per ton, the fixture would be reported as worldscale 80, which is to say 80 percent (12/15) of the nominal rate.

All worldscale rates are based upon movement of a fully loaded vessel of 19,500 long tons from loading port to discharging port and back to loading port without regard to geographical rotation. Certain other factors, such as fuel consumption, summer draft in salt water, and average speed, are used to calculate the standard vessel upon which the nominal rate is predicated.

Originally, worldscale rates were quoted in both U.S. dollars and pounds sterling; from January 1, 1972, all rates are quoted in dollars only. Worldscale replaces the International Tanker Nominal Freight Scale issued in London and the American Tanker Rate Schedule issued in New York.

Worldscale is published by Worldscale Association, with offices in New York and London.

WORLD TRADE DATA REPORT. A service provided to American manufacturers by the International Trade Administration of the U.S. Department of Commerce as a stimulus to exports. For a fee of forty dollars, an American exporter may secure from the International Trade Administration a report on a potential trading partner. The report typically includes background information on the firm, including year established and number of employees; area and volume of sales activity; list of products offered; and U.S. embassy commercial officer's comments.

World trade data reports may be obtained by completing Department of Commerce form ITA-431, available from any office of the International Trade Administration. Reports are not available for firms in the United States, Puerto Rico, or U.S. possessions, or any Soviet bloc country. *See* Appendix C2 for a full list of district offices of the International Trade Administration.

WOWO. *See* WALK-ON/WALK-OFF.

Y

YANKEE BONDS. U.S.-dollar-denominated debt obligations issued by entities outside the United States.

YORK-ANTWERP RULES. An organized body of rules relating to the adjustment of claims arising in GENERAL AVERAGE *(q.v.).* The rules were originally promulgated by world shipping interests in 1890, with revisions and supplements in 1924, 1950, and 1974. The York-Antwerp rules do not enjoy formal status as law but are incorporated into virtually all bills of lading.

YO-YO EFFECT. A condition that arises under the rules of FINANCIAL ACCOUNTING STANDARDS BOARD STATEMENT NO. 8 *(q.v.)* when a foreign company's total monetary assets differ from its total monetary liabilities. Specifically, FASB 8 requires that non-monetary assets (e.g., plant and equipment) be translated at the *historical* rate, i.e., the exchange values in effect at the time assets were acquired. Monetary assets and liabilities, such as cash, receivables, payables, et cetera, are converted as current exchange rates.

Inasmuch as exchange rates are fluctuating continuously, and different rates are used in translating monetary and nonmonetary items, a yo-yo effect may occur in valuing a company's foreign position. Changes in value resulting from exchange rate fluctuations are incorporated into the firm's income statement as a gain or loss.

See also FINANCIAL ACCOUNTING STANDARDS BOARD STATEMENT NO. 52.

YUGEN KAISHA. A form of limited company organization used in Japan for small or family-controlled corporations. This form, usually identified by the letters *YK*, resembles the American closed corporation and usually includes restrictions on the transfer of stock. A large or public company is usually organized as a KABUSHIKI KAISHA *(q.v.).*

Z

ZAIBATSU. Industrial and financial combines that arose in Japan in the late nineteenth century and dominated the Japanese economy until the end of World War II. Prior to their dissolution by the Allied powers after the war, the four big *zaibatsu* (Mitsui, Mitsubishi, Sumitomo, and Yasuda) collectively controlled almost 25 percent of the paid-up capital of all firms, including more than 32 percent of heavy industries and almost 50 percent of all financial institutions.

As part of a program of democratization and as a stimulus to Japanese industry, the *zaibatsu* were broken up by the occupation authorities. The Antimonopoly Law of 1947 was adopted to prevent a recurrence of *zaibatsu*-type combines; the act precluded interlocking directorates and significant certified holding companies, and prohibited domination of the financial sector by any firm or group of firms. The act has since been relaxed, giving rise to corporate families, known as *keiritsu*.

ZERO HAVEN. A tax haven country that levies no taxes (or virtually no taxes) on income. Examples of such jurisdictions are the Bahamas, Cayman Islands, and Saint Vincent.

ZONE DELIVERED PRICING. A pricing strategy whereby a supplier equalizes freight on shipments to all customers within a defined geographic area. This mechanism, by applying a uniform FOB delivered price to all customers, or by granting a freight allowance to each customer, effectively offsets differences in freight costs within the defined zone.

ZONE RESTRICTED STATUS. A condition accorded to goods entered into a FOREIGN TRADE ZONE *(q.v.)* solely for destruction or exportation to another country. These goods may not be manipulated or processed in any way; re-entry into the customs territory of the United States for consumption is prohibited except upon a finding by the Foreign Trade Zones Board that such a re-entry is in the public interest.

Entry of merchandise into a foreign trade zone as zone-restricted merchandise is the full legal equivalent of exportation, and the goods may remain in the zone pending actual disposal. The status may be conveyed upon application to the district director of customs.

Z THEORY. *See* THEORY Z.

APPENDICES

APPENDIX A: STATUTES

1. LIMITED LIABILITY STATUTE (46 U.S.C. §§ 181, 183-189); FIRE STATUTE (46 U.S.C. § 182)

§ 181 Liability of masters as carriers.

If any shipper of platina, gold, gold dust, silver, bullion, or other precious metals, coins, jewelry, bills of any bank or public body, diamonds, or other precious stones, or any gold or silver in a manufactured or unmanufactured state, watches, clocks, or timepieces of any description, trinkets, orders, notes, or securities for payment of money, stamps, maps, writings, title deeds, printings, engravings, pictures, gold or silver plate or plated articles, glass, china, silks in a manufactured or unmanufactured state, and whether wrought up or not wrought up with any other material, furs, or lace, or any of them, contained in any parcel, or package, or trunk, shall lade the same as freight or baggage, on any vessel, without at the time of such lading giving to the master, clerk, agent, or owner of such vessel receiving the same a written notice of the true character and value thereof, and having the same entered on the bill of lading therefor, the master and owner of such vessel shall not be liable as carriers thereof in any form or manner; nor shall any such master or owner be liable for any such goods beyond the value and according to the character thereof so notified and entered. (R. S. § 4281.)

§ 182 Loss by fire.

No owner of any vessel shall be liable to answer for or make good to any person any loss or damage, which may happen to any merchandise whatsoever, which shall be shipped, taken in, or put on board any such vessel, by reason or by means of any fire happening to or on board the vessel, unless such fire is caused by the design or neglect of such owner. (R. S. § 4282.)

§ 183 Amount of liability; loss of life or bodily injury; privity imputed to owner; "seagoing vessel."

(a) The liability of the owner of any vessel, whether American or foreign, for any embezzlement, loss, or destruction by any person of any property, goods, or merchandise shipped or put on board of such vessel, or for any loss, damage, or injury by collision, or for any act, matter, or thing, loss, damage, or forfeiture, done, occasioned, or incurred, without the privity or knowledge of such owner or owners, shall not, except in the cases provided for in subsection (b) of this section, exceed the amount or value of the interest of such owner in such vessel, and her freight then pending.

(b) In the case of any seagoing vessel, if the amount of the owner's liability as limited under subsection (a) of this section is insufficient to pay all losses in full, and the portion of such amount applicable to the payment of losses in respect of loss of life or bodily injury is less than $60 per ton of such vessel's tonnage, such portion shall be increased to an amount equal to $60 per ton, to be available only for the payment of losses in respect of loss of life or bodily injury. If such portion so increased is insufficient to pay such losses in full, they shall be paid therefrom in proportion to their respective amounts.

(c) For the purposes of this section the tonnage of a seagoing steam or motor vessel shall be her gross tonnage without deduction on account of engine room, and the tonnage of a seagoing sailing vessel shall be her registered tonnage: *Provided*, That there shall not be included in such tonnage any space occupied by seamen or apprentices and appropriated to their use.

(d) The owner of any such seagoing vessel shall be liable in respect of loss of life or bodily injury arising on distinct occasions to the same extent as if no other loss of life or bodily injury had arisen.

(e) In respect of loss of life or bodily injury the privity or knowledge of the master of a seagoing vessel or of the superintendent or managing agent of the owner thereof, at or prior to the commencement of each voyage, shall be deemed conclusively the privity or knowledge of the owner of such vessel.

(f) As used in subsections (b), (c), (d), and (e) of this section and in section 183b of this title, the term "seagoing vessel" shall not include pleasure yachts, tugs, towboats, towing vessels, tank vessels, fishing vessels or their tenders, self-propelled lighters, nondescript self-propelled vessels, canal boats, scows, car floats, barges, lighters, or nondescript non-self-propelled vessels, even though the same may be seagoing vessels within the meaning of such term as used in section 188 of this title.

§ 183b   Stipulations limiting time for filing claims and commencing suit.

(a) It shall be unlawful for the manager, agent, master, or owner of any sea-going vessel (other than tugs, barges, fishing vessels and their tenders) transporting passengers or merchandise or property from or between ports of the United States and foreign ports to provide by rule, contract, regulation, or otherwise a shorter period for giving notice of, or filing claims for loss of life or bodily injury, than six months, and for the institution of suits on such claims, than one year, such period for institution of suits to be computed from the day when the death or injury occurred.

(b) Failure to give such notice, where lawfully prescribed in such contract, shall not bar any such claim—

(1) If the owner or master of the vessel or his agent had knowledge of the injury, damage, or loss and the court determines that the owner has not been prejudiced by the failure to give such notice; nor

(2) If the court excuses failure on the ground that for some satisfactory reason such notice could not be given; nor

(3) Unless objection to such failure is raised by the owner.

(c) If a person who is entitled to recover on any such claim is mentally incompetent or a minor, or if the action is one for wrongful death, any lawful limitation of time prescribed in such contract shall not be applicable so long as no legal representative has been appointed for such incompetent, minor, or decedent's estate, but shall be applicable from the date of the appointment of such legal representative: *Provided, however,* That such appointment be made within three years after the date of such death or injury.

§ 183c   Stipulations limiting liability for negligence invalid.

It shall be unlawful for the manager, agent, master, or owner of any vessel transporting passengers between ports of the United States or between any such port and a foreign port to insert in any rule, regulation, contract, or agreement any provision or limitation (1) purporting, in the event of loss of life or bodily injury arising from the negligence or fault of such owner or his servants, to relieve such owner, master, or agent from liability, or from liability beyond any stipulated amount, for such loss or injury, or (2) purporting in such event to lessen, weaken, or avoid the right of any claimant to a trial by court of competent jurisdiction on the question of liability for such loss or injury, or the measure of damages therefor. All such provisions or limitations contained in any such rule, regulation, contract, or agreement are declared to be against public policy and shall be null and void and of no effect.

§ 184   Apportionment of compensation.

Whenever any such embezzlement, loss, or destruction is suffered by several freighters or owners of goods, wares, merchandise, or any property whatever, on the same voyage, and the whole value of the vessel, and her freight for the voyage, is not sufficient to make compensation to each of them, they shall receive compensation from the owner of the vessel in proportion to their respective losses; and for that purpose the freighters and owners of the property, and the owner of the vessel, or any of them, may take the appropriate proceedings in any court, for the purpose of apportioning the sum for which the owner of the vessel may be liable among the parties entitled thereto.

§ 185   Petition for limitation of liability; deposit of value of interest in court; transfer of interest to trustee.

The vessel owner, within six months after a claimant shall have given to or filed with such owner written notice of claim, may petition a district court of the United States of competent jurisdiction for limitation of liability within the provisions of this chapter and the owner (a) shall deposit with the court, for the benefit of claimants, a sum equal to the amount or value of the interest of such owner in the vessel and freight, or approved security therefor, and in addition such sums, or approved security therefor, as the court may from time to time fix as necessary to carry out the provisions of section 183 of this title, or (b) at his option shall transfer, for the benefit of claimants, to a trustee to be appointed by the court his interest in the vessel and freight, together with such sums, or approved security therefor, as the court may from time to time fix as necessary to carry out the provisions of section 183 of this title. Upon compliance with the requirements of this section all claims and proceedings against the owner with respect to the matter in question shall cease.

§ 186   Charterer may be deemed owner.

The charterer of any vessel, in case he shall man, victual, and navigate such vessel at his own expense, or by his own procurement, shall be deemed the owner of such vessel within the meaning of the provisions of this chapter relating to the limitation of the liability of the owners of vessels; and such vessel, when so chartered, shall be liable in the same manner as if navigated by the owner thereof.

§ 187   Remedies reserved.

Nothing in sections 182, 183, 184, 185 and 186 of this title shall be construed to take away or affect the remedy to which any party may be entitled, against the master, officers, or seamen, for or on account of any embezzlement, injury, loss, or destruction of merchandise, or property, put on board any vessel, or on account of any negligence, fraud, or other malversation of such master, officers, or seamen, respectively, nor to lessen or take away any responsibility to which any master or seaman of any vessel may by law be liable, notwithstanding such master or seaman may be an owner or part owner of the vessel.

§ 188   Limitation of liability of owners applied to all vessels.

Except as otherwise specifically provided therein, the provisions of sections 182, 183, 183b to 187, and 189 of this title shall apply to all seagoing vessels, and also to all vessels used on lakes or rivers or in inland navigation, including canal boats, barges, and lighters.

§ 189   Limitation of liability of owners of vessels for debts.

The individual liability of a shipowner shall be limited to the proportion of any or all debts and liabilities that his individual share of the vessel bears to the whole; and the aggregate liabilities of all the owners of a vessel on account of the same shall not exceed the value of such vessels and freight pending: *Provided,* That this provision shall not prevent any claimant from joining all the owners in one action; nor shall the same apply to wages due to persons employed by said shipowners.

2. THE HARTER ACT (46 U.S.C. §§190-196)

§ 190 Stipulations relieving from liability for negligence.

It shall not be lawful for the manager, agent, master, or owner of any vessel transporting merchandise or property from or between ports of the United States and foreign ports to insert in any bill of lading or shipping document any clause, covenant, or agreement whereby it, he, or they shall be relieved from liability for loss or damage arising from negligence, fault, or failure in proper loading, stowage, custody, care, or proper delivery of any and all lawful merchandise or property committed to its or their charge. Any and all words or clauses of such import inserted in bills of lading or shipping receipts shall be null and void and of no effect.

§ 191 Stipulations relieving from exercise of due diligence in equipping vessels.

It shall not be lawful for any vessel transporting merchandise or property from or between ports of the United States of America and foreign ports, her owner, master, agent, or manager, to insert in any bill of lading or shipping document any covenant or agreement whereby the obligations of the owner or owners of said vessel to exercise due diligence, [to] properly equip, man, provision, and outfit said vessel, and to make said vessel seaworthy and capable of performing her intended voyage, or whereby the obligations of the master, officers, agents, or servants to carefully handle and stow her cargo and to care for and properly deliver same, shall in any wise be lessened, weakened, or avoided.

§ 192 Limitation of liability for errors of navigation, dangers of the sea and acts of God.

If the owner of any vessel transporting merchandise or property to or from any port in the United States of America shall exercise due diligence to make the said vessel in all respects seaworthy and properly manned, equipped, and supplied, neither the vessel, her owner or owners, agent, or charterers, shall become or be held responsible for damage or loss resulting from faults or errors in navigation or in the management of said vessel nor shall the vessel, her owner or owners, charterers, agent, or master be held liable for losses arising from dangers of the sea or other navigable waters, acts of God,

or public enemies, or the inherent defect, quality, or vice of the thing carried, or from insufficiency of package, or seizure under legal process, or for loss resulting from any act or omission of the shipper or owner of the goods, his agent or representative, or from saving or attempting to save life or property at sea, of from any deviation in rendering such service.

§ 193 Bills of lading to be issued; contents.

It shall be the duty of the owner or owners, masters, or agent of any vessel transporting merchandise or property from or between ports of the United States and foreign ports to issue to shippers of any lawful merchandise a bill of lading, or shipping document, stating, among other things, the marks necessary for identification, number of packages, or quantity, stating whether it be carrier's or shipper's weight, and apparent order or condition of such merchandise or property delivered to and received by the owner, master, or agent of the vessel for transportation, and such document shall be prima facie evidence of the receipt of the merchandise therein described.

§ 194 Penalties; liens; recovery.

For a violation of any of the provisions of sections 190 to 193 of this title the agent, owner, or master of the vessel guilty of such violation, and who refuses to issue on demand the bill of lading provided for, shall be liable to a fine not exceeding $2,000. The amount of the fine and costs for such violation shall be a lien upon the vessel, whose agent, owner, or master is guilty of such violation, and such vessel may be libeled therefor in any district court of the United States, within whose jurisdiction the vessel may be found. One-half of such penalty shall go to the party injured by such violation and the remainder to the Government of the United States.

§ 195 Certain provisions inapplicable to transportation of live animals.

Sections 190 and 193 of this title shall not apply to the transportation of live animals.

§ 196 Certain laws unaffected.

Sections 190 to 195 of this title shall not be held to modify or repeal sections 181 to 183 of this title, or any other statute defining the liability of vessels, their owners, or representatives.

3. CARRIAGE OF GOODS BY SEA ACT (COGSA) (46 U.S.C. §§ 1300-1315)

§ 1300   Bills of lading subject to chapter.

Every bill of lading or similar document of title which is evidence of a contract for the carriage of goods by sea to or from ports of the United States, in foreign trade, shall have effect subject to the provisions of this chapter.

§ 1301   Definitions.

When used in this chapter—

(a) The term "carrier" includes the owner or the charterer who enters into a contract of carriage with a shipper.

(b) The term "contract of carriage" applies only to contracts of carriage covered by a bill of lading or any similar document of title, insofar as such document relates to the carriage of goods by sea, including any bill of lading or any similar document as aforesaid issued under or pursuant to a charter party from the moment at which such bill of lading or similar document of title regulates the relations between a carrier and a holder of the same.

(c) The term "goods" includes goods, wares, merchandise, and articles of every kind whatsoever, except live animals and cargo which by the contract of carriage is stated as being carried on deck and is so carried.

(d) The term "ship" means any vessel used for the carriage of goods by sea.

(e) The term "carriage of goods" covers the period from the time when the goods are loaded on to the time when they are discharged from the ship.

§ 1302   Duties and rights of carrier.

Subject to the provisions of section 1306 of this title, under every contract of carriage of goods by sea, the carrier in relation to the loading, handling, stowage, carriage, custody, care, and discharge of such goods, shall be subject to the responsibilities and liabilities and entitled to the rights and immunities set forth in sections 1303 and 1304 of this title.

§ 1303   Responsibilities and liabilities of carrier and ship.

[1]—Seaworthiness.

The carrier shall be bound, before and at the beginning of the voyage, to exercise due diligence to—

(a) Make the ship seaworthy;

(b) Properly man, equip, and supply the ship;

(c) Make the holds, refrigerating and cooling chambers, and all other parts of the ship in which goods are carried, fit and safe for their reception, carriage, and preservation.

[2]—Cargo.

The carrier shall properly and carefully load, handle, stow, carry, keep, care for, and discharge the goods carried.

[3]—Contents of bill.

After receiving the goods into his charge the carrier, or the master or agent of the carrier, shall, on demand of the shipper, issue to the shipper a bill of lading showing among other things—

(a) The leading marks necessary for identification of the goods as the same are furnished in writing by the shipper before the loading of such goods starts, provided such marks are stamped or otherwise shown clearly upon the goods if uncovered, or on the cases or coverings in which such goods are contained, in such a manner as should ordinarily remain legible until the end of the voyage.

(b) Either the number of packages or pieces, or the quantity or weight, as the case may be, as furnished in writing by the shipper.

(c) The apparent order and condition of the goods: *Provided,* That no carrier, master, or agent of the carrier, shall be bound to state or show in the bill of lading any marks, number, quantity, or weight which he has reasonable ground for suspecting not accurately to represent the goods actually received, or which he has had no reasonable means of checking.

[4]—Bill as prima facie evidence.

Such a bill of lading shall be prima facie evidence of the receipt by the carrier of the goods as therein described in accordance with paragraphs (3) (a), (b), and (c), of this section: *Provided,* That nothing in this chapter shall be construed as repealing or limiting the application of any part of sections 81 to 124 of Title 49.

[5]—Guaranty of statements.

The shipper shall be deemed to have guaranteed to the carrier the accuracy at the time of shipment of the marks, number, quantity, and weight, as furnished by him; and the shipper shall indemnify the carrier against all loss, damages, and expenses arising or resulting from inaccuracies in such particulars. The right of the carrier to such indemnity shall in no way limit his responsibility and liability under the contract of carriage to any person other than the shipper.

[6]—Notice of loss or damage; limitation of actions.

Unless notice of loss or damage and the general nature of such loss or damage be given in writing to the carrier or his agent at the port of discharge before or at the time of the removal of the goods into the custody of the person entitled to delivery thereof under the contract of carriage, such removal shall be prima facie evidence of the delivery by the carrier of the goods as described in the bill of lading. If the loss or damage is not apparent, the notice must be given within three days of the delivery.

Said notice of loss or damage may be endorsed upon the receipt for the goods given by the person taking delivery thereof.

The notice in writing need not be given if the state of the goods has at the time of their receipt been the subject of joint survey or inspection.

In any event the carrier and the ship shall be discharged from all liability in respect of loss or damage unless suit is brought within one year after delivery of the goods or the date when the goods should have been delivered: *Provided*, That if a notice of loss or damage, either apparent or concealed, is not given as provided for in this section, that fact shall not affect or prejudice the right of the shipper to bring suit within one year after the delivery of the goods or the date when the goods should have been delivered.

In the case of any actual or apprehended loss or damage the carrier and the receiver shall give all reasonable facilities to each other for inspecting and tallying the goods.

[7]—"Shipped" bill of lading.

After the goods are loaded the bill of lading to be issued by the carrier, master, or agent of the carrier to the shipper shall, if the shipper so demands, be a "shipped" bill of lading: *Provided*, That if the shipper shall have previously taken up any document of title to such goods, he shall surrender the same as against the issue of the "shipped" bill of lading, but at the option of the carrier such document of title may be noted at the port of shipment by the carrier, master, or agent with the name or names of the ship or ships upon which the goods have been shipped and the date or dates of shipment, and when so noted the same shall for the purpose of this section be deemed to constitute a "shipped" bill of lading.

[8]—Limitation of liability for negligence.

Any clause, covenant, or agreement in a contract of carriage relieving the carrier or the ship from liability for loss or damage to or in connection with the goods, arising from negligence, fault, or failure in the duties and obligations provided in this section, or lessening such liability otherwise than as provided in this chapter, shall be null and void and of no effect. A benefit of insurance in favor of the carrier, or similar clause, shall be deemed to be a clause relieving the carrier from liability.

§ 1304 Rights and immunities of carrier and ship.

[1]—Unseaworthiness.

Neither the carrier nor the ship shall be liable for loss or damage arising or resulting from unseaworthiness unless caused by want of due diligence on the part of the carrier to make the ship seaworthy, and to secure that the ship is properly manned, equipped, and supplied, and to make the holds, refrigerating and cool chambers, and all other parts of the ship in which goods are carried fit and safe for their reception, carriage, and preservation in accordance with the provisions of paragraph (1) of section 1303 of this title. Whenever loss or damage has resulted from unseaworthiness, the burden of proving the exercise of due diligence shall be on the carrier or other persons claiming exemption under this section.

[2]—Uncontrollable causes of loss.

Neither the carrier nor the ship shall be responsible for loss or damage arising or resulting from—

(a) Act, neglect, or default of the master, mariner, pilot, or the servants of the carrier in the navigation or in the management of the ship;

(b) Fire, unless caused by the actual fault or privity of the carrier;

(c) Perils, dangers, and accidents of the sea or other navigable waters;

(d) Act of God;

(e) Act of war;

(f) Act of public enemies;

(g) Arrest or restraint of princes, rulers, or people, or seizure under legal process;

(h) Quarantine restrictions;

(i) Act or omission of the shipper or owner of the goods, his agent or representative;

(j) Strikes or lockouts or stoppage or restraint of labor from whatever cause, whether partial or general: *Provided*, That nothing herein contained shall be construed to relieve a carrier from responsibility for the carrier's own acts;

(k) Riots and civil commotions;

(l) Saving or attempting to save life or property at sea;

(m) Wastage in bulk or weight or any other loss or damage arising from inherent defect, quality, or vice of the goods;

(n) Insufficiency of packing;

(o) Insufficiency or inadequacy of marks;

(p) Latent defects not discoverable by due diligence; and

(q) Any other cause arising without the actual fault and privity of the carrier and without the fault or neglect of the agents or servants of the carrier, but the burden of proof shall be on the person claiming the benefit of this exception to show that neither the actual fault or privity of the carrier nor the fault or neglect of the agents or servants of the carrier contributed to the loss or damage.

[3]—Freedom from negligence.

The shipper shall not be responsible for loss or damage sustained by the carrier or the ship arising or resulting from any cause without the act, fault, or neglect of the shipper, his agents, or his servants.

[4]—Deviations.

Any deviation in saving or attempting to save life or property at sea, or any reasonable deviation shall not be deemed to be an infringement or breach of this chapter or of the contract of carriage, and the carrier shall not be liable for any loss or damage resulting therefrom: *Provided, however*, That if the deviation is for the purpose of loading or unloading cargo or passengers it shall, prima facie, be regarded as unreasonable.

[5]—Amount of liability; valuation of cargo.

Neither the carrier nor the ship shall in any event be or become liable for any loss or damage to or in connection with the transportation of goods in an amount exceeding $500 per package lawful money of the United States, or in case of goods not shipped in packages, per customary freight unit, or the equivalent of that sum in other currency, unless the nature and value of such goods have been declared by the shipper before shipment and inserted in the bill of lading. This declaration, if embodied in the bill of lading, shall be prima facie evidence, but shall not be conclusive on the carrier.

By agreement between the carrier, master, or agent of the carrier, and the shipper another maximum amount than that mentioned in this paragraph may be fixed: *Provided,* That such maximum shall not be less than the figure above named. In no event shall the carrier be liable for more than the amount of damage actually sustained.

Neither the carrier nor the ship shall be responsible in any event for loss or damage to or in connection with the transportation of the goods if the nature or value thereof has been knowlingly and fraudulently misstated by the shipper in the bill of lading.

[6]—Inflammable, explosive, or dangerous cargo.

Goods of an inflammable, explosive, or dangerous nature to the shipment whereof the carrier, master or agent of the carrier, has not consented with knowledge of their nature and character, may at any time before discharge be landed at any place or destroyed or rendered innocuous by the carrier without compensation, and the shipper of such goods shall be liable for all damages and expenses directly or indirectly arising out of or resulting from such shipment. If any such goods shipped with such knowledge and consent shall become a danger to the ship or cargo, they may in like manner be landed at any place, or destroyed or rendered innocuous by the carrier without liability on the part of the carrier except to general average, if any.

§ 1305 Surrender of rights; increase of liabilities; charter parties; general average.

A carrier shall be at liberty to surrender in whole or in part all or any of his rights and immunities or to increase any of his responsibilities under this chapter, provided such surrender or increase shall be embodied in the bill of lading issued to the shipper.

The provisions of this chapter shall not be applicable to charter parties; but if bills of lading are issued to a shipper under a charter party, they shall comply with the terms of this chapter. Nothing in this chapter shall be held to prevent insertion in a bill of lading any lawful provision regarding general average.

2§ 1306 Special agreement as to particular goods.

Notwithstanding the provisions of sections 1303 to 1305 of this title, a carrier, master or agent of the carrier, and a shipper shall, in regard to any particular goods be at liberty to enter into any agreement in any terms as to the responsibility and liability of the carrier for such goods, and as to the rights and immunities of the carrier in respect of such goods, or his obligation as to seaworthiness (so far as the stipulation regarding seaworthiness is not contrary to public policy), or the care or diligence of his servants or agents in regard to the loading, handling, stowage, carriage, custody, care, and discharge of the goods carried by sea: *Provided,* That in this case no bill of lading has been or shall be issued and that the terms agreed shall be embodied in a receipt which shall be a nonnegotiable document and shall be marked as such.

Any agreement so entered into shall have full legal effect: *Provided,* That this section shall not apply to ordinary commercial shipments made in the ordinary course of trade but only to other shipments where the character or condition of the property to be carried or the circumstances, terms, and conditions under which the carriage is to be performed are such as reasonably to justify a special agreement.

§ 1307 Agreement as to liability prior to loading or after discharge.

Nothing contained in this chapter shall prevent a carrier or a shipper from entering into any agreement, stipulation, condition, reservation, or exemption as to the responsibility and liability of the carrier or the ship for the loss or damage to or in connection with the custody and care and handling of goods prior to the loading on and subsequent to the discharge from the ship on which the goods are carried by sea.

§ 1308 Rights and liabilities under other provisions.

The provisions of this chapter shall not affect the rights and obligations of the carrier under the provisions of the Shipping Act, 1916, or under the provisions of sections 175, 181 to 183, and 183b to 188 of this title or of any amendments thereto; or under the provisions of any other enactment for the time being in force relating to the limitation of the liability of the owners of seagoing vessels.

§ 1309 Discrimination between competing shippers.

Nothing contained in this chapter shall be construed as permitting a common carrier by water to discriminate between competing shippers similarly placed in time and circumstances, either (a) with respect to their right to demand and receive bills of lading subject to the provisions of this chapter; or (b) when issuing such bills of lading, either in the surrender of any of the carrier's rights and immunities or in the increase of any of the carrier's responsibilities and liabilities pursuant to section 1305 of this title: or (c) in any other way prohibited by the Shipping Act, 1916, as amended.

§ 1310 Weight of bulk cargo.

Where under the customs of any trade the weight of any bulk cargo inserted in the bill of lading is a weight ascertained or accepted by a third party other than the carrier or the shipper, and the fact that the weight is so ascertained or accepted is stated in the bill of lading, then, notwithstanding anything in this chapter, the bill of lading shall not be deemed to be prima facie evidence against the carrier of the receipt of goods of the weight so inserted in the bill of lading, and the accuracy thereof at the time of shipment shall not be deemed to have been guaranteed by the shipper.

§ 1311 Liabilities before loading and after discharge; effect on other laws.

Nothing in this chapter shall be construed as superseding any part of sections 190 to 196 of this title, or of any other law which would be applicable in the absence of this chapter, insofar as they relate to the duties, responsibilities, and liabilities of the ship or carrier prior to the time when the goods are loaded on or after the time they are discharged from the ship.

§ 1312   Scope of chapter; "United States"; "foreign trade."

This chapter shall apply to all contracts for carriage of goods by sea to or from ports of the United States in foreign trade. As used in this chapter the term "United States" includes its districts, territories, and possessions. The term "foreign trade" means the transportation of goods between the ports of the United States and ports of foreign countries. Nothing in this chapter shall be held to apply to contracts for carriage of goods by sea between any port of the United States or its possessions, and any other port of the United States or its possessions: *Provided, however*, That any bill of lading or similar document of title which is evidence of a contract for the carriage of goods by sea between such ports, containing an express statement that it shall be subject to the provisions of this chapter, shall be subjected hereto as fully as if subject hereto by the express provisions of this chapter: *Provided further,* That every bill of lading or similar document of title which is evidence of a contract for the carriage of goods by sea from ports of the United States, in foreign trade, shall contain a statement that it shall have effect subject to the provisions of this chapter.

§ 1313   Suspension of provisions by President.

Upon the certification of the Secretary of Transportation that the foreign commerce of the United States in its competition with that of foreign nations is prejudiced by the provisions, or any of them, of sections 1301 to 1308 of this title, or by the laws of any foreign country or countries relating to the carriage of goods by sea, the President of the United States may, from time to time, by proclamation, suspend any or all provisions of said sections for such periods of time or indefinitely as may be designated in the proclamation. The President may at any time rescind such suspension of said sections, and any provisions thereof which may have been suspended shall thereby be reinstated and again apply to contracts thereafter made for the carriage of goods by sea. Any proclamation of suspension or rescission of any such suspension shall take effect on a date named therein, which date shall be not less than ten days from the issue of the proclamation.

Any contract for the carriage of goods by sea, subject to the provisions of this chapter, effective during any period when sections 1301 to 1308 of this title, or any part thereof, are suspended, shall be subject to all provisions of law now or hereafter applicable to that part of said sections which may have thus been suspended.

§ 1314   Effective date; retroactive effect.

This chapter shall take effect ninety days after April 16, 1936; but nothing in this chapter shall apply during a period not to exceed one year following April 16, 1936, to any contract for the carriage of goods by sea, made before April 16, 1936, nor to any bill of lading or similar document of title issued, whether before or after such date in pursuance of any such contract as aforesaid.

§ 1315   Short title.

This chapter may be cited as the "Carriage of Goods by Sea Act."

4. FEDERAL BILLS OF LADING ACT (POMERENE ACT)
(49 U.S.C. §§ 81-124)

§ 81   Transportation included.

Bills of lading issued by any common carrier for the transportation of goods in any Territory of the United States, or the District of Columbia, or from a place in a State to a place in a foreign country, or from a place in one State to a place in another State, or from a place in one State to a place in the same State through another State or foreign country, shall be governed by this chapter.

§ 82   Straight bill of lading.

A bill in which it is stated that the goods are consigned or destined to a specified person is a straight bill.

§ 83   Order bill of lading; negotiability.

A bill in which it is stated that the goods are consigned or destined to the order of any person named in such bill is an order bill. Any provision in such a bill or in any notice, contract, rule, regulation, or tariff that is nonnegotiable shall be null and void and shall not affect its negotiability within the meaning of this chapter unless upon its face and in writing agreed to by the shipper.

§ 84   Order bills in parts or sets; liability of carrier.

Order bills issued in a State for the transportation of goods to any place in the United States on the Continent of North America, except Alaska and Panama, shall not be issued in parts or sets. If so issued, the carrier issuing them shall be liable for failure to deliver the goods described therein to anyone who purchases a part for value in good faith, even though the purchase be after the delivery of the goods by the carrier to a holder of one of the other parts: *Provided, however,* That nothing contained in this section shall be interpreted or construed to forbid the issuing of order bills in parts or sets for such transportation of goods to Alaska, Panama, Puerto Rico, Hawaii, or foreign countries, or to impose the liabilities set forth in this section for so doing.

§ 85   Indorsement on duplicate bill; liability.

When more than one order bill is issued in a State for the same goods to be transported to any place in the United States on the Continent of North America, except Alaska and Panama, the word "duplicate", or some other word or words indicating that the document is not an original bill, shall be placed plainly upon the face of every such bill except the one first issued. A carrier shall be liable for the damage caused by his failure so to do to anyone who has purchased the bill for value in good faith as an original, even though the purchase be after the delivery of the goods by the carrier to the holder of the original bill: *Provided, however,* That nothing contained in this section shall in such case for such transportation of goods to Alaska, Panama, Puerto Rico, Hawaii, or foreign countries be interpreted or construed so as to require the placing of the word "duplicate" thereon, or to impose the liabilities set forth in this section for failure so to do.

§ 86   Indorsement on straight bill.

A straight bill shall have placed plainly upon its face by the carrier issuing it "nonnegotiable" or "not negotiable."

This section shall not apply, however, to memoranda or acknowledgments of an informal character.

§ 87   Effect of insertion of name of person to be notified.

The insertion in an order bill of the name of a person to be notified of the arrival of the goods shall not limit the negotiability of the bill or constitute notice to a purchaser thereof of any rights or equities of such person in the goods.

§ 88   Duty to deliver goods on demand; refusal.

A carrier, in the absence of some lawful excuse, is bound to deliver goods upon a demand made either by the consignee named in the bill for the goods or, if the bill is an order bill, by the holder thereof, if such a demand is accompanied by—

(a) An offer in good faith to satisfy the carrier's lawful lien upon the goods;

(b) Possession of the bill of lading and an offer in good faith to surrender, properly indorsed, the bill which was issued for the goods, if the bill is an order bill; and

(c) A readiness and willingness to sign, when the goods are delivered, an acknowledgment that they have been delivered, if such signature is requested by the carrier.

In case the carrier refuses or fails to deliver the goods, in compliance with a demand by the consignee or holder so accompanied, the burden shall be upon the carrier to establish the existence of a lawful excuse for such refusal or failure.

§ 89   Delivery; when justified.

A carrier is justified, subject to the provisions of sections 90 to 92 of this title, in delivering goods to one who is—

(a) A person lawfully entitled to the possession of the goods, or

(b) The consignee named in a straight bill for the goods, or

(c) A person in possession of an order bill for the goods, by the terms of which the goods are deliverable to his order; or which has been indorsed to him, or in blank by the consignee, or by the mediate or immediate indorsee of the consignee.

§ 90   Liability for delivery to person not entitled thereto.

Where a carrier delivers goods to one who is not lawfully entitled to the possession of them, the carrier shall be liable to anyone having a right of property or possession in the goods if he delivered the goods otherwise than as authorized by subdivisions (b) and (c) of section 89 of this title; and, though he delivered the goods as authorized by either of said subdivisions, he shall be so liable if prior to such delivery he—

(a) Had been requested, by or on behalf of a person having a right of property or possession in the goods, not to make such delivery, or

(b) Had information at the time of the delivery that it was to a person not lawfully entitled to the possession of the goods.

Such request or information, to be effective within the meaning of this section, must be given to an officer or agent of the carrier, the actual or apparent scope of whose duties includes action upon such a request or information, and must be given in time to enable the officer or agent to whom it is given, acting with reasonable diligence, to stop delivery of the goods.

§ 91   Liability for delivery without cancellation of bill.

Except as provided in section 106 of this title, and except when compelled by legal process, if a carrier delivers goods for which an order bill had been issued, the negotiation of which would transfer the right to the possession of the goods, and fails to take up and cancel the bill, such carrier shall be liable for failure to deliver the goods to anyone who for value and in good faith purchases such bill, whether such purchaser acquired title to the bill before or after the delivery of the goods by the carrier and notwithstanding delivery was made to the person entitled thereto.

§ 92   Liability in case of delivery of part of goods.

Except as provided in section 106 of this title, and except when compelled by legal process, if a carrier delivers part of the goods for which an order bill had been issued and fails either—

(a) To take up and cancel the bill, or

(b) To place plainly upon it a statement that a portion of the goods has been delivered with a description which may be in general terms either of the goods or packages that have been so delivered or of the goods or packages which still remain in the carrier's possession, he shall be liable for failure to deliver all the goods specified in the bill to anyone who for value and in good faith purchases it, whether such purchaser acquired title to it before or after the delivery of any portion of the goods by the carrier, and notwithstanding such delivery was made to the person entitled thereto.

§ 93   Alteration of bill.

Any alteration, addition, or erasure in a bill after its issue without authority from the carrier issuing the same either in writing or noted on the bill, shall be void whatever be the nature and purpose of the change, and the bill shall be enforceable according to its original tenor.

§ 94   Loss, etc., of bill; delivery of goods on order of court.

Where an order bill has been lost, stolen, or destroyed a court of competent jurisdiction may order the delivery of the goods upon satisfactory proof of such loss, theft, or destruction and upon the giving of a bond, with sufficient surety, to be approved by the court, to protect the carrier or any person injured by such delivery from any liability or loss incurred by reason of the original bill remaining outstanding. The court may also in its discretion order the payment of the carrier's reasonable costs and counsel fees: *Provided,* A voluntary indemnifying bond without order of court shall be binding on the parties thereto.

The delivery of the goods under an order of the court, as provided in this section, shall not relieve the carrier from liability to a person to whom the order bill has been or shall be negotiated for value without notice of the proceedings or of the delivery of the goods.

§ 95   Liability on bill marked "duplicate."

A bill, upon the face of which the word "duplicate" or some other word or words indicating that the document is not an original bill is placed, plainly shall impose upon the carrier issuing the same the liability of one who represents and warrants that such bill is an accurate copy of an original bill properly issued, but no other liability.

§ 96   Claim of title as excuse for refusal to deliver.

No title to goods or right to their possession asserted by a carrier for his own benefit shall excuse him from liability for refusing to deliver the goods according to the terms of a bill issued for them, unless such title or right is derived directly or indirectly from a transfer made by the consignor or consignee after the shipment, or from the carrier's lien.

§ 97   Interpleader of conflicting claimants.

If more than one person claim the title or possession of goods, the carrier may require all known claimants to interplead, either as a defense to an action brought against him for nondelivery of the goods or as an original suit, whichever is appropriate.

§ 98   Reasonable time for procedure allowed in case of adverse claim.

If someone other than the consignee or the person in possession of the bill has a claim to the title or possession of the goods, and the carrier has information of such claim, the carrier shall be excused from liability for refusing to deliver the goods, either to the consignee or person in possession of the bill or to the adverse claimant, until the carrier has had a reasonable time to ascertain the validity of the adverse claim or to bring legal proceedings to compel all claimants to interplead.

§ 99   Failure to deliver; claim of third person as defense.

Except as provided in sections 89, 97, and 98 of this title, no right or title of a third person, unless enforced by legal process, shall be a defense to an action brought by the consignee of a straight bill or by the holder of an order bill against the carrier for failure to deliver the goods on demand.

§ 100   Loading by carrier; counting packages, etc.; contents of bill.

When goods if loaded by a carrier, such carrier shall count the packages of goods if package freight, and ascertain the kind and quantity if bulk freight, and such carrier shall not, in such cases, insert in the bill of lading or in any notice, receipt, contract, rule, regulation, or tariff, "Shipper's weight, load, and count", or other words of like purport, indicating that the goods were loaded by the shipper and the description of them made by him, or in case of bulk freight and freight not concealed by packages the description made by him. If so inserted contrary to the provisions of this section, said words shall be treated as null and void and as if not inserted therein.

§ 101   Loading by shipper; contents of bill; ascertainment of kind and quantity on request.

When package freight or bulk freight is loaded by a shipper and the goods are described in a bill of lading merely by a statement of marks or labels upon them or upon packages containing them, or by a statement that the goods are said to be goods of a certain kind or quantity, or in a certain condition, or it is stated in the bill of lading that packages are said to contain goods of a certain kind or quantity or in a certain condition, or that the contents or condition of the contents of packages are unknown, or words of like purport are contained in the bill of lading, such statements, if true, shall not make liable the carrier issuing the bill of lading, although the goods are not of the kind or quantity or in the condition which the marks or labels upon them indicate, or of the kind or quantity or in the condition they were said to be by the consignor. The carrier may also by inserting in the bill of lading the words "Shipper's weight, load, and count," or other words of like purport, indicate that the goods were loaded by the shipper and the description of them made by him; and if such statement be true, the carrier shall not be liable for damages caused by the improper loading or by the nonreceipt or by the misdescription of the goods described in the bill of lading: *Provided, however,* Where the shipper of bulk freight installs and maintains adequate facilities for weighing such freight, and the same are available to the carrier, then the carrier, upon written request of such shipper and when given a reasonable opportunity so to do, shall ascertain the kind and quantity of bulk freight within a reasonable time after such written request, and the carriers shall not in such cases insert in the bill of lading the words "Shipper's weight," or other words of like purport, and if so inserted contrary to the provisions of this section, said words shall be treated as null and void and as if not inserted therein.

§ 102   Liability for nonreceipt or misdescription of goods.

If a bill of lading has been issued by a carrier or on his behalf by an agent or employee the scope of whose actual or apparent authority includes the receiving of goods and issuing bills of lading therefor for transportation in commerce among the several States and with foreign nations, the carrier shall be liable to (a) the owner of goods covered by a straight bill subject to existing right of stoppage in transitu or (b) the holder of an order bill, who has given value in good faith, relying upon the description therein of the goods, or upon the shipment being made upon the date therein shown, for damages caused by the nonreceipt by the carrier of all or part of the goods upon or prior to the date therein shown, or their failure to correspond with the description thereof in the bill at the time of its issue.

§ 103   Attachment, etc., of goods delivered to carrier.

If goods are delivered to a carrier by the owner or by a person whose act in conveying the title to them to a purchaser for value in good faith would bind the owner, and an order bill is issued for them, they can not thereafter, while in the possession of the carrier, be attached by garnishment or otherwise or be levied upon under an execution unless the bill be first surrendered to the carrier or its negotiation enjoined. The carrier shall in no such case be compelled to deliver the actual possession of the goods until the bill is surrendered to him or impounded by the court.

§ 104   Remedies of creditor of owner of order bill.

A creditor whose debtor is the owner of an order bill shall be entitled to such aid from courts of appropriate jurisdiction by injunction and otherwise in attaching such bill or in satisfying the claim by means thereof as is allowed at law or in equity in regard to property which cannot readily be attached or levied upon by ordinary legal process.

§ 105   Lien of carrier.

If an order bill is issued the carrier shall have a lien on the goods therein mentioned for all charges on those goods for freight, storage, demurrage and terminal charges, and expenses necessary for the preservation of the goods or incident to their transportation subsequent to the date of the bill and all other charges incurred in transportation and delivery, unless the bill expressly enumerates other charges for which a lien is claimed. In such case there shall also be a lien for the charges enumerated so far as they are allowed by law and the contract between the consignor and the carrier.

§ 106   Liability after sale to satisfy lien, etc.

After goods have been lawfully sold to satisfy a carrier's lien, or because they have not been claimed, or because they are perishable or hazardous, the carrier shall not thereafter be liable for failure to deliver the goods themselves to the consignee or owner of the goods, or to a holder of the bill given for the goods when they were shipped, even if such bill be an order bill.

§ 107   Negotiation of order bill by delivery.

An order bill may be negotiated by delivery where, by the terms of the bill, the carrier undertakes to deliver the goods to the order of a specified person, and such person or a subsequent indorsee of the bill has indorsed it in blank.

§ 108   Negotiation of order bill by indorsement.

An order bill may be negotiated by the indorsement of the person to whose order the goods are deliverable by the tenor of the bill. Such indorsement may be in blank or to a specified person. If indorsed to a specified person, it may be negotiated again by the indorsement of such person in blank or to another specified person. Subsequent negotiation may be made in like manner.

§ 109 Transfer of bill by delivery; negotiation of straight bill.

A bill may be transferred by the holder by delivery, accompanied with an agreement, express or implied, to transfer the title to the bill or to the goods represented thereby. A straight bill can not be negotiated free from existing equities, and the indorsement of such a bill gives the transferee no additional right.

§ 110 Negotiation of order bill by person in possession.

An order bill may be negotiated by any person in possession of the same, however such possession may have been acquired, if by the terms of the bill the carrier undertakes to deliver the goods to the order of such person, or if at the time of negotiation the bill is in such form that it may be negotiated by delivery.

§ 111 Title and right acquired by transferee of order bill.

A person to whom an order bill has been duly negotiated acquires thereby—

(a) Such title to the goods as the person negotiating the bill to him had or had ability to convey to a purchaser in good faith for value, and also such title to the goods as the consignee and consignor had or had power to convey to a purchaser in good faith for value; and

(b) The direct obligation of the carrier to hold possession of the goods for him according to the terms of the bill as fully as if the carrier had contracted directly with him.

§ 112 Rights of transferee of bill without negotiation; notice to carrier.

A person to whom a bill has been transferred, but not negotiated, acquires thereby as against the transferor the title to the goods, subject to the terms of any agreement with the transferor. If the bill is a straight bill such person also acquires the right to notify the carrier of the transfer to him of such bill and thereby to become the direct obligee of whatever obligations the carrier owed to the transferor of the bill immediately before the notification.

Prior to the notification of the carrier by the transferor or transferee of a straight bill the title of the transferee to the goods and the right to acquire the obligation of the carrier may be defeated by garnishment or by attachment or execution upon the goods by a creditor of the transferor, or by a notification to the carrier by the transferor or a subsequent purchaser from the transferor of a subsequent sale of the goods by the transferor.

A carrier has not received notification within the meaning of this section unless an officer or agent of the carrier, the actual or apparent scope of whose duties includes action upon such a notification, has been notified; and no notification shall be effective until the officer or agent to whom it is given has had time, with the exercise of reasonable diligence, to communicate with the agent or agents having actual possession or control of the goods.

§ 113 Compelling indorsement of order bill transferred by delivery.

Where an order bill is transferred for value by delivery, and the indorsement of the transferor is essential for negotiation, the transferee acquires a right against the transferor to compel him to indorse the bill, unless a contrary intention appears. The negotiation shall take effect as of the time when the indorsement is actually made. This obligation may be specifically enforced.

§ 114 Warranties arising out of transfer of bill.

A person who negotiates or transfers for value a bill by indorsement or delivery, unless a contrary intention appears, warrants—

(a) That the bill is genuine;

(b) That he has a legal right to transfer it;

(c) That he has knowledge of no fact which would impair the validity or worth of the bill;

(d) That he has a right to transfer the title to the goods, and that the goods are merchantable or fit for a particular purpose whenever such warranties would have been implied if the contract of the parties had been to transfer without a bill the goods represented thereby.

§ 115 Liability of indorser of bill.

The indorsement of a bill shall not make the indorser liable for any failure on the part of the carrier or previous indorsers of the bill to fulfill their respective obligations.

§ 116 Warranties by mortgagee, etc., receiving payment of bill.

A mortgagee or pledgee or other holder of a bill for security who in good faith demands or receives payment of the debt for which such bill is security, whether from a party to a draft drawn for such debt or from any other person, shall not be deemed by so doing to represent or warrant the genuineness of such bill or the quantity or quality of the goods therein described.

§ 117 Negotiation of bill; impairment of validity.

The validity of the negotiation of a bill is not impaired by the fact that such negotiation was a breach of duty on the part of the person making the negotiation, or by the fact that the owner of the bill was deprived of the possession of the same by fraud, accident, mistake, duress, loss, theft, or conversion, if the person to whom the bill was negotiated, or a person to whom the bill was subsequently negotiated, gave value therefor in good faith, without notice of the breach of duty, or fraud, accident, mistake, duress, loss, theft, or conversion.

§ 118 Negotiation of bill by seller, mortgagor, etc., to person without notice.

Where a person, having sold, mortgaged, or pledged goods which are in a carrier's possession and for which an order bill has been issued, or having sold, mortgaged, or pledged the order bill representing such goods, continues in possession of the order bill the subsequent negotiation thereof by that person under any sale, pledge, or other disposition thereof to any person receiving the same in good faith, for value and without notice of the previous sale, shall have the same effect as if the first purchaser of the goods or bill had expressly authorized the subsequent negotiation.

§ 119 Rights of bona fide purchaser as affected by seller's lien or right of stoppage.

Where an order bill has been issued for goods no seller's lien or right of stoppage in transitu shall defeat the rights of any purchaser for value in good faith to whom such bill has been negotiated, whether such negotiation be prior or subsequent to the notification to the carrier who issued such bill of the seller's claim to a lien or right of stoppage in transitu. Nor shall the carrier be obliged to deliver or justified in delivering the goods to an unpaid seller unless such bill is first surrendered for cancellation.

§ 120   Rights of mortgagee or lien holder; limitation.

Except as provided in section 119 of this title, nothing in this chapter shall limit the rights and remedies of a mortgagee or lien holder whose mortgage or lien on goods would be valid, apart from this chapter, as against one who for value and in good faith purchased from the owner, immediately prior to the time of their delivery to the carrier, the goods which are subject to the mortgage or lien and obtained possession of them.

§ 121   Offenses; penalty.

Any person who, knowingly or with intent to defraud, falsely makes, alters, forges, counterfeits, prints or photographs any bill of lading purporting to represent goods received for shipment among the several States or with foreign nations, or with like intent utters or publishes as true and genuine any such falsely altered, forged, counterfeited, falsely printed or photographed bill of lading, knowing it to be falsely altered, forged, counterfeited, falsely printed or photographed, or aids in making, altering, forging, counterfeiting, printing or photographing, or uttering or publishing the same, or issues or aids in issuing or procuring the issue of, or negotiates or transfers for value a bill which contains a false statement as to the receipt of the goods, or as to any other matter, or who, with intent to defraud, violates, or fails to comply with, or aids in any violation of, or failure to comply with any provision of this chapter, shall be guilty of a misdemeanor, and, upon conviction, shall be punished for each offense by imprisonment not exceeding five years, or by a fine not exceeding $5,000, or both.

§ 122   Terms defined.

In this chapter, unless the context of subject matter otherwise requires—

"Action" includes counterclaim, set-off, and suit in equity.

"Bill" means bill of lading, governed by this chapter.

"Consignee" means the person named in the bill as the person to whom delivery of the goods is to be made.

"Consignor" means the person named in the bill as the person from whom the goods have been received for shipment.

"Goods" means the merchandise or chattels in course of transportation or which have been or are about to be transported.

"Holder" of a bill means a person who has both actual possession of such bill and a right of property therein.

"Order" means an order by indorsement on the bill.

"Person" includes a corporation or partnership, or two or more persons having a joint or common interest.

To "purchase" includes to take as mortgagee and to take as pledgee.

"State" includes any Territory, District, insular possession, or isthmian possession.

§ 123   Retroactive effect.*

§ 124   Invalidity of part of chapter.

The provisions and each part therof and the sections and each part thereof of this chapter are independent and severable, and the declaring of any provision or part thereof, or provisions or part therof, or section or part thereof, or sections or part thereof, unconstitutional shall not impair or render unconstitutional any other provision or part thereof or section or part thereof

*Section, act Aug. 29, 1916, ch. 415, § 43, 39 Stat. 545, provided that provisions of this chapter should not apply to bills made and delivered prior to January 1, 1917.

Omitted as obsolete.

5. SHIPPING ACT OF 1916, as amended

(46 U.S.C. Appendix §§ 801-842)

Including amendments made by the Shipping Act of 1984 and PL 98-595

§ 801   Terms defined.

When used in this Act:

The term "common carrier by water in interstate commerce" means a common carrier engaged in the transportation by water of passengers or property on the high seas or the Great Lakes on regular routes from port to port between one State, Territory, District, or possession of the United States and any other State, Territory, District, or possession of the United States, or between places in the same Territory, District, or possession.

The term "other person subject to this chapter" means any person not included in the term "common carrier by water in interstate commerce," carrying on the business of forwarding or furnishing wharfage, dock, warehouse, or other terminal facilities in connection with a common carrier by water in interstate commerce.

The term "person" includes corporations, partnerships, and associations, existing under or authorized by the laws of the United States, or any State, Territory, District, or possession thereof, or of any foreign country.

The term "vessel" includes all water craft and other artificial contrivances of whatever description and at whatever stage of construction, whether on the stocks or launched, which are used or are capable of being or are intended to be used as a means of transportation on water.

The term "documented under the laws of the United States," means "registered, enrolled, or licensed under the laws of the United States."

The term "carrying on the business of forwarding" means the dispatching of shipments by any person on behalf of others, by oceangoing common carriers in commerce between the United States and its Territories or possessions, or between such Territories and possessions, and handling the formalities incident to such shipments.

The term "maritime labor agreement" means any collective bargaining agreement between an employer subject to this chapter, or a group of such employers and a labor organization representing employees in the maritime or stevedoring industry, or any agreement preparatory to such a collective bargaining agreement among members of a multiemployer bargaining group, or any agreement specifying provisions of such a collective bargaining agreement or providing for the formation, financing, or administration of a multiemployer bargaining group.

§ 802   Corporation, partnership, or association as citizen.

(a) Within the meaning of this chapter no corporation, partnership, or association shall be deemed a citizen of the United States unless the controlling interest therein is owned by citizens of the United States, and, in the case of a corporation, unless its president or other chief executive officer and the chairman of its board of directors are citizens of the United States and unless no more of its directors than a minority of the number necessary to constitute a quorum are noncitizens and the corporation itself is organized under the laws of the United States or of a State, Territory, District, or possession thereof, but in the case of a corporation, association, or partnership operating any vessel in the coastwise trade the amount of interest required to be owned by citizens of the United States shall be 75 per centum.

(b) The controlling interest in a corporation shall not be deemed to be owned by citizens of the United States (a) if the title to a majority of the stock thereof is not vested in such citizens free from any trust or fiduciary obligation in favor of any person not a citizen of the United States; or (b) if the majority of the voting power in such corporation is not vested in citizens of the United States; or (c) if through any contract or understanding it is so arranged that the majority of the voting power may be exercised, directly or indirectly, in behalf of any person who is not a citizen of the United States; or (d) if by any other means whatsoever control of the corporation is conferred upon or permitted to be exercised by any person who is not a citizen of the United States.

(c) Seventy-five per centum of the interest in a corporation shall not be deemed to be owned by citizens of the United States (a) if the title to 75 per centum of the shares is not vested in such citizens free from any trust or fiduciary obligation in favor of any person not a citizen of the United States; or (b) if 75 per centum of the voting power in such corporation is not vested in such citizens of the United States; or (c) if, through any contract or understanding, it is so arranged that more than 25 per centum of the voting power in such corporation may be exercised,

directly or indirectly, in behalf of any person who is not a citizen of the United States; or (d) if by any other means whatsoever control of any interest in the corporation in excess of 25 per centum is conferred upon or permitted to be exercised by any person who is not a citizen of the United States.

§ 803   Applicability to receivers and trustees.

The provisions of this Act shall apply to receivers and trustees of all persons to whom the Act applies, and to the successors or assignees of such persons.

§ 804   Federal Maritime Commission; rules and regulations for filing of rates and charges for barging and affreighting of containers or containerized cargo by barges within the United States.

Notwithstanding part III of the Interstate Commerce Act, as amended (49 U.S.C. 901 et seq. [former 49 USCS §§901 et seq.]), or any other provision of law, rates and charges for the barging and affreighting of containers or containerized cargo by barge between points in the United States, shall be filed solely with the Federal Maritime Commission in accordance with rules and regulations promulgated by the Commission where (a) the cargo is moving between a point in a foreign country or a non-contiguous State, territory, or possession and a point in the United States, (b) the transportation by barge between points in the United States is furnished by a terminal operator as a service substitute in lieu of a direct vessel call by the common carrier by water transporting the containers or containerized cargo under a through bill of lading, (c) such terminal operator is a Pacific Slope State, municipality, or other public body or agency subject to the jurisdiction of the Federal Maritime Commission, and the only one furnishing the particular circumscribed barge service in question as of the date of enactment hereof [enacted Jan. 2, 1975], and (d) such terminal operator is in compliance with the rules and regulations of the Federal Maritime Commission for the operation of such barge service. The terminal operator providing such services shall be subject to the provisions of the Shipping Act, 1916 [46 USCS §§ 801 et seq.].

§§ 805, 806   [Repealed].

§ 807   [Repealed].

§ 808   Registration, enrollment, and licensing of vessels purchased, chartered, or leased; regulations; coastwise trade.

Any vessel purchased, chartered, or leased from the Secretary of Transportation, by persons who are citizens of the United States, may be registered or enrolled and licensed, or both registered and enrolled and licensed, as a vessel of the United States and entitled to the benefits and privileges appertaining thereto: Provided, That foreign-built vessels admitted to American registry or enrollment and license under this Act, and vessels owned by any corporation in which the United States is a stockholder, and vessels sold, leased, or chartered by the Secretary of Transportation to any person a citizen of the United States, as provided in this Act, may engage in the coastwise trade of the United States while owned, leased, or chartered by such a person.

Every vessel purchased, chartered, or leased from the Secretary of Transportation shall, unless otherwise authorized by the Secretary of Transportation be operated only under such registry or enrollment and license. Such vessels while employed solely as merchant vessels shall be subject to all laws, regulations, and liabilities governing merchant vessels, whether the United States be interested therein as owner, in whole or in part, or hold any mortgage, lien, or other interest therein.

Except as provided in section 61 of the Merchant Marine Act, 1936, as amended [49 USCS §1181], it shall be unlawful, without the approval of the Secretary of Transportation, to sell, mortgage, lease, charter, deliver, or in any manner transfer, or agree to sell, mortgage, lease, charter, deliver, or in any manner transfer, to any person not a citizen of the United States, or transfer or place under foreign registry or flag, any vessel or any interest therein owned in whole or in part by a citizen of the United States and documented under the laws of the United States, or the last documentation of which was under the laws of the United States.

The issuance, transfer, or assignment of a bond, note, or other evidence of indebtedness which is secured by a mortgage of a vessel to a trustee or by an assignment to a trustee of the owner's right, title, or interest in a vessel under construction, to a person not a citizen of the United States, without the approval of the Secretary of Transportation, is unlawful unless the trustee or a substitute trustee of such mortgage or assignment is approved by the Secretary of Transportation. The Secretary of Transportation shall grant his approval if such trustee or a substitute trustee is a bank or trust company which (1) is organized as a corporation, and is doing business, under the laws of the United States or any State thereof, (2) is authorized under such laws to exercise corporate trust powers, (3) is a citizen of the United States, (4) is subject to supervision or examination by Federal or State authority, and (5) has a combined capital and surplus (as set forth in its most recent published report of condition) of at least $3,000,000. If such trustee or a substitute trustee at any time ceases to meet the foregoing qualifications, the Secretary of Transportation shall disapprove such trustee or substitute trustee, and after such disapproval the transfer or assignment of such bond, note, or other evidence of indebtedness to a person not a citizen of the United States, without the approval of the Secretary of Transportation, shall be unlawful. The trustee or substitute trustee approved by the Secretary of Transportation shall not operate the vessel under the mortgage or assignment without the approval of the Secretary of Transportation. If a bond, note, or other evidence of indebtedness which is secured by a mortgage of a vessel to a trustee or by an assignment to a trustee of the owner's right, title, or interest in a vessel under construction, is issued, transferred, or assigned to a person not a citizen of the United States in violation of this section, the issuance, transfer, or assignment shall be void.

Any such vessel, or any interest therein, chartered, sold, transferred, or mortgaged to a person not a citizen of the United States or placed under a foreign registry or flag, or operated, in violation of any provision of this section shall be forfeited to the United States, and whoever violates any provision of this section shall be guilty of a misdemeanor and subject to a fine of not more than $5,000, or to imprisonment for not more than five years, or both.

§§ 809, 810 [Repealed].

§ 811 Investigations as to cost of merchant vessels.

The Secretary of Transportation shall investigate the relative cost of building merchant vessels in the United States and in foreign maritime countries, and the relative cost, advantages, and disadvantages of operating in the foreign trade vessels under United States registry and under foreign registry. The Secretary shall examine the rules under which vessels are constructed abroad and in the United States, and the methods of classifying and rating same, and the Secretary shall examine into the subject of marine insurance, the number of companies in the United States, domestic and foreign, engaging in marine insurance, the extent of the insurance on hulls and cargoes placed or written in the United States, and the extent of reinsurance of American maritime risks in foreign companies, and ascertain what steps may be necessary to develop an ample marine insurance system as an aid in the development of an American merchant marine. The Secretary shall examine the navigation laws of the United States and the rules and regulations thereunder, and make such recommendations to the Congress as the Secretary deems proper for the amendment, improvement, and revision of such laws, and for the development of the American merchant marine. The Secretary shall investigate the legal status of mortgage loans on vessel property, with a view to means of improving the security of such loans and of encouraging investment in American shipping.

The Secretary shall, on or before the first day of December in each year, make a report to the Congress, which shall include his recommendations and the results of his investigations, a summary of his transactions, and a statement of all expenditures and receipts under this Act, and of the operations of any corporation in which the United States is a stockholder, and the names and compensation of all persons employed by the Secretary of Transportation.

§ 812 Rebates and discriminations by carriers by water prohibited; use of "fighting ship."

No common carrier by water in interstate commerce shall, directly or indirectly, in respect to the transportation by water of passengers or property between a port of a State, Territory, District, or possession of the United States and any other such port—

First. Pay or allow, or enter into any combination, agreement, or understanding, express or implied, to pay or allow a deferred rebate to any shipper. The term "deferred rebate" in this Act means a return of any portion of the freight money by a carrier to any shipper as a consideration for the giving of all or any portion of his shipments to the same or any other carrier, or for any other purpose, the payment of which is deferred beyond the completion of the service for which it is paid, and is made only if, during both the period for which computed and the period of deferment, the shipper has complied with the terms of the rebate agreement or arrangement.

Second. Use a fighting ship either separately or in conjunction with any other carrier, through agreement or otherwise. The term "fighting ship" in this Act means a vessel used in a particular trade by a carrier or group of carriers for the purpose of excluding, preventing, or reducing competition by driving another carrier out of said trade.

Third. Retaliate against any shipper by refusing, or threatening to refuse, space accommodations when such are available, or resort to other discriminating or unfair methods, because such shipper has patronized any other carrier or has filed a complaint charging unfair treatment, or for any other reason.

Fourth. Make any unfair or unjustly discriminatory contract with any shipper based on the volume of freight offered, or unfairly treat or unjustly discriminate against any shipper in the matter of (a) cargo space accommodations or other facilities, due regard being had for the proper loading of the vessel and the available tonnage; (b) the loading and landing of freight in proper condition; or (c) the adjustment and settlement of claims.

§ 813   [Repealed].

§ 813a   [Repealed].

§ 814   **Contracts between carriers filed with Commission; definition of "agreement"; approval, disapproval, etc., by Commission; unlawful execution of agreements; conference agreements and antitrust laws exemptions; civil actions for penalties; terminal leases exemption.**

Every common carrier by water in interstate commerce, or other person subject to this Act, shall file immediately with the Commission a true copy, or, if oral, a true and complete memorandum, of every agreement with another such carrier or other person subject to this Act, or modification or cancellation thereof, to which it may be a party or conform in whole or in part, fixing or regulating transportation rates or fares; giving or receiving special rates, accommodations, or other special privileges or advantages; controlling, regulating, preventing, or destroying competition; pooling or apportioning earnings, losses, or traffic; allotting ports or restricting or otherwise regulating the number and character of sailings between ports; limiting or regulating in any way the volume or character of freight or passenger traffic to be carried; or in any manner providing for an exclusive, preferential, or cooperative working arrangement. The term "agreement" in this section includes understandings, conferences, and other arrangements.

The Commission shall by order, after notice and hearing, disapprove, cancel or modify any agreement, or any modification or cancellation thereof, whether or not previously approved by it, that it finds to be unjustly discriminatory or unfair as between carriers, shippers, exporters, importers, or ports, or between exporters from the United States and their foreign competitors, or to operate to the detriment of the commerce of the United States, or to be contrary to the public interest, or to be in violation of this Act, and shall approve all other agreements, modifications, or cancellations. No such agreement shall be approved, nor shall continued approval be permitted for any agreement (1) between carriers not members of the same conference or conferences or carriers serving different trades that would otherwise be naturally competitive, unless in the case of agreements between carriers, each carrier, or in the case of agreements between conferences, each conference, retains the right of independent action, or (2) in respect to any conference agreement, which fails to provide reasonable and equal terms and conditions for admission and readmission to conference membership of other qualified carriers

in the trade, or fails to provide that any member may withdraw from membership upon reasonable notice without penalty for such withdrawal.

The Commission shall disapprove any such agreement, after notice and hearing, on a finding of inadequate policing of the obligations under it, or of failure or refusal to adopt and maintain reasonable procedures for promptly and fairly hearing and considering shippers' requests and complaints.

Any agreement and any modification or cancellation of any agreement not approved, or disapproved, by the Commission shall be unlawful, and agreements, modifications, and cancellations shall be lawful only when and as long as approved by the Commission; before approval or after disapproval it shall be unlawful to carry out in whole or in part, directly or indirectly, any such agreement, modification, or cancellation; except that tariff rates, fares, and charges, and classifications, rules, and regulations explanatory thereof agreed upon by approved conferences, and changes and amendments thereto, if otherwise in accordance with law, shall be permitted to take effect without prior approval upon compliance with the provisions of any regulations the Commission may adopt.

Every agreement, modification, or cancellation lawful under this section shall be excepted from the provisions of the Act approved July 2, 1980, entitled "An Act to protect trade and commerce against unlawful restraints and monopolies", and amendments and Acts supplementary thereto, and the provisions of sections 73 to 77, both inclusive, of the Act approved August 27, 1894, entitled "An Act to reduce taxation, to provide revenue for the Government, and for other purposes", and amendments and Acts supplementary thereto.

Whoever violates any provision of this section shall be subject to a civil penalty of not more than $1,000 for each day such violation continues: Provided, however, That the penalty provisions of this section shall not apply to leases, licenses, assignments, or other agreements of similar character for the use of terminal property or facilities which were entered into before the date of enactment of this Act [enacted Feb. 29, 1964], and, if continued in effect beyond said date, submitted to the Federal Maritime Commission for approval prior to or within ninety days after the enactment of this Act [enacted Feb. 29, 1964], unless such leases, licenses, assignments, or other agreements for the use of terminal facilities are disapproved, modified, or canceled by the Commission and are continued in operation without regard to the Commission's action thereon. The Commission shall promptly approve, disapprove, cancel, or modify each such agreement in accordance with the provisions of this section.

§ 815   **Discriminatory acts prohibited; penalties.**

It shall be unlawful for any shipper, consignor, consignee, forwarder, broker, or other person, or any officer, agent, or employee thereof, knowingly and willfully, directly or indirectly, by means of false billing, false classification, false weighing, false report of weight, or by any other unjust or unfair device or means to obtain or attempt to obtain transportation by water in interstate commerce for property at less than the rates or charges which would otherwise be applicable.

It shall be unlawful for any common carrier by water in interstate commerce, or other person subject to this Act either alone or in conjunction with any other person, directly or indirectly—

First. To make or give any undue or unreasonable preference or advantage to any particular person, locality, or description of traffic in any respect whatsoever, or to subject any particular person, locality, or description of traffic to any undue or unreasonable prejudice whatsoever: Provided, That within thirty days after enactment of this Act, or within thirty days after the effective date or the filing with the Commission, whichever is later, of any conference freight rate, rule, or regulation in the foreign commerce of the United States, the Governor of any State, Commonwealth, or possession of the United States may file a protest with the Commission upon the ground that the rate, rule, or regulation unjustly discriminates against that State, Commonwealth, or possession of the United States, in which case the Commission shall issue an order to the conference to show cause why the rate, rule, or regulation should not be set aside. Within one hundred and eighty days from the date of the issuance of such order, the Commission shall determine whether or not such rate, rule, or regulation is unjustly discriminatory and issue a final order either dismissing the protest, or setting aside the rate, rule, or regulation.

Second. To allow any person to obtain transportation for property at less than the regular rates or charges then established and enforced on the line of such carrier by means of false billing, false classification, false weighing, false report of weight, or by any other unjust or unfair device or means.

Third. To induce, persuade, or otherwise influence any marine insurance company or underwriter, or agent thereof, not to give a competing carrier by water as favorable a rate of insurance on vessel or cargo, having due regard to the class of vessel or cargo, as is granted to such carrier or other person subject to this Act.

Whoever violates any provision of this section other than paragraphs First and Third hereof shall be subject to a civil penalty of not more than $5,000 for each such violation.

Whoever violates paragraphs First and Third hereof shall be guilty of a misdemeanor punishable by a fine of not more than $5,000 for each offense.

§ 816   Discriminatory rates prohibited; supervision by Commission.

Every every other person subject to this Act shall establish, observe, and enforce just and reasonable regulations and practices relating to or connected with the receiving, handling, storing, or delivering of property. Whenever the Federal Maritime Commission finds that any such regulation or practice is unjust or unreasonable it may determine, prescribe, and order enforced a just and reasonable regulation or practice.

§ 817   Carriers in interstate commerce to establish, observe, and enforce reasonable rates and regulations; carriers in foreign commerce to file tariffs of rates and charges.

(a) Every common carrier by water in interstate commerce shall establish, observe, and enforce just and reasonable rates, fares, charges, classifications, and tariffs, and just and reasonable regulations and practices relating thereto and to the issuance, form, and substances of tickets, receipts, and bills of lading, the manner and method of presenting, marking, packing and delivering property for transportation, the carrying of personal, sample, and excess baggage, the facilities for transportation, and all other matters relating to or connected with the receiving, handling, transporting, storing, or delivering of property.

Every such carrier shall file with the Commission and keep open to public inspection, in the form and manner and within the time prescribed by the Commission the maximum rates, fares, and charges for or in connection with transportation between points on its own route; and if a through route has been established, the maximum rates, fares, and charges for or in connection with transportation between points on its own route and points on the route of any other carrier by water.

No such carrier shall demand, charge, or collect a greater compensation for such tranportation than the rates, fares, and charges filed in compliance with this section, except with the approval of the Commission and after ten days' public notice in the form and manner prescribed by the Commission stating the increase proposed to be made; but the Commission for good cause shown may waive such notice.

Whenever the Commission finds that any rate, fare, charge, classification, tariff, regulation, or practice, demanded, charged, collected, or observed by such carrier is unjust or unreasonable, it may determine, prescribe, and order enforced a just and reasonable maximum rate, fare, or charge, or a just and reasonable classification, tariff, regulation, or practice.

(b) (1) From and after ninety days following enactment hereof [enacted Oct. 3, 1961] every common carrier by water in foreign commerce and every conference of such carriers shall file with the Commission and keep open to public inspection tariffs showing all the rates and charges of such carrier or conference of carriers for transportation to and from United States ports and foreign ports between all points on its own route and on any through route which has been established. Such tariffs shall plainly show the places between which freight will be carried, and shall contain the classification of freight in force, and shall also state separately such terminal or other charge, privilege, or facility under the control of the carrier or conference of carriers which is granted or allowed, and any rules or regulations which in anywise change, affect, or determine any part or the aggregate of such aforesaid rates, or charges, and shall include specimens of any bill of lading, contract of affreightment, or other document evidencing the transportation agreement. Copies of such tariffs shall be made available to any person and a reasonable charge may be made therefor. The requirements of this section shall not be applicable to cargo loaded and carried in bulk without mark or count, or to cargo which is softwood lumber. As used in this paragraph, the term "softwood lumber" means softwood lumber not further manufactured than passing lengthwise through a standard planing machine and crosscut to length, logs, poles, piling, and ties, including such articles preservatively treated, or bored, or framed, but not including plywood or finished articles knocked down or set up.

(2) No change shall be made in rates, charges, classifications, rules or regulations, which results in an increase in cost to the shipper, nor shall any new or initial rate of any common carrier by water in foreign commerce or conference of such carriers be instituted, except by the publication, and filing, as

aforesaid, of a new tariff or tariffs which shall become effective not earlier than thirty days after the date of publication and filing thereof with the Commission, and each such tariff or tariffs shall plainly show the changes proposed to be made in the tariff or tariffs then in force and the time when the rates, charges, classifications, rules or regulations as changed are to become effective: Provided, however, That the Commission may, in its discretion and for good cause, allow such changes and such new or initial rates to become effective upon less than the period of thirty days herein specified. Any change in the rates, charges, or classifications, rules or regulations which results in a decreased cost to the shipper may become effective upon the publication and filing with the Commission. The term "tariff" as used in this paragraph shall include any amendment, supplement or reissue.

(3) No common carrier by water in foreign commerce or conference of such carriers shall charge or demand or collect or receive a greater or less or different compensation for the transportation of property or for any service in connection therewith than the rates and charges which are specified in its tariffs on file with the Commission and duly published and in effect at the time; nor shall any such carrier rebate, refund, or remit in any manner or by any device any portion of the rates or charges so specified, nor extend or deny to any person any privilege or facility, except in accordance with such tariffs: Provided, however, That the Federal Maritime Commission may in its discretion and for good cause shown permit a common carrier by water in foreign commerce or conference of such carriers to refund a portion of freight charges collected from a shipper or waive the collection of a portion of the charges from a shipper where it appears that there is an error in a tariff of a clerical or administrative nature or an error due to inadvertence in failing to file a new tariff and that such refund or waiver will not result in discrimination among shippers: Provided further, That the common carrier by water in foreign commerce or conference of such carriers has, prior to applying for authority to make refund, filed a new tariff with the Federal Maritime Commission which sets forth the rate on which such refund or waiver would be based: Provided further, That the carrier or conference agrees that if permission is granted by the Federal Maritime Commission, an appropriate notice will be published in the tariff, or such other steps taken as the Federal Maritime Commission may require, which give notice of the rate on which such refund or waiver would be based, and additional refunds or waivers as appropriate shall be made with respect to other shipments in the manner prescribed by the Commission in its order approving the application: And provided further, That application for refund or waiver must be filed with the Commission within one hundred and eighty days from the date of shipment.

(4) The Commission shall by regulations prescribe the form and manner in which the tariffs required by this section shall be published and filed; and the Commission is authorized to reject any tariff filed with it which is not in conformity with this section and with such regulations. Upon rejection by the Commission, a tariff shall be void and its use unlawful.

(5) The Commission shall disapprove any rate or charge filed by a common carrier by water in the foreign commerce of the United States or conference of carriers which, after hearing, it finds to be so unreasonably high or low as to be detrimental to the commerce of the United States.

(6) Whoever violates any provision of this section shall be subject to a civil penalty of not more than $1,000 for each day such violation continues.

(7) Whoever violates subsection (b) (3) hereof by means of rebates or refunds, shall be subject to a civil penalty of not more than $25,000 for each shipment on which a rebate or refund was paid and to suspension by the Commission of any or all tariffs filed by or on behalf of such carrier, or suspension of that carrier's right to utilize any or all tariffs of conferences of which that carrier may be a member, for a period not to exceed twelve months. Any carrier whose tariffs or rights of use thereof have been suspended pursuant to this paragraph and who accepts cargo for carriage during the suspension period which cargo would otherwise have been governed by the provisions of the suspended tariff(s) shall be subject to a civil penalty of not more than $50,000 for each shipment so accepted.

For purposes of this subsection and section 821(c) of this title, a shipment shall mean all of that cargo, the carriage of which is evidenced by a single bill of lading.

(c) (1) No controlled carrier subject to this chapter shall maintain rates or charges in its tariffs filed with the Commission that are below a level which is just and reasonable, nor shall any carrier establish or maintain unjust or unreasonable classifications, rules, or regulations in such tariffs. An unjust or unreasonable classification, rule, or regulation means one which results or is likely to result in the carriage or handling of cargo at rates or charges which are below a level which is just and reasonable. The Commission may at any time, after notice and hearing, disapprove any rates, charges, classifications, rules, or regulations that have failed to demonstrate to be just and reasonable. In any proceeding under this subsection, the burden of proof shall be on the controlled carrier to demonstrate that its rates, charges, classifications, rules or regulations are just and reasonable. Rates, charges, classifications, rules, or regulations filed by a controlled carrier which have been rejected, suspended, or disapproved by the Commission are void and their use is unlawful.

(2) For the purpose of this subsection, in determining whether rates, charges, classifications, rules, or regulations by a controlled carrier are just and reasonable, the Commission may take into account the appropriate factors, including, but not limited to, whether: (i) the rates or charges which have been filed or which would result from the pertinent classifications, rules, or regulations are below a level which are fully compensatory to the controlled carrier based upon that carrier's actual costs or upon its constructive costs, which are hereby defined as the costs of another carrier, other than the controlled carrier, operating the same or simi-

lar vessels in the same or similar trade; (ii) the rates, charges, classifications, rules, or regulations are the same as or similar to those filed or assessed by other carriers in the same trade; (iii) the rates, charges, classifications, rules, or regulations are required to assure movement of particular cargo in the trade; (iv) the rates, charges, classifications, rules, or regulations are required to maintain acceptable continuity, level, or quality of common carrier service to or from affected ports.

(3) Notwithstanding the provisions of subsection (b) (2) of this section, rates, charges, classifications, rules, or regulations of controlled carriers shall not, without special permission of the Commission, become effective within less than thirty days following the date of filing with the Commission. Following the effective date of this subsection, each controlled carrier shall, upon request of the Commission, file within twenty days of request, with respect to its existing or proposed rates, charges, classifications, rules, or regulations a statement of the justification which sufficiently details the controlled carrier's need and purpose for such rates, charges, classifications, rules, or regulations, upon which the Commission may reasonably base its determination of the lawfulness thereof.

(4) Whenever the Commission is of the opinion that the rates, charges, classifications, rules, or regulations filed by a controlled carrier may be unjust or unreasonable, the Commission may issue an order to the controlled carrier to show cause why such rates, charges, classifications, rules, or regulations should not be disapproved. Pending a determination as to their lawfulness in such a proceeding, the Commission may suspend such rates, charges, classifications, rules, or regulations at any time prior to their effective date. In the case of any rates, charges, classifications, rules, or regulations which may have already become effective, the Commission may, upon the issuance of an order to show cause, suspend such rates, charges, classifications, rules, or regulations on not less than sixty days notice to the controlled carrier. No period of suspension hereunder may be greater than one hundred eighty days. Whenever the Commission has suspended any rates, charges, classifications, rules, or regulations under this provision, the affected carrier may file new rates, charges, classifications, rules, or regulations to take effect immediately during the suspension period in lieu of the suspended rates, charges, classifications, rules, or regulations: Provided, however, That the Commission may reject such new rates, charges, classifications, rules, or regulations if it is of the opinion that they are unjust and unreasonable.

(5) Concurrently with the publication thereof, the Commission shall transmit to the President any order of suspension or final order of disapproval of rates, charges, classifications, rules, or regulations of a controlled carrier subject to the provisions of this subsection. Within ten days after the receipt or the effective date of such Commission order, whichever is later, the President may request the Commission in writing to stay the effect of the Commission's order if he finds that such stay is required for reasons of national defense or foreign policy which reasons shall be specified in the re-

port. Notwithstanding any other provision of law, the Commission shall immediately grant such request by issuance of an order in which the President's request shall be described. During any such stay, the President shall, whenever practicable, attempt to resolve the matter in controversy by negotiation with representatives of the applicable foreign governments.

(6) The provisions of this subsection shall not apply to: (i) any controlled carrier of a state whose vessels are entitled by a treaty of the United States to receive national or most-favored-nation treatment; (ii) any controlled carrier of a state which, on the effective date of this subsection, has subscribed to the statement of shipping policy contained in note 1 to Annex A of the Code of Liberalization of Current Invisible Operations, adopted by the Council of the Organization for Economic Cooperation and Development; (iii) rates, charges, classifications, rules, or regulations of any controlled carrier in any particular trade which are covered by an agreement approved under section 814 of this title, other than an agreement in which all of the members are controlled carriers not otherwise excluded from the provisions of this subsection; (iv) rates, charges, classifications, rules, or regulations governing the transportation of cargo by a controlled carrier between the country by whose government it is owned or controlled, as defined herein, and the United States, or any of its districts, territories, or possessions; or (v) a trade served exclusively by controlled carriers.

§ 817b   [Repealed].

§ 817c   [Repealed].

§ 817d   Financial responsibility of owners and charterers for death or injury to passengers or other persons.

(a) **Amount; method of establishment.** Each owner or charterer of an American or foreign vessel having berth or stateroom accommodations for fifty or more passengers, and embarking passengers at United States ports, shall establish, under regulations prescribed by the Federal Maritime Commission, his financial responsibility to meet any liability he may incur for death or injury to passengers or other persons on voyages to or from United States ports, in an amount based upon the number of passenger accommodations aboard the vessel, calculated as follows:

$20,000 for each passenger accommodation up to and including five hundred; plus

$15,000 for each additional passenger accommodation between five hundred and one and one thousand; plus

$10,000 for each additional passenger accommodation between one thousand and one and one thousand five hundred; plus

$5,000 for each passenger accommodation in excess of one thousand five hundred:

Provided, however, That if such owner or charterer is operating more than one vessel subject to this section, the foregoing amount shall be based upon the number of passenger accommodations on the vessel being so operated which has the largest number of passenger accommodations. This amount shall be available to pay any judgment for damages, whether in amount less than or more than $20,000 for death or injury occurring on such voyages to any passenger or other person. Such financial responsibility may be established by any one of, or a combination of, the following methods which is acceptable to the Commission: (1) policies of insurance, (2) surety bonds, (3) qualifications as a self-insurer, or (4) other evidence of financial responsibility.

(b) Issuance of bond when filed with Commission. If a bond is filed with the Commission, then such bond shall be issued by a bonding company authorized to do business in the United States or any State thereof or the District of Columbia, the Commonwealth of Puerto Rico, the Virgin Islands, or any territory or possession of the United States.

(c) Civil penalties for violations; remission or mitigation of penalties. Any person who shall violate this section shall be subject to a civil penalty of not more than $5,000 in addition to a civil penalty of $200 for each passage sold, such penalties to be assessed by the Federal Maritime Commission. These penalties may be remitted or mitigated by the Federal Maritime Commission upon such terms as they in their discretion shall deem proper.

(d) Rules and regulations. The Federal Maritime Commission is authorized to prescribe such regulations as may be necessary to carry out the provisions of this section. The provisions of the Shipping Act shall apply with respect to proceedings conducted by the Commission under this section.

(e) Refusal of departure clearance. The collector of customs at the port or place of departure from the United States of any vessel described in subsection (a) of this section shall refuse the clearance required by section 4197 of the Revised Statutes (46 U.S.C. 91) [USCS § 91] to any such vessel which does not have evidence furnished by the Federal Maritime Commission that the provisions of this section have been complied with.

§ 817e   Financial responsibility for indemnification of passengers for nonperformance of transportation.

(a) Filing of information or bond with Commission. No person in the United States shall arrange, offer, advertise, or provide passage on a vessel having berth or stateroom accommodations for fifty or more passengers and which is to embark passengers at United States ports without there first having been filed with the Federal Maritime Commission such information as the Commission may deem necessary to establish the financial responsibility of the person arranging, offering, advertising, or providing such transportation, or in lieu thereof a copy of a bond or other security, in such form as the Commission, by rule or regulation, may require and accept, for indemnification of passengers for nonperformance of the transporation.

(b) Issuance of bond when filed with Commission; amount of bond. If a bond is filed with the Commission, such bond shall be issued by a bonding company authorized to do business in the United States or any State thereof, or the District of Columbia, the Commonwealth of Puerto Rico, the Virgin Islands or any territory or possession of the United States and such bond or other security shall be in an amount paid equal to the estimated total revenue for the particular transportation.

(c) Civil penalties for violations; remission or mitigation of penalties. Any person who shall violate this section shall be subject to a civil penalty of not more than $5,000 in addition to a civil penalty of $200 for each passage sold, such penalties to be assessed by the Federal Maritime Commission. These penalties may be remitted

or mitigated by the Federal Maritime Commission upon such terms as they in their discretion shall deem proper.

(d) Rules and regulations. The Federal Maritime Commission is authorized to prescribe such regulations as may be necessary to carry out the provisions of this section. The provisions of the Shipping Act shall apply with respect to proceedings conducted by the Commission under this section.

(e) Refusal of departure clearance. The collector of customs at the port or place of departure from the United States of any vessel described in subsection (a) of this section shall refuse the clearance required by section 4197 of the Revised Statutes (46 U.S.C. 91) [46 USCS § 91] to any such vessel which does not have evidence furnished by the Federal Maritime Commission that the provisions of this section have been complied with.

§ 818   Rates reduced not to be increased without approval.

Whenever a common carrier by water in interstate commerce reduces its rates on the carriage of any species of freight to or from competitive points below a fair and remunerative basis with the intent of driving out or otherwise injuring a competitive carrier by water, it shall not increase such rates unless after hearing the Federal Maritime Commission finds that such proposed increase rests upon changed conditions other than the elimination of said competition.

§ 819   Disclosure of confidential information prohibited.

It shall be unlawful for any common carrier by water in interstate commerce or other person subject to this Act, or any officer, receiver, trustee, lessee, agent, or employee of such carrier or person, or for any other person authorized by such carrier or person to receive information, knowingly to disclose to or permit to be acquired by any person other than the shipper or consignee, without the consent of such shipper or consignee, any information concerning the nature, kind, quantity, destination, consignee, or routing of any property tendered or delivered to such common carrier or other person subject to this Act for transportation in interstate or foreign commerce, which information may be used to the detriment or prejudice of such shipper or consignee, or which may improperly disclose his business transactions to a competitor, or which may be used to the detriment or prejudice of any carrier, and it shall also be unlawful for any person to solicit or knowingly receive any such information which may be so used.

Nothing in this Act shall be construed to prevent the giving of such information in response to any legal process issued under the authority of any court, or to any officer or agent of the government of the United States, or of any State, Territory, District, or possession thereof, in the exercise of his powers, or to any officer or other duly authorized person seeking such information for the prosecution of persons charged with or suspected of crime, or to another carrier, or its duly authorized agent, for the purpose of adjusting mutual traffic accounts in the ordinary course of business of such carriers; or to prevent any common carrier by water in interstate commerce which is a party to a conference agreement approved pursuant to section 814 of this title, or any other person subject to this Act, or any receiver, trustee, lessee, agent, or employee of such carrier or person, or any other person authorized by such carrier to receive information, from giving information to the conference or any person, firm, corporation, or agency designated by the conference or to prevent the conference or its designee from soliciting or receiving information for the purpose of determining whether a shipper or consignee has breached an agreement with the conference or its member lines or of determining whether a member of the conference has breached the conference agreement, or for the purpose of compiling statistics of cargo movement, but the use of such information for any other purpose prohibited by this Act or any other Act shall be unlawful.

§ 820   Reports by carriers required.

(a) The Federal Maritime Commission and Secretary of Transportation may require any common carrier by water in interstate commerce, or other person subject to this Act, or any officer, receiver, trustee, lessee, agent, or employee thereof, to file with it [or him] any periodical or special report, or any account, record, rate, or charge, or any memorandum of any facts and transactions appertaining to the business of such carrier or other person subject to this Act. Such report, account, record, rate, charge, or memorandum shall be under oath whenever the Commission or Secretary so requires, and shall be furnished in the form and within the time prescribed by the Commission or Secretary. Whoever fails to file any report, account, record, rate, charge, or memorandum as required by this section shall forfeit to the United States the sum of $100 for each day of such default.

Whoever wilfully falsifies, destroys, mutilates, or alters any such report, account, record, rate, charge, or memorandum, or wilfully files a false report, account, record, rate, charge, or memorandum shall be guilty of a misdemeanor, and subject upon conviction to a fine of not more than $1,000, or imprisonment for not more than one year, or to both such fine and imprisonment.

(b) The Commission shall require any common carrier and, to the extent it deems feasible, may require any shipper, shipper's association, maritime terminal operator, ocean freight forwarder, or broker, to file a periodic, written certification under oath with the Commission attesting to—

    (1) a policy prohibiting the payment, solicitation, or receipt of any rebate which is unlawful under the provisions of this chapter;

    (2) the fact that such policy has been promulgated recently to each owner, officer, employee, and agent thereof;

    (3) the details of the efforts made, within the company or otherwise, to prevent or correct illegal rebating; and

    (4) full cooperation with the Commission in its investigation of illegal rebating or refunds in the United States foreign trades, and its efforts to end such illegal practices.

Whoever fails to file a certification required by the Commission under this subsection is liable to the United States for a civil penalty of not more than $5,000 for each day such violation continues.

§ 821   Complaints and investigations.

(a) Any person may file with the Federal Maritime Commission a sworn complaint setting forth any violation of this Act by a common carrier by water in interstate commerce, or other person subject to this Act, and asking reparation for the injury, if any, caused thereby. The Federal Maritime Commission shall furnish a copy of the complaint to such carrier or other person, who shall, within a reasonable time specified by the Federal Maritime Commission, satisfy the complaint or answer it in writing. If the complaint is not satisfied the Federal Maritime Commission shall, except as otherwise provided in this Act, investigate it in such manner and by such means, and make such order as it deems proper. The Federal Maritime Commission, if the complaint is filed within two years after the cause of action accrued, may direct the payment, on or before a day named, of full reparation to the complainant for the injury caused by such violation.

(b) The Federal Maritime Commission upon its own motion, may in like manner and, except as to orders for the payment of money, with the same powers, investigate any violation of this Act.

§ 822   Orders made only after full hearing.

Orders of the Commission relating to any violation of this Act or any violation of any rule or regulation issued pursuant to this Act shall be made only after full hearing, and upon a sworn complaint or in proceedings instituted of its own motion.

All orders of the Federal Maritime Commission, other than for the payment of money, made under this Act, as amended or supplemented, shall continue in force until its further order, or for a specified period of time, as shall be prescribed in the order, unless the same shall be suspended, or modified, or set aside by the Commission, or be suspended or set aside by a court of competent jurisdiction.

§ 823   Records; copies; publication of reports; evidence.

The Federal Maritime Commission shall enter of record a written report of every investigation made in which a hearing has been held, stating its conclusions, decision, and order, and, if reparation is awarded, the findings of fact on which the award is made, and shall furnish a copy of such report to all parties to the investigation.

The Federal Maritime Commission may publish such reports in the form best adapted for public information and use, and such authorized publications shall, without further proof or authentication, be competent evidence of such reports in all courts of the United States and of the States, Territories, Districts, and possessions thereof.

§ 824   Reversal, suspension, or modification of orders.

The Federal Maritime Commission may reverse, suspend, or modify, upon such notice and in such manner as it deems proper, any order made by it. Upon application of any party to a decision or order it may grant a rehearing of the same or any matter determined therein, but no such application for or allowance of a rehearing shall, except by special order of the Federal Maritime Commission, operate as a stay of such order.

§ 825   [Repealed].

§ 826   Depositions, interrogatories, and discovery procedure; compelling testimony.

(a) In all proceedings under section 821 of this title, depositions, written interrogatories, and discovery procedure shall be available under rules and regulations issued by the Federal Maritime Commission, which rules and regulations shall, to the extent practicable, be in conformity with the rules applicable in civil proceedings in the district courts of the United States. In such proceedings, the Commission may by subpena compel the attendance of witnesses and the production of books, papers, documents, and other evidence, in such manner and to such an extent as the Commission may by rule or regulation require. Attendance of witnesses and the production of books, papers, documents, and other evidence in response to subpena may be required from any place in the United States at any designated place of hearing, and persons so acting under the direction of the Commission and witnesses shall, unless employees of the Commission, be entitled to the same fees and mileage as in the courts of the United States.

(b) Obedience to this section shall, on application by the Commission, be enforced as are orders of the Commission.

§ 827   [Repealed].

§ 828   Enforcement of orders.

In case of violation of any order of the Federal Maritime Commission under this Act, other than an order for the payment of money, the Commission, or any party injured by such violation, or the Attorney General, may apply to a district court having jurisdiction of the parties; and if, after hearing, the court determines that the order was regularly made and duly issued, it shall enforce obedience thereto by a writ of injunction or other proper process, mandatory or otherwise.

§ 829   Violation of orders for payment of money.

In case of violation of any order of the Federal Maritime Commission under this Act for the payment of money the person to whom such award was made may file in the district court for the district in which such person resides, or in which is located any office of the carrier or other person to whom the order was directed, or in which is located any point of call on a regular route operated by the carrier, or in any court of general jurisdiction of a State, Territory, District, or possession of the United States having jurisdiction of the parties, a petition or suit setting forth briefly the causes for which he claims damages and the order of the Federal Maritime Commission in the premises.

In the district court the findings and order of the Federal Maritime Commission shall be prima facie evidence of the facts therein stated, and the petitioner shall not be liable for costs, nor shall he be liable for costs at any subsequent stage of the proceedings unless they accrue upon his appeal. If a petitioner in a district court finally prevails, he shall be allowed a reasonable attorney's fee, to be taxed and collected as part of the costs of the suit.

All parties in whose favor the Federal Maritime Commission has made an award of reparation by a single order may be joined as plaintiffs, and all other parties to such order may be joined as defendants, in a single suit in any district in which any one such plaintiff could maintain a suit against any one such defendant. Service of process against any such defendant not found in that district may be made in any district in which is located any office of, or point of call on a regular route operated by, such defendant. Judgment may be entered in favor of any plaintiff against the defendant liable to that plaintiff.

No petition or suit for the enforcement of an order for the payment of money shall be maintained unless filed within one year from the date of the order.

§ 830   Venue and procedure in suits to enforce, suspend, or set aside orders.

The venue and procedure in the courts of the United States in suits brought to enforce, suspend, or set aside, in whole or in part, any order of the Federal Maritime Commission shall, except as otherwise provided, be the same as in similar suits in regard to orders of the Interstate Commerce Commission, but such suits may also be maintained in any district court having jurisdiction of the parties.

§ 831   Civil and criminal penalties.

(a) Whoever violates any provision of sections 812 through 817 and 818 through 820 of this title, except where a different penalty is provided, shall be subject to a civil penalty not to exceed $5,000 for each such violation.

(b) Whoever violates any provision of any other section of this Act, except where a different penalty is provided, shall be guilty of a misdemeanor, punishable by a fine not to exceed $5,000.

(c) Whoever violates any order, rule, or regulation of the Federal Maritime Commission made or issued in the exercise of its powers, duties, or functions under this Act, shall be subject to a civil penalty of not more than $1,000 for each day such violation continues.

(d) No penalty shall be imposed on any person for conspiracy after August 29, 1972: (1) to rebate or refund in violation of the initial paragraph or paragraph Second of section 815 of this title, or under section 817(b)(3)[*] of this title; or (2) to defraud the Commission by concealment of such rebates or refunds in any manner.

(e) Notwithstanding any other provision of law, the Commission shall have the authority to assess or compromise all civil penalties provided in this chapter: Provided, however, That, in order to assess such penalties a formal proceeding under section 821 of this title shall be commenced within five years from the date when the violation occurred.

§ 832   Powers of Interstate Commerce Commission not affected; intrastate commerce.

This Act shall not be construed to affect the power or jurisdiction of the Interstate Commerce Commission, nor to confer upon the Federal Maritime Commission concurrent power or jurisdiction over any matter within the power or jurisdiction of such commission; nor shall this Act be construed to apply to intrastate commerce.

§ 833   Separability of provisions.

If any provision of this Act, or the application of such provision to certain circumstances, is held unconstitutional, the remainder of the act, and the application of such provision to circumstances other than those as to which it is held unconstitutional, shall not be affected thereby.

§ 833a   Exemption of agreements where exemption will not substantially impair effective regulation, be unjustly discriminatory, or detrimental to commerce; conditions; hearings.

The Federal Maritime Commission, upon application or on its own motion, may by order or rule exempt for the future any class of agreements between persons subject to this Act or any specified activity of such persons from any

---

*Although the section cited has been repealed, this reference remains within the text of the new act.

requirement of the Shipping Act, 1916, or Intercoastal Shipping Act, 1933 [46 USCS §§ 843 et seq.], where it finds that such exemption will not substantially impair effective regulation by the Federal Maritime Commission, be unjustly discriminatory, or be detrimental to commerce.

The Commission may attach conditions to any such exemptions and may, by order, revoke any such exemption.

No order or rule of exemption or revocation of exemption shall be issued unless opportunity for hearing has been afforded interested persons.

§ 834   Refusal of clearance to vessel refusing to accept freight.

The Secretary of the Treasury is authorized to refuse a clearance to any vessel or other vehicle laden with merchandise destined for a foreign or domestic port whenever he shall have satisfactory reason to believe that the master, owner, or other officer of such vessel or other vehicle refuses or declines to accept or receive freight or cargo in good condition tendered for such port of destination or for some intermediate port of call, together with the proper freight or transportation charges therefor, by any citizen of the United States, unless the same is fully laden and has no space accommodations for the freight or cargo so tendered, due regard being had for the proper loading of such vessel or vehicle, or unless such freight or cargo consists of merchandise for which such vessel or vehicle is not adaptable.

§ 835   Restrictions on transfer of shipping facilities during war or national emergency.

When the United States is at war or during any national emergency, the existence of which is declared by proclamation of the President, it shall be unlawful, without first obtaining the approval of the Secretary of Transportation:

(a) To transfer to or place under any foreign registry or flag any vessel owned in whole or in part by any person a citizen of the United States or by a corporation organized under the laws of the United States, or of any State, Territory, District, or possession thereof; or

(b) To sell, mortgage, lease, charter, deliver, or in any manner transfer, or agree to sell, mortgage, lease, charter, deliver, or in any manner transfer, to any person not a citizen of the United States, (1) any such vessel or any interest therein, or (2) any vessel documented under the laws of the United States, or any interest therein, or (3) any shipyard, dry dock, ship-building or ship-repairing plant or facilities, or any interest therein; or

(c) To issue, transfer, or assign a bond, note, or other evidence of indebtedness which is secured by a mortgage of a vessel to a trustee or by an assignment to a trustee of the owner's right, title, or interest in a vessel under construction, or by a mortgage to a trustee on a shipyard, drydock, or ship-building or ship-repairing plant or facilities, to a person not a citizen of the United States, unless the trustee or a substitute trustee of such mortgage or assignment is approved by the Secretary of Transportation: Provided, however, That the Secretary of Transportation shall grant his approval if such trustee or a substitute trustee is a bank or trust company which (1) is organized as a corporation, and is doing business, under the laws of the United States or any State thereof, (2) is authorized under such laws to exercise corporate trust powers, (3) is a citizen of the United States, (4) is subject to supervision or examination by Federal or State authority, and (5) has a combined capital and surplus (as set forth in its most recent published report of condition) of at least $3,000,000; or for the trustee or substitute trustee approved by the Secretary of Transportation to operate said vessel under the mortgage or assignment: Provided further, That if such trustee or substitute trustee at any time ceases to meet the foregoing qualifications, the Secretary of Transportation shall disapprove such trustee or substitute trustee, and after such disapproval the transfer or assignment of such bond, note, or other evidence of indebtedness to a person not a citizen of the United States, without the approval of the Secretary of Transportation, shall be unlawful; or

(d) To enter into any contract, agreement, or understanding to construct a vessel within the United States for or to be delivered to any person not a citizen of the United States, without expressly stipulating that such construction shall not begin until after the war or emergency proclaimed by the President has ended; or

(e) To make any agreement or effect any understanding whereby there is vested in or for the benefit of any person not a citizen of the United States, the controlling interest or a majority of the voting power in a corporation which is organized under the laws of the United States, or of any State, Territory, District, or possession thereof, and which owns any vessel, shipyard, dry dock, or ship-building or ship-repairing plant or facilities; or

(f) To cause or procure any vessel constructed in whole or in part within the United States, which has never cleared for any foreign port, to depart from a port of the United States before it has been documented under the laws of the United States.

Whoever violates, or attempts or conspires to violate, any of the provisions of this section shall be guilty of a misdemeanor, punishable by a fine of not more than $5,000 or by imprisonment for not more than five years, or both.

If a bond, note, or other evidence of indebtedness which is secured by a mortgage of a vessel to a trustee or by an assignment to a trustee of the owner's right, title, or interest in a vessel under construction, or by a mortgage to a trustee on a shipyard, drydock or ship-building or ship-repairing plant or facilities, is issued, transferred, or assigned to a person not a citizen of the United States in violation of subsection (c) of this section, the issuance, transfer or assignment shall be void.

Any vessel, shipyard, dry dock, ship-building or ship-repairing plant or facilities, or interest therein, sold, mortgaged, leased, chartered, delivered, transferred, or documented, or agreed to be sold, mortgaged, leased, chartered, delivered, transferred, or documented, in violation of any of the provisions of this section, and any stocks, bonds, or other securities sold or transferred, or agreed to be sold or transferred, in violation of any of such provisions, or any vessel departing in violation of the provisions of subsection (f) of this section shall be forfeited to the United States.

Any such sale, mortgage, lease, charter, delivery, transfer, documentation, or agreement therefor shall be void, whether made within or without the United States, and any consideration paid therefor or deposited in connection therewith shall be recoverable at the suit of the person who has paid or deposited the same, or of his successors or assigns, after the tender of such vessel, shipyard, dry dock, shipbuilding or ship-repairing plant or facilities, or interest therein, or of such stocks, bonds, or other securities, to the person entitled thereto, or after forfeiture thereof to the United States, unless the person to whom the consideration was paid, or in whose interest it was deposited, entered into the transaction in the honest belief that the person who paid or deposited such consideration was a citizen of the United States.

§ 836   Forfeitures.

All forfeitures incurred under the provisions of this Act may be prosecuted in the same court, and may be disposed of in the same manner, as forfeitures incurred for offenses against the law relating to the collection of duties.

§ 837   Prima facie evidence.

In any action or proceeding under the provisions of this Act to enforce a forfeiture the conviction in a court of criminal jurisdiction of any person for a violation thereof with respect to the subject of the forfeiture shall constitute prima facie evidence of such violation against the person so convicted.

§ 838   Record of sale or other disposition of vessels.

Whenever any bill of sale, mortgage, hypothecation, or conveyance of any vessel, or part thereof, or interest therein, is presented to any collector of the customs to be recorded, the vendee, mortgagee, or transferee shall file therewith a written declaration in such form as the Secretary of Transportation may by regulation prescribe, setting forth the facts relating to his citizenship, and such other facts as the Secretary of Transportation requires, showing that the transaction does not involve a violation of any of the provisions of sections 808 or 835 of this title.

Unless the Secretary of Transportation, before such presentation, has failed to prescribe such form, no such bill of sale, mortgage, hypothecation, or conveyance shall be valid against any person whatsoever until such declaration has been filed. Any declaration filed by or in behalf of a corporation shall be signed by the president, secretary, or treasurer thereof, or any other official thereof duly authorized by such corporation to execute any such declaration.

Whoever knowingly makes any false statement of a material fact in any such declaration shall be guilty of a misdemeanor and subject to a fine of not more than $5,000, or to imprisonment for not more than five years, or both.

§ 839   Approvals.

Whenever by sections 808 or 835 of this title the approval of the Secretary of Transportation is required to render any act or transaction lawful, such approval may be accorded either absolutely or upon such conditions as the Secretary of Transportation prescribes. Whenever the approval of the Secretary of Transportation is accorded upon any condition a statement of such condition shall be entered upon its records and incorporated in the same document or paper which notifies the applicant of such approval. A violation of such condition so incorporated

shall constitute a misdemeanor and shall be punishable by fine and imprisonment in the same manner, and shall subject the vessel, stocks, bonds, or other subject matter of the application conditionally approved to forfeiture in the same manner, as though the act conditionally approved had been done without the approval of the Secretary of Transportation, but the offense shall be deemed to have been committed at the time of the violation of the condition.

Whenever by this Act the approval of the Secretary of Transportation is required to render any act or transaction lawful, whoever knowingly makes any false statement of a material fact to the Secretary of Transportation, or to any officer, attorney, or agent of the Department of Transportation, for the purpose of securing such approval, shall be guilty of a misdemeanor and subject to a fine of not more than $5,000 or to imprisonment for not more than five years, or both.

§ 840   Documented vessels.

Any vessel registered, enrolled, or licensed under the laws of the United States shall be deemed to continue to be documented under the laws of the United States within the meaning of subdivision (b) of section 835 of this title, until such registry, enrollment, or license is surrendered with the approval of the Secretary of Transportation, the provisions of any other Act of Congress to the contrary notwithstanding.

§ 841a   Rules and regulations.

The Commission shall make such rules and regulations as may be necessary to carry out the provisions of this Act.

§ 841b   [Repealed].

§ 841c

The provisions of this chapter and of the Intercoastal Shipping Act, 1933 [46 U.S.C. 843, et seq.] shall not apply to maritime labor agreements and all provisions of such agreements except to the extent that such provisions provide for the funding of collectively bargained fringe benefit obligations on other than a uniform man-hour basis, regardless of the cargo handled or the type of vessel or equipment utilized. Notwithstanding the preceding sentence, nothing in this section shall be construed as providing an exemption from the provisions of this chapter or the Intercoastal Shipping Act, 1933 or any rates, charges, regulations, or practices of a common carrier by water in interstate commerce or other person subject to this chapter which are required to be set forth in a tariff, whether or not such rates, charges, regulations, or practices arise out of or are otherwise related to a maritime labor agreement.

§ 842.   Short title

This Act may be cited as "Shipping Act, 1916."

6. SHIPPING ACT OF 1984

Public Law 98–237
98th Congress

An Act

To improve the international ocean commerce transportation system of the United States.

Be it enacted by the Senate and House of Representatives of the United States of America in Congress assembled, That this Act may be cited as the "Shipping Act of 1984".

TABLE OF CONTENTS

SEC. 2. DECLARATION OF POLICY.

The purposes of this Act are—
(1) to establish a nondiscriminatory regulatory process for the common carriage of goods by water in the foreign commerce of the United States with a minimum of government intervention and regulatory costs;
(2) to provide an efficient and economic transportation system in the ocean commerce of the United States that is, insofar as possible, in harmony with, and responsive to, international shipping practices; and
(3) to encourage the development of an economically sound and efficient United States-flag liner fleet capable of meeting national security needs.

SEC. 3. DEFINITIONS.

As used in this Act—
(1) "agreement" means an understanding, arrangement, or association (written or oral) and any modification or cancellation thereof; but the term does not include a maritime labor agreement.
(2) "antitrust laws" means the Act of July 2, 1890 (ch. 647, 26 Stat. 209), as amended; the Act of October 15, 1914 (ch. 323, 38 Stat. 730), as amended; the Federal Trade Commission Act (38 Stat. 717), as amended; sections 73 and 74 of the Act of August 27, 1894 (28 Stat. 570), as amended; the Act of June 19, 1936 (ch. 592, 49 Stat. 1526), as amended; the Antitrust Civil Process Act (76 Stat. 548), as amended; and amendments and Acts supplementary thereto.
(3) "assessment agreement" means an agreement, whether part of a collective-bargaining agreement or negotiated separately, to the extent that it provides for the funding of collectively bargained fringe benefit obligations on other than a uniform man-hour basis, regardless of the cargo handled or type of vessel or equipment utilized.
(4) "bulk cargo" means cargo that is loaded and carried in bulk without mark or count.
(5) "Commission" means the Federal Maritime Commission.
(6) "common carrier" means a person holding itself out to the general public to provide transportation by water of passengers or cargo between the United States and a foreign country for compensation that—
(A) assumes responsibility for the transportation from the port or point of receipt to the port or point of destination, and

(B) utilizes, for all or part of that transportation, a vessel operating on the high seas or the Great Lakes between a port in the United States and a port in a foreign country.
(7) "conference" means an association of ocean common carriers permitted, pursuant to an approved or effective agreement, to engage in concerted activity and to utilize a common tariff; but the term does not include a joint service, consortium, pooling, sailing, or transshipment arrangement.
(8) "controlled carrier" means an ocean common carrier that is, or whose operating assets are, directly or indirectly, owned or controlled by the government under whose registry the vessels of the carrier operate; ownership or control by a government shall be deemed to exist with respect to any carrier if—
(A) a majority portion of the interest in the carrier is owned or controlled in any manner by that government, by any agency thereof, or by any public or private person controlled by that government; or
(B) that government has the right to appoint or disapprove the appointment of a majority of the directors, the chief operating officer, or the chief executive officer of the carrier.
(9) "deferred rebate" means a return by a common carrier of any portion of the freight money to a shipper as a consideration for that shipper giving all, or any portion, of its shipments to that or any other common carrier, or for any other purpose, the payment of which is deferred beyond the completion of the service for which it is paid, and is made only if, during both the period for which computed and the period of deferment, the shipper has complied with the terms of the rebate agreement or arrangement.
(10) "fighting ship" means a vessel used in a particular trade by an ocean common carrier or group of such carriers for the purpose of excluding, preventing, or reducing competition by driving another ocean common carrier out of that trade.
(11) "forest products" means forest products in an unfinished or semifinished state that require special handling moving in lot sizes too large for a container, including, but not limited to, lumber in bundles, rough timber, ties, poles, piling, laminated beams, bundled siding, bundled plywood, bundled core stock or veneers, bundled particle or fiber boards, bundled hardwood, wood pulp in rolls, wood pulp in unitized bales, paper board in rolls, and paper in rolls.
(12) "inland division" means the amount paid by a common carrier to an inland carrier for the inland portion of through transportation offered to the public by the common carrier.
(13) "inland portion" means the charge to the public by a common carrier for the nonocean portion of through transportation.
(14) "loyalty contract" means a contract with an ocean common carrier or conference, other than a service contract or contract based upon time-volume rates, by which a shipper obtains lower rates by committing all or a fixed portion of its cargo to that carrier or conference.
(15) "marine terminal operator" means a person engaged in the United States in the business of furnishing wharfage, dock, warehouse, or other terminal facilities in connection with a common carrier.
(16) "maritime labor agreement" means a collective-bargaining agreement between an employer subject to this Act, or group of such employers, and a labor organization representing employees in the maritime or stevedoring industry, or an agreement preparatory to such a collective-bargaining agreement among members of a multiemployer bargaining group, or an agreement specifically implementing provisions of such a collective-bargaining agreement or providing for the formation, financing, or administration of a multiemployer bargaining group; but the term does not include an assessment agreement.
(17) "non-vessel-operating common carrier" means a common carrier that does not operate the vessels by which the ocean transportation is provided, and is a shipper in its relationship with an ocean common carrier.
(18) "ocean common carrier" means a vessel-operating common carrier; but the term does not include one engaged in ocean transportation by ferry boat or ocean tramp.

(19) "ocean freight forwarder" means a person in the United States that—

(A) dispatches shipments from the United States via common carriers and books or otherwise arranges space for those shipments on behalf of shippers; and

(B) processes the documentation or performs related activities incident to those shipments.

(20) "person" includes individuals, corporations, partnerships, and associations existing under or authorized by the laws of the United States or of a foreign country.

(21) "service contract" means a contract between a shipper and an ocean common carrier or conference in which the shipper makes a commitment to provide a certain minimum quantity of cargo over a fixed time period, and the ocean common carrier or conference commits to a certain rate or rate schedule as well as a defined service level—such as, assured space, transit time, port rotation, or similar service features; the contract may also specify provisions in the event of nonperformance on the part of either party.

(22) "shipment" means all of the cargo carried under the terms of a single bill of lading.

(23) "shipper" means an owner or person for whose account the ocean transportation of cargo is provided or the person to whom delivery is to be made.

(24) "shippers' association" means a group of shippers that consolidates or distributes freight on a nonprofit basis for the members of the group in order to secure carload, truckload, or other volume rates or service contracts.

(25) "through rate" means the single amount charged by a common carrier in connection with through transportation.

(26) "through transportation" means continuous transportation between origin and destination for which a through rate is assessed and which is offered or performed by one or more carriers, at least one of which is a common carrier, between a United States point or port and a foreign point or port.

(27) "United States" includes the several States, the District of Columbia, the Commonwealth of Puerto Rico, the Commonwealth of the Northern Marianas, and all other United States territories and possessions.

SEC. 4. AGREEMENTS WITHIN SCOPE OF ACT.

(a) OCEAN COMMON CARRIERS.—This Act applies to agreements by or among ocean common carriers to—

(1) discuss, fix, or regulate transportation rates, including through rates, cargo space accommodations, and other conditions of service;

(2) pool or apportion traffic, revenues, earnings, or losses;

(3) allot ports or restrict or otherwise regulate the number and character of sailings between ports;

(4) limit or regulate the volume or character of cargo or passenger traffic to be carried;

(5) engage in exclusive, preferential, or cooperative working arrangements among themselves or with one or more marine terminal operators or non-vessel-operating common carriers;

(6) control, regulate, or prevent competition in international ocean transportation; and

(7) regulate or prohibit their use of service contracts.

(b) MARINE TERMINAL OPERATORS.—This Act applies to agreements (to the extent the agreements involve ocean transportation in the foreign commerce of the United States) among marine terminal operators and among one or more marine terminal operators and one or more ocean common carriers to—

(1) discuss, fix, or regulate rates or other conditions of service; and

(2) engage in exclusive, preferential, or cooperative working arrangements.

(c) ACQUISITIONS.—This Act does not apply to an acquisition by any person, directly or indirectly, of any voting security or assets of any other person.

SEC. 5. AGREEMENTS.

(a) FILING REQUIREMENTS.—A true copy of every agreement entered into with respect to an activity described in section 4 of this Act shall be filed with the Commission, except agreements related to transportation to be performed within or between foreign countries and agreements among common carriers to establish, operate, or maintain a marine terminal in the United States. In the case of an oral agreement, a complete memorandum specifying in detail the substance of the agreement shall be filed. The Commission may by regulation prescribe the form and manner in which an agreement shall be filed and the additional information and documents necessary to evaluate the agreement.

(b) CONFERENCE AGREEMENTS.—Each conference agreement must—

(1) state its purpose;

(2) provide reasonable and equal terms and conditions for admission and readmission to conference membership for any ocean common carrier willing to serve the particular trade or route;

(3) permit any member to withdraw from conference membership upon reasonable notice without penalty;

(4) at the request of any member, require an independent neutral body to police fully the obligations of the conference and its members;

(5) prohibit the conference from engaging in conduct prohibited by section 10(c) (1) or (3) of this Act;

(6) provide for a consultation process designed to promote—

(A) commercial resolution of disputes, and

(B) cooperation with shippers in preventing and eliminating malpractices;

(7) establish procedures for promptly and fairly considering shippers' requests and complaints; and

(8) provide that any member of the conference may take independent action on any rate or service item required to be filed in a tariff under section 8(a) of this Act upon not more than 10 calendar days' notice to the conference and that the conference will include the new rate or service item in its tariff for use by that member, effective no later than 10 calendar days after receipt of the notice, and by any other member that notifies the conference that it elects to adopt the independent rate or service item on or after its effective date, in lieu of the existing conference tariff provision for that rate or service item.

(c) INTERCONFERENCE AGREEMENTS.—Each agreement between carriers not members of the same conference must provide the right of independent action for each carrier. Each agreement between conferences must provide the right of independent action for each conference.

(d) ASSESSMENT AGREEMENTS.—Assessment agreements shall be filed with the Commission and become effective on filing. The Commission shall thereafter, upon complaint filed within 2 years of the date of the agreement, disapprove, cancel, or modify any such agreement, or charge or assessment pursuant thereto, that it finds, after notice and hearing, to be unjustly discriminatory or unfair as between carriers, shippers, or ports. The Commission shall issue its final decision in any such proceeding within 1 year of the date of filing of the complaint. To the extent that an assessment or charge is found in the proceeding to be unjustly discriminatory or unfair as between carriers, shippers, or ports, the Commission shall remedy the unjust discrimination or unfairness for the period of time between the filing of the complaint and the final decision by means of assessment adjustments. These adjustments shall be implemented by prospective credits or debits to future assessments or charges, except in the case of a complainant who has ceased activities subject to the assessment or charge, in which case reparation may be awarded. Except for this subsection and section 7(a) of this Act, this Act, the Shipping Act, 1916, and the Intercoastal Shipping Act, 1933, do not apply to assessment agreements.

(e) MARITIME LABOR AGREEMENTS.—This Act, the Shipping Act, 1916, and the Intercoastal Shipping Act, 1933, do not apply to maritime labor agreements. This subsection does not exempt from this Act, the Shipping Act, 1916, or the Intercoastal Shipping Act, 1933, any rates, charges, regulations, or practices of a common carrier that are required to be set forth in a tariff, whether or not those rates, charges, regulations, or practices arise out of, or are otherwise related to, a maritime labor agreement.

SEC. 6. ACTION ON AGREEMENTS.

(a) NOTICE.—Within 7 days after an agreement is filed, the Commission shall transmit a notice of its filing to the Federal Register for publication.

(b) REVIEW STANDARD.—The Commission shall reject any agreement filed under section 5(a) of this Act that, after preliminary review, it finds does not meet the requirements of section 5. The Commission shall notify in writing the person filing the agreement of the reason for rejection of the agreement.

(c) REVIEW AND EFFECTIVE DATE.—Unless rejected by the Commission under subsection (b), agreements, other than assessment agreements, shall become effective—

(1) on the 45th day after filing, or on the 30th day after notice of the filing is published in the Federal Register, whichever day is later; or

(2) if additional information or documentary material is requested under subsection (d), on the 45th day after the Commission receives—

(A) all the additional information and documentary material requested; or

(B) if the request is not fully complied with, the information and documentary material submitted and a statement of the reasons for noncompliance with the request. The period specified in paragraph (2) may be extended only by the United States District Court for the District of Columbia upon an application of the Commission under subsection (i).

(d) ADDITIONAL INFORMATION.—Before the expiration of the period specified in subsection (c)(1), the Commission may request from the person filing the agreement any additional information and documentary material it deems necessary to make the determinations required by this section.

(e) REQUEST FOR EXPEDITED APPROVAL.—The Commission may, upon request of the filing party, shorten the review period specified in subsection (c), but in no event to a date less than 14 days after notice of the filing of the agreement is published in the Federal Register.

(f) TERM OF AGREEMENTS.—The Commission may not limit the effectiveness of an agreement to a fixed term.

(g) SUBSTANTIALLY ANTICOMPETITIVE AGREEMENTS.—If, at any time after the filing or effective date of an agreement, the Commission determines that the agreement is likely, by a reduction in competition, to produce an unreasonable reduction in transportation service or an unreasonable increase in transportation cost, it may, after notice to the person filing the agreement, seek appropriate injunctive relief under subsection (h).

(h) INJUNCTIVE RELIEF.—The Commission may, upon making the determination specified in subsection (g), bring suit in the United States District Court for the District of Columbia to enjoin operation of the agreement. The court may issue a temporary restraining order or preliminary injunction and, upon a showing that the agreement is likely, by a reduction in competition, to produce an unreasonable reduction in transportation service or an unreasonable increase in transportation cost, may enter a permanent injunction. In a suit under this subsection, the burden of proof is on the Commission. The court may not allow a third party to intervene with respect to a claim under this subsection.

(i) COMPLIANCE WITH INFORMATIONAL NEEDS.—If a person filing an agreement, or an officer, director, partner, agent, or employee thereof, fails substantially to comply with a request for the submission of additional information or documentary material within the period specified in subsection (c), the United States District Court for the District of Columbia, at the request of the Commission—

(1) may order compliance;

(2) shall extend the period specified in subsection (c)(2) until there has been substantial compliance; and

(3) may grant such other equitable relief as the court in its discretion determines necessary or appropriate.

(j) NONDISCLOSURE OF SUBMITTED MATERIAL.—Except for an agreement filed under section 5 of this Act, information and documentary material filed with the Commission under section 5 or 6 is exempt from disclosure under section 552 of title 5, United States Code and may not be made public except as may be relevant to an administrative or judicial action or proceeding. This section does not prevent disclosure to either body of Congress or to a duly authorized committee or subcommittee of Congress.

(k) REPRESENTATION.—Upon notice to the Attorney General, the Commission may represent itself in district court proceedings under subsections (h) and (i) of this section and section 11(h) of this Act. With the approval of the Attorney General, the Commission may represent itself in proceedings in the United States Courts of Appeal under subsections (h) and (i) of this section and section 11(h) of this Act.

SEC. 7. EXEMPTION FROM ANTITRUST LAWS.

(a) IN GENERAL.—The antitrust laws do not apply to—

(1) any agreement that has been filed under section 5 of this Act and is effective under section 5(d) or section 6, or is exempt under section 16 of this Act from any requirement of this Act;

(2) any activity or agreement within the scope of this Act, whether permitted under or prohibited by this Act, undertaken or entered into with a reasonable basis to conclude that (A) it is pursuant to an agreement on file with the Commission and in effect when the activity took place, or (B) it is exempt under section 16 of this Act from any filing requirement of this Act;

(3) any agreement or activity that relates to transportation services within or between foreign countries, whether or not via the United States, unless that agreement or activity has a direct, substantial, and reasonably foreseeable effect on the commerce of the United States;

(4) any agreement or activity concerning the foreign inland segment of through transportation that is part of transportation provided in a United States import or export trade;

(5) any agreement or activity to provide or furnish wharfage, dock, warehouse, or other terminal facilities outside the United States; or

(6) subject to section 20(e)(2) of this Act, any agreement, modification, or cancellation approved by the Commission before the effective date of this Act under section 15 of the Shipping Act, 1916, or permitted under section 14b thereof, and any properly published tariff, rate, fare, or charge, classification, rule, or regulation explanatory thereof implementing that agreement, modification, or cancellation.

(b) EXCEPTIONS.—This Act does not extend antitrust immunity—

(1) to any agreement with or among air carriers, rail carriers, motor carriers, or common carriers by water not subject to this Act with respect to transportation within the United States;

(2) to any discussion or agreement among common carriers that are subject to this Act regarding the inland divisions (as opposed to the inland portions) of through rates within the United States; or

(3) to any agreement among common carriers subject to this Act to establish, operate, or maintain a marine terminal in the United States.

(c) LIMITATIONS.—(1) Any determination by an agency or court that results in the denial or removal of the immunity to the antitrust laws set forth in subsection (a) shall not remove or alter the antitrust immunity for the period before the determination.

(2) No person may recover damages under section 4 of the Clayton Act (15 U.S.C. 15), or obtain injunctive relief under section 16 of that Act (15 U.S.C. 26), for conduct prohibited by this Act.

SEC. 8. TARIFFS.

(a) IN GENERAL.—

(1) Except with regard to bulk cargo, forest products, recycled metal scrap, waste paper, and paper waste, each common carrier and conference shall file with the Commission, and keep open to public inspection, tariffs showing all its rates, charges, classifications, rules, and practices between all points or ports on its own route and on any through transportation route that has been established. However, common carriers shall not be required to state separately or otherwise reveal in tariff filings the inland divisions of a through rate. Tariffs shall—

(A) state the places between which cargo will be carried;

(B) list each classification of cargo in use;

(C) state the level of ocean freight forwarder compensation, if any, by a carrier or conference;

(D) state separately each terminal or other charge, privilege, or facility under the control of the carrier or conference and any rules or regulations that in any way change, affect, or determine any part or the aggregate of the rates or charges; and

(E) include sample copies of any loyalty contract, bill of lading, contract of affreightment, or other document evidencing the transportation agreement.

(2) Copies of tariffs shall be made available to any person, and a reasonable charge may be assessed for them.

(b) TIME-VOLUME RATES.—Rates shown in tariffs filed under subsection (a) may vary with the volume of cargo offered over a specified period of time.

(c) SERVICE CONTRACTS.—An ocean common carrier or conference may enter into a service contract with a shipper or shippers' association subject to the requirements of this Act. Except for service contracts dealing with bulk cargo, forest products, recycled metal scrap, waste paper, or paper waste, each contract entered into under this subsection shall be filed confidentially with the Commission, and at the same time, a concise statement of its essential terms shall be filed with the Commission and made available to the general public in tariff format, and those essential terms shall be available to all shippers similarly situated. The essential terms shall include—

(1) the origin and destination port ranges in the case of port-to-port movements, and the origin and destination geographic areas in the case of through intermodal movements;

(2) the commodity or commodities involved;

(3) the minimum volume;

(4) the line-haul rate;

(5) the duration;

(6) service commitments; and

(7) the liquidated damages for nonperformance, if any.

The exclusive remedy for a breach of a contract entered into under this subsection shall be an action in an appropriate court, unless the parties otherwise agree.

(d) RATES.—No new or initial rate or change in an existing rate that results in an increased cost to the shipper may become effective earlier than 30 days after filing with the Commission. The Commission, for good cause, may allow such a new or initial rate or change to become effective in less than 30 days. A change in an existing rate that results in a decreased cost to the shipper may become effective upon publication and filing with the Commission.

(e) REFUNDS.—The Commission may, upon application of a carrier or shipper, permit a common carrier or conference to refund a portion of freight charges collected from a shipper or to waive the collection of a portion of the charges from a shipper if—

(1) there is an error in a tariff of a clerical or administrative nature or an error due to inadvertence in failing to file a new tariff and the refund will not result in discrimination among shippers, ports, or carriers;

(2) the common carrier or conference has, prior to filing an application for authority to make a refund, filed a new tariff with the Commission that sets forth the rate on which the refund or waiver would be based;

(3) the common carrier or conference agrees that if permission is granted by the Commission, an appropriate notice will be published in the tariff, or such other steps taken as the Commission may require that give notice of the rate on which the refund or waiver would be based, and additional refunds or waivers as appropriate shall be made with respect to other shipments in the manner prescribed by the Commission in its order approving the application; and

(4) the application for refund or waiver is filed with the Commission within 180 days from the date of shipment.

(f) FORM.—The Commission may by regulation prescribe the form and manner in which the tariffs required by this section shall be published and filed. The Commission may reject a tariff that is not filed in conformity with this section and its regulations. Upon rejection by the Commission, the tariff is void and its use is unlawful.

SEC. 9. CONTROLLED CARRIERS.

(a) CONTROLLED CARRIER RATES.—No controlled carrier subject to this section may maintain rates or charges in its tariffs filed with the Commission that are below a level that is just and reasonable, nor may any such carrier establish or maintain unjust or unreasonable classifications, rules, or regulations in those tariffs. An unjust or unreasonable classification, rule, or regulation means one that results or is likely to result in the carriage or handling of cargo at rates or charges that are below a just and reasonable level. The Commission may, at any time after notice and hearing, disapprove any rates, charges, classifications, rules, or regulations that the controlled carrier has failed to demonstrate to be just and reasonable. In a proceeding under this subsection, the burden of proof is on the controlled carrier to demonstrate that its rates, charges, classifications, rules, or regulations are just and reasonable. Rates, charges, classifications, rules, or regulations filed by a controlled carrier that have been rejected, suspended, or disapproved by the Commission are void and their use is unlawful.

(b) RATE STANDARDS.—For the purpose of this section, in determining whether rates, charges, classifications, rules, or regulations by a controlled carrier are just and reasonable, the Commission may take into account appropriate factors including, but not limited to, whether—

(1) the rates or charges which have been filed or which would result from the pertinent classifications, rules, or regulations are below a level which is fully compensatory to the controlled carrier based upon that carrier's actual costs or upon its constructive costs, which are hereby defined as the costs of another carrier, other than a controlled carrier, operating similar vessels and equipment in the same or a similar trade;

(2) the rates, charges, classifications, rules, or regulations are the same as or similar to those filed or assessed by other carriers in the same trade;

(3) the rates, charges, classifications, rules, or regulations are required to assure movement of particular cargo in the trade; or

(4) the rates, charges, classifications, rules, or regulations are required to maintain acceptable continuity, level, or quality of common carrier service to or from affected ports.

(c) EFFECTIVE DATE OF RATES.—Notwithstanding section 8(d) of this Act, the rates, charges, classifications, rules, or regulations of controlled carriers may not, without special permission of the Commission, become effective sooner than the 30th day after the date of filing with the Commission. Each controlled carrier shall, upon the request of the Commission, file, within 20 days of request (with respect to its existing or proposed rates, charges, classifications, rules, or regulations), a statement of justification that sufficiently details the controlled carrier's need and purpose for such rates, charges, classifications, rules, or regulations upon which the Commission may reasonably base its determination of the lawfulness thereof.

(d) DISAPPROVAL OF RATES.—Whenever the Commission is of the opinion that the rates, charges, classifications, rules, or regulations filed by a controlled carrier may be unjust and unreasonable, the Commission may issue an order to the controlled carrier to show cause why those rates, charges, classifications, rules, or regulations should not be disapproved. Pending a determination as to their lawfulness in such a proceeding, the Commission may suspend the rates, charges, classifications, rules, or regulations at any time before their effective date. In the case of rates, charges, classifications, rules, or regulations that have already become effective, the Commission may, upon the issuance of an order to show cause, suspend those rates, charges, classifications, rules, or regulations on not less than 60 days' notice to the controlled carrier. No period of suspension under this subsection may be greater than 180 days. Whenever the Commission has suspended any rates, charges, classifications, rules, or regulations under this subsection, the affected carrier may file new rates, charges, classifications, rules, or regulations to take effect immediately during the suspension period in lieu of the suspended rates, charges, classifications, rules, or regulations—except that the Commission may reject the new rates, charges, classifications, rules, or regulations if it is of the opinion that they are unjust and unreasonable.

(e) PRESIDENTIAL REVIEW.—Concurrently with the publication thereof, the Commission shall transmit to the President each order of suspension or final order of disapproval of rates, charges, classifications, rules, or regulations of a controlled carrier subject to this section. Within 10 days after the receipt or the effective date of the Commission order, the President may request the Commission in writing to stay the effect of the Commission's order if the President finds that the stay is required for reasons of national defense or foreign policy, which reasons shall be specified in the report. Notwithstanding any other law, the Commission shall immediately grant the request by the issuance of an order in which the President's request shall be described. During any such stay, the President shall, whenever practicable, attempt to resolve the matter in controversy by negotiation with representatives of the applicable foreign governments.

(f) EXCEPTIONS.—This section does not apply to—

(1) a controlled carrier of a state whose vessels are entitled by a treaty of the United States to receive national or most-favored-nation treatment;

(2) a controlled carrier of a state which, on the effective date of this section, has subscribed to the statement of shipping policy contained in note 1 to annex A of the Code of Liberalization of Current Invisible Operations, adopted by the Council of the Organization for Economic Cooperation and Development;

(3) rates, charges, classifications, rules, or regulations of a controlled carrier in any particular trade that are covered by an agreement effective under section 5 of this Act, other than an agreement in which all of the members are controlled carriers not otherwise excluded from the provisions of this subsection;

(4) rates, charges, classifications, rules, or regulations governing the transportation of cargo by a controlled carrier between the country by whose government it is owned or controlled, as defined herein and the United States; or

(5) a trade served exclusively by controlled carriers.

SEC. 10. PROHIBITED ACTS.

(a) IN GENERAL.—No person may—

(1) knowingly and willfully, directly or indirectly, by means of false billing, false classification, false weighing, false report of weight, false measurement, or by any other unjust or unfair device or means obtain or attempt to obtain ocean transportation for property at less than the rates or charges that would otherwise be applicable;

(2) operate under an agreement required to be filed under section 5 of this Act that has not become effective under section 6, or that has been rejected, disapproved, or canceled; or

(3) operate under an agreement required to be filed under section 5 of this Act except in accordance with the terms of the agreement or any modifications made by the Commission to the agreement.

(b) COMMON CARRIERS.—No common carrier, either alone or in conjunction with any other person, directly or indirectly, may—

(1) charge, demand, collect, or receive greater, less, or different compensation for the transportation of property or for any service in connection therewith than the rates and charges that are shown in its tariffs or service contracts;

(2) rebate, refund, or remit in any manner, or by any device, any portion of its rates except in accordance with its tariffs or service contracts;

(3) extend or deny to any person any privilege, concession, equipment, or facility except in accordance with its tariffs or service contracts;

(4) allow any person to obtain transportation for property at less than the rates or charges established by the carrier in its tariff or service contract by means of false billing, false classification, false weighing, false measurement, or by any other unjust or unfair device or means;

(5) retaliate against any shipper by refusing, or threatening to refuse, cargo space accommodations when available, or resort to other unfair or unjustly discriminatory methods because the shipper has patronized another carrier, or has filed a complaint, or for any other reason;

(6) except for service contracts, engage in any unfair or unjustly discriminatory practice in the matter of—

(A) rates;

(B) cargo classifications;

(C) cargo space accommodations or other facilities, due regard being had for the proper loading of the vessel and the available tonnage;

(D) the loading and landing of freight; or

(E) the adjustment and settlement of claims;

(7) employ any fighting ship;

(8) offer or pay any deferred rebates;

(9) use a loyalty contract, except in conformity with the antitrust laws;

(10) demand, charge, or collect any rate or charge that is unjustly discriminatory between shippers or ports;

(11) except for service contracts, make or give any undue or unreasonable preference or advantage to any particular person, locality, or description of traffic in any respect whatsoever;

(12) subject any particular person, locality, or description of traffic to an unreasonable refusal to deal or any undue or unreasonable prejudice or disadvantage in any respect whatsoever;

(13) refuse to negotiate with a shippers' association; or

(14) knowingly disclose, offer, solicit, or receive any information concerning the nature, kind, quantity, destination, consignee, or routing of any property tendered or delivered to a common carrier without the consent of the shipper or consignee if that information—

(A) may be used to the detriment or prejudice of the shipper or consignee;

(B) may improperly disclose its business transaction to a competitor; or

(C) may be used to the detriment or prejudice of any common carrier.

Nothing in paragraph (14) shall be construed to prevent providing such information, in response to legal process, to the United States, or to an independent neutral body operating within the scope of its authority to fulfill the policing obligations of the parties to an agreement effective under this Act. Nor shall it be prohibited for any ocean common carrier that is a party to a conference agreement approved under this Act, or any receiver, trustee, lessee, agent, or employee of that carrier, or any other person authorized by that carrier to receive information, to give information to the conference or any person, firm, corporation, or agency designated by the conference, or to prevent the conference or its designee from soliciting or receiving information for the purpose of determining whether a shipper or consignee has breached an agreement with the conference or its member lines or for the purpose of determining whether a member of the conference has breached the conference agreement, or for the purpose of compiling statistics of cargo movement, but the use of such information for any other purpose prohibited by this Act or any other Act is prohibited.

(c) CONCERTED ACTION.—No conference or group of two or more common carriers may—

(1) boycott or take any other concerted action resulting in an unreasonable refusal to deal;

(2) engage in conduct that unreasonably restricts the use of intermodal services or technological innovations;

(3) engage in any predatory practice designed to eliminate the participation, or deny the entry, in a particular trade of a common carrier not a member of the conference, a group of common carriers, an ocean tramp, or a bulk carrier;

(4) negotiate with a nonocean carrier or group of nonocean carriers (for example, truck, rail, or air operators) on any matter relating to rates or services provided to ocean common carriers within the United States by those nonocean carriers: *Provided,* That this paragraph does not prohibit the setting and

publishing of a joint through rate by a conference, joint venture, or an association of ocean common carriers;

(5) deny in the export foreign commerce of the United States compensation to an ocean freight forwarder or limit that compensation to less than a reasonable amount; or

(6) allocate shippers among specific carriers that are parties to the agreement or prohibit a carrier that is a party to the agreement from soliciting cargo from a particular shipper, except as otherwise required by the law of the United States or the importing or exporting country, or as agreed to by a shipper in a service contract.

(d) COMMON CARRIERS, OCEAN FREIGHT FORWARDERS, AND MARINE TERMINAL OPERATORS.—

(1) No common carrier, ocean freight forwarder, or marine terminal operator may fail to establish, observe, and enforce just and reasonable regulations and practices relating to or connected with receiving, handling, storing, or delivering property.

(2) No marine terminal operator may agree with another marine terminal operator or with a common carrier to boycott, or unreasonably discriminate in the provision of terminal services, to any common carrier or ocean tramp.

(3) The prohibitions in subsection (b) (11), (12), and (14) of this section apply to marine terminal operators.

(e) JOINT VENTURES.—For purposes of this section, a joint venture or consortium of two or more common carriers but operated as a single entity shall be treated as a single common carrier.

SEC. 11. COMPLAINTS, INVESTIGATIONS, REPORTS, AND REPARATIONS.

(a) FILING OF COMPLAINTS.—Any person may file with the Commission a sworn complaint alleging a violation of this Act, other than section 6(g), and may seek reparation for any injury caused to the complainant by that violation.

(b) SATISFACTION OR INVESTIGATION OF COMPLAINTS.—The Commission shall furnish a copy of a complaint filed pursuant to subsection (a) of this section to the person named therein who shall, within a reasonable time specified by the Commission, satisfy the complaint or answer it in writing. If the complaint is not satisfied, the Commission shall investigate it in an appropriate manner and make an appropriate order.

(c) COMMISSION INVESTIGATIONS.—The Commission, upon complaint or upon its own motion, may investigate any conduct or agreement that it believes may be in violation of this Act. Except in the case of an injunction granted under subsection (h) of this section, each agreement under investigation under this section remains in effect until the Commission issues an order under this subsection. The Commission may by order disapprove, cancel, or modify any agreement filed under section 5(a) of this Act that operates in violation of this Act. With respect to agreements inconsistent with section 6(g) of this Act, the Commission's sole remedy is under section 6(h).

(d) CONDUCT OF INVESTIGATION.—Within 10 days after the initiation of a proceeding under this section, the Commission shall set a date on or before which its final decision will be issued. This date may be extended for good cause by order of the Commission.

(e) UNDUE DELAYS.—If, within the time period specified in subsection (d), the Commission determines that it is unable to issue a final decision because of undue delays caused by a party to the proceedings, the Commission may impose sanctions, including entering a decision adverse to the delaying party.

(f) REPORTS.—The Commission shall make a written report of every investigation made under this Act in which a hearing was held stating its conclusions, decisions, findings of fact, and order. A copy of this report shall be furnished to all parties. The Commission shall publish each report for public information, and the published report shall be competent evidence in all courts of the United States.

(g) REPARATIONS.—For any complaint filed within 3 years after the cause of action accrued, the Commission shall, upon petition of the complainant and after notice and hearing, direct payment of reparations to the complainant for actual injury (which, for purposes of this subsection, also includes the loss of interest at commercial rates compounded from the date of injury) caused by a violation of this Act plus reasonable attorney's fees. Upon a showing that the injury was caused by activity that is prohibited by section 10(b) (5) or (7) or section 10(c) (1) or (4) of this Act, or that violates section 10(a) (2) or (3), the Commission may direct the payment of additional amounts; but the total recovery of a complainant may not exceed twice the amount of the actual injury. In the case of injury caused by an activity that is prohibited by section 10(b)(6) (A) or (B) of this Act, the amount of the injury shall be the difference between the rate paid by the injured shipper and the most favorable rate paid by another shipper.

(h) INJUNCTION.—

(1) In connection with any investigation conducted under this section, the Commission may bring suit in a district court of the United States to enjoin conduct in violation of this Act. Upon a showing that standards for granting injunctive relief by courts of equity are met and after notice to the defendant, the court may grant a temporary restraining order or preliminary injunction for a period not to exceed 10 days after the Commission has issued an order disposing of the issues under investigation. Any such suit shall be brought in a district in which the defendant resides or transacts business.

(2) After filing a complaint with the Commission under subsection (a), the complainant may file suit in a district court of the United States to enjoin conduct in violation of this Act. Upon a showing that standards for granting injunctive relief by courts of equity are met and after notice to the defendant, the court may grant a temporary restraining order or preliminary injunction for a period not to exceed 10 days after the Commission has issued an order disposing of the complaint. Any such suit shall be brought in the district in which the defendant has been sued by the Commission under paragraph (1); or, if no suit has been filed, in a district in which the defendant resides or transacts business. A defendant that prevails in a suit under this paragraph shall be allowed reasonable attorney's fees to be assessed and collected as part of the costs of the suit.

SEC. 12. SUBPENAS AND DISCOVERY.

(a) IN GENERAL.—In investigations and adjudicatory proceedings under this Act—

(1) depositions, written interrogatories, and discovery procedures may be utilized by any party under rules and regulations issued by the Commission that, to the extent practicable, shall be in conformity with the rules applicable in civil proceedings in the district courts of the United States; and

(2) the Commission may by subpena compel the attendance of witnesses and the production of books, papers, documents, and other evidence.

(b) WITNESS FEES.—Witnesses shall, unless otherwise prohibited by law, be entitled to the same fees and mileage as in the courts of the United States.

SEC. 13. PENALTIES.

(a) ASSESSMENT OF PENALTY.—Whoever violates a provision of this Act, a regulation issued thereunder, or a Commission order is liable to the United States for a civil penalty. The amount of the civil penalty, unless otherwise provided in this Act, may not exceed $5,000 for each violation unless the violation was willfully and knowingly committed, in which case the amount of the civil penalty may not exceed $25,000 for each violation. Each day of a continuing violation constitutes a separate offense.

(b) ADDITIONAL PENALTIES.—

(1) For a violation of section 10(b) (1), (2), (3), (4), or (8) of this Act, the Commission may suspend any or all tariffs of the common carrier, or that common carrier's right to use any or all tariffs of conferences of which it is a member, for a period not to exceed 12 months.

(2) For failure to supply information ordered to be produced or compelled by subpena under section 12 of this Act, the Commission may, after notice and an opportunity for hearing, suspend any or all tariffs of a common carrier, or that common carrier's right to use any or all tariffs of conferences of which it is a member.

(3) A common carrier that accepts or handles cargo for carriage under a tariff that has been suspended or after its right to utilize that tariff has been suspended is subject to a civil penalty of not more than $50,000 for each shipment.

(4) If, in defense of its failure to comply with a subpena or discovery order, a common carrier alleges that documents or information located in a foreign country cannot be produced because of the laws of that country, the Commission shall immediately notify the Secretary of State of the failure to comply and of the allegation relating to foreign laws. Upon receiving the notification, the Secretary of State shall promptly consult with the government of the nation within which the documents or information are alleged to be located for the purpose of assisting the Commission in obtaining the documents or information sought.

(5) If, after notice and hearing, the Commission finds that the action of a common carrier, acting alone or in concert with any person, or a foreign government has unduly impaired access of a vessel documented under the laws of the United States to ocean trade between foreign ports, the Commission shall take action that it finds appropriate, including the imposition of any of the penalties authorized under paragraphs (1), (2), and (3) of this subsection.

(6) Before an order under this subsection becomes effective, it shall be immediately submitted to the President who may, within 10 days after receiving it, disapprove the order if the President finds that disapproval is required for reasons of the national defense or the foreign policy of the United States.

(c) ASSESSMENT PROCEDURES.—Until a matter is referred to the Attorney General, the Commission may, after notice and an opportunity for hearing, assess each civil penalty provided for in this Act. In determining the amount of the penalty, the Commission shall take into account the nature, circumstances, extent, and gravity of the violation committed and, with respect to the violator, the degree of culpability, history of prior offenses, ability to pay, and such other matters as justice may require. The Commission may compromise, modify, or remit, with or without conditions, any civil penalty.

(d) REVIEW OF CIVIL PENALTY.—A person against whom a civil penalty is assessed under this section may obtain review thereof under chapter 158 of title 28, United States Code.

(e) FAILURE TO PAY ASSESSMENT.—If a person fails to pay an assessment of a civil penalty after it has become final or after the appropriate court has entered final judgment in favor of the Commission, the Attorney General at the request of the Commission may seek to recover the amount assessed in an appropriate district court of the United States. In such an action, the court shall enforce the Commission's order unless it finds that the order was not regularly made or duly issued.

(f) LIMITATIONS.—

(1) No penalty may be imposed on any person for conspiracy to violate section 10 (a)(1), (b)(1), or (b)(4) of this Act, or to defraud the Commission by concealment of such a violation.

(2) Each proceeding to assess a civil penalty under this section shall be commenced within 5 years from the date the violation occurred.

SEC. 14. COMMISSION ORDERS.

(a) IN GENERAL.—Orders of the Commission relating to a violation of this Act or a regulation issued thereunder shall be made, upon sworn complaint or on its own motion, only after opportunity for hearing. Each order of the Commission shall continue in force for the period of time specified in the order or until suspended, modified, or set aside by the Commission or a court of competent jurisdiction.

(b) REVERSAL OR SUSPENSION OF ORDERS.—The Commission may reverse, suspend, or modify any order made by it, and upon application of any party to a proceeding may grant a rehearing of the same or any matter determined therein. No rehearing may, except by special order of the Commission, operate as a stay of that order.

(c) ENFORCEMENT OF NONREPARATION ORDERS.—In case of violation of an order of the Commission, or for failure to comply with a Commission subpena, the Attorney General, at the request of the Commission, or any party injured by the violation, may seek enforcement by a United States district court having jurisdiction over the parties. If, after hearing, the court determines that the order was properly made and duly issued, it shall enforce the order by an appropriate injunction or other process, mandatory or otherwise.

(d) ENFORCEMENT OF REPARATION ORDERS.—(1) In case of violation of an order of the Commission for the payment of reparation, the person to whom the award was made may seek enforcement of the order in a United States district court having jurisdiction of the parties.

(2) In a United States district court the findings and order of the Commission shall be prima facie evidence of the facts therein stated, and the petitioner shall not be liable for costs, nor for the costs of any subsequent stage of the proceedings, unless they accrue upon his appeal. A petitioner in a United States district court who prevails shall be allowed reasonable attorney's fees to be assessed and collected as part of the costs of the suit.

(3) All parties in whose favor the Commission has made an award of reparation by a single order may be joined as plaintiffs, and all other parties in the order may be joined as defendants, in a single suit in a district in which any one plaintiff could maintain a suit against any one defendant. Service of process against a defendant not found in that district may be made in a district in which is located any office of, or point of call on a regular route operated by, that defendant. Judgment may be entered in favor of any plaintiff against the defendant liable to that plaintiff.

(e) STATUTE OF LIMITATIONS.—An action seeking enforcement of a Commission order must be filed within 3 years after the date of the violation of the order.

SEC. 15. REPORTS AND CERTIFICATES.

(a) REPORTS.—The Commission may require any common carrier, or any officer, receiver, trustee, lessee, agent, or employee thereof, to file with it any periodical or special report or any account, record, rate, or charge, or memorandum of any facts and transactions appertaining to the business of that common carrier. The report, account, record, rate, charge, or memorandum shall be made under oath whenever the Commission so requires, and shall be furnished in the form and within the time prescribed by the Commission. Conference minutes required to be filed with the Commission under this section shall not be released to third parties or published by the Commission.

(b) CERTIFICATION.—The Commission shall require the chief executive officer of each common carrier and, to the extent it deems feasible, may require any shipper, shippers' association, marine terminal operator, ocean freight forwarder, or broker to file a periodic written certification made under oath with the Commission attesting to—

(1) a policy prohibiting the payment, solicitation, or receipt of any rebate that is unlawful under the provisions of this Act;

(2) the fact that this policy has been promulgated recently to each owner, officer, employee, and agent thereof;

(3) the details of the efforts made within the company or otherwise to prevent or correct illegal rebating; and

(4) a policy of full cooperation with the Commission in its efforts to end those illegal practices.

Failure to file a certification shall result in a civil penalty of not more than $5,000 for each day the violation continues.

SEC. 16. EXEMPTIONS.

The Commission, upon application or on its own motion, may by order or rule exempt for the future any class of agreements between persons subject to this Act or any specified activity of those persons from any requirement of this Act if it finds that the exemption will not substantially impair effective regulation by the Commission, be unjustly discriminatory, result in a substantial reduction in competition, or be detrimental to commerce. The Commission may attach conditions to any exemption and may, by order, revoke any exemption. No order or rule of exemption or revocation of exemption may

be issued unless opportunity for hearing has been afforded interested persons and departments and agencies of the United States.

SEC. 17. REGULATIONS.

(a) The Commission may prescribe rules and regulations as necessary to carry out this Act.

(b) The Commission may prescribe interim rules and regulations necessary to carry out this Act. For this purpose, the Commission is excepted from compliance with the notice and comment requirements of section 553 of title 5, United States Code. All rules and regulations prescribed under the authority of this subsection that are not earlier superseded by final rules shall expire no later than 270 days after the date of enactment of this Act.

SEC. 18. AGENCY REPORTS AND ADVISORY COMMISSION.

(a) COLLECTION OF DATA.—For a period of 5 years following the enactment of this Act, the Commission shall collect and analyze information concerning the impact of this Act upon the international ocean shipping industry, including data on:

(1) increases or decreases in the level of tariffs;

(2) changes in the frequency or type of common carrier services available to specific ports or geographic regions;

(3) the number and strength of independent carriers in various trades; and

(4) the length of time, frequency, and cost of major types of regulatory proceedings before the Commission.

(b) CONSULTATION WITH OTHER DEPARTMENTS AND AGENCIES.—The Commission shall consult with the Department of Transportation, the Department of Justice, and the Federal Trade Commission annually concerning data collection. The Department of Transportation, the Department of Justice, and the Federal Trade Commission shall at all times have access to the data collected under this section to enable them to provide comments concerning data collection.

(c) AGENCY REPORTS.—

(1) Within 6 months after expiration of the 5-year period specified in subsection (a), the Commission shall report the information, with an analysis of the impact of this Act, to Congress, to the Advisory Commission on Conferences in Ocean Shipping established in subsection (d), and to the Department of Transportation, the Department of Justice, and the Federal Trade Commission.

(2) Within 60 days after the Commission submits its report, the Department of Transportation, the Department of Justice, and the Federal Trade Commission shall furnish an analysis of the impact of this Act to Congress and to the Advisory Commission on Conferences in Ocean Shipping.

(3) The reports required by this subsection shall specifically address the following topics:

(A) the advisability of adopting a system of tariffs based on volume and mass of shipment;

(B) the need for antitrust immunity for ports and marine terminals; and

(C) the continuing need for the statutory requirement that tariffs be filed with and enforced by the Commission.

(d) ESTABLISHMENT AND COMPOSITION OF ADVISORY COMMISSION.—

(1) Effective 5½ years after the date of enactment of this Act, there is established the Advisory Commission on Conferences in Ocean Shipping (hereinafter referred to as the "Advisory Commission").

(2) The Advisory Commission shall be composed of 17 members as follows:

(A) a cabinet level official appointed by the President;

(B) 4 members from the United States Senate appointed by the President pro tempore of the Senate, 2 from the membership of the Committee on Commerce, Science, and Transportation and 2 from the membership of the Committee on the Judiciary;

(C) 4 members from the United States House of Representatives appointed by the Speaker of the House, 2 from the membership of the Committee on Merchant Marine and Fisheries, and 2 from the membership of the Committee on the Judiciary; and

(D) 8 members from the private sector appointed by the President.

(3) The President shall designate the chairman of the Advisory Commission.

(4) The term of office for members shall be for the term of the Advisory Commission.

(5) A vacancy in the Advisory Commission shall not affect its powers, and shall be filled in the same manner in which the original appointment was made.

(6) Nine members of the Advisory Commission shall constitute a quorum, but the Advisory Commission may permit as few as 2 members to hold hearings.

(e) COMPENSATION OF MEMBERS OF THE ADVISORY COMMISSION.—

(1) Officials of the United States Government and Members of Congress who are members of the Advisory Commission shall serve without compensation in addition to that received for their services as officials and Members, but they shall be reimbursed for reasonable travel, subsistence, and other necessary expenses incurred by them in the performance of the duties vested in the Advisory Commission.

(2) Members of the Advisory Commission appointed from the private sector shall each receive compensation not exceeding the maximum per diem rate of pay for grade 18 of the General

Schedule under section 5332 of title 5, United States Code, when engaged in the performance of the duties vested in the Advisory Commission, plus reimbursement for reasonable travel, subsistence, and other necessary expenses incurred by them in the performance of those duties, notwithstanding the limitations in sections 5701 through 5733 of title 5, United States Code.

(3) Members of the Advisory Commission appointed from the private sector are not subject to section 208 of title 18, United States Code. Before commencing service, these members shall file with the Advisory Commission a statement disclosing their financial interests and business and former relationships involving or relating to ocean transportation. These statements shall be available for public inspection at the Advisory Commission's offices.

(f) ADVISORY COMMISSION FUNCTIONS.—The Advisory Commission shall conduct a comprehensive study of, and make recommendations concerning, conferences in ocean shipping. The study shall specifically address whether the Nation would be best served by prohibiting conferences, or by closed or open conferences.

(g) POWERS OF THE ADVISORY COMMISSION.—

(1) The Advisory Commission may, for the purpose of carrying out its functions, hold such hearings and sit and act at such times and places, administer such oaths, and require, by subpena or otherwise, the attendance and testimony of such witnesses, and the production of such books, records, correspondence, memorandums, papers, and documents as the Advisory Commission may deem advisable. Subpenas may be issued to any person within the jurisdiction of the United States courts, under the signature of the chairman, or any duly designated member, and may be served by any person designated by the chairman, or that member. In case of contumacy by, or refusal to obey a subpena to, any person, the Advisory Commission may advise the Attorney General who shall invoke the aid of any court of the United States within the jurisdiction of which the Advisory Commission's proceedings are carried on, or where that person resides or carries on business, in requiring the attendance and testimony of witnesses and the production of books, papers, and documents; and the court may issue an order requiring that person to appear before the Advisory Commission, there to produce records, if so ordered, or to give testimony. A failure to obey such an order of the court may be punished by the court as a contempt thereof. All process in any such case may be served in the judicial district whereof the person is an inhabitant or may be found.

(2) Each department, agency, and instrumentality of the executive branch of the Government, including independent agencies, shall furnish to the Advisory Commission, upon request made by the chairman, such information as the Advisory Commission deems necessary to carry out its functions.

(3) Upon request of the chairman, the Department of Justice, the Department of Transportation, the Federal Maritime Commission, and the Federal Trade Commission shall detail staff personnel as necessary to assist the Advisory Commission.

(4) The chairman may rent office space for the Advisory Commission, may utilize the services and facilities of other Federal agencies with or without reimbursement, may accept voluntary services notwithstanding section 1342 of title 31, United States Code, may accept, hold, and administer gifts from other Federal agencies, and may enter into contracts with any public or private person or entity for reports, research, or surveys in furtherance of the work of the Advisory Commission.

(h) FINAL REPORT.—The Commission shall, within 1 year after its establishment, submit to the President and to the Congress a final report containing a statement of the findings and conclusions of the Advisory Commission resulting from the study undertaken under subsection (f), including recommendations for such administrative, judicial, and legislative action as it deems advisable. Each recommendation made by the Advisory Commission to the President and to the Congress must have the majority vote of the Advisory Commission present and voting.

(i) EXPIRATION OF THE COMMISSION.—The Advisory Commission shall cease to exist 30 days after the submission of its final report.

(j) AUTHORIZATION OF APPROPRIATION.—There is authorized to be appropriated $500,000 to carry out the activities of the Advisory Commission.

SEC. 19. OCEAN FREIGHT FORWARDERS.

(a) LICENSE.—No person may act as an ocean freight forwarder unless that person holds a license issued by the Commission. The Commission shall issue a forwarder's license to any person that—

(1) the Commission determines to be qualified by experience and character to render forwarding services; and

(2) furnishes a bond in a form and amount determined by the Commission to insure financial responsibility that is issued by a surety company found acceptable by the Secretary of the Treasury.

(b) SUSPENSION OR REVOCATION.—The Commission shall, after notice and hearing, suspend or revoke a license if it finds that the ocean freight forwarder is not qualified to render forwarding services or that it willfully failed to comply with a provision of this Act or with a lawful order, rule, or regulation of the Commission. The Commission may also revoke a forwarder's license for failure to maintain a bond in accordance with subsection (a)(2).

(c) EXCEPTION.—A person whose primary business is the sale of merchandise may forward shipments of the merchandise for its own account without a license.

(d) COMPENSATION OF FORWARDERS BY CARRIERS.—

(1) A common carrier may compensate an ocean freight forwarder in connection with a shipment dispatched on behalf of others only when the ocean freight forwarder has certified in writing that it holds a valid license and has performed the following services:

(A) Engaged, booked, secured, reserved, or contracted directly with the carrier or its agent for space aboard a vessel or confirmed the availability of that space.

(B) Prepared and processed the ocean bill of lading, dock receipt, or other similar document with respect to the shipment.

(2) No common carrier may pay compensation for services described in paragraph (1) more than once on the same shipment.

(3) No compensation may be paid to an ocean freight forwarder except in accordance with the tariff requirements of this Act.

(4) No ocean freight forwarder may receive compensation from a common carrier with respect to a shipment in which the forwarder has a direct or indirect beneficial interest nor shall a common carrier knowingly pay compensation on that shipment.

SEC. 20. REPEALS AND CONFORMING AMENDMENTS.

(a) REPEALS.—The laws specified in the following table are repealed:

Shipping Act, 1916:	
Sec. 13	39 Stat. 732
Sec. 14a	46 App. U.S.C. 813
Sec. 14b	46 App. U.S.C. 813a
Sec. 18(b)	46 App. U.S.C. 817(b)
Sec. 18(c)	46 App. U.S.C. 817(c)
Sec. 26	46 App. U.S.C. 825
Sec. 44	46 App. U.S.C. 841b
Merchant Marine Act, 1920:	
Sec. 20	41 Stat. 996
Merchant Marine Act, 1936:	
Sec. 212(e)	46 App. U.S.C. 1122(e)
Sec. 214	46 App. U.S.C. 1124, wherever that section applies to the Federal Maritime Commission (Commission), any member of the Commission or any member, officer or employee designated by the Commission.
Omnibus Budget Reconciliation Act of 1981:	
Sec. 1608	95 Stat. 752

(b) CONFORMING AMENDMENTS.—The Shipping Act, 1916 (46 App. U.S.C. 801 et seq.), is amended as follows:

(1) in section 1 by striking the definitions "controlled carrier" and "independent ocean freight forwarder";

(2) in sections 14, 15, 1 ̂ 20, 21(a), 22, and 45 by striking "common carrier by water" wherever it appears in those sections and substituting "common carrier by water in interstate commerce";

(3) in section 14, first paragraph, by striking "or a port of a foreign country";

(4) in section 14, last paragraph, by striking all after the words "for each offense" and substituting a period;

(5) in section 15, fourth paragraph, by striking "(including changes in special rates and charges covered by section 14b of this Act which do not involve a change in the spread between such rates and charges and the rates and charges applicable to noncontract shippers)" and also "with the publication and filing requirements of section 18(b) hereof and";

(6) in section 15, sixth paragraph, by striking ", or permitted under section 14b," and in the seventh paragraph, by striking "or of section 14b";

(7) in section 16, in the paragraph designated "First", by striking all after "disadvantage in any respect" and substituting "whatsoever.";

(8) in section 17 by striking the first paragraph, and in the second paragraph, by striking "such carrier and every";

(9) in section 21(b) by striking "The Commission shall require the chief executive officer of every vessel operating common carrier by water in foreign commerce and to the extent it deems feasible, may require any shipper, consignor, consignee, forwarder, broker, other carrier or other person subject to this Act," and substituting "The Commission may, to the extent it deems feasible, require any shipper, consignor, consignee, forwarder, broker, or other person subject to this Act.";

(10) in section 22 by striking subsection (c);

(11) in section 25, at the end of the first sentence, by adding "under this Act";

(12) in section 29 by striking "any order of the board, the board," and substituting "any order of the Federal Maritime Commission under this Act, the Commission,";

(13) in sections 30 and 31, after the words "any order of the board", by adding "under this Act,";

(14) in section 32(a) by striking "and section 44"; and

(15) in section 32(c), after the words "or functions,", by adding "under this Act,".

(c) TECHNICAL AMENDMENTS.—Section 212 of the Merchant Marine Act, 1936 (46 App. U.S.C. 1122) is amended by—

(1) striking after subsection (d) the following undesignated paragraph:

"The Federal Maritime Commission is authorized and directed—"; and

(2) striking after subsection (e) the following undesignated paragraph:

"The Secretary of Transportation is authorized and directed—".

(d) EFFECTS ON CERTAIN AGREEMENTS AND CONTRACTS.—All agreements, contracts, modifications, and exemptions previously approved or licenses previously issued by the Commission shall continue in force and effect as if approved or issued under this Act; and all new agreements, contracts, and modifications to existing, pending, or new contracts or agreements shall be considered under this Act.

(e) SAVINGS PROVISIONS.—

(1) Each service contract entered into by a shipper and an ocean common carrier or conference before the date of enactment of this Act may remain in full force and effect and need not comply with the requirements of section 8(c) of this Act until 15 months after the date of enactment of this Act.

(2) This Act and the amendments made by it shall not affect any suit—

(A) filed before the date of enactment of this Act; or

(B) with respect to claims arising out of conduct engaged in before the date of enactment of this Act, filed within 1 year after the date of enactment of this Act.

SEC. 21. EFFECTIVE DATE.

This Act shall become effective 90 days after the date of its enactment, except that sections 17 and 18 shall become effective upon enactment.

SEC. 22. COMPLIANCE WITH BUDGET ACT.

Any new spending authority (within the meaning of section 401 of the Congressional Budget and Impoundment Control Act of 1974) which is provided under this Act shall be effective for any fiscal year only to the extent or in such amounts as provided in advance in appropriations Acts. Any provision of this Act that authorizes the enactment of new budget authority shall be effective only for fiscal years beginning after September 30, 1984.

Approved March 20, 1984.

APPENDIX **B** : SYMBOLS

1. ABBREVIATIONS AND ACRONYMS

a	Area
A	Ampere
A/	I (we) credit (Spanish)
A-1	First-class condition
A.A.	Average adjusters
AAA	American Arbitration Association
AAPA	American Association of Port Authorities
a.a.r.	Against all risks
AAR	Association of American Railroads
AB	*Aktiebolag* (Swedish)
abb	Illustration
ABI	Automated broker interface
ABS	American Bureau of Shipping
abt.	Department (German)
AC	Alternating current
ACP	African, Caribbean, and Pacific countries
A. cta.	Debit of (Spanish)
ACU	African currency unit
ACU	Asian clearing unit
a.d.	After date
a.d.	From today (German)
A.D.	Air dried
ADA	Anti-Dumping Act of 1921, as amended
ADAB	Australian Development Assistance Bureau
ADB	Asian Development Bank
ADBF	African Development Bank and Fund
adcom	Address commission
ADR	American depository receipt
AD VAL	Ad valorem
a/f	In favor of (Spanish)
a.f.	In favor of (French)
Affr.	Paid as used (French)
AG	Corporation (German)
AG	Arabian Gulf
AGC	African Groundnut Council
AGR	American goods returned
AGRICOLA	Agricultural on-line access system
A.H.	Aft hatch
AID	Agency for International Development
AIMU	American Institute of Marine Underwriters
AIOEC	Association of Iron-Ore Exporting Countries
AITA	International Air Transport Association (French/German)

Akc Dvo.	Joint stock company (Czech/Polish)
AMC	*American Maritime Cases*
Am M.	On the River Main (German)
AMO	Associated Marine Officers
AMVER	Automated Mutual Assistance Vessel Rescue System
ANCOM	Andean Common Market
ANRPC	Association of Natural Rubber Producing Countries
ANSI	American National Standards Institute
APHIS	Animal and Plant Health Inspection Service
APIC	African petroleum importing countries
APS	Arrival at pilot station
AQ	Any quantity
AR	American Tanker Rate Schedule, Revised
A/R	All risks
A/S	Joint stock company (Danish, Finnish, Norwegian)
A.S.A.	American Standards Association
ASEAN	Association of Southeast Asian Nations
ASOF	Australian Steamship Owners Federation
A.S.P.	American selling price
A spol.	And company (Czech)
ATA	*Admission Temporaire*/Temporary Admission
A.T.A.	American Trucking Association
ATRS	American Tanker Rate Schedule
A/V	Ad valorem
A/V	At sight (Spanish)
AWB	Air waybill
B.A.	Buenos Aires
BAD	African Development Bank or Asian Development Bank (in French)
BADEA	Banque Arab de Development Eco-nomique en Afrique
b.b.	Below bridges
B/B	Break-bulk
bbl.	Barrel
BCEAO	Central Bank of West Africa
bd. ft.	Board foot
b.d.	Bar draught
BD	Bill discounted
B.D.I.	Both dates inclusive
Bdls.	Bundles

Bds.	Boards
B/E	Bill of exchange
BEA	Bureau of Economic Analysis
BENDS	Both ends
B/G.	Bonded goods
bg.	Bag
B/H	Bill of health
B.I.	Purchasing cooperative (Swedish)
BIE	Bureau of Industrial Economics
BIMCO	Baltic & International Maritime Conference
B.I.P.M.	International Bureau of Weights and Measures (French)
BIRPI	United International Bureau for the Protection of International Property
B/L	Bill of lading
BLEU	Belgium-Luxembourg Economic Union
B.M.	Board measure
BOAD	Banque Ouest Africaine de Developpment
B.O.P.	Balance of payments
B.O.T.	Balance of trade
B.P.	British Pharmacopoeia
bq.	Barque
B/s.	Bags, bales
B.S.	Bill of sale
BSI	British Standards Institute
Bs/L	Bills of lading
B.S.T.	British summer time
B.T.	Berth terms
BTN	Brussels Tariff Nomenclature
bu.	Bushel
BWI	British West Indies
bx.	Box
c	Carat
c.c.	Current costs
C.	Degrees Celsius
C.	One hundred
C.C.	Civil commotions
Ca.	Company (Italian)
C/a	Capital account
CAB	Civil Aeronautics Board
CABEI	Central American Bank for Economic Integration
CACM	Central American Common Market
CAD	Cash against documents
CAF	Central African franc
C & F	Cost and freight
CAP	Common Agricultural Policy
CARICOM	Caribbean Community
CARIFTA	Caribbean Free Trade Association
CB	*Customs Bulletin*
CBD	Cash before delivery
CBT	Chicago Board of Trade
CC	Carrier's certificate
CCC	Commodity Credit Corporation
CCC	Customs Cooperation Council
CCCN	Customs Cooperation Council Nomenclature
CCT	Common Customs Tariff (of the European Economic Community)
cd	Candela
C&D	Collected and delivered
CDB	Caribbean Development Bank
CDC	Commonwealth Development Corporation
C/E	Country of exportation
C.E.	Consumption entry
CEA	Council of Economic Advisors

CEAO	West African Economic Community
CENSA	Council of European & Japanese National Shipowners Associations
CENTO	Central Treaty Organization
certs.	Certificates
CET	Common external tariff
c.f.	Cubic foot
C.F.	Customs form
CFA	African Financial Community
C.F.R.	Code of Federal Regulations
C.F.S.	Container freight station
CFTC	Commodity Futures Trading Commission
cg.	Centigram
C.G.A.	Cargo's (proportion of) general average
C.G.A.	Portion of general average attributable to cargo
CGFPI	Consultative Group for Food Production and Investment
CGPM	General Conference on Weights and Measures
ch.	Chain
CHL	Customhouse broker's license
CH & H	Continent between Havre and Hamburg
c/i	Certificate of insurance
c.i.	Cost and insurance
C/I	Consular invoice
Cia.	Company (Spanish/Portuguese)
CIAP	Inter-American Committee for the Alliance for Progress
CIDA	Canadian International Development Agency
Cie.	Company (French)
C.I.E.	Customs Information Exchange
CIEP	Committee for International Economic Cooperation
C.I.F.	Cost, insurance, and freight
C.I.F.C.	Cost, insurance, freight, and commission
C.I.F.E.	Cost, insurance, freight, and exchange
CIM	International Convention Concerning Carriage of Goods By Rail
CIPEC	Intergovernmental Council of Copper Exporting Countries (French)
CITA	Committee for Implementation of Textile Agreements
cl.	Centiliter
C.L.	Carload
CLC	Convention on Civil Liability for Oil Pollution Damages
cm.	Centimeter
C.M.	Customs Manual
C.M.A.	Customs Manual Amendment
CME	Chicago Mercantile Exchange
CMEA	Council for Mutual Economic Assistance
CMI	Comité Maritime International (Antwerp)
COFA	Contract of Freight Agreement
COGSA	Carriage of Goods by Sea Act
COLREGS	Convention on the International Regulations for Preventing Collisions at Sea
COMECON	Council for Mutual Economic Assistance
COMEX	Commodity Exchange, Inc.
COPAL	Cocoa Producers Alliance
Cord	Unit of measure equal to 128 cubic feet
COTP	Captain of the port
COW	Crude oil washing
C/P	Customs of the port
C/P	Charter party
C.P.	Customs of the port

C.P.	Charter party
C.P.D.	Charterers pay dues
CPI	Consumer price index
CPI-U	Consumer price index—all urban consumers
C.Q.D.	Customary quick despatch
c.r.	Current rate
C.R.	Carrier's risk
C.R.	Customs Regulations
C.R.A.	Customs Regulations Amendment
CREW	Combined rewarehouse and withdrawal (entry)
CRR	Contemporaneous reserve accounting
C.S.A.	Customs Simplification Act
C.S.C.	International Convention for Safe Containers
CSCE	Coffee, Sugar, and Cocoa Exchange
CSI	International Convention Relating to Intervention on the High Seas in Cases of Oil Pollution Casualties
ctge.	Cartage
C.T.L.	Constructive total loss
c.t.l.o.	Constructive total loss only
CTO	Combined Transport Operator
cu.	Cubic
C.U.L.	Canadian Underwriters Laboratory
CWB	Canadian Wheat Board
C.W.O.	Cash (or check) with order
cwt.	Hundredweight
CXL	Cancelled order
CXT	Common External Tariff
C.Y.	Container yard
C.Z.	Canal Zone
D/A	(Vessel must) discharge afloat
D/A	Documents against acceptance
DA	Department of Agriculture
DA	Department of the Army
dal.	Dekaliter
dam.	Dekameter
DANIDA	Danish International Development Agency
D.A.T.	Dangerous Articles Tariff
d/b/a	Doing business as
d.b.b.	Deals, battens and boards
D/C	Deviation clause
DC	Direct current
D.C.	Dutiable charge
D/d	Days after date
D/D	Demand draft
D.D.	District director
d.d.o.	Despatch discharging only
D/E	Date of exportation
DEC	District Export Council
deg.	Dekagram
d/f	Days from the date (Spanish)
D.F.	Dead freight
Dft.	Draft
dg.	Dekagram
DIN	Deutsche Institut für Normung
Dis.	Discount
DISC	Domestic International Sales Corporation
dl.	Dekaliter
d.l.o.	Despatch loading only
dm.	Decimeter
do	Diesel oil
DoD	Department of Defense
D/O	Delivery
DOE	Department of Energy

DOHSA	Death on the High Seas Act (U.S.)
D.O.P.	Documents on payment
D.O.P.	Dropping outward pilot
DOT	Department of Transportation
doz.	Dozen
d.p.	Direct payment
d.p.	Direct port
D/P	Documents against payment
d.p.p.	Dirty petroleum products
dr.	Dram
D.R.	Dock receipt
D/S	Days after sight
D/TR	Documents against trust receipt
d/v	Days after sight (Spanish)
d.w.	Deadweight (in tons)
d.w.a.t.	Deadweight all told
d.w.c.	Deadweight (capacity) for cargo
dwt.	Pennyweight
d.w.t.	Deadweight ton
D/W	Dock warrant
D/y	Delivery
EADB	East African Development Bank
E. & O.E.	Errors and omissions excepted
E.A.O.N.	Except as otherwise noted
E.B.	Eastbound
EC	European Communities
E.C.	East coast
ECA	Economic Commission for Africa
ECCA	East Caribbean Currency Authority
E.C.C.P.	East coast coal port
E.C.I.	East coast of Ireland
ECLA	Economic Commission for Latin America
ECCM	East Caribbean Common Market
ECT	Europa Container Terminal
ECOWAS	Economic Community of West African States
ECSC	European Coal and Steel Community
ECU	European currency unit
EDF	European Development Fund
E.E.	Errors excepted
EEC	European Economic Community
EFTA	European Free Trade Association
e.g.	For example *(exempli gratia)*
E.I.A.	Equipment Interchange Association
EMA	European Monetary Agreement
EMC	Export Management Company
EMS	European monetary system
E.O.	Executive order
e.o.h.p.	Except as otherwise herein provided
EPC	European Patent Convention
ESCAP	Economic and Social Commission for Asia and the Pacific
Est.	Estimate
Est. wt.	Estimated weight
et al.	And others
EURATOM	European Atomic Energy Community
E.U.S.C.	Effective United States Control
Ex	Out of; from (point of origin)
Ex.	Excluding
EXIMBANK	Export-Import Bank of the United States
Ex Int.	Without interest
Exp.	Export
F/A	Free astray
FAA	Federal Aviation Administration
f.a.c.	Fast as can
FAC	Foreign assets control
FACS	Federation of American Controlled Shipping

FAL	Convention on Facilitation of International Maritime Traffic	F.R.C.C.	Free of riot and civil commotions
F.a.m.	Free at mill	f.r.o.f.	Fire risk on freight
F. & D.	Freight and demurrage	FSC	Foreign Sales Corporation
FAO	Food and Agriculture Organization	ft.	Foot
F.a.q.	Fair average quality	f.t.	Full terms
F.A.S.	Free alongside ship	FTC	Federal Trade Commission
FASB	Financial Accounting Standards Board	F.T.W.	Free trade wharf
fath.	Fathom	FTZ	Foreign trade zone
F.B.	Freight bill	f.w.d.	Fresh water damage
F.b.H.	Free on board (harbor)	FX	Foreign exchange
F.B.M.	Feet, in board measure	g.	Gram
F.B.T.	Full berth terms	G/A	General average
FC	Frozen concentrate	G.A.	General average
F.C. & S.	Free of capture and seizure	GAB	General agreements to borrow
FCFA	Central African Financial Cooperation Franc	gal.	Gallon
		GATT	General Agreement on Tariffs and Trade
FCIA	Foreign Credit Insurance Association	GBq	Gigabecquerel
FCN	Treaty of friendship, commerce, and navigation	GCBS	General Council of British Shipping
		G.C.T.	Greenwich civil time
F.c.s.	Free of capture and seizure	Ges.	Company (German)
F.C.S.	Foreign Commercial Service (U.S. Department of Commerce)	Gesch-Z	Trademarked (Germany)
		GF	Government form
F/d	Free at dock	g.f.a.	Good, fair, average
f.d.	Free discharge	GmbH	Corporation (German)
F&D	Freight and demurrage	GMP	Global Mediterranean Policy
f. desp.	Free despatch	G.M.T.	Greenwich mean time
f. dis.	Free discharge	G.O.	General order
FEOGA	Agricultural Guidance and Guarantee Fund	Grs. T.	Gross ton
		Gr. Wt.	Gross Weight
F.f.a.	Free from alongside	GSP	Generalized system of preferences
F.G.	Flat grain (lumber)	G.T.	Gross ton
F.g.a.	Free of general average	GTB	General term bond
f.i.a.	Full interest admitted	G.T.C.	Good till canceled
FIATA	International Federation of Forwarding Agents Assns.	Gtd.	Guaranteed
		G.W.	Gross weight
F.i.b.	Free in bundles; free into bunkers; free into barge	ha.	Hectare
		H.B.	Trading company (Swedish)
		HCWM	High capacity washing machines
f.i.o.	Free in and out	hf.	Half
F.I.O.	Free in and out	hg.	Hectogram
F.I.O.S.	Free in, out, and stowed	hhd.	Hogshead
F.I.O.T.	Free in, out, and trimmed	HHS	Department of Health and Human Services
FMC	Federal Maritime Commission	hl	Hectoliter
F.o.	For orders	hl.	Hectoliter
F.O.	Free out	hm.	Hectometer
F.O.B.	Free on board	H.M.C.	Her Majesty's Customs
F.O.C.	Free of charges	H. mij.	Trading company (Dutch)
F.o.d.	Free of damage	H.P.S.	Hazardous polluting substance (other than petroleum)
f.o.k.	Fill or kill		
F.o.q.	Free on quay	H.T.	High tension
F.o.r.	Free on rail	H.W.	High water
F.o.s.	Free on steamer	H.W.M.	High water mark
F.o.t.	Free on truck	H.W.O.S.T.	High water ordinary spring tides
F.o.w.	Free on wagon	IADB	Inter-American Development Bank
F.o.w.	First open water	IAEA	International Atomic Energy Agency
F.P.A.	Free of particular average	IATA	International Air Transport Association
F.P.A.A.C.	Free of particular average—American conditions	IATTC	Inter-American Tropical Tuna Association
F.p.a. (A.C.)	Free of particular average—American conditions	IBA	International Bauxite Association
		IBRD	International Bank for Reconstruction and Development
F.P.A.E.C.	Free of particular average—English conditions		
		ICAC	International Cotton Advisory Committee
F/R	Freight release	I.C. & C.	Invoice, cost, and charges
F.R.	Full registered	ICAO	International Civil Aviation Organization
fr.	Franc	I.C.C.	International Chamber of Commerce
F.r. & c.c.	Free of riot and civil commotions	I.C.C.	Interstate Commerce Commission
FRB	Federal Reserve Bank	ICCAT	International Commission for the Conservation of Atlantic Tuna

ICCO	International Cocoa Organization	ISO	International Organization for Standard-ization
ICFTU	International Confederation of Free Trade Unions	ISO	International Sugar Organization
ICO	International Coffee Organization	IT	Immediate Transportation Entry
ICS	International Chamber of Shipping	I.T.	In transit (entry)
ICSID	International Centre for Settlement of Investment Disputes	ITA	International Trade Administration
ID	Immediate delivery	ITC	International Tin Council
I.D.	Immediate delivery	ITC	U.S. International Trade Commission
IDA	International Development Association	ITIA	International Tanker Indemnity Association
IDB	Islamic Development Bank	ITU	International Telecommunications Union
IDR	International depository receipt	IUMI	International Union of Marine Insurers
i. drug.	And company (Yugoslavia)	IWC	International Whaling Council
IE	Immediate export	j. & w.o.	**Jettison and washing overboard**
IE	Informal entry	K	Kelvin
IFAD	International Fund for Agricultural Development	k.	Company (Danish, German, Japanese)
IFAP	International Federation of Agricultural Producers	ka.	Company (Finnish)
		KCBT	Kansas City Board of Trade
IFC	International Convention on the Establishment of an International Fund for Compensation for Oil Pollution Damage	K.D.	Knocked down
		K.D.F.	Knocked down flat
		KFAED	Kuwait Fund for Arab Economic Development
IFC	International Finance Corporation	kg.	Kilogram
IGA	International Grains Agreement	K.G.	Limited partnership (German)
i.h.p.	Indicated horsepower	kl.	Kiloliter
IIB	International Patent Institute	Km.	Kilometer
IIB	International Investment Bank	kV	Kilovolt
IIC	International Institute for Cotton	kVA	Kilovolt ampere
ILO	International Labour Organization	L/A	Letter of authority
IMAO	International Maritime Arbitration Organization	LAFTA	Latin American Free Trade Association
		L & D	Lost and damaged
IMCO	Inter-Governmental Maritime Consultative Organization	LDC	Convention on the Prevention of Marine Pollution by Dumping of Waste and Other Matter
IMF	International Monetary Fund		
IMM	International Monetary Market	LDC	Less (least) developed country
IMO	International Maritime Organization	LDDC	Landlocked, least developed and island states
Inc.	Incorporated		
Ince.	Insurance	LDDC	Least developed developing country
INM	International nautical mile	L.d.t.	Loss during transit
INMARSAT	International Maritime Convention on Communication by Satellite	LFL	Low flammable limit
		lat.	Latitude
INN	International Non-Proprietary Names	lb.	Pound
INNM	International Non-Proprietary Names, Modified	Lbp	Length between perpendiculars
		L/C	Letter of credit
INPADOC	International Patent Documentation Centre	LCL	Less than carload
		LCL	Less than containerload
Int.	Interest	l.c.r.	Lowest current rate
INTELSAT	International Telecommunications Satellite Organization	LIBOR	London interbank offered rate
		lin.	Linear
INTERCARGO	International Association of Dry Cargo Shipowners	liq.	Liquid
		LIQ.	Liquidated (entry)
INTERTANKO	International Association of Independent Tanker Owners	LL	International Convention on Load Lines
		LLMC	Convention on Limitation of Liability for Marine Claims
Inv.	Invoice		
IOOC	International Olive Oil Council	L.L.T	London landed terms
i.p.a.	Including particular average	Lloyd's Rep.	*Lloyd's Law List Reports*
IPC	International Patent Classification	L.M.C.	Lloyd's Machinery Certificate
i.p.f.	Intaken piled fathom	L.M.E.	London Metals Exchange
I.R.	Inland Revenue	LNM	Convention Relating to Civil Liability in the Field of Maritime Carriage of Nuclear Material
I.R.C.	Internal Revenue Code		
IRS	Internal Revenue Service		
IRT	Internal Revenue Tax	Loa	Length overall
IRU	International Road Transport Union	Loco	On the spot
ISAC	Industry Services Advisory Committee	LOF	Lloyds Open Form (of salvage)
ISF	International Shipping Federation	Long.	Longitude
ISGOTT	International Safety Guide for Oil Tankers and Terminals	l.o.w.	Last open water
		LPG	Liquefied petroleum gas

l.s.	Lump sum	MTO	Multimodal transport operator
L.R.M.C.	Lloyd's Refrigerating Machinery Certificate	M/V	Motor vessel
L.S.	Place of the seal	MW	Minimum weight
LT	Long ton	N/A	Nonacceptance
l.t.	Liner terms	n.a.a.	Not always afloat
l.t.	Long ton	NAEGA	North American Export Grain Association
Ltda.	Limited company (Spanish and Portuguese)	NAM	National Association of Manufacturers
ltge.	Lighterage	NATO	North Atlantic Treaty Organization
LTL	Less than truckload	N.B.	Northbound
l.w.	Low water	NBS	National Bureau of Standards
l.w.o.s.t.	Low water, ordinary spring tides	N.C.B.	National Cargo Bureau, Inc.
m.	Meter	NCITD	National Committee for International Trade Documentation
M.	One thousand	N.C.V.	No commercial value
MARPOL	International Convention for the Prevention of Pollution from Ships, 1973	NDC	Nondutiable charge
MARPOL 78	1978 Protocol modifying MARPOL	n.E.	Not east of
max.	Maximum	N.E.C.	Not elsewhere classified
m.b.	Merchant's broker	n.e.i.	Not elsewhere included
M. bd. ft.	Thousand board feet	n.e.m.	Not elsewhere mentioned
mc.	Millicurie	n/exc.	Not exceeding
MCA	Monetary compensation amounts	N/F	No funds
MCA	Monetary Control Act of 1980	NGO	Nongovernmental organization
MCE	Mid-America Commodity Exchange	N.H.P.	Nominal horsepower
mdse.	Merchandise	NI	National income
MEBA	Marine Engineers Beneficial Association	NI	Negotiable instrument
M.E.C.	Marine extension clause	NIB	Nordic Investment Bank
Med.	Mediterranean	NIC	Newly industrializing country
MEPC	Marine Environment Protection Committee (of the IMO)	NIMEXE	Nomenclature for External Trading Statistics
MFA	Multifiber Agreement	NLM	Not legally marked
MFN	Most favored nation	NMFC	National Motor Freight Classification
MFU	Marine Firemen's Union	NMU	National Maritime Union
mg.	Milligram	n.N.	Not north of
MGE	Minneapolis Grain Exchange	No.	Number
M.H.	Main hatch	NOCE	New Orleans Commodity Exchange
M.H.W.S.	Mean high water springs	N.O.E.	Not otherwise enumerated
mi.	Mile	N.O.I.B.N.	Not otherwise indicated by name
MIDAM	Mid-America Commodity Exchange	nom.	Nominally
Mij.	Company (Dutch)	N.o.m.	Norwegian official measure
Min.	Minimum	NORAD	Norwegian Agency for Development
Min. B/L	Minimum bill of lading	nom. std.	Nominal standard
min. wt.	Minimum weight	n.o.n.	Not otherwise named
M.I.P.	Minimum insurance policy	nor	Notice of readiness
MITI	Ministry of International Trade and Industry (Japan)	N.O.S.	Not otherwise specified
		n/p	Net proceeds
Mkt.	Market	N.P.	National Pharmacopoeia
ml.	Milliliter	N.P.	No proceeds
M/L	Legal tender (Spanish)	N.P.N.A.	No protest for nonacceptance
M.L.W.S.	Mean low water springs	N.P.V.	No par value
MMP	Masters, mates, and pilots	N.R.	No risk
MNC	Multinational corporation	n.r.a.d.	No risk after discharge
MNE	Multinational enterprise	n/s.	Not sufficient
MOA	Memorandum of agreement	n.s.	Not specified
mol	More or less	n.S.	Not south of
molco	More or less, charterer's option	N.S.F.	Not sufficient funds
moloo	More or less, owner's option	NSPA	National Soybean Processors Association
MOT	Ministry of Transport	N.T.	Net tons
M/R	Mate's receipt	NTB	Nontariff barrier
MSO	Marine staff officers	NVOCC	Nonvessel operating common carrier
mst.	Measurement	n.W.	Not west of
MT	Metric ton	NYCE	New York Cotton Exchange
M/T	Mail transfer	NYFE	New York Futures Exchange
M/T	Metric ton	NYMEX	New York Mercantile Exchange
M.T.	Mean time	NYPE	New York Produce Exchange
MTN	Multilateral trade negotiations	o.a.	Over all
		O/a	On account
		OAPEC	Organization of Arab Petroleum Exporting Countries

OAS	Organization of American States
OAU	Organization of African Unity
OBO	Oil/bulk/ore combination vessel
O/c	Open charter
o.c.c.	One cancels the other
OCIMF	Oil Companies International Marine Forum
O.C.P.	Overland common point
O/d	On demand
O.D.	Outside diameter
ODA	Official Development Assistance
ODL	Overdimensional load
OECD	Organization for Economic Cooperation and Development
O/H	Foreign trade company (Dutch)
OILPOL	International Convention for the Prevention of Pollution of the Sea by Oil
OMB	Office of Management and Budget
O/N	Order notify
O/o	Order of
OO	Oil/ore
O.P.	Open policy
OPEC	Organization of Petroleum Exporting Countries
OPOL	Off-shore pollution liability agreement
O.R.	Owner's risk
O.R.B.	Owner's risk of breakage
O.R.C.	Owner's risk of chaffing
O.R.D.	Owner's risk of damage
O.R.Det.	Owner's risk of deterioration
O.R.F.	Owner's risk of fire (or freezing)
O.R.L.	Owner's risk of leakage
O.R.S.	Owner's risk of shifting
ORM	Other restricted material
O.R.W.	Owner's risk of water damage
o.t.	On truck
O/Y	Stock company (Finnish)
OS & D	Over, short, and damaged
oz.	Ounce
oz. avdp.	Ounce, avoirdupois
oz. tr.	Ounce, troy
p.a.	Per annum
P.A.	Particular average
P & I	Property and indemnity
PAL	Athens Convention Relating to the Carriage of Passengers and Their Luggage by Sea
PATU	Pan African Telecommunications Union
P. B.	Permanent bunkers
pcs.	Pieces
PCT	Patent Cooperation Treaty
P.D.	Per diem
PEFCO	Private Export Funding Company
% mas	Alcoholic strength by mass
per pro.	Per procuration (by authority)
pes.	Pieces
p.f.	Pro forma
Pfd.	Preferred
pf. gal	Proof gallon
PG	Persian Gulf
PIOPIC	P & I oil pollution indemnity clause
P.L.	Partial loss
P.L.	Public law
pm.	Premium
P/N	Promissory note
P.O.D.	Pay on delivery
P.O.P.	Point of purchase

P.O.R.	Pay on receipt
P.O.R.	Price on request
p.p.	Per procuration (by authority)
P/P	Postpaid
ppd.	Prepaid
p.p.i.	Policy proof of interest
prs.	Pairs
psi	Pounds per square inch
PTA	Preferential Trade Area of East and Southern Africa
PTE	Private trading entity
P.W.	Packed weight
q.c.	Quantity at captain's option
Q.C.	Queen's counselor
RA	Rate advance
R/A	Refer to acceptor
r. & c.c.	Riots and civil commotions
R. & L.	Rail and lake
R. & O.	Rail and ocean
RC	Regional commissioner
R.C.L.	River, canal, and lake
r.d.	Running days
Refg.	Refrigerate
R.I.T.	Refining in transit
RMEA	World Bank Regional Mission for East Africa
RMWA	World Bank Regional Mission for West Africa
r.o.b.	Remaining on board
R.o.D.	Refused on delivery
roe	Rate of exchange
ROI	Return on investment
ROS	Return on sales
ROU	Radio Officers Union
R/R	Railroad
s	Second (unit of time)
S.A.	Stock company (French/Spanish)
S.Acc.	Limited partnership (Italian)
SADCC	Southern Africa Development Coordination Conference
S.A.p.A.	Stock company (Romanian)
SAR	International Convention on Maritime Search and Rescue
SARC	South Asian Regional Council
SARL	Limited liability company (Spanish)
S.B.	Southbound
sbe	Standard brick equivalent
SBM	Single buoy mooring
S.C.&S.	Strapped, corded, and sealed
S.C.I.	Special customs invoice
S.d.	Short delivery
S.D.	Single deck
S.D.B.L.	Sight draft, bill of lading attached
sdg.	Siding (rail)
S.D.H.	Still in drawee's hands
SDR	Special drawing rights
SE	Single entry (bond)
SEATO	South East Asia Treaty Organization
s.f.	Superficial feet
SFTC	Standard Foreign Trade Classification
SHEX	Sundays and holidays excluded
SHINC	Sundays and holidays included
SI	Internatinal System of Units
SIDA	Swedish International Development Agency
S.I.T.	Stop in transit
SITC	Standard International Trade Classification

SITC-2	Standard International Trade Classification, Revision 2	UMOA	West African Monetary Union
SITPRO	Simplified International Trade Procedures	UNCDF	United Nations Capital Development Fund
SIU	Seafarers International Union	UNCLOS	United Nations Conference on the Law of the Sea
S.L. & C.	Shipper's load and count	UNCTAD	United Nations Conference on Trade and Development
S.L. & T.	Shipper's load and tally		
S/L. C.	Sue and labor clause	UNDP	United Nations Development Programme
SOLAS	International Convention for the Safety of Life at Sea	UNEP	United Nations Environment Programme
S.o.m.	Swedish official measure	UNGA	United Nations General Assembly
SpA.	Limited liability company (Italian)	UNITAR	United Nations Institute for Training and Research
SPARTECA	South Pacific Regional Trade and Cooperation Agreement	UPEB	Union of Banana Exporting Countries
s.p.d.	Steamer pays dues	UPU	Universal Postal Union
SPR	Strategic Petroleum Reserve (U.S.)	USAC	U.S. Atlantic coast
SPRL	Limited liability company (Belgian)	USAID	United States Agency for International Development
Sp.Z.P.	Limited liability company (Polish)		
SS	Shipside	U.S.C.	United States Code
s.s. & c.	Same sea and country coast	U.S.C.A.	United States Code, Annotated
S/S	Steamship	U.S.C.G.	United States Coast Guard
S.S.	Steamship	U.S.D.A.	United States Department of Agriculture
s.t.c.	Said to Contain	USG	U.S. Gulf Coast
STCW	International Convention on Standards of Training, Certification and Watchkeeping for Seafarers	U.S.P.	United States Pharmaacopoeia
		U.S.N.H.	United States, north of Cape Hatteras
		USPHS	United States Public Health Service
Stds.	Standards	USTR	United States Trade Representative
s. ton	Short ton	U.S.T.S.	United States Treaty Series
str.	Steamer	U/w	Underwriters
STR	Special Trade Representative	u/w.	Underwater
S.U.C.L.	Set up carload	V	Volt
S.U.L.C.L.	Set up less than carload	V/	Sight (Spanish)
SUP	Sailors' Union of the Pacific	val	Value
s.v.	Sailing vessel	V.A.T.	Value added tax
T.A. 1930	Tariff Act of 1930	VER	Voluntary export restraints
TB	Term bond	ves.	Vessel
T.B.L.	Through bill of lading	viz.	Namely, or specifically
T.C.	Till countermanded	VLCC	Very large crude carrier
TCM	Convention for the International Combined Transport of Goods	v.o.p.	Value in original policy
		VRA	Voluntary restraint agreement
T/D	Time draft	W	Watt
t/d/b/a	Trading and doing business as	W.A.	With average
TDW	Tons deadweight	WAEC	West African Economic Community
T.E.	Trade expense	W & F	Water and feed
T.F.	Till forbidden	W. & I.	Weight and inspection
T.I.P.	Taking inward pilot	W & R	Water and rail
T.I.R.	International Road Transport Carnet (French)	W/B	Waybill
		W.B.	Westbound
t.l.o.	Total loss only	W.B./E.I.	West Britain/East Ireland
TM	International Convention on Tonnage Measurement of Ships	w.b.s.	Without benefit of salvage
		W.C.	West coast
TNC	Transnational corporation	WCARRD	World Conference on Agrarian Reform and Rural Development
TOVALOP	Tanker Owners' Voluntary Agreement Concerning Liability for Oil Pollution		
		Wd.	Warranted
T.T.	Telegraphic transfer (of funds)	WD Ex.	Withdrawal for export
TTS rate	Telegraphic transfer selling rate	WDIT	Warehouse withdrawal for immediate transportation without appraisement
TVA	Value added tax		
u.a.	Units of account	WDT	Withdrawal for transportation
UCP	Uniform Customs and Practices	WDT & E	Withdrawal for transportation and exportation
UDEAC	Central African Customs and Economic Union		
		WDT Rew.	Withdrawal for transportation and rewarehousing
UIC	International Union of Railways	W.E.N.	Waive exchange if necessary
UKC	United Kingdom/Continent	WFP	World Food Programme
UL	Underwriters Laboratories	w.g.	Weight guaranteed
ULCC	Ultra large crude carrier	WHO	World Health Organization
ULD	Unit load device	Whse	Warehouse
UMAC	Central African Monetary Union		

Whse E.	Warehouse entry	WS	Worldscale
Whse W.	Warehouse withdrawal	WSG	International Wool Study Group
W.I.	West Indies	wt.	Weight
WIBON	Whether in berth or not	WTO	Warsaw Treaty Organization
WIPO	World Intellectual Property Organization	W/W	Warehouse warrant
WIPON	Whether in free pratique or not	W.W.	Weather working
W/M	Weight or measurement	W.W.D.	Weather working days
w.p.	Weather permitting.	X-Heavy	Extra heavy
W.P.	Wire payment	X-W	Without warrants
W.P.A.	With particular average	XX Heavy	Double extra heavy
WPG	Winnipeg exchange	XX Strong	Double extra strong
W/R	Warehouse receipt	Y/A	York-Antwerp Rules
W.R.	War risk	yd	Yard
w.r.o.	War risk only	YK	Limited liability company (Japanese)

2. FLAG ABBREVIATIONS

The following are the abbreviations of country names used in bills of lading and similar documents to designate a vessel's country of registration:

Listed by Abbreviation

Ab	Abu Dhabi	Da	Denmark	Is	Israel
Ag	Algeria	Db	Dubai	It	Italy
Al	Albania	Do	Dominican Republic	Iv	Ivory Coast
Am	United States of America	Du	Netherlands	Ja	Japan
An	Angola	Ec	Ecuador	Jm	Jamaica
Ar	Argentina	EG	German Democratic Republic	Jo	Jordan
As	Austria	Eg	Egypt	Ke	Kenya
Au	Australia	ES	El Salvador	Ko	Korea (South)
Bb	Barbados	Et	Ethiopia	Ku	Kuwait
Be	Belgium	Fa	Faroes	Le	Lebanon
Bh	Bangladesh	Fi	Finland	Li	Liberia
Bm	Burma	Fj	Fiji	Ly	Libya
Bn	Benin	Fr	France	Ma	Malta
Bo	Bolivia	Ga	Gabon	Me	Mexico
Br	United Kingdom & Colonies	Ge	German Federal Republic	Mg	Madagascar
Bs	Bahamas	Gh	Ghana	Mn	Monaco
Bu	Bulgaria	Gm	Gambia	Mo	Morocco
Bz	Brazil	Gn	Guinea	Ms	Mauritius
Ca	Canada	Gr	Greece	Mt	Mauritania
Ce	Sri Lanka (Ceylon)	Gu	Guatemala	Mv	Maldives
Ch	Chile	Ha	Haiti	My	Malaysia
Cm	Comoro Islands	Ho	Honduras	Mz	Mozambique
Cn	Cameroun	Hu	Hungary	Na	Nauru
Co	Colombia	Ia	Indonesia	NA	Netherlands Antilles
CR	Costa Rica	Ic	Iceland	Ng	Nigeria
Cu	Cuba	Ih	Ireland	Ni	Nicaragua
CV	Cape Verde	In	India	No	Norway
Cy	Cyprus	Iq	Iraq	Nz	New Zealand
Cz	Czechoslovakia	Ir	Iran	Pa	Panama

PG	Papua New Guinea	Se	Senegal	Th	Thailand
Ph	Poland	Sg	Singapore	Tn	Tunisia
Pi	Philippines	Sh	Sharjah	To	Tonga
Pk	Pakistan	Si	Saudi Arabia	Tr	Trinidad & Tobago
Po	Portugal	SL	Sierra Leone	Tu	Turkey
Pu	Peru	Sn	Surinam	Ug	Uganda
Py	Paraguay	So	Somalia	Ur	Uruguay
Qt	Qatar	Sp	Spain	Va	Vanuatu
RC	China	Ss	Switzerland	Ve	Venezuela
RK	Korea (North)	Su	Sudan	Vn	Vietnam
Rn	Romania	Sw	Sweden	WS	Western Samoa
Ru	USSR	Sy	Syria	Ye	Yemen (Arab Republic)
SA	South Africa	Ta	Tanzania	Ys	Yugoslavia
Sc	Seychelles	Tg	Togo	Zr	Zaire

Flag Abbreviations, Listed by Country

Abu Dhabi	Ab	Greece	Gr	Panama	Pa
Albania	Al	Guatemala	Gu	Papua New Guinea	PG
Algeria	Ag	Guinea	Gn	Paraguay	Py
Angola	An	Haiti	Ha	Peru	Pu
Argentina	Ar	Honduras	Ho	Philippines	Pi
Australia	Au	Hungary	Hu	Poland	Ph
Austria	As	Iceland	Ic	Portugal	Po
Bahamas	Bs	India	In	Qatar	Qt
Bangladesh	Bh	Indonesia	Ia	Romania	Rn
Barbados	Bb	Iran	Ir	Saudi Arabia	Si
Belgium	Be	Iraq	Iq	Senegal	Se
Benin	Bn	Ireland	Ih	Seychelles	Sc
Bolivia	Bo	Israel	Is	Sharjah	Sh
Brazil	Bz	Italy	It	Sierra Leone	SL
Bulgaria	Bu	Ivory Coast	Iv	Singapore	Sg
Burma	Bm	Jamaica	Jm	Somalia	So
Canada	Ca	Japan	Ja	South Africa	SA
Cameroun	Cn	Jordan	Jo	Spain	Sp
Cape Verde	CV	Kenya	Ke	Sri Lanka	Ce
Chile	Ch	Korea (North)	RK	Sudan	Su
China	RC	Korea (South)	KO	Surinam	Sn
Colombia	Co	Kuwait	Ku	Sweden	Sw
Comoro Islands	Cm	Lebanon	Le	Switzerland	Ss
Costa Rica	CR	Liberia	Li	Syria	Sy
Cuba	Cu	Libya	Ly	Tanzania	Ta
Cyprus	Cy	Madagascar	Mg	Thailand	Th
Czechoslovakia	Cz	Malaysia	My	Togo	Tg
Denmark	Da	Maldives	Mv	Tonga	To
Dominican Republic	Do	Malta	Ma	Trinidad & Tobago	Tr
Dubai	Db	Mauritania	Mt	Tunisia	Tn
Ecuador	Ec	Mauritius	Ms	Turkey	Tu
Egypt	Eg	Mexico	Me	Uganda	Ug
El Salvador	ES	Monaco	Mn	United Kingdom	Br
Ethiopia	Et	Morocco	Mo	United States	Am
Faroes	Fa	Mozambique	Mz	Uruguay	Ur
Finland	Fi	Nauru	Na	USSR	Ru
Fiji	Fj	Netherlands	Du	Vanuatu	Va
France	Fr	Netherlands Antilles	NA	Venezuela	Ve
Gabon	Ga	New Zealand	Nz	Vietnam	Vn
Gambia	Gm	Nicaragua	Ni	Western Samoa	WS
German Democratic Republic	EG	Nigeria	Ng	Yemen (Arab Republic)	Ye
German Federal Republic	Ge	Norway	No	Yugoslavia	Ys
Ghana	Gh	Pakistan	Pk	Zaire	Zr

3. SYMBOLS FOR PRINCIPAL TRADING CURRENCIES

The following symbols are used by the SWIFT system:

Country	Currency	Symbol	Country	Currency	Symbol
Austria	Austrian schilling	ATS	Liechtenstein	Swiss franc	CHF
Belgium	Common Belgian franc	BEF	Luxembourg	Common Belgian franc	BEF
	Convertible Belgian franc	BEC		Convertible Belgian franc	BEC
	Financial Belgian franc	BEL		Financial Belgian franc	BEL
Canada	Canadian dollar	CAD	Netherlands	Netherlands guilder	NLG
Denmark	Danish krone	DKK	Norway	Norwegian krone	NOK
Finland	Markka	FIM	Singapore	Singapore dollar	SGD
German Fed. Rep.	Deutsche mark	DEM	Spain	Spanish peseta	ESP
Greece	Drachma	GRD		Spanish peseta (Acc. A)	ESA
				Spanish peseta (Acc. B)	ESB
Hong Kong	Hong Kong dollar	HKD	Sweden	Swedish krona	SEK
Ireland	Irish pound	IRP	Switzerland	Swiss franc	CHF
Italy	Italian lira	ITL	United Kingdom	Pound sterling	GBP
Japan	Japanese yen	JPY	United States	Dollar	USD

4. CURRENCY SYMBOLS (COMMERCIAL USAGE)

Currency Abbreviation	Monetary Unit	Country	Currency Abbreviation	Monetary Unit	Country
฿	Baht	Thailand	£S	Sudanese Pound	Sudan
¢	Colon	El Salvador	Q̸	Quetzal	Guatemala
$	U. S. dollar	United States	¥	Yen	Japan
$b	Peso	Bolivia	A$	Australian dollar	Australia, Kiribati, & Nauru
$Bz.	Belize dollar	Belize			
$F	Fiji dollar	Fiji	Af	Afghani	Afghanistan
₲	Guarani	Paraguay	₳	Austral	Argentina
₱	Philippine peso	Philippines	AS	Schilling	Austria
£	Pound sterling	United Kingdom	B/.	Balboa	Panama
£E	Egyptian pound	Egypt	Ba$	Bahamian dollar	Bahamas
£M	Maltese pound	Malta	BD	Bahrain dinar	Bahrain

Currency Abbreviation	Monetary Unit	Country	Currency Abbreviation	Monetary Unit	Country
BD$	Bermuda dollar	Bermuda	Ft	Forint	Hungary
BDS$	Barbados dollar	Barbados	G	Gourde	Haiti
Bfr.	Belgian franc	Belgium	G¢	Cedi	Ghana
BK	Kyat	Burma	G$	Guyana dollar	Guyana
Br	Birr	Ethiopia	Gib.£	Gibraltar pound	Gibraltar
Br$	Brunei dollar	Brunei	Hfl.	Guilder (florin)	Netherlands
Bs	Bolivar	Venezuela	HK$	Hong Kong dollar	Hong Kong
C¢	Colon	Costa Rica	ID	Iraqi dinar	Iraq
C$	Cordoba	Nicaragua	IKr	(New) Icelandic krona	Iceland
C£	Cyprus pound	Cyprus	iR.	Indian rupee	India
can$	Canadian dollar	Canada	Ir£	Irish punt	Ireland
chil.$	Peso	Chile	IS	Sheqel	Israel
CI$	Cayman Islands dollar	Cayman Islands	J$	Jamaica dollar	Jamaica
col.$	Colombian peso	Colombia	JD	Jordan dinar	Jordan
Cr$	Cruzeiro	Brazil	K	Kina	Papua New Guinea
cub$	Cuban peso	Cuba	Kcs	Czechoslovakian koruna	Czechoslovakia
C.V.Esc	Cape Verde escudo	Cape Verde	KD	Kuwaiti dinar	Kuwait
CFA-Fr	CFA-franc	Benin, Cammeroon, Central African Republic, Chad, Comoros, Congo, Gabon, Ivory Coast, Niger, Senegal, Togo, & Upper Volta	Kz	Kwanza	Angola
			L	Lempira	Honduras
			L£	Lebanese pound	Lebanon
			LD	Libyan dinar	Libya
			Le	Leone	Sierra Leone
			Lib$	Liberian dollar	Liberia
CFP-Fr	CFP-franc	New Caledonia, & Tahiti	Lit	Lira	Italy, & San Marino
			LK	Kip	Laos
D	Dalasi	Gambia	Lw	Lev	Bulgaria
DA	Dinar	Algeria	M	Loti	Lesotho
Db	Dobra	São Tomé & Príncipe	M$	Ringgit	Malaysia
DH	Dirham	Morocco	M-DDR	Mark	German Democratic Republic
Dh	Dirham	United Arab Emirates	MKw..	Malawi kwacha	Malawi
Din	Dinar	Yugoslavia	mR	Maldivian rupee	Maldives
DKr	Morocco	Dh	mR	Mauritian rupee	Mauritius
Dirham	United Arab		MT	Metical	Mozambique
DM	Deutsche mark	German Federal Republic	N	Naira	Nigeria
Dr	Drachma	Greece	NAfl	Netherlands Antilles Guilder	Netherlands Antilles
E	Lilangeni	Swaziland	NKr	Norwegian crown	Norway
EC$	East Caribbean dollar	Leeward Islands (Montserrat, Antigua, St. Kitts-Nevis-Anguilla), & Windward Islands (Dominica, Grenada, St. Lucia, & St. Vincent)	NR	Nepalese rupee	Nepal
			NT$	New Taiwan dollar	Taiwan
			NZ$	New Zealand dollar	Cook Islands, & New Zealand
			P	Pula	Botswana
			Pat	Pataca	Macao
			PG	Peso guineano	Guinea-Bissau
			Pos	Mexican peso	Mexico
			PR	Pakistan rupee	Pakistan
Esc	Escudo	Portugal	Ptas	Pesetas	Andorra, & Spain
F.Bu.	Burundi franc	Burundi	QDR	Qatar riyal	Qatar
FD	Djibouti franc	Djibouti	R	Rand	Namibia & South Africa
FF	French franc	France, French Guiana, Guadeloupe, Martinique, Monaco, Reunion, & St. Pierre et Miquelon	Rbl.	Rouble	USSR
			RD$	Dominican peso	Dominican Republic
			Ri	Rial	Iran
			Riel	Riel	Kampuchea
			RL	Lei	Romania
FLUX	Luxembourg franc	Luxembourg	RMB	Renminbi (yuan)	China
F.M.	Mali franc	Mali	RO	Rial Omani	Oman
FMG	Franc Malgache	Madagascar	Rp	Rupiah	Indonesia
FMK	Finmark	Finland	S	Sol	Peru
Fr	Swiss franc	Liechtenstein, & Switzerland	S$	Singapore dollar	Singapore
			Sf	Suriname guilder	Suriname
F.Rw.	Rwanda franc	Rwanda	S/	Sucre	Ecuador

Currency Abbreviation	Monetary Unit	Country	Currency Abbreviation	Monetary Unit	Country
Sh	Kenya shilling	Kenya	urug $	Uruguayan peso	Uruguay
ShSo	Somali shilling	Somalia	U.S.$	United States dollar	British Virgin Islands, United States, United States Dependencies
SI$	Solomon Islands dollar	Solomon Islands			
Skr	Swedish crown	Sweden			
SL Re.	Sri Lanka rupee	Sri Lanka			
sR	Seychelles rupee	Seychelles	U.Sh	Uganda shilling	Uganda
S.Rl.	Riyal	Saudi Arabia	VD	Vietnam dong	Vietnam
SY	Syli	Guinea	VT	Vatu	Vanuatu
syr£	Syrian pound	Syria	W	Won	Korea (South)
T$	Pa'anga	Tonga	WS$	Samoan tala	Western Samoa
T & T$	Trinidad & Tobago dollar	Trinidad & Tobago	YD	Yemeni dinar	Yemen, Peoples Dem. Rep.
TD	Tunisian dinar	Tunisia	YRl	Rial	Yemen
TK	Taka	Bangladesh	Z	Zaire	Zaire
TL	Turkish lira	Turkey	Z$	Zimbabwe dollar	Zimbabwe
T Sh	Tanzania shilling	Tanzania	ZK	Kwacha	Zambia
Tug.	Tugrik	Mongolia	Zl	Zloty	Poland
UM	Ouguiya	Mauritania			

5. WEIGHTS & MEASURES

Apothecaries' Weight

20 grains	= 1 scruple
8 scruples	= 1 dram
8 drams	= 1 ounce
12 ounces	= 1 pound

Avoirdupois Weight

27 11/32 grains	= 1 dram
16 drams	= 1 ounce
16 ounces	= 1 pound
25 pounds	= 1 quarter
4 quarters	= 1 hundredweight
2000 pounds	= 1 short ton
2240 pounds	= 1 long ton

Troy Weight

24 grains	= 1 pennyweight
20 pennyweights	= 1 ounce
12 ounces	= 1 ounce

Cloth Measure

2¼ inches	= 1 nail
4 nails	= 1 quarter
4 quarters	= 1 yard

Cubic Measure

1728 cu. inches	= 1 cu. foot
27 cu. feet	= 1 cu. yard
128 cu. feet	= 1 cord (wood)
40 cu. feet	= 1 shipping ton
231 cu. inches	= 1 U. S. gallon
1.24456 cu. feet	= 1 standard bushel

Dry Measure

2 pints	= 1 quart
8 quarts	= 1 peck
4 pecks	= 1 bushel
36 bushels	= 1 chaldron

Liquid Measure

4 gills	= 1 pint
2 pints	= 1 quart
4 quarts	= 1 gallon
31.5 gallons	= 1 barrel
42 gallons	= 1 barrel (petroleum)
2 barrels	= 1 hogshead

Linear Measure

12 inches	= 1 foot
3 feet	= 1 yard
5.5 yards	= 1 rod
40 rods	= 1 furlong
8 furlongs	= 1 statute mile
3 miles	= 1 league
6 feet	= 1 fathom
120 fathoms	= 1 cable length
6080.2 feet	= 1 nautical mile

Surveyors' Measure

7.92 inches	= 1 link
25 links	= 1 rod
4 rods	= 1 chain
10 sq. chains	= 1 acre
640 acres	= 1 sq. mile
36 sq. miles	= 1 township

Miscellaneous Measures

144 sq. inches	= 1 sq. foot
9 sq. feet	= 1 sq. yard
30¼ sq. yards	= 1 sq. rod
40 sq. rods	= 1 rood
4 roods	= 1 acre
3 inches	= 1 palm
4 inches	= 1 hand
6 inches	= 1 span
18 inches	= 1 cubit
21.8 inches	= 1 Bible cubit
2½ feet	= 1 military pace

6. METRIC EQUIVALENTS

Linear Measure

1 centimeter	0.3937 inches
1 inch	2.54 centimeters
1 decimeter	3.937 inches
1 foot	3.048 decimeters
1 meter	39.37 inches
1 yard	0.9144 meter
1 dekameter	1.9884 rods
1 rod	0.5029 dekameter
1 kilometer	0.621 mile
1 mile	1.609 kilometers

Square Measure

1 square centimeter	0.1550 square inch
1 square inch	6.452 square centimeters
1 square decimeter	0.1076 square foot
1 square foot	9.2903 square decimeters
1 square meter	1.196 square yards
1 square yard	0.8361 square meter
1 acre	160 square rods
1 square rod	0.00625 acre
1 hectare	2.47 acres

Square Measure

1 acre	0.4047 hectare
1 square kilometer	0.386 square mile
1 square mile	2.59 square kilometers

Measure of Volume

1 cubic centimeter	0.061 cubic inch
1 cubic inch	16.39 cubic centimeters
1 cubic decimeter	0.0353 cubic foot
1 cubic foot	28.317 cubic decimeters
1 cubic meter	1.308 cubic yards
1 cubic yard	0.7646 cubic meter
1 stere	0.2759 cord
1 cord	3.624 steres
1 liter	1.0567 quarts liquid
1 quart dry	1.101 liters
1 quart liquid	0.9463 liter
1 dekaliter	1.135 pecks
1 gallon	0.3785 dekaliter
1 peck	0.881 dekaliter
1 hektoliter	2.8375 bushels
1 bushel	0.3524 hektoliter

7. INTERNATIONAL SYSTEM OF UNITS

The following designate multiples and submultiples of units.

Multiplying Factor	Prefix	Symbol			
1,000,000,000,000,000,000	peta	P	.1	deci	d
1,000,000,000,000,000	exa	E	.01	centi	c
1,000,000,000,000	tera	T	.001	milli	m
1,000,000,000	giga	G	.000001	micro	μ
1,000,000	mega	M	.000000001	nano	n
1,000	kilo	k	.000000000001	pico	p
100	hecto	h	.000000000000001	femto	f
10	deka	da	.000000000000000001	atto	a

8. INTERNATIONAL PACKING SYMBOLS AND CAUTIONARY MARKS

English	Spanish	French	German	Portuguese
Glass, handle with care.	Vidrio, manéjese con cuidado.	Fragile—attention!	Zerbrechich—Vorsicht!	Fragil—Cuida do!
When empty return to.	Cuando esté vacío, devuélvase a.	Vide, retourner à.	Wenn leer, zurück an.	Quando vazio devolva-se a.
Keep dry.	Manténgase seco.	Protéger contre l'humidité.	Trocken halten.	Afaste da humidade.
Use no hooks.	No use ganchos.	Manier sans crampons.	Ohne Haken handhaben.	Nao use ganchos.
This side up.	Este lado para arriba.	Cette face en haut.	Diese Seite nach oben.	Este lado para cima.
Top.	Encima.	Dessus.	Oberseite.	Tampa.
Weight, net, legal, gross, tare.	Peso, neto, legal, bruto, tara.	Poids, net, légal, brut, tare.	Gewicht, Netto-, geselzliches, Brutto-, Tara.	Peso, neto, legal, bruto, tara.
Do not place near boilers.	No se ponga cerca de calderas.	Tenir loin de chaudières.	Vom Dampfkessel fernhalten.	Nao colloque perto das caldeiras.
Do not store in a damp place.	No se ponga en un lugar húmedo.	Pas emmagasiner en lieu humide.	Nicht an feuchter Stelle lagern.	Teme humidade.
Keep in cool place.	Guárdese en un lugar fresco.	Garder en lieu frais.	Kühl aufbewahren.	Teme calor.

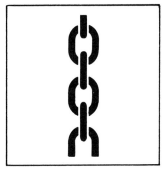

Sling here

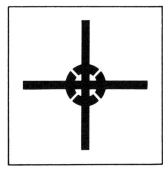

Center of gravity

This way up

Fragile. Handle with care.

Use no hooks

Keep dry

Keep away from heat.

APPENDIX C: DIRECTORIES

1. DIRECTORY OF COMMODITY EXCHANGES

UNITED STATES

Board of Trade of the City of Chicago
141 W. Jackson Blvd.
Chicago, IL 60604
(312) 435-3500

Board of Trade Kansas City
4800 Main Street
Suite 274
Kansas City, MO 64112
(816) 753-7363

Chicago Mercantile Exchange
444 W. Jackson Blvd.
Chicago, IL 60606
(312) 648-1000

Coffee, Sugar and Cocoa Exchange
4 World Trade Center
New York, NY 10048
(212) 938-2800

Commodity Exchange, Inc.
4 World Trade Center
New York, NY 10048
(212) 938-2900

MidAmerica Commodity Exchange
175 W. Jackson Blvd.
Suite A-220
Chicago, IL 60604
(312) 435-0606

Minneapolis Grain Exchange
150 Grain Exchange Building
Minneapolis, MN 55415
(612) 338-6212

New Orleans Commodity Exchange
308 Board of Trade Place
New Orleans, LA 70130
(504) 524-2184

New York Cotton Exchange
4 World Trade Center
New York, NY 10048
(212) 938-2650

New York Futures Exchange
20 Broad St.
New York, NY 10005
(212) 623-4949

New York Mercantile Exchange
4 World Trade Center
New York, NY 10048
(212) 938-2222

AUSTRALIA

Sydney Futures Exchange
7th Level, Australia Square Tower
Sydney 2000

BRAZIL

Bolsa de Mercadorias de Sao Paulo
Rua Libero Bardaro 471 - 5th Floor
Sao Paulo

CANADA

Montreal Stock Exchange (Financial Futures)
P. O. Box 61
Stock Exchange Tower
Montreal, Quebec H4Z 1A9

Toronto Stock Exchange Futures Market
234 Bay St.
Toronto, Ontario M5J 1R1

The Winnipeg Commodity Exchange
687-167 Lombard Ave.
Winnipeg, Manitoba R3B 047

FRANCE

Cocoa Terminal Market on the Paris Commodity Exchange
Bourse de Commerce
2 rue de Viarmes
Paris 75040

International Market of Robusta Coffee
Bourse de Commerce
2 rue de Viarmes
Paris 75040

International Market of White Sugar of Paris
Bourse de Commerce
2 rue de Viarmes
Paris 75040

GREAT BRITAIN

International Petroleum Exchange
Cereal House
58 Mark Lane
London EC3R 7NE

The London Commodity Exchange
Cereal House
58 Mark Lane
London EC3R 7NE

The London International Financial Futures Exchange
66 Cannon Street
London EC4N 6AE

The London Grain Futures Market
The Grain and Feed Trade Association, Ltd.
28 St. Mary Axe
London EC3A 8EP

The London Metal Exchange
Whittington Ave.
London EC3V 1LB

The London Soya Bean Meal Futures Market
GAFTA Soya Bean Meal Futures Association Ltd.
28 St. Mary Axe
London EC3 8EP

HONG KONG

Hong Kong Commodity Exchange
Hutchinson House
Second Floor, Harcourt Rd.
Hong Kong

JAPAN

Japan Federation of Commodity Exchanges, Inc.
Magyokaikan, Nihonbashi-Ningyocho 1-1-0
Chuo-Ku, Tokyo 103

MALAYSIA

Kuala Lumpur Commodity Exchange
Kuala Lumpur, Malaysia

SINGAPORE

Gold Exchange of Singapore
28th Floor
Clifford Centre
Raffles Place
Singapore 0104

2. DISTRICT OFFICES, INTERNATIONAL TRADE ADMINISTRATION
UNITED STATES DEPARTMENT OF COMMERCE

Albuquerque, 87102, 505 Marquette Ave. NW., Rm 1015 (505) 766-2386.

Anchorage, 99513, P.O. Box 32, 701 C St. (907) 271-5041.

Atlanta, 30309, Suite 600, 1365 Peachtree St., NE. (404) 881-7000.

Baltimore, 21202, 415 U.S. Customhouse, Gay and Lombard Sts. (301) 962-3560.

Birmingham, 35205, Suite 200-201, 908 S. 20th St. (205) 254-1331.

Boston, 02116, 10th Floor, 441 Stuart St. (617) 223-2312.

Buffalo, 14202, 1312 Federal Bldg., 111 W. Huron St. (716) 846-4191.

Charleston, W.Va., 25301, 3000 New Federal Office Bldg., 500 Quarrier St.(304) 343-6181, Ext. 375.

Cheyenne, 82001, 6022 O'Mahoney Federal Center, 2120 Capitol Ave. (307) 778-2220, Ext. 2151.

Chicago, 60603, Room 1406, Mid-Continental Plaza Bldg., 55 E. Monroe St. (312) 353-4450.

Cincinnati, 45202, 10504 Fed. Bldg., 550 Main St. (513) 684-2944.

Cleveland, 44114, Room 600, 666 Euclid Ave. (216) 522-4750.

Columbia, S.C., 29201, Fed. Bldg., 1835 Assembly St. (803) 765-5345.

Dallas, 75242, Room 7A5, 1100 Commerce St. (214) 749-1515.

Denver, 80202, Room 165, New Custom House, 19th and Stout Sts. (303) 837-3246.

Des Moines, 50309, 817 Federal Bldg., 210 Walnut St. (515) 284-4222.

Detroit, 48226, 445 Federal Bldg., 231 W. Lafayette (313) 226-3650.

Greensboro, N.C., 27402, 203 Federal Bldg., W. Market St., P.O. Box 1950 (919) 378-5345.

Hartford, 06103, Room 610-B, Fed. Bldg., 450 Main St. (203) 244-3530.

Honolulu, 96850, 4106 Federal Bldg., 300 Ala Moana Blvd., P.O. Box 50026 (808) 546-8694.

Houston, 77002, 2625 Federal Bldg., 515 Rusk Ave. (713) 226-4231.

Indianapolis, 46204, 357 U.S. Court-House & Federal Office Bldg., 46 E. Ohio St. (317) 269-6214.

Los Angeles, 90049, Rm. 800, 11777 San Vicente Blvd. (213) 824-7591.

Memphis, 38103, Room 710, 147 Jefferson Ave. (901) 521-3213.

Miami, 33130, Rm. 821, City National Bank Bldg., 25 W. Flagler St. (305) 350-5267.

Milwaukee, 53202, 605 Federal Office Bldg., 517 E. Wisconsin Ave. (414) 291-3473.

Minneapolis, 55401, 218 Federal Bldg., 110 S. 4th St. (612) 725-2133.

New Orleans, 70130, Room 432, International Trade Mart, 2 Canal St. (504) 589-6546.

New York, 10007, 37th Floor, Federal Office Bldg., 26 Federal Plaza, Foley Sq. (212) 264-0634.

Newark, 07102, Gateway Bldg. (4th floor) Market St. & Penn Plaza (201) 645-6214.

Omaha, 68102, 1815 Capitol Ave., Suite 703A (402) 221-3665.

Philadephia, 19106, 9448 Federal Bldg., 600 Arch St. (215) 597-2850.

Phoenix, 85073, 2950 Valley Bank Center, 201 N. Central Ave. (602) 261-3285.

Pittsburgh, 15222, 2002 Fed. Bldg., 1000 Liberty Ave. (412) 644-2850.

Portland, Ore., 97204, Room 618, 1220 S.W. 3rd Ave. (503) 221-3001.

Reno, Nev., 89503, 777 W. 2nd St., Room 120 (702) 784-5203.

Richmond, 23240, 8010 Federal Bldg., 400 N. 8th St. (804) 782-2246.

St. Louis, 63105, 120 S. Central Ave. (314) 425-3302.

Salt Lake City, 84138, 1203 Federal Bldg., 125 S. State St. (801) 524-5116.

San Francisco, 94102, Federal Bldg., Box 36013, 450 Golden Gate Ave. (415) 556-5860.

San Juan, P.R., 00918, Room 659, Federal Bldg., Chardon Ave. (809) 753-4555.

Savannah, 31402, 222 U.S. Courthouse, P.O. Box 9746, 125-29 Bull St. (912) 232-4321, Ext. 204.

Seattle, 98109, 706 Lake Union Bldg., 1700 Westlake Ave. North (206) 442-5615.

3. STATE TAX AND REVENUE AUTHORITIES. Taxes of Interest to Merchandise Importers and Foreign Exporters

State of Alabama
  Department of Revenue Services
  Montgomery, AL 36130
      Alcoholic beverage
      Franchise
      General income
      Lubricating oil
      Motor fuels
      Sales
      Severance
      Tobacco stamp

State of Alaska
  Department of Revenue
  Juneau, AK 99811
      Alcoholic beverage
      Cigarette
      Fisheries
      Gasoline
      Income
      Mining license
      Oil and gas production

State of Arizona
  Department of Revenue
  Phoenix, AZ 85007
      Alcoholic beverage
      Cigarette and tobacco
      Income
      Sales
      Severance

State of Arkansas
  Department of Finance and
      Administration
  Little Rock, AR 72203
      Alcoholic beverage
      Gasoline
      Gross receipts
      Income
      Tobacco

State of California
  State Board of Equalization
  Sacramento, CA 98514
      Alcoholic beverage
      Cigarette
      Gasoline
      Income
      Sales and use

State of Colorado
  Department of Revenue
  Denver, CO 80261
      Alcoholic beverage
      Gasoline fuels
      Income
      Oleomargarine
      Sales and use
      Severance

State of Connecticut
Department of Revenue Services
Hartford, CT 06115
    Alcoholic beverage
    Cigarette
    Motor fuels
    Sales and use

State of Delaware
Department of Finance
Wilmington, DE 19801
    Alcoholic beverage
    Income
    Manufacturers and
      merchants
    Tobacco products
    Use

District of Columbia
Office of the Mayor
Washington, D.C. 20001
    Alcoholic beverage
    Cigarette
    Gasoline
    Income
    Motor fuels
    Sales and use

State of Florida
Department of Revenue
Tallahassee, FL 32304
    Corporate franchise
    Documentary stamp
    Oil and gas conservation
    Pollutant terminal excise
    Sales and use
    Solid minerals
Department of Business
  Regulation
Tallahassee, FL 32304
    Alcoholic beverage
    Cigarette

State of Georgia
Department of Revenue
  Commissioner
Atlanta, GA 30334
    Alcoholic beverage
    Corporate franchise
    Gasoline
    General income
    Sales and use
    Tobacco

State of Hawaii
Department of Taxation
Honolulu, HI 96804
    Alcoholic beverage
    Fuel
    General excise
    Tobacco
    Use

State of Idaho
State Tax Commission
Boise, ID 83722
    Alcoholic beverage
    Cigarette
    Gasoline
    General income
    Sales and use
    Severance
    Special fuel use
    Tobacco products

State of Illinois
Department of Revenue
Springfield, IL 46204
    Gasoline
    Gross income
    Intangibles
    Petroleum production
Alcoholic Beverage Commission
Springfield, IL 46204
    Alcoholic beverage
    Cigarette

State of Iowa
Department of Revenue
Des Moines, IA 50319
    Alcoholic beverage
    Cigarette and tobacco
    Gasoline
    Income
    Oleomargarine
    Sales and use

State of Kansas
Department of Revenue
Topeka, KS 66625
    Alcoholic beverage
    Cigarette
    Gasoline
    Grain handling
    Income
    Liquefied petroleum gas
    Sales and use
    Tobacco products

Commonwealth of Kentucky
Revenue Cabinet
Department of Processing
  and Enforcement
Frankfort, KY 40620
    Alcoholic beverage
    Cigarette
    Coal severance
    Gasoline
    General income
    Intangibles
    Oil Production
    Natural resources
      severance
    Sales and use

State of Louisiana
Department of Revenue and
  Taxation
Baton Rouge, LA 78021
    Beverage
    General income
    Petroleum products
    Sales and use
    Severance
    Tobacco

State of Maine
Bureau of Taxation
Augusta, ME 04330
    Alcoholic beverage
    Cigarette
    Gasoline
    Income
    Mining excise
    Sales and use

State of Maryland
State Comptroller
Annapolis, MD 21401
    Alcoholic beverage
    Cigarette
    Gasoline
    Income
    Sales and use

Commonwealth of Massachusetts
Department of Revenue
Boston, MA 02204
    Alcoholic beverage
    Cigarette
    Gasoline
    Income
    Insurance
    Sales and use

State of Michigan
Department of Treasury
Revenue Division
Lansing, MI 48922
    Cigarette
    Fuel
    Gas and oil severance
    Intangibles
    Personal income
    Sales and use
Liquor Control Commission
Lansing, MI 48909
    Alcoholic beverage

State of Minnesota
Department of Revenue
Saint Paul, MN 55145
    Alcoholic beverage
    Cigarette
    Gasoline
    Income
    Occupation and royalty
    Sales and use

State of Mississippi
State Tax Commission
Jackson, MS 39205
    Alcoholic beverage
    Amusement
    Compressed gas
    Gas and oil severance
    Gasoline and oil excise
    General income
    Lubricating oils
    Malt
    Occupations
    Sales and use
    Timber and timber
      products
    Tobacco

State of Missouri
Department of Revenue
Jefferson City, MO 65105
    Alcoholic beverage
    Cigarette
    Fuel use
    Gasoline
    Sales and use
Department of Social Services
Division of Health
Jefferson City, MO 65105
    Soft drinks

State of Montana
Department of Revenue
Helena, MT 59620
    Alcoholic beverage
    Cement
    Cigarette
    Coal severance
    Gasoline
    General income
    Metalliferous mines
    Oil and gas producers
    Tobacco products

State of Nebraska
Department of Revenue
Lincoln, NE 68509
    Aircraft fuels
    Cigarette
    General income
    Sales and use
    Special fuels
Liquor Control Commission
Lincoln, NE 68509
    Alcoholic beverage

State of Nevada
Department of Taxation
Carson City, NV 89710
    Alcoholic beverage
    Cigarette
    Gasoline
    Sales and use

State of New Hampshire
Department of Revenue
  Administration
Concord, NH 03301
    Cigarette
    Corporate gross profit
    Intangible income
    Refined petroleum
      products
State Liquor Commission
Concord, NH 03301
    Alcoholic beverage

State of New Jersey
Department of the Treasury
Trenton, NJ 08625
    Alcoholic beverage
    Business personal property
    Financial excise
    Gasoline
    Hazardous substances
    Income
    Sales and use
    Utilities excise

State of New Mexico
Taxation and Revenue Department
Santa Fe, NM 87509
    Cigarette
    Conservation
    Gasoline
    Gross receipts
    Income
    Liquor excise
    Mining property
    Oil and gas ad valorem
    Oil and gas equipment ad
      valorem
    Resources excise

State of New York
Department of Taxation and
  Finance
Albany, NY 12226
    Alcoholic beverage
    Cigarette
    Gasoline
    Income
    Intangibles
    Primary forest products
      assessment
    Sales and use
    Soft drinks

State of North Dakota
State Tax Commissioner
Bismarck, ND 58505
    Cigarette and snuff
    Coal conversion plant
    Coal severance
    Fuel use
    Gasoline
    Grain
    Oil and gas production
    Oil extraction
    Sales and use

State of Ohio
Department of Taxation
Columbus, OH 43215
    Alcoholic beverage
    Cigarette and tobacco
    Gasoline
    Income
    Resource severance
State Treasurer
Columbus, OH 43216
    Sales and use

State of Oklahoma
Tax Commission
Oklahoma City, OK 73194
    Beverage
    Cigarette and tobacco
      products
    Conservation excise
    Income
    Motor fuels
    Sales and use
Alcoholic Beverage Control Board
Oklahoma City, OK 73194
    Alcoholic beverage

State of Oregon
Department of Revenue
Salem, OR 97310
    Forest products
    Income
    Reforestation
    Timber
Department of Transportation
Salem, OR 97310
    Fuel use
    Gasoline
Liquor Control Commission
Salem, OR 97310
    Alcoholic beverage
Department of Geology and Min-
  eral Industries
Salem, OR 97310
    Oil
State Wheat Commission
Salem, OR 97310
    Wheat

Commonwealth of Pennsylvania
Department of Revenue
Harrisburg, PA 17105
    Alcoholic beverage
    Cigarette
    Corporate loans
    Gasoline
    Income
    Insurance
    Sales and use

State of Rhode Island
Department of Administration
Providence, RI 02908
 Alcoholic beverage
 Bank deposits
 Gasoline
 Income
 Sales and use

State of South Carolina
Tax Commission
Columbia, SC 29414
 Alcoholic beverage
 Cigarette and tobacco
 Gasoline
 Income
 Malt extract
 Playing card
 Sales and use
 Soft drinks

State of South Dakota
Secretary of Revenue
Pierre, SD 57501
 Alcoholic beverage
 Cigarette
 Contractors excise
 Fuel use
 Gasoline
 Oil and gas severance
 Precious metals severance
 Sales and use

State of Tennessee
Department of Revenue
Nashville, TN 37242
 Alcoholic beverage
 Cigarette and tobacco
 Coal severance
 Corporate excise
 Fuel use
 Gasoline
 Sales and use

State of Texas
Comptroller of Public Accounts
Austin, TX 78774
 Cement
 Cigarette
 Gasoline
 Natural gas
 Oil production
 Petroleum
 Sales and use
 Sulfur
Alcoholic Beverage Commission
Austin, TX 78711
 Alcoholic beverage

State of Utah
Tax Commission
Salt Lake City, UT 84134
 Alcoholic beverage
 Cigarette
 Fuel use
 Gasoline
 Income
 Sales and use

State of Vermont
Commissioner of Taxes
Montpelier, VT 05602
 Alcoholic beverage
 Cigarette
 Electric energy
 Income
 Sales and use

Commissioner of Motor Vehicles
Montpelier, VT 05602
 Diesel fuels
 Gasoline

Commonwealth of Virginia
Department of Taxation
Richmond, VA 23282
 Beer
 Cigarette
 Forest products
 Income
 Intangibles
 Sales and use
 Soft drinks
Division of Motor Vehicles
Richmond, VA 23220
 Motor fuels
 Oil company excise
 Special fuel
Alcoholic Beverage Control
 Commission
Richmond, VA 23261
 Liquor and wine

State of Washington
Department of Revenue
Olympia, WA 98504
 Business and occupation
 Cigarette
 Fish and shellfish
 Sales and use
 Stumpage on timber
State Liquor Control Board
Olympia, WA 98504
 Alcoholic beverage
Department of Licensing
Olympia, WA 98504
 Fuel

State of West Virginia
State Tax Department
Charleston, WV 25305
 Business and occupation
 Cigarette
 Income
 Motor fuels
 Sales and use
 Soft drinks
Alcoholic Beverage Control
 Commission
Charleston, WV 25304
 Alcoholic beverage
Nonintoxicating Beer Commission
Charleston, WV 25305
 Excise on beer with
  alcoholic contents
  below 3.2%

State of Wisconsin
Department of Revenue
Madison, WI 53708
 Alcoholic beverage
 Cigarette
 Gasoline
 Income
 Metalliferous mineral
  occupation
 Sales and use

State of Wyoming
Department of Revenue and
 Taxation
Cheyenne, WY 82002
 Cigarette
 Gasoline
 Mining severance
 Sales and use
State Liquor Commission
Cheyenne, WY 82002
 Alcoholic beverage
Secretary of State
Cheyenne, WY 82001
 Corporate income
Oil and Gas Conservation
 Commission
Cheyenne, WY 82001
 Oil and gas production

4. FOREIGN CHAMBERS OF COMMERCE IN THE UNITED STATES

NEW YORK

African-American Chamber of Commerce, Inc.
65 Liberty Street
New York, NY 10005
(212) 766-1343

U.S.-Arab Chamber of Commerce
One World Trade Center
New York, NY 10048
(212) 432-0655

American-Arab Association for Commerce and Industry, Inc.
342 Madison Avenue
New York, NY 10017
(212) 986-7229

Argentine-American Chamber of Commerce, Inc.
11 Broadway
New York, NY 10004
(212) 943-8753

United States-Australian Chamber of Commerce, Inc.
165 West 46th Street
New York, NY 10036
(212) 757-0117

Belgian-American Chamber of Commerce in the United States, Inc.
50 Rockefeller Plaza
New York, NY 10020
(212) 247-7613

Brazilian-American Chamber of Commerce, Inc.
22 West 48th Street
New York, NY 10036
(212) 575-9030

British-American Chamber of Commerce
10 East 40th Street
New York, NY 10016
(2120 889-0680

Central American Chamber of Commerce in the United States, Inc.
65 Liberty Street
New York, NY 10005
(212) 766-1348

North American-Chilean Chamber of Commerce, Inc.
220 East 81st Street
New York, NY 10028
(212) 288-5691

Chinese Chamber of Commerce of New York, Inc.
33 Bowery
New York, NY 10002
(212) 226-2795

Ecuadorean-American Association Inc.
115 Broadway
New York, NY 10006
(212) 233-7776

Finnish-American Chamber of Commerce
540 Madison Avenue
New York, NY 10022
(212) 832-2588

French-American Chamber of Commerce in the United States, Inc.
1350 Avenue of the Americas
New York, NY 10019
(212) 581-4554

German-American Chamber of Commerce, Inc.
666 Fifth Avenue
New York, NY 10019
(212) 974-8330

Hellenic-American Chamber of Commerce
29 Broadway
New York, NY 10004
(212) 943-8594

American-Indonesian Chamber of Commerce, Inc.
120 Wall Street
New York, NY 10005
(212) 344-1808

American-Israel Chamber of Commerce and Industry, Inc.
500 Fifth Avenue
New York, NY 10036
(212) 354-6510

Ireland-United States Council for Commerce and Industry , Inc.
460 Park Avenue
New York, NY 10022
(212) 751-2660

Italy-America Chamber of Commerce, Inc.
350 Fifth Avenue
New York, NY 10118
(212) 279-5520

Japanese Chamber of Commerce of New York, Inc.
39 Broadway
New York, NY 10006
(212) 425-2513

United States-Korea Economic Council, Inc.
88 Morningside Drive
New York, NY 10027
(212) 749-4200

Chamber of Commerce of Latin America in the United States, Inc.
One World Trade Center
New York, NY 10048
(212) 432-9313

United States-Lebanese Chamber of Commerce, Inc.
One World Trade Center
New York, NY 10048
(212) 432-1133

Mexican Chamber of Commerce in the United States, Inc.
One World Trade Center
New York, NY 10048
(212) 432-9332

Netherlands Chamber of Commerce in the United States, Inc.
One Rockefeller Plaza
New York, NY 10020
(212) 265-6460

Nigerian-American Chamber of Commerce
65 Liberty Street
New York, NY 10005
(212) 766-1342

Norwegian-American Chamber of Commerce, Inc.
800 Third Avenue
New York, NY 10022
(212) 421-9210

Peruvian-American Association, Inc.
11 Broadway
New York, NY 10004
(212) 943-8753

Philippine-American Chamber of Commerce, Inc.
565 Fifth Avenue
New York, NY 10017
(212) 972-9326

Portugal-United States Chamber of Commerce
5 West 45th Street
New York, NY 10036
(212) 354-4627

Puerto Rico Chamber of Commerce in the United States, Inc.
65 Liberty Street
New York, NY 10005
(212) 766-1348

Spain-United States Chamber of Commerce, Inc.
500 Fifth Avenue
New York, NY 10036
(212) 354-7848

Swedish-American Chamber of Commerce, Inc.
1 Dag Hammarskjold Plaza
New York, NY 10017
(212) 838-5530

Trinidad and Tobago Chamber of Commerce of the United States of America, Inc.
One Battery Park Plaza
New York, NY 10004
(212) 742-3350

Venezuelan-American Association of the United States, Inc.
115 Broadway
New York, NY 10006
(212) 233-7776

United States-Yugoslav Economic Council, Inc.
51 East 42nd Street
New York, NY 10017
(212) 687-7797

CHICAGO

Mid-America-Arab Chamber of Commerce
135 South LaSalle Street
Chicago, IL 60603
(312) 782-4654

Belgian-American Chamber of Commerce in the United States, Inc.
Midwest Chapter
112 South Michigan Avenue
Chicago, IL 60603
(312) 236-0399

Ecuadorian Chamber of Commerce and Industry of Chicago
2804 West Belmont Avenue
Chicago, IL 60618
(312) 478-3993

Finnish-American Chamber of Commerce of the Midwest
35 East Wacker Drive
Chicago, IL 60611
(312) 346-1150

French-American Chamber of Commerce in the United States, Inc.
Midwest Chapter
Banque Nationale de Paris
33 North Dearborn Street
Chicago, IL 60602
(312) 977-2221

German-American Chamber of Commerce of Chicago
77 East Monroe Street
Chicago, IL 60603
(312) 782-8557

American-Israel Chamber of Commerce and Industry, Inc.
180 North Michigan Avenue
Chicago, IL 60601
(312) 641-2937

Italian Chamber of Commerce of Chicago
327 South LaSalle Street
Chicago, IL 60604
(312) 427-3014

Japanese Chamber of Commerce and Industry of Chicago
230 North Michigan Avenue
Chicago, IL 60601
(312) 332-6199

Mexican-American Chamber of Commerce and Industry of Chicago
4539 South Ashland Avenue
Chicago, IL 60609
(312) 523-5721

Netherlands Chamber of Commerce in the United States, Inc.
303 East Wacker Drive
Chicago, IL 60601
(312) 938-9050

Norwegian-American Chamber of Commerce, Inc.
360 North Michigan Avenue
Chicago, IL 60601
(312) 782-7751

Spain-U.S. Chamber of Commerce of the Middle West
180 North Michigan Avenue
Chicago, IL 60601
(312) 782-7663

Mid-American Swedish Trade Association
333 North Michigan Avenue
Chicago, IL 60601
(312) 372-1680

LOS ANGELES AREA

African-American Chamber of Commerce
16130 Ventura Boulevard
Encino, CA 91436
(213) 788-3720

British-American Chamber of Commerce
350 South Figueroa Street
Los Angeles, CA 90071
(213) 622-7124

Finnish-American Chamber of Commerce of the Pacific Coast, Inc.
3600 Wilshire Boulevard
Los Angeles, CA 90010
(213) 385-1779

German-American Chamber of Commerce of Los Angeles
3250 Wilshire Boulevard
Los Angeles, CA 90010
(213) 381-2236

Western States-Israel Chamber of Commerce
6399 Wilshire Boulevard
Los Angeles, CA 90048
(213) 653-7910

Japanese Chamber of Commerce of Southern California
244 Pedro Street
Los Angeles, CA 90012
(213) 626-5116

Mexican Chamber of Commerce of Southern California
125 Paseo de la Raza
Los Angeles, CA 90012
(213) 688-7330

Norwegian-American Chamber of Commerce, Inc.
350 South Figueroa Street
Los Angeles, CA 90071

SAN FRANCISCO

U.S.-Arab Chamber of Commerce (Pacific), Inc.
433 California Street
San Francisco, CA 94104
(415) 397-5663

Australian-American Association
P.O. Box 3450
San Francisco, CA 94119
(415) 772-9200

British-American Chamber of Commerce
111 Pine Street
San Francisco, CA 94111
(415) 397-0250

Chile-Northern California Chamber of Commerce, Inc.
303 World Trade Center
San Francisco, CA 94111
(415) 986-5698

Chinese Chamber of Commerce of San Francisco
730 Sacramento Street
San Francisco, CA 94108
(415) 982-3000

German-American Chamber of Commerce of the Pacific Coast
465 California Avenue
San Francisco, CA 94104
(415) 392-2262

Pacific-Indonesia Chamber of Commerce
303 World Trade Center
San Francisco, CA 94111
(415) 433-2491

Japanese Chamber of Commerce of Northern California
312 Sutter Street
San Francisco, CA 94108
(415) 986-6140

Korean-American Chamber of Commerce
160 Indian Road
Piedmont, CA 94610
(415) 547-4371

Norwegian-American Chamber of Commerce
One Embarcadero Center
San Francisco, CA 94111
(415) 986-0766

Philippine-American Chamber of Commerce
447 Sutter Street
San Francisco, CA 94108
(415) 391-3655

Swedish-American Chamber of Commerce of the Western United States
World Trade Center
San Francisco, CA 94111
(415) 781-4188

OTHER CITIES

Chamber of Commerce of the Americas
P.O. Box 1056
Seffner, FL 33584
(813) 681-3105

Arab-United States Chamber of Commerce
6420 Richmond Avenue
Houston, TX 77057
(713) 977-7124

United States-Arab Chamber of Commerce
1625 I Street, N.W.
Washington, DC 20006
(202) 293-6975

Brazilian-American Chamber of Commerce
2800 ITM Building
New Orleans, LA 70130
(504) 588-9187

Finnish-American Chamber of Commerce of the Rocky Mountains
P.O. Box 1556
Boulder, CO 80306

French-American Chamber of Commerce
4940 Viking Drive
Minneapolis, MN 55435
(612) 835-1900

German-American Chamber of Commerce
233 Peachtree Street, N.E.
Atlanta, GA 30303
(404) 577-7228

German-American Chamber of Commerce
Two Houston Center
Houston, TX 77002
(713) 658-8230

German-American Chamber of Commerce
One Farragut Square South
Washington, DC 20006
(202) 327-0247

American-Israel Chamber of Commerce and Industry
10800 Brookpark Road
Cleveland, OH 44130
(216) 267-1200

American-Israel Chamber of Commerce and Industry
1901 Walnut Street
Phildelphia, PA 19103

American-Israel Chamber of Commerce
  3950 Biscayne Boulevard
  Miami, FL 33137
  (305) 573-0668
Italian Chamber of Commerce of Houston, Inc.
  209 World Trade Center
  Houston, TX 77002
  (713) 222-7860
United States-Mexico Chamber of Commerce
  1800 K Street, N.W.
  Washington, DC 20006
  (202) 296-5198

Norwegian-American Chamber of Commerce
  800 Foshay Tower
  Minneapolis, MN 55402
Norwegian-American Chamber of Commerce
  2727 Rainier Bank Tower
  Seattle, WA 98101
  (206) 683-5250

5. INTERNAL REVENUE SERVICE CENTERS, BY REGION

New Jersey, New York (counties of Kings, Queens, Nassau, Suffolk, Richmond, New York, Rockland, Westchester)	Holtsville, NY 00501	Arkansas, Kansas, Louisiana, New Mexico, Oklahoma, Texas	Austin, TX 73301
New York (all other counties), Connecticut, Maine, Massachusetts, New Hampshire, Rhode Island, Vermont	Andover, MA 05501	Alaska, Arizona, Colorado, Idaho, Minnesota, Montana, Nebraska, Nevada, North Dakota, Oregon, South Dakota, Utah, Washington, Wyoming	Ogden, UT 84201
District of Columbia, Delaware, Maryland, Pennsylvania	Philadelphia, PA 19255	Illinois, Iowa, Missouri, Wisconsin	Kansas City, MO 64999
		California, Hawaii	Fresno, CA 93883
Alabama, Florida, Georgia, Mississippi, South Carolina	Atlanta, GA 31101	Indiana, Kentucky, North Carolina, Tennessee, Virginia, West Virginia	Memphis, TN 37501
Michigan, Ohio	Cincinnati, OH 45999		

6. NATIONAL STANDARDS BODIES
* "Enquiry Points" under Article 10 of GATT
[1]Sources of governmental standards; [2]Sources of nongovernmental standards

Algeria
Institut Algérien de Normalisation et de Propriété
  Industrielle
5 rue Abou Hamou Moussa
B.P. 1021, Centre de Tri
Algiers

Argentina
*Ministerio de Comercio e Intereses Maritimos
Subsecretaria de Negociaciones Comerciales
  Internacionales
Av. Julio A. Roca 651
1322 Buenos Aires
Telephone: (011) + 54 + 1 +34-6826
Telex: 1622, 17065, 18055

Australia
Standards Association of Australia
80-86 Arthur Street
North Sydney, N.S.W. 2060

Austria
*[1]Bundesministerium für Handel, Gewerbe, und
  Industrie
Abteilung II/7
Stubenring 1-3
A-1010 Vienna
Telephone: (011) + 43 + 222-7500, ext. 5238
Telex: 111780, 111145
*[2]Österreiches Normungsinstitut
Postfach 130
A-1021 Vienna
Telephone: (011) + 43 + 222 + 33 55 19
Telex: 75960
Cable: Austrianorm

Bangladesh
Bangladesh Standards Institution
3-DIT (Extension) Avenue
Motijheel Commercial Area
Dacca 2

Barbados
Barbados National Standards Institution
Flodden, Culloden Road
St. Michael

Belgium
*Centre d'Information belge sur les normes et les régle-
  ments techniques
Avenue de la Brabancconne 29
B-1040 Bruxelles
Telephone: 02-734-9205
Telex: 23877

Bolivia
Direccion General de Normas y Technologia
Ministerio de Industria, Comercio y Turismo
Casilla 4430, Piso 9
La Paz

Brazil
*[1] Divisao de Politica Comercial
Sala 536
Ministerio das Reclacoes Exteriores
Palacio Itamaraty
Brasilia
Telephone: (011) + 55 + 226-0962
Telex: 61-1311, 63-1319
[2]Associacao Brasiliera de Normas Technicas
Av. 13 de Maio, no. 13-28 andar
Caixa Postal 1680
Rio de Janeiro

Bulgaria
State Committee for Standardization
Council of Ministers
21, Sixth of September Street
Sofia

Cameroun
Service de Normalisation
Direction de l'Industrie
Ministère de l'Économie et du Plan
B.P. 1604
Yaoundé

Canada
*Standards Information Service
Standards Council of Canada
350 Sparks Street
Ottawa, Ontario K1R 7S8
Telephone: (613) 238-3222
Telex: 053-4403

Chile
[1]Instituto Nacional de Normalisation
Matias Cousino 64-6 piso
Casilla 995-Correo 1
Santiago

*Delegación Permanente de Chile
Case Postal 211
1211 Geneva 19 (Switzerland)
Telephone: (011) + 41 + 22 + 345130
Telex: 22142

*Dirección de Asuntos Económicos Multilaterales
Ministerio de Relaciones Exteriores
Bandera 52, 3er Piso
Santiago
Telephone: (011) + 56 + 2 + 71-1142
Telex: 94642

China, People's Republic
China Association for Standardization
P. O. Box 820
Beijing

Colombia
Instituto Colombiano de Normas Technicas
Carrera 37, No. 52-56
P. O. Box 14237
Bogotá

Costa Rica (see Guatemala)

Cyprus
Cyprus Organization for Standards & Quality Control
Ministry of Commerce and Industry
Nicosia

Czechoslovakia
Československy Inštitút Technickej Normalizácie a Akosti
Mierová 139, PSČ: 827 08
Bratislava
Telephone: 292 234

Denmark
*Dansk Standardiseringsraad
Aurehojvaj 12
Postbox 77
DK-2900 Hellerup
Telephone: (011) + 45 + 2 + 62 93 15
Telex: 15615 Dansta DK
Cable: Danskstandard

Dominican Republic
Dirección General de Normas y Systemas de Calidad
Secretaria de Industria y Comercio
Av. Mexico 30
Santo Domingo

Ecuador
Instituto Ecuadoriano de Normalisation
Casilla 3999
Universitaria 784
Quito

Egypt
Egyptian Organization for Standardization
2 Latin America Street
Garden City
Cairo

El Salvador (see Guatemala)

European Economic Community
(a) Industrial Products
*GATT Enquiry Point
DG III/F/I
Rond Point R. Schuman 6
1049 Brussels
Telephone: (011) + 32 + 235-8257
Telex: 21877 COMEU-B
(b) Agricultural Products
*GATT Enquiry Point
DG VI/H
Berlaymont Building
Rue de la Loi 200
1049 Brussels
Telephone: (011) + 32 + 235-6827

Ethiopia
Ethiopian Standards Institution
P. O. Box 2310
Addis Ababa

Finland
*Suomen Standardisoimisliitto
P. O. Box 205
SF-00121 Helsinki 12
Telephone: (011) + 358 + 9 + 645 601
Telex: 122303 stand sf
Cable: Finnstandard

France
*CINORTECH—AFNOR
Tour Europe Cedex 07
92080 Paris La Défense
Telephone: (011) + 33 + 1 + 778-1326
Telex: 611974 Afnor F

German Federal Republic
*Deutsche Informationszentrum für Technische Regeln
Postfach 11 07
Burgraffenstrasse 4-10
D 1000 Berlin 30
Telephone: (011) + 49 + 30 + 260-1600
Telex: 185 269 DITR-D
Cable: Deutschnormen Berlin

Ghana
Ghana Standards Board
P. O. Box M-245
Accra

Greece
*Ministry of Commerce
Directorate of International Organizations & Conventions
Canningos Square
Athens
[2]Hellenic Organization for Standardization
Didotou 15
Athens 144

Guatemala
Instituto Centroamericano de Investigaciones y Technologica Industrial
4a Calle y Avenida la Reforma
Zona 10
Guatemala City

Honduras (see Guatemala)

Hong Kong
*Department of Trade, Industry & Customs
Ocean Centre
Canton Road, Kowloon
Hong Kong
Telex: 50151 IND HK

Hungary
Magyar Szabvanyugyi Hivatal
Ulloi ut 25
1450 Budapest
Telephone: (011) + 36 + 1 + 183 011
Telex: 035/225723 Norm H

Iceland
Technological Institute of Iceland
Division of Standards
Skipholt 37
IS-105 Reykjavik

India
Indian Standards Institution
Manak Bhavan
9 Bahadur Shah Zafar Marg 9
New Delhi 110 002
Telephone: 270131, 266021
Telex: 031-3970 ISI/ND

Indonesia
Yavasan Dana Normalisasi Indonesia
Jalan Teuku Chik Ditiro No. 43
P. O. Box 250
Jakarta

Iran
Ministry of Industry and Mines
Institute of Standards and Industrial Research
P. O. Box 2937, Tehran

Iraq
Central Organization for Standardization & Quality
  Control
P. O. Box 13032 Aljadiria
Baghdad

Ireland
  (a) Technical Regulations and Certification
*GATT Section
International Trade Division
Department of Industry, Commerce & Tourism
Kildare Street
Dublin 2
Telephone: (011) + 35 + 31 + 78 94 11
Telex: 24651
  (b) Standards
*Institute for Industrial Research and Standards
Ballymun
Dublin 9
Telephone: (011) + 35 + 31 + 37 01 01
Telex: 25449

Israel
Standards Institution of Israel
42 University Street
Tel Aviv 69977

Italy
*Consiglio Nazionale delle Ricerche
Servizio Transferimento Innovazioni-Brevetti-Normativa
  Tecnica
Viale Liegi 48
I 00198 Rome
Telephone: 06 864883
Telex: 620623 CNRSTI I
2 Ente Nazionale Italiano di Unificazione
Piazza Armando Diaz 2
I 20123 Rome

Ivory Coast
Bureau Ivoirien de Normalisation
01 B.P. 1318
Abidjan 01

Jamaica
Jamaica Bureau of Standards
6 Winchester Road
Box 113
Kingston 10

Japan
  (a) Standards for food, drugs, cosmetics, telecommuni-
    cations and transport equipment (including
    automobiles)
*Standards Information Service
First International Organizations Division
Economic Affairs Bureau
Ministry of Foreign Affairs
2-2-1, Kasumagaseki, Chiyoda-ku
Tokyo
Telephone: (011) + 81 + 3 + 580-3311
Telex: J22350
  (b) Standards for products other than those above
*Standards Information Service
Information Service Department
Japan External Trade Organization
2-2-5 Toranomon, Minato-ku
Tokyo
Telephone: (011) + 81 + 3 + 582 + 5511
Telex: J24378

Kenya
Kenya Bureau of Standards
P. O. Box 54974
Nairobi

Korea, Republic of
  (a) Industrial Products
*Bureau of Standards
Office of Industrial Advancement Administration
94-267 Youngdungpo-dong
Youngdungpo-ku
Seoul
Telephone: (011) + 82 + 2 + 633-9559
  (b) Agricultural Products
*Division of Inspection Management
National Agricultural Products Inspection Office
Kwanhun-dong, chongro-ku 117-2
Seoul
Telephone: (011) + 82 + 2 + 700-4518
  (c) Fisheries Products
*National Fishery Inspection Office
Central Fishery Products Inspection Station
Wonnam-dong, chongro-ku 203
Telephone: (011) + 82 + 2 + 762-9214

Kuwait
Standards and Meteorology Department
Ministry of Commerce and Industry
P. O. Box 2944
Kuwait

Lebanon
Institut Libanais de Normalisation
B.P. 195144
Beirut

Liberia
Division of Standards
Ministry of Commerce, Industry and Transportation
Monrovia

Libya
Libyan Standards and Patent Section
Department of Industrial Organization and Services
Secretariat of Light Industry
Tripoli

Luxembourg
*Inspection du Travail et des Mines
26 rue Zithe, B.P. 27
2010 Luxembourg
Telephone: (011) + 35 + 2 + 44 92 11

Madagascar
Ministère de Developpment Rural et de la Réforme Agraire
Direction de l'Agriculture
Service du Contrôle des Qualités et du Conditionnement
B.P. 1-316
Antananarivo

Malawi
Malawi Bureau of Standards
P. O. Box 946
Blantyre

Malaysia
Standards and Industrial Research Institute
Lot 108, Phase 3, Federal Highway
P. O. Box 35
Shah Alam, Selangor

Mauritius
Mauritius Bureau of Standards
Ministry of Commerce and Industry
Reduit

Mexico
Direccion General de Normas
Tuxpan No. 2
Mexico 7, D.F.

Mongolian People's Republic
State Committee for Prices and Standardization
Council of Ministers
Marshal Zhukov Avenue 51
Ulan Bator

Morocco
Service de Normalistion Industrielle Marocain
Direction de l'Industrie
Ministère du Comerce, de l'Industrie, de la Marine
    Marchande et des Péches Maritimes
Rabat

Mozambique
National Information and Documentation Center
P. O. Box 4116
Maputo

Netherlands
*Dienst voor Economische Voorlichting en Exportbe-
    vordering Afdeling Overheidsmaatregelen
Bezuidenhoutseweg 151
2594 AG The Hague
Telephone: (011) + 31 + 70 + 79 89 11
Telex: 31099

*Stichting Raad voor de Certificatie
Kalfjeslaan 2
2623 AA Delft
Telephone: (011) + 31 + 15 + 61 10 61
Telex: 38144

New Zealand
*Department of Trade and Industry
Private Bag
Wellington
Telephone: (011) + 64 + 4 + 720 030
Telex: WN 315 30
[2]Standards Association of New Zealand
Private Bag
Wellington
Telephone: (011) + 64 + 4 + 842 + 108
Telex: NZ 3850 SANZ

Nicaragua (see Guatemala)

Nigeria
Nigerian Standards Organization
Federal Ministry of Industries
4 Club Road, P. O. Box 550
Enugu

Norway
*Norges Standardiseringsforbund
Hegdenaugsveien 31
Postboks 7020, Homansbyen
N-Oslo 3
Telephone: (011) + 47 + 2 + 46 60 94
Telex: 19050 NSF N

Oman
Directorate General for Specifications and Measurements
Ministry of Commerce and Industry
P. O. Box 550, Muscat

Pakistan
Pakistan Standards Institution
39 Garden Road, Saddar
Karachi 3

*Standards Consultant
Ministry of Commerce
Islamabad
Telephone: (011) + 92 + 51 + 208 52
Telex: COMDN PAK-5859

Panama (see Guatemala)

Philippines
*GATT-TBT Enquiry Point
Product Standards Agency
Ministry of Trade and Industry
361 Sen. Gil J. Payant Avenue, Makati
Metro Manila 3117
Telex: 14830 MOTF

Peru
Instituto de Investigacion Technologia Industrial y
    de Normas Technicas
Jr. Morelli - 2da Cuadra
Urbanizacion San Borja
Lima 34

Poland
Polish Committee for Standardization, Measures
    and Quality Control
U1. Elektoralna 2
00-139 Warsaw

Portugal
Direccao-Geral da Qualidade
Rua Jose Estevao 83-A
1199 Lisbon Codex

Romania
*Romanian Institute for Standardization
Roma Street No. 24, Sector I
Bucharest 7000
Telex: 11-312 CNSTR

Saudi Arabia
Saudi Arabian Standards Organization
P. O. Box 3437
Riyadh

Singapore
    (a) Industrial Standards
*Singapore Institute of Standards & Industrial Research
179 River Valley Road
Singapore 0617
Telephone: (011) + 65 + 336-0933
    (b) Electrical Standards
*Public Utilities Board
Somerset Road
Singapore 0923
Telephone: (011) + 65 + 235-8888
    (c) Processed Food Standards
*Ministry of the Environment
Princess House, Alexandra Road
Singapore 0315
Telephone: (011) + 65 + 635 111
Telex: MOERS 34365
    (d) Standard for fish, meats, fruits, and vegetables
*Primary Production Department
National Development Building
Maxwell Road
Singapore 0106
Telephone: (011) + 65 + 222-1211
Telex: AGRIVET

Sweden
*1Kommerskollegium
Gatt Enquiry Point
Box 1209
S-111 82 Stockholm
Telephone: (011) + 46 + 8 + 22 36 00
Telex: 11835 komkol S
Cable: Tradeboard Stockholm

*2Standardiseringskommissionen i Sverge
SIS Enquiry Services
Box 3295
S-103 66 Stockholm
Telephone: (011) + 46 + 8 + 23 04 00
Telex: 17453 SIS-S
Cable: Standardis Stockholm

Switzerland
*Office Fédéral des Affaires Économiques Extérieures
Palais Fédéral Est
3003 Berne
Telephone: (011) + 41 + 31 + 61 23 09
Telex: 911340 EDA/CH
2Association Suisse de Normalisation
Kirchenweg 4
8032 Zurich

Syria
Syrian Arab Organization for Standardization &
    Meteorology
P. O. Box 11836
Damascus

Tanzania
Tanzania Bureau of Standards
P. O. Box 9524
Dar es Salaam

Thailand
Thai Industrial Standards Institute
Ministry of Industry
Rama VI Street
Bangkok 4

Trinidad & Tobago
Trinidad & Tobago Bureau of Standards
318 Salvatori Building
P. O. Box 288
Port of Spain

Tunisia
Le Directeur de l'Environment et de la Normalisation et
    du Control de la Qualité
Direction Général de l'Industrie
Ministère de l'Économie Nationale
Le Casbah
Tunis

Turkey
Turk Standard'ari Enstitusu
Necatibey Cad. 112
Bakanlikiar
Ankara

United Arab Emirates
Directorate of Standardization and Meteorology
P. O. Box 433
Abu Dhabi

United Kingdom
*1Department of Trade and Industry
Standards and Quality Policy Unit
Ashdown House
124 Victoria Street
London SW1E 6RB
Telephone: (011) + 44 + 1 + 215-3092
Telex: 88 11 084 DTHQ G
*2British Standards Institution
Linford Wood
Milton Keynes MK14 6LE
Telephone: (011) + 44 + 1 + 629-9000
Telex: 82577 BSIMKG

Union of Soviet Socialist Republics
USSR State Committee for Standards
Leninsky Prospekt 9
Moscow 117049

United States
*Standards Code and Information Center
Office of Product Standards Policy
National Bureau of Standards
Gaithersburg, Maryland 20899
Telephone: (301) 921-2092
Telex: 898493 GARG

Venezuela
Comisión Venezolana de Normas Industriales
Av. Bovaca (Cota Mil.)
Edf. Fundacion La Salle 5 piso
Caracas 105

Yugoslavia
Savezni zavod za Standardizaciju
Slobodana Penezica-Krcuna 35
11000 Belgrade
Telephone: (011) + 38 + 11 + 644 066
Telex: 12089 YUJUS

7. U. S. FOREIGN TRADE ZONES
Listed by State and Community

Customs Port of Entry is given when names of zone community and POE do not coincide.

ALABAMA

FTZ No. 82	Mobile
FTZ No. 83	Huntsville
FTZ No. 98	Birmingham

ALASKA

FTZ No. 108	Valdez

ARIZONA

FTZ No. 48	Pima County (Tucson)
FTZ No. 60	Nogales
FTZ No. 75	Phoenix

ARKANSAS

FTZ No. 14	Little Rock

CALIFORNIA

FTZ No. 3	San Francisco
FTZ No. 18	San Jose (San Francisco)
FTZ No. 50	Long Beach
FTZ No. 56	Oakland

COLORADO

FTZ No. 112	El Paso County (Denver)

CONNECTICUT

FTZ No. 71	Windsor Locks (Hartford)
FTZ No. 76	Bridgeport

DELAWARE

FTZ No. 99	Wilmington & Kent County (Wilmington)

FLORIDA

FTZ No. 25	Broward County (Port Everglades)
FTZ No. 32	Miami
FTZ No. 42	Orlando
FTZ No. 64	Jacksonville
FTZ No. 65	Panama City
FTZ No. 79	Tampa

GEORGIA

FTZ No. 26	Coweta County (Atlanta)
FTZ No. 104	Savannah

HAWAII

FTZ No. 9	Honolulu

ILLINOIS

FTZ No. 22	Chicago
FTZ No. 31	Granite City (St. Louis)

INDIANA

FTZ No. 72	Indianapolis

IOWA

FTZ No. 107	Polk County (Des Moines)

KANSAS

FTZ No. 17	Kansas City

KENTUCKY

FTZ No. 29	Jefferson County (Louisville)
FTZ No. 47	Campbell County (Cincinnati)

LOUISIANA

FTZ No. 2	New Orleans
FTZ No. 87	Calcasieu Parish (Lake Charles)

MAINE

FTZ No. 58	Bangor

MARYLAND

FTZ No. 63	Prince George's County (Washington, D.C.)
FTZ No. 73	BWI Airport (Baltimore)
FTZ No. 74	Baltimore

MASSACHUSETTS

FTZ No. 27	Boston
FTZ No. 28	New Bedford

MICHIGAN
FTZ No. 16	Sault Ste. Marie
FTZ No. 43	Battle Creek
FTZ No. 70	Detroit

MINNESOTA
FTZ No. 51	Duluth
FTZ No. 119	Mineapolis-St. Paul

MISSISSIPPI
FTZ No. 92	Harrison County (Gulfport)

MISSOURI
FTZ No. 15	Kansas City
FTZ No. 102	St. Louis

MONTANA
FTZ No. 88	Great Falls

NEBRASKA
FTZ No. 19	Omaha
FTZ No. 59	Lincoln (Omaha)

NEVADA
FTZ No. 89	Clark County (Las Vegas)

NEW HAMPSHIRE
FTZ No. 81	Portsmouth

NEW JERSEY
FTZ No. 44	Morris County (New York City)
FTZ No. 49	Newark/Elizabeth (New York City)

NEW YORK
FTZ No. 1	New York City
FTZ No. 23	Buffalo (Buffalo-Niagara Falls)
FTZ No. 34	Niagara County
FTZ No. 37	Orange County (New York City)
FTZ No. 52	Suffolk Country (New York City)
FTZ No. 54	Clinton County (Champlain-Rouses Point)
FTZ No. 90	County of Onondaga (Syracuse)
FTZ No. 109	Jefferson (Alexandria Bay)
FTZ No. 111	JFK Int'l. Airport
FTZ No. 118	Ogdensburg
FTZ No. 121	Albany

NORTH CAROLINA
FTZ No. 57	Mecklenburg County (Charlotte)
FTZ No. 66	Wilmington
FTZ No. 67	Morehead City (Beaufort-Morehead City)
FTZ No. 93	Raleigh/Durham (Durham)

NORTH DAKOTA
FTZ No. 103	Grand Forks (Pembina)

OHIO
FTZ No. 8	Toledo
FTZ No. 40	Cleveland
FTZ No. 46	Butler County (Cincinnati)
FTZ No. 100	Dayton
FTZ No. 101	Clinton (Dayton)

OKLAHOMA
FTZ No. 53	Rogers County (Tulsa)
FTZ No. 106	Oklahoma City

OREGON
FTZ No. 45	Portland

PENNSYLVANIA
FTZ No. 24	Pittston (Wilkes-Barre/Scranton)
FTZ No. 33	Allegheny County (Pittsburgh)
FTZ No. 35	Philadelphia

PUERTO RICO
FTZ No. 7	Mayaguez
FTZ No. 61	Guaynabo (San Juan)

RHODE ISLAND
FTZ No. 105	Providence & North Kingstown (Providence)

SOUTH CAROLINA
FTZ No. 21	Dorchester County (Charleston)
FTZ No. 38	Spartanburg County (Greenville-Spartanburg)

TENNESSEE
FTZ No. 77	Memphis
FTZ No. 78	Nashville

TEXAS
FTZ No. 12	McAllen (Hidalgo)
FTZ No. 36	Galveston
FTZ No. 39	Dallas/Ft. Worth
FTZ No. 62	Brownsville
FTZ No. 68	El Paso
FTZ No. 80	San Antonio
FTZ No. 84	Harris County (Houston)
FTZ No. 94	Webb County (Laredo)
FTZ No. 95	Starr County (Rio Grande City & Roma)
FTZ No. 96	Maverick County (Eagle Pass)
FTZ No. 97	Val Verde County (Del Rio)
FTZ No. 113	Ellis County
FTZ No. 115	Beaumont
FTZ No. 116	Jefferson County (Port Arthur)
FTZ No. 117	Orange County

UTAH
FTZ No. 30	Salt Lake City

VERMONT
FTZ No. 55	Burlington
FTZ No. 91	Newport (Derby Line)

VIRGINIA
FTZ No. 20	Suffolk (Norfolk-Newport News)

WASHINGTON
FTZ No. 5	Seattle
FTZ No. 85	Everett (Puget Sound)
FTZ No. 86	Tacoma (Puget Sound)
FTZ No. 120	Cowlitz (Longview)

WISCONSIN
FTZ No. 41	Milwaukee

U. S. Foreign Trade Zones, Listed by Number*

Zone No. 1, New York City
Operator: S & F Warehouse Inc.
Brooklyn Navy Yard, Brooklyn, NY 11205
Sol Braun (718) 834-0400
Grantee: City of New York

Zone No. 2, New Orleans
Grantee/Operator: Board of Commissioners of the
Port of New Orleans, P. O. Box 60046,
New Orleans, LA 70160
Robert Dee (504) 897-0189

Zone No. 3, San Francisco
Operator: Foreign Trade Services, Inc.
Pier 23, San Francisco, CA 94111
Ed Osgood (415) 391-0176
Grantee: San Francisco Port Commission

Zone No. 5, Seattle
Grantee/Operator: Port of Seattle Commission
P. O. Box 1209, Seattle, WA 98111
Jack Fox (206) 382-3257

Zone No. 7, Mayaguez, Puerto Rico
Grantee/Operator: Puerto Rico Industrial Develop-
ment Co., G.P.O. Box 2350,
San Juan, PR 00936
Jose Cobian (809) 765-2784

Zone No. 8, Toledo
Operator: Toledo World Industry
3332 St. Lawrence Drive, Toledo, OH 43605
Frank E. Miller (419) 698-8026
Grantee: Toledo-Lucas Port Authority

Zone No. 9, Honolulu
Grantee/Operator: State of Hawaii
Pier 2, Honolulu, HI 96813
Homer Maxey (808) 548-5435

Zone No. 12, McAllen, Texas
Grantee/Operator: McAllen Trade Zone, Inc.
6401 S. 33rd Street, McAllen, TX 78501
Frank Birkhead (512) 682-4306

Zone No. 14, Little Rock
Operator: Little Rock Port Authority
7500 Lindsey Rd., Little Rock, AR 72206
Robert Brave (501) 490-1468
Grantee: Arkansas Dept. of Industrial Development

Zone No. 15, Kansas City, Missouri
Grantee/Operator: Greater Kansas City FTZ, Inc.
600 CharterBank Center, 920 Main St.,
Kansas City, MO 64105
Robert Drost (816) 421-7666

Zone No. 16, Sault Ste. Marie, Michigan
Grantee/Operator: Economic Development Corp. of
Sault Ste. Marie, 1301 W. Easterday,
Sault Ste. Marie, MI 49783
James F. Hendricks (906) 635-9131

Zone No. 17, Kansas City, Kansas
Grantee/Operator: Greater Kansas City FTZ, Inc.
600 CharterBank Center, 920 Main St.,
Kansas City, MO 64105
Robert Drost (816) 421-7666

Zone No. 18, San Jose, California
Grantee: City of San Jose
801 North First St., Rm. 408, City Hall,
San Jose, CA 95110
Ted Daigle (408) 277-4744
Operator: Chris Koelfgen (408) 263-6200

Zone No. 19, Omaha
Grantee/Operator: Dock Board of the City of Omaha
Omaha-Douglas Civic Center, 1819 Farnam St.,
Rm. 701, Omaha, NE 68183
Irvin H. Smith (402) 444-5921

Zone No. 20, Suffolk, Virginia
Grantee: Virginia Port Authority
600 World Trade Center, Norfolk, VA 23510
John Hunter (804) 623-8080

Zone No. 21, Dorchester County, South Carolina
Operator: Carolina Trade Zone
2725 W. 5th North St., Summerville, SC 29483
A.M. Quattlebaum (803) 871-4870
Grantee: South Carolina State Ports Authority

Zone No. 22, Chicago
Operator: Industrial America Corporation
12700 Butler Drive, Chicago, IL 60633
Frank Albert (312) 646-4400
Grantee: Chicago Regional Port District

Zone No. 23, Buffalo
Operator: Buffalo Foreign Trade Zone Operators, Inc.
901 Fuhrman Blvd., Buffalo, NY 14203
George Keitner (716) 856-4436
Grantee: County of Erie

Zone No. 24, Pittston, Pennsylvania
Grantee/Operator: Eastern Distribution Center, Inc.
P. O. Box 31, Avoca, PA 18641
James G. Pettinger (717) 655-5581

Zone No. 25, Port Everglades, Florida
Grantee/Operator: Port Everglades Port Authority
P. O. Box 13136, Port Everglades, FL 33316
Thomas E. Ezzo (305) 523-3404

Zone No. 26, Shenandoah, Georgia
Operator: Georgia Foreign Trade Zone, Inc.
230 Peachtree St. N.W., Atlanta, GA 30301
James R. Steele (404) 656-6338
Grantee: Georgia Foreign Trade Zone, Inc.

Zone No. 27, Boston
Grantee: Massachusetts Port Authority
99 High Street, Boston, MA 02110
Elliot K. Friedman (617) 482-2930 x222

Zone No. 28, New Bedford, Massachusetts
Grantee/Operator: City of New Bedford
Industrial Dev. Commission, 1213 Purchase St.,
New Bedford, MA 02740
Norman Bergeron (617) 997-6501

Zone No. 29, Louisville
Grantee/Operator: Louisville & Jefferson County
Riverport Authority, 6219 Cane Run Road,
Louisville, KY 40258
Robert M. Timmerman (502) 935-6024

*This list gives the address and phone number of the contact person for each zone project, with the city or county location appearing after the zone number. When the contact person is not an employee of the grantee, the name of the grantee organization is given. Further information on any particular zone can be obtained from the contact person. If assistance is needed from FTZ Staff, U. S. Department of Commerce, please call (202) 377-2862.

Zone No. 30, Salt Lake City
Grantee: Salt Lake City Corporation
351 S. State St.
Salt Lake City, UT 84111
Michael Chitwood (801) 328-3211

Zone No. 31, Granite City, Illinois
Grantee/Operator: Tri-City Regional Port District
2801 Rock Road, Granite City, IL 62040
Robert Wydra (618) 877-8444

Zone No. 32, Miami
Grantee: Greater Miami Foreign Trade Zone, Inc.
1601 Biscayne Blvd., Miami, FL 33132
Sandra Gonzalez (305) 350-7700

Zone No. 33, Pittsburgh
Grantee/Operator: Regional Industrial Dev. Corp. of
Southwestern Pennsylvania, 534 Union Trust Bldg.,
Pittsburgh, PA 15219
Frank Brooks Robinson (412) 471-3939

Zone No. 34, Niagara County, New York
Grantee/Operator: County of Niagara
County Office Bldg., 59 Park Ave.,
Lockport, NY 14094
Theodore J. Belling (716) 439-6033

Zone No. 35, Philadelphia
Operator: Delaware Valley Foreign Trade Zone, Inc.
1020 Public Ledger Bldg., Philadelphia, PA 19106
John J. Malone (215) 928-9100
Grantee: The Philadelphia Port Corporation
Vince Di Paloto

Zone No. 36, Galveston
Operator: Port of Galveston
Galveston Wharves, P. O. Box 328,
Galveston, TX 77550
John Massey, Jr. (409) 766-6112
Grantee: City of Galveston

Zone No. 37, Orange County, New York
Operator: Foreign Trade Dev. Co. of Orange Cty., Inc.
P. O. Box 6147, Stewart Airport,
Newburgh, NY 12550
Albert Randall (914) 564-7700
Grantee: County of Orange

Zone No. 38, Spartanburg County, South Carolina
Operator: Carolina Trade Zone
2725 W. 5th North St., Summerville, SC 29483
A. M. Quattlebaum (803) 871-4870
Grantee: South Carolina State Ports Authority

Zone No. 39, Dallas/Fort Worth
Grantee: Dallas/Fort Worth Regional Airport Board
P. O. Drawer DFW,
Dallas/Fort Worth Airport, TX 75261
James Alderson (214) 574-6720

Zone No. 40, Cleveland
Grantee: Cleveland Port Authority
101 Erieside Avenue, Cleveland, OH 44114
John Desmond (216) 241-8004

Zone No. 41, Milwaukee
Grantee: Foreign Trade Zone of Wisconsin, Ltd.
2150 E. College Avenue, Cudahy, WI 53110
Vincent J. Boever (414) 764-2111

Zone No. 42, Orlando
Grantee/Operator: Greater Orlando Aviation Authority
4101 East 9th Street, Orlando, FL 32812
William Blood (305) 859-9485

Zone No. 43, Battle Creek, Michigan
Grantee/Operator: BC/CAL/KAL Inland Port Author-
ity of S. Central Michigan Development Corp.,
P. O. Box 1438, Battle Creek, MI 49016
Marilyn E. Parks (616) 968-8197

Zone No. 44, Morris County, New Jersey
Grantee: N. J. Dept. of Commerce & Economic Dev.
Office of Int'l Trade, 744 Broad St., Newark NJ 07102
Joseph Brady (201) 648-3518

Zone No. 45, Portland, Oregon
Grantee/Operator: Port of Portland
P. O. Box 3529, Portland, OR 97208
Peggy J. Krause (503) 231-5000

Zone No. 46, Cincinnati
Grantee/Operator: Greater Cincinnati FTZ, Inc.
120 W. 5th Street, Cincinnati, OH 45203
Joe Kramer (513) 579-3143

Zone No. 47, Campbell County, Kentucky
Operator: Northern Kentucky Port Authority
400 Licking Pike, Wilder, KY 41071
Robert Vogt (606) 581-1444
Grantee: Greater Cincinnati FTZ, Inc.

Zone No. 48, Tucson, Arizona
Grantee/Operator: Papago-Tucson FTZ Corp.
San Xavier Development Authority, P. O. Box 11246,
Mission Station, AZ 85734
William Tatom (602) 792-6862

Zone No. 49, Newark/Elizabeth, New Jersey
Grantee/Operator: Port Authority of NY and NJ
One World Trade Center, Rm. 64 West,
New York, NY 10048
Catherine Durda (212) 466-7985

Zone No. 50, Long Beach, California
Grantee: Board of Harbor Commissioners of the Port of
Long Beach, P. O. Box 570, Long Beach, CA 90801
Michael R. Powers (213) 437-0041

Zone No. 51, Duluth, Minnesota
Grantee/Operator: Seaway Port Authority of Duluth
1200 Port Terminal Drive, P. O. Box 8677,
Duluth, MN 55808
Henry K. Hanka (218) 727-8525

Zone No. 52, Suffolk County, New York
Grantee/Operator: County of Suffolk
4175 Veterans Memorial Hwy.,
Ronkonkoma, NY 11779
Joseph C. Giacalone (516) 588-1000

Zone No. 53, Rogers County, Oklahoma
Grantee/Operator: City of Tulsa-Rogers City Port Auth.
Tulsa Port of Catoosa, 5350 Cimarron Road,
Catoosa, OK 74105
Robert W. Portiss (918) 266-2291

Zone No. 54, Clinton County, New York
Grantee/Operator: Clinton County Area Dev. Corp.
P. O. Box 19, Plattsburgh, NY 12901
Francis Lapham (518) 561-8800

Zone No. 55, Burlington, Vermont
Grantee/Operator: Greater Burlington Industrial Corp.
P. O. Box 786, Burlington, VT 05402
C. Harry Behney (802) 862-5726

Zone No. 56, Oakland, California
Operator: Oakland International Trade Center, Inc.
633 Hagenburger Rd, Oakland, CA 94607
Dayton Ballenger (415) 639-7405
Grantee: City of Oakland

Zone No. 57, Mecklenburg County, North Carolina
Operator: Piedmont Distribution Center
P. O. Box 7123, Charlotte, NC 28217
Richard Primm (704) 588-2868
Grantee: North Carolina Department of Commerce

Zone No. 58, Bangor, Maine
Grantee/Operator: City of Bangor
Economic Dept., City Hall, Bangor, ME 04401
Edward McKeon (207) 947-0341

Zone No. 59, Lincoln, Nebraska
Grantee/Operator: Lincoln Chamber of Commerce
1221 North Street, Suite 606, Lincoln, NE 68508
Duane Vicary (402) 476-7511

Zone No. 60, Nogales, Arizona
Operator: Rivas Realty
3450 Tucson-Nogales Highway, Nogales, AZ 85621
Herman Rivas (602) 287-3411
Grantee: Border Industrial Development, Inc.

Zone No. 61, San Juan, Puerto Rico
Grantee/Operator: Puerto Rico Commercial Dev. Co.
Commonwealth of Puerto Rico, G.P.O. Box 4943,
San Juan, PR 00936
Miguel Figueroa (809) 721-1273

Zone No. 62, Brownsville, Texas
Grantee/Operator: Brownsville Navigation District
Port of Brownsville, P. O. Box 3070,
Brownsville, TX 78520
Al Cisneros (512) 831-4592

Zone No. 63, Prince George's County, Maryland
Operator: International Commerce Management, Inc.
12301 Old Columbia Pike, Silver Spring, MD 20904
Peter B. Crouch (301) 622-9000
Grantee: Prince George's County Government

Zone No. 64, Jacksonville, Florida
Grantee: Jacksonville Port Authority
P. O. Box 3005, 2701 Talleyrand Avenue,
Jacksonville, FL 32206
Bruce Cashon (904) 633-5250

Zone No. 65, Panama City, Florida
Grantee/Operator: Panama City Port Authority
P. O. Box 15095, Panama City, FL 32406
Tommy L. Berry (904) 763-8471

Zone No. 66, Wilmington, North Carolina
Operator: N. C. State Port Authority
2202 Burnett Blvd., Wilmington, NC 28402
Patsy Jackson (919) 763-1621
Grantee: North Carolina Dept. of Commerce

Zone No. 67, Morehead City, North Carolina
Operator: N.C. State Port Authority
2202 Burnett Blvd., Wilmington, NC 28402
Patsy Jackson (919) 763-1621
Grantee: North Carolina Dept. of Commerce

Zone No. 68, El Paso, Texas
Operator: El Paso International Airport
El Paso, TX 79925
James R. Mettler (915) 772-4271
Grantee: City of El Paso

Zone No. 70, Detroit
Grantee/Operator: Greater Detroit Foreign-Trade
18800 Sunnybrook, Lathrup Village, MI 48076
Joseph T. Auwers (313) 259-8077

Zone No. 71, Windsor Locks, Connecticut
Grantee: Industrial Development Commission of
Windsor Locks, Town Office Building, Church Street,
Windsor Locks, CT 06096
Richard Blackburn (203) 623-3458

Zone No. 72, Indianapolis
Grantee: Indianapolis Airport Authority
Indianapolis International Airport, 2500 South High
School Road, Indianapolis, IN 46251
David P. Bennett (317) 236-6246

Zone No. 73, Baltimore/Washington Int'l Airport
Grantee: Maryland Dept. of Transportation
BWI Airport, P. O. Box 28673,
BWI Airport, MD 21240
Robert J. Schott (301) 859-4449
Operator: All Cargo Expediting Services, Inc.

Zone No. 74, Baltimore
Grantee: City of Baltimore
c/o Baltimore Economic Development Corp.,
36 South Charles St., Baltimore, MD 21201
Paul Gilbert (301) 837-9305

Zone No. 75, Phoenix
Grantee: City of Phoenix
Community & Economic Dev. Adm., Suite D,
920 E. Madison St., Phoenix, AZ 85034
Edward R. Standage (602) 261-8707

Zone No. 76, Bridgeport, Connecticut
Grantee/Operator: City of Bridgeport
City Hall, 45 Lyon Terrace, Bridgeport, CT 06604
Tom Corso (203) 576-7221

Zone No. 77, Memphis
Grantee/Operator: Memphis & Shelby Cty. Office of
Planning and Dev., City Hall, 125 North Main Street,
Memphis, TN 38103
Jimmie Covington (901) 528-3307

Zone No. 78, Nashville
Grantee: Metropolitan Nashville-Davidson
County Port Authority, 601 Stahlman Building,
Nashville, TN 37201
Ed J. Johnson (615) 259-6121

Zone 79, Tampa
Grantee: City of Tampa
Office of Economic Dev., Int'l Trade, City Hall,
315 E. Kennedy Blvd., Tampa, FL 33602
Tony Collins (813) 223-8381

Zone No. 80, San Antonio
Grantee: City of San Antonio
P. O. Box 9066, San Antonio, TX 78285
Kenneth W. Daly (512) 299-8080

Zone No. 81, Portsmouth, New Hampshire
Grantee/Operator: New Hampshire State Port Authority
555 Market Street, P. O. Box 506,
Portsmouth, NH 03801
George Smith (603) 436-8500

Zone No. 82, Mobile
Operator: Mobile Airport Authority
Bldg. 11, Brookley Complex, Mobile, AL 36615
Dan Dupont (205) 438-7334
Grantee: City of Mobile

Zone No. 83, Huntsville, Alabama
Grantee/Operator: Huntsville-Madison County Airport
Authority, P. O. Box 6006, Huntsville, AL 35806
J. E. Mitchell, Jr. (205) 772-9395

Zone No. 84, Harris County, Texas
Grantee: Port of Houston Authority
P. O. Box 2562, Houston, TX 77001
Richard P. Leach (713) 226-2100

Zone No. 85, Everett, Washington
Grantee: Puget Sound Foreign-Trade Zone Association
c/o Economic Development Council of Puget Sound,
1900 Seattle Tower, 1218 Third Avenue,
Seattle, WA 98101
Lawrence W. Blackett (206) 433-1629

Zone No. 86, Tacoma, Washington
Grantee: Puget Sound Foreign-Trade Zone Association
c/o Economic Development Council of Puget Sound,
1900 Seattle Tower, 1218 Third Avenue,
Seattle, WA 98101
Lawrence W. Blackett (206) 433-1629

Zone No. 87, Lake Charles, Louisiana
Grantee/Operator: Lake Charles Harbor & Terminal
District, P.O. Box AAA,
Lake Charles, LA 70602
James E. Sudduth (318) 439-3661

Zone No. 88, Great Falls, Montana
Grantee/Operator: Economic Growth Council of Great
Falls, P.O. Box 1273,
Great Falls, MT 59403
Joseph C. Mudd (406) 761-5036

Zone No. 89, Clark County, Nevada
Grantee/Operator: Nevada Development Authority
McCarran Int'l Airport, P. O. Box 11128,
Las Vegas, NV 89111
Al Dague (702) 739-8222

Zone No. 90, Onondaga, New York
Grantee: County of Onondaga
c/o Greater Syracuse Chamber of Commerce,
100 E. Onondaga Street, Syracuse, NY 13202
Joseph W. Louis (315) 470-1343

Zone No. 91, Newport, Vermont
Grantee/Operator: Northeastern Vermont Dev. Assoc.
44 Main Street, St. Johnsbury, VT 05819
Henry W. Merrill, Jr. (802) 748-5181

Zone No. 92, Harrison County, Mississippi
Grantee: Greater Gulfport/Biloxi Foreign-Trade
Zone, Inc., c/o Mississippi Research & Dev. Center,
P. O. Drawer 2470, Jackson, MS 39205
Noel Guthrie (601) 982-6606

Zone No. 93, Raleigh/Durham, North Carolina
Grantee: Triangle J Council of Governments
100 Park Drive, P. O. Box 12276,
Research Triangle Park, NC 27709
Lee H. Capps (919) 549-0551

Zone No. 94, Laredo, Texas
Grantee/Operator: City of Laredo
c/o Laredo Development Foundation, P. O. Box 1435,
Laredo, TX 78040
Frank E. Leach (512) 722-0563

Zone No. 95, Starr County, Texas
Grantee/Operator: Starr County Industrial Foundation
P. O. Drawer H, Rio Grande City, TX 78582
Sam Vale (512) 487-5606

Zone No. 96, Eagle Pass, Texas
Grantee/Operator: City of Eagle Pass
P. O. Box C, City Manager's Office,
Eagle Pass, TX 78852
Roberto Barrientos (512) 773-1111

Zone No. 97, Del Rio, Texas
Grantee/Operator: City of Del Rio
City Manager's Office, P. O. Drawer DD,
Del Rio, TX 78840
Jim Miceli (512) 744-2781

Zone No. 98, Birmingham, Alabama
Grantee/Operator: City of Birmingham
Mayors Office, City Hall
Birmingham, AL 35203
Virginia Riley (205) 254-2277

Zone No. 99, Wilmington, Delaware
Grantee/Operator: State of Delaware
Delaware Development Office, Dover, DE 19901
Dorothy Sbriglia (302) 736-4271

Zone No. 100, Dayton, Ohio
Grantee/ Operator: Greater Dayton Foreign-Trade
Zone, Inc., 1880 Kettering Tower,
Dayton, OH 45423-1880
Gary D. Geisel (513) 226-1444

Zone No. 101, Clinton County, Ohio
Grantee/Operator: Airborne FTZ, Inc.
145 Hunter Drive, Wilmington, OH 45177
Mike Kuli (513) 382-5591

Zone No. 102, St. Louis
Grantee/Operator: St. Louis County Port Authority
130 South Bemiston, Clayton, MO 63105
Wayne Weidemann (314) 721-0900

Zone No. 103, Grand Forks, North Dakota
Grantee/Operator: Grand Forks Dev. Foundation
P. O. Box 1177, 204 North 3rd,
Grand Forks, ND 58201
Robert W. Nelson (701) 772-7271

Zone No. 104, Savannah, Georgia
Grantee/Operator: Savannah Airport Commission
P. O. Box 2723, Savannah, GA 31402
Don Fishero (912) 964-0514

**Zone No. 105, Providence and North Kingstown,
Rhode Island**
Grantee: Rhode Island Port Authority and
Economic Dev. Corp., 7 Jackson Walkway,
Providence, RI 02903
Joseph D. Lombardo (401) 277-2601

Zone No. 106, Oklahoma City, Oklahoma
Grantee: The Oklahoma City Port Authority
100 N. Walker
Oklahoma City, OK 73102
Ed McGee (405) 231-2285

Zone No. 107, Des Moines, Iowa
Operator: Centennial Warehouse Corporation
10400 Hickman Rd., Des Moines, IA 50322
Fred Caruthers (515) 278-9517
Grantee: The Iowa Foreign Trade Zone Corporation

Zone No. 108, Valdez, Alaska
Grantee: The City of Valdez, Alaska
Port of Valdez, 1 S.W. Columbia St., Suite 1620,
Portland, OR 97258
Vern Chase (503) 227-4567

Zone No. 109, Watertown, New York
Grantee: The County of Jefferson
c/o Jefferson Industrial Dev. Agency
175 Arsenal St., Watertown, NY 13601
Kenneth W. Steblen (315) 785-3226

Zone No. 110, Albuquerque, New Mexico
Operator: Foreign-Trade Zone of New Mexico
FTZ Operators, Inc., 1617 Broadway N.E.,
P. O. Box 26928, Albuquerque, NM 87125
Bob Wittington (505) 842-0088
Grantee: The City of Albuquerque

Zone No. 111, JFK Int'l Airport, New York
Operator: Port Authority of New York and New Jersey
Kennedy Int'l Airport, Business Admin. Div.,
Bldg. 141, Jamaica, NY 11430
Gerald Drasheff (212) 656-4402
Grantee: The City of New York

Zone No. 112, Colorado Springs, Colorado
Operator: Front Range Foreign Trade Zone Inc.
3300 E. First Ave.
Denver, Co 80206
Leon Bronfin (303) 320-5313
Grantee: Colorado Springs Foreign-Trade Zone, Inc.

Zone No. 113, Ellis County, Texas
Operator: Trade Zone Operations, Inc.
  100 Center Drive, Midlothian, TX 76065
  Larry White (214) 299-6301
Grantee: Midlothian Chamber of Commerce
Zone No. 114, Peoria, Illinois
Grantee: Economic Development Council, Inc.
  230 S. W. Adams, Peoria, IL 61602
  Donald Shoenheider (309) 676-0755
Zone No. 115, Beaumont, Texas
Grantee: Foreign-Trade Zone of Southeast Texas, Inc.
  2748 Viterbo Road, P. O. Box 9
  Beaumont, TX 77705
  Mitzi Vorachek (409) 722-7831
Zone No. 116, Port Arthur, Texas
Grantee: Foreign-Trade Zone of Southeast Texas, Inc.
  2748 Viterbo Road, P. O. Box 9
  Beaumont, TX 77705
  Mitzi Vorachek (409) 722-7831
Zone No. 117, Orange, Texas
Grantee: Foreign-Trade Zone of Southeast Texas, Inc.
  2748 Viterbo Road, P. O. Box 9
  Beaumont, TX 77705
  Mitzi Vorachek (409) 722-7831

Zone No. 118, Ogdensburg, New York
Grantee: Ogdensburg Bridge and Port Authority
  Ogdensburg, NY 13669
  Salvatore Pisani (315) 393-4080
Zone No. 119, Minneapolis-St. Paul, Minnesota
Grantee: Greater Metropolitan Foreign-Trade
  Zone Commission
  331 Second Ave. S., Midland Square Bldg.,
  Minneapolis, MN 55401
  Charles E. Riesenberg (612) 370-5028
Zone No. 120, Cowlitz County, Washington
Grantee: Cowlitz Economic Development Council
  1338 Commerce, Suite 211, Longview, WA 98632
  John C. Thompson (206) 423-9921
Zone No. 121, Albany, New York
Grantee: Capital District Regional Planning
  Commission, 251 River St., Monument Square
  Troy, NY 12180
  Chungchin Chen (518) 272-1414

APPENDIX D : TEXTUAL MATERIALS

1. REVISED AMERICAN FOREIGN TRADE DEFINITIONS—1941

Courtesy of National Foreign Trade Council, Inc.

(I) Ex (Point of Origin)

"EX FACTORY", "EX MILL", "EX MINE", "EX PLANTATION", "EX WAREHOUSE", etc. (named point of origin)

Under this term, the price quoted applies only at the point of origin, and the seller agrees to place the goods at the disposal of the buyer at the agreed place on the date or within the period fixed.

Under this quotation—
Seller must:
(1) bear all costs and risks of the goods until such time as the buyer is obliged to take delivery thereof.
(2) render the buyer, at the buyer's request and expense, assistance in obtaining the documents issued in the country of origin, or of shipment, or of both, which the buyer may require either for purposes of exportation, or of importation at destination.

Buyer must:
(1) take delivery of the goods as soon as they have been placed at his disposal at the agreed place on the date or within the period fixed.
(2) pay export taxes, or other fees or charges, if any, levied because of exportation.
(3) bear all costs and risks of the goods from the time when he is obligated to take delivery thereof.
(4) pay all costs and charges incurred in obtaining the documents issued in the country of origin, or of shipment, or of both, which may be required either for purposes of exportation, or of importation at destination.

(II) F.O.B. (Free On Board)

Note: *Seller and buyer should consider not only the definitions but also the "Comments on All F.O.B. Terms" given at end of this section in order to understand fully their respective responsibilities and rights under the several classes of "F.O.B." terms.*

(II-A) "F.O.B. (named inland carrier at named inland point of departure)"*

Under this term, the price quoted applies only at inland shipping point, and the seller arranges for loading of the goods on, or in, railway cars, trucks, lighters, barges, aircraft, or other conveyance furnished for transportation.

Under this quotation—
Seller must:
(1) place goods on, or in, conveyance, or deliver to inland carrier for loading.
(2) provide clean bill of lading or other transportation receipt, freight collect.
(3) be responsible for any loss or damage, or both, until goods have been placed in, or on, conveyance at loading point, and clean bill of lading or other transportation receipt has been furnished by the carrier.
(4) render the buyer, at the buyer's request and expense, assistance in obtaining the documents issued in the country of origin, or of shipment, or of both, which the buyer may require either for purposes of exportation, or of importation at destination.

Buyer must:
(1) be responsible for all movement of the goods from inland point of loading, and pay all transportation costs.
(2) pay export taxes, or other fees or charges, if any, levied because of exportation.
(3) be responsible for any loss or damage, or both, incurred after loading at named inland point of departure.
(4) pay all costs and charges incurred in obtaining the documents issued in the country of origin, or of shipment, or of both, which may be required either for purposes of exportation, or of importation at destination.

* See Note this page, and Comments on all F.O.B. Terms

(II-B) "F.O.B. (named inland carrier at named inland point of departure) FREIGHT PREPAID TO (named point of exportation)"*

Under this term, the seller quotes a price including transportation charges to the named point of exportation and prepays freight to named point of exportation, without assuming responsibility for the goods after obtaining a clean bill of lading or other transportation receipt at named inland point of departure.

Under this quotation—
Seller must:
(1) assume the seller's obligations under II-A, except that under
(2) he must provide clean bill of lading or other transportation receipt, freight prepaid to named point of exportation.

Buyer must:
(1) assume the same buyer's obligations as under II-A , except that he does not pay freight from loading point to named point of exportation.

(II-C) "F.O.B. (named inland carrier at named inland point of departure) FREIGHT ALLOWED TO (named point)"*

Under this term, the seller quotes a price including the transportation charges to the named point, shipping freight collect and deducting the cost of transportation, without assuming responsibility for the goods after obtaining a clean bill of lading or other transportation receipt at named inland point of departure.

Under this quotation—
Seller must:
(1) assume the same seller's obligations as under II-A, but deducts from his invoice the transportation cost to named point.

Buyer must:
(1) assume the same buyer's obligations as under II-A, including payment of freight from inland loading point to named point, for which seller has made deduction.

(II-D) "F.O.B. (named inland carrier at named point of exportation)"*

Under this term, the seller quotes a price including the costs of transportation of the goods to named point of exportation, bearing any loss or damage, or both, incurred up to that point.

Under this quotation—

Seller must:

(1) place goods on, or in, conveyance, or deliver to inland carrier for loading.

(2) provide clean bill of lading or other transportation receipt, paying all transportation costs from loading point to named point of exportation.

(3) be responsible for any loss or damage, or both, until goods have arrived in, or on, inland conveyance at the named point of exportation.

(4) render the buyer, at the buyer's request and expense, assistance in obtaining the documents issued in the country of origin, or of shipment, or of both, which the buyer may require either for purposes of exportation, or of importation at destination.

Buyer must:

(1) be responsible for all movement of the goods from inland conveyance at named point of exportation.

(2) pay export taxes, or other fees or charges, if any, levied because of exportation.

(3) be responsible for any loss or damage, or both, incurred after goods have arrived in, or on, inland conveyance at the named point of exportation.

(4) pay all costs and charges incurred in obtaining the documents issued in the country of origin, or of shipment, or of both, which may be required, for either purposes of exportation or of importation at destination.

(II-E) "F.O.B. VESSEL (named port of shipment)"*

Under this term, the seller quotes a price covering all expenses up to, and including, delivery of the goods upon the overseas vessel provided by, or for, the buyer at the named port of shipment.

Under this quotation—

Seller must:

(1) pay all charges incurred in placing goods actually on board the vessel designated and provided by, or for, the buyer on the date or within the period fixed.

(2) provide clean ship's receipt or on board bill of lading.

(3) be responsible for any loss or damage, or both, until goods have been placed on board the vessel on the date or within the period fixed.

(4) render the buyer, at the buyer's request and expense, assistance in obtaining the documents issued in the country of origin, or of shipment, or of both, which the buyer may require either for purposes of exportation, or of importation at destination.

Buyer must:

(1) give seller adequate notice of name, sailing date, loading berth of, and delivery time to, the vessel.

(2) bear the additional costs incurred and all risks of the goods from the time when the seller has placed them at his disposal if the vessel named by him fails to arrive or to load within the designated time.

(3) handle all subsequent movement of the goods to destination.

(a) provide and pay for insurance;

(b) provide and pay for ocean and other transportation.

(4) pay export taxes, or other fees or charges, if any, levied because of exportation.

(5) be responsible for any loss or damage, or both, after goods have been loaded on board the vessel.

(6) pay all costs and charges incurred in obtaining the documents, other than clean ship's receipt or bill of lading, issued in the country of origin, or of shipment, or of both, which may be required either for purposes of exportation, or of importation at destination.

(II-F) "F.O.B. (named inland point in country of importation)"*

Under this term, the seller quotes a price including the cost of the merchandise and all costs of transportation to the named inland point in the country of importation.

Under this quotation—

Seller must:

(1) provide and pay for all transportation to the named inland point in the country of importation.

(2) pay export taxes, or other fees or charges, if any, levied because of exportation.

(3) provide and pay for marine insurance.

(4) provide and pay for war risk insurance, unless otherwise agreed upon between the seller and buyer.

(5) be responsible for any loss or damage, or both, until arrival of goods on conveyance at the named inland point in the country of importation.

(6) pay the costs of certificates of origin, consular invoices, or any other documents issued in the country of origin, or of shipment, or of both, which the buyer may require for the importation of goods into the country of destination and, where necessary, for their passage in transit through another country.

(7) pay all costs of landing, including wharfage, landing charges, and taxes, if any.

(8) pay all costs of customs entry in the country of importation.

(9) pay customs duties and all taxes applicable to imports, if any, in the country of importation.

Note: The seller under this quotation must realize that he is accepting important responsibilities, costs, and risks, and should therefore be certain to obtain adequate

insurance. On the other hand, the importer or buyer may desire such quotations to relieve him of the risks of the voyage and to assure him of his landed costs at inland point in country of importation. When competition is keen, or the buyer is accustomed to such quotations from other sellers, seller may quote such terms, being careful to protect himself in an appropriate manner.

Buyer must:

(1) take prompt delivery of goods from conveyance upon arrival at destination.

(2) bear any costs and be responsible for all loss or damage, or both, after arrival at destination.

Comments On All F.O.B. Terms

In connection with F.O.B. terms, the following points of caution are recommended.

1. The method of inland transportation, such as trucks, railroad cars, lighters, barges, or aircraft should be specified.

2. If any switching charges are involved during the inland transportation, it should be agreed, in advance, whether these charges are for account of the seller or the buyer.

3. The term "F.O.B. (named port)", without designating the exact point at which the liability of the seller terminates and the liability of the buyer begins, should be avoided. The use of this term gives rise to disputes as to the liability of the seller or the buyer in the event of loss or damage arising while the goods are in port, and before delivery to or on board the ocean carrier. Misunderstandings may be avoided by naming the specific point of delivery.

4. If lighterage or trucking is required in the transfer of goods from the inland conveyance to ship's side, and there is a cost therefore, it should be understood, in advance, whether this cost is for account of the seller or the buyer.

5. The seller should be certain to notify the buyer of the minimum quantity required to obtain a carload, a truckload, or a bargeload freight rate.

6. Under F.O.B. terms, excepting "F.O.B. (named inland point in country of importation)", the obligation to obtain ocean freight space, and marine and war risk insurance, rests with the buyer. Despite this obligation on the part of the buyer, in many trades the seller obtains the ocean freight space, and marine and war risk insurance, and provides for shipment on behalf of the buyer. Hence, seller and buyer must have an understanding as to whether the buyer will obtain the ocean freight space, and marine and war risk insurance, as is his obligation, or whether the seller agrees to do this for the buyer.

7. For the seller's protection, he should provide in his contract of sale that marine insurance obtained by the buyer include standard warehouse to warehouse coverage.

(III) F.A.S. (Free Along Side)

Note: Seller and buyer should consider not only the definitions but also the "Comments" given at the end of this section in order to understand fully their respective responsibilities and rights under "F.A.S." terms.

"F.A.S. VESSEL (named port of shipment)"

Under this term, the seller quotes a price including delivery of the goods along side overseas vessel and within reach of its loading tackle.

Under this quotation—
Seller must:
(1) place goods along side vessel or on dock designated and provided by, or for, buyer on the date or within the period fixed; pay any heavy lift charges, where necessary, up to this point.
(2) provide clean dock or ship's receipt.
(3) be responsible for any loss or damage, or both. until goods have been delivered along side the vessel or on the dock.
(4) render the buyer, at the buyer's request and expense, assistance in obtaining the documents issued in the country of origin, or of shipment, or of both, which the buyer may require either for purposes of exportation, or of importation at destination.
Buyer must:
(1) give seller adequate notice of name, sailing date, loading berth of and delivery time to, the vessel.
(2) handle all subsequent movement of the goods from along side the vessel:
    (a) arrange and pay for demurrage or storage charges, or both, in warehouse or on wharf, where necessary.
    (b) provide and pay for insurance.
    (c) provide and pay for ocean and other transportation.
(3) pay export taxes, or other fees or charges, if any, levied because of exportation.
(4) be responsible for any loss or damage, or both, while the goods are on a lighter or other conveyance along side vessel within reach of its loading tackle, or on the dock awaiting loading, or until actually loaded on board the vessel, and subsequent thereto.
(5) pay all costs and charges incurred in obtaining the documents, other than clean dock or ship's receipt, issued in the country of origin, or of shipment, or cf both, which may be required either for purposes of exportation, or of importation at destination.

F.A.S. Comments

1. Under F.A.S. terms, the obligation to obtain ocean freight space, and marine and war risk insurance, rests with the buyer. Despite this obligation on the part of the buyer, in many trades the seller obtains ocean freight space, and marine and war risk insurance, and provides for shipment on behalf of the buyer. In others, the buyer notifies the seller to make delivery along side a vessel designated by the buyer and the buyer provides his own marine and war risk insurance. Hence, seller and buyer must have an understanding as to whether the buyer will obtain the ocean freight space, and marine and war risk insurance, as is his obligation, or whether the seller agrees to do this for the buyer.
2. For the seller's protection, he should provide in his contract of sale that marine insurance obtained by the buyer include standard warehouse to warehouse coverage.

(IV) C.&F. (Cost & Freight)

Note: *Seller and buyer should consider not only the definitions but also the "C. & F. Comments" and the "C. & F. and C.I.F. Comments", in order to understand fully their respective responsibilities and rights under "C. & F." terms.*

"C. & F. (named point of destination)"
Under this term, the seller quotes a price including the cost of transportation to the named point of destination.
Under this quotation—
Seller must:
(1) provide and pay for transportation to named point of destination.
(2) pay export taxes, or other fees or charges, if any, levied because of exportation.
(3) obtain and dispatch promptly to buyer, or his agent, clean bill of lading to named point of destination.
(4) where received-for-shipment ocean bill of lading may be tendered, be responsible for any loss or damage, or both, until the goods have been delivered into the custody of the ocean carrier.
(5) where on-board ocean bill of lading is required, be responsible for any loss or damage, or both, until the goods have been delivered on board the vessel.
(6) provide, at the buyer's request and expense, certificates of origin, consular invoices, or any other documents issued in the country of origin or of shipment, or of both, which the buyer may require for importation of goods into country of destination and, where necessary, for their passage in transit through another country.
Buyer must:
(1) accept the documents when presented.
(2) receive goods upon arrival, handle and pay for all subsequent movement of the goods, including taking delivery from vessel in accordance with bill of lading clauses and terms; pay all costs of landing, including any duties, taxes, and other expenses at named point of destination.
(3) provide and pay for insurance.
(4) be responsible for loss of, or damage to goods, or both, from time and place at which seller's obligations under (4) or (5) above have ceased.
(5) pay the costs of certificates of origin, consular invoices, or any other documents issued in the country of origin, or of shipment, or of both, which may be required for the importation of goods into the country of destination and, where necessary, for their passage through another country.

C. & F. Comments

1. For the seller's protection, he should provide in his contract of sale that marine insurance obtained by the buyer include standard warehouse to warehouse coverage.
2. The comments listed under the following C.I.F. terms in many cases apply to C.&F. terms as well, and should be read and understood by the C. & F. seller and buyer.

(V) C.I.F. (Cost, Insurance, Freight)

Note: *Seller and buyer should consider not only the definitions, but also the "Comments", at the end of this section, in order to understand fully their respective responsibilities and rights under "C.I.F." terms.*

"C.I.F. (named point of destination)"
Under this term, the seller quotes a price including the cost of the goods, the marine insurance, and all transportation charges to the named point of destination.
Under this quotation—
Seller must:
(1) provide and pay for transportation to named point of destination.
(2) pay export taxes, or other fees or charges, if any, levied because of exportation.
(3) provide and pay for marine insurance.
(4) provide war risk insurance as obtainable in seller's market at time of shipment at buyer's expense, unless seller has agreed that buyer provide for war risk coverage. (See Comment 10 (c).)
(5) obtain and dispatch promptly to buyer, or his agent, clean bill of lading to named point of destination, and also insurance policy or negotiable insurance certificate.
(6) where received-for-shipment ocean bill of lading may be tendered, be responsible for any loss or damage, or both, until the goods have been delivered into the custody of the ocean carrier.
(7) where on-board ocean bill of lading is required, be responsible for any loss or damage, or both, until the goods have been delivered on board the vessel.
(8) provide, at buyer's request and expense, certificates of origin, consular invoices, or any other documents issued in the country of origin, or of shipment, or both, which the buyer may require for importation of goods into country of destination and, where necessary, for their passage in transit through another country.
Buyer must:
(1) accept the documents when presented.
(2) receive the goods upon arrival, handle and pay for all subsequent movement of the goods, including taking delivery from vessel in accordance with bill of lading clauses and terms; pay all costs of landing, including any duties, taxes, and other expenses at named point of destination.
(3) pay for war risk insurance provided by seller.
(4) be responsible for loss of/or damage to goods, or both, from time and place at which seller's obligations under (6) or (7) above have ceased.
(5) pay the cost of certificates of origin, consular invoices, or any other documents issued in the country of origin, or of shipment, or both, which may be required

for importation of the goods into the country of destination and, where necessary, for their passage in transit through another country.

C. & F. and C.I.F. Comments

Under C. & F. and C.I.F. contracts there are the following points on which the seller and the buyer should be in complete agreement at the time that the contract is concluded:

1. It should be agreed upon, in advance, who is to pay for miscellaneous expenses, such as weighing or inspection charges.

2. The quantity to be shipped on any one vessel should be agreed upon, in advance, with a view to the buyer's capacity to take delivery upon arrival and discharge of the vessel; within the free time allowed at the port of importation.

3. Although the terms C. & F. and C.I.F. are generally interpreted to provide that charges for consular invoices and certificates of origin are for the account of the buyer, and are charged separately, in many trades these charges are included by the seller in his price. Hence, seller and buyer should agree, in advance whether these charges are part of the selling price, or will be invoiced separately.

4. The point of final destination should be definitely known in the event the vessel discharges at a port other than the actual destination of the goods.

5. When ocean freight space is difficult to obtain, or forward freight contracts cannot be made at firm rates, it is advisable that sales contracts, as an exception to regular C. & F. or C.I.F. terms, should provide that shipment within the contract period be subject to ocean freight space being available to the seller, and should also provide that changes in the cost of ocean transportation between the time of sales and the time of shipment be for account of the buyer.

6. Normally, the seller is obligated to prepay the ocean freight. In some instances, shipments are made freight collect and the amount of the freight is deducted from the invoice rendered by the seller. It is necessary to be in agreement on this, in advance, in order to avoid misunderstanding which arises from foreign exchange fluctuations which might affect the actual cost of transportation, and from interest charges which might accrue under letter of credit financing. Hence, the seller should always prepay the ocean freight unless he has a specific agreement with the buyer, in advance, that goods can be shipped freight collect.

7. The buyer should recognize that he does not have the right to insist on inspection of goods prior to accepting the documents. The buyer should not refuse to take delivery of goods on account of

delay in the receipt of documents, provided the seller has used due diligence in their dispatch through the regular channels.

8. Sellers and buyers are advised against including in a C.I.F. contract any indefinite clause at variance with the obligations of a C.I.F. contract as specified in these Definitions. There have been numerous court decisions in the United States and other countries invalidating C.I.F. contracts because of the inclusion of indefinite clauses.

9. Interest charges should be included in cost computations and should not be charged as a separate item in C.I.F. contracts, unless otherwise agreed upon, in advance, between the seller and buyer; in which case, however, the term C.I.F. and I (Cost, Insurance, Freight, and Interest) should be used.

10. In connection with insurance under C.I.F. sales, it is necessary that seller and buyer be definitely in accord upon the following points:

(a) The character of the marine insurance should be agreed upon in so far as being W.A. (With Average) or F.P.A. (Free of Particular Average), as well as any other special risks that are covered in specific trades, or against which the buyer may wish individual protection. Among the special risks that should be considered and agreed upon between seller and buyer are theft, pilferage, leakage, breakage, sweat, contact with other cargoes, and others peculiar to any particular trade. It is important that contingent or collect freight and customs duty should be insured to cover Particular Average losses, as well as total loss after arrival and entry but before delivery.

(b) The seller is obligated to exercise ordinary care and diligence in selecting an underwriter that is in good financial standing. However, the risk of obtaining settlement of insurance claims rests with the buyer.

(c) War risk insurance under this term is to be obtained by the seller at the expense and risk of the buyer. It is important that the seller be in definite accord with the buyer on this point, particularly as to the cost. It is desirable that the goods be insured against both marine and war risk with the same underwriter, so that there can be no difficulty arising from the determination of the cause of the loss.

(d) Seller should make certain that in his marine or war risk insurance, there be included the standard protection against strikes, riots and civil commotions.

(e) Seller and buyer should be in accord as to the insured valuation, bearing in mind that merchandise contributes in General Average on certain bases of valuation which differ in various trades. It is desirable that a competent insurance broker be consulted, in order that full value be covered and trouble avoided.

(VI) Ex Dock

Note: *Seller and buyer should consider not only the definitions but also the "Ex Dock Comments" at the end of this section in order to understand fully their respective responsibilities, and rights under "Ex Dock" terms.*

Under this term, seller quotes a price including the cost of the goods and all additional costs necessary to place the goods on the dock at the named port of importation, duty paid, if any.

"EX DOCK (named port of importaton)"

Under this quotation—

Seller must:

(1) provide and pay for transportation to named port of importation.

(2) pay export taxes, or other fees or charges, if any, levied because of exportation.

(3) provide and pay for marine insurance.

(4) provide and pay for war risk insurance, unless otherwise agreed upon between the buyer and seller.

(5) be responsible for any loss or damage, or both, until the expiration of the free time allowed on the dock at the named port of importation.

(6) pay the costs of certificates of origin, consular invoices, legalization of bill of lading, or any other documents issued in the country of origin, or of shipment, or of both, which the buyer may require for the importation of goods into the country of destination and, where necessary, for their passage in transit through another country.

(7) pay all costs of landing, including wharfage, landing charges, and taxes, if any.

(8) pay all costs of customs entry in the country of importation.

(9) pay customs duties and all taxes applicable to imports, if any, in the country of importation, unless otherwise agreed upon.

Buyer must:

(1) take delivery of the goods on the dock at the named port of importation within the free time allowed.

(2) bear the cost and risk of the goods if delivery is not taken within the free time allowed.

Ex Dock Comments

This term is used principally in United States import trade. It has various modifications, such as "Ex Quay", "Ex Pier", etc., but it is seldom, if ever, used in American export practice. Its use in quotations for export is not recommended.

2. MERCHANT'S AGREEMENT

(Text of Trans-Pacific Freight Conference of Japan/Korea, Tariff No. 36 FMC-7, by permission)

For their mutual benefit in the stabilization of rates, services, and practices and for the development of international maritime commerce in the trade defined in Article 1 of this Agreement, the parties hereby agree as follows:

1. The Conference undertakes, throughout the period of this Agreement, to maintain common carrier service which shall, so far as concerns the frequency of sailings and the carrying capacity of the vessels of the Carriers, be adequate to meet all the reasonable requirements of the Merchant for the movement of goods in the trade from Japan and Korea to Pacific Coast ports of California, Oregon, Washington, Hawaii and Alaska (hereinafter called the "Trade"); and the Conference further agrees that, subject to the availability of suitable space in the vessels of the Carriers at the time when the Merchant applies therefor, said vessels shall transport the goods of the Merchant in the Trade upon the terms and conditions herein set forth. Ports from and to which service is offered by the Carriers shall be set forth in the Conference tariff.

2. (a) The Merchant shall ship or cause to be shipped all of his ocean shipments moving in the Trade on vessels of the Carriers unless otherwise provided in this Agreement.

(b) The term "Merchant" shall include the party signing this Agreement as shipper and any of his parent, subsidiary, or other related companies or entities who may engage in the shipment of commodities in the Trade covered by this Agreement and over whom he regularly exercises direction and working control (as distinguished from the possession of the power to exercise such direction and control) in relation to shipping matters, whether the shipments are made by or in the name of the "Merchant," any such related company or entity, or an agent or shipping representative acting on their behalf. The names of such related companies and entities, all of whom shall have the unrestricted benefits of this Agreement and be fully bound thereby, are listed at the beginning of this Agreement. The party signing this Agreement as "Merchant" warrants and represents that the list is true and complete, that he will promptly notify the Carriers in writing of any future changes in the list, and that he has authority to enter into this Agreement on behalf of the said related companies and entities so listed.

(c) In agreeing to confine the carriage of its shipments to the vessels of the Carriers the Merchant promises and declares that it is his intent to do so without evasion or subterfuge either directly or indirectly by any means, including the use of intermediaries or persons, firms or entities affiliated with or related to the Merchant.

(d) The Carriers agree that they will not provide contract rates to anyone not bound by a Merchant's Rate Agreement with the Carriers. The Merchant agrees that he will not obtain contract rates for any person not entitled to them, including related companies not bound by this Agreement, by making shipments under this Agreement on behalf of any such person.

3. (a) If the Merchant has the legal right at the time of shipment to select a carrier for the shipment of any goods subject to this Agreement, whether by the expressed or implied terms of an agreement for the purchase, sale or transfer of such goods, shipment for his own account, operation of law, or otherwise, the Merchant shall select one or more of the Carriers.

(b) If Merchant's vendor or vendee has the legal right to select the carrier and fails to exercise that right or otherwise permits Merchant to select the carrier, Merchant shall be deemed to have the legal right to select the carrier.

(c) It shall be deemed a breach of this Agreement, if before the time of shipment, the Merchant, with the intent of avoiding his obligation hereunder, divests himself, or with the same intent permits himself to be divested, of the legal right to select the carrier and the shipment is carried by a carrier not a party hereto.

(d) For the purposes of this Article, the Merchant shall be deemed prima facie to have the legal right at the time of shipment to select the carrier for any shipment:

(1) with respect to which the Merchant arranged or participated in the arrangements for ocean shipment, or selected or participated in the selection of the ocean carrier, or

(2) with respect to which the Merchant's name appears on the bill of lading or export declaration as shipper or consignee.

(e) Nothing contained in this Agreement shall require the Merchant to refuse to purchase, sell or transfer any goods on terms which vest the legal right to select the carrier in any other person.

(f) In order that the Conference may investigate the facts as to any shipment of the Merchant that has moved, or that the Conference believes has moved, via a non-conference carrier, and upon written request clearly so specifying, the Merchant, at his option,

(1) will furnish to the Conference chairman, secretary, or other duly authorized Conference representative or attorney, such information or copies of such documents which relate thereto and are in his possession or reasonably available to him, or

(2) allow the foregoing persons to examine such documents on the premises of the Merchant where they are regularly kept.

Pricing data and similar information may be deleted from the documents at the option of the Merchant, and there shall be no disclosure of such information without the consent of the Merchant except that nothing herein shall be construed to prevent the giving of such information

(1) in response to any legal process issued under the authority of any court, or

(2) to any officer or agent of any government in the exercise of his powers, or

(3) to any officer or other duly authorized person seeking such information for the prosecution of persons charged with or suspected of crime, or

(4) to arbitrators appointed pursuant to this Agreement.

(g) Within ten (10) days after the event in any transaction in which the Merchant is a party and the legal right to select the carrier is vested in a person other than the Merchant, and if he has knowledge that the shipment has been made via a non-conference carrier, the Merchant shall notify the Conference in writing of this fact, giving the names of the Merchant and his customer, the commodity involved and the quantity thereof, and the name of the non-conference carrier; Provided, however, that where the activities of Merchants are so extensive in area or the nature or volume of his sales makes it impracticable to give notice within ten (10) days, the Merchant shall give notice as promptly as possible after the event.

4. This Agreement excludes:

(1) cargo of the Merchant which is loaded and carried in bulk without mark or count except liquid bulk cargoes (other than chemicals and petroleum products) in less than full shipload lots;

(2) shipments on vessels owned by the Merchant or chartered solely by the Merchant where the term of the charter is for six months or longer, and the chartered vessels are used exclusively for the carriage of the Merchant's commodities; and

(3) shipments of cargoes for which no contract rate is provided.

5. The Merchant has the option of selecting any of the vessels operated by the Carriers, subject to agreement with the particular Carrier as to quantity, and agrees to make application for space as early as

possible before the selected vessel's advertised sailing date. In the event that the Merchant is unable to secure space on the selected vessel, he may request the assistance of the Conference in securing space on the selected vessel or on a vessel sailing from the chosen port at or about the same time as the selected vessel. If within three (3) business days of such request, the Conference fails to secure space on a vessel scheduled to sail within fifteen (15) days of the date of the request from the Merchant as aforesaid, the Merchant shall be at liberty to secure such space on any vessel whatsoever.

6. This Agreement does not require the Merchant to divert shipments of goods from natural transportation routes not served by Conference vessels where direct carriage is available. Provided, however, that where the Carriers provide service between any two ports within the scope of this contract which constitute a natural transportation route between the origin and destination of such shipment, the Merchant shall be obligated to select the Carrier's service. A natural transportation route is a traffic path reasonably warranted by economic criteria such as costs, time, available facilities, the nature of the shipment and any other economic criteria appropriate in the circumstances. Whenever Merchant intends to assert his rights under this Article, to use a carrier who is not a party hereto, and the port through which Merchant intends to ship or receive his goods is within the scope of this Agreement, Merchant shall first so notify the Conference in accordance with the provisions of Article 5 hereof.

7. The rates applicable to shipments made under this Agreement shall be the contract rates lawfully in effect at the time of shipment as set forth in the tariff or tariffs of the Conference. Contract rates on every commodity or class of commodities shall be lower than the ordinary rates set forth in the Carriers' tariff by a fixed percentage of nine and a half (9-1/2) per centum of the non-contract or ordinary rates. The rates may be rounded out to the nearest multiple of five (5) cents (not including additional handling or accessorial charges) which will not result in the difference between the rates exceeding nine and a half (9-1/2) per centum of the ordinary rates.

8. (a) The rates of the freight under this Agreement are subject to increase from time to time and the Carriers, insofar as such increases are under the control of the Carriers, will give notice thereof not less than ninety (90) calendar days in advance in the Trans-Pacific Freight Conference of Japan/Korea Conference tariff. Should circumstances necessitate increasing the rates by notice as aforesaid and should such increased rates be not acceptable to the Merchant, the Merchant may tender notice of termination of this Agreement to become effective as of the effective date of the proposed increase by giving written notice of such intention to the Conference within thirty (30) calendar days after the date of notice, as aforesaid of the proposed increase: Further provided, however, that the Carriers may, within thirty (30) calendar days subsequent to the expiration of the aforesaid thirty (30) calendar day period, notify the Merchant in writing that they elect to continue this Agreement under the existing effective rates, and, in the event the Carriers give such notice, this Agreement shall remain in full force and effect as if the proposed increase had never been made and the Merchant's notice of termination had never been given.

(b) The Conference shall offer to the Merchant a subscription to its tariffs at a reasonably compensatory price; however, the Merchant shall be bound by all notices accomplished as aforesaid without regard to whether he subscribes to the Conference tariff. Tariffs shall be open to the Merchant's inspection at the Conference offices and at each of the offices of the Carriers during regular business hours.

(c) The rates initially applicable under this Agreement shall be deemed to have become effective with their original effective date rather than to have become effective with the signing of this Agreement and notices of proposed rate increases which are outstanding at the time this contract becomes effective shall run from the date of publication in the tariff rather than from the date of this Agreement.

(d) The Merchant and the Carriers recognize that mutual benefits are derived from freedom on the part of the Carriers to open rates, where conditions in the Trade require such action, without thereby terminating the dual-rate system as applicable to the commodity involved; therefore, it is agreed that the Conference, to meet the demands of the Merchants and of the Trade may suspend the application of the contract as to any commodity through the opening of the rate on such commodity (including opening subject to maximum or minimum rates) provided that none of the Carriers during a period of ninety (90) days after the date when the opening of such rate becomes effective shall quote a rate in excess of the Conference contract rate applicable to such commodity on the effective date of the opening of the rate, and provided further that the rate shall not thereafter be closed and the commodity returned to the application of the contract system on less than ninety (90) days' notice by the Carriers through the filing of contract/non-contract rates in their tariff.

9.   (a) The Merchant may terminate this Agreement at any time without penalty upon the expiration of ninety (90) calendar days following written notice to the Conference of intent to so terminate. Provided, however, that the Merchant may terminate this Agreement upon less than said ninety (90) days' notice pursuant to Article 8(a) hereof.

(b) The Conference may terminate this Agreement at any time without penalty upon the expiration of ninety (90) calendar days following written notice to the Merchant. Termination by the Conference may be in whole or with respect to any commodity; provided, however, that Agreements with similarly situated Merchants are also so terminated.

(c) Termination as provided in this Article shall not abrogate any obligation of any party or parties to any other party or parties hereto which shall have accrued prior to termination.

10.   (a) In the event of breach of this Agreement by either party, the damages recoverable shall be the actual damages determined after breach in accordance with the principles of contract law; Provided, however, that where the Merchant has made or has permitted a shipment on a vessel of a carrier not a party hereto in violation of this Agreement, and whereas actual damages resulting from such a violation would be uncertain in amount and not readily calculable, the parties hereby agree that a fair measure of damages in such circumstances shall be an amount equal to the lesser of:

(1) fifty (50) percent of the freight charges on such shipment computed at the Carriers' contract rates in effect at the time of shipment, or

(2) one hundred (100) percent of the freight charges on such shipment computed at the Carriers' contract rates in effect at the time of shipment, less the estimated costs of loading and unloading which would have been incurred had the shipment been made on a vessel of a Carrier party hereto.

Such amount, and no more, shall be recoverable as liquidated damages.

(b) Upon the failure of the Merchant to pay or dispute his liability to pay liquidated damages as herein specified for breach of the contract within thirty (30) days after receipt of notice by registered mail from the Conference that they are due and payable, the Carriers shall suspend the Merchant's rights and obligations under the contract until he pays such damages. If within thirty (30) days after receipt of such notice the Merchant notifies the Conference by registered mail that he disputes the claim, the Conference shall within ninety (90) days thereafter proceed in accordance with Article 14, to adjudicate its claim for damages, and if it does not do so, said claim shall be forever barred. If the adjudication is in the Conference's favor, and the damages are not paid within thirty (30) days after the adjudication becomes final, the Conference shall suspend the Merchant's rights and obligations under the contract until he pays the damages. No suspension shall abrogate any cause of action which shall have arisen prior to the suspension. Payment of damages shall automatically terminate suspension. The Conference shall notify the Federal Maritime Commission of each suspension and of each termination of suspension, within ten (10) days after the event.

11.   (a) This Agreement is not and shall not be construed to be a contract of carriage with the Carriers or any one of them. Shipments under this Agreement are subject to all the terms and conditions and exceptions of the then current Conference tariff, and of the permits, dock receipts, bills of lading and other shipping documents regularly in use by the individual Carriers and to all laws and regulations of the appropriate authorities.

(b) It shall be a breach of this Agreement for the Merchant or any person, firm, or company acting or purporting to act on behalf thereof, to make a false declaration or representation in respect of the kind, quantity, weight, measurement, or value of the cargo covered by this Agreement, unless the Merchant shows that such false declaration or representation was made accidentally and without the intent to avoid the payment of the proper amount of freight on such cargo and that, immediately upon learning of such false declaration or representation, the Merchant tendered the balance (if any) of the amount of freight properly due to the Carrier concerned.

12.   Receipt and carriage of dangerous, hazardous, or obnoxious commodities shall be subject to the special facilities and requirements of the individual Carriers.

13. The Conference shall promptly notify Merchant of changes in the Conference membership, and any additional carriers which become members of said Conference shall thereupon become parties to this Agreement, and the Merchant shall thereupon have the right to avail himself of their services under the terms of this Agreement. Any Carrier, party to this Agreement, which for any reason ceases to be a member of the Conference shall thereupon cease to be a party to or participate in this Agreement and the Merchant shall not be entitled to ship over said Carrier under this Agreement after such Carrier ceases to be a member of the Conference or after having fifteen (15) calendar days' written notice of the termination of such Carrier's membership, whichever is later. The Merchant may, at any time after notice that a Carrier has ceased to be a member of the Conference, cancel without penalty or liability for damages any outstanding forward booking with such withdrawing Carrier.

14. All disputes arising in connection with this Agreement shall be submitted to arbitration by any party and any dispute so submitted to arbitration shall be finally settled under the Commercial Arbitration Rules of the Japan Commercial Arbitration Association. At the time a party makes a demand for arbitration to the Japan Commercial Arbitration Association it shall also submit the name of its arbitrator, and the other party shall have fourteen (14) calendar days thereafter to name its arbitrator and file same with the Japan Commercial Arbitration Association. The Japan Commercial Arbitration Association shall, within fourteen (14) calendar days thereafter, or within such other period as the parties may agree, name the third arbitrator, who shall act as chairman. Any sum required to be paid by an award of the arbitrators shall be paid within thirty (30) calendar days after a copy of the award has been mailed by the arbitrators to the parties. Judgment upon the arbitration award may be rendered in any court having jurisdiction thereof or application may be made to such court for a judicial acceptance of the award and an order of enforcement, as the case may be. In the event an action for judgment of execution is brought in a court of competent jurisdiction on the arbitration award or on the judgment rendered thereon, the parties waive all rights to object thereto insofar as permissible under the laws of the place where the enforcement action is instituted. The place of arbitration referred to in this paragraph shall be Tokyo, Japan, unless otherwise mutually agreed upon by parties concerned. The foregoing provisions regarding arbitrations shall apply unless the parties mutually agree to have any dispute settled pursuant to the rules of any other arbitration society and at any other place, or in any other manner.

If the intention with which any party hereto did or omitted, or caused or permitted to be done or omitted, any act or thing shall be an issue in any arbitration proceedings hereunder, and such party shall have failed, refused, or omitted to furnish to any other party or to the arbitrators any information, document, or data, required to be furnished by it in accordance with this Agreement, the arbitrators may draw from such failure, refusal, or omission, the inference that the information, documents or data contain facts adverse to the position of the party who so failed, refused or omitted.

15. (a) In the event of war, hostilities, warlike operations, embargoes, blockades, currency devaluation by governmental action, regulations of any governmental authority pertaining thereto, or any other official interferences with commercial intercourse arising from the above conditions, which affect the operations of any of the Carriers in the Trade covered by this Agreement, the Carriers may suspend the effectiveness of this Agreement with respect to the operations affected, and shall notify the Merchant of such suspension. Upon cessation of any cause or causes of suspension set forth in this Article and invoked by the Carriers, said Carriers shall forthwith reassume their rights and obligations hereunder and notify the Merchant on fifteen (15) days' written notice that the suspension is terminated.

(b) In the event of any of the conditions enumerated in Article 15(a), the Carriers may increase any rate or rates affected thereby, in order to meet such conditions, in lieu of suspension. Such increase or increases shall be on not less than fifteen (15) days' written notice to the Merchant, who may notify the Carriers in writing not less than ten (10) days before increases are to become effective of its intention to suspend this Agreement insofar as such increase or increases is or are concerned, and in such event, the Agreement shall be suspended as of the effective date of such increase or increases, unless the Carriers shall give written notice that such increase or increases have been rescinded and cancelled.

(c) In the event of any extraordinary conditions not enumerated in Article 15(a), which conditions may unduly impede, obstruct, or delay the obligations of the Carriers, the Carriers may increase any rate or rates affected thereby, in order to meet such conditions; provided, however, that nothing in this Article shall be construed to limit the provisions of Section 18(b) of the Shipping Act, 1916, in regard to the notice provisions of rate changes. The Merchant may, not less than ten (10) days before increases are to become effective, notify the Carriers that this Agreement shall be suspended insofar as the increases are concerned, as of the effective date of the increases, unless the Carriers shall give notice that such increase or increases have been rescinded and cancelled.

3. THE U. S. MUNITIONS LIST
(Incorporating the U. S. Munitions Import List)

Special Note: The U.S. Munitions Import List consists of the articles enumerated in the U.S. Munitions List, with the exception of certain items deemed unsuitable for commercial importation into the United States. The items which have deemed unsuitable (and therefore not included in the U.S. Munitions Import List) consist of the following categories:

IV (e), (f)
V all
VII (d), (e)
VIII all, other than (a)
X all
XI all
XII all
XIII all
XVII all
XVIII all

CATEGORY I—FIREARMS

(a) Nonautomatic and semiautomatic firearms, to caliber .50 inclusive, shotguns with barrels less than 18 inches in length, and all components and parts therefor.

(b) Automatic firearms and all components and parts therefor to caliber .50 inclusive.

(c) Insurgency-counterinsurgency type firearms or other weapons having a special military application regardless of caliber; and all components and parts therefor.

(d) Firearms silencers.

(e) Bayonets and specifically designed components therefor.

(f) Riflescopes (except sporting type sights including optical) and specifically designed components therefor.

CATEGORY II—ARTILLERY AND PROJECTORS

(a) Guns over caliber .50, howitzers, mortars, and recoilless rifles.

(b) Military flame throwers and projectors.

(c) Components and parts including, but not limited to, mounts and carriages for the articles in paragraphs (a) and (b) of this category.

CATEGORY III—AMMUNITION

(a) Ammunition for the arms in Categories I and II of this section.

(b) The following components, parts, accessories, and attachments: cartridge cases, powder bags, bullets, jackets, cores, shells (excluding shotgun), projectiles, boosters, fuzes and components therefor, primers, and other detonating devices for such ammunition.

(c) Ammunition belting and linking machines.

(d) Ammunition manufacturing machines, and ammunition loading machines (except hand loading).

CATEGORY IV—LAUNCH VEHICLES, GUIDED MISSILES, BALLISTIC MISSILES, ROCKETS, TORPEDOES, BOMBS, AND MINES

(a) Rockets (except meteorological sounding rockets), bombs, grenades, torpedoes, depth charges, land and naval mines, and demolition blocks and blasting caps.

(b) Launch vehicles, guided missiles, and ballistic missiles, tactical and strategic.

(c) Apparatus, devices, and materials for the handling, control, activation, detection, protection, discharge, or detonation of the articles in paragraphs (a) and (b) of this category.

(d) Missile and space vehicle powerplants.

(e) Military explosive excavating devices.

(f) Ablative materials fabricated or semifabricated from advanced composites (e.g., silica, graphite, carbon, and boron filaments) for the articles in this category when clearly identifiable as arms, ammunition, and implements of war, including the tape wrapping and other techniques for their production.

(g) All specifically designed components, parts, accessories, attachments, and associated equipment for the articles in this category.

Note: The term "military demolition blocks and blasting caps" as used in category IV(a) does not include the following articles:

(a) Electric squibs.

(b) No. 6 and No. 8 blasting caps, including electric.

(c) Delay electric blasting caps (including No. 6 and No. 8 millisecond).

(d) Seismograph electric blasting caps (including SSS, Static-Master, Vibrocap SR, and SEISMO SR).

(e) Oil well perforating devices.

Category IV(b) includes inter alia the following : Fuzes and components therefor, bomb racks and shackes, bomb shackle release units, bomb ejectors, torpedo tubes, torpedo and guided missile boosters, guidance system materials (except those having a commercial application), launching racks and projectors, pistols (exploders), igniters, fuze arming devices, intervalometers, and components therefor, guided missile launchers and specialized handling equipment and hardened missile launching facilities.

CATEGORY V—PROPELLANTS, EXPLOSIVES, AND INCENDIARY AGENTS

(a) Propellants for the articles in Categories III and IV of this section.

(b) Military explosives

(c) Military fuel thickeners

(d) Military pyrotechnics except (i) nonirritant smoke and (ii) other pyrotechnic materials having dual military and commercial use.

Category VI—Vessels of War and Special Naval Equipment

(a) Warships, amphibious warfare vessels, landing craft, mine warfare vessels, patrol vessels, auxiliary vessels, service craft, floating dry docks, and experimental types of naval ships.

(b) Turrets and gun mounts, missile systems, arresting gear, special weapons systems, protective systems, submarine storage batteries, catapults and other components, parts, attachments, and accessories specifically designed for combatant vessels, including but not limited to, battleships, command ships, guided missile ships, cruisers, aircraft carriers, destroyers, frigates, escorts, minesweepers, and submarines.

(c) Submarine and torpedo nets, and mine sweeping equipment. Components, parts, attachments and accessories specifically designed therefor.

Note: The term "vessels of war" includes, but is not limited to the following:

(a) Combatant:

(1) Warships (including nuclear-powered versions):

Aircraft carriers (CVA, CVE, CVHE, CVL, CVS).

Battleships (BB, BBG).

Command Ships (CBC, CLC).

Cruisers (CA, CAG, CB, CG, CLAA, CLG).

Destroyers (DD, DDC,DDE, DDG, DDR, DL, DLG).

Submarines (SS, SSB, SSG, SSK, SSR).

(2) Amphibious warfare vessels:

Amphibious assault ship (LPH).

Amphibious force flagship (AGC).

Assault helicopter aircraft carrier (CVHA).

Attack cargo ship (AKA).

Control escort vessel (DEC).

Cargo submarine (AK(SS)).

Inshore fire support ship (IFS).

Landing ships (LDS, LSMR, LST, LPD).

Transport submarine (AP(SS)).

(3) Landing craft (LCM, LCU, LCVP, ATC, CCB).

(4) Landing vehicle, tracked (LVT).

(5) Mine warfare vessels:

Mine hunter, coastal (MHC).

Mine countermeasures support ship (MSC).

Minelayers (DM, MMA, MMC, MMF).

Minesweepers (DMS, MSC, MSC(O), MSF, MSO, MSI, MSB, MDA, YMS, MSL, Ub/MS).

(6) Patrol vessels:

Escort vessels (DE, DER, PCS, PCER, PF, DEG).

Gunboats (PCM,PR).

Submarine chasers (PC, PCS, SC).

(b) Auxiliary vessels and service craft:

(1) Advanced aviation base ship (AVB).

(2) Auxiliary submarine (AG (SS)).

(3) Drone aircraft catapult control craft (YV).

(4) Guided Missile ship (AVM).

(5) Harbor utility craft (YFU).

(6) Icebreaker (AGB).

(7) Logistic support ships (AE, AF, AK, AKS, AO, ACE, AOG, AOR, AO(SS), AVS).

(8) Miscellaneous auxiliary (AG, IX, YAG).

(9) Patrol craft (PT, YP).

(10) Target and training submarine (SST).

(11) Ocean radar picket ship (AGR).

(12) Submersible craft (X). (See Category XX.)

(13) Utility aircraft carrier (CVU).

(c) Coast Guard patrol and service vessels and craft:

(1) Submarine repair and berthing barge (YRB).

(2) Labor transportation barracks ship (APL).

(3) Coast Guard cutter (CGC).

(4) Gunboat (WPG).

(5) Patrol craft (WPC, WSC).

(6) Seaplane tender (WAVP).

(7) Icebreaker (WAGB).

(8) Radio Ship (WAGR).

(9) Special Vessel (WIX).

(10)Auxiliary vessels (WAG, WAGE).

Note: Other Coast Guard patrol or rescue craft (i) of over 300 horsepower when equipped with a gas turbine engine or engines, and (ii) of over 600 horsepower when equipped with an engine or engines of the internal combustion, reciprocating type.

Category VII—Tanks and Military Vehicles

(a) Military type armed or armored vehicles, military railway trains, and vehicles fitted with, designed or modified to accommodate mountings for arms or other specialized military equipment.

(b) Military tanks, tank recovery vehicles, half-tracks and gun carriers.

(c) Self-propelled guns and howitzers.

(d) Military trucks, trailers, hoists, and skids specifically designed for carrying and handling the articles in paragraph (a) of Categories III and IV; military mobile repair shops specifically designed to service military equipment.

(e) Military recovery vehicles.

(f) Amphibious vehicles.

(g) All specifically designed components, parts, accessories, attachments, and associated equipment, including military bridging and deep water fording kits for the articles in this Category.

Note: As used in Category VII(f), the term "amphibious vehicles" includes, but is not limited to, automotive vehicles or chassis embodying all-wheel drive and equipped to meet special military requirements, with adaptation features for deep water fording and sealed electrical systems.

Category VIII—Aircraft, Spacecraft, and Associated Equipment

(a) Aircraft including helicopters designed, modified, or equipped for military purposes, including but not limited to the following: Gunnery, bombing, rocket, or missile launching, electronic surveillance, reconnaissance, refueling, aerial mapping, military liaison, cargo carrying or dropping, personnel dropping, military trainers, drones, and lighter-than-air aircraft.

(b) Spacecraft including manned and unmanned, active and passive satellites.

(c) Military aircraft engines, except reciprocating engines, and spacecraft engines specifically designed or modified for the aircraft and spacecraft in paragraphs (a) and (b) of this category.

(d) Airborne equipment, including but not limited to airborne refueling equipment, specifically designed for use with the aircraft, spacecraft, and engines of the types in paragraphs (a), (b), and (c) of this category.

(e) Launching, arresting, and recovery equipment for the articles in paragraphs (a) and (b) of this category.

(f) Nonexpansive balloons in excess of 3,000 cubic feet capacity, except such types as are in normal sporting use.

(g) Power supplies and energy sources specifically designed for spacecraft.

(h) Components, parts, accessories, attachments, and associated equipment specifically designed or modified for the articles in paragraphs (a) through (g) of this category, excluding propellors used with reciprocating engines and aircraft tires.

(i) Developmental aircraft components known to have a significant military application, excluding aircraft components concerning which Federal Aviation Agency certification is scheduled.

(j) Parachutes, except such types as are in normal sporting use, and complete canopies, harnesses, and platforms, and electronic release mechanisms therefor.

(k) Ground effect machines (GEMS), including surface effect machines and other air cushion vehicles, except such machines as are in normal commercial use, and all components, parts, accessories, attachments, and associated equipment specifically designed or modified for use with such machines.

(l) Inertial systems, and specifically designed components therefor, inherently capable of yielding accuracies of better than 1 to 2 nautical miles per hour circular error of probability (c.e.p.).

Note: (a) The term "aircraft" used in Category VIII means aircraft designed, modified, or equipped for military purposes as specified in Category VIII, including so-called "demilitarized" aircraft.

(b) Regardless of demilitarization, all aircraft bearing an original military designation are included in Category VIII, except the following aircraft which have not been specifically equipped, re-equipped, or modified for military operations:

(1) Cargo aircraft bearing "C" designations C-45 through C-118 inclusive, and C-121.

(2) Trainer aircraft bearing "T" designations and using reciprocating engines only.

(3) Utility aircraft bearing "U" designations and using reciprocating engines only.

(4) All liaison aircraft bearing an "L" designation.

CATEGORY IX—MILITARY TRAINING EQUIPMENT

(a) Military training equipment includes but is not limited to attack trainers, radar target trainers, radar target generators, gunnery training devices, anti-submarine warfare trainers, target equipment, armament training units, flight simulation devices, operational flight trainers, flight simulators, radar trainers, instrument flight trainers and navigation trainers.

(b) Components, parts, accessories, attachments, and associated equipment specifically designed or modified for the articles in paragraph (a) of this Category.

CATEGORY X—PROTECTIVE PERSONNEL EQUIPMENT

(a) Military body armor (including armored vests), flak suits and components and parts specifically designed therefor; military helmets, including liners.

(b) Partial pressure suits, pressurized breathing equipment, military oxygen masks, anti-"G" suits, protective clothing for handling guided missile fuel, military crash helmets, liquid oxygen converters used for aircraft (enumerated in Category VIII (a)), missiles, catapults, and cartridge-actuated devices utilized in emergency escape of personnel from aircraft (enumerated in Category VIII(a)).

(c) Protective apparel and equipment specifically designed for use with the articles in paragraphs (a) through (d) in Category XIV.

(d) Components, parts, accessories, attachments, and associated equipment specifically designed for use with the articles in paragraphs (a), (b) and (c) of this category.

CATEGORY XI—MILITARY AND SPACE ELECTRONICS

(a) Electronic equipment assigned a military designation including, but not limited to, the following items: Radar, active and passive countermeasures, counter countermeasures, underwater sound, computers, navigation, guidance, electronic fuzes, object-locating methods and means, displays that represent signals of military use, identification systems, missile and antimissile systems, telemetering and communications electronic equipment; and regardless of designation, any experimental or developmental electronic equipment specifically designed or modified for military application, or for use with a military system.

(b) Electronic equipment specifically designed or modified for spacecraft and spaceflight.

(c) Electronic systems or equipment designed, configured, used, or intended for use in search, reconnaissance, collection, monitoring, direction-finding, display, analysis, and production of information from the electromagnetic spectrum for intelligence or security purposes.

(d) Components, parts, accessories, attachments, and associated equipment specifically designed for use or currently used with the equipment in paragraphs (a) through (c) of this category, except such items as are in normal commercial use.

CATEGORY XII—FIRE CONTROL, RANGE FINDER, OPTICAL AND GUIDANCE AND CONTROL EQUIPMENT

(a) Fire control systems; gun and missile tracking and guidance systems; military infrared, image intensifier and other night sighting and night viewing equipment; military masers and military lasers; gun laying equipment; range, position and height finders and spotting instruments; aiming devices (electronic, gyroscopic, optic, and acoustic); bomb sights, bombing computers, military television sighting and viewing units, inertial platforms, and periscopes for the articles of this section.

(b) Inertial and other weapons or space vehicle guidance and control systems; spacecraft guidance, control and stabilization systems; astro compasses; and star trackers.

(c) Components, parts, accessories, attachments, and associated equipment specifically designed or modified for the articles in paragraphs (a) and (b) of this category, except such items as are in normal commercial use.

CATEGORY XIII—AUXILIARY MILITARY EQUIPMENT

(a) Aerial cameras, space cameras, special purpose military cameras, and specialized processing equipment therefor; military photointerpretation, stereoscopic plotting, and photogrammetry equipment, and specifically designed components therefor.

(b) Speech scramblers, privacy devices, cryptographic devices (encoding and decoding), and specifically designed components therefor, ancillary equipment, and especially devised protective apparatus for such devices, components, and equipment.

(c) Self-contained diving and underwater breathing apparatus designed for a military purpose and specifically designed components therefor.

(d) Armor plate.

(e) Concealment and deception equipment, including but not limited to, special paints, decoys, and simulators, components, parts and accessories specifically designed therefor.

(f) Energy conversion devices for producing electrical energy from nuclear, thermal, or solar energy, or from chemical reaction, specifically designed or modified for military application.

(g) Chemiluminescent compounds and solid state devices specifically designed or modified for military application.

CATEGORY XIV—TOXICOLOGICAL AGENTS AND EQUIPMENT; RADIOLOGICAL EQUIPMENT

(a) Chemical agents, including lung irritants, vesicants, lachrymators, and tear gases, sternutators and irritant smoke, and nerve gases and incapacitating agents.

(b) Biological agents adapted for use in war to produce death or disablement in human beings or animals, or to damage crops and plants.

(c) Equipment for dissemination, detection, and identification of, and defense against the articles in paragraphs (a) and (b) of this Category.

(d) Nuclear radiation detection and measuring devices, except such devices as are in normal commercial use.

(e) Components, parts, accessories, attachments, and associated equipment specifically designed or modified for the articles in paragraphs (c) and (d) of this category.

CATEGORY XV—[RESERVED]

CATEGORY XVI—NUCLEAR WEAPONS DESIGN AND TEST EQUIPMENT

(a) Any article, material, equipment, or device, which is specifically designed or specifically modified for use in the design, development, or fabrication of nuclear weapons or nuclear explosive devices.

(b) Any article, material, equipment, or device, which is specifically designed or specifically modified for use in the devising, carrying out, or evaluating of nuclear weap-ons tests or any other nuclear explosions except such items as are in normal commercial use for other purposes.

(c) Cold cathode tubes such as krytrons and sprytrons.

CATEGORY XVII—CLASSIFIED ARTICLES

All articles including technical data relating thereto, not enumerated herein, containing information which is classified as requiring protection in the interests of national defense.

CATEGORY XVIII—TECHNICAL DATA

Technical data relating to the articles designated in this subchapter as arms, ammunition, and implements of war (see 27 CFR 125.01 for definition and 27 CFR 125.11 for exemptions; see also 27 CFR 123.38).

CATEGORY XIX—[RESERVED]

CATEGORY XX—SUBMERSIBLE VESSELS, OCEANO-GRAPHIC AND ASSOCIATED EQUIPMENT

(a) Submersible vessels, manned and unmanned, designed for military purposes or having independent capability to maneuver vertically or horizontally at depths below 1,000 feet or powered by nuclear propulsion plants.

(b) Submersible vessels, manned or unmanned, designed in whole or in part from technology developed by or for the U.S. Armed Forces.

(c) Any of the articles in Categories VI, IX, XI, XIII, and elsewhere in 27 CFR 121.01 of this subchapter that may be used with submersible vessels.

(d) Equipment, components, parts, accessories, and attachments designed specifically for any of the articles in paragraphs (a) and (b) of this Category.

CATEGORY XXI—[RESERVED]

CATEGORY XXII—MISCELLANEOUS ARTICLES

Any article and technical data relating thereto not enumerated herein having significant military applicability, determined by the Director, Office of Munitions Control, Department of State, in consultation with appropriate agencies of the Government and having the concurrence of the Department of Defense.

4. PROPERTY AND IDEMNITY POLICY

Assessable—1963

S P E C I M E N

Policy No. A

AMERICAN STEAMSHIP OWNERS
MUTUAL PROTECTION AND INDEMNITY ASSOCIATION, INC.

NEW YORK, N. Y.

(Herein called the Association)

and of

Dollars being Premium at the rate of

per gross registered ton

DOES INSURE

, Policyholder

and

Additional Assured

(Herein called collectively the Assured)

who in accepting this policy agree that the party described above as "Policyholder" shall exclusively be entitled to the rights of a policyholder and member as set forth in the charter and by-laws of the Association;

LOSS, IF ANY, PAYABLE TO

IN THE INSURED SUM OF .... DOLLARS

at and from the .... day of .... 19 , at .... time

until the .... day of .... 19 , at .... time

against the risks and subject to the terms and conditions hereunder set forth in respect of the vessel called the

of .... gross registered tons or by

whatsoever other names the said vessel is or shall be named or called.

IN CONSIDERATION OF THE STIPULATIONS HEREIN NAMED

ASSESSABILITY. The Assured are subject to a contingent liability hereunder for assessment without limit of amount for their proportionate share of any deficiency or impairment as provided by law and fixed in accordance with the by-laws of the Association: provided, however, that any such assessment shall be for the exclusive benefit of holders of policies which provide for such a contingent liability, and the holders of policies subject to assessment shall not be liable to assessment in an amount greater in proportion to the total deficiency than the ratio that the deficiency attributable to the assessable business bears to the total deficiency.

THE ASSOCIATION AGREES TO INDEMNIFY THE ASSURED AGAINST ANY LOSS, DAMAGE OR EXPENSE WHICH THE ASSURED SHALL BECOME LIABLE TO PAY AND SHALL PAY BY REASON OF THE FACT THAT THE ASSURED IS THE OWNER (OR OPERATOR, MANAGER, CHARTERER, MORTGAGEE, TRUSTEE, RECEIVER OR AGENT, AS THE CASE MAY BE) OF THE INSURED VESSEL AND WHICH SHALL RESULT FROM THE FOLLOWING LIABILITIES, RISKS, EVENTS, OCCURRENCES AND EXPENDITURES:

(1) LIABILITY FOR LIFE SALVAGE, LOSS OF LIFE OF, OR PERSONAL INJURY TO, OR ILLNESS OF ANY PERSON, NOT INCLUDING, HOWEVER, UNLESS OTHERWISE AGREED BY ENDORSEMENT HEREON, LIABILITY TO AN EMPLOYEE (OTHER THAN HEREAFTER EXCEPTED) OF THE ASSURED, OR IN CASE OF HIS DEATH TO HIS BENEFICIARIES, UNDER ANY COMPENSATION ACT. LIABILITY HEREUNDER WITH RESPECT TO A MEMBER OF THE CREW SHALL INCLUDE LIABILITY ARISING ASHORE OR AFLOAT. LIABILITY HEREUNDER SHALL ALSO INCLUDE BURIAL EXPENSES NOT EXCEEDING $500. WHERE REASONABLY INCURRED BY THE ASSURED FOR THE BURIAL OF ANY SEAMAN.

LOSS OF LIFE, INJURY AND ILLNESS.

(a) Liability hereunder shall include the liability of the Assured for claims under any Compensation Act (other than hereafter excepted), in respect of an employee (i) who is a member of the crew of the insured vessel, or (ii) who is on board the insured vessel with the intention of becoming a member of her crew, or (iii) who, in the event of the vessel being laid up and out of commission, is engaged in the upkeep, maintenance or watching of the insured vessel, or (iv) who is engaged by the insured vessel or its Master to perform stevedoring work in connection with the vessel's cargo at ports in Alaska and ports outside the Continental United States where contract stevedores are not readily available. This insurance, however, shall not be considered as a qualification under any Compensation Act, but, without diminishing in any way the liability of the Association under this policy, the Assured may have in effect policies covering such liabilities. All claims under such Compensation Acts for which the Association is liable under the terms of this policy are to be paid without regard to such other policies.

(b) Liability hereunder shall not cover any liability under the provisions of the Act of Congress approved September 7th, 1916 and as amended, Public Act No. 267. Sixty-fourth Congress, known as the U. S. Employees Compensation Act.

(c) Liability hereunder in connection with the handling of cargo for the insured vessel shall commence from the time of receipt by the Assured of the cargo on dock or wharf, or on craft alongside for loading, and shall continue until due delivery thereof from dock or wharf of discharge or until discharge from the insured vessel on to a craft alongside.

(d) Liability hereunder may, by endorsement hereon, be made payable to an employee of the Assured or in the event of his death to his beneficiaries or estate.

(e) Claims hereunder, other than for burial expenses, are subject to a deduction of $ .... with respect to each accident or occurrence.

REPATRIATION EXPENSES.

(2) LIABILITY FOR EXPENSES REASONABLY INCURRED IN NECESSARILY REPATRIATING ANY MEMBER OF THE CREW OR ANY OTHER PERSON EMPLOYED ON BOARD THE INSURED VESSEL: PROVIDED, HOWEVER, THAT THE ASSURED SHALL NOT BE ENTITLED TO RECOVER ANY SUCH EXPENSES INCURRED BY REASON OF THE EXPIRATION OF THE SHIPPING AGREEMENT, OTHER THAN BY SEA PERILS, OR BY THE VOLUNTARY TERMINATION OF THE AGREEMENT. WAGES SHALL BE RECOVERABLE HEREUNDER ONLY WHEN PAYABLE UNDER STATUTORY OBLIGATION DURING UNEMPLOYMENT DUE TO THE WRECK OR LOSS OF THE INSURED VESSEL.

(a) Claims hereunder are subject to a deduction of $ _____ with respect to each accident or occurrence.

COLLISION.

(3) LIABILITY FOR LOSS OR DAMAGE ARISING FROM COLLISION OF THE INSURED VESSEL WITH ANOTHER SHIP OR VESSEL WHERE THE LIABILITY IS OF A TYPE, CHARACTER, OR KIND WHICH WOULD NOT BE COVERED IN ANY RESPECT BY THE FOLLOWING PORTIONS OF THE FOUR-FOURTHS COLLISION CLAUSE IN THE AMERICAN-INSTITUTE HULL CLAUSES (JUNE 2, 1977) FORM.

"And it is further agreed that:

(a) if the Vessel shall come into collision with any other ship or vessel, and the Assured or the Surety in consequence of the Vessel being at fault shall become liable to pay and shall pay by way of damages to any other person or persons any sum or sums in respect of such collision, the Underwriters will pay the Assured or the Surety, whichever shall have paid, such proportion of such sum or sums so paid as their respective subscriptions hereto bear to the Agreed Value, provided always that their liability in respect to any one such collision shall not exceed their proportionate part of the Agreed Value:

(b) in cases where, with the consent in writing of a majority (in amount) of Hull Underwriters, the liability of the Vessel has been contested, or proceedings have been taken to limit liability, the Underwriters will also pay a like proportion of the costs which the Assured shall thereby incur or be compelled to pay.

When both vessels are to blame, then, unless the liability of the owners or charterers of one or both such vessels becomes limited by law, claims under the Collision Liability clause shall be settled on the principle of Cross-Liabilities as if the owners or charterers of each vessel had been compelled to pay to the owners or charterers of the other of such vessels such one-half or other proportion of the latter's damages as may have been properly allowed in ascertaining the balance or sum payable by or to the Assured in consequence of such collision.

The principles involved in this clause shall apply to the case where both vessels are the property, in part or in whole, of the same owners or charterers, all questions of responsibility and amount of liability as between the two vessels being left to the decision of a single Arbitrator, if the parties can agree upon a single Arbitrator, or failing such agreement, to the decision of Arbitrators, one to be appointed by the Assured and one to be appointed by the majority (in amount) of Hull Underwriters interested; two Arbitrators chosen to choose a third Arbitrator before entering upon the reference, and the decision of such single Arbitrator, or of any two of such three Arbitrators, appointed as above, to be final and binding.

Provided that this clause shall in no case extend to any sum which the Assured or the Surety may become liable to pay or shall pay in consequence of, or with respect to:

(a) removal or disposal of obstructions, wrecks or their cargoes under statutory powers or otherwise pursuant to law:

(b) injury to real or personal property of every description:

(c) the discharge, spillage, emission or leakage of oil, petroleum products, chemicals or other substances of any kind or description whatsoever:

(d) cargo or other property on or the engagements of the Vessel:

(e) loss of life, personal injury or illness.

Provided further that exclusions (b) and (c) above shall not apply to injury to other vessels or property thereon except to the extent that such injury arises out of any action taken to avoid, minimize or remove any discharge, spillage, emission or leakage described in (c) above."

PROVIDED, HOWEVER, THAT INSURANCE HEREUNDER SHALL NOT EXTEND TO ANY LIABILITY, WHETHER DIRECT OR INDIRECT, IN RESPECT OF THE ENGAGEMENTS OF OR THE DETENTION OR LOSS OF TIME OF THE INSURED VESSEL.

(a) Claims hereunder shall be settled on the principles of Cross-Liabilities to the same extent only as provided in the four-fourths Collision Clause above mentioned.

(b) Where both vessels are the property, in part or in whole, of the same Owners or Charterers, claims hereunder shall be settled on the basis of the principles set forth in the four-fourths Collision Clause above mentioned.

(c) Claims hereunder shall be separated among and take the identity of the several classes of liability for loss, damage, and expense enumerated in this policy and each class shall be subject to the deductions, inclusions, exclusions and special conditions applicable in respect to such class.

(d) Notwithstanding the foregoing, the Association shall not be liable for any claims hereunder where the various liabilities resulting from such collision, or any of them, have been compromised, settled or adjusted without the written consent of the Association.

DAMAGE CAUSED OTHERWISE THAN BY COLLISION.

(4) LIABILITY FOR LOSS OF OR DAMAGE TO ANY OTHER VESSEL OR CRAFT, OR TO PROPERTY ON BOARD SUCH OTHER VESSEL OR CRAFT, CAUSED OTHERWISE THAN BY COLLISION OF THE INSURED VESSEL WITH ANOTHER VESSEL OR CRAFT.

(a) Where such other vessel or craft or property on board such other vessel or craft belongs to the Assured, claims hereunder shall be adjusted as if it belonged to a third person: provided, however, that if such vessel, craft or property be insured, the Association shall be liable hereunder only in so far as the loss or damage, but for the insurance herein provided, is not or would not be recoverable by the Assured under such other insurance.

(b) Claims hereunder are subject to a deduction of $ _____ with respect to each accident or occurrence.

DAMAGE TO DOCKS, BUOYS, ETC.

(5) LIABILITY FOR DAMAGE TO ANY DOCK, PIER, JETTY, BRIDGE, HARBOR, BREAKWATER, STRUCTURE, BEACON, BUOY, LIGHTHOUSE, CABLE, OR TO ANY FIXED OR MOVABLE OBJECT OR PROPERTY WHATSOEVER, EXCEPT ANOTHER VESSEL OR CRAFT OR PROPERTY ON AN-OTHER VESSEL OR CRAFT, OR TO PROPERTY ON THE INSURED VESSEL UNLESS PROPERTY ON THE INSURED VESSEL IS ELSEWHERE COVERED HEREIN.

(a) Where any such object or property belongs to the Assured, claims hereunder shall be adjusted as if it belonged to a third person; provided, however, that if such object or property be insured, the Association shall be liable hereunder only in so far as the damage, but for the insurance herein provided, is not or would not be recoverable by the Assured under such other insurance.

(b) Claims hereunder are subject to a deduction of $ _____ with respect to each accident or occurrence.

(6) LIABILITY FOR COSTS OR EXPENSES OF OR INCIDENTAL TO THE REMOVAL OF THE WRECK OF THE INSURED VESSEL: PROVIDED, HOWEVER, THAT:

WRECK REMOVAL.

(a) From such costs and expenses shall be deducted the value of any salvage from or which might have been recovered from the wreck inuring, or which might have inured, to the benefit of the Assured;

(b) The Association shall not be liable for any costs or expenses of a type, character or kind which would be payable under the terms of a policy written on the American Institute Hull Clauses (June 2, 1977) Form and a policy written on the American Institute Increased Value and Excess Liabilities Clauses (November 3, 1977) Form;

(c) In the event that the wreck of the insured vessel is upon property owned, leased, rented, or otherwise occupied by the Assured, the Association shall be liable for any liability for removal of the wreck which would be imposed upon the Assured by law in the absence of contract if the wreck had been upon the property belonging to another, but only for the excess over any amount recoverable under any other insurance applicable thereto;

(d) Each claim hereunder is subject to a deduction of $

(7) LIABILITY FOR LOSS OF OR DAMAGE TO OR IN CONNECTION WITH CARGO OR OTHER PROPERTY (EXCEPT MAIL OR PARCELS POST), INCLUDING BAGGAGE AND PERSONAL EFFECTS OF PASSENGERS, TO BE CARRIED, CARRIED OR WHICH HAS BEEN CARRIED ON BOARD THE INSURED VESSEL: PROVIDED, HOWEVER, THAT NO LIABILITY SHALL EXIST HEREUNDER FOR:

CARGO.

(a) Loss, damage or expense incurred in connection with the custody, carriage or delivery of specie, bullion, precious metals, precious stones, jewelry, silks, furs, currency, bonds or other negotiable documents, or similar valuable property, unless specially agreed to and accepted for transporation under a form of contract approved, in writing, by the Association;

SPECIE, BULLION, JEWELRY, ETC.

(b) Loss, damage or expense arising out of or in connection with the care, custody, carriage or delivery of cargo requiring refrigeration, unless the spaces, apparatus and means used for the care, custody and carriage thereof have been surveyed by a classification or other competent disinterested surveyor under working conditions before the commencement of each round voyage and found in all respects fit, and unless the Association has approved in writing the form of contract under which such cargo is accepted for transportation;

REFRIGERATION.

(c) Loss or damage to any passenger's baggage or personal effects, unless the form of ticket issued to the passenger shall have been approved, in writing, by the Association;

PASSENGERS' EFFECTS.

(d) Loss, damage or expense arising from any deviation in breach of the Assured's obligation to cargo, known to the Assured in time to enable him specifically to insure his liability therefor, unless notice thereof has been given the Association, and the Association has agreed, in writing, that such insurance was unnecessary;

DEVIATION.

(e) Loss, damage or expense arising from stowage of under deck cargo on deck, or stowage of cargo in spaces not suitable for its carriage, unless the Assured shall show that every reasonable precaution has been taken by him to prevent such improper stowage;

STOWAGE IN IMPROPER SPACES.

(f) Loss, damage or expense arising from issuance of clean bills of lading for goods known to be missing, unsound or damaged;

BILLS OF LADING.

(g) Loss, damage or expense arising from the intentional issuance of bills of lading prior to receipt of the goods described therein, or covering goods not received at all;

(h) Loss, damage or expense arising from delivery of cargo without surrender of bills of lading;

(i) Freight on cargo short-delivered, whether or not prepaid, or whether or not included in the claim and paid by the Assured;

FREIGHT.

AND PROVIDED FURTHER THAT:

(j) Liability hereunder shall in no event exceed that which would be imposed by law in the absence of contract:

(k) Liability hereunder shall be limited to such as would exist if the charter party, bill of lading or contract of affreightment contained (A) a negligence general average clause in the form hereinafter specified under Paragraph (12); (B) a clause providing that any provision of the charter party, bill of lading or contract of affreightment to the contrary notwithstanding, the Assured and the insured vessel shall have the benefit of all limitations and exemptions from liability accorded to the owner or chartered owner of vessels by any statute or rule of law for the time being in force; (C) such clauses, if any, as are required by law to be stated therein; (D) and such other protective clauses as are commonly in use in the particular trade;

PROTECTIVE CLAUSES REQUIRED IN CONTRACT OF AFFREIGHTMENT.

(l) When cargo carried by the insured vessel is under a bill of lading or similar document of title subject or made subject to the Carriage of Goods by Sea Act of the United States or a law of any other country of similar import, liability hereunder shall be limited to such as is imposed by said Act or law, and if the Assured or the insured vessel assumes any greater liability or obligation, either in respect of the valuation of the cargo or in any other respect, than the minimum liabilities and obligations imposed by said Act or law, such greater liability or obligation shall not be covered hereunder;

CARRIAGE OF GOODS BY SEA ACT.

(m) When cargo carried by the insured vessel is under a charter party, bill of lading or contract of affreightment not subject or made subject to the Carriage of Goods by Sea Act of the United States or a law of any other country of similar import, liability hereunder shall be limited to such as would exist if said charter party, bill of lading or contract of affreightment contained a clause exempting the Assured and the insured vessel from liability for losses arising from unseaworthiness provided that due diligence shall have been exercised to make said vessel seaworthy and properly manned, equipped and supplied, and a clause effectively limiting the Assured's liability for total loss or damage to goods shipped to $500. per package, or in case of goods not shipped in packages, per customary freight unit, and providing for pro rata adjustment on such basis for partial loss or damage;

LIMIT OF $500. PER PACKAGE.

(n) In the event cargo is carried under an arrangement not reduced to writing, the Association's liability hereunder shall be no greater than if such cargo had been carried under a charter party, bill of lading or contract of affreightment containing the clauses referred to herein;

ORAL CONTRACT.

(o) Where cargo on board the insured vessel is the property of the Assured, such cargo shall be deemed to be carried under a contract containing the protective clauses described in clauses (k), (l), and (m) herein; and such cargo shall be deemed to be fully insured under the usual form of cargo policy, and in case of loss of or damage to such cargo the Assured shall be deemed hereunder in respect of such loss or damage only to the extent that he would have been if the cargo had belonged to another, but only in the event and to the extent that the loss or damage would not be recoverable from marine insurers under a cargo policy as above specified;

ASSURED'S OWN CARGO.

(p) No liability shall exist hereunder for any loss, damage or expense in respect of cargo, or baggage and personal effects of passengers being transported on land or while on another vessel or craft unless such loss, damage or expense is caused directly by the insured vessel, her master, officers or crew;

TRANSPORTATION ON LAND OR OTHER CRAFT.

(q) No liability shall exist hereunder for any loss, damage or expense in respect of cargo, or baggage and personal effects of passengers before loading on or after discharge from the insured vessel caused by flood, tide, windstorm, earthquake, fire, explosion, heat, cold, deterioration, collapse of wharf, leaky shed, theft or pilferage unless such loss, damage or expense is caused directly by the insured vessel, her master, officers or crew:

CARGO ON DOCK.

(r) A deduction of $ _____ shall be made from any claim or claims with respect to each cargo carried, including passengers' baggage and personal effects.

(8) LIABILITY FOR FINES AND PENALTIES FOR THE VIOLATION OF ANY LAWS OF THE UNITED STATES, OR OF ANY STATE THEREOF, OR OF ANY FOREIGN COUNTRY: PROVIDED, HOWEVER, THAT THE ASSOCIATION SHALL NOT BE LIABLE TO INDEMNIFY THE ASSURED AGAINST ANY SUCH FINES OR PENALTIES RESULTING DIRECTLY OR INDIRECTLY FROM THE FAILURE, NEGLECT OR FAULT OF THE ASSURED OR ITS MANAGING OFFICERS TO EXERCISE THE HIGHEST DEGREE OF DILIGENCE TO PREVENT A VIOLATION OF ANY SUCH LAWS.

FINES AND PENALTIES.

(a) Claims hereunder are subject to a deduction of $ _____ with respect to each fine or penalty.

(9) LIABILITY FOR EXPENSES INCURRED IN RESISTING ANY UNFOUNDED CLAIM BY A SEAMAN OR OTHER PERSON EMPLOYED ON BOARD THE INSURED VESSEL, OR IN PROSECUTING SUCH PERSON OR PERSONS IN CASE OF MUTINY OR OTHER MISCONDUCT: NOT INCLUDING, HOWEVER, COSTS OF SUCCESSFULLY DEFENDING CLAIMS ELSEWHERE PROTECTED IN THIS POLICY.

MUTINY, MISCONDUCT.

(a) Claims hereunder are subject to a deduction of $ _____ with respect to each occurrence.

(10) LIABILITY FOR EXTRAORDINARY EXPENSES INCURRED IN CONSEQUENCE OF THE OUTBREAK OF PLAGUE OR OTHER DISEASE ON THE INSURED VESSEL, FOR DISINFECTION OF THE VESSEL OR OF PERSONS ON BOARD, OR FOR QUARANTINE EXPENSES, NOT BEING THE ORDINARY EXPENSES OF LOADING OR DISCHARGING, NOR THE ORDINARY WAGES OR PROVISIONS OF CREW OR PASSENGERS: PROVIDED, HOWEVER, THAT NO LIABILITY SHALL EXIST HEREUNDER IF THE VESSEL BE ORDERED TO PROCEED TO A PORT WHERE IT IS KNOWN THAT SHE WILL BE SUBJECTED TO QUARANTINE.

QUARANTINE EXPENSES.

(a) Each claim hereunder is subject to a deduction of $ _____

(11) LIABILITY FOR PORT CHARGES INCURRED SOLELY FOR THE PURPOSE OF PUTTING IN TO LAND AN INJURED OR SICK SEAMAN OR PASSENGER, AND THE NET LOSS TO THE ASSURED IN RESPECT OF BUNKERS, INSURANCE, STORES AND PROVISIONS AS THE RESULT OF THE DEVIATION.

PUTTING IN EXPENSES.

(12) LIABILITY FOR CARGO'S PROPORTION OF GENERAL AVERAGE, INCLUDING SPECIAL CHARGES, SO FAR AS THE ASSURED IS NOT ENTITLED TO RECOVER THE SAME FROM ANY OTHER SOURCE: PROVIDED, HOWEVER, THAT IF THE CHARTER PARTY, BILL OF LADING OR CONTRACT OF AFFREIGHTMENT DOES NOT CONTAIN THE NEGLIGENCE GENERAL AVER-

CARGO'S PROPN. G/A.

AGE CLAUSE QUOTED BELOW, THE ASSOCIATION'S LIABILITY HEREUNDER SHALL BE LIMITED TO SUCH AS WOULD EXIST IF SUCH CLAUSE WERE CONTAINED THEREIN: VIZ.

NEGLIGENCE G/A CLAUSE.

"In the event of accident, danger, damage or disaster, before or after commencement of the voyage resulting from any cause whatsoever, whether due to negligence or not, for which, the Carrier is not responsible, by statute, contract, or otherwise, the goods, the shipper and the consignee shall contribute with the Carrier in general average to the payment of any sacrifices, losses, or expenses of a general average nature that may be made or incurred, and shall pay salvage and special charges incurred in respect of the goods. If a salving ship is owned or operated by the Carrier, salvage shall be paid for as fully and in the same manner as if such salving ship or ships belonged to strangers."

(a) Claims hereunder are subject to a deduction of $ _____ with respect to each accident or occurrence.

(13) LIABILITY FOR EXPENSES ARISING OUT OF ACTION TAKEN IN COMPLIANCE WITH THE LAWS OF THE UNITED STATES OR ANY STATE OR SUBDIVISION THEREOF OR OF ANY COUNTRY TO AVOID DAMAGE FROM, OR TO MINIMIZE OR REMOVE, ANY DISCHARGE, SPILLAGE, EMISSION OR LEAKAGE OF OIL, PETROLEUM PRODUCTS, CHEMICALS OR OTHER SUBSTANCES.

DISCHARGE OF OIL OR OTHER SUBSTANCE.

(a) Claims hereunder are subject to a deduction of $ _____ with respect to each accident or occurrence.

(14) LIABILITY FOR COSTS, CHARGES AND EXPENSES REASONABLY INCURRED AND PAID BY THE ASSURED IN CONNECTION WITH ANY LIABILITY INSURED UNDER THIS POLICY, SUBJECT, HOWEVER, TO THE SAME DEDUCTION THAT WOULD BE APPLICABLE UNDER THIS POLICY TO THE LIABILITY DEFENDED: PROVIDED THAT IF ANY LIABILITY IS INCURRED AND PAID BY THE ASSURED AS AFORESAID, THE DEDUCTION SHALL BE APPLIED TO THE AGGREGATE OF THE CLAIM AND EXPENSES; AND PROVIDED FURTHER THAT THE ASSURED SHALL NOT BE ENTITLED TO INDEMNITY FOR EXPENSES UNLESS THEY WERE INCURRED WITH THE APPROVAL IN WRITING OF THE ASSOCIATION, OR THE ASSOCIATION SHALL BE SATISFIED THAT SUCH APPROVAL COULD NOT HAVE BEEN OBTAINED UNDER THE CIRCUMSTANCES WITHOUT UNREASONABLE DELAY, OR THAT THE EXPENSES WERE REASONABLY AND PROPERLY INCURRED; AND PROVIDED FURTHER THAT ANY SUGGESTION OR APPROVAL OF COUNSEL, OR INCURRING OF EXPENSES IN CONNECTION WITH LIABILITIES NOT INSURED UNDER THIS POLICY, SHALL NOT BE DEEMED AN ADMISSION OF THE ASSOCIATION'S LIABILITY.

EXPENSES OF INVESTIGATION AND DEFENSE.

(a) It is understood and agreed that the Association may undertake the investigation of any occurrence which might develop into a claim against the Assured, and may undertake the investigation and defense of any claim made against the Assured with respect to which the Assured shall be or may claim to be indemnified by the Association, and that during such investigation and/or defense the Association may incur expenses, which expenses shall be for the account of the Assured, and such investigation and/or defense shall not be considered as an admission of the Association's liability for such claim or expenses, and the liability of the Association to the Assured for any loss, damage or expense shall not be affected by any acts of the Association prior to formal presentation to the Association of the Assured's claim for reimbursement or indemnity.

(15) EXPENSES WHICH THE ASSURED MAY INCUR UNDER AUTHORIZATION OF THE ASSOCIATION IN THE INTEREST OF THE ASSOCIATION.

(24) The Association shall not be liable for any loss, damage or expense against which, but for the insurance herein provided, the Assured is or would be insured under existing insurance.

(25) If and when the Assured under this policy has any interest other than as an owner or bareboat charterer of the insured vessel, in no event shall the Association be liable hereunder to any greater extent than if such Assured were the owner or bareboat charterer and were entitled to all the rights of limitation to which a shipowner is entitled.

(26) If an insured vessel shall be and remain in any safe port for a period of thirty (30) or more consecutive days after finally mooring there (such period being computed from the day of arrival to the day of departure, one only being included) the Association is to return _____ per cent of the initial annual premium, prorated daily, for the period the insured vessel shall be laid up without cargo and without crew (other than a skeleton crew) and to return _____ per cent of the initial annual premium, prorated daily, for the period the insured vessel shall be laid up with cargo or crew on board, provided the Assured give written notice to the Association as soon as practicable after the commencement and termination of such lay up period. The Association shall have absolute discretion to determine whether a port is safe and how many crew members constitute a skeleton crew within the meaning of this paragraph.

(27) Liability hereunder in respect of any one accident or occurrence is limited to the amount hereby insured.

CANCELLATION PROVISIONS:

(28) (a) If the insured vessel should be sold or requisitioned, the Association shall have the option to cancel insurance hereunder with respect to the insured vessel, the Association to return _____ per cent of the gross annual premium for each thirty (30) consecutive days of the unexpired term of the insurance with respect to said vessel. If the entire management, control and possession of the insured vessel be transferred whether by demise charter or by change in corporate ownership or control of the insured owner, the Association shall have the option to cancel insurance hereunder with respect to the insured vessel, the Association to return three (3) percent of the gross annual premium for each thirty (30) consecutive days of the unexpired term of the insurance with respect to said vessel. Cancellation shall not relieve the Assured from liability for premiums under this policy and for assessments levied and to be levied for deficiencies and impairments in respect to the insurance year for which the policy was originally written.

(b) In the event of non-payment of the full premium within sixty (60) days after attachment, or, if installment payment of the premium has been arranged, in the event of non-payment of any installment thereof within twenty (20) days after it is due, this policy may be cancelled by the Association upon five (5) days' written notice being given the Assured. Should this policy be cancelled under the provisions of this clause or otherwise or should the Assured fail to pay any assessment within ten (10) days after it is due or should the Assured or any of them become insolvent or bankrupt or assign its property for the benefit of creditors or suffer the appointment of a receiver

GENERAL CONDITIONS AND LIMITATIONS

(16) In the event of any happening which may result in loss, damage or expense for which the Association may become liable, prompt notice thereof, on being known to the Assured, shall be given by the Assured to the Association.

(17) The Association shall not be liable for any claim not presented to the Association with proper proofs of loss within one year after payment by the Assured.

(18) In no event shall suit on any claim be maintainable against the Association unless commenced within two years after the loss, damage or expense resulting from liabilities, risks, events, occurrences and expenditures specified under this policy shall have been paid by the Assured.

(19) If the Assured shall fail or refuse to settle any claim as authorized or directed by the Association, the liability of the Association to the Assured shall be limited to the amount for which settlement could have been made, or, if the amount is unknown, to the amount which the Association authorized.

(20) Whenever required by the Association, the Assured shall aid in securing information and evidence and in obtaining witnesses and shall cooperate with the Association in the defense of any claim or suit or in the appeal from any judgment, in respect of any occurrence as hereinbefore provided.

(21) Unless otherwise agreed by endorsement hereon, the Association's liability shall in no event exceed that which would be imposed on the Assured by law in the absence of contract; provided, however, that the Assured's right of indemnity from the Association shall include any loss, damage or expense covered under the provisions of this policy arising as a result of any contract for the employment of tugs where such contract is one which is substantially similar to those customarily in use or in force during the currency of this policy. The Assured's right of indemnity hereunder shall not include any liability for loss, damage or expense arising from collision between the insured vessel and another vessel or craft, other than liability consequent on such collision, (a) for removal of obstructions under statutory powers, (b) for damage to any dock, pier, jetty, bridge, harbor, breakwater, structure, beacon, buoy, lighthouse, cable or similar structures, (c) in respect of the cargo of the insured vessel and (d) for loss of life, personal injury and illness.

(22) No claim or demand against the Association shall be assigned or transferred without the written consent of the Association, and unless otherwise specifically agreed by endorsement hereon no person other than the Assured or Loss Payee named herein, or a receiver of the property or estate thereof, shall acquire any right against the Association hereunder.

(23) The Association shall be subrogated to all the rights which the Assured may have against any other person or entity, in respect of any payment made under this policy, to the extent of such payment, and the Assured shall, upon the request of the Association, execute all documents necessary to secure to the Association such rights.

for its property or any part thereof or the institution of dissolution proceedings by or against it, the Association shall not be liable for any claims whatsoever under this policy unless within sixty (60) days from the date of such cancellation or the occurrence of such insolvency, bankruptcy, assignment, receivership or dissolution proceedings, there are paid to the Association by or on behalf of the Assured all premiums due, and the payment of any premiums to become due as well as all possible assessments is unconditionally guaranteed by a responsible surety.

(c) In the event that Sections 182 to 189, both inclusive, of U. S. Code, Title 46, or any other existing law or laws determining or limiting liability of shipowners and carriers, or any of them, shall, while this policy is in force, be modified, amended or repealed, or the liabilities of shipowners or carriers be increased in any respect by legislative enactment, the Association shall have the right to cancel said insurance upon giving thirty (30) days' written notice of their intention so to do, and in the event of such cancellation, make return of premium upon a pro rata daily basis.

RISKS EXCLUDED.

(29) NOTWITHSTANDING ANYTHING TO THE CONTRARY CONTAINED IN THIS POLICY, THE ASSOCIATION SHALL NOT BE LIABLE FOR ANY LOSS, DAMAGE OR EXPENSE SUSTAINED, DIRECTLY OR INDIRECTLY, BY REASON OF:

(a) Loss, damage or expense to hull, machinery, equipment or fittings of the insured vessel, including refrigerating apparatus and wireless equipment, whether or not owned by the Assured;

(b) Cancelment or breach of any charter or contract, detention of the vessel, bad debts, insolvency, fraud of agents, loss of freight, passage money, hire, demurrage or any other loss of revenue;

(c) Any loss, damage, sacrifice or expense of a type, character or kind which would be payable under the terms of a policy written on the American Institute Hull Clauses (June 2, 1977) Form and a policy written on the American Institute Increased Value and Excess Liabilities Clauses (November 3, 1977) Form whether or not the insured vessel is fully covered under those policies by insurance and excess insurance sufficient in amount to pay in full and without limit all such loss, damage, sacrifice or expense;

(d) The insured vessel towing any other vessel or craft, unless such towage was to assist such other vessel or craft in distress to a port or place of safety; provided, however, that this exception shall not apply to claims covered under Paragraph (1) of this policy;

(e) For any claim for loss of life, personal injury or illness in relation to the handling of cargo where such claim arises under a contract of indemnity between the Assured and his sub-contractor.

TUGS.

(30) In every case where this policy insures tugs, Clause (b) of Paragraph (6) and Clause (c) of Paragraph (29) shall be deemed to refer to the American Institute Tug Form, August 1, 1976 instead of the American Institute Hull Clauses (June 2, 1977) Form and Paragraph (3) shall be deemed to incorporate the Collision Clause contained in said policy (American Institute Tug Form, August 1, 1976) instead of the Collision Clause quoted in said Paragraph (3) and the following clause shall be substituted for and supersede Clause (d) of Paragraph (29) namely

"Loss of or damage to any vessel or vessels in tow and/or their cargoes, whether such loss or damage occurs before, during or after actual towage; provided, that this exception shall not apply to claims under Paragraph (1) of this policy."

WAR RISKS.

(31) Notwithstanding anything to the contrary contained in this policy, the Association shall not be liable for or in respect of any loss, damage or expense sustained by reason of capture, seizure, arrest, restraint or detainment, or the consequences thereof or of any attempt thereat; or sustained in consequence of military, naval or air action by force of arms, including mines and torpedoes or other missiles or engines of war, whether of enemy or friendly origin; or sustained in consequence of placing the vessel in jeopardy as an act or measure of war taken in the actual process of a military engagement, including embarking or disembarking troops or material of war in the immediate zone of such engagement; and any such loss, damage and expense shall be excluded from this policy without regard to whether the Assured's liability therefor is based on negligence or otherwise, and whether before or after a declaration of war.

IN WITNESS WHEREOF the Association has caused this Policy to be signed in its behalf this .... day of .... 19......

AMERICAN STEAMSHIP OWNERS MUTUAL
PROTECTION AND INDEMNITY ASSOCIATION, INC.

By Shipowners Claims Bureau, Inc., Manager.

....
Authorized Signature

5. SALVAGE AGREEMENT
Courtesy of the Society of Lloyd's, by permission

LOF 1980

LLOYD'S

STANDARD FORM OF

SALVAGE AGREEMENT

(APPROVED AND PUBLISHED BY THE COMMITTEE OF LLOYD'S)

NO CURE—NO PAY

On board the

Dated   19

IT IS HEREBY AGREED between Captain†   for and on behalf of the Owners of the "   " her cargo freight bunkers and stores and   for and on behalf of (hereinafter called "the Contractor"*):—

1. (a) The Contractor agrees to use his best endeavours to salve the and/or her cargo bunkers and stores and take them to ‡   or other place to be hereafter agreed or if no place is named or agreed to a place of safety. The Contractor further agrees to use his best endeavours to prevent the escape of oil from the vessel while performing the services of salving the subject vessel and/or her cargo bunkers and stores. The services shall be rendered and accepted as salvage services upon the principle of "no cure—no pay" except that where the property being salved is a tanker laden or partly laden with a cargo of oil and without negligence on the part of the Contractor and/or his Servants and/or Agents (1) the services are not successful or (2) are

only partially successful or (3) the Contractor is prevented from completing the services the Contractor shall nevertheless be awarded solely against the Owners of such tanker his reasonably incurred expenses and an increment not exceeding 15 per cent of such expenses but only if and to the extent that such expenses together with the increment are greater than any amount otherwise recoverable under this Agreement. Within the meaning of the said exception to the principle of "no cure—no pay" expenses shall in addition to actual out of pocket expenses include a fair rate for all tugs craft personnel and other equipment used by the Contractor in the services and oil shall mean crude oil fuel oil heavy diesel oil and lubricating oil.

(b) **The Contractor's remuneration shall be fixed by arbitration in London in the manner herein prescribed and any other difference arising out of this Agreement or the operations thereunder shall be referred to arbitration in the same way. In the event of the services referred to in this Agreement or any part of such services having been already rendered at the date of this Agreement by the Contractor to the said vessel and/or her cargo bunkers and stores the provisions of this Agreement shall apply to such services.**

(c) **It is hereby further agreed that the security to be provided to the Committee of Lloyd's the Salved Values the Award and/or Interim Award and/or Award on Appeal of the Arbitrator and/or Arbitrator(s) on Appeal shall be in‡   currency. If this Clause is not completed then the security to be provided and the Salved Values the Award and/or Interim Award and/or Award on Appeal of the Arbitrator and/or Arbitrator(s) on Appeal shall be in Pounds Sterling.**

(d) **This Agreement shall be governed by and arbitration thereunder shall be in accordance with English law.**

2.   The Owners their Servants and Agents shall co-operate fully with the Contractor in and about the salvage including obtaining entry to the place named in Clause 1 of this Agreement or such other place as may be agreed or if applicable the place of safety to which the salved property is taken. The Owners shall promptly accept redelivery of the salved property at such place. The Contractor may make reasonable use of the vessel's machinery gear equipment anchors chains stores and other appurtenances during and for the purpose of the operations free of expense but shall not unnecessarily damage abandon or sacrifice the same or any property the subject of this Agreement.

3.   The Master or other person signing this Agreement on behalf of the property to be salved is not authorised to make or give and the Contractor shall not demand or take any payment draft or order as inducement to or remuneration for entering into this Agreement.

PROVISIONS AS TO SECURITY

4.   The Contractor shall immediately after the termination of the services or sooner in appropriate cases notify the Committee of Lloyd's and where practicable the Owners of the amount for which he requires security (inclusive of costs expenses and interest). Unless otherwise agreed by the parties such security shall be given to the Committee of Lloyd's and security so given shall be in a form approved by the Committee and shall be given by persons firms or corporations resident in the United Kingdom either satisfactory to the Committee of Lloyd's or agreed by the Contractor. The Committee of Lloyd's shall not be responsible for the sufficiency (whether in amount or otherwise) of any security which shall be given nor for the default or insolvency of any person firm or corporation giving the same.

5.   Pending the completion of the security as aforesaid the Contractor shall have a maritime lien on the property salved for his remuneration. Where the aforementioned exception to the principle of "no cure—no pay" becomes likely to be applicable the Owners of the vessel shall on demand of the Contractor provide security for the Contractor's remuneration under the aforementioned exception in accordance with Clause 4 hereof. The salved property shall not without the consent in writing of the Contractor be removed from the place (within the terms of Clause 1) to which the property is taken by

the Contractor on the completion of the salvage services until security has been given as aforesaid. The Owners of the vessel their Servants and Agents shall use their best endeavours to ensure that the Cargo Owners provide security in accordance with the provisions of Clause 4 of this Agreement before the cargo is released. The Contractor agrees not to arrest or detain the property salved unless (a) the security be not given within 14 days (exclusive of Saturdays and Sundays or other days observed as general holidays at Lloyd's) after the date of the termination of the services (the Committee of Lloyd's not being responsible for the failure of the parties concerned to provide the required security within the said 14 days) or (b) the Contractor has reason to believe that the removal of the property is contemplated contrary to the above agreement. In the event of security not being provided or in the event of (1) any attempt being made to remove the property salved contrary to this agreement or (2) the Contractor having reasonable grounds to suppose that such an attempt will be made the Contractor may take steps to enforce his aforesaid lien. The Arbitrator appointed under Clause 6 or the person(s) appointed under Clause 13 hereof shall have power in their absolute discretion to include in the amount awarded to the Contractor the whole or such part of the expense incurred by the Contractor in enforcing or protecting by insurance or otherwise or in taking reasonable steps to enforce or protect his lien as they shall think fit.

PROVISIONS AS TO ARBITRATION

6. (a) Where security within the provisions of this Agreement is given to the Committee of Lloyd's in whole or in part the said Committee shall appoint an Arbitrator in respect of the interests covered by such security.

   (b) Whether security has been given or not the Committee of Lloyd's shall appoint an Arbitrator upon receipt of a written or telex or telegraphic notice of a claim for arbitration from any of the parties entitled or authorised to make such a claim.

7. Where an Arbitrator has been appointed by the Committee of Lloyd's and the parties do not wish to proceed to arbitration the parties shall jointly notify the said Committee in writing or by telex or by telegram and the said Committee may thereupon terminate the appointment of such Arbitrator as they may have appointed in accordance with Clause 6 of this Agreement.

8. Any of the following parties may make a claim for arbitration viz.: — (1) The Owners of the ship. (2) The Owners of the cargo or any part thereof. (3) The Owners of any freight separately at risk or any part thereof. (4) The Contractor. (5) The Owners of the bunkers and/or stores. (6) Any other person who is a party to this Agreement.

9. If the parties to any such Arbitration or any of them desire to be heard or to adduce evidence at the Arbitration they shall give notice to that effect to the Committee of Lloyd's and shall respectively nominate a person in the United Kingdom to represent them for all the purposes of the Arbitration and failing such notice and nomination being given the Arbitrator or Arbitrator(s) on Appeal may proceed as if the parties failing to give the same had renounced their right to be heard or adduce evidence.

10. The remuneration for the services within the meaning of this Agreement shall be fixed by an Arbitrator to be appointed by the Committee of Lloyd's and he shall have power to make an Interim Award ordering such payment on account as may seem fair and just and on such terms as may be fair and just.

CONDUCT OF THE ARBITRATION

11. The Arbitrator shall have power to obtain call for receive and act upon any such oral or documentary evidence or information (whether the same be strictly admissible as evidence or not) as he may think fit and to conduct the Arbitration in such manner in all respects as he may think fit and shall if in his opinion the amount of the security demanded is excessive have power in his absolute discretion to

condemn the Contractor in the whole or part of the expense of providing such security and to deduct the amount in which the Contractor is so condemned from the salvage remuneration. Unless the Arbitrator shall otherwise direct the parties shall be at liberty to adduce expert evidence at the Arbitration. Any Award of the Arbitrator shall (subject to appeal as provided in this Agreement) be final and binding on all the parties concerned. The Arbitrator and the Committee of Lloyd's may charge reasonable fees and expenses for their services in connection with the Arbitration whether it proceeds to a hearing or not and all such fees and expenses shall be treated as part of the costs of the Arbitration. Save as aforesaid the statutory provisions as to Arbitration for the time being in force in England shall apply.

12.   Interest at a rate per annum to be fixed by the Arbitrator from the expiration of 21 days (exclusive of Saturdays and Sundays or other days observed as general holidays at Lloyd's) after the date of publication of the Award and/or Interim Award by the Committee of Lloyd's until the date payment is received by the Committee of Lloyd's both dates inclusive shall (subject to appeal as provided in this Agreement) be payable upon any sum awarded after deduction of any sums paid on account.

PROVISIONS AS TO APPEAL

13.   Any of the persons named under Clause 8 may appeal from the Award but not without leave of the Arbitrator(s) on Appeal from an Interim Award made pursuant to the provisions of Clause 10 hereof by giving written or telegraphic or telex Notice of Appeal to the Committee of Lloyd's within 14 days (exclusive of Saturdays and Sundays or other days observed as general holidays at Lloyd's) after the date of the publication by the Committee of Lloyd's of the Award and may (without prejudice to their right of appeal under the first part of this Clause) within 14 days (exclusive of Saturdays and Sundays or other days observed as general holidays at Lloyd's) after receipt by them from the Committee of Lloyd's of notice of such appeal (such notice if sent by post to be deemed to be received on the day following that on which the said notice was posted) give written or telegraphic or telex Notice of Cross-Appeal to the Committee of Lloyd's. As soon as practicable after receipt of such notice or notices the Committee of Lloyd's shall refer the Appeal to the hearing and determination of a person or persons selected by it. In the event of an Appellant or Cross-Appellant withdrawing his Notice of Appeal or Cross-Appeal the hearing shall nevertheless proceed in respect of such Notice of Appeal or Cross-Appeal as may remain. Any Award on Appeal shall be final and binding on all the parties concerned whether such parties were represented or not at either the Arbitration or at the Arbitration on Appeal.

CONDUCT OF THE APPEAL

14.   No evidence other than the documents put in on the Arbitration and the Arbitrator's notes of the proceedings and oral evidence if any at the Arbitration and the Arbitrator's Reasons for his Award and Interim Award if any and the transcript if any of any evidence given at the Arbitration shall be used on the Appeal unless the Arbitrator(s) on the Appeal shall in his or their discretion call for or allow other evidence. The Arbitrator(s) on Appeal may conduct the Arbitration on Appeal in such manner in all respects as he or they may think fit and may act upon any such evidence or information (whether the same be strictly admissible as evidence or not) as he or they may think fit and may maintain increase or reduce the sum awarded by the Arbitrator with the like power as is conferred by Clause 11 on the Arbitrator to condemn the Contractor in the whole or part of the expense of providing security and to deduct the amount disallowed from the salvage remuneration. And he or they shall also make such order as he or they shall think fit as to the payment of interest on the sum awarded to the Contractor. The Arbitrator(s) on the Appeal may direct in what manner the costs of the Arbitration and of the Arbitration on Appeal shall be borne and paid and he or they and the Committee of Lloyd's may charge reasonable fees and expenses for their services in connection with the Arbitration on Appeal whether it proceeds to a hearing or not and all such fees and expenses shall be treated as part of the costs of the Arbitration on Appeal. Save as aforesaid the statutory provisions as to Arbitration for the time being in force in England shall apply.

PROVISIONS AS TO PAYMENT

15. (a) In case of Arbitration if no Notice of Appeal be received by the Committee of Lloyd's within 14 days (exclusive of Saturdays and Sundays or other days observed as general holidays at Lloyd's) after the date of the publication by the Committee of the Award and/or Interim Award the Committee shall call upon the party or parties concerned to pay the amount awarded and in the event of non-payment shall realize or enforce the security and pay therefrom to the Contractor (whose receipt shall be a good discharge to it) the amount awarded to him together with interest as hereinbefore provided but the Contractor shall reimburse the parties concerned to such extent as the final Award is less than the Interim Award.

(b) If Notice of Appeal be received by the Committee of Lloyd's in accordance with the provisions of Clause 13 hereof it shall as soon as but not until the Award on Appeal has been published by it call upon the party or parties concerned to pay the amount awarded and in the event of non-payment shall realize or enforce the security and pay therefrom to the Contractor (whose receipt shall be a good discharge to it) the amount awarded to him together with interest if any in such manner as shall comply with the provisions of the Award on Appeal.

(c) If the Award and/or Interim Award and/or Award on Appeal provides or provide that the costs of the Arbitration and/or of the Arbitration on Appeal or any part of such costs shall be borne by the Contractor such costs may be deducted from the amount awarded before payment is made to the Contractor by the Committee of Lloyd's unless satisfactory security is provided by the Contractor for the payment of such costs.

(d) If any sum shall become payable to the Contractor as remuneration for his services and/or interest and/or costs as the result of an agreement made between the Contractor and the parties interested in the property salved or any of them the Committee of Lloyd's in the event of non-payment shall realize or enforce the security and pay therefrom to the Contractor (whose receipt shall be a good discharge to it) the amount agreed upon between the parties.

(e) Without prejudice to the provisions of Clause 4 hereof the liability of the Committee of Lloyd's shall be limited in any event to the amount of security held by it.

GENERAL PROVISIONS

16.   Notwithstanding anything hereinbefore contained should the operations be only partially successful without any negligence or want of ordinary skill and care on the part of the Contractor his Servants or Agents and any portion of the vessel her appurtenances bunkers stores and cargo be salved by the Contractor he shall be entitled to reasonable remuneration and such reasonable remuneration shall be fixed in case of difference by Arbitration in the manner hereinbefore prescribed.

17.   The Master or other person signing this Agreement on behalf of the property to be salved enters into this Agreement as Agent for the vessel her cargo freight bunkers and stores and the respective owners thereof and binds each (but not the one for the other or himself personally) to the due performance thereof.

18.   In considering what sums of money have been expended by the Contractor in rendering the services and/or in fixing the amount of the Award and/or Interim Award and/or Award on Appeal the Arbitrator or Arbitrator(s) on Appeal shall to such an extent and in so far as it may be fair and just in all the circumstances give effect to the consequences of any change or changes in the value of money or rates of exchange which may have occurred between the completion of the services and the date on which the Award and/or Interim Award and/or Award on Appeal is made.

19.   Any Award notice authority order or other document signed by the Chairman of Lloyd's or any person authorised by the Committee of Lloyd's for the purpose shall be deemed to have been duly made or given by the Committee of Lloyd's and shall have the same force and effect in all respects as if it had been signed by every member of the Committee of Lloyd's.

20.   The Contractor may claim salvage and enforce any Award or agreement made between the Contractor and the parties interested in the property salved against security provided under this Agreement if any in the name and on behalf of any Sub-Contractors Servants or Agents including Masters and members of the Crews of vessels employed by him in the services rendered hereunder provided that he first indemnifies and holds harmless the Owners of the property salved against all claims by or liabilities incurred to the said persons. Any such indemnity shall be provided in a form satisfactory to such Owners.

21.   The Contractor shall be entitled to limit any liability to the Owners of the subject vessel and/or her cargo bunkers and stores which he and/or his Servants and/or Agents may incur in and about the services in the manner and to the extent provided by English law and as if the provisions of the Convention on Limitation of Liability for Maritime Claims 1976 were part of the law of England.

For and on behalf of the Contractor

For and on behalf of the Owners of property to be salved.

. . . .

. . . .

(To be signed either by the Contractor personally or by the Master of the salving vessel or other person whose name is inserted in line 3 of this Agreement.)

(To be signed by the Master or other person whose name is inserted in line 1 of this Agreement.)

6. J-LIST ITEMS

Art, works of

Articles classifiable under items 850.40, 850.70, 851.30, and 853.30, Tariff Schedules of the United States

Articles entered in good faith as antiques and rejected as unauthentic

Bagging, waste

Bags, jute

Bands, steel

Beads, unstrung

Bearings, ball, ⅝-inch or less in diameter

Blanks, metal, to be plated

Bodies, harvest hat

Bolts, nuts, and washers

Briarwood in blocks

Briquettes, coal or coke

Buckles, 1 inch or less in greatest dimension

Burlap

Buttons

Cards, playing

Cellophane and celluloid in sheets, bands, or strips

Chemicals, drugs, medicinal, and similar substances, when imported in capsules, pills, tablets, lozenges, or troches

Cigars and cigarettes

Covers, straw bottle

Dies, diamond wire, unmounted

Dowels, wooden

Effects, theatrical

Eggs

Feathers

Firewood

Flooring, not further manufactured when planed, tongued, and grooved

Flowers, artificial, except bunches

Flowers, cut

Glass, cut to shape and size for use in clocks, hand, pocket, and purse mirrors, and other glass of similar shapes and sizes, not including lenses or watch crystals

Glides, furniture, except glides with prongs
Hairnets
Hides, raw
Hooks, fish (except snell fish hooks)
Hoops (wood), barrel
Laths
Leather, except finished
Livestock
Lumber, sawed
Metal bars, except concrete reinforcement bars; billets, blocks, blooms; ingots, pigs; plates; sheets; except galvanized sheets; shafting; slabs; and metal in similar forms
Mica, not further manufactured than cut or stamped to dimensions, shape or form
Monuments
Nails, spikes, and staples
Natural products, such as vegetables, fruits, nuts, berries, and live or dead animals, fish and birds; all the foregoing which are in their natural state or not advanced in any manner further than is necessary for their safe transportation
Nets, bottle, wire
Paper, newsprint
Paper, stencil
Paper, stock
Parchment and vellum
Parts for machines imported from same country as parts
Pickets (wood)
Pins, tuning
Pipes, iron or steel, and pipe fittings of cast or malleable iron (except cast iron soil pipe and fittings)*
Plants, shrubs, and other nursery stock

Plugs, tie
Poles, bamboo
Post (wood), fence
Pulpwood
Rags (including wiping rags)
Rails, joint bars, and tie plates covered by item 601.20 through 610.26, Tariff Schedules of the United States
Ribbon
Rivets
Rope, including wire rope; cordage; cords, twines, threads, and yarns
Scrap and waste
Screws
Shims, track
Shingles (wood), bundles of (except bundles of red-cedar shingles)
Skins, fur, dressed or dyed
Skins, raw fur
Sponges
Springs, watch
Stamps, postage and revenue, and other articles covered in item 274.40, Tariff Schedules of the United States
Staves (wood), barrel
Steel, hoop
Sugar, maple
Ties (wood), railroad
Tiles, not over 1 inch in greatest dimension
Timbers, sawed
Tips, penholder
Trees, Christmas
Weights, analytical and precision in sets
Wicking, candle
Wire, except barbed

---

*Pursuant to section 207 of the Trade and Tariff Act of 1984, amending 19 U.S.C. 1304, the referenced products will be subject to individual country of origin marking requirements, with effect for shipments after November 14, 1984. Pipe fittings of iron or steel (of the kind classified under items 610.62-610.93, inclusive, and 688.32, Tariff Schedules of the U.S.) must be marked with the country of origin by means of die stamping, cast-in-mold lettering, etching, or engraving, unless the nature of the article will not permit such marking. Notwithstanding the foregoing, pipe fittings of iron or steel (except for cast or malleable iron) which the exporter or manufacturer certifies were manufactured prior to November 14, 1984 may be marked by tagging or stencilling of packages. Pipes of iron or steel (as defined Headnote 3(e), Schedule 6, Part 2, Tariff Schedules of the U.S. [excepting items 607.05-607.09, inclusive]) must be marked by means of die stamping, cast-in-mold lettering, etching, or engraving.

One marking per piece of pipe shall be sufficient. Fittings must be marked independently, whether or not attached to pipe.

7. INTERNATIONAL MARITIME ORGANIZATION

Agreements in Effect on January 1, 1984

Title of Convention	Date of adoption	Requirements for entry into force	Time from fulfillment to entry into force	Date of entry into force	Contracting Parties at 1.1.84	AMENDMENTS AND PROTOCOLS				
						Is tacit acceptance procedure included?	Year of adoption	Date of entry into force	Contracting Parties at 1.1.84	Notes
International Convention for the Safety of Life at Sea (SOLAS)	1 Nov. 1974	25 States whose combined merchant fleets constitute not less than 50% of world gt.	1 year	25 May 1980	78 / 93.70%	Yes	1978 (P) / 1981 / 1983	1 May 1981 / 1 Sept. 1984* / 1 July 1986*	46‡ / - / -	The adopted amendments to Solas 1960 are incorporated in this instrument. *Unless rejected by ⅓ contracting parties with 50% of world gt. ‡84.96%
International Convention on Load Lines (LL)	5 Apr. 1966	15 States including 7 with not less than 1 million gt. of shipping.	1 year	21 July 1968	100 / 98.14%	No	1971 / 1975 / 1979		37 / 34 / 27	The amendments will enter into force 12 months after being ratified by two-thirds of Contracting Parties (67)
Special Trade Passenger Ships Agreement (STP)	6 Oct. 1971	3 States (including at least 2 in whose territory are registered ships engaged in special trades or whose nationals are carried in ships engaged in these trades)	6 months	2 Jan. 1974	13	No	1973 (P)	2 June 1977	11	
International Convention for Safe Containers (CSC)	2 Dec. 1972	10 States	1 year	6 Sept. 1977	38	No	1981 / 1983	Dec. 1981 / 1 Jan. 1984*	-	The amendments are concerned with Annex 1. regulations for testing inspection, approval and maintenance of containers *Unless rejected by 5 Contracting Parties

Title of Convention	Date of adoption	Requirements for entry into force	Time from fulfillment to entry into force	Date of entry into force	Contracting Parties at 1.1.84	Is tacit acceptance procedure included?	AMENDMENTS AND PROTOCOLS			Notes
							Year of adoption	Date of entry into force	Contracting Parties at 1.1.84	
Convention on the International Regulations for Preventing Collisions at Sea (COLREG)	20 Oct. 1972	15 States with not less than 65% of world fleet by number of ships or gross tonnage	1 year	15 July 1977	86 97.27%	Yes	1981	1 June 1983	–	These regulations replace those adopted in 1960 and annexed to The Final Act of the 1960 SOLAS conference.
Convention on the International Maritime Satellite Organization (INMARSAT) and Operating Agreement	3 Sept. 1976	States representing 95% of initial investment shares	60 days	16 July 1979	40	No	–	–	–	
Torremolinos International Convention for the Safety of Fishing Vessels (SFV)	2 Apr. 1977	15 States with not less than 50% of world fishing fleet of 24 m in length and over	1 year	–	11	Yes	–	–	–	
International Convention on Standards of Training, Certification and Watchkeeping for Seafarers (STCW)	7 July 1978	25 States with not less than 50% of world gross tonnage	1 year	28 Apr. 1984	30 63.84%	Yes	–	–	–	
International Convention on Maritime Search and Rescue (SAR)	27 Apr. 1979	15 States	1 year	–	14	Yes	–	–	–	
International Convention Relating to Intervention on the High Seas in Cases of Oil Pollution Casualties (CSI)	29 Nov. 1969	15 States	90 days	6 May 1975	46	No	1973 (P)	30 Mar 1983	17	

Convention	Date of adoption	Entry into force requirements		Date of entry into force	No. of States		Protocol	Date	No.	Notes
Convention on the Prevention of Marine Pollution by Dumping of Wastes and Other Matter (LDC)	29 Dec. 1972	15 States	30 days	30 Aug. 1975	53	Yes	1978* 1978† 1980‡	- 11 Mar. 1979 11 Mar. 1981	8	This Convention was adopted under the auspices of the United Kingdom but IMO performs Secretariat functions. *Disputes †Incineration ‡List of substances
International Convention for the Prevention of Pollution from Ships, 1973 as modified by the Protocol of 1978 (MARPOL 73/78)	2 Nov. 1973 (Conv) 17 Feb. 1978 (Prot)	15 States with not less than 50% of world gross tonnage of merchant shipping. As above	1 year As above	2 Oct. 1983	25 67.52%	Yes	1978 (P)	(See note)		The 1978 Protocol absorbs the parent convention: States which ratify the Protocol automatically ratify the Convention as modified, but are able to defer implementation of Annex II until 2 Oct. 1986

LIABILITY AND COMPENSATION

Convention	Date of adoption	Entry into force requirements		Date of entry into force	No. of States		Protocol	Date	No.	Notes
International Convention on Civil Liability for Oil Pollution Damage (CLC)	29 Nov. 1969	8 States including 5 with not less than 1 million gt of tanker tonnage each	90 days	19 June 1975	54	No	1976 (P)	8 Apr. 1981	17	
Convention Relating to Civil Liability in the Field of Maritime Carriage of Nuclear Material (LNM)	17 Dec. 1971	5 States	90 days	15 July 1975	11	No	-	-	-	
International Convention on the Establishment of an International Fund for Compensation for Oil Pollution Damage (IFC)	18 Dec. 1971	8 States, which have received at least 750 m tons of contributing oil during previous calendar year	90 days	16 Oct. 1978	29	No	1976 (P)	-	12	
Athens Convention Relating to the Carriage of Passengers and Their Luggage by Sea (PAL)	13 Dec. 1974	10 States	90 days		9	No	1976 (P)	-	-	

Title of Convention	Date of adoption	Requirements for entry into force	Time from fulfillment to entry into force	Date of entry into force	Contracting Parties at 1.1.84	Is tacit acceptance procedure included?	AMENDMENTS AND PROTOCOLS			
							Year of adoption	Date of entry into force	Contracting Parties at 1.1.84	Notes
Convention on Limitation of Liability for Maritime Claims (LLMC)	19 Nov. 1976	12 States	1 year	-	7	No	-	-	-	
OTHER MATTERS										
Convention on Facilitation of International Maritime Traffic (FAL)	9 Dec. 1965	10 States	60 days	5 Mar. 1967	53	No	1969 1977 1973	1971 1978 2 June 1984	37	The 1969 and 1977 amendments only concern the Annex. Those adopted in 1973 affect Article VII, and are designed to introduce 'tacit acceptance'.
International Convention on Tonnage Measurement of Ships (TM)	23 June 1969	25 States with not less than 65% of world gross tonnage of merchant ships	2 years	18 July 1982	63 92.48%	No				
Instruments which are in force or applicable but which are no longer fully operational because they have been superseded by later Instruments										
PREVENTION OF MARINE POLLUTION										
International Convention for the Prevention of Pollution of the Sea by Oil (OILPOL)	12 May 1954	10 States including 5 with not less than 500,000 gt of tanker tonnage	1 year	26 July 1958	71 88.63%	No	1962 1969 1971* 1971†	1967 1978 - -	26 25	This Convention was adopted under the auspices of the United Kingdom but depositary functions were transferred to IMO when the Organization came into being in 1959. As far as Parties to MARPOL 73/78 are concerned, this Convention has been superseded. *Great Barrier Reef †Tank Size

MARITIME SAFETY

										Remarks
International Convention for the Safety of Life at Sea (SOLAS)	17 June 1960	15 States including 7 with not less than 1 million gt of merchant shipping each	1 year	26 May 1965	101	No	1966 1967 1968 1969 1971 1973* 1973†	46 36 37 26 18 9 10		The amendments to this instrument have been incorporated in SOLAS 1974. It has been superseded as far as Contracting Parties to SOLAS 1974 are concerned. *General †Grain
International Regulations for Preventing Collisions at Sea 1960	17 June 1960	Individual acceptances	-	Applied from 1 Sept. 1965	73	No				The regulations were adopted at the 1960 SOLAS Conference and annexed to the Final Act

8. STATUS OF TOKYO ROUND MTN AGREEMENT SIGNATURES AND ACCEPTANCES

(GATT and Non-GATT Members as of January 1, 1985)

GATT Member	Tariff Protocol	Supplement	Standards	Procurement	Subsidies	Meat	Dairy	Customs Valuation	Cus. Val. Protocol	Licensing	Aircraft	Anti-dumping
Argentina	1		3			1	1	2	2	3		
Australia		1			2	1	1	1	1	1		1
Austria	1		1	1	1	1	1	1	1	1	1	1
Brazil		1	1		1	1		2	1			1
Canada	1	1	1	1	1	1		2	1	1	2	1
Chile		1	1		1					1		
Czechoslovakia	1		1							1		1
Dominican Republic		1										
Egypt		1	3		1	3	3			1	3	3
European Economic Community:	1	1	1	4	4	4	4	4	4	4	1	4
Belgium	1	1	1								1	
Denmark	5		5								5	
France	1		1								1	
Germany	1		1								1	
Greece			3								3	
Ireland	1		1								1	
Italy	1		1								3	
Luxembourg	1		1								1	
Netherlands	6		1								1	
United Kingdom	1		1	1	1	7		1	1	1	1	1
Finland	1		1	1	1	1	1	1	1	1		1
Haiti		1										
Hong Kong			1	1	1			1	1	1	1	1
Hungary	1		1			1	1	1	1	1		1
Iceland	1											
India		1	1		1			2	2	1		1
Indonesia		1										
Israel	3	1		1								
Ivory Coast		1										
Jamaica	1											
Japan	1		1	1	1	1	1	1	1	1	1	1
Korea		1	1		1			2	2			
Malaysia		1										
New Zealand	1		1		2	1	1	2	2	1		
Norway	1		1	1	1	1	1	1	1	1	1	1
Pakistan		1	1		1					1		
Peru		1										
Philippines		1								1		
Poland	1					1	1					1
Romania	1		1		1		1	1	1	1	1	1
Rwanda			1									
Singapore		1	1	1						1		1
South Africa	1					1	1	1	1	1		
Spain	1	1	1		2			1	1			1
Sweden	1		1	1	1	1	1	1	1	1	1	1
Switzerland	1		1	1	1	1	1	1	1	1	1	1
United States	1		1	1	1	1	1	1	1	1	1	1
Uruguay		1			1	1	1					
Yugoslavia	1		1		3	1		1	1	1		1
Zaire		1										
Non-GATT Member												
Bulgaria					1	1						
Guatemala						1						
Paraguay						3						
Tunisia			1			1						

1. Accepted.
2. Accepted with reservation.
3. Subject to ratification.
4. Accepted for member states.
5. Accepted except with respect to Faroe Islands.
6. Accepted except with respect to Netherlands Antilles.
7. Accepted with respect to Belize.

APPENDIX E: STATISTICAL AND FINANCIAL DATA

1. U. S. EXPORTS OF DOMESTICALLY PRODUCED MERCHANDISE, SELECTED PRODUCTS: 1970-83

[**In millions of dollars.** Totals and subtotals include data for commodities not shown separately. Beginning 1975, exports include nonmonetary gold. Commodity data beginning 1978 are not strictly comparable with previous years due to changes in export classifications; see source for changes. For 1977, adjustments have been made to the subtotals and to certain commodities to provide greater comparability with later years; and beginning 1980, includes trade of Virgin Islands with foreign countries (see footnote 1 for exception). "N.e.c." means not elsewhere classified. See also *Historical Statistics, Colonial Times to 1970*, series U 274-294]

COMMODITY GROUP	1970	1975	1976	1977	1978	1979	1980	1981	1982	1983
U.S. merchandise	**42,590**	**106,561**	**113,666**	**119,005**	**141,126**	**178,578**	[1] **216,668**	**228,961**	**207,158**	**195,969**
Food and live animals	**4,356**	**15,484**	**15,710**	**14,116**	**18,311**	**22,245**	**27,744**	**30,291**	**23,950**	**24,166**
Meat and preparations	175	528	798	797	958	1,127	1,293	1,482	1,285	1,191
Meat, fresh, chilled, or frozen	147	491	759	750	894	1,057	1,217	1,389	1,194	1,110
Dairy products and eggs	137	134	128	189	190	161	255	433	409	373
Grains and preparations	2,596	11,642	10,911	8,755	11,634	14,450	18,079	19,457	14,747	15,152
Wheat and wheat flour	1,112	5,293	4,040	2,883	4,532	5,491	6,586	8,073	6,869	6,509
Rice	314	858	629	730	929	850	1,285	1,526	997	926
Coarse grains	1,072	5,272	6,023	4,913	5,920	7,804	9,866	9,501	6,420	7,231
Corn	824	4,448	5,223	4,139	5,301	7,022	8,570	8,014	5,682	6,480
Grain sorghums	196	699	642	604	531	686	1,080	1,174	720	747
Fruits and nuts	406	871	976	1,080	1,335	1,525	1,938	1,983	1,778	1,701
Fruit, fresh	164	404	434	458	530	624	716	802	730	761
Vegetables	178	406	559	517	554	605	992	1,131	937	744
Feed for animals	497	987	1,358	1,572	1,921	2,317	2,878	2,739	2,473	2,802
Beverages and tobacco	**702**	**1,308**	**1,524**	**1,847**	**2,293**	**2,337**	**2,663**	**2,915**	**3,026**	**2,813**
Tobacco and manufactures	679	1,253	1,457	1,732	2,125	2,148	2,426	2,723	2,845	2,647
Leaf tobacco	481	852	922	1,094	1,358	1,184	1,334	1,457	1,547	1,462
Cigarettes	159	368	510	615	749	909	1,055	1,229	1,235	1,126
Crude materials, inedible, exc. fuels	**4,605**	**9,784**	**10,891**	**13,086**	**15,555**	**20,755**	**23,791**	**20,993**	**19,248**	**18,596**
Hides and skins, except fur skins	145	295	522	578	695	992	694	700	778	807
Soybeans	1,216	2,865	3,315	4,393	5,210	5,708	5,883	6,200	6,240	5,925
Synthetic rubber	176	261	329	327	369	578	695	624	553	543
Wood in the rough [2]	366	751	945	1,178	1,376	1,782	2,002	1,426	1,522	1,366
Wood shaped or simply worked	193	413	563	551	618	1,015	1,060	933	811	914
Lumber, softwood	162	342	471	444	452	778	778	653	576	602
Woodpulp	464	875	844	875	817	1,104	1,652	1,661	1,415	1,432
Textile fibers and wastes	543	1,345	1,426	1,899	2,302	3,046	3,929	3,402	2,817	2,593
Raw cotton, excluding linters	372	991	1,049	1,530	1,740	2,198	2,864	2,260	1,955	1,817
Ores and metal scrap	940	1,355	1,284	1,290	1,839	3,325	4,518	2,718	2,174	2,276
Iron and steel scrap	447	780	634	413	698	1,142	1,226	639	610	637
Ores and scrap, nonferrous base	397	461	499	600	893	1,920	1,223	899	690	451
Mineral fuels and related materials	**1,595**	**4,470**	**4,226**	**4,184**	**3,881**	**5,616**	**7,982**	**10,279**	**12,729**	**9,500**
Coal	962	3,259	2,910	2,655	2,046	3,328	4,621	5,909	5,987	4,051
Petroleum and products	488	908	998	1,280	1,564	1,914	2,833	3,696	5,947	4,557
Lubricating oils	175	275	292	305	467	639	733	799	345	667
Animal and vegetable oils and fats	**493**	**944**	**978**	**1,309**	**1,521**	**1,845**	**1,946**	**1,750**	**1,541**	**1,459**
Tallow, inedible	176	299	377	504	516	655	677	645	572	568
Soybean oil	192	266	238	440	560	776	689	474	486	447
Chemicals and related products	**3,826**	**8,691**	**9,959**	**10,812**	**12,623**	**17,306**	**20,740**	**21,187**	**19,890**	**19,751**
Chemical elements and compounds	1,642	3,623	4,408	4,811	5,297	7,704	2,106	2,285	1,969	1,838
Dyeing, tanning, coloring materials	137	244	310	352	386	450	490	524	494	491
Medicinal, pharmaceutical prod	420	866	997	1,081	1,404	1,591	1,932	2,165	2,275	2,494
Fertilizers, manufactured	178	1,083	613	704	1,091	1,404	2,265	1,735	1,386	1,267
Plastic materials and resins [3]	653	1,166	1,672	1,838	2,088	3,241	3,884	3,809	3,650	3,732
Machinery and transport equip	**17,882**	**45,668**	**49,501**	**50,248**	**59,268**	**70,491**	**84,628**	**95,736**	**87,148**	**82,578**
Machinery [4]	11,685	29,215	32,113	32,630	38,105	45,914	57,263	64,426	59,821	54,695
Power generating machinery	1,405	3,551	3,662	3,619	4,797	6,839	8,428	9,465	9,461	8,718
Agricultural machinery	182	704	707	717	844	1,088	1,295	1,420	1,127	832
Tractors and parts	750	2,126	2,223	2,064	2,316	2,720	2,150	2,296	1,760	1,389
Electronic computers, parts and accessories	1,236	2,228	2,588	3,264	4,359	5,671	7,763	8,741	9,159	10,599
Other office machines [5]	311	411	349	621	647	804	946	1,069	1,048	1,070
Metalworking machinery	396	922	953	730	1,188	1,391	1,756	2,158	1,611	1,121
Metalcutting machines	213	344	290	258	338	350	397	574	345	204
Textile, leather machinery	273	486	457	423	485	628	693	685	554	453
Construction, excavating, and maintenance equipment	434	1,277	1,381	1,352	1,318	1,234	2,076	2,189	1,553	762
Materials handling equipment	607	1,846	1,859	1,664	1,457	1,744	2,243	2,438	1,592	946
Air-conditioning and refrigerating equipment	397	928	1,055	1,245	1,562	1,468	1,523	1,694	1,487	1,268
Pumping equipment, incl. parts	241	543	606	630	729	893	1,091	1,248	1,246	1,003
Pipe valves and parts	196	458	518	548	610	657	829	936	854	716
Power machinery, switchgear	611	1,709	2,139	2,301	2,690	3,140	3,254	3,835	3,624	3,221
Generators, generating sets	117	548	800	889	569	487	619	745	686	376
Transforming, converting, transmission apparatus	156	417	487	518	609	553	914	1,116	1,325	926
Telecommunications apparatus	660	1,574	1,997	2,360	2,689	2,957	3,454	3,856	3,864	3,804
Radio, television apparatus	576	1,339	1,729	1,827	1,831	2,148	2,238	2,525	2,430	590
Domestic electrical equipment	119	359	463	523	610	666	796	841	673	611
Transport equipment [6]	6,197	16,452	17,388	17,619	21,163	24,577	27,366	31,310	26,668	27,298
Railway vehicles	91	462	392	305	305	384	452	488	433	402
Road motor vehicles, parts [6]	3,245	9,290	10,132	10,887	12,150	13,904	13,117	14,733	12,751	13,492
Automobiles, nonmilitary, new	822	2,852	3,228	3,568	3,573	4,611	3,919	3,919	2,860	4,200
Trucks and tractor trucks, commercial, new	452	1,712	1,509	1,513	1,504	1,583	1,467	1,618	1,186	1,042
Parts, accessories, commercial	1,603	3,620	4,213	4,673	5,682	6,147	6,058	7,395	6,939	7,531
Aircraft, parts, and accessories	2,656	6,136	6,104	5,874	8,204	9,719	12,816	14,738	11,775	12,189
Civilian aircraft	1,528	3,169	3,204	2,747	3,616	6,177	8,256	8,613	4,848	7,531
Other manufactured goods	**7,636**	**16,592**	**17,781**	**19,091**	**22,644**	**28,879**	**38,602**	**37,381**	**32,700**	**30,097**
Tires and tubes	186	544	491	338	280	353	511	584	372	304
Paper and manufactures	622	1,447	1,624	1,517	1,597	1,967	2,831	2,961	2,653	2,553
Paper and paperboard	526	1,131	1,291	1,162	1,187	1,430	2,162	2,192	1,877	1,843
Nonmetallic mineral mfrs., n.e.c.	475	964	1,166	1,275	1,597	1,949	2,209	2,194	1,804	1,770
Metals and manufactures	2,978	5,661	5,180	5,149	6,101	5,583	8,948	7,363	6,075	5,477
Iron and steelmill products [7]	1,188	2,382	1,833	1,608	1,646	2,227	2,998	2,801	2,101	1,415
Plates and sheets	335	327	338	272	402	567	936	663	372	295
Tubes, pipes, and fittings	226	1,412	778	677	798	1,077	1,080	1,252	1,214	731
Silver bullion, refined	31	104	33	39	56	238	1,327	181	106	169
Nonferrous base metals	893	1,090	1,088	1,058	1,048	1,745	2,964	2,046	1,768	1,606
Copper	358	333	282	196	310	425	434	388	322	386
Aluminum	358	433	469	480	555	899	2,022	1,297	1,026	1,010
Metal manufactures, n.e.c.	744	1,891	2,089	2,399	3,103	3,431	4,205	4,769	3,981	3,443
Tools for hand or machine	204	480	498	558	603	693	856	932	810	671
Textiles, other than clothing	603	1,624	1,971	1,970	2,225	3,189	3,632	3,619	2,784	2,368
Textile yarn and thread	145	298	374	417	370	621	753	902	711	533
Cotton broad-woven fabrics	103	376	499	438	426	626	566	349	253	201
Textile fabrics, woven, exc. cotton	151	386	423	399	472	721	832	797	522	430
Clothing	198	403	510	608	677	931	1,183	1,208	931	796
Professional, scientific, and controlling instruments [8]	857	1,792	1,951	3,241	3,904	4,289	5,256	5,980	6,003	5,856
Photographic supplies	250	606	703	813	1,073	1,227	1,507	1,501	1,396	1,366
Printed matter	327	548	607	668	812	956	1,097	1,297	1,341	1,324
Other transactions	**1,496**	**3,621**	**3,097**	**4,314**	**5,030**	**9,103**	**8,496**	**8,428**	**6,924**	**7,009**
Firearms of war and ammunition	682	1,361	1,261	1,617	1,951	1,854	2,006	2,165	3,261	3,092
Shipments of $500 or less, estimates	692	1,572	1,190	1,244	1,487	1,796	2,119	2,368	1,698	1,597

[1] Includes revisions not carried to commodity groups; therefore commodity groups will not add to total. [2] Beginning 1977, includes pulp wood chips, formerly classified in "Other manufactured goods" under "Wood and manufactures." [3] Beginning 1977, includes rubber materials, formerly classified in "Other manufactured goods" under "Rubber manufactures." [4] Includes parts for tractors. [5] Beginning 1978, includes photocopy apparatus, formerly classified in "Other manufactured goods" under "Photographic and motion picture equipment." [6] Excludes parts for tractors. [7] Excludes pig iron. [8] Beginning 1977, electric measuring and controlling instruments are included in "Other manufactured goods" under "Professional, scientific, and controlling instruments"; formerly classified under "Machinery."

Source: U.S. Bureau of the Census, *Highlights of U.S. Export and Import Trade*, Report FT 990, monthly. Also in U.S. Dept. of Commerce, International Trade Administration, *Overseas Business Reports, U.S. Foreign Trade*, annual.

2. DISTRIBUTION OF U. S. DOMESTIC EXPORTS AND GENERAL IMPORTS BY BROAD COMMODITY GROUPS: 1960-83

COMMODITY GROUP	1960	1965	1970	1975	1976	1977	1978	1979	1980	1981	1982	1983
Exports:												
Food and live animals	13.2	14.7	10.2	14.6	13.9	11.9	13.0	12.5	12.8	13.2	11.6	12.1
Beverages and tobacco	2.4	1.9	1.6	1.2	1.3	1.6	1.6	1.3	1.2	1.3	1.5	1.4
Crude materials, inedible [1]	13.7	10.5	10.8	9.2	9.6	11.0	11.0	11.6	11.0	9.2	9.3	9.3
Mineral fuels and related materials	4.1	3.5	3.7	4.2	3.7	3.5	2.8	3.1	3.7	4.5	6.1	4.7
Chemicals	8.7	8.8	9.0	8.2	8.8	9.1	8.9	9.7	9.6	9.3	9.6	9.8
Machinery and transport equipment	34.3	37.3	42.0	43.0	43.7	42.2	42.0	39.5	39.1	41.8	42.1	41.2
Other manufactured goods	18.7	18.0	17.9	15.6	15.7	16.0	16.1	16.2	17.8	16.3	15.8	15.2
General imports:												
Food and live animals	19.9	16.1	13.5	8.8	8.5	8.5	7.9	7.4	6.4	5.8	5.9	6.0
Beverages and tobacco	2.6	2.6	2.1	1.5	1.3	1.1	1.3	1.2	1.1	1.2	1.4	1.3
Crude materials, inedible [1]	18.3	14.5	8.3	5.8	5.8	5.7	5.4	5.2	4.3	4.3	3.5	3.7
Mineral fuels and related materials	10.5	10.4	7.7	27.5	28.2	30.2	24.5	29.1	33.9	31.2	26.8	22.5
Chemicals	5.3	3.6	3.6	3.8	4.0	3.4	3.7	3.6	3.5	3.6	3.9	4.2
Machinery and transport equipment	9.7	13.8	28.0	24.4	24.7	24.7	27.7	26.0	24.7	26.6	30.1	33.4
Other manufactured goods	30.3	35.1	33.3	24.9	25.0	23.8	26.9	24.8	22.9	24.3	25.1	31.7

[1] Excludes fuels.

Source: U.S. Bureau of the Census, *Highlights of U.S. Export and Import Trade*, Report FT 990, monthly. Also in U.S. Dept. of, Commerce, International Trade Administration, *Overseas Business Reports, U.S. Foreign Trade*, annual.

3. U. S. MERCHANDISE EXPORTS AND IMPORTS FOR CONSUMPTION BY CUSTOMS REGION AND DISTRICT: 1970-83

[**In billions of dollars.** Exports are f.a.s. (free alongside ship) value all years; imports are on customs value basis for years 1982 to present; f.a.s. value basis prior to 1982. *See Historical Statistics, Colonial Times to 1970,* series U 264-273, for related data]

CUSTOMS REGION AND DISTRICT	EXPORTS						IMPORTS FOR CONSUMPTION					
	1970	1975	1980	1981	1982	1983	1970	1975	1980	1981	1982	1983
Total [1]	**43.2**	**107.6**	**220.8**	**233.7**	**212.3**	**200.5**	**40.0**	**96.5**	**244.0**	**259.0**	**242.3**	**258.0**
Boston, MA region	**3.3**	**7.8**	**14.3**	**15.4**	**13.7**	**14.9**	**5.7**	**9.9**	**21.6**	**24.4**	**24.3**	**27.5**
Portland, ME	.1	.3	4.3	4.2	.5	.7	.3	.8	1.6	2.2	11.8	1.8
St. Albans, VT	.2	.4	.7	.7	.7	.7	.4	.6	1.6	1.8	1.8	2.0
Boston, MA	.4	.8	.8	.9	2.7	2.6	1.0	2.2	5.0	5.8	5.4	6.4
Providence, RI	(Z)	(Z)	2.5	2.4	.2	.1	.1	.2	.6	.8	1.0	1.0
Bridgeport, CT	(Z)	(Z)	.2	.1	.1	.1	.2	.4	.9	1.2	1.1	1.2
Ogdensburg, NY	.9	2.3	3.8	4.0	3.1	3.7	1.1	1.8	4.6	4.7	4.7	5.6
Buffalo, NY	1.7	3.9	6.3	11.2	6.3	7.0	2.7	3.7	7.4	7.9	8.4	9.2
New York, NY region	**10.0**	**18.7**	**38.9**	**35.8**	**31.2**	**29.0**	**10.1**	**18.1**	**43.4**	**44.1**	**41.2**	**46.5**
Baltimore, MD region	**3.9**	**12.5**	**21.5**	**22.2**	**21.5**	**16.8**	**3.9**	**11.9**	**26.8**	**26.9**	**24.3**	**23.3**
Philadelphia, PA	.7	2.2	3.2	3.5	3.1	2.3	1.9	6.5	15.6	16.5	14.3	13.4
Baltimore, MD	1.3	4.8	9.0	9.0	8.6	7.1	1.4	3.2	6.0	5.8	5.4	5.5
Norfolk, VA	1.8	5.0	8.9	9.3	9.3	7.1	.6	1.8	4.7	4.3	4.3	4.1
Washington, DC	.1	.5	.3	.5	.5	.4	.1	.2	.4	.4	.4	.3
Miami, FL region	**2.0**	**6.2**	**17.6**	**19.8**	**18.5**	**15.7**	**2.4**	**6.4**	**19.0**	**20.3**	**19.7**	**21.3**
Wilmington, NC	.2	.5	1.3	1.6	1.6	1.3	.2	.7	1.1	1.3	1.3	1.3
Charleston, SC	.2	.8	3.1	3.7	2.8	2.5	.3	.8	1.8	2.2	1.8	2.3
Savannah, GA	.4	.9	2.4	2.7	2.7	2.9	.3	.8	2.2	2.9	2.9	3.5
Tampa, FL	.2	1.3	2.8	2.7	2.2	2.1	.6	1.4	3.7	4.4	4.1	4.6
San Juan, PR	.1	.4	.9	1.0	1.3	1.3	.6	1.9	3.7	3.5	2.9	3.5
Virgin Islands	(NA)	(NA)	.1	.1	.5	.2	(NA)	(NA)	4.1	3.6	4.0	2.6
Miami, FL	.7	2.3	6.9	7.9	7.4	5.5	.4	1.0	2.6	2.8	3.1	3.3
New Orleans, LA region	**3.9**	**11.3**	**22.0**	**23.3**	**21.3**	**19.6**	**1.6**	**6.8**	**25.5**	**26.1**	**20.4**	**16.3**
Mobile, AL	.5	1.4	2.6	2.4	2.1	1.4	.3	1.0	3.0	3.9	2.3	3.2
New Orleans, LA	3.5	9.9	19.5	20.9	19.2	18.2	1.4	5.9	22.5	22.2	18.1	13.0
Houston, TX region	**4.0**	**12.9**	**28.3**	**31.5**	**27.3**	**22.5**	**1.8**	**8.8**	**34.7**	**36.2**	**30.0**	**28.1**
Port Arthur, TX	.5	1.1	2.0	2.0	2.0	1.5	.1	1.6	9.4	7.6	4.2	5.0
Galveston, TX	.7	2.0	3.6	3.7	(²)	(²)	.2	2.2	10.1	10.2	(²)	(²)
Laredo, TX	1.1	3.1	8.3	9.9	6.1	4.4	.4	1.1	2.7	3.0	3.2	4.0
El Paso, TX	.1	.6	1.8	1.8	1.3	1.4	.2	.5	1.4	1.7	1.8	1.9
Houston/Galveston, TX	1.7	6.1	12.1	13.5	17.5	14.6	1.0	3.5	10.0	12.5	19.8	15.7
Dallas/Fort Worth, TX	(NA)	(NA)	.5	.5	.5	.6	(NA)	(NA)	1.2	1.4	1.3	1.5
Los Angeles, CA region	**2.5**	**6.4**	**17.0**	**19.6**	**18.4**	**18.7**	**3.3**	**8.6**	**22.2**	**24.4**	**24.6**	**28.3**
San Diego, CA	.3	.7	1.4	1.9	1.4	.9	.2	.6	1.0	1.1	1.1	1.2
Nogales, AZ	.1	.3	.8	.9	.7	.6	.2	.4	1.2	1.4	1.7	1.7
Los Angeles, CA	2.1	5.4	14.8	16.9	16.3	17.1	2.9	7.6	20.0	21.9	22.0	25.4
San Francisco, CA region	**4.9**	**11.5**	**29.3**	**30.6**	**26.6**	**27.6**	**3.6**	**10.6**	**25.0**	**26.6**	**26.5**	**30.2**
San Francisco, CA	1.8	4.2	10.6	11.3	11.4	11.3	1.3	3.5	8.3	8.7	9.5	11.2
Portland, OR	.8	2.0	3.8	3.9	3.3	3.7	.4	.8	2.6	2.8	2.6	2.8
Seattle, WA	1.9	4.2	12.0	12.3	8.9	10.0	1.3	4.0	9.2	10.0	9.3	9.9
Anchorage, AK	.1	.3	1.0	1.2	1.3	1.1	.1	.4	.2	.2	.3	.4
Honolulu, HI	.1	.1	.2	.2	.2	.2	.2	.8	1.8	1.5	1.7	1.8
Great Falls, MT	.2	.7	1.8	1.7	1.4	1.2	.3	1.3	3.2	3.6	3.4	3.8
Chicago, IL region	**6.2**	**15.3**	**25.2**	**28.2**	**24.8**	**27.6**	**7.3**	**15.1**	**25.6**	**29.7**	**31.0**	**35.7**
Pembina, ND	.4	1.5	2.3	2.7	2.1	2.0	.5	1.3	3.0	3.3	3.1	2.5
Minneapolis, MN	(Z)	(Z)	.1	.1	.1	.2	.1	.1	.3	.4	.5	.5
Duluth, MN	.3	1.0	1.5	1.4	1.0	1.0	.5	1.5	3.0	2.8	2.6	2.9
Milwaukee, WI	.1	.2	.4	.3	.2	.2	.1	.2	.4	.4	.5	.8
Detroit, MI	4.1	9.8	14.6	17.1	15.1	17.9	4.2	8.2	12.7	15.2	16.3	19.9
Chicago, IL	.8	1.5	4.2	4.6	4.3	4.7	1.2	2.2	4.1	4.5	5.2	5.8
Cleveland, OH	.5	1.3	1.8	1.8	1.8	1.7	.6	.9	1.5	2.0	1.7	2.1
St. Louis, MO	(Z)	.1	.2	.2	.1	.1	.1	.3	.9	1.1	1.1	.8

NA Not available. Z Less than $50 million. [1] Includes data on low-value shipments not distributed by customs region. [2] Beginning 1982, included with Houston.

Source: U.S. Bureau of the Census, *Highlights of U.S. Export and Import Trade,* FT 990, monthly.

4. EXPORTS AND IMPORTS OF SELECTED NATIONS, BETWEEN 1965 AND 1984

[Billions of U.S. dollars]

Area and country	1965	1970	1975	1980	1981	1982	1983	1984 [1]
	Exports, f.o.b. [2]							
Developed countries [3]	131.3	226.6	584.9	1,284.5	1,259.3	1,192.9	1,179.8	1,288.9
United States	27.5	43.2	108.1	220.8	233.7	212.3	200.5	218.0
Canada	8.4	16.7	34.1	67.7	72.7	70.5	76.7	89.6
Japan	8.5	19.3	55.8	130.4	151.5	138.4	147.0	168.8
European Community [4]	65.2	113.5	299.6	665.8	612.4	590.0	575.2	615.5
France	10.2	18.1	53.1	116.0	106.4	96.7	94.9	100.1
West Germany	17.9	34.2	90.2	192.9	176.1	176.4	169.4	170.1
Italy	7.2	13.2	34.8	77.7	75.3	73.5	72.7	72.7
United Kingdom	13.8	19.4	43.4	110.1	102.2	97.0	91.6	92.7
Other developed countries	21.7	33.8	87.4	199.7	188.9	181.8	180.3	197.0
Developing countries	34.5	52.5	207.8	557.1	541.3	462.8	431.1	470.6
OPEC [5]	10.3	16.9	111.5	298.9	278.1	215.4	176.4	185.2
Other	24.2	35.6	96.3	258.2	263.2	247.4	254.8	285.3
Communist countries [6]	23.2	34.9	90.3	201.7	205.2	223.9	235.7	244.6
U.S.S.R.	8.2	12.8	33.4	76.4	79.4	87.2	91.7	93.5
Eastern Europe	11.8	18.2	45.3	86.2	83.8	91.4	96.7	100.0
China	2.0	2.2	7.1	18.9	21.5	22.9	23.7	26.6
TOTAL	189.0	314.0	883.0	2,043.3	2,005.8	1,879.6	1,846.6	2,004.1
	Imports, c.i.f. [7]							
Developed countries [3]	138.7	238.0	618.9	1,428.9	1,361.5	1,278.7	1,254.5	1,405.0
United States	23.2	42.7	105.9	257.0	273.4	254.9	269.9	327.1
Canada	8.7	14.3	36.2	62.8	70.3	58.4	65.1	77.6
Japan	8.2	18.9	57.9	141.3	142.9	131.5	126.4	138.4
European Community [4]	70.5	118.7	306.6	729.1	645.4	615.4	590.7	626.1
France	10.4	19.1	54.0	134.9	121.0	115.7	105.4	105.9
West Germany	17.6	29.9	74.9	188.0	163.9	155.4	152.9	155.6
Italy	7.4	15.0	38.5	99.7	91.1	86.2	80.4	81.6
United Kingdom	16.1	21.9	53.3	115.5	102.7	99.7	100.2	106.2
Other developed countries	28.2	43.4	112.4	238.7	229.6	218.5	202.5	235.8
Developing countries	36.0	53.1	180.1	440.8	488.6	463.1	421.8	432.5
OPEC [5]	6.4	9.9	52.1	133.0	156.5	166.1	140.2	132.9
Other	29.6	43.2	128.0	307.8	332.1	297.0	281.6	299.6
Communist countries [6]	22.5	34.1	100.8	200.4	200.0	203.1	213.0	220.2
U.S.S.R.	8.0	11.7	37.1	68.5	73.2	77.8	80.4	80.5
Eastern Europe	11.6	18.5	51.3	91.2	87.5	87.1	91.7	95.8
China	1.8	2.2	7.4	20.7	19.3	17.9	19.6	21.9
TOTAL	197.2	325.2	899,8	2,070.1	2,050.1	1,944.9	1,889.3	2,057.7

[1] Preliminary estimates.
[2] Free-on-board ship value.
[3] Includes the OECD countries, South Africa, Israel, and non-OECD Europe.
[4] Includes Belgium-Luxembourg, Denmark, Greece, Ireland, and the Netherlands, not shown separately.
[5] Includes Algeria, Ecuador, Gabon, Indonesia, Iran, Iraq, Kuwait, Libya, Nigeria, Qatar, Saudi Arabia, United Arab Emirates, and Venezuela.
[6] Includes North Korea, Vietnam, Albania, Cuba, Mongolia, and Yugoslavia, not shown separately.
[7] Cost, insurance, and freight value, except Eastern Europe (except Hungary) and U.S.S.R., which are f.o.b. (free on board).

Sources: International Monetary Fund, Organization for Economic Cooperation and Development, and Council of Economic Advisers.

5. EXPORTS AND IMPORTS OF LEADING COMMODITIES: 1983

[**In millions of dollars.** Includes nonmonetary gold. Exports are f.a.s. (free alongside ship) transaction value basis; imports are customs value basis]

SELECTED COMMODITIES	Total [1]	WESTERN HEMISPHERE			WESTERN EUROPE			ASIA	
		Total [1]	Canada	Mexico	Total [1]	Germany, Fed. Rep. of	United Kingdom	Total	Japan
Domestic exports, total	**195,969**	**62,007**	**36,917**	**8,757**	**54,497**	**8,444**	**10,270**	**62,813**	**21,520**
Agricultural commodities	36,108	7,042	1,830	1,942	10,116	1,529	812	13,977	6,241
Nonagricultural commodities	159,862	54,964	35,087	6,815	44,381	6,915	9,457	48,835	15,279
Food and live animals	24,166	5,599	1,496	1,424	5,009	777	488	9,597	4,294
Meat and meat preparations	1,199	247	97	26	177	11	27	711	574
Grain and cereal preparation	15,152	3,129	143	1,148	1,821	73	112	6,777	2,493
Wheat and wheat flour	6,509	1,222	1	-	301	11	1	2,913	589
Corn	6,480	1,085	37	676	1,255	54	98	3,064	1,764
Beverages and tobacco	2,813	225	68	9	1,169	187	86	1,113	442
Crude materials, excluding fuels	18,596	2,973	1,588	790	7,064	1,135	777	7,579	1,485
Soybeans	5,925	399	61	239	3,176	423	123	2,014	1,210
Logs and lumber	2,104	373	275	157	355	100	39	1,300	900
Metal ores and scrap	2,276	536	393	108	884	85	283	842	527
Mineral fuels and related materials	9,500	2,942	1,692	262	2,976	113	174	3,134	1,994
Bituminous coal	4,008	1,118	886	7	1,620	82	66	1,194	1,002
Chemicals and related products	19,751	6,123	2,546	1,068	5,893	902	830	6,243	2,607
Manufactured goods	14,852	6,365	3,777	910	3,173	518	739	4,323	1,360
Textile yarn, fabric, articles	2,368	1,042	591	88	562	66	133	539	98
Iron and steel mill products	1,415	724	423	147	157	16	40	422	33
Machinery	54,309	16,539	9,754	2,698	16,622	2,875	4,184	16,829	3,251
Power generating	8,718	3,254	2,321	345	2,629	280	408	2,084	517
Agricultural [2]	1,589	858	754	282	256	45	44	236	24
General industrial	7,980	2,895	1,757	403	1,705	309	391	2,663	319
Office machinery and computers	11,669	2,303	1,560	228	6,103	1,115	1,699	2,533	905
Telecommunications	3,804	1,130	442	358	1,017	194	294	1,325	208
Electrical [3]	11,936	3,416	1,741	989	2,801	606	767	5,305	738
Transport equipment	28,269	13,139	10,912	818	5,120	699	1,063	5,883	1,543
Automobile, motor vehicles [4]	14,463	11,352	10,136	549	1,059	229	190	1,353	145
Aircraft and parts	12,189	1,424	685	182	3,904	445	852	3,967	1,345
Professional, scientific, and controlling instruments	5,856	1,240	793	154	2,253	414	575	1,819	583
General imports, total	**258,048**	**93,872**	**52,130**	**16,776**	**53,884**	**12,695**	**12,470**	**91,464**	**41,183**
Agricultural commodities	16,534	7,598	1,502	1,279	3,645	453	155	2,621	169
Nonagricultural commodities	241,514	86,275	50,628	15,339	50,240	12,243	12,315	88,843	41,014
Food and live animals	15,412	8,709	1,983	1,554	2,096	206	136	2,140	337
Meat and meat preparations	2,034	668	333	4	306	3	2	12	6
Fish, including shellfish	3,594	1,995	806	417	529	5	30	786	219
Vegetables and fruit	2,920	1,911	125	644	347	63	5	560	44
Coffee	2,590	1,843	(Z)	277	46	26	(Z)	248	(Z)
Beverages and tobacco	3,408	809	465	98	2,408	208	551	102	24
Crude materials, excluding fuels	9,590	6,543	5,276	257	711	96	71	1,064	75
Paper base stocks	1,508	1,442	1,398	6	43	(Z)	(Z)	(Z)	(Z)
Wood	2,719	2,664	2,610	6	34	1	(Z)	49	(Z)
Metal ores and scrap	2,500	1,459	694	94	102	31	16	76	9
Mineral fuels and related materials	57,952	28,707	8,321	8,569	6,579	94	4,170	11,491	11
Crude petroleum	36,809	13,686	2,665	7,521	4,762	(Z)	3,931	10,149	-
Petroleum products	15,517	10,147	1,330	520	1,800	94	232	1,296	11
Natural gas	5,530	4,801	4,264	507	17	(Z)	7	44	(Z)
Chemicals and related products	10,779	3,474	2,390	352	5,020	1,255	1,036	1,627	1,099
Manufactured goods	34,833	12,130	8,512	1,183	9,295	1,676	1,882	11,541	5,222
Paper, paperboard	3,813	3,381	3,323	121	474	79	58	65	71
Iron and steel	6,338	1,493	853	191	2,076	554	164	2,523	1,931
Nonferrous metals	7,422	3,597	2,082	412	2,085	291	1,037	810	393
Machinery	46,975	9,393	5,141	3,232	10,465	3,674	2,110	26,952	15,323
Power generating	5,274	2,475	1,603	589	1,837	437	643	953	834
General industrial	4,837	933	784	163	1,993	671	323	1,867	1,194
Telecommunications	11,278	1,647	438	1,076	334	68	77	9,295	5,697
Electrical [3]	12,499	2,442	791	1,222	1,937	715	289	8,085	2,912
Office machinery and data processing equipment	6,759	832	617	178	886	272	152	5,027	3,247
Transport equipment	39,156	15,452	14,983	342	8,142	4,102	1,000	15,499	14,819
Automobiles, buses, trucks	28,736	10,330	10,315	14	5,534	3,566	420	12,867	12,845
New passenger cars	22,934	7,276	7,263	13	5,357	3,429	405	10,301	10,294
Motor vehicle parts	6,299	4,216	3,836	297	1,083	329	155	968	865
Clothing	9,583	809	103	189	613	40	96	8,035	340
Footwear	4,010	623	28	58	1,111	17	17	2,214	22

- Represents zero. Z Less than $500,000. [1] Includes countries and regions not shown separately. [2] Agricultural machinery and parts and tractors, excluding tractor parts. [3] Electrical machinery, apparatus, appliances, and parts. [4] Includes motor vehicle and tractor parts, except tires, engines, and electrical parts.

Source: U.S. Bureau of the Census, *Highlights of U.S. Export and Import Trade,* Report FT 990, December issue.

6. INDICES OF TOTAL VALUE, UNIT VALUE (AVERAGE PRICE), AND QUANTITY OF U. S. EXPORTS AND IMPORTS: 1970-83

[**1977 average = 100.** See headnote, table 1444. See also *Historical Statistics, Colonial Times to 1970,* series U 225-248]

ECONOMIC CLASS	INDEX OF EXPORTS OF U.S. MERCHANDISE							INDEX OF GENERAL IMPORTS						
	1970-1975, avg.	1975	1979	1980	1981	1982	1983	1970-1975, avg.	1975	1979	1980	1981	1982	1983
Total value	**57.3**	**89.7**	**151.3**	**183.6**	**194.1**	**175.6**	**166.2**	**46.6**	**66.5**	**142.1**	**165.5**	**179.1**	**167.4**	**177.1**
Foods:														
Crude	70.8	125.0	167.2	205.2	223.3	174.7	175.0	44.7	51.5	108.8	108.5	102.0	102.4	107.2
Manufactured	56.7	78.8	141.5	177.7	191.3	159.5	159.7	73.6	88.4	142.5	153.9	160.7	145.9	156.6
Materials, crude	78.8	116.5	143.7	170.0	166.2	160.7	139.4	25.0	57.8	137.5	180.5	179.7	136.8	114.3
Manufactures:														
Semi	64.9	90.8	219.4	266.5	245.0	218.2	208.7	52.5	69.1	136.9	150.8	161.2	144.0	165.9
Finished	55.1	87.9	138.6	168.2	186.3	171.6	162.5	54.4	70.2	150.5	169.1	195.6	204.2	229.6
Unit value	**67.4**	**92.8**	**121.6**	**138.1**	**150.8**	**152.5**	**154.1**	**59.8**	**89.4**	**128.7**	**161.4**	**170.3**	**167.5**	**160.6**
Foods:														
Crude	84.1	128.2	125.6	140.0	146.6	127.9	134.9	39.2	46.1	96.6	103.8	97.1	92.2	88.9
Manufactured	76.7	99.8	118.8	121.4	127.3	118.0	117.7	87.5	122.1	133.8	169.5	164.5	149.6	151.8
Materials, crude	58.3	88.4	115.5	122.1	125.0	116.7	117.0	46.1	86.0	137.7	224.2	249.0	232.4	210.4
Manufactures:														
Semi	69.7	100.9	133.6	167.6	166.2	154.7	150.5	57.4	91.9	142.0	171.3	172.6	157.9	152.8
Finished	67.0	87.4	119.4	134.8	154.2	165.7	168.4	66.6	92.8	123.1	134.9	142.2	147.6	143.5
Quantity	**82.3**	**96.6**	**124.5**	**132.9**	**128.8**	**115.1**	**107.8**	**77.4**	**74.4**	**110.4**	**102.5**	**105.2**	**99.9**	**110.3**
Foods:														
Crude	78.4	97.5	133.1	146.6	152.3	136.6	129.7	114.5	112.0	112.7	104.5	105.0	111.1	120.6
Manufactured	73.1	79.0	119.2	146.3	150.3	135.2	135.8	84.7	72.4	106.5	90.8	97.7	97.5	103.1
Materials, crude	88.8	88.1	124.5	139.3	132.9	137.7	119.1	53.3	67.3	99.8	80.5	72.2	58.9	54.3
Manufactures:														
Semi	92.0	90.0	164.3	159.1	147.4	141.0	138.6	92.4	75.2	96.5	88.1	93.4	91.2	108.6
Finished	79.9	100.6	116.1	124.7	120.8	103.6	96.5	81.0	75.7	122.2	125.4	137.6	138.3	160.0

Source: U.S. Bureau of the Census, *Indexes of U.S. Exports and Imports by Economic Class, 1919-1971,* and unpublished data.

7. U. S. MERCHANDISE TRADE BALANCE, BY COUNTRY: 1975-83

[**In millions of dollars, except percent.** Includes silver ore and bullion. Beginning 1980, data include nonmonetary gold and beginning 1981, data include trade of Virgin Islands with foreign countries, see footnote 2 for exception. Minus sign (−) denotes an excess of imports over exports. See *Historical Statistics, Colonial Times to 1970*, series U 317-352, for selected countries]

CONTINENT, AREA, AND COUNTRY	EXPORTS, DOMESTIC AND FOREIGN					GENERAL IMPORTS					MERCHANDISE TRADE BALANCE				
	1975	1980	1981	1982	1983	1975	1980	1981	1982	1983	1975	1980	1981	1982	1983
Total [1]	**107,592**	**[2] 220,783**	**233,739**	**212,275**	**200,538**	**96,902**	**244,871**	**261,305**	**243,952**	**258,048**	**+10,690**	**−24,088**	**−27,566**	**−31,677**	**−57,510**
Developed countries [3]	64,780	130,848	135,840	122,541	122,822	56,700	125,306	141,506	141,594	152,177	+8,080	+5,542	−5,666	−19,053	−29,355
Percent of total	60.2	59.3	58.1	57.7	61.2	58.5	51.2	54.2	58.0	59.0	(x)	(x)	(x)	(x)	(x)
Developing countries [3]	39,215	81,125	88,972	82,674	72,342	39,311	117,025	116,343	99,002	102,266	−96	−35,900	−27,371	−16,328	−29,924
Communist areas, total	3,092	7,616	7,951	6,554	5,085	891	2,496	3,452	3,354	3,604	+2,201	+5,120	+4,499	+3,200	+1,481
Africa	4,949	9,060	11,448	10,271	8,768	8,299	34,410	27,071	17,770	14,425	−3,350	−25,350	−15,623	−7,499	−5,657
Asia	28,223	60,168	63,849	64,822	63,813	27,252	80,299	92,033	85,170	91,464	+971	−20,131	−28,184	−20,348	−27,651
Oceania	2,340	4,876	6,436	5,700	4,827	1,508	3,392	3,353	3,131	3,044	+832	+1,484	+3,083	+2,569	+1,783
Europe	32,732	71,372	69,715	63,664	58,871	21,623	48,039	53,410	53,413	55,243	+11,109	+23,333	+16,305	+10,251	+3,628
North America	30,040	56,737	63,934	52,057	53,450	30,976	64,287	69,909	70,022	77,880	−936	−7,550	−5,975	−18,037	−24,430
South America	8,803	17,377	17,732	15,257	10,520	7,232	14,400	15,527	14,444	15,992	+1,571	+2,977	+2,205	+884	−5,472
Western Hemisphere	**38,843**	**74,114**	**81,667**	**67,312**	**63,970**	**38,209**	**78,687**	**85,436**	**84,467**	**93,873**	**+634**	**−4,573**	**−3,769**	**−17,155**	**−29,903**
Canada	21,744	35,395	39,564	33,720	38,244	22,151	41,459	46,414	46,477	52,130	−407	−6,064	−6,850	−12,757	−13,886
20 Latin American countries	15,655	36,030	38,950	30,086	22,618	11,847	29,952	32,023	32,513	35,683	+3,808	+6,078	+6,927	−2,427	−13,065
Other Western Hemisphere	1,444	2,688	3,152	3,506	3,108	4,210	7,277	6,999	5,477	6,060	−2,766	−4,589	−3,847	−1,971	−2,952
Central American Common Market	968	1,951	1,773	1,405	1,494	810	1,849	1,546	1,467	1,585	+158	+102	+227	−62	−91
Costa Rica	212	498	373	330	382	179	356	365	358	387	+33	+142	+8	−28	−5
El Salvador	194	272	308	292	365	182	427	259	319	348	+12	−155	+49	−27	+17
Guatemala	255	552	559	390	316	173	435	349	336	371	+82	+117	+210	+54	−55
Honduras	151	379	349	275	299	145	419	433	365	381	+6	−40	−84	−90	−82
Nicaragua	156	250	184	119	132	131	211	140	90	97	+25	+39	+44	+29	+35
Latin American Free Trade Association	13,773	32,274	35,260	26,879	19,378	10,100	26,735	28,981	29,850	32,611	+3,673	+5,539	+6,279	−2,971	−13,233
Argentina	628	2,625	2,192	1,294	965	215	741	1,124	1,128	853	+413	+1,884	+1,068	+166	+112
Bolivia	138	172	189	99	102	89	182	177	109	166	+49	−10	+12	−10	−64
Brazil	3,056	4,343	3,798	3,423	2,557	1,467	3,715	4,475	4,285	4,946	+1,589	+628	−677	−862	−2,389
Chile	533	1,353	1,465	925	729	138	515	604	666	969	+395	+838	+861	+259	−240
Colombia	643	1,736	1,771	1,903	1,514	596	1,241	819	801	970	+47	+495	+952	+1,102	+544
Ecuador	410	864	854	828	597	463	876	1,021	1,131	1,429	−53	−12	−167	−303	−832
Mexico	5,141	15,145	17,789	11,817	9,082	3,066	12,580	13,765	15,566	16,776	+2,075	+2,565	+4,024	−3,749	−7,694
Paraguay	33	109	108	78	37	19	81	48	39	32	+14	+28	+60	+39	+5
Peru	896	1,171	1,486	1,117	900	397	1,386	1,224	1,099	1,151	+499	−215	+262	+18	−251
Uruguay	51	183	163	190	86	24	97	158	258	381	+27	+86	+5	−68	−295
Venezuela	2,243	4,573	5,445	5,206	2,811	3,625	5,321	5,566	4,768	4,938	−1,382	−748	−121	+438	−2,127
Other Latin America	914	1,805	1,917	1,803	1,747	937	1,368	1,496	1,195	1,487	−23	+437	+421	+608	+267
Cuba	(z)	(z)	1	1	8	(z)	(z)	(z)	2	(z)	(z)	(z)	(z)	−1	+8
Dominican Republic	453	795	772	664	632	634	787	926	629	814	−181	+8	−154	+35	−182
Haiti	144	311	301	299	366	107	252	274	310	335	+37	+59	+27	−11	+30
Panama	317	699	844	839	748	196	330	297	255	337	+121	+369	+547	+584	+411
Other Western Hemisphere	**1,444**	**2,688**	**3,152**	**3,506**	**3,108**	**4,210**	**7,277**	**6,999**	**5,477**	**6,060**	**−2,766**	**−4,589**	**−3,847**	**−1,971**	**−2,952**
Bahamas	208	396	441	590	452	880	1,469	1,262	1,050	1,687	−672	−1,073	−791	−460	−1,235
Barbados	36	136	150	155	195	34	96	80	107	202	+2	+40	+90	+48	−7
Belize	26	58	69	64	36	34	60	43	36	27	−6	−2	+26	+28	+9
Bermuda	63	136	149	172	185	3	13	18	12	11	+60	+123	+131	+160	+174
French West Indies	26	67	69	51	38	1	7	20	9	22	+25	+60	+49	+42	+16
Greenland	8	3	1	3	1	7	14	15	16	15	+1	−11	−14	−13	−14
Guyana	89	96	106	56	36	87	120	104	71	69	+2	−24	+2	−15	−33
Jamaica	381	305	479	468	452	307	383	366	294	273	+74	−78	+113	+174	+179
Leeward and Windward Islands	41	152	282	177	166	15	36	32	27	39	+26	+116	+250	+150	+127
Netherlands Antilles	228	448	499	660	553	1,559	2,564	2,626	2,117	2,291	−1,331	−2,116	−2,127	−1,457	−1,738
Suriname	79	136	138	128	117	108	109	180	60	63	−29	+27	−42	+68	+54
Trinidad and Tobago	256	680	688	894	728	1,171	2,383	2,215	1,627	1,318	−915	−1,703	−1,527	−733	−590
Other	3	74	81	88	149	4	23	38	51	43	−1	+51	−7	+37	+106
Western Europe	**29,945**	**67,512**	**65,377**	**60,054**	**55,980**	**20,892**	**46,602**	**51,855**	**52,346**	**53,884**	**+9,053**	**+20,910**	**+13,522**	**+7,708**	**+2,096**
OECD [4]	29,575	66,654	64,548	59,378	55,261	20,627	46,137	51,399	51,966	53,468	+8,948	+20,517	+13,149	+7,412	+1,793
European Economic Community [5]	23,315	54,601	52,363	47,932	44,311	16,843	36,384	41,624	42,509	43,892	+6,472	+18,217	+10,739	+5,423	+419
Belgium and Luxembourg	2,417	6,661	5,765	5,229	5,049	1,199	1,914	2,297	2,396	2,412	+1,218	+4,747	+3,468	+2,833	+2,637
Denmark	445	863	887	732	649	464	727	850	904	1,067	−19	+136	+37	−172	−418
France	3,031	7,485	7,341	7,110	5,961	2,164	5,265	5,851	5,545	6,025	+867	+2,220	+1,490	+1,565	−64
Germany, Fed. Rep. of	5,194	10,960	10,277	9,291	8,737	5,410	11,693	11,379	11,975	12,695	−216	−733	−1,102	−2,684	−3,958
Greece [5]	450	922	676	721	503	110	292	359	242	238	+340	+630	+317	+479	+265
Ireland	190	836	1,025	983	1,115	178	413	498	556	560	+12	+423	+527	+427	+555
Italy	2,867	5,511	5,360	4,616	3,908	2,457	4,325	5,189	5,301	5,455	+410	+1,186	+171	−685	−1,547
Netherlands	4,193	8,669	8,595	8,604	7,767	1,089	1,913	2,366	2,494	2,970	+3,104	+6,756	+6,229	+6,110	+4,797
United Kingdom	4,527	12,694	12,439	10,645	10,621	3,773	9,842	12,835	13,095	12,470	+754	+2,852	−396	−2,450	−1,849
Other OECD [4]	6,260	12,053	12,185	11,445	10,950	3,784	9,753	9,776	9,457	9,576	+2,476	+2,300	+2,409	+1,988	+1,374
Austria [6]	181	447	484	371	371	243	389	382	491	447	−62	+58	+102	−120	−76
Finland [6]	261	505	613	489	413	149	439	525	414	496	+112	+66	+88	+75	−83
Iceland	32	79	71	77	53	85	200	198	184	219	−53	−121	−127	−107	−166
Norway	510	843	892	950	813	403	2,632	2,477	1,973	1,358	+107	−1,789	−1,585	−1,023	−545
Portugal	427	911	1,075	838	1,212	157	278	238	283	280	+270	+633	837	+555	+932
Spain	2,164	3,179	3,397	3,456	2,763	836	1,220	1,533	1,505	1,533	+1,328	+1,959	1,864	+1,951	+1,230
Sweden [6]	925	1,767	1,842	1,689	1,581	887	1,617	1,714	1,993	2,429	+38	+150	128	−304	−848
Switzerland [6]	1,153	3,781	3,022	2,707	2,960	879	2,803	2,448	2,340	2,494	+274	+978	577	+367	+466
Turkey	608	540	789	868	783	145	175	261	274	320	+463	+365	528	+594	+463
Other Western Europe	**369**	**858**	**829**	**677**	**720**	**265**	**464**	**455**	**380**	**416**	**+104**	**+394**	**374**	**+297**	**+304**
Yugoslavia	328	756	648	494	572	261	446	437	360	386	+67	+310	+211	+134	+186
Other and Special Category	41	102	180	183	148	4	18	18	20	30	+37	+84	+162	+163	+118
Communist areas in Europe	**2,787**	**3,860**	**4,338**	**3,610**	**2,891**	**731**	**1,437**	**1,555**	**1,067**	**1,359**	**+2,056**	**+2,423**	**+2,783**	**+2,543**	**+1,532**
Bulgaria	30	161	258	107	66	20	25	34	28	28	+10	+136	+224	+79	+38
Czechoslovakia	53	185	83	84	59	31	69	67	62	62	+22	+116	+16	+22	−3
German Dem. Rep	17	479	296	223	139	11	44	48	54	58	+6	+435	+248	+169	+81
Hungary	76	80	78	68	111	35	107	129	133	156	+41	−27	−51	−65	−45
Poland	583	714	682	295	324	243	416	365	212	189	+340	+298	+317	+83	+135
Romania	191	722	504	224	186	133	312	561	348	513	+58	+410	−57	−124	−327
Soviet Union	1,835	1,513	2,431	2,587	2,003	255	454	348	228	347	+1,580	+1,059	+2,083	+2,359	+1,656
Other	2	7	6	22	3	3	10	3	2	6	−1	−3	+3	+20	−3
Asia	**28,223**	**60,168**	**63,849**	**64,822**	**63,813**	**27,252**	**80,299**	**92,033**	**85,170**	**91,464**	**+971**	**−20,131**	**−28,184**	**−20,348**	**−27,651**
Japan	**9,563**	**20,790**	**21,823**	**20,966**	**21,894**	**11,425**	**30,714**	**37,612**	**37,744**	**41,183**	**−1,862**	**−9,924**	**−15,789**	**−16,778**	**−19,289**
Communist areas	**305**	**3,756**	**3,613**	**2,945**	**2,194**	**160**	**1,059**	**1,897**	**2,287**	**2,245**	**+145**	**+2,697**	**+1,716**	**+658**	**−51**
Near East Asia	**8,263**	**11,900**	**14,964**	**15,950**	**13,796**	**5,401**	**18,672**	**18,543**	**11,812**	**7,135**	**+2,862**	**−6,772**	**−3,579**	**+4,138**	**+6,661**
Bahrain	90	197	297	220	136	100	16	35	31	23	−10	+181	+262	+189	+113
Iran	3,244	23	300	122	190	1,398	458	64	585	1,130	+1,846	−435	+236	−463	−940
Iraq	310	724	914	846	512	19	460	164	39	59	+291	+264	+750	+807	+453
Israel	1,551	2,045	2,521	2,271	2,017	314	950	1,243	1,164	1,255	+1,237	+1,095	+1,278	+1,107	+762
Jordan	195	407	727	620	436	1	3	2	7	5	+194	+404	+725	+613	+431
Kuwait	366	886	976	941	741	111	494	86	40	130	+255	+392	+890	+901	+611
Lebanon	368	303	296	294	484	33	33	19	19	17	+335	+270	+277	+275	+467
Saudi Arabia	1,502	5,768	7,327	9,026	7,903	2,623	12,648	14,391	7,443	3,627	−1,121	−6,880	−7,064	+1,583	+4,276
Syria	128	239	143	138	112	7	26	83	10	8	+121	+213	+60	+128	+104
Other	508	1,307	1,464	1,472	1,265	796	3,584	2,456	2,474	881	−288	−2,277	−994	−1,002	+384
East and South Asia	**10,095**	**23,722**	**23,448**	**24,962**	**25,930**	**10,267**	**29,854**	**33,980**	**33,328**	**40,901**	**−172**	**−6,132**	**−10,532**	**−8,366**	**−14,971**
Afghanistan	19	11	6	10	5	8	6	13	11	8	+11	+5	−7	−1	−3
Burma	10	29	34	34	16	2	9	15	17	11	+8	+20	+19	+17	+5
China: Taiwan	1,659	4,337	4,305	4,367	4,667	1,946	6,854	8,049	8,893	11,204	−287	−2,517	−3,744	−4,526	−6,537
Hong Kong	808	2,686	2,635	2,453	2,564	1,573	4,739	5,428	5,540	6,394	−765	−2,053	−2,793	−3,087	−3,830
India	1,290	1,689	1,748	1,599	1,828	549	1,098	1,202	1,404	2,191	+741	+591	+546	+195	−363

See footnotes at end of table.

[**In millions of dollars, except percent.** See headnote, p. 816]

CONTINENT, AREA, AND COUNTRY	EXPORTS, DOMESTIC AND FOREIGN					GENERAL IMPORTS [1]					MERCHANDISE TRADE BALANCE				
	1975	1980	1981	1982	1983	1975	1980	1981	1982	1983	1975	1980	1981	1982	1983
Indonesia	810	1,545	1,302	2,025	1,466	2,222	5,217	6,022	4,224	5,285	−1,412	−3,672	−4,720	−2,199	−3,819
Kampuchea	66	26	12	2	3	1	(z)	1	(z)	(z)	+65	+26	+11	+2	+3
Korea, Republic of	1,762	4,685	5,116	5,529	5,925	1,442	4,147	5,227	5,637	7,148	+320	+538	−111	−108	−1,223
Laos	4	(z)	1	(z)	(z)	(z)	1	1	(z)	3	(z)	(z)	-	(z)	−1
Malaysia	393	1,337	1,537	1,736	1,684	772	2,577	2,183	1,885	2,124	−379	−1,240	−646	−149	−440
Pakistan	372	642	492	700	812	49	128	174	165	167	+323	+514	+318	+535	+645
Philippines	832	1,999	1,787	1,854	1,807	756	1,731	1,964	1,806	2,001	+76	+268	−177	+48	−194
Singapore	994	3,033	3,003	3,214	3,759	534	1,921	2,114	2,195	2,868	+460	+1,112	+889	+1,019	+891
Sri Lanka	38	62	91	198	75	40	126	154	175	185	−2	−64	−63	+23	−110
Thailand	357	1,263	1,170	915	1,063	217	816	946	884	967	+140	+447	+224	+31	+96
Other and Special Category	681	378	211	326	258	154	484	487	490	344	+527	−106	−276	−164	−86
Oceania	**2,340**	**4,876**	**6,436**	**5,700**	**4,827**	**1,508**	**3,392**	**3,353**	**3,131**	**3,044**	**+832**	**+1,484**	**+3,083**	**+2,569**	**+1,783**
Australia	1,815	4,093	5,242	4,535	3,954	1,147	2,509	2,465	2,287	2,222	+668	+1,584	+2,777	+2,248	+1,732
New Zealand and W. Samoa	411	599	940	900	625	245	703	718	777	737	+166	−104	+222	+123	−112
Other	114	184	254	265	248	116	180	170	67	85	−2	+4	+84	+198	+163
Africa	**4,949**	**9,060**	**11,448**	**10,271**	**8,768**	**8,299**	**34,410**	**27,071**	**17,770**	**14,425**	**−3,350**	**−25,350**	**−15,623**	**−7,499**	**−5,657**
Algeria	632	542	717	909	594	1,359	6,577	5,038	2,673	3,551	−727	−6,035	−4,321	−1,764	−2,957
Angola	53	111	268	159	91	425	742	904	697	911	−372	−631	−636	−538	−820
Cameroon	30	93	152	85	93	18	605	625	790	515	+12	−512	−473	−705	−422
Central African Republic	1	1	1	1	1	5	9	6	5	4	−4	−8	−5	−4	−3
Egypt	683	1,874	2,159	2,875	2,813	28	539	397	547	303	+655	+1,335	+1,762	+2,328	+2,510
Ethiopia	70	72	62	43	43	49	87	83	102	87	+21	−15	−21	−59	−44
Gabon	59	48	128	110	63	197	343	432	610	657	−138	−295	−304	−500	−594
Ghana	100	127	154	116	119	151	206	246	362	120	−51	−79	−92	−246	−1
Ivory Coast	78	185	130	97	61	157	288	344	303	343	−79	−103	−214	−206	−282
Kenya	49	141	150	98	69	36	54	52	71	65	+13	+87	+98	+27	+4
Liberia	90	113	128	113	110	96	128	113	91	91	−6	−15	+15	+22	+19
Libya	232	509	813	301	191	1,045	8,595	5,301	512	1	−813	−8,086	−4,488	−211	+190
Madagascar	7	7	16	24	22	46	91	69	63	71	−39	−84	−53	−39	−49
Mauritania	14	20	27	26	28	(z)	(z)	(z)	1	1	13	19	26	+25	+27
Morocco	200	344	429	397	440	10	35	36	45	31	+190	+309	+393	+352	+409
Mozambique	18	69	35	27	20	36	105	83	51	29	−18	−36	−48	−24	−9
Nigeria	536	1,150	1,523	1,295	864	3,281	11,105	9,249	7,045	3,736	−2,745	−9,955	−7,726	−5,750	−2,872
South Africa, Republic of	1,302	2,463	2,912	2,368	2,129	840	3,321	2,445	1,967	2,027	+462	−858	+467	+401	+102
Sudan	103	142	208	270	157	8	17	58	16	19	+95	+125	+150	+254	+138
Tanzania	66	62	48	41	32	29	32	19	29	14	+37	+30	+29	+12	+18
Tunisia	90	173	222	213	216	26	60	10	59	33	+64	+113	+212	+154	+183
Uganda	15	12	7	9	4	61	126	101	156	104	−46	−114	−94	−147	−100
Zaire	188	155	141	91	83	67	418	423	407	366	+121	−263	−282	−316	−283
Zambia	86	98	68	69	35	(z)	200	114	30	52	86	−102	−46	+39	−17
Other	251	549	950	534	490	331	727	923	1,139	1,294	−80	−178	+27	−605	−804

- Represents zero. Z Less than $500,000. [1] 1975, 1982, and 1983 imports are customs value basis; f.a.s. basis other years. Exports are f.a.s. value. [2] Includes revisions not carried to area values; therefore, area values will not add to total. [3] Developed countries include Canada, Western Europe, Japan, Australia, New Zealand, and South Africa; developing countries include rest of the world excluding Communist areas in Europe and Asia. Assignment of countries generally follows that made by United Nations. (See table 1475.) [4] OECD=Organization of Economic Cooperation and Development. [5] As of 1981, Greece, became a member of EEC. For consistency, data for all years are shown on same basis. [6] Includes Special Category exports, if any.

Source: U.S. Bureau of the Census, *Highlights of U.S. Export and Import Trade,* FT 990, monthly; and unpublished data.

8. AGRICULTURAL EXPORTS, BY PRINCIPAL COMMODITIES, VALUE, AND IMPORTING COUNTRY: 1970-83

[See headnote, table 1159. Data by country of destination not adjusted for transshipments]

COMMODITY AND COUNTRY	VALUE (mil. dol.)								PERCENT		
	1970	1975	1978	1979	1980	1981	1982	1983	1970	1980	1983
Total agricultural exports [1]	**7,259**	**21,859**	**29,384**	**34,749**	**41,233**	**43,339**	**36,623**	**36,098**	**100.0**	**100.0**	**100.0**
Grains and preparations [2]	2,582	11,619	11,585	14,406	17,991	19,390	14,649	15,021	35.6	43.6	41.6
Feed grains and products	1,093	5,283	5,909	7,796	9,831	9,494	6,527	7,352	15.1	23.8	20.4
Corn	818	4,422	5,257	6,977	8,492	7,935	5,582	6,367	11.3	20.6	17.6
Wheat and products	1,136	5,353	4,602	5,586	6,660	8,150	6,928	6,561	15.6	16.2	18.2
Rice	313	858	932	854	1,289	1,527	997	926	4.3	3.1	2.6
Oilseeds and products [2]	1,931	4,452	8,175	8,887	9,393	9,555	9,141	8,716	26.6	22.8	24.1
Soybeans	1,228	2,865	5,208	5,701	5,880	6,186	6,218	5,913	16.9	14.3	16.4
Soybean oil cake and meal	344	639	1,242	1,416	1,665	1,589	1,411	1,527	4.7	4.0	4.2
Vegetable oils and waxes	295	635	970	1,155	1,216	1,077	952	888	4.1	2.9	2.5
Soybean oil	194	269	569	769	689	474	486	424	2.7	1.7	1.2
Animals and animal products [2]	865	1,686	3,032	3,765	3,768	4,239	3,935	3,785	11.9	9.1	10.5
Hides and skins, incl. furskins	187	407	914	1,332	1,046	1,024	1,022	1,010	2.6	2.5	2.8
Cattle hides	130	260	629	906	623	617	704	742	1.8	1.5	2.1
Meats and meat products	132	432	743	853	890	997	978	916	1.8	2.2	2.5
Fats, oils, and greases	246	360	599	740	769	760	663	600	3.4	1.9	1.7
Poultry and poultry products	82	157	341	409	603	770	515	428	1.1	1.5	1.2
Cotton, excluding linters	372	991	1,740	2,198	2,864	2,260	1,955	1,817	5.1	6.9	5.0
Tobacco, unmanufactured	517	852	1,356	1,183	1,334	1,457	1,547	1,462	7.1	3.2	4.1
Fruits and preparations	334	699	1,014	1,127	1,335	1,497	1,376	1,349	4.6	3.2	3.7
Fresh fruits	164	404	565	646	739	855	796	829	2.3	1.8	2.3
Feeds and fodders	138	313	609	838	1,126	1,066	1,037	1,230	1.9	2.7	3.4
Vegetables and preparations	219	505	703	764	1,188	1,553	1,174	980	3.0	2.9	2.7
Nuts and preparations	69	169	324	584	757	581	541	496	1.0	1.8	1.4
Other	232	573	846	997	1,477	1,741	1,268	1,242	3.2	3.6	3.4
Asia [1]	2,670	7,620	10,295	12,109	14,886	15,777	13,616	14,025	36.8	36.1	38.9
Japan	1,214	3,082	4,435	5,255	6,111	6,562	5,547	6,240	16.7	14.8	17.3
Korea, Rep. of	224	830	1,148	1,441	1,797	2,008	1,581	1,840	3.1	4.4	5.1
China:											
Mainland	(z)	80	573	990	2,210	1,956	1,498	544	(z)	5.4	1.5
Taiwan	134	565	825	1,074	1,095	1,145	1,155	1,308	1.8	2.7	3.6
Western Europe [1] [3]	2,532	7,164	9,115	9,912	11,744	11,905	11,104	9,854	34.9	28.5	27.3
European Economic Community [4]	2,133	5,704	7,312	7,849	9,236	9,059	8,273	7,298	29.4	22.4	20.2
Netherlands	526	1,722	2,346	2,624	3,412	3,301	3,042	2,530	7.2	8.3	7.0
Germany, Fed. Rep. of	529	1,564	1,497	1,399	1,831	1,759	1,448	1,529	7.3	4.4	4.2
United Kingdom	411	588	1,023	1,057	928	960	896	812	5.7	2.3	2.2
Italy	210	798	995	1,005	1,094	1,181	941	713	2.9	2.7	2.0
France	164	406	565	726	748	624	612	485	2.3	1.8	1.3
Spain	143	776	822	930	1,129	1,267	1,458	1,138	2.0	2.7	3.2
Portugal	35	261	372	485	608	757	576	660	.5	1.5	1.8
Latin America [1]	688	2,274	3,158	3,687	6,150	6,367	4,438	5,211	9.5	14.9	14.4
Mexico	155	586	903	1,024	2,468	2,432	1,156	1,942	2.1	6.0	5.4
Venezuela	98	277	387	494	701	893	671	665	1.4	1.7	1.8
Soviet Union	16	1,133	1,687	2,855	1,047	1,665	1,855	1,457	.2	2.5	4.0
Eastern Europe	169	616	1,120	1,933	2,071	1,654	833	819	2.3	5.0	2.3
Canada	826	1,304	1,621	1,650	1,852	1,989	1,805	1,829	11.4	4.5	5.1
Africa	254	1,134	1,556	1,581	2,179	2,766	2,195	2,398	3.5	5.3	6.6
Egypt	26	425	554	601	770	967	800	943	.4	1.9	2.6

Z Less than $500,000 or .05 percent. [1] Includes areas not shown separately. [2] Includes commodities not shown separately. [3] As of Jan. 1, 1982, includes Canary Islands and Madeira Islands. For consistency, data for all years are shown on same basis. [4] Includes data for Belgium, Luxembourg, Denmark, Greece, and Ireland. As of Jan. 1, 1973, United Kingdom, Denmark, and Ireland became members of EEC. As of Jan. 1, 1981, Greece became a member of EEC. For consistency, data for all years are shown on same basis.

Source: U.S. Dept. of Agriculture, Economic Research Service, *U.S. Foreign Agricultural Trade Statistical Report,* annual. Also in *Agricultural Statistics,* annual.

9. WORLD TRADE BALANCE AND CURRENT ACCOUNT BALANCE FOR SELECTED YEARS AND COUNTRIES

[Billions of U.S. dollars]

Area and country	1965	1970	1975	1980	1981	1982	1983	1984 [1]
	World trade balance [2]							
Developed countries [3]	−7.4	−11.4	−34.0	−144.4	−102.2	−85.7	−74.7	−116.1
United States	4.3	.5	2.2	−36.2	−39.6	−42.6	−69.3	−109.1
Canada	−.2	2.5	−2.1	4.9	2.4	12.1	11.7	12.1
Japan	.3	.4	−2.0	−10.9	8.6	6.9	20.5	30.3
European Community [4]	−5.3	−5.3	−7.0	−63.3	−32.9	−25.4	−15.5	−10.7
France	−.2	−1.0	−.8	−18.9	−14.5	−19.0	−10.5	−5.8
West Germany	.3	4.3	15.2	4.9	12.2	21.1	16.5	14.6
Italy	−.2	−1.8	−3.7	−22.0	−15.8	−12.7	−7.7	−9.0
United Kingdom	−2.3	−2.4	−9.9	−5.4	−.5	−2.7	−8.5	−13.4
Other developed countries	−6.5	−9.6	−25.0	−39.0	−40.7	−36.7	−22.2	−38.8
Developing countries	−1.5	−.6	27.7	116.2	52.7	−.3	9.3	38.1
OPEC [5]	3.9	7.0	59.4	165.9	121.6	49.3	36.1	52.3
Other	−5.4	−7.6	−31.7	−49.6	−68.9	−49.6	−26.8	−14.3
Communist countries [6]	.7	.8	−10.5	1.3	5.2	20.8	22.7	24.4
U.S.S.R.	.2	1.1	−3.7	7.9	6.2	9.4	11.3	13.0
Eastern Europe	.2	−.3	−6.0	−5.0	−3.7	4.3	5.0	4.2
China	.2	.0	−.3	−1.8	2.2	5.1	4.0	4.7
TOTAL [7]	−8.2	−11.2	−16.8	−26.9	−44.3	−65.2	−42.7	−53.6
	Current account balances [8]							
Developed countries [3]	3.2	4.7	0.2	−64.5	−30.4	−33.1	−26.8	−75.5
United States	5.4	2.3	18.1	1.9	6.3	−9.2	−41.6	−102.4
Canada	−1.1	1.1	−4.7	−1.0	−5.1	2.2	1.4	1.0
Japan	.9	2.0	−.7	−10.7	4.8	6.9	20.8	32.3
European Community [4]	.8	2.8	3.4	−35.4	−11.8	−9.5	3.6	−1.0
France	.4	.1	2.7	−4.2	−4.7	−12.1	−4.4	−.3
West Germany	−1.6	.9	4.0	−15.7	−5.8	3.8	4.1	2.3
Italy	2.2	.8	−.6	−9.7	−8.1	−5.5	.8	−1.0
United Kingdom	−.1	2.0	−3.3	8.4	14.5	9.1	4.4	−1.5
Other developed countries	−2.9	−3.4	−15.9	−19.3	−24.6	−23.5	−11.0	−5.4
Developing countries	...	−8.5	−.9	48.8	−28.6	−80.8	−56.8	−30.0
OPEC [5]	...	−.5	27.0	109.8	49.8	−15.4	−18.1	2.0
Other	...	−8.0	−27.9	−61.0	−78.4	−65.4	−38.7	−32.0
Communist countries [9]	...	−.8	−11.1	−4.6	−.4	11.6	12.5	...
U.S.S.R.	−.2	.1	−4.6	1.9	−.2	4.3	4.7	4.8
Eastern Europe	...	−.8	−6.4	−5.5	−3.7	1.7	3.8	2.9
China	...	−.1	−.1	−1.0	3.5	5.6	4.0	...
TOTAL	...	−4.6	−11.8	−20.3	−59.4	−102.3	−71.1	...

[1] Preliminary estimates.
[2] Exports f.o.b. (free-on-board ship value) less imports c.i.f. (cost, insurance, and freight).
[3] Includes the OECD countries, South Africa, Israel, and non-OECD Europe.
[4] Includes Belgium-Luxembourg, Denmark, Greece, Ireland, and the Netherlands, not shown separately.
[5] Includes Algeria, Ecuador, Gabon, Indonesia, Iran, Iraq, Kuwait, Libya, Nigeria, Qatar, Saudi Arabia, United Arab Emirates, and Venezuela.
[6] Includes North Korea, Vietnam, Albania, Cuba, Mongolia, and Yugoslavia, not shown separately.
[7] Asymmetries arise in global payments aggregations because of discrepancies in coverage, classification, timing, and valuation in the recording of transactions by the countries involved and because freight charges are attributed to the cost of imports.
[8] OECD basis.
[9] Includes only countries listed.

Sources: International Monetary Fund, Organization for Economic Cooperation and Development, and Council of Economic Advisers.

10. WORLD BANK STRUCTURE

PAID-IN SUBSCRIPTIONS

Member	World Bank (000s SDRs)	IDA (000s USDs)	IFC (000s USDs)
Afghanistan	3,000	1,175	111
Algeria	39,605	4,553	---
Antigua & Barbuda	200	---	---
Argentina	53,610	45,998	9,821
Australia	109,777	586,368	12,191
Austria	45,882	199,309	5,085
Bahamas	1,710	---	---
Bahrain	2,777	---	---
Bangladesh	12,420	6,044	2,328
Barbados	2,365	---	93
Belgium	109,430	385,817	13,723
Belize	390	208	26
Benin	1,000	524	---
Bhutan	90	52	---
Bolivia	2,640	1,154	490
Botswana	715	181	29
Brazil	91,922	60,227	10,169
Burkina Faso	1,000	558	245
Burma	5,910	2,306	666
Burundi	1,500	868	100
Cameroun	2,000	1,117	490
Canada	164,215	1,460,017	20,952
Cape Verde	160	84	---
Central African Republic	1,000	558	---
Chad	1,000	544	---
Chile	12,400	3,854	2,328
China	204,240	33,981	4,154
Colombia	11,750	9,231	2,083
Comoros	160	89	---
Congo	1,000	553	67
Costa Rica	1,300	224	245
Cyprus	4,730	863	551
Denmark	42,955	276,019	4,779
Djibouti	310	170	21
Dominica	160	86	11
Dominican Republic	2,980	534	306
Ecuador	3,680	883	674
Egypt	28,080	5,789	3,124
El Salvador	1,200	358	11
Equatorial Guinea	640	348	---
Ethiopia	2,488	602	33
Fiji	1,890	609	74
Finland	28,915	144,252	4,043
France	258,898	1,316,808	29,528
Gabon	1,200	548	429
Gambia	530	301	35
German Federal Republic	299,757	3,413,426	33,204
Ghana	8,560	2,577	1,306
Greece	9,450	5,298	1,777
Grenada	170	104	21
Guatemala	1,670	465	306
Guinea	2,000	1,165	134
Guinea-Bissau	270	147	18
Guyana	2,895	920	368
Haiti	1,740	884	306
Honduras	840	350	184
Hungary	20,420	---	---
Iceland	3,780	2,408	11
India	198,972	50,604	19,788
Indonesia	66,173	12,472	7,351
Iran	15,800	5,817	372
Iraq	9,560	867	67

PAID-IN SUBSCRIPTIONS

Member	World Bank (000s SDRs)	IDA (000s USDs)	IFC (000s USDs)
Ireland	21,548	32,034	332
Israel	11,080	2,390	550
Italy	172,240	778,337	19,114
Ivory Coast	5,480	1,117	913
Jamaica	4,460	---	1,103
Japan	298,518	4,065,230	25,546
Jordan	2,330	392	429
Kampuchea	2,140	1,117	---
Kenya	5,500	1,906	1,041
Korea, Republic of	23,710	4,519	2,450
Kuwait	54,515	508,535	4,533
Laos	1,000	550	---
Lebanon	900	501	50
Lesotho	985	181	18
Liberia	2,130	884	83
Libya	19,150	1,136	55
Luxembourg	4,642	13,003	551
Madagascar	2,190	1,059	111
Malawi	1,500	862	368
Malaysia	35,165	2,929	3,921
Maldives	105	34	4
Mali	1,730	980	116
Malta	1,630	---	---
Mauritania	1,000	560	55
Mauritius	2,210	1,001	429
Mexico	53,715	13,529	6,004
Morocco	20,765	3,966	2,328
Nepal	2,488	570	306
Netherlands	130,700	755,243	14,458
New Zealand	25,485	29,230	923
Nicaragua	910	416	184
Niger	1,000	563	67
Nigeria	29,410	3,735	5,575
Norway	24,100	270,841	4,533
Oman	1,920	372	306
Pakistan	25,190	11,618	4,411
Panama	2,160	26	344
Papua New Guinea	2,460	988	490
Paraguay	1,195	342	123
Peru	9,280	1,856	1,777
Philippines	29,398	5,664	3,247
Portugal	13,240	---	2,144
Qatar	3,270	---	---
Romania	20,010	---	---
Rwanda	1,740	878	306
St. Lucia	290	173	19
St. Vincent	130	73	---
Sao Tome & Principe	140	73	---
Saudi Arabia	96,370	903,880	9,251
Senegal	3,620	1,892	707
Seychelles	110	---	7
Sierra Leone	1,500	853	83
Singapore	3,200	---	177
Solomon Islands	170	96	11
Somalia	1,890	844	83
South Africa	34,630	45,520	4,108
Spain	45,510	66,418	6,004
Sri Lanka	9,610	3,382	1,838
Sudan	6,000	1,140	111
Suriname	1,620	---	---
Swaziland	1,670	363	184
Sweden	62,658	806,549	6,923

PAID-IN SUBSCRIPTIONS

Member	World Bank (000s SDRs)	IDA (000s USDs)	IFC (000s USDs)
Syria	8,642	1,068	72
Tanzania	3,500	1,884	724
Thailand	25,152	3,496	2,818
Togo	1,500	856	368
Trinidad & Tobago	6,670	1,416	1,059
Tunisia	3,730	1,645	919
Turkey	27,762	6,394	3,063
Uganda	3,300	1,833	735
United Arab Emirates	9,800	136,464	1,838
United Kingdom	328,445	2,950,842	37,900
United States	1,025,338	9,643,966	146,661
Uruguay	4,110	---	919
Vanuatu	643	198	25
Venezuela	64,265	---	7,106
Viet Nam	5,430	1,651	166
Western Samoa	1,730	100	9
Yemen Arab Republic	1,802	495	184
Yemen People's Republic	3,360	---	---
Yugoslavia	15,090	20,527	2,879
Zaire	9,600	3,290	1,929
Zambia	11,510	3,008	1,286
Zimbabwe	8,170	4,364	546
TOTAL	4,818,842	29,186,461	544,238

11. SUMMARY FEATURES OF EXCHANGE AND TRADE SYSTEMS

Summary Features of Exchange and Trade Systems in Member Countries[1]
(as of date shown on first country page)[2]

	Afghanistan	Algeria	Antigua and Barbuda	Argentina	Australia	Austria	Bahamas	Bahrain	Bangladesh	Barbados	Belgium and Luxembourg	Belize	Benin	Bhutan	Bolivia	Botswana	Brazil	Burma	Burundi	Cameroon	Canada	Cape Verde	Central African Rep.	Chad
A. Acceptance of Article Status																								
1. Article VIII status	—	—	●	●	●	●	●	●	—	—	●	●	—	—	●	—	—	—	—	—	●	—	—	—
2. Article XIV status	●	●	—	—	—	—	—	—	●	●	—	—	●	●	—	●	●	●	●	●	—	●	●	●
B. Exchange Arrangement[3]																								
1. Exchange rate determined on the basis of:																								
(a) A peg to:																								
(i) the U.S. dollar	—	—	●	—	—	—	●	—	—	●	—	●	—	—	●	—	—	—	—	—	—	—	—	—
(ii) pound sterling	—	—	—	—	—	—	—	—	—	—	—	—	—	—	—	—	—	—	—	—	—	—	—	—
(iii) the French franc	—	—	—	—	—	—	—	—	—	—	—	—	●	—	—	—	—	—	—	●	—	—	●	●
(iv) other currencies[4]	—	—	—	—	—	—	—	—	—	—	—	—	—	●	—	—	—	—	—	—	—	—	—	—
(v) a composite of currencies	—	●	—	—	—	●	—	—	●	—	—	—	—	—	—	●	□	□	—	—	—	●	—	—
(b) Limited flexibility with respect to:																								
(i) single currency	●	—	—	—	—	—	—	●	—	—	—	—	—	—	—	—	—	—	—	—	—	—	—	—
(ii) cooperative arrangement	—	—	—	—	—	—	—	—	—	—	●	—	—	—	—	—	—	—	—	—	—	—	—	—
(c) More flexible arrangements:																								
(i) adjusted according to a set of indicators	—	—	—	—	—	—	—	—	—	—	—	—	—	—	—	—	●	—	—	—	—	—	—	—
(ii) other managed floating	—	—	—	●	—	—	—	—	—	—	—	—	—	—	—	—	—	—	—	—	—	—	—	—
(iii) independently floating	—	—	—	—	●	—	—	—	—	—	—	—	—	—	—	—	—	—	—	—	●	—	—	—
2. Separate exchange rate(s) for some or all capital transactions and/or some or all invisibles	●	●	—	—	—	—	●	—	●	—	●	—	—	—	—	—	●	—	—	—	—	—	—	—
3. Import rate(s) different from export rate(s)	●	—	—	●	—	—	●	—	—	—	—	—	—	—	—	—	●	—	—	—	—	—	—	—
4. More than one rate for imports	●	—	—	—	—	—	●	—	—	—	—	—	—	—	—	—	●	—	—	—	—	—	—	—
5. More than one rate for exports	●	—	—	●	—	—	●	—	—	—	—	—	—	—	—	—	●	—	—	—	—	—	—	—
C. Prescription of Currency	●	●	—	●	●	—	—	—	●	●	●	●	●	—	—	●	●	●	●	●	—	●	●	●
D. Bilateral Payments Arrangements																								
1. with members	●	●	—	—	—	—	●	—	—	—	—	●	—	—	—	—	●	—	—	—	—	●	—	—
2. with nonmembers	●	●	—	—	—	—	●	—	—	—	—	—	—	—	—	—	●	—	—	—	—	●	—	—
E. Payments Restrictions																								
1. Restrictions on payments for current transactions[5]	●	●	—	●	—	—	—	—	●	●	—	●	—	●	●	●	●	●	●	—	—	●	●	●
2. Restrictions on payments for capital transactions[5,6]	●	●	—	●	●	●	●	—	●	●	—	—	●	●	●	●	●	●	●	●	—	●	●	●
F. Cost-Related Import Restrictions																								
1. Import surcharges	—	—	—	●	—	—	—	—	—	—	—	●	—	—	●	—	—	—	●	—	—	—	—	—
2. Advance import deposits	●	—	—	—	—	—	—	—	—	—	—	—	—	—	—	—	—	—	—	—	—	—	—	—
G. Surrender Requirement for Export Proceeds	●	●	—	●	●	—	●	—	●	●	●	●	●	●	●	●	●	●	●	●	—	●	●	●

For key and notes, see page 385

Chile	China, People's Rep.	Colombia	Comoros	Congo	Costa Rica	Cyprus	Denmark	Djibouti	Dominica	Dominican Republic	Ecuador	Egypt	El Salvador	Equatorial Guinea	Ethiopia	Fiji	Finland	France	Gabon	The Gambia	Germany, Fed. Rep. of	Ghana	Greece	Grenada	Guatemala	Guinea	Guinea-Bissau	Guyana	Haiti	Honduras	Hong Kong	Hungary	Iceland
●	—	—	—	—	●	—	●	●	●	●	●	—	●	—		●	●	●	—		●	—	—	—	●	—	—	●	●	●	●	—	●
—	●	●	●	●	—	●	—	—	—	—	—	●	—	●	●	—	—	—	●	●	—	●	●	●	—	●	●	—	—	—	—	●	—
—	—	—	—	—	—	—	●	●	●	●	—	●	●	—	—	—	—	—	—	—	—	—	—	—	●	●	—	—	●	●	—	—	—
—	—	—	—	—	—	—	—	—	—	—	—	—	—	—	—	—	—	—	—	—	●	—	—	—	—	—	—	—	—	—	—	—	—
—	—	—	●	●	—	—	—	—	—	—	—	—	—	—	—	—	—	—	●	—	—	—	—	—	—	—	—	—	—	—	—	—	—
—	—	—	—	—	—	—	—	—	—	—	—	—	—	●	—	—	—	—	—	—	—	—	—	—	—	—	—	—	—	—	—	—	—
—	●	—	—	—	—	●	—	—	—	—	—	—	—	—	—	●	●	—	—	—	—	—	—	—	—	□	□	—	—	—	—	●	—
—	—	—	—	—	—	—	—	—	—	—	—	—	—	—	—	—	—	—	—	—	—	—	●	—	—	—	—	●	—	—	—	—	—
—	—	—	—	—	—	—	●	—	—	—	—	—	—	—	—	—	—	—	●	—	—	—	—	—	—	—	—	—	—	—	—	—	—
●	—	●	—	—	—	—	—	—	—	—	—	—	—	—	—	—	—	—	—	—	—	—	—	—	—	—	—	—	—	—	—	—	—
—	—	—	—	—	●	—	—	—	—	—	●	—	—	—	—	—	—	—	—	—	—	—	●	—	—	—	—	—	—	—	●	—	●
—	—	—	—	—	—	—	—	—	—	—	—	—	—	—	—	—	—	—	—	—	—	—	—	—	—	—	—	—	—	—	—	—	—
●	●	●	—	—	●	—	—	—	●	●	●	●	●	—	—	—	—	—	●	—	●	—	●	—	—	—	—	—	—	—	—	●	—
—	—	●	—	—	●	—	—	—	●	●	●	●	—	—	—	—	—	—	—	—	—	—	—	●	—	●	—	●	—	—	—	●	—
—	—	●	—	—	●	—	—	—	●	●	●	●	—	—	—	—	—	—	●	—	—	—	—	—	●	—	●	—	—	—	—	●	—
—	—	●	—	—	●	—	—	—	●	●	●	●	—	—	—	—	—	—	—	—	—	—	—	—	●	—	●	—	—	—	—	●	—
●	●	●	●	●	●	●	—	—	●	●	●	●	●	●	●	—	●	●	●	—	●	—	●	●	●	●	●	●	—	—	—	●	●
—	●	●	—	—	—	—	—	—	—	●	●	●	—	—	—	●	—	—	—	—	●	—	—	—	●	●	—	●	●	—	—	●	—
—	●	●	—	—	—	—	—	—	—	●	●	—	—	—	—	●	—	—	—	—	—	—	—	—	●	—	●	—	—	—	—	●	—
●	●	●	●	●	●	●	—	—	—	●	●	●	●	●	—	—	—	—	●	—	●	●	●	●	●	●	●	—	—	—	—	●	●
●	●	●	●	●	●	●	●	—	●	●	—	●	●	●	●	●	●	●	●	●	—	●	●	●	●	●	●	●	●	●	—	●	●
—	—	●	—	—	●	●	—	●	—	●	●	●	●	—	—	—	—	—	—	—	—	●	●	●	●	—	—	●	●	●	—	●	●
—	—	●	—	—	—	—	—	—	—	●	●	●	●	—	—	—	—	—	—	—	—	—	—	—	●	—	—	—	—	—	—	—	—
●	●	●	●	●	●	●	●	—	●	●	●	●	●	●	●	●	—	●	●	●	—	●	●	●	●	●	●	●	●	●	—	●	●

	India	Indonesia	Iran, Islamic Rep.	Iraq	Ireland	Israel	Italy	Ivory Coast	Jamaica	Japan	Jordan	Kenya	Korea	Kuwait	Lao People's Dem. Rep.	Lebanon	Lesotho	Liberia	Libyan Arab Jamahiriya	Madagascar	Malawi	Malaysia	Maldives	Mali
A. Acceptance of Article Status																								
1. Article VIII status	–	–	–	–	●	–	●	–	●	●	–	–	–	●	–	–	–	–	–	–	–	●	–	–
2. Article XIV status	●	●	●	●	–	●	–	●	–	–	●	●	●	–	●	●	●	●	●	●	●	–	●	●
B. Exchange Arrangement[3]																								
1. Exchange rate determined on the basis of:																								
(a) A peg to:																								
(i) the U.S. dollar	–	–	–	●	–	–	–	–	–	–	–	–	–	–	●	–	–	●	●	–	–	–	–	–
(ii) pound sterling	–	–	–	–	–	–	–	–	–	–	–	–	–	–	–	–	–	–	–	–	–	–	–	–
(iii) the French franc	–	–	–	–	–	–	–	●	–	–	–	–	–	–	–	–	–	–	–	–	–	–	–	●
(iv) other currencies[4]	–	–	–	–	–	–	–	–	–	–	–	–	–	–	–	–	–	–	●	–	–	–	–	–
(v) a composite of currencies	–	–	□ ●	–	–	–	–	–	–	–	□ ●	□ ●	–	●	–	–	–	–	–	–	●	□	●	–
(b) Limited flexibility with respect to:																								
(i) single currency	–	–	–	–	–	–	–	–	–	–	–	–	–	–	–	–	–	–	–	–	–	●	–	–
(ii) cooperative arrangement	–	–	–	–	●	–	●	–	–	–	–	–	–	–	–	–	–	–	–	–	–	–	–	–
(c) More flexible arrangements:																								
(i) adjusted according to a set of indicators	–	–	–	–	–	–	–	–	–	–	–	–	–	–	–	–	–	–	–	–	–	–	–	–
(ii) other managed floating	●	●	–	–	–	–	–	–	●	–	–	●	–	–	–	–	–	–	–	–	–	–	–	–
(iii) independently floating	–	–	–	–	–	●	–	–	●	–	–	–	–	–	–	●	–	–	–	–	–	–	–	–
2. Separate exchange rate(s) for some or all capital transactions and/or some or all invisibles	–	–	●	–	–	–	–	–	–	–	–	–	–	–	–	●	–	–	–	–	–	–	–	–
3. Import rate(s) different from export rate(s)	–	–	●	–	–	–	–	–	–	–	–	●	–	–	–	–	–	–	–	–	–	–	–	–
4. More than one rate for imports	–	–	–	–	–	–	–	–	–	–	–	–	–	–	–	–	–	–	–	–	–	–	–	–
5. More than one rate for exports	–	–	●	–	–	–	–	–	–	–	–	●	–	–	–	–	–	–	–	–	–	–	–	–
C. Prescription of Currency	●	●	●	●	●	●	●	●	●	–	–	●	–	●	–	●	–	●	–	●	●	–	–	●
D. Bilateral Payments Arrangements																								
1. with members	●	–	●	–	–	–	–	–	–	–	–	–	–	–	–	●	●	–	–	–	–	–	–	●
2. with nonmembers	●	–	●	–	–	–	–	–	–	–	–	–	–	–	–	●	●	–	–	–	–	–	–	●
E. Payments Restrictions																								
1. Restrictions on payments for current transactions[5]	●	–	●	●	–	–	–	–	●	–	–	●	●	–	●	–	–	●	–	●	●	●	–	–
2. Restrictions on payments for capital transactions[5,6]	●	–	●	●	●	●	–	●	●	–	●	●	●	–	●	–	●	–	●	●	●	–	–	●
F. Cost-Related Import Restrictions																								
1. Import surcharges	●	–	●	●	–	●	–	●	–	●	●	●	●	–	–	●	–	●	●	–	–	–	–	–
2. Advance import deposits	–	–	●	–	–	●	–	–	–	–	–	●	–	–	–	–	–	–	–	–	–	–	–	–
G. Surrender Requirement for Export Proceeds	●	–	●	●	●	●	●	●	●	–	●	●	●	–	●	–	●	–	●	●	●	–	●	●

For key and notes, see page 385

Malta	Mauritania	Mauritius	Mexico	Morocco	Nepal	Netherlands	Netherlands Antilles	New Zealand	Nicaragua	Niger	Nigeria	Norway	Oman	Pakistan	Panama	Papua New Guinea	Paraguay	Peru	Philippines	Portugal	Qatar	Romania	Rwanda	St. Lucia	St. Vincent and Grenadines	São Tomé and Principe	Saudi Arabia	Senegal	Seychelles	Sierra Leone	Singapore	Solomon Islands	Somalia
–	–	–	•	–	–	•	•	•	•	–	•	•	•	–	•	•	–	•	–	–	•	–	–	•	•	–	•	–	•	–	•	•	–
•	•	•	–	•	•	–	–	–	–	•	•	–	–	•	–	–	•	–	•	•	–	•	•	–	•	–	•	–	–	•	–	–	•
–	–	–	–	–	–	–	•	–	•	–	–	–	–	•	•	–	•	–	–	–	–	–	–	–	–	–	–	–	–	–	•	–	–
–	–	–	–	–	–	–	–	–	–	–	•	–	–	–	–	–	–	–	–	–	–	–	–	–	–	–	–	•	–	–	–	–	–
–	–	–	–	–	–	–	–	–	–	–	–	–	–	–	–	–	–	–	–	–	–	–	–	–	–	–	–	–	–	–	–	–	–
•	•	•	–	–	•	–	–	–	–	–	–	–	•	–	–	•	–	–	–	–	•	•	□	–	–	□	•	–	□	•	•	•	–
–	–	–	–	–	–	–	–	–	–	–	–	–	–	–	–	–	–	–	–	•	–	–	–	–	–	–	–	•	–	–	–	–	–
–	–	–	–	–	–	–	•	–	–	–	–	–	–	–	–	–	–	–	–	–	–	–	–	–	–	–	–	–	–	–	–	–	–
–	–	–	–	–	–	–	–	–	–	–	–	–	–	–	–	–	–	–	–	•	–	–	–	–	–	–	–	–	–	–	–	–	•
–	–	–	•	•	–	–	–	•	–	–	•	–	–	•	–	–	–	•	•	–	–	–	–	–	–	–	–	–	–	–	–	–	–
–	–	–	–	–	–	–	–	–	–	–	–	–	–	–	–	–	–	–	–	–	–	–	–	–	–	–	–	–	–	–	–	–	–
–	–	•	•	•	–	–	–	–	•	–	–	–	–	–	•	–	–	•	•	–	–	•	–	–	–	–	–	–	–	–	–	–	•
–	–	–	•	–	–	–	–	–	•	–	–	–	–	–	•	–	–	•	•	–	–	•	–	–	–	–	–	–	–	–	–	–	–
–	–	–	•	–	–	–	–	–	•	–	–	–	–	–	•	–	–	•	•	–	–	•	–	–	–	–	–	–	–	–	–	–	–
–	–	–	–	–	–	–	–	–	•	–	–	–	–	–	•	–	–	•	•	–	–	•	–	–	–	–	–	–	–	–	–	–	–
–	•	•	–	•	•	–	•	–	–	•	•	–	–	–	–	–	•	•	•	–	•	•	•	•	•	•	•	–	•	–	•	–	•
–	–	–	•	•	–	–	–	–	–	–	–	–	•	–	–	–	–	•	•	–	–	•	–	–	•	–	–	•	–	–	•	–	–
–	–	–	–	•	•	–	–	–	–	–	–	–	•	–	–	–	–	•	•	–	–	•	–	–	•	–	–	–	–	–	–	–	•
•	•	•	•	•	•	–	•	–	•	•	•	–	•	–	•	–	•	•	•	•	–	•	•	•	•	•	–	•	–	•	–	–	•
•	•	•	•	•	•	–	•	•	•	•	•	•	•	–	•	–	•	–	•	–	•	•	•	•	•	•	–	•	–	•	–	•	•
–	–	•	•	–	•	–	•	–	•	–	–	–	–	•	–	•	–	•	•	•	•	–	–	•	–	–	–	–	–	•	–	–	•
–	–	–	–	•	•	–	–	–	–	–	•	–	–	•	–	–	•	–	•	–	–	•	–	–	•	–	–	–	–	–	–	–	•
•	•	•	•	•	•	–	•	•	•	–	•	–	•	–	•	–	–	•	•	•	•	•	•	•	•	–	•	–	•	–	•	•	•

	South Africa	Spain	Sri Lanka	Sudan	Suriname	Swaziland	Sweden	Syrian Arab Rep.	Tanzania	Thailand	Togo	Trinidad and Tobago	Tunisia	Turkey	Uganda	United Arab Emirates	United Kingdom	United States	Upper Volta	Uruguay	Vanuatu	Venezuela	Viet Nam	Western Samoa
A. Acceptance of Article Status																								
1. Article VIII status	•	–	–	–	•	–	•	–	–	–	–	–	–	–	–	•	•	•	–	•	•	•	–	–
2. Article XIV status	–	•	•	•	–	•	–	•	•	•	•	•	•	•	•	–	–	–	•	–	–	–	•	•
B. Exchange Arrangement[3]																								
1. Exchange rate determined on the basis of:																								
(a) A peg to:																								
(i) the U.S. dollar	–	–	–	•	•	–	–	•	–	–	–	•	–	–	–	–	–	–	–	–	–	•	–	–
(ii) pound sterling	–	–	–	–	–	–	–	–	–	–	–	–	–	–	–	–	–	–	–	–	–	–	–	–
(iii) the French franc	–	–	–	–	–	–	–	–	–	–	•	–	–	–	–	–	–	–	•	–	–	–	–	–
(iv) other currencies[4]	–	–	–	–	–	•	–	–	–	–	–	–	–	–	–	–	–	–	–	–	–	–	–	–
(v) a composite of currencies	–	–	–	–	–	–	•	–	•	–	–	–	•	–	–	–	–	–	–	□	•	–	□	–
(b) Limited flexibility with respect to:																								
(i) single currency	–	–	–	–	–	–	–	–	–	•	–	–	–	–	•	–	–	–	–	–	–	–	–	–
(ii) cooperative arrangement	–	–	–	–	–	–	–	–	–	–	–	–	–	–	–	–	–	–	–	–	–	–	–	–
(c) More flexible arrangements:																								
(i) adjusted according to a set of indicators	–	–	–	–	–	–	–	–	–	–	–	–	–	–	–	–	–	–	–	–	–	–	–	–
(ii) other managed floating	–	•	•	–	–	–	–	–	–	–	–	–	–	•	–	–	–	–	–	–	–	–	–	•
(iii) independently floating	•	–	–	–	–	–	–	–	–	–	–	–	–	–	–	•	•	•	–	•	–	–	–	–
2. Separate exchange rate(s) for some or all capital transactions and/or some or all invisibles	–	–	–	•	–	–	–	•	–	–	–	–	–	•	–	–	–	–	–	–	–	•	•	–
3. Import rate(s) different from export rate(s)	–	–	–	•	–	–	–	•	•	–	–	–	–	•	–	–	–	–	–	–	–	•	–	•
4. More than one rate for imports	–	–	–	•	–	–	–	•	–	–	–	–	–	•	–	–	–	–	–	–	–	•	–	–
5. More than one rate for exports	–	–	–	•	–	–	–	•	•	–	–	–	–	•	–	–	–	–	–	–	–	•	–	–
C. Prescription of Currency	•	•	•	•	•	•	•	–	•	•	–	•	•	•	•	–	–	–	•	–	–	•	–	–
D. Bilateral Payments Arrangements																								
1. with members	–	–	•	•	–	–	–	•	–	–	–	–	•	•	–	–	–	–	–	–	–	–	•	–
2. with nonmembers	–	–	–	•	–	–	–	•	–	–	–	–	–	–	–	–	–	–	–	–	–	–	•	–
E. Payments Restrictions																								
1. Restrictions on payments for current transactions[5]	•	–	•	•	•	–	–	•	•	–	•	•	–	•	•	–	–	–	•	–	–	•	•	•
2. Restrictions on payments for capital transactions[5,6]	•	•	•	•	•	•	•	•	•	•	•	•	•	•	•	–	–	–	•	–	–	•	•	•
F. Cost-Related Import Restrictions																								
1. Import surcharges	–	–	–	•	•	–	–	•	–	•	–	–	–	•	–	–	–	–	•	•	•	–	–	–
2. Advance import deposits	–	–	–	•	•	–	–	•	–	–	–	–	–	•	–	–	–	–	–	–	–	•	–	–
G. Surrender Requirement for Export Proceeds	•	•	•	•	•	•	–	•	•	•	•	•	•	•	•	–	–	–	•	•	–	•	•	•

For key and notes, see page 385

Yemen Arab Rep.	Yemen, P. D. R. of	Yugoslavia	Zaïre	Zambia	Zimbabwe
−	−	−	−	−	−
●	●	●	●	●	●
●	●	−	−	−	−
−	−	−	−	−	−
−	−	−	−	−	−
−	−	−	−	−	−
−	−	−	−	●	●
−	−	−	−	−	−
−	−	−	−	−	−
−	−	●	●	−	−
−	−	−	−	−	−
−	−	−	●	●	●
−	−	−	●	−	−
−	−	−	●	−	−
−	−	−	−	−	−
−	●	●	●	−	●
−	−	−	●	−	−
−	−	●	−	−	−
−	●	●	●	●	●
−	●	●	●	●	●
●	●	●	−	●	●
●	−	−	−	−	−
−	●	●	●	●	●

Key and Footnotes

● indicates that the specified practice is a feature of the exchange and trade system.

− indicates that the specified practice is not a feature of the system.

□ indicates that the composite is the SDR.

[1] The listing includes a nonmetropolitan territory (Hong Kong) for which the United Kingdom has accepted the Fund's Articles of Agreement, and the Netherland Antilles, which is a part of the Kingdom of the Netherlands. Exchange practices indicated in individual countries do not necessarily apply to all external transactions.

[2] Usually December 31, 1983.

[3] It should be noted that existence of a separate rate does not necessarily imply a multiple currency practice under Fund jurisdiction. Exchange arrangements involving transactions at a unitary rate with a second group of countries are considered, from the viewpoint of the overall economy, to involve two separate rates for similar transactions.

[4] Indian rupee, South African rand, and Spanish peseta.

[5] Restrictions (i.e., official action directly affecting the availability or cost of exchange, or involving undue delay) on payments to member countries, other than restrictions imposed for security reasons under Executive Board Decision No. 144-(52/51) adopted August 14, 1952.

[6] Resident-owned funds.

APPENDIX F: TAXES

1. EXCISE TAXES

The following taxes are imposed on domestically produced merchandise as well as imports. Excise taxes imposed on retail sales, services, and other transactions not likely to directly affect exporters or importers, and special occupational taxes have been omitted.

Alcoholic Beverages and Preparations

Distilled Spirits	$12.50 proof gal[1]
including: whiskey, gin, vodka, rum, tequila, brandy, and other alcoholic beverages having an alcoholic content of more than 24% by volume, and dilutions thereof, and ethyl alcohol which has not been denatured	
Still Wine	
under 14% alcohol	.17 wine gal.
14-21% alcohol	.67 wine gal.
21-24% alcohol	2.25 wine gal.
Sparkling Wine	
naturally carbonated	3.40 wine gal.
artificially carbonated	2.40 wine gal.
Beer	9.00 bbl.[2]
Perfume	12.50 wine gal.

Sporting Goods

Bows and Arrows	11%[3]
Fishing Equipment	10%
including: rods, reels, creels, artificial lures, baits, flies, and parts and accessories thereof	
Pistols and Revolvers	10%
Other Firearms	11%
Shells and Cartridges	11%

Fuels

Gasoline	$0.09 gal.
Gasohol[4]	.045 gal.
Diesel Fuel	.15 gal.
Special Motor Fuel[5]	.09 gal.
Reprocessed Fuel Alcohol	
190 proof or over	.50 gal.
more than 150 but less than 190 proof	.375 gal.

Aviation Fuel–other than gasoline[6]	.14 gal.
Aviation Fuel–gasoline[6]	.12 gal.

Tobacco

Small cigars[7]	$0.75 per M
Large cigars[8]	8½% of whole-sale price, not to exceed $20. per M
Small cigarettes[9]	4.00 per M
Large cigarettes[10]	8.40 per M
Cigarette papers[11]	.005 per 50 papers
Cigarette tubes[12]	.01 per 50 tubes

Automotive and Related Items

Tires (highway type only)	
weighing 40 lbs. or less	no tax
weighing 41–70 lbs.	$0.15 lb. over 40 lbs.
weighing 71–90 lbs.	4.50 ea. plus .30 per lb. over 70 lbs.
weighing over 90 lbs.	10.50 ea. plus .50 per lb. over 90 lbs.

Gas Guzzler Automobiles[13]	
1985 model year cars, having fuel economy, in miles per gallon:	
at least 21 mpg	no tax
at least 20 but less than 21	$ 500
at least 19 but less than 20	600
at least 18 but less than 19	800
at least 17 but less than 18	1,000
at least 16 but less than 17	1,200
at least 15 but less than 16	1,500
at least 14 but less than 15	1,800
at least 13 but less than 14	2,200
less than 13	2,650
model year 1986	
at least 22.5 miles per gallon	no tax
at least 21.5 but less than 22.5	$ 500
at least 20.5 but less than 21.5	650

at least 19.5 but less than 20.5	850
at least 18.5 but less than 19.5	1,050
at least 17.5 but less than 18.5	1,300
at least 16.5 but less than 17.5	1,500
at least 15.5 but less than 16.5	1,850
at least 14.5 but less than 15.5	2,250
at least 13.5 but less than 14.5	2,700
at least 12.5 but less than 13.5	3,200
less than 12.5	3,850

Environmental Taxes

Deep seabed hard mineral removal[14]	3¾% of the imputed value of the resource removed
Petroleum[15]	$0.79 bbl.
Chemicals[15]	per ton
Acetylene	4.87
Benzene	4.87
Butane	4.87
Butylene	4.87
Butadiene	4.87
Ethylene	4.87
Methane	3.44
Naphthalene	4.87
Propylene	4.87
Toluene	4.87
Xylene	4.87
Ammonia	2.64
Antimony	4.45
Antimony trioxide	3.75
Arsenic	4.45
Arsenic trioxide	3.41
Barium sulfide	2.30
Bromine	4.45
Cadmium	4.45
Chlorine	2.70
Chromium	4.45
Chromite	1.52
Potassium dichromate	1.69
Sodium dichromate	1.87
Cobalt	4.45
Cupric sulfate	1.87
Cupric oxide	3.59
Cuprous oxide	3.97
Hydrochloric acid	.29
Hydrogen fluoride	4.23
Lead oxide	4.14
Mercury	4.45
Nickel	4.45
Phosphorus	4.45
Stannous chloride	2.85
Stannic chloride	2.12
Zinc chloride	2.22
Zinc sulfate	1.90
Potassium hydroxide	.22
Sodium hydroxide	.28
Sulfuric acid	.26
Nitric acid	.24
Hazardous waste[15]	2.13 dry ton

Notes to Excise Tax Tables

1. Rate is $10.50 per proof gallon until October 1, 1985.

2. Barrel of 31 gallons.

3. Exempt from the tax are bows with a draw weight of less than ten pounds and arrows having an overall length of less than 18 inches. The tax is imposed on parts or accessories suitable for inclusion or use with taxable bows and arrows, including quivers for arrows over 18 inches in length. A special exemption is granted to Indians on reservations, in Indian schools, or under Federal jurisdiction in Alaska, or for traditional bows and arrows, their parts and accessories.

4. Gasohol must consist of at least 10 percent alcohol of not less than 190 proof, determined without regard to denaturants. The alcohol used may be methanol or ethanol, but must not have been produced from petroleum, coal, or natural gas.

5. Special motor fuel includes such products as benzol, benzene, naphtha, liquid petroleum gas, casinghead, natural gasoline, or any other liquid, other than gasoline, kerosene, gas oil, or fuel oil, used to propel a motor vehicle or motorboat.

6. Tax applies only to aviation fuel used in non-commercial aircraft.

7. Cigars weighing not more than three pounds per thousand.

8. Cigars weighing more than three pounds per thousand.

9. Cigarettes weighing not more than three pounds per thousand. The rate on this product is $8 per thousand until October 1, 1985.

10. Cigarettes weighing more than three pounds per thousand; except, that if the cigarettes are more than 6½ inches in length, they shall be taxable at the rate for cigarettes weighing not more than three pounds per thousand, counting each 2¾ inches, or fraction thereof, of the length of each as one cigarette. The rate for large cigarettes is $16.80 per thousand until October 1, 1985.

11. Rate applies on "each book or set of cigarette papers containing more than 25 papers." Where the papers measure more than 6½ inches in length, they are taxable at the rate prescribed counting each 2¾ inches, or fraction thereof, of the length of each as one paper.

12. Where tubes measure more than 6½ inches in length, they are taxable at the prescribed rate counting each 2¾ inches, or each fraction thereof, of the length of each as one tube.

13. The gas guzzler tax has been applied on automobiles for model years beginning 1980.

14. Tax expires June 28, 1990, or the date when an international seabed treaty takes effect for the United States, whichever is earlier.

15. Tax expires September 30, 1985; the tax could expire earlier, depending upon the unobligated balance of the Hazardous Substance Response Fund.

2. LIST OF TAX TREATIES

Country	Official text symbol	Effective date	Citation	Applicable Treasury decisions
Australia	[1]TIAS 2880	Jan. 1, 1953	1958-2 C.B. 1029	6108, 1954-2 C.B. 614.
Australia (new treaty)	TIAS	Dec. 1, 1983		
Austria	TIAS 3923	Jan. 1, 1957	1957-2 C.B. 985	6322, 1958-2 C.B. 1038.
Belgium	TIAS 7463	Jan. 1, 1971	1973-1 C.B. 619	None issued.
Belgium[2]				
Supplemental	TIAS 2833	Jan. 1, 1953	1954-2 C.B. 626	6056, 1954-1 C.B. 132; 6160, 1956-1 C.B. 815.
Supplemental[3]	TIAS 4280	Jan. 1, 1959	1960-1 C.B. 740 & 753	6438 1960-1 C.B. 739; 6469 1960-1 C.B. 752.
Canada[5]	[4]TS 983	Jan. 1, 1941	1943 C.B. 526	5206, 1943 C.B. 526.
Supplemental	TIAS 2347	Jan. 1, 1951	1955-1 C.B. 624	6047, 1953-2 C.B. 59.
Supplemental	TIAS 3916	Jan. 1, 1957	1957-2 C.B. 1014	
Supplemental	TIAS 6415	Dec. 20, 1967	1968-1 C.B. 628	
China, People's Republic of	TIAS	Jan. 1, 1981		
Denmark	TIAS 1854	Jan. 1, 1948	1950-1 C.B. 77	5692, 1949-1 C.B. 104; 5777, 1950-1 C.B. 76.
Egypt	TIAS 10149	Jan. 1, 1982	1982-1 C.B. 219	None issued.
Finland	TIAS 7042	Feb. 28, 1971	1971-1 C.B. 513	None issued.
France	TIAS 6518	Jan. 1, 1967	1968-2 C.B. 691	6986, 1969-1 C.B. 365.
Protocol	TIAS 7270	Jan. 1, 1970	1972-1 C.B. 438	
Protocol	TIAS 9500	Jan. 1, 1979	1979-2 C.B. 411	
Germany	TIAS 3133	Jan. 1, 1954	1955-1 C.B. 635	6122, 1955-1 C.B. 641.
Protocol	TIAS 5920	Various	1966-1 C.B. 360	
Greece	TIAS 2902	Jan. 1, 1953	1958-2 C.B. 1054	6109, 1954-2 C.B. 638.
Protocol	TIAS 2902	Jan. 1, 1953	1958-2 C.B. 1059	
Hungary	TIAS 9560	Jan. 1, 1980	1980-1 C.B. 333	None issued.
Iceland	TIAS 8151	Jan. 1, 1976	1976-1 C.B. 442	None issued.
Ireland	TIAS 2356	Jan. 1, 1951	1958-2 C.B. 1060	5897, 1952-1 C.B. 89.
Italy	TIAS 3679	Jan. 1, 1956	1956-2 C.B. 1096	6215, 1956-2 C.B. 1105.
Jamaica	TIAS 10207	Jan. 1, 1982	1982-1 C.B. 257	None issued.
Japan	TIAS 7365	Jan. 1, 1973	1973-1 C.B. 630	None issued.
Korea	TIAS 9506	Jan. 1, 1980	1979-2 C.B. 435	None issued.
Luxembourg	TIAS 5726	Jan. 1, 1964	1965-1 C.B. 615	None issued.
Malta	TIAS 10567	Jan. 1, 1982		None issued.
Morocco	TIAS 10195	Jan. 1, 1981	1982-2 C.B. 405	None issued.
Netherlands	TIAS 1855	Jan. 1, 1947	1950-1 C.B. 93	5690, 1949-1 C.B. 92; 5778, 1950-1 C.B. 92.
Supplemental	TIAS 3366	Nov. 10, 1955	1956-2 C.B. 1116	6153, 1955-2 C.B. 777.
Supplemental	TIAS 6051	Jan. 1, 1967	1967-2 C.B. 472	
Netherlands Antilles	TIAS 3367	Jan. 1, 1955	1956-2 C.B. 1116	6153, 1955-2 C.B. 777.
Protocol	TIAS 5665	Various	1965-1 C.B. 624	
New Zealand	TIAS 2360	Jan. 1, 1951	1958-2 C.B. 1071	5957, 1953-1 C.B. 238.
New Zealand (new treaty)	TIAS	Generally, Jan. 1, 1984		
Norway	TIAS 7474	Jan. 1, 1971	1973-1 C.B. 669	None issued.
Protocol	TIAS 10205	Various	1982-2 C.B. 440	
Pakistan	TIAS 4232	Jan. 1, 1959	1960-2 C.B. 646	6431, 1960-1 C.B. 755.
Philippines	TIAS 10417	Jan. 1, 1983		None issued.
Poland	TIAS 8486	Jan. 1, 1974	1977-1 C.B. 416	None issued.
Romania	TIAS 8228	Jan. 1, 1974	1976-2 C.B. 492	None issued.
South Africa	TIAS 2510	July 1, 1946	1954-2 C.B. 651	None issued.
Protocol	TIAS 2510	July 1, 1948	1954-2 C.B. 655	
Sweden	TS 958	Jan. 1, 1940	1940-2 C.B. 43	4975, 1940-2 C.B. 43.
Supplemental	TIAS 5656	Various	1965-1 C.B. 626	
Switzerland	TIAS 2316	Jan. 1, 1951	1955-2 C.B. 815	5867, 1951-2 C.B. 75; 6149, 1955-2 C.B. 814.
Trinidad and Tobago	TIAS 7047	Jan. 1, 1970	1971-2 C.B. 479	None issued.
Union of Soviet Socialist Republics	TIAS 8225	Jan. 1, 1976	1976-2 C.B. 463	None issued.
United Kingdom	TIAS 9682	Jan. 1, 1975	1980-1 C.B. 394	None issued.
United Kingdom[6]	TIAS 1546	Jan. 1, 1945	1947-1 C.B. 209	5532, 1946-2 C.B. 73; 5569, 1947-2 C.B. 100.
Supplemental	TIAS 3165	Jan. 19, 1955	1957-1 C.B. 665	
Supplemental	TIAS 4124	Jan. 1, 1956	1958-2 C.B. 1078	
Supplemental[3]	TIAS 4141	Jan. 1, 1959	1960-2 C.B. 653	6437, 1960-1 C.B. 767.
Supplemental	TIAS 6089	Jan. 1, 1966	1966-2 C.B. 582	6898, 1966-2 C.B. 567.

[1] Treaties and Other International Agreements Series.
[2] Applies only to the following former Belgian overseas territories: Democratic Republic of the Congo (Zaire), Republic of Rwanda, and Republic of Burundi. The United States announced termination of this treaty, effective January 1, 1984.
[3] As extended to overseas territories or former territories.
[4] Treaty Series.
[5] The Canadian Treaty also may be found in Publication 597, *Information on the United States—Canada Income Tax Treaty.*
[6] Applies only to British overseas territories and former territories. The United States announced termination of this treaty, effective January 1, 1984.

3. TAX RATES ON INCOME OTHER THAN PERSONAL SERVICE INCOME

Name	Code	Interest paid by U.S. obligors general	Interest on real property mortgages	Interest paid to a controlling foreign corporation	Tax-free covenant bonds: If obligor assumes more than 2% of tax	Tax-free covenant bonds: If obligor assumes 2% or less of tax	Maturity date extended after 1933 and obligor assumes over 27½% of tax	Dividends: U.S. corporation general	Dividends: U.S. subsidiary to foreign parent corporation	Capital gains	Industrial royalties	Copyright royalties: Motion pictures and television	Copyright royalties: Other	Real property income and natural resources royalties	Pensions and annuities	Social security payments
Anguilla*	AV	30	30	30	2	30	27½	c.h15	b.c.h5	30	c.h0	c.h0	c.h0	c.h15	d0	15
Antigua and Barbuda*	AC	30	30	30	2	30	27½	c.h15	b.c.h5	30	c.h0	c.h0	c.h0	c.h15	d0	15
Australia	AS	30	30	30	2	30	27½	c.h15	c.h5	30	30	30	h0	30	0	—
Australia (eff. 12-1-83)	AS	g10	g10	g10	2	g10	g10	915	915	30	g10	g10	g10	30	d0	15
Austria	AU	g0	30	h0	2	h0	h0	h15	b.h5	30	h0	h0	h0	30	d0	15
Barbados*	BB	30	30	30	2	30	27½	c.h15	b.c.h5	30	c.h0	c.h0	c.h0	30	d0	15
Belgium	BE	915	915	915	2	915	915	915	915	e.g.m0	90	h0	90	30	d0	15
Belize (British Honduras)*	BH	30	30	30	2	30	27½	c.h15	b.c.h5	30	c.h0	c.h0	c.h0	c.h15	d0	15
Burundi	BY	h15	h15	h15	2	h15	h15	h15	h15	30	h0	h0	h0	30	d0	15
Canada	CA	h15	h15	h15	2	h15	h15	c.h15	b.c.h5	h0	h15	h0	h0	h15	0	15
Denmark	DA	h0	h0	h0	h0	h0	h0	h15	b5	30	h0	h0	h0	30	d0	15
Egypt	EG	h15	30	h15	2	h15	h15	h15	b.h5	e.h.m0	h0	h0	915	30	d.t0	0
Falkland Islands*	FA	30	30	30	2	30	27½	c.h15	b.c.h5	30	c.h0	c.h0	c.h0	c.h15	d0	15
Finland	FI	90	g.q10	90	90	90	90	915	b95	e.g.m0	90	90	90	30	d.t0	15
France	FR	g.q10	g.q10	g.q10	2	g.q10	g.q10	915	b95	e.g.m0	95	90	90	30	d.t0	15
Gambia*	GA	30	30	30	2	30	27½	c.h15	b.c.h5	30	c.h0	c.h0	c.h0	c.h15	d0	15
Germany, Fed. Rep. of	GE	90	90	90	90	90	90	915	915	e.g.m0	90	90	90	30	d0	15
Greece	GR	h0	h0	30	h0	h0	h0	30	30	30	h0	30	h0	30	d0	15
Grenada*	GJ	30	30	30	2	30	27½	c.h15	b.c.h5	30	90	c.h0	c.h0	c.h15	d0	15
Hungary	HU	90	90	90	90	90	90	915	b95	g.m0	90	90	90	30	d0	15
Iceland	IC	90	90	90	90	90	90	915	b95	e.g.m0	90	90	90	30	d.t0	15
Ireland	EI	c.h0	c.h0	30	c.h0	c.h0	c.h0	c.h15	b.c.h5	30	c.h0	c.h0	c.h0	c.h15	d0	0
Italy	IT	30	30	30	2	30	27½	915	b.h5	30	h0	h0	h0	30	d0	15
Jamaica	JM	912½	912½	912½	2	912½	912½	c.h15	b.c.h5	g.m0	910	910	910	30	d0	15
Japan	JA	910	910	910	2	910	910	915	b.g10	e.g.m0	910	910	910	30	d.f.r0	0
Korea, Rep. of	KS	912	912	912	2	912	912	915	b.g10	e.g.m0	915	910	910	30	d0	15
Luxembourg	LU	h0	30	h0	h0	h0	h0	h15	b95	30	h0	h0	h0	30	d0	15
Malawi*	MI	30	30	30	2	30	27½	c.h15	b.c.h5	30	c.h0	c.h0	c.h0	c.h15	d0	15
Malta	MT	912½	912½	912½	2	912½	912½	915	b95	g.m0	912½	912½	90	30	d0	0
Montserrat*	MH	30	30	30	2	30	27½	c.h15	b.c.h5	30	c.h0	c.h0	c.h0	30	0	15
Morocco	MO	915	915	915	2	915	915	915	b.g10	e.g.m0	910	910	910	30	d0	15
Netherlands	NL	90	90	90	90	90	90	915	b95	e.g.m0	90	90	90	30	d0	15
Netherlands Antilles	NA	h0	30	30	h0	h0	h0	h15	b.h5	30	h0	h0	h0	30	d0	15
New Zealand	NZ	30	30	30	2	30	27½	h15	b.h5	30	30	30	30	30	30	—
New Zealand (eff. 1-1-84)	NZ	910	g10	g10	2	g10	g10	915	915	30	g10	g10	g10	30	d0	15

Country	Code														
Norway	NO	g0	g0	g0	g0	g0	g15	90	g0	h0	90	90	30	d,0	15
Pakistan[i]	PK	30	30	2	30	30	b,h15	30	30	h0	90	h0	e,g,m0	d,0	0
Philippines	RP	915	915	2	915	915	b,g20	915	915	915	915	915	g,m0	s,30	15
Poland	PL	90	90	90	90	90	b,95	90	90	910	910	910	e,g,m0	30	15
Romania	RO	910	910	90	910	910	910	910	910	910	910	910	30	30	0
Rwanda[u]	RW	h15	h15	2	h15	h15	h15	h15	h15	h0	h0	h0	30	d,0	15
St. Christopher-Nevis*	SC	30	30	2	30	30	b,c,h5	27½	30	c,h0	c,h0	c,h0	30	g0	15
Seychelles*	SE	30	30	2	30	30	b,c,h5	27½	30	c,h0	c,h0	c,h0	30	g0	15
Sierra Leone*	SL	30	30	2	30	30	b,c,h5	27½	30	c,h0	c,h0	c,h0	30	g0	15
South Africa	SF	30	30	2	30	30	30	27½	30	30	30	30	30	30	15
Sweden	SW	h0	h0	h0	h0	h0	b,h5	h0	h0	h0	h0	0	h,m0	30	15
Switzerland	SZ	h5	h5	2	h5	h5	b,h5	h5	h5	h0	h0	30	30	g0	15
Trinidad & Tobago	TD	30	30	2	30	30	30	27½	30	915	90	30	30	d,0	15
Union of Soviet Socialist Republics	UR	30	30	2	30	30	30	27½	30	p,0	0	0	0	30	15
United Kingdom	UK	90	90	90	90	90	b,95	90	915	h,0	0	90	30	d,0	0
Zaire[u]	CG	h15	2	h15	h15	h15	h15	h15	h0	h0	h0	h0	30	d,0	15
Zambia*	ZA	c,h0	c,h0	c,h0	c,h0	c,h0	b,c,h5	c,h0	c,h0	c,h0	c,h0	c,h0	30	g0	15
Other countries		30	30	2	30	30	30	27½	30	30	30	30	30	30	15

a No U.S. tax is imposed on a dividend paid by a U.S. corporation that has less than 20% of its gross income from U.S. sources for the 3-year period before the dividend is declared. (See section 861(a)(2)(A) of the Internal Revenue Code.)

b The reduced rate applies to dividends paid by a subsidiary to a foreign parent corporation that has the required percentage of stock ownership. In some cases, the income of the subsidiary must meet certain requirements (e.g. a certain percentage of its total income must consist of income other than dividends and interest).

c The exemption or reduction in rate applies only if the recipient is subject to tax on this income in the country of residence. Otherwise a 30% rate applies. For Canada, this requirement applies to intercorporate dividends only.

d Exemption does not apply to U.S. Government (federal, state, or local) pensions and annuities; a 30% rate applies to these pensions and annuities.

e The treaty exemption that applies to U.S. source capital gains includes capital gains under section 871(a)(2) if they are received by a nonresident alien who is in the U.S. for no more than 183 days. (182 days for Belgium and Egypt.)

f Includes alimony.

g Under the treaty, the exemption or reduction in rate does not apply if the recipient has a permanent establishment in the United States and the property giving rise to the income is effectively connected with this permanent establishment. In the case of Australia, Hungary, Jamaica, Malta, New Zealand, Philippines, and the United Kingdom, the exemption or reduction in rate also does not apply if the property giving rise to the income is effectively connected with a fixed base in the United States from which the recipient performs independent personal services (professional services or royalties paid to a Philippines resident). Even with the treaty, if the income is not effectively connected with a trade or business in the United States by the recipient, the recipient will be considered as not having a permanent establishment in the United States under section 894(b). I.R.C.

h Under the treaty the exemption or reduction in rate does not apply if the recipient is engaged in a trade or business in the United States through a permanent establishment that is in the United States. However, if the income is not effectively connected with a trade or business in the United States recipient, the recipient will be considered as not having a permanent establishment in the United States for the purpose of applying the reduced treaty rate to that item of income. Section 894(b), I.R.C.

i Bangladesh has not indicated that it wishes to assume the responsibilities or exercise the rights of the United States—Pakistan income tax treaty.

j Exemption is not available when paid from a fund under an employees' pension or annuity plan, if contributions to it are deductible under U.S. tax laws in determining taxable income of the employer.

k The former United Kingdom treaty (proclaimed by the President of the United States on July 30, 1946) as it was in effect before the Supplementary Protocol of September 9, 1966, applied to British overseas territories and former territories. Dominica, St. Lucia, St. Vincent and the Grenadines, and Yemen (Aden) have not indicated that they wish to assume the responsibilities or exercise the rights of the United States—United Kingdom income tax treaty. The United States ended the extension of the treaty to Southern Rhodesia (now Zimbabwe), effective January 1, 1974, and the British Virgin Islands, effective January 1, 1983. Nigeria ended its participation in the United States—United Kingdom income tax treaty for tax years beginning after 1978. Antigua and Barbuda ended its participation in the treaty, effective August 26, 1983. The United States announced termination of this treaty, effective January 1, 1984.

l Exemption from or reduction in rate of tax does not apply to income of holding companies entitled to special tax benefits under the laws of Luxembourg.

m Exemption does not apply to gains from the sale of real property; a 30% rate applies to these sales.

n The exemption or reduced rates that apply to U.S. source dividends, interest, industrial, and literary royalties do not apply if these items are paid to a Netherlands Antilles investment or holding company entitled to special tax benefits under Netherlands Antilles law and owned by persons or corporations not resident in the Netherlands.

o The exemption applies only to interest on credits, loans, and other indebtedness connected with the financing of trade between the United States and the Union of Soviet Socialist Republics. It does not include interest from the conduct of a general banking business.

p The exemption applies only to gains from the sale or other disposition of property acquired by gift or inheritance.

q Interest paid on a loan granted by a U.S. bank is exempt from U.S. tax, except when footnote (g) applies.

r The exemption does not apply if the recipient was a resident of the United States when the pension was earned or when the annuity was purchased.

s Annuities paid in return for other than the recipient's services are exempt.

t Applies to social security payments received from the U.S. Government after 1983. Payments received before 1984 are not subject to U.S. tax. The 15% effective rate shown is the result of applying a 30% withholding rate to half the social security benefits.

u The United States announced termination of this treaty, effective January 1, 1984.

ABOUT THE AUTHOR

William J. Miller, a graduate of the State University of New York, has been actively involved in import/export management for many years. He has been a director of the American Association of Exporters and Importers, has served on the Shipper's Advisory Board of the National Maritime Council, and has taught international business subjects at the university level. He is president of Infotrade International, Ltd., a research and consulting firm specializing in international trade, with offices in Washington, D.C., and New York.